PROFITS, PROGRESS AND POVERTY

PROFITS, PROGRESS AND POVERTY

Case Studies of International Industries in Latin America

Edited by
Richard S. Newfarmer

UNIVERSITY OF NOTRE DAME PRESS
NOTRE DAME, INDIANA 46556

Library of Congress Cataloging in Publication Data

Main entry under title:

Profits, progress, and poverty.

Bibliography: p.
Includes indexes.
1. International business enterprises—Latin
America—Case studies.   2. Investments, Foreign—
Latin America—Case studies. I. Newfarmer, Richard S.
HD2810.5.P76   1984   338.8'888   83-40115
ISBN 0-268-01152-4
ISBN 0-268-01153-2 (pbk.)

Manufactured in the United States of America

Table of Contents

List of Tables

ix

PREFACE

The process which produced this volume has been long and arduous—and immensely rewarding. Each study began with field experience in Latin America. All of the authors had already lived and worked in Latin America prior to the initiation of the project. This shared field experience was crucial in providing common ground for a group that was otherwise extremely diverse in disciplinary backgrounds and theoretical perspective. Even though our disciplinary training often led us in different directions, we would often agree as to what we had found to be important "on the ground". Achieving consensus on a common perspective that would transform individual research into an integrated volume proved more exciting—and time-consuming—than any of us had imagined when we began.

The group was originally constituted as "The Continuing Working Group on the Study of Transnational Corporations in Latin America in an International Context." It was sponsored by the Joint Committee on Latin American Studies of the Social Science Research Council and the American Council of Learned Societies, and was led originally by Alfred C. Stepan. We met periodically from 1975 to 1980. The meetings were small and intense, and always included outside scholars whose comments and criticisms prevented the group from becoming in grown and losing perspective on its own ideas. This volume is only one of the group's products. The interchange among members of the group also provided invaluable inputs for several individually authored research monographs on Latin America produced over the course of the group's five year life. This volume does represent, however, the group's most ambitious undertaking, one which would not have been possible without the leadership of Richard Newfarmer. From 1978 to the present, Richard worked tirelessly, shaping drafts through extensive comments and suggestions, bringing out the best in each contribution while molding them into a coherent whole. The group's debt to Richard is hard to overstate.

We hope that this volume will be valued for its substantive contributions and theorectical insights regarding the role of international oligopolies in Latin American industrialization. For participants, it provided another kind of insight which may be less clear to those reading the final product. It taught us the value of producing collab-

xi

oratively rather than in the isolation that is the normal scholarly rule. Many of us came to feel that participation in the group was a more effective form of research training than we had encountered in our long years of formal education. We are glad to be able to share the written results of our work, but regret that the experience which went into producing it cannot be more fully shared. We can only hope that readers will also be stimulated to experiment with the kind of collaborative process which lies behind it.

Peter Evans and Louis W. Goodman
Past Coordinators
Continuing Working Group on
Transnational Corporations in
Latin America

ACKNOWLEDGEMENTS

This book grew out of the Social Science Research Council's Working Group on Transnational Corporations. Louis Goodman, as the director of the SSRC's Latin American program, provided the spark to initiate the project; he, together with Peter Evans, were the primary architects in designing the project and in putting the group together. As the group coalesced around a series of ideas for this book, both continued to play guiding intellectual roles over the course of more than two years of meetings in its creation. To these talented scholars, we are greately indebted.

When Lou left the SSRC for new challenges in Washington, Reid Andrews and later Brooke Larson continued with enthusiastic support as Lou's successors at the SSRC.

Several people joined our discussions and offered helpful insight and criticisms: Alice Amsden, Thomas Birstecker, Carlos Dias Alejandro, Arthur Domike, Albert Fishlow, Gerry Helliener, Sylvia Ann Hewlett, Al Litvak, Christopher Maule, Theodore Moran, David Moore, Ronald Mueller, Lynn Mytelka, Andrew Richter, Alfred Stepan, Paul Streeten, Michael Tanzer, Richard Weinert, and Louis Wells.

But the project awaited a final push. Victoria Morss, an accomplished social scientist in her own right, deserves thanks for editing what was in earlier draft a burdensomely long manuscript. With a quick mastery of our political-economic approach and an eagle eye for repetition, she made innumerable insightful suggestions for tightening presentations. We are enormously grateful for her generous commitment to the book. Kathy Lynn produced an exceptional index to the book and handled with admirable efficiency some of the administrative burden of the project.

Special thanks is also due to the Helen Kellogg Institute for International Studies under the able leadership of Father Ernest Bartell at the University of Notre Dame. The Institute's intellectual enthusiasm and generous financial support was instrumental in publishing the book.

Richard Newfarmer
Washington, D.C.
July 1984

Richard S. Newfarmer

1.

An Introduction to the Issues

THE NEW INTEREST IN FOREIGN INVESTMENT

Latin America during 1981-1983 was plunged into its gravest economic difficulties since the Great Depression. Growth rates plummeted, unemployment reached levels of 20 percent or more in many countries, and inflation at times raged out of control. Country after country was forced to suspend payments on its debt and seek last-resort funding from the International Monetary Fund.

The crisis renewed interest in foreign direct investment and transnational corporations among many policymakers in the United States. Some see foreign direct investment as filling the void left by the ebbing flows of commercial bank capital. Those flows, which had been enormous in the years after the first oil crisis as petrodollars were recycled, slowed to a trickle after 1981. Transnational corporations (TNCs), according to this argument, can bring in large amounts of new capital to help fill foreign exchange gaps. Moreover, equity capital may be preferable to debt capital since equity assumes risk; future claims on foreign exchange are made on the basis of domestic profitability, not fluctuating world interest rates.

Nonetheless, foreign investment in the region slowed perceptibly after 1981. The underlying cause of this slowdown was the declining profitability of new investment because of the recession itself, but many policymakers also feel that regulations have stifled the interest of TNCs in investing in the region. Indeed, the United States has recently placed the regulations facing U.S. and other foreign investors in the Third World on the center stage of international commercial relations. The Reagan Administration, with its private sector, free-market orientation, has produced several policy initiatives. First,

1

multilateral foreign aid—most of which goes to the poorest countries—has been cut on the theory that it has been ineffective and that private capital flows were sufficient and preferable. Second, the administration has sought to bring foreign investment into the system of multilateral rules governing trade, the General Agreement on Tariffs and Trade (GATT). The United States launched its major effort at the November 1982 ministerial meeting of the GATT. The initiative proposed action on trade in services (including investment-related capital flows), trade in high-technology products (where developing countries are especially restrictive), and investment performance requirements, which mandate specific behavior for foreign firms as a condition of doing business. One objective of the new multilateral effort is to restrict the power of national governments to impose conditions on foreign direct investment, since these conditions frequently spill over into the markets of other countries, or create government-to-government competition in subsidizing local industrial development, or constitute increased levels of trade protection. Developing countries generally opposed the initiative (as did some developed countries), and the meeting made little headway on these issues. Third, the United States has also pursued bilateral measures. In December 1981 the Reagan Administration introduced "bilateral investment treaties," which include reciprocal arrangements: (a) to extend national treatment to investors; (b) to restrict performance requirements; (c) to permit free movement of earnings and capital in and out of signatory countries; (d) to provide prompt and adequate compensation in cases of expropriation; and, (e) to provide provisions for settling investment disputes. Business groups in the United States have urged the government to grant trade preferences—such as those contained in the Caribbean Basin Initiative—to only those developing countries that have concluded a bilateral investment treaty with the United States. Among Latin American governments, however, only a few small countries have signed bilateral investment treaties.

What explains the remarkable lack of success in either of these two initiatives? Multilaterally, it is clearly in the interest of all nations to see that governments do not engage in costly bidding wars by offering incentives and subsidies to investors. It is also in the interest of all that countries do not engage in investment practices that injure their foreign trading partners. Moreover, most governments need capital inflows now more than ever; the international recession followed by the debt crisis has produced balance of payments difficulties for almost all countries in Latin America. To the extent that stable bilateral and multilateral rules encourage investment flows, they are certainly in the interests of the developing countries. What then explains the lack of receptivity among developing countries to the U.S. approach?

Aside from the natural reluctance of governments everywhere to give up national sovereignty to multilateral rules, even when gains can accrue to all, the issues surrounding investment flows raise additional complex problems. Investment flows between developed and developing countries are asymmetrical: most investment originates in the former and goes to the latter. Even though outward investment is increasingly common from the advanced developing countries, such flows are miniscule when compared to North-South investment. This asymmetry is coupled with a disparity in economic power between large TNCs operating in imperfect markets and relatively poor (though increasingly sophisticated) nations. It is not always clear that free markets in these circumstances do result in development that benefits everyone—at least with the sense of equity implicit in orthodox trade theory.

The issue of the distribution of the gains from TNC-related trade and investment between host country and home country as well as the internal distributional effects have been the subject of heated political and academic controversy during much of the 1960s and 1970s. Many developing countries argue that international markets are systematically biased against developing countries in their distribution of gains from trade and investment. These biases are traceable in part to the existence of nation-states, which put restrictions on product, capital, and labor flows, and the global distribution of wealth, as well as to the failure of markets to be competitive. This is not to say that trade and investment do not produce economic gains for buying and selling countries. At issue is the distribution of gains between developing countries and developed countries. After reviewing several categories of international markets, G.K. Helleiner concluded that ". . . developing countries do rather badly under the existing market system" (1979c, p. 383). Leaving aside the question of whether this conclusion is correct for all markets, do developing countries "do rather badly" in TNC-related markets?

Another reason that developing countries are reluctant to accept international rules curbing their powers to regulate foreign investment is the perceived influence of TNCs upon the path of development—which products are produced, which technologies are employed, and how industries insert into an increasingly interdependent global system. Because the equity relationship is one of control, foreign managers make decisions affecting the level, rate, and activity of domestic business expansion. To be sure, they respond to market signals and to government regulation, but foreign investment also

3

reflects the global interests of the corporation itself. Moreover, foreign investment is far more invasive than international trade because it is more integral to all economic activity—foreign companies employ workers, advertise, create networks of suppliers and buyers, and may even participate in economic policymaking or domestic politics. These aspects of investment raise considerably more obstacles to reaching international accords. On the other hand, these concerns about foreign investment may not be well founded: Do TNCs exert an independent influence on development or is their behavior neutral and no different from other firms?

These two issues—the distributional biases among countries that may be present as a result of foreign investment and the identifiable influences that TNCs have on the nature of growth itself—are the subject of this book. In examining these issues, authors contributing to this book focus on four broad areas of dispute. These are: the economic reasons for transnational expansion and dominance of an industry; the nature and consequences of oligopolistic rivalry among TNCs; the consequences of transnational control of investment in developing countries for industrial growth; and the relative power of TNCs and governments to affect the course of development.

As a prerequisite for understanding the effects of TNCs on the fairness of international transactions or on development, it is necessary to find out why TNCs have expanded abroad and assumed positions of lasting stature in several markets around the world. That is, we must answer the question, "What is the advantage that TNCs have over other purely domestic firms in the world's markets?" If the answer were based solely on technological or capital advantages, then foreign investment might well have benign consequences; if advantages stem from monopolistic practices the social consequences might be less benign. Understanding this, it is possible to proceed to the second area: how transnational firms with similar advantages compete with each other in world markets and whether this rivalry benefits developing countries in their international dealing with TNCs. For example, has the rise of Western European and Japanese firms undermined the advantages traditionally enjoyed by the U.S. firms, and has this produced more price competition and advantageous terms of international exchange for products and technology going to developing countries? The third area turns to the effects of transnational growth and rivalry upon developing countries. Has international rivalry resulted in new types of investments in developing countries or new products and technologies sold at lower prices? Fourth, do states have enough power, skill, and the "political will" to regulate effectively the activities of TNCs to insure the realization of multiple social goals?

4

TOWARD AN ANALYTICAL FRAMEWORK: METHOD AND SOME CAVEATS

To study these questions, we have undertaken case studies of transnationally controlled and oligopolistic industries—what we have called "international oligopolies." This approach allowed us to proceed historically and inductively and to expand beyond the conventional methodologies and biases of our various disciplines. Industries were chosen as the unit of analysis, rather than firms or countries, because international rivalry among firms in an industry seemed to be fundamental to addressing the four sets of issues. Moreover, they offered a vehicle to capture the essence of the economic reality of foreign investment which is not merely a capital flow or a transfer of technology, but a package of factors, products, and dynamic strategies. To evaluate the economic power of transnational corporations contributors turned to that branch of economics that puts economic power at the center of its analysis: industrial organization.

Industrial organization economics locates the roots of a firm's power in the structure of markets. For example, if only one firm serves the market, it probably will behave like a monopolist by charging higher prices, resulting in income transfers from consumers to producers. Market structure thus affects conduct options open to the firm and these conduct choices affect industrial performance. Applying the methodology is complex. Industries have several types of market structures—concentration, barriers to entry, product differentiation, conglomerate size, etc. Even when market structure is known, firms can exercise different choices in their behavior, so studies strive for probabilistic statements about the relationship of market structure to conduct and performance.

Applied to an international context, the complexity of the framework increases geometrically with the addition of each national market. The analyst now must consider not only market structures in several countries but the links among them. For example, if a firm operates in a monopolistic market at home and a competitive market abroad, will it behave like a monopolist in the first and a competitive firm in the foreign market? What about the effects of the policies of different governments on the conduct options open to a firm in both markets? To handle this complexity, these studies analyze an industry on two levels: First, the home and international markets, then in domestic markets of selected developing countries. The idea is to capture the influence of the international organization of an industry on the domestic growth of that industry in peripheral countries. This means tracing the international organization of the industry to its

5

structural roots in the advanced home countries and then looking at how that structure shapes their international rivalry. Then it is possible to see how international rivalry affects the structure of markets in developing countries, the conduct within local oligopolies, and the consequences for industrial performance. This method permits: (1) a qualitative analysis of the sources and consequences of economic power; and, (2) an analysis of the principal ways TNCs can influence or shape development, i.e.,—capturing domestic surplus, investing it in certain economic activities rather than others, and interacting with local groups and political actors. For example, if TNCs enter an industry with new product designs that entail a capital-intensive technology and convince enough consumers of the superiority of their differentiated product they may expand their market share rapidly and therefore compel other firms to invest in the same technologies and product. In the process their share of economic surplus may increase and the employment-creation potential of the industry may diminish. While this may enhance the welfare of some consumers, it may qualitatively and quantitatively change the entire performance of the industry—altering the path of development. When such changes increase efficiency and help realize other performance goals for an industry, the overall impact of TNC-induced changes may bring substantial benefits to a host economy; when the resulting industrial performance does not match up to development objectives, such changes can entail considerable social costs.

Although this way of analyzing the role of TNCs in development offers several advantages over conventional approaches, the reader should be aware of some of the caveats that the authors have in applying traditional industrial organization analysis. These concern the role of the state, the "power of the market" (as distinct from the market power of firms), and the method for evaluating industrial performance.

The State

The state policies can affect nearly every category of the industrial organization framework—market structure, conduct, and industrial performance. These case studies raise three distinct questions about the state: How does the state affect industrial structure, conduct, and performance—and with what degree of efficiency and effectiveness? What power does the state have to enact its policies? Why does the state enact the policy that it does?

Of these questions the third poses the greatest difficulty. Neither the industrial organization analytical framework nor the bilateral mo-

6

nopoly approach explains why the state assumes the "political will" to bargain with TNCs or why it chooses to establish controls over TNCs. As a general rule, it is precisely because the industry is not performing up to the expectation of policymakers that the state chooses to intervene. But how are policymakers' expectations and, more importantly, goals for an industry formed? All states with similar power bases and performance difficulties do not respond in the same way. To resolve this issue, we deal with the state inductively, and examine empirically the ways both home and host governments affect industrial organization and performance. This means charting the effects of public policy in an industry, being careful to not generalize from goals of policymakers to the national interest, and, where possible and relevant, exploring the politics of key political decisions.

Basic Conditions and the Power of the Market

A second issue in applying industrial organization methods to development, concerns the basic conditions in a country within which market structures were formed. Basic conditions include the level of development, technological capabilities, income distribution, and class structure of a country—factors that determined market size, the attractiveness of markets to TNCs, and demand patterns as well as the politics of the state. The "power of the market" stemming from the distribution of wealth may overshadow the "market power" of transnationals in shaping development. The relationship of market structures and TNCs to basic conditions is complex. Consider the example of income distribution. To explain contemporary wealth and therefore income distribution, it is necessary to reach outside of the industrial organization model to look for deeper, historical-structural causes. Prominant among these causes are the historical expansion of the international economy and the particular role of colonialism. However, the concern of most industrial organization studies is narrower and temporally defined; taking income distribution as a parameter of the analysis, these studies ask how firms and market structures shape subsequent industrial performance, including effects on income. Thus, a skewed income distribution may explain in the first round why a poor country has any potential demand at all for motorized transportation while market imperfections and the investment decisions of firms explain why that demand will be satisfied by differentiated autos produced by foreign companies. The presence of powerful foreign firms controlling investment may explain in the second round why the ground transportation industry continues to invest in autos with its consequences for income distribution. One could consider the basic conditions, such as technology and class structure, in much the same way.

The absence of an elegant and ultimately determinant solution to this system of multicausality is bound to leave some readers uncomfortable, but it is important to avoid rigid interpretations of the industrial organization model. Economic relationships are not immutable, but subject to constant change and these case studies try to incorporate relevant forces into a dynamic framework.

Evaluating Industrial Performance

A third set of issues concerns the evaluation of industrial performance. These case studies use three standards for judging industrial performance: that of conventional economics, declared government objectives, and normative standards.

Conventional Economics. Conventional industrial organization theory uses market performance under workable competition as its standard for allocative and technical efficiency. The analyst can evaluate the effects of power by comparing market performance in pricing, technological progress, advertising, and equity with what happens when power is absent. These are the conditions of workable competition. This comparison between "power present" and "power absent" can be undertaken counterfactually based upon a substantial body of existing theory, or studied through intertemporal or international comparisons of the same market or through cross-sectional comparisons with other markets in the same country. The case studies that follow often do a bit of each.

The application of this standard is undertaken with some qualms. First, it must be clear that using workable competition is a method of economic analysis and does not imply a policy prescription favoring antitrust remedies of breaking up monopolies. In fact, host governments may condone or even facilitate economic power to achieve other social goals (such as in the case of tariffs, natural monopolies or patent-based monopolies). Breaking up centers of economic power is only one policy option open to planners; alternatively, they may choose to do nothing, to regulate the powerful firms, to establish a state-owned competitor, to nationalize the industry, to reduce effective protection, or to enact some mix of policies aimed at improving industrial performance. A second qualm concerns the measurement of the distributional effects of market power which are usually analyzed by measuring the extent to which market prices exceed long run marginal and averaged costs of production. This excess profit is generated in the simplest case because powerful producers not subject to the discipline of the market are able to set higher prices; consumers must pay more to the owners of capital and valuable societal resources are misallocated.

This may be sufficient for a first-round statement about efficiency and distributional fairness, but it is important to be aware of the implicit values in using only this measure. Such a definition assumes that market transactions in competitive markets are fair. However, fairness in competitive market transactions cannot be separated analytically from the distribution of income and wealth. That distribution determines the allocation of purchasing power among citizens and hence what goods a society as a whole will produce. One could envision a society with a set of nearly perfect markets and a highly skewed distribution of income in which products satisfying the needs of the poor were under produced for lack of effective demand. Although such market transactions may be efficient, are they fair? The answer is of course normative, although most among us would say no. Even if market power were eliminated in inegalitarian developing countries, and with it the monopoly advantage of TNCs, the market-based economy would probably continue to produce inappropriate, though not necessarily foreign, products so long as income distribution remained highly concentrated. That understood, our interest is in examining how the dynamic insertion of transnational corporate market power into developing economies ameliorates or exacerbates social inequalities and facilities or impedes reform.

A third and related issue concerns the concept of economic surplus. In neoclassical theory, the conventional concept of "economic profits" or "excess profits" is a monopoly rent generated through use of market power, or the difference between the selling price and the long run average costs of production. Under conditions of competition, market forces will keep prices down to just cover the costs of production and so excess profits disappear. Thus, the implicit comparison between monopolistic and competitive markets is used to obtain the value of excess profits. The main distributional effects of market power is seen to be the transfer of value from consumers to producers in the form of monopoly pricing.

The neoclassical definition is narrower than the concept of economic surplus used in the Cambridge (or "Post Keynesian") school. The term refers to the physical output of an economic system over and above that going to workers to provide for their daily consumption. Once income distribution is specified, economic surplus is reflected in the accounts of firms as all return over and above prime costs (namely, wages, materials, other variable costs, and depreciation). The market power of firms is thus central to this school because it determines the ability of the firm to raise prices above variable costs, the height of the "mark-up." There are, however, at least two important differences in the treatment of the distributional effects of market power. In the Cambridge scheme, the surplus generated by the firm is not distributed among labor and capital according to the "marginal productivity" of each, but is decided by a variety of economic conditions such as the rate of investment and institutional forces (colonialism, land tenure, class struggles, the control of technology, etc.). More importantly, the Cambridge tradition is interested in analysis of long term development and therefore focuses on the level, rates, and form of investment as having important distributive consequences in the long process of development. Investment in one productive structure, for example a food system based on extensive food processing, has subsequent effects for the relative prices of labor, agricultural products to satisfy basic needs, and so forth that are different from investment in a food system emphasizing basic need commodities. Each have different consequences for income distribution. Indeed, it is exactly these consequences which the case studies seek to analyze.

The Marxian concepts of surplus are even more broadly defined. Marx himself defined surplus value as the difference between the value of the final product and the value of the amount of labor power required to produce it.[1] This of course is founded on the labor theory of value, a difference from the Cambridge school, which generally recognizes both labor and capital (but not necessarily capitalists) as productive. This reduces the importance of market power per se as a subject of inquiry because value emanates from labor, not through market but through the labor process. Monopoly simply redistributes surplus from the competitive sector to the monopolistic sector in the circulation of commodities. On the other hand, market power accelerates the centralization of capital and therefore is important to this school since it may strengthen the capitalist class, particularly that segment linked to international capital.

Declared Government Objectives. An industry's performance can be judged by its effects upon government goals with regard to the balance of payments, inflation, growth, employment, technology, absorption, and dependence. There are two problems here. First, it is virtually impossible to assess rigorously the priorities governments may establish among conflicting objectives. For example, how can the analyst adequately weigh the trade-off at the industry level between technological absorption and employment when government policy itself is often ambiguous and changing? The best one can do is evaluate the industry's performance in the relevant categories and define trade-offs between conflicting goals. The second problem concerns using state policies as representative of national interests. In most cases, it is a fair assumption that politically dominant groups and state technocrats have aims and interests at least distinct from the interests of the large majority of the population, if not opposed to their interests on many policy issues. Although this is not always true, state policy should not be taken axiomatically as an adequate proxy for the national interest.

Normative Standards. The inadequacies of the above two standards suggests that explicitly normative standards must ultimately be adopted. The authors in this volume opt for using a standard of reducing absolute poverty, income inequities, and unemployment. The concluding chapter addresses these delicate problems of performance evaluation on three levels of historical and analytical abstraction. First, using the method of comparative statics taken from conventional industrial organization, conclusions are drawn about the impact of market power upon inter- and intra-country income distribution and technological progress. Second, by comparing the behavior of foreign to domestic firms, it is possible to evaluate the contribution and distortions of TNCs to the dynamic development of an industry, and their effects of trade, technology, advertising, market structure, and industrial performance. Finally, with a slightly longer view of history, it is possible to consider how TNCs, in interaction with domestic actors, invest in certain activities and therefore implant a structure of production that, while opening up some avenues of development, forecloses or restricts investment in alternative forms of production.

ORGANIZATION OF THE STUDY

Although the organization of a collection of case studies is somewhat transparent, it is helpful to call the reader's attention to their order. The opening chapter reviews the existing literature to show how the international system plays a strong role in determining or influencing industrial development in single national economies. Subsequent chapters take the general model and apply it to industrial studies. These are presented more or less in order of their historical transformation into international industries in order to illustrate contrasting historical patterns of oligopolistic rivalry.

11

Notes

[1] Some putative Marxists have altered the definition of surplus for the sake of measurement using firm accounting data; and the result is nearly identical to the Cambridge school (e.g., contrast Baran 1957 and Robinson 1979; see also Baran and Sweejy 1964).

Richard S. Newfarmer

2.

International Industrial Organization and Development: A Survey

INTRODUCTION*

A central assertion of developing countries in North-South discussions is that power and exchange relations between developed and developing countries are asymmetric and unequal. As a consequence, the international economic system is seen as constraining, even impeding, growth and development in peripheral countries. Transnational corporations are seen as potent actors in the international system. They are usually portrayed as shaping, if not controlling, market development in many countries around the globe. This perspective raises two fundamental questions about the way TNCs and the international system affect the growth of industry in developing countries: First, what are the sources of, and limits to, TNC power? Second, how can the effects of this economic power that link developing countries to the international system be analyzed and even measured?

The first section of this chapter shows how concepts taken from industrial organization theory can shed some light on these questions by providing an analytical framework and presents the central proposition of this book: that the organization of industry in the home countries has a direct, often quantifiable, influence on industrial

* The author wishes to thank Rhona Boardman-Free who provided valuable research assistance on an earlier draft of this paper.

organization and performance in open developing countries. A second section discusses this proposition by using this analytical framework to review the vast literature on TNCs and development, focusing first on their rivalry in home markets and its implications for the international system, then on their expansion in developing countries. A final section draws together some preliminary conclusions about the way that TNCs, as part of the international economic system, appear to use their power to shape market development. Some of these conclusions are: First, monopolistic markets in the developed countries tend to give rise to foreign direct investment activity of large firms, leading to increases in foreign activity in developing countries. Second, transnationals tend to link oligopolistic markets at home with those in developing countries and, because of attendant market power, these markets tend to be the most profitable. TNCs are thus often able to capture a greater share of locally generated surplus. Third, transnational subsidiaries appear to use this surplus to grow differently from independent domestically controlled firms and so the spread of TNCs has implications for development performance.[1] Transnational corporations generally evidence different strategies from local enterprises in acquisitions, advertising, trade, technology, and trade pricing. Their behavior has implications for control of industry investment capital, growth, and technological dependence.

TOWARDS AN INTERNATIONAL INDUSTRIAL ORGANIZATION METHOD AND MODEL

The conventional industrial organization model traces the roots of economic power of firms to monopolistic advantages inherent in industrial market structure. Given the basic conditions of an economy at any point in its development (that is, its level of technology, distribution of income, class structure, etc.), the theory posits a set of causal and measurable relationships running from *market structure* through firm *conduct* to industrial *performance*. For example, the degree of monopoly or conglomerate bigness are variables of market structure, and they may result in monopoly pricing or predation. This in turn can contribute to a less efficient industrial performance such as income transfers from consumers to producers and from the competitive sector to the monopolistic sector. Industrial organization has explored this intellectual terrain with great care for domestic markets such as the United States (Scherer 1980; Greer 1980) and, to a lesser extent, Western Europe (Jacquemin and de Jong 1976) and Japan

14

(Caves and Uekusa 1976). This exploration has at times taken place amid considerable controversy, (Craven 1983) and mechanistic application of the framework are to be avoided.

Diagram 1 shows how transnational corporations might fit into the industrial organization taxonomy of causal relationships encompassing the many hypotheses about the determinants of economic performance. On the lower level, there is the more conventional national environment, for our purposes, the host country. Our hypothesis here is that TNCs will probably behave quite differently from domestically-controlled firms, private or public. This is so because, in accord with Hymer's (1960) insight, their market advantage is based upon a unique package of intangible assets not readily available to national firms, whose superior knowledge of local conditions would otherwise give them the upper hand. TNCs exhibit different patterns of conduct, e.g., earnings repatriation, marketing behavior, and transfer pricing, with consequences for performance. Examining these differences systematically is one way for seeing how TNCs influence development. Second, there is another level of analysis—that connected with the home country and international market, shown as the upper tier. Following Caves (1974a), TNCs germinate in concentrated home markets and this leads to the possibility of oligopolistic rivalry that "spills across national boundaries." International oligopolistic rivalry, he suggests, might influence various dimensions of firm behavior in markets around the world, the lower tier of analysis.

Sufficient work has been done on the relationships between home country industrial structure and foreign investment and between foreign investment and development that we can now begin to integrate these into a more general formulation which suggests a strong causal link between the structure of international industries based in the developed countries and the structure and performance of industries in developing countries. The crucial link in the relation between international industrial structure and host country industrial organization is the global behavior of transnational companies—international oligopolistic rivalry.

The Special Problem of State

One problem of conventional industrial organization deserves special mention: It is the often determinant role of public policy, a problem accentuated in the international environment. As with governments in home countries, host governments potentially exercise considerable influence over all categories of the industrial organiza-

15

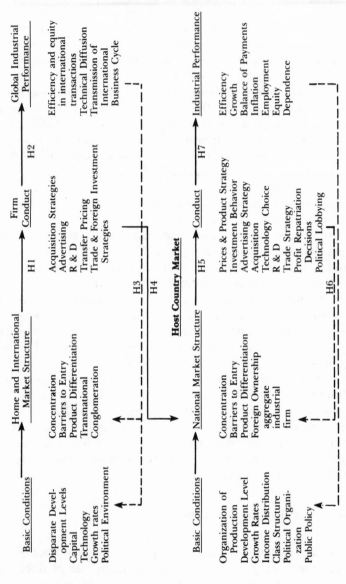

DIAGRAM 1

A Schematic Representation of International Industrial Organization Hypotheses

International Environment

<u>Basic Conditions</u> → <u>Home and International Market Structure</u> —H1→ <u>Firm Conduct</u> —H2→ <u>Global Industrial Performance</u>

Disparate Development Levels
Capital
Technology
Growth rates
Political Environment

Concentration
Barriers to Entry
Product Differentiation
Transnational
Conglomeration

Acquisition Strategies
Advertising
R & D
Transfer Pricing
Trade & Foreign Investment Strategies

Efficiency and equity in international transactions
Technical Diffusion
Transmission of International Business Cycle

H3
H4

Host Country Market

<u>Basic Conditions</u> → <u>National Market Structure</u> —H5→ <u>Conduct</u> —H7→ <u>Industrial Performance</u>

Organization of Production
Development Level
Growth Rates
Income Distribution
Class Structure
Political Organization
Public Policy

Concentration
Barriers to Entry
Product Differentiation
Foreign Ownership
aggregate industrial firm

Prices & Product Strategy
Investment Behavior
Advertising Strategy
Acquisition
Technology Choice
R & D
Trade Strategy
Profit Repatriation Decisions
Political Lobbying

Efficiency
Growth
Balance of Payments
Inflation
Employment
Equity
Dependence

H6

Note: Numbers refer to hypothesized relationships treated in the text. H1 hypotheses are discussed on pages 18-24: H2 hypotheses appear on pages 30-40; H3 on 24-30; H4 on 32-37; H5 on 37-50; H6 on 37-41; and H7 on pages 50-57.

* All page numbers refer to thise chapter and these galleys.

16

tion model (Baer 1973). They set the policy parameters that form part of the slow-to-change basic conditions, such as tariff policies, ownership requirements, profit repatriation rules, etc. Governments may intervene directly to alter market structures; for example, they may establish state-owned firms, encourage mergers, finance selected firms, break up monopolies, or nationalize an industry. Political authorities routinely regulate various aspects of firm conduct through price controls, import-export requirements, and consumer protection.

While acknowledging the powerful role of government in influencing TNC behavior, one insight of dependency theory should not be lost. The dependency approach recognizes limits to autonomous state activity because governments are accountable in varying degrees to elites, classes, and changing coalitions of political power. Governments, like corporations, do not have infinite power capabilities. In fact, the growth of foreign corporations in developing economies may create new powerful social groups working for and benefiting from foreign investment. These groups may ally with other elites to constrain and/or create state policy. Thus, Evans (1979), while acknowledging some conflicts between national and foreign capitalism, sees a more fundamental alliance between the state, domestic producers and foreign corporations and sees this as a parameter establishing limits to any bargaining between the state and TNCs.

In general, the existence of an alliance is not necessarily inconsistent with vigorous host country bargaining with TNCs according to the literature on the subject. Some writers have hypothesized that the bargaining position of developing countries has rather consistently improved *vis-a-vis* the international corporations, though not without short-term set-backs.[2] The great bulk of the bargaining literature focuses on vertical investments of TNCs in raw material industries and obsolescing bargaining (Vernon 1971; Moran 1974 and 1977). The argument of these writers is that as the cost of TNC investments becomes sunk and governments learn more about the industry in developing countries, the initial bargaining advantage slowly passes from TNCs to the developing country. Oligopolistic rivalry among TNCs can accelerate this process as host governments learn to play one oligopolist off another. As bargaining power over time in TNC-state negotiations has generally swung in favor of host governments, developing countries have taken advantage of this to secure a greater share of the mutual gains from foreign investment. This conclusion is seconded in studies of legislations (Robinson 1976), and in the views expressed by the companies themselves (Frank 1980).

On the other hand, few detailed studies of this hypothesis have been advanced for the manufacturing sector, where the bases for

17

bargaining power are considerably different than in manufacturing as well as the impact on class formation (Stepan 1978; Goodman 1981). Bennett and Sharpe (1979b) presented evidence from the auto case in Mexico of a much more complex situation in which bargaining power shifted back and forth, depending on the historical phase and issues being negotiated, but ultimately with most bargains, TNCs emerged in a more profitable, stronger position than prior to the negotiations.

Second, writings that have focused on horizontal investments of TNCs in manufacturing show that, for the most part, these negotiations often deal with bargaining over the terms of technology transfers, export promotion, or other forms of TNC behavior (Vaitsos 1974a; Bennett and Sharpe 1979a and b), and rarely with the full gamut of structural and performance dimensions of the industry, such as employment, investment, and particularly control. Thus, state-TNC bargaining in manufacturing has tended to dwell upon certain forms of TNC conduct rather than the structural fact of foreignness. There are some exceptions to this: Mexico's 1972 Foreign Investment Law; the Andean Pact's Decision 24; India's legislation on foreign investment; and finally, the prohibitions many countries have placed upon foreign entry into selected national industries (Robinson 1976). However, many of these legislations have been weakened in their structural applications—though some have been interpreted with flexibility in exchange for specific changes in TNC conduct. It is not surprising that cross-national studies of the manufacturing sectors have found considerable structural similarities in open capitalist economies, even in different policy environments affecting conduct (Newfarmer and Mueller 1975; Connor and Mueller 1977b; Mellor 1977; Evans and Gereffi 1979). While industry studies can deal with the state on a case-by-case basis, this review will concentrate on generalized findings among countries with similar policy environments.

THE LITERATURE IN THE PERSPECTIVE OF THE MODEL

Home Market Structure and International Conduct

Stephen Hymer (1960) challenged the prevailing notion in orthodox theory that foreign direct investment was analogous to portfolio capital flows. He argued that foreign direct investment was a form of corporate behavior associated with imperfections in home country markets, particularly high entry barriers. Firms in these industries usually possess a combination of intangible assets, such as patented technology, a differentiated product, and marketing experience. Hymer saw these assets as the source of a monopolistic advantage at home and abroad. The way to maximize the profit from this package of assets is to exercise direct management control over the foreign assets. For the investment to be attractive, the package has to yield a return abroad higher than further applications at home (to outweight risks and communication costs) and higher than nationally-owned competitors in the foreign market who would otherwise be induced to make the investment themselves. The power of this analysis is that it explained three phenomena that portfolio theories of direct investment could not: first, why some industries exhibited high foreign investment proclivities and others had almost no foreign operations; second, the emergence of the transnational corporate organization itself, centrally administered and hierarchical; and third, the tendency for TNCs to invest in each others' market and for investments to be "cross-penetrating."

Charles Kindleberger (1969) formalized Hymer's discussion by distinguishing four general sources of the monopolistic advantages of TNCs: (1) imperfect market structures in the final goods market through introduction of a new or differentiated product; (2) departures from perfect competition in factor markets, including patented technology, access to capital or managerial skill; (3) economies of scale; and, (4) governmental limitations on output, trade, or entry. Kindleberger showed theoretically that foreign investment would not occur without these sources of market imperfections.

Richard Caves (1971) extended Hymer's analysis in a systematic way. He recognized that not all barriers to entry lead to foreign investment or foreign investment of the same variety. Product differentiation, usually based on technology or product design, was predicted to give rise to horizontal investments abroad—that is, investments abroad in the same product line as the parent—because the technology or design could be readily transferred to the subsidiary. The product differentiation barrier is unimportant in many raw material industries; but high seller concentration when combined with control over overseas resources raises additional barriers to new competitors in the home market. Thus, high concentration in undifferentiated, primary industries is likely to spawn vertical foreign investments. Caves further suggested that the home base of the foreign investor provides certain advantages over domestic competitors in the foreign market. TNCs thus represent an entry threat that is less sensitive to local barriers to entry.

Several authors have reviewed and extended the Hymer-Kindleberger-Caves formulation. One of the most comprehensive theoretical reviews is John Connor's (1977) that compares "five bodies of

19

thought" explaining foreign investment: analogies with portfolio capital flows, pure trade theory, adaptions of the theory of the firm, the intangible asset theory, and the industrial organization approach. He concluded that:

> . . . the industrial organization model is the most comprehensive and consistent theory of the five surveyed. [It] explains why foreign direct investment is corporate, concentrated, mostly horizontal and vertical backward, oligopolistic, crosshauled, and available mainly as a bundle of complementary inputs (1977, p. 30).

Lall and Streeten (1977) in their review elaborated in some detail the monopolistic or oligopolistic advantages that TNCs have relative to their local competitors in the host country market, our second tier of analysis. These include privileged access to capital, management, technology, marketing, raw materials, economies of scale, bargaining, and political power. Bergsten, Horst, and Moran (1977), after a review of the theoretical and empirical evidence concluded that, "several authors show that foreign investment is the product of domestic industry structure." Another strand of theory of investment increasingly associated with the industrial organization school are extensions of the theory of the firm. This is an extension of the Coase (1937) insight that a firm internalizes markets when it can handle administratively the costs of the transactions more cheaply than the market itself. The idea is that market imperfections raise the cost of transferring the factors or inputs abroad through normal market channels and so firms internalize the market through foreign direct investment to lower these costs. For example, weak patent protection in host countries does not assure inventors the full return of their rents from technology, and so foreign investment is seen as a result of the failure of technology markets to adequately protect proprietary rights. Economies of interdependent activities might also lower administrative transactions costs compared to the market and provide an incentive for internalization (Buckley and Casson 1976; Casson 1979). John Dunning (1979) recently proposed an eclectic theory of international investment to unite the industrial organization approach, the theory of the firm approach, and location theory. Foreign investment, he posits, can be explained by ownership-specific advantages, incentives to internalize markets within the firm, and location-specific variables. Ownership advantages are the possession of a package of intangible assets; incentives to internalize exist when firms find it more profitable to extend their own activities rather than sell the assets through external transactions such as licensing technology; finally, there must

20

be some locational advantage to deploying the assets in the foreign country, otherwise the firm would service the foreign market through exports.

Four noteworthy econometric studies have tested the hypotheses that imperfect home country market structure is a determinant of foreign direct investment. Horst (1972) studied both the firm- and industry-specific determinants of the decision of U.S. TNCs to invest abroad. Within a given industry, large size was found to be the crucial determinant of the foreign investment decision; across industries, the research and development intensity (which Horst took as a proxy for international product differentiation) and the concentration—resource interaction (a proxy to test Cave's vertical integration hypothesis) were positively associated with the ratio of foreign to domestic assets. Caves found that the principal determinants of foreign investment in Canada and the U.K. were "intangible-asset variables— chiefly the industry's advertising and research intensity" (1974b, p. 272). He also found that the foreign share was related to the size of firms and the degree of multiplant production. Sanjaya Lall attempted to measure the separate influences of product differentiation and research and development intensities in explaining total foreign involvement. He concluded that: "The combination of technology and product-differentiation factors exercises the largest effects on foreign involvement: . . . they seem to be the main 'engines of growth' behind overseas expansion of U.S. industries" (1980, p. 120). When foreign involvement was broken down into export propensities and foreign production, research and development were closely associated with both foreign activities while product differentiation was only linked to foreign production. These findings, he concluded, are more transferable abroad through foreign production than others, such as technology intensity. Buckley and Dunning (1980) evaluated three approaches to explaining the industrial structure of U.S. investments in U.K. manufacturing. They tested hypotheses derived from the theory of the firm, industrial organization theory, and traditional investment determinants and concluded that "the most successful formulation . . . is based on industrial organization theory" (1980, p. 11). They found a high proportion of the variance in the industrial structure of U.S. investment in the U.K. could be explained by examining entry barriers facing the U.S. as compared to domestic firms.

Oligopolistic Interdependence

The Hymer-Kindleberger-Caves formulation places some emphasis on "recognized oligopolistic interdependence," the mutual recognition among firms that the actions of one firm have a perceptible effect on those of another.[3] Two kinds of oligopolistic interdependence extending internationally have been suggested in the literature, one originating in the home country oligopoly and the other based on globally recognized interdependence.

The first is the hypothesis that oligopolists based in the same home country may react to each others' foreign investment activity and follow each other into foreign markets. For example, Ford might follow General Motors into Brazil whether or not immediate profit opportunities dictate the move. This type of international oligopolistic behavior, dubbed *oligopolistic reaction*, is a form of non-price competition rooted in the home country market. Knicherbocker (1973) tested this hypothesis in his study of U.S. companies that invested abroad in the 1947-1968 period. Calculating an "entry concentration index," which measures the closeness in time that firms in the same 3-digit industry establish an overseas subsidiary, Knicherbocker found a positive correlation between the home country industrial concentration and time "bunching" of rivals' entry into the same market. The reaction was found to be less typical of stable, highly concentrated oligopolies.

Although the study has been rightly acclaimed, further evidence is necessary to fill in unexplored areas. First, as Stevens suggested, the evidence does not preclude "the hypothesis that the bunching was merely the result of business responding—independently—to profitable opportunities" (1974, p. 75). Also, industry-specific variables besides profitability may push firms abroad simultaneously; for example, in 1973 the Occupational Safety and Health Administration issued new regulations governing working conditions in the U.S. asbestos industry and within twenty-four months industry leaders had all established plants in Mexico. West (1977) advances a second criticism: to calculate the industry concentration index, Knicherbocker had to discard cases where there were fewer than two entrants in the three- to five-year base period; this would seem to bias upwards his result. Third, the measure does not capture reactive investment behavior in the same region but not country, although it is perfectly plausible that, for example, Westinghouse might enter Venezuela in response to General Electric's entrance into Colombia. Finally, the Knicherbocker study assumed that oligopolistic reaction is determined solely by the home country oligopoly, though it is conceivable that oligopolists could respond to actions of rivals from other countries. All in all, the burden of proof would still seem to be on those who argue that interdependence is not a factor in the foreign investment decision.

A second type of international interdependence involves, in the words of Caves, "the possibility that interdependence runs across national boundaries" involving oligopolists based in different countries (1974d, p. 11). He discounts this *a priori* for two reasons: First, producers of a given nationality share a common cultural background, making it easier to achieve mutual understanding; and second, national governments are likely to vigorously support home-based firms in their dealings with foreign firms, "reducing the credibility (because of ease of abrogation) of any collusive arrangement that entails continued access to the foreign partners' national market" (1974d, p. 12). Neither reason sufficiently compel to discard the hypothesis without empirical investigation. It is evident that common cultural and ideological backgrounds facilitate mutual accords, but this hardly precludes international understandings, especially in the age of such high cultural, political, and economic intercourse among western countries. The second reason assumes that collusive arrangements entail access to foreign partners' home bases; yet the history of international collusion evident from the literature on cartels in the 1930s is that producers often join cartels precisely to protect home markets by agreement.

Whatever the value of *a priori* reasoning, the researcher suddenly encounters an empirical void in the literature on the question of international interdependence. One manifestation of global interdependence is collusive price agreements, and so the old pre-1950 literature on international cartels assumes a new relevance (Stocking and Watkins 1948; Hexner 1945; Baldwin 1948; United Kingdom Board of Trade 1947; League of Nations 1947). Writings after 1950 on the subject are increasingly rare, undoubtedly because formal, international private cartels, especially those visible to the public, are increasingly rare (Edwards 1964 and 1971; OECD 1974). In some industries, private agreements facilitating international price collusion and other arrangements have been replaced by state sponsored, public cartel-like arrangements, such as in the oil and steel industry (Rahl 1979).

Reading the old and new literature one is struck by two facts: the comprehensiveness of agreements in many industries on export prices, quantities and territorial allocation schemes (although many agreements were unsuccessful in controlling prices and short-lived), and the fact that many of the manufacturing industries that were cartelized at some time in the decades before the war, e.g., chemicals, electrical machinery, pharmaceuticals, tires, etc., now have a heavy component of foreign direct investment. In the post-war period, foreign direct investment of course became the primary form of organizing foreign markets rather than exports. This is not to say that international trade is insignificant, but a large share of it consists of intra-firm trade between parents and subsidiaries (Helleiner 1979a and b; Vaitsos 1979; Murray 1979; UNCTAD 1978).

The fact that global interdependence in export sales was so widely recognized in the 1920s and 1930s suggests that one cannot easily write off the possibility that this same recognition carries over into foreign investment activities. What forms of behavior might such a recognition take? The old cartels almost always had rules protecting the territorial spheres of influence of members (including home countries). One might expect that at least in some industries the modern extension would be some mutual forbearance in investment location as TNCs "respect" *spheres of influence*. The more competitive version of international interdependence in investment location is *oligopolistic reaction* among rivals based in different countries. This might assume a "hostage-taking" character to maintain global stability or oligopolistic market sharing tactics. A third form of international interdependence is *joint ventures* among large transnational rivals to share markets, such as one sees in the cable industries of Africa, Asia, and Latin America (Newfarmer 1978a). Finally, recognized global interdependence could carry over into foreign markets where rivals meet as *local interdependence*, and be manifest in the response of existing foreign oligopolists producing locally to new foreign entrants or in local pricing and investment strategies. The empirical literature on this question of international interdependence is surprisingly silent. Raymond Vernon says it well: "Concepts of oligopoly pricing behavior, which heretofore have been treated within a single national market, must be applied in an international setting" (1974, p. 100).

International Rivalry and Changes in Global Market Power

At this point, there is a sharp theoretical division in the literature over the consequences of international rivalry for the economic power of the dominant TNCs. At issue is whether the foreign activities of TNCs increase or decrease concentration and whether they enhance or diminish international competition in markets. Three not mutually exclusive views are found here: a first that contends TNCs promote global competition and decrease concentration, the workable competition view; a second view contending that TNCs adopt strategies to mute global competition and raise concentration, the conglomerate power model; and a third that argues the outcome of either workable competition or constrained rivalry is increased concentration. The views can usefully be summarized by presenting these models of international oligopolistic rivalry in a stylized form.

The first view of international oligopolistic rivalry is a composite of themes found in the writings of various scholars, particularly in the work of Raymond Vernon (1977). The theoretical foundation of Vernon's model is the product life cycle of international trade. It assumes that economies of scale exist in production, that information flows are imperfect across national boundaries, that barriers to entry tend to fall, usually because of the spread of innovation, and that TNCs experience competitive advantages in innovation and marketing because of their huge research and development (R&D) effort and sales experience in their home countries. Most products, it is argued, pass through a relatively rapid cycle of "life stages"—birth, rapid growth, spread and maturation, and finally senescence. During the early stages of the product's life, the innovating corporation possesses some degree of monopoly power. As the product and its technologies become widely known, barriers preventing the entry of new firms in the market begin to fall. In the latter stages, most product markets tend to pass through a transition from "monopoly to oligopoly to workable competition" (Vernon 1977, p. 91).

Transnationals, according to this view, generally accelerate these natural market forces. As oligopolists, their competition often takes non-price forms, especially in innovation and marketing, and so their economic activities of introducing new products to stay ahead of their rivals accelerate the product life cycle. Desiring growth but not wishing to disturb home country oligopolistic price equilibriums, oligopolists undertake another form of non-price competition: foreign investment. This behavior makes them strong potential competitors that can hurdle the entry barriers shielding other TNCs abroad, accelerating the product cycle abroad. Consequently, TNCs are seen as a strong competitive force because their non-price competition leads to changes in product market structure—if not at home at least abroad—since barriers to entry fall and concentration is reduced, resulting finally in a workably price-competitive market.

In industrialized countries, this cross-penetrating foreign investment is seen as reducing market concentration and increasing competition, hence reducing global market power. In developing countries, as TNCs substitute direct production for their exports, they develop local skills, suppliers, and new marketing channels. Ironically, this ultimately facilitates the deterioration of their monopolistic advantage. First, other TNCs see the profit opportunities created in the new market and soon enter. Then, as barriers fall with market expansion, local producers jump in as well. After some time, the level of market concentration and foreign control in a market tends to decline (Vernon 1977, pp. 91-98), and subsequent TNC leadership in the industry depends largely on their ability to "roll over" into new products.

In sum, this model—which we can term the workable competition model of international oligopolistic behavior—predicts that TNCs will bring several benefits to developing countries. First, they will transmit rapidly the latest products and technologies to the host country. Second, their international rivalry will propel many into profitable markets in developing countries, reducing market concentration and speeding the deterioration of entry barriers—ultimately resulting in more price-competitive markets. Third, as markets expand, local entrepreneurs will be stimulated and domestic firms will soon capture a substantial share of the market, making complete the transfer of technology, capital, and income gains to the developing country.

A second model of international oligopolistic rivalry comes from the literature on industrial organization and focuses on the conduct of TNCs in their non-price competition. Transnational corporations are seen as having the power to influence those economic factors which the product cycle model takes as assumptions, and hence to protect their monopolistic advantage. For example, rather than simply assuming information flows are imperfect across boundaries, corporations may make information flows more imperfect through restrictions on technology transfers, excessive product differentiation, and so forth. Similarly, while barriers to entry in some markets may indeed tend to fall, this perspective assumes TNCs can adopt strategies that raise barriers to outside competition such as controlling material supplies and technology. The model suggests that TNCs, individually and collectively, exert some degree of control over the product price in specific markets, and may, within limits, gear their innovations and marketing activities to speed up or slow down the rate of product innovation and maturation.

The individual multimarket transnational by itself has several advantages over its smaller, single market competitor, much like large conglomerates domestically. The subsidiary can call upon the substantial financial reserves of the parent to enter a market through the takeover of existing large firms. The TNC has a global fund of legal, technical, and administrative personnel. The centralization of strategic decisionmaking affecting multiple markets confers upon the firm the ability to influence the structure and performance of any of its

26

single markets. For example, the transnational conglomerate can quickly introduce a new line of business or double or triple plant size to maintain market share in times of booming demand; it can take advantage of tax and legal options not open to single market competitors; it can absorb extended losses to restructure any single market; it can cultivate or buy political influence.

Transnational corporations also mobilize market power by recognizing their collective interdependence. In specific oligopolies, experience suggests this recognition leads to noncompetitive pricing and excess profits. However TNCs are not only oligopolists, but multimarket oligopolists; they meet in several product and national markets. Consequently, aggressive actions in any one market that adversely affect a rival may trigger reprisals in another; this recognition may result in a live-and-let-live philosophy, and attempts to channel aggressive expansion into other markets. Such mutual competitive forbearance can be extended to the creation of spheres of influence, emerging informally or formally through licensing contracts, patent pools, and cartel agreements. Thus, in this view, the transnational conglomerate adopts international strategies, including non-price competition such as foreign investment, on the basis of global interdependent rivalry as well as oligopolistic rivalry at home.

The implications of this conglomerate power model of international oligopolistic rivalry are quite different from those of the workable competition model. First, TNC rivalry is not likely to lead to competitive industrial structures because new entry in most markets will stop short of disruptive aggression that results in vigorous price-competition. New entry may be via acquisition and thus not increase the number of competitors at all. While many markets may pass from monopoly to oligopoly, few are predicted to become workably price-competitive. Within most oligopolies, corporate rivalry is likely to be restricted to non-price competition, especially product differentiation, and this behavior raises barriers to new entry rather than speeding their erosion. Second, this view implies that increasing the foreign share of ownership in industrial countries will merely heighten the power of the large corporations and that developing countries will receive only limited benefits from TNC rivalry. While development of local markets may occur, concentration may start and remain high since barriers to entry do not automatically fall. On the one hand, this insures above normal returns when oligopolistic pricing tactics are adopted; on the other hand, the level of foreign ownership can remain high indefinitely if market forces are left to themselves. Both of these consequences imply that the distribution of international gains, both in present and future earnings, will be biased in favor of the TNCs to a far greater extent than predicted under the workable competition model.

A third perspective argues that the outcome of either workable competition or oligopolistic non-price rivalry is increased global concentration. This view takes an agnostic position on changes in competitive structure and behavior in any given market, preferring to view them as short-term phenomena subordinate in importance to long-run structural changes. This perspective has the potential disadvantage of overlooking what may be essential immediate changes that affect consumers such as higher or lower prices.

Let us consider the evidence on two questions raised by these models: how the transnationalization of production affects global concentration within an industry, and how it affects market concentration and competition in specific home countries. The evidence on empirical global concentration trends is woefully inadequate. Vernon (1977, pp. 80, 81) presented information showing dramatic declines in global Herfindahl indices of concentration for eight product classes from about 1950 to 1975. Likewise, Dunning and Pierce (1975) calculated three-firm concentration ratios as a percent of the largest 70-20 firms in an industry taken from the *Fortune 500* lists for 1962 and 1972; they found that the share of the top three declined in 12 to 14 industries, though in only 7 industries does the decline exceed two percentage points. Both findings, however, are of limited value. The Herfindahl index, since it is weighted by size, is extremely sensitive to the market shares of the largest one or two firms; any shift of market share from the very largest firms to the next echelon of firms will dominate the index. The measure that Dunning and Pierce employ is inadequate because of the small universe definition; the interesting question is not shifts of output shares among the largest 20 firms, but rather the share of the largest 8 to 20 firms as a percent of the worldwide universe. The proper relevant measure of global concentration in an industry is, for our purpose, the share of the largest 8 to 20 firms in total assets or sales. This provides one meaningful index of the power of a select group of firms to influence business decisions and control price-competition in the industry around the world. (Industries with firms producing in several highly diversified product lines might use more firms in the numerator because specialization tends to raise actual concentration.) These data unfortunately are not usually available. Nonetheless, it is probably a safe bet, as these studies indicate, that the market share of the largest one or two firms in many global industries is declining relative to the next six or eight firms. In

28

this narrow sense, rivalry appears to be becoming more equally based among giants.

On a broader level, however, data on aggregate and market concentration in home countries call into question the assertion that concentration is declining or that it is doing so as a consequence of transnational investment. Aggregate concentration in all manufacturing, the share of business accounted for by the largest 50-200 firms in an economy, has apparently increased in most industrialized countries.[4] Trends in market concentration (measured with three- or four-firm concentration ratios) in the industrialized countries have also generally been upward, though in varying degrees. In the U.S. concentration tended to remain stable between 1958 and 1972, though substantial increases apparently took place in highly differentiated industries (Mueller and Rogers 1980). European countries generally experienced greater increases in market concentration than the U.S. If foreign investment activities have mitigated concentration, they have not had sufficient impact to offset these larger economic trends.

Understanding the TNC role in these trends is difficult in the absence of careful studies, though a few generalizations are possible. First, TNCs are among the largest firms in their domestic markets and are thus usually key actors in the process of increasing concentration. Second, expansion abroad may reduce market and aggregate concentration in the recipient economy at the same time it increases aggregate concentration in the global industry. This is generally the case if foreign investors are among the largest firms in their home market, if the largest firms grow faster than the universe because of their global opportunities, and when they enter the foreign market *de novo*. Third, many of the new entries into foreign markets by TNCs have not been *de novo* but via acquisition of existing, often large firms. When this occurs, concentration in the recipient economy will remain unaffected, but concentration in the global industry will increase, and more sharply than in the case of *de novo* growth. If the acquired firm in the recipient economy is among the largest, a long-term consequence of the takeover may be to entrench the position of the dominant firm because of its access to the resources of the new parent.

Increases in global and market concentration associated with transnational investment do not necessarily preclude strong inter-firm rivalry, of course. In fact, the emergence of such sharp international oligopolistic rivalry may raise concentration over the long-run as firms are driven out of business. If this is the case, two questions are immediately germane: What is the nature of the competitive forces, and are they enduring into the foreseeable future? The first implicitly

29

recognizes that competition through product differentiation, take-overs, innovation, and expansion of market share through other non-price mechanisms has different implications for social welfare than does price-competition. The second recognizes that strong price and non-price-competition in the near term may restructure international markets in ways that reduce price-competition in the long-term. Both questions, fundamental to understanding changes in global market power, can only be answered through industrial case studies.

TNCs, Trade, and International Equity

Orthodox models of international trade based upon general equilibrium theories and perfectly functioning markets generally predict a narrowing of wage and income differentials between countries and the rapid, even diffusion of technical progress. That this has not occurred in reality is usually attributed to market imperfections. Although it would be an onerous task to critique orthodox trade theory in light of the literature on TNCs and market imperfections, two recent articles are worthy of brief mention because of their integration of monopolistic pricing and other forms of international oligopolistic behavior into international trade theory. They show how international exchange can be asymmetric and the gains from international trade can be biased in favor of the developed countries.

Richard Cooper (1977) attempts to analyze "exploitative" trade relations and the inequalities stemming from the uneven distribution of economic power in global markets. He focuses on the earning of supranormal profits—that is, profit rates in excess of the competitive rate of return. He distinguishes three types of transactions: (1) international economic transactions in which one party gains while the other loses; (2) those in which both parties gain from such transactions but the first gains more than the second; and, (3) those in which the first party earns profits above competitive levels in its own economy on its transactions with the second, whereas the second does not enjoy above normal rates of profits on transactions with the first. The first case, Cooper argues, arises only when the losing party is forced into the transaction or is ignorant of the distribution of benefits. Since in Cooper's view ignorance is deemed to be the fault of the losing party, the first case involves no exploitation except when force is involved. The second case may arise because of differences in resource endowments, bargaining strengths, etc., or use of monopolistic powers. Only when monopoly power is used to extract supranormal profits does the exchange involve exploitation for Cooper. The third type of transaction, wherein companies based in one country continuously earn excess profits on transactions with parties in another country and the reverse is not true, is seen as unequivocably exploitative. The result of such exploitative relations is to bias the distribution of trade gains in favor of the developed countries and widen income gaps rather than narrow them. This approach provides the theoretical starting point for an analysis of monopoly and excess profits in trade relations.

G. K. Helleiner (1979c) starts where Cooper leaves off. He begins by adding to the list of Cooper's "exploitative" situations, asking "when advantage is taken of an ignorant partner to a transaction in order to attain merely 'normal' profits, is this not exploitative? And can one really isolate the 'voluntariness' of economic transactions from their social and political context? He also questions Cooper's use of the domestic rate of return as the basis for the competitive norm: Rates of return in a rich and growing country are likely to be higher than in a poor and stagnant one and the former is likely to demand a higher return from trade than the latter, arguably an exploitative situation. Furthermore, Emmanuel's (1973) argument deserves greater attention in Helleiner's view. Even if rates of return on capital were the same in all corners of the globe (thus eliminating that source of exploitation), wage earners in rich countries producing for export earn much more than those in poor countries producing for export. ". . . it is quite obvious that something inequitable is taking place" (Helleiner 1979c, p. 359).

No matter how one treats these latter problems, the roots of the Cooper-style exploitation are found in "market imperfections," seen in orthodox trade theory as the occasional exceptions to the rule and presumably without bias in affecting rich-poor country trade. Helleiner poses the question: "Do market imperfections systematically work against developing countries?" He considers market imperfections in: (a) the immobility of labor across national boundaries," (b) the uneven access to information; (c) the inequitable international division of labor between primary and secondary production and its effects on exports from developing countries; and, (d) imports to developing countries in the form of restrictive trade practices in goods markets and of limited access to technology and capital.

Transnational corporations, he contends, tend to heighten market imperfections in all but the first category. In primary exports, for example, vertically integrated TNCs will, in the words of Diaz-Alejandro, "routinely erect and protect barriers to entry, including hoarding mineral deposits, limiting technological diffusion and establishing exclusive marketing networks" (Diaz-Alejandro 1976, p. 14, as quoted in Helleiner 1979c, p. 369). This, when combined with other imperfections, tends to reduce the developing country's income share in its primary exports. As an example on the import side, TNCs selling on world markets to developing countries may engage in restrictive practices such as cartelization of some product and technology markets, thus reducing income accruing in developing countries. Or more generally, TNCs' control of much of world trade of developing countries accords them the power through transfer pricing to allocate income where it benefits them most, regardless of market signals. From his survey of the issues, Helleiner concludes that "there does seem to be a strong presumption that the developing countries do rather badly under the existing market system" (1979c, p. 383), and makes the challenge that: "those concerned with the development prospects of the world's poor nations should seek to identify and put the spotlight upon those particular market imperfections which are of greatest consequence to these prospects" (1979c, p. 364). Industry studies are perhaps the best way to take up Helleiner's challenge.

International Conduct and Concentration in Developing Countries

The stylized models of international oligopolistic rivalry presented above highlight one important debate about TNCs and market imperfections: As TNCs expand into the markets of developing countries, do they increase or decrease the level of competition and concentration in the host market?

There is ample evidence that the level of foreign investment is positively associated with the level of market concentration in developing countries. Fajnzylber and Martinez-Tarrago (1976, p. 180) showed that TNCs in Mexico in 1970 made 61 percent of their total sales in markets with four-firm concentration ratios of 50 or greater and less than 10 percent in markets with four-firm concentration ratios of less than 25; by comparison Mexican firms sold only 29 percent in the highly concentrated markets and 33 percent in low concentration industries. Newfarmer and Marsh (1981b), in their cross-sectional econometric study of Brazil's manufacturing sector, found a positive correlation between foreign ownership of an industry and industrial concentration. The measures for minimum efficient scale, industry advertising, and concentration in the U.S. also were positively related, controlling for other factors. Connor and Mueller (1977b) found in Brazil and Mexico that there was a strong positive relationship, after controlling for other factors, between market concentration and two other measures of market imperfection (product differentiation and relative market share) and the level of foreign ownership in industry. In addition, they found a strong direct correlation between the level of market concentration in Mexico, Brazil, and the U.S. Market concentration was found to be slightly lower in the U.S. than in either of the smaller markets of the two developing countries. Tironi (1978), using a much simpler model than Connor and Mueller, found in the Andean countries that "There is a positive association between the participation of foreign firms in an industry and its concentration . . . ." He reported that in Chile two-thirds of the industries dominated by foreign firms are among those where the top four firms control between 95 and 100 percent activity. Wilmore (1976) in Central America found that there is no simple correlation between concentration and foreign control. However, in the group of 22 industries where at least one of the leading firms is a foreign owner, the correlation did hold. He took this as an indication that an increase in foreign direct investment increases the extent of monopoly and lessens competition. Chudnovsky (1974), looking at the structure of Colombian industry, found that foreign-dominated industries have unusually high concentration ratios, ranging from 60 to 80 percent. In an econometric study of Malaysia, Lall (1979) found a strong association between foreign firms' share of the market and level of concentration, controlling for scale barriers, size, and other characteristics of firms and markets.

Yet the association of foreign investment with industrial concentration does not define clearly the direction of causality nor the direction of change between the two variables. Does foreign investment cause industrial concentration or is it attracted to concentrated markets? If TNCs cause concentration, they may decrease competition; if they are merely attracted to concentrated markets, they may increase competition. The issues are clouded by complexities of simultaneous changes in technology, scales, and market size. John Dunning (1975) suggested the structural effects of TNC entrance will occur in two conceptually distinct stages. The first effects are the direct, at-entry consequences of foreign investment on the number and size of distribution firms in the market, product and process technologies, and barriers to entry. The second, post-entry effects concern the reaction of other international rivals and the behavior of other foreign affiliates and other rivals in the domestic market.

At-Entry Effects on Structure. The initial impacts of the foreign entry depend on the existing structure of the industry and the mode of entry. If seller concentration is high, new foreign based entry can reduce concentration and disrupt local oligopolistic patterns (Reuber 1973, p. 1978). For new entry to reduce in seller concentration, entry must be *de novo* (via new plant construction) and must not displace producers in the market, either through acquisition or the creation of

33

excess industrial capacity, the cost of which established firms must shoulder.

Knicherbocker (1976) and Vernon (1977) presented some evidence that cross-penetrating investment behavior has increased the number of firms competing in Western Europe and the United States. They calculated the number of foreign subsidiaries established in foreign countries in three-digit industries in 1950, 1966, and 1970, and found that in every industry it has grown remarkably. They took this as an indication that market concentration had fallen and competition had increased. However, these calculations did not fully account for the effect of acquisitions at-entry; assuming that one-third of the new subsidiaries are established through takeovers, the final number of new competing subsidiaries should presumably be reduced by a comparable amount. Moreover, takeovers are most likely to occur in the more concentrated industries where barriers to entry are highest. Entry by acquisition severely reduces the destabilizing impact of new entry because continuity in local management is not broken, new capacity is not added to the industry, and changes in products and technologies are likely to be incremental if they occur at all.[6] At the heart of the Knicherbocker-Vernon argument is the idea that the market share of the leading established foreign and domestic firms should decline as a function of new, foreign-based entry. Yet Connor and Mueller (1977b) found that between 1966 and 1972 the average market share of U.S. subsidiaries in Brazil and Mexico did not decline; to the contrary, it increased slightly. This suggests that the bulk of new entry is either by acquisition, involves displacement of local business, or takes place in non-competing product lines.[7]

Acquisitions obviously cannot be a factor in new import-substitution industries where no local producers are present. After the first firm, any additional entry will reduce seller concentration, provided it is *de novo* and not via acquisition. Vernon (1977, pp. 89-95) has suggested the monopoly position of the initial TNC is likely to be eroded as market conditions become known and additional TNCs enter the market. Oligopolistic reaction among TNCs may accelerate the process, and national firms may even enter if barriers to entry fall. According to Vernon, the dynamics of the product cycle in conjunction with strong international rivalry and falling barriers to entry are likely to propel the market through a rapid transition from "monopoly to oligopoly to workable competition." In the process, domestic firms are predicted to eventually gain ascendance in the market.

The nature and degree of international oligopolistic rivalry is therefore a crucial determinant of the net impact on domestic industrial structure. In the case of oligopolistic reaction, new TNC entry

34

may reduce concentration, a tendency which is accentuated if firms from other countries join in the move to the developing country. The bandwagon effect inflates rates of entry beyond those expected by rates of return, and the low death rate of unprofitable subsidiaries keeps concentration low. In fact, if such non-price competition is strong, the number of subsidiaries high, and the scale barrier present, some TNCs may be forced to cross-subsidize losses while subsidiaries operate at less than minimum efficient scale and the industry experiences wasteful excess capacity. This case is most likely when perceived international interdependence limits price-competition, but non-price oligopolistic rivalry is vigorous and aggressive. The auto industry is the archetypical example, as studies by the Latin American Institute for Transnational Studies (ILET) have shown (Gonzales-Vigil et al., 1979).

However, this may be the rare industrial case rather than the rule. If international rivalry entails a heavy component of tacit collusion, spheres of influence and mutual forbearance, international interdependence does not necessarily produce entry beyond that which the market can bear or even beyond the profit maximization point. In fact, informal or formal market sharing arrangements may emerge which insure that orderly growth and investment occur and profits remain stable at high noncompetitive levels. This may be one of the reasons why Knicherbocker (1973) finds that his entry concentration index actually begins to decline after the level of market concentration reaches moderate levels.[8] In this case, new entry stops short of creating workable competitive markets and international oligopoly is entrenched in the local market.

Second-Stage, Post-Entry. Once in the market, TNCs' conduct may raise or lower market concentration over the medium- and long-term. Here again we encounter competing hypotheses: Vernon (1977) seems to suggest that market concentration is likely to fall because of the dynamics of the product cycle. As TNCs develop a product locally as well as technology, and supply and distribution channels, barriers preventing entry of other TNCs and national firms into the market fall. Eventually, the market becomes less concentrated and less foreign-dominated. Lall (1979) holds the opposite hypothesis. Transnational corporations may be expected to increase concentration because of their behavior. They introduce larger scale and more capital-intensive technology and produce a wider, more differentiated product mix; they have better access to financial, technical, and marketing resources; they have higher propensities to acquire domestic firms (perhaps because of their large capital pools); they may even prompt

35

"defensive" mergers among domestic firms struggling to survive. Defensive mergers in Western Europe have often enjoyed official government sponsorship in an attempt to create "national champions" (Vernon 1974b).

The empirical findings on the post-entry effects of new foreign investment for developing countries are limited indeed. Lall's (1979) conclusions for Malaysia, although based on cross-sectional data, are relevant:

> In general, the findings suggest that foreign investment serves to raise concentration over and above the level accounted for by other industrial variables [e.g., advertising, capital intensiveness, market size, and market growth]. However, it also serves to raise concentration via the industrial variables by raising capital-intensity and minimum capital requirements, and, rather less so, through local advertising (1979, p. 15).

A few studies contain findings that seem to support the notion that oligopolistic reaction leads to lower levels of concentration than those found at home. Evans' (1977a) study of the Brazilian pharmaceutical industry found entry beyond levels of market concentration in the U.S. Likewise, Fajnzylber and Martinez-Tarrago (1976) reached similar conclusions when comparing concentration ratios in Mexico, Brazil, and the U.S. Both studies conclude that oligopolistic reaction and "over entry" of TNCs explain the findings. While both of these studies are invaluable in other respects, this particular conclusion may be on tenuous ground. Given the difficulties of specifying the "relevant market" in the pharmaceutical industry, slight changes in industrial classifications will produce great variation in product concentration. In Brazil, the classification systems are broader, hence concentration appears to be less than it actually is. Maria da Conceicao Tavares (1978) also shows that plant concentration declined in Brazil from 1970 to 1973, attributable to new entry and rapid growth, though the exact role of TNCs is not clear.[9]

In sum, the relation of TNCs to the changing structure of domestic markets is clear on some points and less clear on others. First, it is clear that there is a strong correlation among the market structures of different nations. Concentrated markets in home countries tend to be concentrated abroad, suggesting a universality about open capitalist development (Connor and Mueller 1977b; Mellor 1978). Also, there seems to be no reason to reject Bain's (1966) conclusion, seconded by Scherer (1975), that smaller markets are likely to experience higher levels of concentration. Second, it is clear that foreign direct investment appears to bridge and link concentrated markets at home and in recipient economies. Several studies have shown a high correlation between foreign direct investment and differentiated, concentrated market structures of various nations. Third, the potentially socially beneficial effects of TNCs in reducing concentration through new entry are significantly watered down, perhaps even negated by take-overs of domestic firms at entry. Case study evidence does suggest that new entry has reduced concentration in very concentrated markets, though there is little evidence that new entry has gone beyond trans-forming near-monopolies into oligopolies. The exception to this may be differentiated industries with high scale barriers, such as autos, where oligopolists suffer short-term low profits or losses in a struggle for long-term control of the market. Finally, the long-term conse-quences of an increased foreign presence for concentration are least conclusive, though the balance of new evidence is shifting in favor of those who argue that foreign companies probably increase concentra-tion.

Market Structure-Conduct Hypotheses in the Host Country

In open capitalist economies, market determines the range of choices available to a firm in its short-run behavior. The single prod-uct firm in an atomistic, competitively structured market is disciplined by the market and *ceteris paribus* has little discretionary power over its short-term prices. The highly diversified firm selling in concentrated, high barrier-to-entry markets has considerably more latitude in behav-ior. The foreign subsidiary, because of its status in a transnational network, has even greater conduct options available to it. If subsidi-aries do behave differently because of their structural status as for-eign-owned, we can begin to test the impact of TNCs on the develop-ment process. Let us consider evidence on conduct options in five areas: advertising, acquisitions, technology, trade, and transfer pric-ing. We consider pricing behavior in a subsequent section.

Advertising and Product Differentiation. The level of product differ-entiation is exceptionally important because it is a variable of market structure independently affecting pricing behavior of a firm as well as a barrier to outside competition, influencing the long-term structure of the market. While the exact effects are a subject of considerable debate (Brozen 1974; Mann 1974; Ornstein 1977; Comanor and Wilson 1979), there is persuasive evidence in the U.S. that promo-tional efforts can be an important source of excess profits (Comanor and Wilson 1974), and a force promoting industrial concentration (Mueller and Rogers 1980). Yet, as James and Lister (1980) note, there

37

has been little research on advertising's effects on consumer demand, prices, and industrial structure in developing countries. In addition to these positive economic relationships, normative questions also arise: Should poor countries be spending huge amounts of social resources in differentiating near substitutes when resources are scarce? Does advertising transmit inappropriate values?

For developing countries, the effect of advertising on prices and profitability is only now being studied. (These studies are discussed at some length below; they generally show a positive relationship in developing countries similar to the developed countries.) The second impact of product differentiation on industrial structure has been virtually neglected, except for Lall's study of Malaysia (1979) and Newfarmer and Marsh's study of Brazil (1981b). Lall finds a positive relationship between level of advertising and industrial concentration, though it is not as strong an influence as other industrial variables— perhaps because of the heavy export component of Malaysian manufacturing. Newfarmer and Marsh (1981b) find a strong relationship between advertising in convenience goods and concentration in Brazil. Moreover, they find high correlations between U.S. and Brazilian levels of industry advertising, this suggests that TNCs are important agents transmitting product differentiation to Brazil.

Do TNCs significantly alter the advertising and promotional norms of an industry, and if so, in what direction? *A priori* one would expect that an increased foreign presence would bring with it an upsurge in product differentiation: One monopolistic advantage of TNCs is their marketing skills, often based on intensive advertising. Yet, most evidence on advertising and TNCs in developing countries does not measure the relative advertising propensity of TNCs. Often it is anecdotal and focuses on the "cultural imperialism" dimensions of advertising (Barnet and Muller 1974; Schiller 1971; Roncaglioli and Janus 1978). These studies commonly link the transnational influence to the spread of foreign advertising agencies such as J. W. Thompson, McCann-Ericson, etc. A recent study from the ILET shows the parallel expansion of transnational advertisers, foreign subsidiary advertising, and stories in local newspapers of Latin America adapted from the major transnational wire services (Roncaglioli and Janus 1978). In a slightly different vein, others who analyzed the advertising-sales ratio of a sample of developed and less developed countries found that the ratio was lower for developing countries but that the differences were much smaller than the disparity in per capita incomes. This suggests a North-South transmission effect. Useful as they are, these studies do not tell us whether TNCs advertise more or differently from their national counterparts or whether increases in foreign direct investment are associated with increases in promotional outlays of firms.

Some fragmentary evidence suggests TNCs might be linked to changes in advertising behavior. In Kenya, Green reported that TNCs sponsored 80 percent of radio ads in Swahili, 75 percent of all newspaper ads in Swahili and English, and controlled 45 percent of all ads placed (Helleiner 1975b, p. 174). Cross-sectional findings are reported for Brazil and Mexico (Connor and Mueller 1977), and Malaysia (Lall 1979), showing that the level of foreign ownership was positively associated with levels of industry advertising. Newfarmer and Marsh (1980), using the industry level selling expenditures as a proxy for product differentiation, found that TNCs were a principal determinant of the level of product differentiation in Brazil's 16 electrical subindustries. Only one study, that by Lall and Streeten (1977, pp. 112-113), found no difference in the behavior of TNCs and domestic firms in their advertising conduct in Columbia; their sample was "admittedly limited" and heavily centered in pharmaceuticals. However, these cross-sectional comparisons may be missing a dynamic relationship: As TNCs move into an industry they may raise the industry level of advertising and compel domestic producers to counter with increases in their own promotional expenditures. Consequently, while economic theory, casual observation, and a handful of studies point to TNCs as an important force promoting product differentiation, the question remains open for further research.

Acquisitions and Mergers. Acquisitions not only occur as a mode of entry into a market but can form part of a subsidiary's domestic expansion strategy. Takeovers of existing firms are among the most important determinants of industrial structure in developing countries, yet it has been the subject of surprisingly little research.

The most commonly cited statistics, from the Harvard Multinational Enterprise project, reveal the significance of the problem. One-third of subsidiaries in developing countries entered the parent system via acquisition. But this only provides a point of departure. The statistics do not reflect all mergers and corporate takeovers: If the parent forms a subsidiary and then the subsidiary acquires ten other firms and absorbs them into its own corporate identity, the ten acquisitions are usually not revealed in the statistics. More importantly, the data say nothing about the size of acquisitions. Finally, the data do not permit thorough analysis of the effects of takeovers on subsidiary growth, host country market structure, or subsequent firm conduct.

There are several separate issues involving foreign takeovers, most of which have not been investigated. First, why do acquisitions of

39

national firms by foreign firms take place? Volume of acquisitions at entry seem to be correlated with level of national income (Vaupel and Curhan 1973) this is to be expected because countries with large GNP have more domestic industry and hence more firms attractive to entering TNCs. Case studies of pharmaceuticals (Evans 1977a), autos (Jenkins 1977), and electrical machinery (Newfarmer 1978b) suggest that some blend of transnational market power, finance, and technology are involved. The financial and technological capacities of the transnational give them a decided market advantage, which explains the higher value TNCs often place on the acquired firm than its domestic owner. But the takeover may also reflect power in markets downstream or upstream from the acquired firm and/or the willingness to use it coercively. Also, many developing countries in Latin America are going through the transition from owner control to management control of corporate enterprise as founding fathers of national firms approach retirement. This transition took place in the U.S. from roughly 1910 to 1930 concomitantly with the rise of a large market in equities. In most developing countries today there are no viable national capital markets. TNCs wait in the wings with their huge pools of investable surplus and so the capital market is in effect "internationalized." The absence of an insulated domestic capital market usually prevents domestic management from assuming control of these corporations in transition.

A second related issue is the structural consequence of TNC acquisition activity. Two structural effects are important: possible increases in concentration and increases in denationalization. Evans (1977b) found that takeovers in Brazil's pharmaceutical industry accounted for a large share of the industry's denationalization during the 1960s, although concentration did not increase because of oligopolistic reaction. Newfarmer (1978b) measured the denationalization effect in Brazil's electrical industry and found that takeovers between 1960 and 1974 explained more than 90 percent of the increase in foreign ownership change; acquisitions also reduced actual or potential competition in several markets. Takeovers also accounted for 20 percent of the growth of U.S. manufacturing subsidiaries in Mexico from 1960 to 1972 and 24 percent in Brazil (Newfarmer and Mueller 1975, pp. 70, 123).

A third issue is the effect of the takeover on the acquired firm's subsequent performance, as measured in its technological progress, growth, and efficiency. Rosenthal's (1975) study of changes in Guatemala's industry is one of the few that attempts to trace the consequences of the takeover on the performance of the acquired firm after takeover. Although his sample is small his findings are

40

surprising: In one-half of the cases studied, the acquiring TNC made virtually no changes in technology, products, or management during the first three years of ownership. The acquired firms thus appear to be generally viable, profitable, and well-situated in markets. This is consistent with other findings for U.S. firms in Brazil and Mexico, showing that nearly three-quarters of the acquired firms between 1960 and 1972 were profitable prior to takeover (Newfarmer and Mueller 1975). Even so, further study is necessary to shed light on managerial, marketing, and technological changes associated with new foreign ownership. It would also be important to know what selling owners do with their financial, capital, and entrepreneurial skills after takeover.

Technology. The complex and hotly debated issues surrounding technology and the conduct of foreign versus domestic firms can be subdivided into three issue-areas: cost of technology, choice of technique, and dynamic implications of TNCs for technological dependence. We leave technological dependence in abeyance to consider subsequently as a performance variable, and discuss here cost and choice of technology.

The cost of imported technology is a classic example of the bilateral monopoly situation envisioned by Vaitsos (1974a). Transnational corporations control much of patented advance technology and host countries control the terms of its application in the host country. The relevant question for our purposes is whether transfer of technology through the TNC is the least-cost way of obtaining the most appropriate, highest quality international technology. One argument is that the legal captivity of the subsidiary reduces its bargaining power *vis-a-vis* the technology supplier, and the parent sets the price of its technology in view of its global strategic objectives which may or may not bear any relation to the marginal cost of the transfer. The independent firm or majority-owned local joint venture, on the other hand, can bargain more vigorously, play one oligopolistic seller off another, and secure the best deal for itself. There is some evidence that independent firms do pay less: Vaitsos (1974a) showed that royalty rates were larger for subsidiaries in Colombia than for independent firms. Shing Fung and Jose Cassiolato (1976) found this for a large sample of firms in Brazil as well. Katz (1973), while not making direct comparisons between TNCs and domestic firms, found that about half of the total bill for technology transfers was accounted for by two foreign-dominated industries, motor vehicles and pharmaceuticals in the early 1970s. Evidence on joint ventures is conflicting: Stopford and Wells (1972, pp. 121-122) and Lall (1971, pp. 93-95)

41

found that joint ventures paid more, presumably because TNCs use royalties to increase their share of profits at the expense of their local partners. Vaitsos (1974a) found joint ventures in Colombia paid less, presumably because local majority owners drive harder bargains with the TNC sellers of technology.

The complexity of the transfer process and the quality of what is being transferred makes it difficult to evaluate the costs of technology in different forms of ownership. Lynn Mytelka (1979) makes this point in her detailed study of the Andean Pact. It may be that know-how, trade secrets, and process as well as product technology are often transferred informally, especially when the costs of registering technology are high. In this case, the royalty payment may understate the value of technology actually transferred for TNCs while it fully reflects the value for domestic firms; it is thus conceivable that TNCs may transfer greater value at a lower reported cost. Much depends on the rate of technical change in the industry and the regulatory framework controlling the rate of payments on technology. If industrial growth is rapid and continuous, spurred by competition in the host country, market forces may compel TNCs to transfer technology at a low royalty rate; if the host government enacts legislation to prohibit royalty payments between related parties the cost of technology can be reduced, as the Brazilians have done with some success (Fung and Cassiolato (1976). Still, there may be positive external economies of learning that affect any monopolistic prices at intrafirm technology transfers; for example, national firms may learn from TNCs, and thus gain access to international technology that they would not have had otherwise (Katz 1976; Wils 1979). All factors considered, the logic of the bargaining situation and empirical findings so far suggest that independent firms are more assertive in their technology purchasing decisions—with greater net positive social benefits—but measurement problems and "nonquantifiables" abound so one leaves the issue far from certain.

Perhaps the area of greatest study of the effects of TNCs on development has been their choice of technology. Sanjaya Lall (1978) in his thorough review of TNCs and industrial structures in developing countries posed three questions related to the influence of TNCs on technological choice: (1) Are the technologies used by TNCs adaptable to the low-wage, labor-abundant condition of developing countries? (2) Do TNCs in fact adapt the technologies they transfer? and (3) Do TNCs adapt better or worse than local firms?

As to the first question, he concluded from his review of about 20 studies that technologies are somewhat flexible, although he expresses some doubt about the degree of flexibility once products, income distribution, and tastes are specified. He writes:

> . . . it does appear that efficient technologies may be fairly 'rigid' in a plausible range of economic conditions in LDCs. This rigidity applies especially to TNC technologies (since they tend to predominate in complex, continuous-process, capital-intensive, and modern industries) . . . (1978, p. 237).

Lall qualified this conclusion by saying that peripheral processes (handling, transport, storage, administration, etc.) may be amenable to substitution of labor for capital. Also, core processes may be adapted through greater machine speeds and more shifts, subcontracting, use of lower quality inputs, and in rapid change in techniques and models (1978, p. 238).

Lawrence White (1976) arrived at slightly more sanguine conclusions in his review of more than 50 studies. He concluded: "There do seem to be plenty of opportunities for more labor-intensive methods to be used" (1976, p. 20). He agreed with Lall that there is a strong link between product type and mix and technical choice and "there do seem to be opportunities for a more appropriate product mix." Although there is considerable divergence of opinion, Lall and White are joined by an impressive array of other economists who have reviewed parts or all of this voluminous literature, including Baer (1976) and Helleiner (1975b). Bruton's (1974) survey is the most optimistic as he proclaims: "Factor substitutability is alive and well in developing countries." Lawrence White expressed the majority opinion, however, in saying that "the ranges of choice are far from complete on both the production and product sides. The economist's smoothly curved production isoquant is rarely present" (1976, p. 20).

If there is some range for factor substitution—a range which becomes wider the less specific the quality and physical conditions defining the product—do TNCs adapt to situations of relatively cheap labor when they transfer technology to developing countries? Theory would suggest that TNCs' special monopolistic advantage are largely based on advanced technology and so it is predicted that they would not undertake major changes to serve the relatively small markets of developing countries. This may occur for two not mutually exclusive reasons even when relative factor prices are sharply different between home and host country: (1) The presumably heavy fixed costs of developing alternative technologies may not be compensated by the savings in marginal costs of productions in developing countries; and (2) imperfect product markets, often characteristic of TNC sales, allow the firm to pass on the higher costs of inappropriate technology to buyers of the product.

Lawrence White (1976) argues that there is some evidence that TNCs do adapt their subsidiaries' technology, but it is not because of simple differences in relative factor prices, a finding seconded by Baer (1976). Rather, TNCs must adapt to smaller scales of production and slightly different raw material inputs. A good example of such behavior is presented in Morley and Smith's (1977) case study of Brazil's machinery industry.

"Are TNCs less responsive to host country economic conditions than domestic firms?" is Lall's third question. Several studies have found that TNCs do employ less labor per unit of capital than domestic firms (Radhu 1973; Cohen 1975; Lall 1978; Wells 1973; Morley and Smith 1974). There are also a handful of studies which show the opposite to be true. Pack (1976), Strassman (1968), and others have found that managers of foreign subsidiaries are alert to ways to cut costs, especially in peripheral processes, and may react more readily to business conditions and adopt a more appropriate and profitable technique. Others find relatively few differences (Mason 1973; Wilmore 1976). Kenneth Flamm's (1979) study of three industries in Mexico is one of the most sophisticated econometric examinations, and he finds no differences in two of the three industries. White concluded in his review that "although the TNCs may not be the heroes of appropriate technology, they are far from the villains that many make them out to be" (1976, p. 18). Lall is agnostic: "The mass of conflicting evidence, the occasional use of imprecise methodology, the inherent problems of definition and measurement, all do not support any strong statement about the relative performance of TNCs and local firms" (1978, p. 241).

A central gap in this literature is some feeling for the dynamic process of technical change and the role of TNCs in pushing factor usage in one direction rather than another. Most studies of relative factor usages between ownership groups are cross-sectional, but TNCs may restructure techniques in an industry in a way not captured by these measures. Does the scale at which TNCs enter push producers in the market into larger size categories, reducing labor-capital ratios, a possibility raised in the important work of Maria da Conceicao Tavares (1978)? When TNCs enter a market with a differentiated product, does that product and its concomitant technology entail a new, more capital-intensive technology (as observed by Mytelka in the Andean Pact (1979)? Does it require a greater ratio of skilled to unskilled labor? One could imagine a circumstance in which evolving technological changes between countries might occur and entail productivity and efficiency gains that would translate into net social benefits overshadowing the loss of employment at the micro level. On the other hand, if such changes are simply part of what Jorge Katz (1973) calls "the product differentiation game" and if demand shifts reflect responses to increasing advertising outlays, one could easily envisage net social losses in conjunction with employment losses. Thorough case studies of the sort White (1981) undertook for joint ventures in Argentina are required—that is, ones that examine the dynamic changes in technology associated with, and attributable to, TNC market penetration. Fertile areas to explore include the effects of changing scale and introducing new differentiated products with different employment structures.

Trade. Besides technology, the most important ties in the world network of subsidiaries are through trade. These ties have implications for a country's foreign exchange, balance of payments position, and its national income. The spread of TNCs into a local economy may change the trading behavior of firms in an industry and consequently the industry's import and export performance.

The dynamics of import substitution industrialization and the product cycle suggest that TNCs will have a higher import coefficient than domestic firms, even when product mix and input prices are held constant. TNCs open manufacturing operations in the wake of exporting into a foreign market. It is customary for TNCs to initiate local production with the assembly of imported components and then gradually to shift to local parts as relative costs and host government policy dictate. Similarly, as each new product is developed in the home country of a TNC, it usually goes through an export phase to the foreign economy, eventually to be produced locally with imported parts and components. Parents profit from the export of parts to the captive subsidiary. Production at home often entails cost advantages due to economies of scale; it facilitates accruing profits at home; and exports please home country governments worried about trade deficits as well as unions worried about jobs. Domestic firms may commence production through assembly, but are less likely to be tied to one overseas supplier; they probably will search more vigorously for reliable local suppliers. In contrast to TNCs, domestic firms have an interest in backwards domestic vertical integration and in generating local suppliers, even if it means producing a product of slightly different quality. By producing parts they had previously imported, domestic firms can capture suppliers' profits; by encouraging local suppliers they may improve their reliability of supply and reduce their fears of foreclosure from imported parts. These differing attitudes are most likely to be present when local costs of production approximate costs in developed countries. On the other hand, if wide cost differences persist in parts production, local producers may join foreign producers in bitterly opposing domestic vertical integration, much as Hirschman (1968) pointed out more than a decade ago. Much depends on the stage of industrialization and industrialization strategies.

These dynamics apparently lead to higher import propensities for foreign subsidiaries than for domestic firms, even when industry, firm size, and product mix are held constant. Using a variety of methodologies, such findings are reported for Canada (Safarian 1966), Korea (Cohen 1973), Costa Rica (Wilmore 1976, although the differences in import propensities were not statistically significant), Peru (Vaitsos 1976), Taiwan (Riedel 1975), India (Subrahamanian and Pillai 1977), Mexico (Jenkins 1977), and Brazil (Fajnzylber 1970).

Fewer studies have reported no significant differences in import propensities. These include Lall and Streeten (1977) for a sample drawn from India, Kenya, Jamaica, Iran, Colombia, and Malaysia, as well as Reuber (1973) for a sample from Indonesia, and Cohen (1975) for Singapore. Only in Taiwan are foreign firms reported to have a lower import propensity than domestically controlled firms (Cohen 1975); yet there is reason to doubt this finding: Cohen's sample is small (19 foreign and 5 local firms) and it conflicts with Riedel's study for Taiwan based on a larger sample. In sum, the balance of evidence suggests TNCs do have a greater import propensity, though in some cases the differences may be minimal.

Cohen's (1975) study of three Asian nations traces the purchasing behavior of firms yet further. Domestic firms tended to buy more from other local firms than do TNCs and they had a higher ratio of value added to sales than TNCs. This suggests a stronger overall linkage and income effect for their behavior.

On the other side of the trade balance—exports of manufactures—TNCs do not seem to be the superior performers that Helleiner (1973) and others had hoped they would become. In fact, studies of the export behavior of TNCs and domestic firms surprisingly reveal domestic firms have a higher export propensity in samples from several countries: Brazil, Argentina, Mexico, Columbia, Peru, Venezuela (Vaitsos 1978), Taiwan (Cohen 1975), Jamaica, Kenya, Iran, Colombia, Malaysia, India (Lall and Stretten 1977), and Mexico (Fajnzylber and Martinez-Tarrago 1976). Nayyar (1978) concluded that the share of manufactured exports of U.S. subsidiaries from all developing countries has fallen from nearly 20 percent in

1966 to about 9 percent in 1974, though it was not clear if domestic firms or other TNCs have made up the difference.

Much of the behavioral difference in exporting may be due to industrial location: Jenkins' (1979) study for Mexico distinguishes among industries (omitting the border industries) and found that TNCs performed less well in traditional industries—textiles, beverages, etc.—and better in engineering industries, including transportation and machinery. One reason that TNCs have done well in these industries is that the Mexican government has put strong pressure on these TNCs to export, often holding their imports hostage, as Bennett and Sharpe (1979a and b) recounted in their case studies of auto exports from Mexico.

There are some exceptions to the findings that domestic firms have a higher export propensity than foreign firms. Cohen (1975) and Jo (1976) both found that in Korea TNCs exported notably more than their local counterparts, though when the effects of industrial location were taken into account the differences narrowed. This was attributed, in part, to generous tax incentive schemes, profit repatriation rules, and import licensing. Two studies for Central America (Wilmore 1976; Rosenthal 1975) found that TNCs exported slightly more than domestic firms. These firms generally exported to neighboring regional markets.

One frequently cited study on the behavior of U.S. firms is that by Herbert May (1970). He found that U.S. subsidiaries increased their exports from 25 percent of Latin America's total manufactured exports in 1957 to 41.4 percent in 1966. Unfortunately, May neglected to correct for differences in U.S. and U.N. industrial classification codes; since data from the U.S. include food processing which the U.N. system does not, his results were overstated. Omitting food processing, the actual U.S. share of Latin America's manufactured exports fell substantially to less than 25 percent. Nayyar (1978) re-estimated the universe to solve this problem and concludes that the 1966 figure of 37 percent was a peak year, after which the U.S. share fell to below 20 percent by 1974.

In sum, the differences in average export behavior at the firm level within an industry are minimal, but because domestically-led industries tend to export more, their total average export ratios are often higher. The advantage of domestic firms mainly resides in more traditional industries. Often these industries find outlets to major distributors such as Sears or Penney's in the U.S., which are willing to experiment with low-price imports (Cohen 1975). However, exports from domestic firms may spill over into more sophisticated industries, as Ablin (1979) showed for engineering exports from Argentina, though the situations where this has occurred have been limited to the more advanced development countries. Helleiner's survey is perhaps the most comprehensive attempt to assess the impact of TNCs' export activities and their effects on national income and employment. He concludes: "Other things being equal, more arms-length and more diversified relations are generally likely to be in the exporting countries' interest" (1976, p. 220).

Transfer pricing. One form of firm conduct related solely to TNCs is the manipulation of prices on international non-market transactions among affiliates in the parent organization. Since the sale of a good or a service from one affiliate to another is not subject to the discipline of the market, the appropriate authority in the corporate hierarchy is free to set prices at the most advantageous level for maximizing corporate profits, subject to effective constraints imposed by governments. Vaitsos (1974a), Lall (1973 and 1977), Robbins and Stobaugh (1973), and Horst (1971) elaborated several reasons why TNCs might find it advantageous to manipulate transfer prices by overpricing imports to host countries or underpricing exports: to avoid controls on profit repatriation, on royalties payments and on local prices (because inflated import prices show up as higher costs), or to circumvent local tax rules, tariffs, or exchange rate controls. Most writers would agree with Lall (1973) and Vaitsos (1974a) that transfer pricing is systematically biased against developing countries because of the desire to accumulate most earnings at home. The bias is accentuated because taxes in developing countries are often higher, import duties on intermediate goods lower, currencies are less stable, and controls on profit remittances more stringent (Lall 1973, p. 179).

Transfer pricing is an option open to TNCs because of the intra-firm character of international trade. Three comprehensive studies have reviewed government sources and independent findings to assess the magnitude of intrafirm trade as a percent of world trade and trade to and from individual countries (UNCTAD 1978; Helleiner 1979a; Murray 1979). The data are far from complete, but the consensus is that from 20 to 40 percent of world trade in manufactures is intrafirm trade outside the discipline of the market. For individual countries and industries the figure is frequently higher. The U.S. Department of Commerce 1970 survey, for example, indicates that 40 percent of U.S. imports were subsidiary to parent sales. Helleiner and Lavergne's (1979) econometric analysis showed that intrafirm trade of the U.S. was highly correlated with firm size and R&D efforts.

48

Whatever the exact magnitude, TNC managers clearly have discretionary control over the prices of billions of dollars of international trade. Robbins and Stobaugh estimated that a 10 percent change in intrafirm sales of U.S. TNCs in 1972 "would substantially exceed all payments of royalties and management fees and would approximate the size of dividend payments" (1973, p. 92). They constructed a simulation model that showed that replacing arms-length pricing with an "optimal" transfer pricing strategy can increase profits by as much as 15 percent in their illustrative model (1973, p. 165). Their interviews of several companies, however, suggested that managers of large TNCs have not taken full advantage of transfer prices, though medium size companies tended to be more aggresive in seeking profits from transfer pricing.

The most comprehensive empirical study of transfer prices is still Constantine Vaitsos' seminal work *Intercountry Income Distribution and Transnational Enterprises* (1974a). By comparing prices of imports with estimates of arms-length world prices, he found that overpricing of intrafirm exports to affiliates ranged between 16 and 155 percent in four industries of Colombia in the 1960s. Few studies have added further empirical data of this scope, largely because of the difficulty in securing information. Lall (1973) provided some additional information for the pharmaceutical industry, finding extensive overpricing on U.K. TNCs' sales to affiliates. The Monopolies Commission indicted Hoffman La Roche of Switzerland for overpricing its intrafirm sales to its affiliates in the U.K. and ordered it to reduce prices by an average of 30 percent or greater (Monopolies Commission 1973). Business International (1973) reported that the U.S. Internal Revenue Service examined prices on intrafirm trade of 700 firms and ordered the reallocation of earnings back to the U.S. in over 400 cases. Because the IRS is concerned only with U.S. tax revenue, it does not compel reallocation of profits to other countries.

Most recently, Roumeliotis and Golemis (1978) reported on efforts of the Greek government to scrutinize transfer prices. They found foreign subsidiaries on average paid 20 percent higher than the world market price in their sample of metallurgical imports and 25.7 percent for chemical imports. Furthermore, they found that exports of "three very important products" of subsidiaries were sold to affiliates abroad for 8 to 17 percent below the world market price. Using low prices on exports to shift earnings abroad was taken to be the cause of findings reported earlier in Muller and Morgenstern's (1974) study of TNC intrafirm exports from Argentina.

With the increasing importance of overseas banking, the possibility arises that financial corporations may engage in transfer pricing on foreign exchange transactions, accentuating the difficulty of controlling non-market financial transactions. *The New York Times,* for example, reported that the enforcement staff of the Security and Exchange Commission after a three year investigation concluded that Citicorp "had directed a scheme for seven years that had circumvented and at one time violated other countries' tax and currency laws." Between 1973 and 1980, "at least $46 million in profits . . . had been improperly shifted from the bank's branches in Europe, where taxes are high, to other branches in the Bahamas, where taxes on profits are much lower." The practices were not limited to Europe. In October 1979 Citibank's comptroller reported to the audit committee of the bank's board of directors that transfer prices—called "off-market rates"—were used in foreign exchange transactions in Japan, Hong Kong, the Philippines, Malaysia, Indonesia, India, and Saudia Arabia. Citicorp does not deny the facts or evidence in the case, according to the *Times,* though it maintains its transactions were "basically proper" (February 18, 1982).

The evidence from these studies and others is summarized succinctly in the UNCTAD 1978 report, written by Emil Herbolzheimer and Colin Greenhill. Robbin Murray (1979) also summarizes the literature and elaborates on the theoretical importance of transfer pricing for the political economies of developing countries; furthermore, his 1981 edition contains an impressive number of useful studies on the growth of intrafirm trade. Hansen (1975) adds a helpful discussion on policies, both for host countries and home countries. Helleiner (1978a and b) presents additional evidence on the extent of intrafirm trade and considers the methodological problems of studying transfer pricing. These studies, despite their necessary fragmentary character, demonstrate the uniqueness of the TNC in being able to take advantage of this structural arrangement. They also indicate the serious magnitude of income losses to developing countries potentially stemming from transfer pricing.

Structure-Conduct-Performance Hypotheses

The studies discussed thus far make it clear that the international organization of and rivalry within an industry have important consequences for the market structure in developing countries. Likewise, the imperfect structure of the local market, including "foreignness," facilitates a variety of behavioral options not open to the single-market firm competing against a large number of sellers. It follows that transnational influence on market structure and conduct should be reflected in firm and industrial performance.[10]

It should be acknowledged that the line between conduct and performance is at best fuzzy; differences in firm conduct in trade, for example, affect the industry's import or export performance and technical choice affects industrial employment. Since some of these areas of firm performance have just been discussed, we will confine the discussion in this section to three areas: profitability, growth, and technological dependence.

Profitability. In an economy unfettered by oligopolistic restrictions on output and other manifestations of market power, profit rates across several industries should fall to some equilibrium rate reflecting the marginal efficiency of capital. In the presence of market imperfections, however, high profits often do not attract new entry because barriers prevent new competition and expanded output. High persistent profits can be taken as an indicator of monopoly power and inefficiency.

Nathaniel Leff (1979) outlined in some detail the importance of this basic concern of industrial organization for development. Concentration facilitates oligopolistic pricing strategies to secure higher-than-average rates of return. This causes some misallocation of productive resources as society exhibits a demand for more of a product than firms employ resources to produce. By pricing in excess of long-run average cost, power wielding firms redistribute income from consumers to themselves through excess profits, in most cases aggravating distributional inequities. Finally, there is some loss in social welfare through underproduction. In addition to Leff's concerns, another problem arises when the firms in the market are transnational. Oligopolists which are transnational in exercising their market power can redistribute income from consumers and workers in developing countries to owners (and managers) of capital in developed countries.

Still, these relationships cannot be put forward without some qualification, especially in the context of developing countries. Demsetz (1973a and 1973b), for example, has argued that positive associations between concentration and profitability are an indicator of efficiency rather than monopoly power because scale economies permit the largest firms to have the lowest costs. A second argument is that the monopoly price may be lower than a competitive price when markets are so small they permit only one or two optimally sized firms. A third argument, is that concentration gives rise to greater R&D efforts which produce lower costs through new production technol-

51

ogy. While these arguments have been rebutted or modified for the developed economies (Greer 1980; Scherer 1980), studies of developing economies have not so far tried to separate out these three counter-arguments to the concentration-profits relationship. An exception is Newfarmer and Marsh's (1981b) study of Brazilian manufacturing.

Profitability is important in a second sense, one not usually a concern for traditional industrial organization. If foreign companies do grow differently from their domestic counterparts, then excess profits attributable to market power provide an important source of funds for that expansion. Not only the excess profits but the entire amount of funds generated for reinvestment can be reinvested along this "different" growth path. Excess profits enhance the influence of powerful firms in the process of growth.

While many studies present evidence about the relationship between imperfect market structures and profitability in developed countries (Weiss 1974), only a handful of studies exist for developing countries. These include House on Kenya (1973 and 1976), White on Pakistan (1974), Sawhney and Sawhney on India (1973 and 1976), Amjad on Pakistan (1977), Nam for Korea (1975), Fajnzylber and Martinez-Tarrago for Mexico (1976), Gan and Tham on Malaysia (1977), Connor and Mueller on Brazil and Mexico (1977), Gupta on India (1968), Lall and Streeten for Colombia and India (1977), and Newfarmer and Marsh for Brazil (1981b). All but one of the econometric studies (Gan and Tham's) show a significant and positive relationship between market concentration and measures for profitability. In addition, Connor and Mueller (1977a) and Lall and Streeten (1977) find that measures for product differentiation are positively associated with profitability. Connor and Mueller also report positive findings for the effects of a firm's relative market share; the greater the relative market share (taking the weighted average of all product lines), the greater on average the firm's profits. Newfarmer and Marsh (1981b) find similar results in their study of all Brazilian manufacturing industries during the 1970s. Concentration, relative market share, and to a lesser extent industrial advertising are strongly associated with increases in profitability. Moreover, their tests suggest that, contrary to the Demsetz (1973a and b) argument, concentration does appear to be a force for inefficiency.

Studies comparing the rates of profitability of TNCs and domestic firms are few in number and contradictory in results. Reuber (1973) found slightly higher rates of profitability for TNCs than domestic firms and takes this as an indication of superior efficiency, though he did not control for domestic market structure. Fajnzylber

52

and Martinez-Tarrago, cross-tabulating industry level data, found that industrial profitability was markedly higher in industries with 75 percent of sales or more controlled by TNCs; some of this was due to the effect of concentration, since most of sales in foreign-dominated industries were also in highly concentrated, highly profitable industries (1976, p. 238). Lall and Streeten (1977), in their sample of Colombian and Indian firms, found no significant differences in profitability, though their data were limited and did not include complete structural measures. Newfarmer and Marsh (1981a) presented 1972 and 1974 data for Brazil's electrical industry showing higher rates of profitability for domestic firms than for foreign subsidiaries after controlling for measures of imperfect market structures which are also positive and significant. In a more sophisticated follow-up study (1981b) they report similar findings for all of Brazilian manufacturing for the period 1971 to 1978. The authors suggested that this may be due to superior efficiency of domestic firms or because of unreported profits of TNCs taken abroad through transfer pricing, or perhaps some combination of the two. In both studies, industrial concentration and product differentiation were positively associated with high profitability for both TNCs and domestic firms.

The relative rates of profitability between the transnational and the domestic sectors are important because they are indicators of control of surplus flows within the economy. Because of the affinity of TNCs for concentrated markets, it is arguable that their market power facilitates capture of greater segments of investment funds than their share of manufacturing assets alone warrants. Controlling a disproportionate share of surplus magnifies the impact of their behavioral decision in profit remittances, choice of technology, trade, and advertising. In short, their use of funds garnered from application of their market power accentuates their influence on development processes exacerbating international income inequities when they repatriate excess profits or altering industrial development by reinvesting them locally.

One consequence of noncompetitive profits in the global organization is that TNCs tend to link the business cycle in developing countries more closely to their own fate in the home country. For example, when recession brings a decline in profits in the home country, parents may repatriate cash from subsidiaries to maintain profits and dividend records at home. These funds would often otherwise be used to expand production in new countries, and so growth abroad is curtailed. Writing of the 1980 recession, *Business Week* discussed the problem:

So far, multinationals have squeezed their subsidiaries only to the point of bringing home a few billion dollars, but an avalanche of money is just waiting to come crashing back to parental headquarters . . . multinationals are poised to squeeze an enormous sum of money out of their overseas subsidiaries in a determined attempt to get the cash to make it through the recession (March 31, 1980, p. 83).

Funds were being shifted in several ways: transfer pricing, higher royalties, lead-lag billing, higher management and engineering fees, and borrowing from local capital markets. This point has not been treated systematically in the literature.

TNCs and Growth in National Income. There have been few comprehensive and adequate studies of the contribution of TNCs to growth using an industrial organization approach. Such an approach would have to control for acquisition effects and market structural changes, and distinguish the effects of foreign firms from domestic firms. There are good reasons for this lacunae. A proper evaluation must make counterfactual assumptions in response to key questions: Would investment have been forthcoming from other sectors had TNCs not undertaken it? Would it have been less or more efficient? Would growth have taken the same "path", as measured in product design, technology, etc.? In our opinion, the most promising evaluation— albeit partially qualitative—of TNCs' role in promoting or impeding growth of whatever form can best be undertaken through case studies of industries. The research can make more realistic counterfactual assumptions, understand the importance of intervening variables, for example, acquisitions, and capture the qualitative essense of the growth process. Nonetheless, let us step outside the industrial organization framework and consider one other approach, the social cost-benefit approach.[11]

Lall and Streeten's (1977) study is the most comprehensive. These authors use firm-level data to calculate the "social income effects" of TNCs, using three cost-benefit procedures (the Little-Mirrlees, financial replacement, and most likely local replacement models). The exercise requires considerable firm-level data. It also requires risky assumptions about shadow prices for non-tradables, weighting for benefits accruing to different income groups, and the extent to which domestic control can be substituted for foreign control. Conscious of these methodological limitations,[12] Lall and Streeten concluded that some 40 percent of foreign investments had net negative effects on social income in the host country. But this outcome was not because the firms were transnational *per se*; the main determinant was the extent of effective protection. State policy was then a principal factor in income losses by this measure. The purely financial contribution of foreign capital was, over a reasonable range of the opportunity cost for local capital, negligible or negative; that is, when technology, capital, and other factors could be obtained separately, it would have been cheaper for the countries concerned to buy out the foreign investments. They estimate that local capital could replace, either wholly or in part, nearly 80 percent of investment projects (Lall and Streeten 1977, pp. 182, 183).

Technological Dependence.[13] Dependency theorists, such as Teotonio dos Santos (1970) and Osvaldo Sunkel (1970), have recognized the fundamental importance of technological dependence, a concern usually not shared by orthodox economists. Technological dependence, as Furtado (1970) uses the term, refers to the continued inability of a developing country to "independently" generate the invention and innovation necessary to propel self-sustaining growth. There are two conceptually separable issues here. First, if a country does not produce its own technology and create a comparative advantage technologically in at least some industries, it probably will suffer slower growth and more disadvantageous terms of trade in the long run. Technological prowess is often the secret to secure shares in fast growing export markets and to some international market power. Thus, prolonged technological dependence probably entails a continuing cost to developing countries in the form of higher prices for imports (Greer 1979) and lower prices for exports. The second issue involves the vulnerability of the national economy to external decisionmakers and market forces; it is the issue of sovereign control over growth and accumulation in the host economy. Although many orthodox economists have dismissed this concern, few developed countries have failed to recognize the importance of technological sovereignty. Japan, for example, although encouraging technological imports, disallowed foreign ownership and control of production, insisting on technological independence (Caves and Uekusa 1976; Tsurumi 1976). Canada is a country with extensive reliance on TNCs and it has vigorously worked to overcome the absence of nationally controlled technology. A country may choose not to reinvent every process or product, but its bargaining power is increased if it can threaten to do so. Developing countries have recognized since the Great Depression and World War II that the inability to produce local technology can hamper economic growth itself.

The insights of Magee (1977) are particularly germane to the argument that TNCs will probably prolong technological dependence and behave differently in their approach to local knowledge creation. Magee asserts that TNCs create "information" with the hope of appropriating some portion of the prospective monopoly rent associated with the application of the patented information in production and marketing. Since patent protection is imperfect, TNCs are predicted to develop technology for markets where barriers to entry supplement patent protection. They may also strive to raise barriers to entry to assure appropriability of monopoly rents, including such activity as licensing restrictions, centralization of R&D, product differentiation, and so forth. It follows from Magee's argument that TNCs will transfer technology to developing countries only within those institutional frameworks that maximize "appropriable" rents (most often the wholly-owned subsidiary) and when business conditions make such a transfer the most profitable, usually in response to tariffs, government demands, or threats to the local markets formerly served by exports. It also follows that TNCs will generally prefer to control tightly research and development activities, the source of new information, in the home country. Centralization of the R&D activities of the global company conflicts directly with the interests of developing countries in domestic technological "parity" or interdependence.

Does experience confirm the hypothesis that independent domestic firms are more likely to invest in local research and development than TNC subsidiaries? First at a general level, the history of technological progress in Japan is relevant. After World War II, the Japanese continued their policy of not permitting foreign direct investment but of spending liberally for imported licensed technology (Tsurumi 1976). Their purchases of technology from abroad were considerable, yet at the same time they spent more than four times that amount on domestic R&D. Within the relatively short period of two decades they transformed themselves into aggressive world leaders in many industries. It is arguable that this would not have occurred had U.S. and European TNCs been allowed to control technology-intensive industries in Japanese manufacturing. Second, studies of subsidiary behavior in developing countries tend to confirm the proposition that TNCs would rather not invest heavily in local R&D. Jorge Katz (1973) found that local expenditures on R&D in Argentine manufacturing, where foreign investment is prevalent, are about one-twentieth of the expenditures on imported technology and are only about one-fifth of U.S. research and development investments on sales. Moreover, much of the local expenditure is devoted to product differentiation, such as researching consumer tastes and redesigning products accordingly. Perhaps for this reason and the fact that payments for technology are often used to transfer profits abroad, Katz found no statistical association between unit royalties paid abroad and technological progress (1973, p. 216).

A more important consequence of the absence of independent locally controlled R&D in developing countries and reliance instead on TNCs follows from Magee's logic: R&D will not be channelled into technologies that are socially efficient and advantageous to developing countries. Francis Stewart (1972) has argued eloquently that new products based on labor intensive techniques and directed at the mass markets of developing countries will not be developed if R&D is confined to the stewardship of TNCs. White (1976) in his review seemed to agree, though he cited studies that show some innovation was occurring in developing countries, largely under the auspices of government institutes, universities and other public agencies.

All in all, technological dependence involves tangible social costs in the long run. Theory and empirical research both seem to indicate that transnational corporate structure tends to institutionalize technological dependence of developing countries on developed countries even while know-how, skills, and technology flow to poor countries. There are policies that can reduce technological dependence, as the Japanese example clearly indicates. These include: national programs aimed at fomenting local innovation, public support for national enterprise, hard bargaining with TNCs, and revision of patent policies (Vaitsos 1976b; Penrose 1973; Greer 1973).

SUMMARY

The industrial organization model facilitates drawing together areas of consensus and controversy about the linkages between industrial organization in the industrialized countries and industrial structure and performance in developing countries. First, theory and evidence strongly support the idea that foreign investment arises out of market imperfections in home markets and in international trade. Transnational corporations investing abroad in manufacturing tend to grow out of differentiated oligopoly while those investing in primary resources tend to grow out of undifferentiated oligopoly. Second, TNCs in their export sales are part of an international market system that is probably biased in favor of the gains from trade being accumulated in the developed countries. We find Helleiner's (1979) argument persuasive in this regard, though undoubtedly there are many who would disagree. Third, the "feedback effects" of foreign

57

investment activity onto industrial structure in the home countries are particularly controversial. Those who argue that foreign investment increases competition in home markets may well be right for many industries, but they have often failed to distinguish between price and non-price competition, with their quite different implications for consumer welfare. More importantly, available trends in market concentration and aggregate concentration in the industrialized countries suggest that foreign investment activity has not caused, on balance, a decline in domestic or global industrial concentration. Fourth, there is a clear link between foreign investment and noncompetitive industrial structure in developing countries. Market structures tend to be highly correlated throughout the capitalist world and TNCs tend to bridge differentiated oligopolies in several national markets. Whether TNCs actually cause increases in concentration, barriers to entry, and product differentiation or are attracted to highly concentrated markets is still open to dispute. Fifth, the hypothesis that "foreignness" is a market structural variable with an independent influence on firm behavior and performance received considerable support from this review. The evidence supports—though with varying degrees of persuasiveness—the idea that TNCs behave differently from domestic firms in their acquisition, advertising, technological, trade, and trade pricing activities. Each of these areas has implications for industrial performance. Sixth, local market structure does appear to be related to profitability, growth, and technological dependence, but evidence was not always consistent on the role of TNCs. Reported profitability does appear to be highly correlated with measures of market imperfections, including concentration, product differentiation, and, less consistently, barriers to entry. Since TNCs are situated in these markets more often than their domestic counterparts, their share of local excess profits is relatively high, transferring locally generated surplus to their control. On the other hand, evidence concerning the reported profitability of firms suggests that TNCs *per se* are not necessarily more profitable than domestic firms, once market structure is taken into account. This finding might not hold if profits repatriated through transfer prices were visible. The evidence on TNCs' role in promoting growth is far less convincing, partly because of methodological difficulties, though what evidence there is suggests a lesser contribution to growth than early neoclassical economists claimed and a somewhat greater contribution than early dependency theorists acknowledged. Finally, there is some strong theoretical and empirical evidence to suppose that TNCs may prolong technological dependence by institutionalizing it in an international corporate organization in which R&D activities are highly centralized in the home country.

Putting these links together, we see strong evidence that the international organization of production—including how an industry is structured in the developed countries, how transnational oligopolists compete with each other, and how home governments affect the dynamics of an industry—has a measurable and rather direct effect on industrial structure and performance in developing countries. This conclusion, however, cannot be left to rest on the limited aggregation of several micro-studies alone. At each stage of analysis, the cross-sectional studies rarely capture the larger backdrop of TNC behavior as well as a sense of TNC interactions with other economic agents in a constantly moving system. International industrial case studies can address both concerns. Richard Caves (1974a) issued the research challenge in these words:

> . . . these extensions of the framework of industrial organization open major opportunities for that homely technique—the industry study. Easily spurned by sophisticated computer buffs, . . . it is not likely that we can uncover the long run effect of the multinational corporation on entry barriers and seller concentration, its impacts on price and product competition, or its innovative performance except through the patient assembly of information on individual industries over time . . . One hopes that the necessary skills have not become entirely passe among economists: a flexible command of simple theoretical tools; foreign languages; and a willingness to grub for obscure and diffuse kinds of information (1974a, pp. 142, 143).

Notes

[1] In making the comparison with domestic firms, we are interested in foreign control of strategic decisions, e.g., investment levels, profit repatriation, technology, output levels, exports, personnel, etc. This is because foreign control indicates decisions are made on the basis of multimarket even global perspectives in contrast to the purely national firm, which makes its decisions on the basis of local prices and other business conditions. Thus, when we use the term TNCs, we mean a transnationally controlled firm, though each study uses a different measure of firms nationality.

Usually, equity participation, especially majority participation, is sufficient to insure control of strategic decisionmaking within the subsidiary. However, there are some cases when foreign firms are sufficiently decentralized that for all intents and purposes one would expect them to behave with only the national market in view. On the other hand, there are some cases when only minority equity participation is sufficient to guarantee control or where a management contract is sufficient to provide control. The complexities of this relationship discussed at length in Louis W. Goodman's (1981) excellent discussion on centralization and decisionmaking and Brooke and Remmer's (1973) extensive study on subsidiary-parent relationships. For an illustration of the importance and difficulties of this problem, Eduardo White's (1981) paper presents carefully done case studies examining the effects of ownership on technology absorptions in different joint venture arrangements. At a broader level, Caves' (1980) survey of the effects and causes of firms' strategic and organizational structures upon market structure can, by extrapolation, offer insight into the complexities of the relation.

[2] Some setbacks are not so short-term; see Girvan's (1976) discussion of the developments in Jamaican bauxite production.

[3] Vernon's (1966) product cycle theory is an important contribution to this theoretical school and is summarized in part in the following section.

Magee's (1977) argument is also relevant and is partially summarized in the last section of this paper on technological dependence. Both Vernon and Magee allow for such interdependence but place the notion of monopolistic advantage of TNCs rather than oligopolistic interdependence at the center of their arguments.

[4] In the U.S., the 200 largest manufacturers have increased their share of manufacturing assets from 45 percent in 1947 to over 66 percent by the mid-1970s. This view of concentration in the U.S., however, is not held by all. L. White (1981) finds that aggregate concentration in U.S. manufacturing has held about stable since 1960, though he notes the effects of the merger wave of the late 1970s may change this. In Japan, the largest 100 firms increased their share of all corporate capital from 35.4 percent in 1958 to 39.4 percent in 1963, though more recent data are not available (Caves and Uekusa 1976, p. 17). In Britain, the 100 largest firms increased their share of industrial net assess from 46.5 percent to 63.7 percent between 1948 and 1968. In Western Europe, the share of the largest 50 firms in gross output of extractive and manufacturing industries rose from 35.1 percent in 1960 to 45.7 percent in 1970 (Jacquemin and de Jong 1977, p. 104).

[5] Substantially more increases than decreases in concentration occurred in markets of Canada, Germany, Japan, and the U.K. In France, the arithmetic mean concentration ratio for a sample of 48 industries showed an absolute increase of 4.2 percent from 1961 - 1969 (OECD 1979).

[6] The Knicherbocker-Vernon calculation has other weaknesses: Newly established subsidiaries may displace local business even without takeovers by inducing aggressive short-term competition. Also, the measure gives no assurance that the newly established subsidiaries are actually competing with each other since the three-digit category includes a plethora of non-competing product groups.

[7] Evidence suggests that acquisitions at entry do mitigate any reduction in seller concentration attributable to TNC entry, although the relation between foreign entry, acquisitions, and changing market concentration has not been studied systematically for developing countries. Vernon found that by the end of the 1960s, 35.3 percent of 3,666 subsidiaries for which entry information was available in developing countries had been set up by acquisitions rather than by new investments (Vernon 1977, p. 72). Independent reports for individual countries, such as Brazil and Mexico (Newfarmer and Mueller 1975), Colombia and Peru (Vaitsos 1974, p. 342), and Guatemala (Wilmore 1977), confirm that acquisitions range from 30 percent to 70 percent of new entries, depending on the country and time period. The pace of acquisition activity as a common form of new entry appears to be increasing in many countries, such as Brazil (Newfarmer and Mueller 1975), although global data on takeovers at entry only for developing countries suggest a leveling off or even decline (UN 1978).

[8] Knicherbocker finds oligopolistic reactions begin to decline when eight-firm concentration ratio reaches 70 percent; this is a relatively "loose oligopoly" since it implies a four-firm concentration ratio of perhaps 45 to 55 percent.

[9] The Fajnzylber and Martinez-Tarrago study and the Conceicao Tavares study are limited by another problem as well. Their concentration ratios are the share of the market produced by the four largest plants, while U.S. concentration ratios are the share of the four largest firms. Since multiplant firms are common in Mexico and Brazil, it is not clear whether firm concentration rose or declined and whether it is higher or lower than the U.S.

[10] The conventional model of industrial organization sees industrial performance as a function of both conduct and structure, since conduct is predicated upon industrial structure. Many economists, such as Bain (1966), have given primacy to structure-performance relationships, while Scherer (1980) has emphasized conduct performance relationships.

[11] For a second method, see Appendix A, p. 437.

[12] Lall and Streeten were careful to point out this method of calculating their net social impact is rife with problems (1977, pp. 181-188). Much depends on the relative values that products command on the free market and these are conditioned by non-market forces, such as income distribution or corporate advertising. It is nearly impossible to reconcile social priorities with market prices without introducing a weighting system that balances the needs of one group against another. This places considerable burden of subjective valuation on the analyst; the valuations are thus likely to change with the interests and values of the analyst.

[13] For a discussion of multicountry statistical analyses of dependence, see Appendix B, p. 439.

Philip L. Shepherd
3.
Transnational Corporations and the International Cigarette Industry

INTRODUCTION*

Mention of the tobacco industry readily brings to mind a variety of images: Jamestown and the exquisitely landscaped colonial plantations in Virginia; the grinding toil of black slaves in hot southern fields; the independent cussedness of the nineteenth century pioneer absorbed in back-breaking work while chewing his ubiquitous "quid" of tobacco; the cigar store Indian; and the colorful syncopation of the auctioneer's unintelligible chant. More recently, however, these images have been partially displaced by dramatic revelations about the health dangers associated with smoking. For the past twenty-five years or so, medical evidence has slowly accumulated, implicating smoking with a wide variety of illnesses, usually terminal: lung, mouth, and throat cancers, emphysema, cardiovascular diseases, and chronic bronchitis. (U.S.DHEW 1979). Public concern about smoking and health has tarnished these images of the tobacco industry in industrialized nations.

What is common to all these images is a curious traditional aura surrounding the industry. Even in Latin America, the tobacco industry is usually viewed as a remnant of the older import substitution industrialization era and associated with old, relatively undynamic industries. The reality of the international tobacco industry is quite different, however.

* Special thanks go to Richard Newfarmer and Louis Wolf Goldman as well as other members of the SSRC Working Group on Multinational Corporations who have commented on various versions of this study.

This study will explore only the cigarette manufacturing part of the international tobacco industry which accounts for over 80 percent of world tobacco production by weight and an even higher proportion by value (UNCTAD 1978b, p. 101). It will begin with a discussion of the development of the industry in the developed world and proceed with an analysis of the implications of the industry in developing nations.

THE STRUCTURE OF THE INTERNATIONAL CIGARETTE OLIGOPOLY

A remarkable fact of the international cigarette industry and tobacco trade in general is the degree to which it is dominated by Anglo-American interests. Of the nine major transnational cigarette producers which dominate the industry, only one is neither American or British in ownership. Six of these firms—British-American, Philip Morris, R.J. Reynolds, American Brands, Imperial, and the Rupert/Rothman's Group—had total sales (excluding taxes) of $24 billion in 1977. Adding the other three, Loew's, Liggett Group, and Reemtsma, a West German firm, boosts aggregate sales to almost $26 billion. These nine TNCs figure among the largest U.S. manufacturing firms and among the largest firms in the world. British-American Tobacco (BAT), the world's largest tobacco firm has long ranked among the top 50 industrial corporations of the world. BAT was the third-largest industrial enterprise in the United Kingdom in 1977, with 82 percent of its assets abroad and manufacturers in 78 nations. (*Fortune* May 1978; *Fortune* August 1978). Philip Morris and R.J. Reynolds are not far behind BAT in size. Although they are somewhat less "transnational" than BAT they have been growing at a more rapid rate through non-tobacco acquisitions and foreign tobacco operations.

World production of cigarettes in highly concentrated (see Table 3.1). Eight TNCs account for a total of 41 percent of total world production of cigarettes. If socialist nations are excluded, 63 percent of the "Free World" production of cigarettes are manufactured by these eight firms. While these figures are rough estimates, they do conform to what TNCs have occasionally revealed about their worldwide sales. For example, BAT claimed it produced one in every five cigarettes sold in the "Free World", which is about 500 billion cigarettes and about 13 percent of world production. Philip Morris produces 7 percent of the world market, almost as much as the entire output of Japan or Eastern Europe.

And international concentration in the industry appears to be increasing. After a brief period of expansive growth in the 1960s, in which virtually all of the U.S. and several of the European firms followed the oligopolistic leaders around the globe, a number of second-level TNCs like Loew's, Liggett, and Reemtsma were weeded out of international cigarette sales as a result of the mergers and acquisitions. In 1977 Loew's sold the rights to its (Lorillard) brands outside the U.S. to BAT; in 1978 Philip Morris acquired all of Liggett's foreign operations; and in 1981 Philip Morris bought a hefty 22 percent (potentially 31 percent) minority share of Rothmans. Several of the smaller TNCs have retired to their domestic markets and emphasized their domestic diversification programs in non-tobacco areas. Thus, the 1974 data presented in Table 3.1 is surely an understatement of concentration at present. By the early 1980s the top six TNCs probably accounted for close to 85 percent of the world cigarette sales in "private enterprise" markets around the world.

As Table 3.2 shows, concentration at the national market level is also rather high. Transnational corporations dominate virtually all the major markets outside the state monopoly and socialist nations. Non-TNCs held only small market shares in most nations, and in only a few did nationally-owned private firms reach even 40 percent of the total national market. In individual nations, market concentration continues apace, strongly toward increased TNC market control.

Barriers to Entry

Such seller concentration is the result of barriers to entry which prevent potential competitors from entering an industry over relatively long periods of time. The existence of barriers to entry and their important impact on industrial structure constitute fundamental insights of industrial organization theory.

The most important contribution is that of Bain (1956), although the phenomena had been recognized by other analysts in earlier case study materials, including early studies of the cigarette industry (Cox 1933; Tennant 1950; Nicholls 1951). Bain identified three basic sets of barriers to entry: (1) absolute cost advantages of existing firms; (2) economies of scale (or other advantages of large-scale production); and, (3) consumer preferences for the products of existing producers. The latter is far and away the most important in the cigarette industry.

Before discussing these barriers, aspects of the industry which do not constitute major constraints to new firms entering the market should be pointed out. Both absolute cost advantages and economies of scale are supply conditions relating to production *process* technology. Process (as opposed to product) technology is not a reason for barriers to entry in the cigarette industry, nor are the supply of raw

Table 3.1

**Estimated World Cigarette Output by Major Producing Groups, 1974
(in billions)**

Socialist Nations		State Monopolies			Major Trans-national corporations			Others[a]		World Total Output	
	#	%		#	%		#	%	#	%	#	%
China	671	17.3	Japan	292	7.5	BAT	500	12.9	—	—	—	
USSR	371	9.6	France	81	2.1	Philip Morris	272	7.1				
E. Europe	292	7.5	Italy	66	1.7	R.J. Reynolds	232	6.0				
N. Korea/N. Vietnam	34	0.8	Turkey	54	1.4	Rupert/Rothmans	200	5.2				
Cuba	23	0.6	S. Korea	49	1.3	American						

			Brands		
Spain	36	0.9	Brands	135	3.5
Maghreb Nations	22	0.6	Imperial	108	2.8
			Reemtsma	61	1.6
Egypt	21	0.5			
Thailand	21	0.5	Loew's	59	1.5
Austria	14	0.4			
Iran	14	0.4			
Subtotals	670	17.3		1569	40.6
	1391	35.8		238	6.2		3868	100

Sources: United States Department of Agriculture, *Foreign Agricultural Circular—Tobacco* FT2-77, July, 1977 and United Nations Conference on Trade and Development, *Marketing and Distribution of Tobacco* (TD/B/D.1/1205), June 16, 1978, UN Publication Sales No. E.78.111.14, Table 8, p. 28.

Note: [a] Includes independent domestic tobacco firms, smaller state monopolies, and transnational companies not shown.

Table 3.2

Cigarette Market Shares[a] of Major Transnational Firms and Affiliates, 1975
(in percent)

Nation	British-American %	Philip Morris %	Rupert/ Rothman's %	R. J. Reynolds %	Reemtsma %	Liggett Group %	American Brands %	Others[b]	Total Sales Sales (millions)
Argentina	Nobleza 42	Massalin 18			Imparciales 12 Particular 11	Piccardo 18		0	38,600
Australia	Wills 36	PM 30	Rothman, Australia 26					8	31,800
Belgium	Warland 12	Weltab 6	Tabacofina 46		Reemtsma 14			22	18,900
Brazil	Souza Cruz 75	PM 5		Lopes[c] 11				9	115,600
Canada	Imasco[d] 42	Benson & Hedges 11	Rothman's of Pall Mall 22	Macdonald 18				7	58,300
Costa Rica	Republic 57	Tabacalera C. Rica 16						27	2,200
Denmark	Scandinavian[f] 100							0	8,800
El Salvador	Morazan 76	Centro-American 15						9	2,100
Finland	Suomen Tupakka 27							73[g]	8,100

West Germany	BAT 25	PM 6	M. Brinkmann 19	R. J. R. 5	Reemtsma 35	10	141,000
Ghana	Pioneer 100					0	2,400
Chile	Chilena[e] de-Tabacos 100					0	8,200
Guatemala	Centra-American 47					53	2,400
India	ITC 37 V. Sultan 24	Godfrey Phillips 5				34	59,700
Jamaica	Machada 27		Carreras 68			5	1,500
Kenya	BAT 100					0	3,600
Malaysia	Malayan 66		Rothman's Pall Mall 17			17	10,900
Mexico	La Moderna[h] 30	Tabacalera Mexicana 14	(h)	(h)		56[g]	45,000
Netherlands	BAT 23	PM 3	Turmac 17 Gruno 1 Laurens 29		T. Niemeyer[i] 12	15	33,600
New Zealand	Wills 16	PM 6	Rothmans 70			8	6,500
Nicaragua	Tabacalera Nicara 96					4	1,600
Nigeria	Nigerian Tob. Co. 66	PM 12				22	10,400
Pakistan	Pakistan Tob, Premier Tob. 35	28				37	26,400
Panama	Tabacalera	Tabacalera National 43				2	1,000

Table 3.2
Cigarette Market Shares[1] of Major Transnational Firms and Affiliates, 1975
(in percent)

Nation	British-American %	Philip Morris %	Rupert/Rothman's %	R. J. Reynolds %	Reemtsma %	Liggett Group %	American Bands %	Others[b]	Total Sales Sales (millions)
Peru				(j)		Tabacalera[j] Valor 14		86[g]	3,700
Sri Lanka	Ceylon Tob. 100							0	3,700
Switzerland	BAT 15	Tabacs Reunies 26	Laurens 5	Reynolds 1				53	26,700
United Kingdom		PM 1	Carreras 6				Gallaher 26	66[k]	157,800
United States	Brown & Williamson 17	PM 25		RJR 32		L&M 4	ATC 15	8[l]	651,200
Venezuela	Biggott Sucs 19	Tabacalera Nacional 76						5	16,500
Zaire	BAT 28							72[m]	4,600
Zambia	Cigarette (n) Man. 100		Cigarette (14) Man. 100					0	1,300

70

Sources: United Nations Conference on Trade and Development, *Marketing and Distribution of Tobacco* (TD/b7b.½₂₀₅), June 16, 1978, UN Publication Sales No. 1.78.11.14, Table 9, p. 31-32 and United States Department of Agriculture, *Foreign Agriculture Circular—Tobacco,* FT2-77, July, 1977.

Notes:

[a] Includes cigarettes produced under licensing arrangements but not those entering under common market rules (EEC and Central American CM).

[b] These may include small shares of brands produced by the listed transnational firms and also includes brands produced under licensing agreements with the listed transnational companies.

[c] R.J. Reynolds bought Lopes in 1975. At that time it held 11% of the market.

[d] Imasco is jointly owned by BAT (44%) and Imperial Group (56%).

[e] La Chilena de Tabacos (BAT 50%) is the sole cigarette producer.

[f] Scandinavian Tobacco (BAT 31%) is the sole cigarette producer.

[g] There is extensive licensing by the transnational firms of locally-owned tobacco companies.

[h] Mexican government forced divestment of majority holdings in the early 1970's which affected RJR, PM, BAT, and Liggett subsidiaries there, with RJR and Liggett apparently pulling out altogether.

[i] Through Gallaher.

[j] In 1975, Tabacalera Valor was acquired by Tabacalera Nacional, a privately-owned firm, which held over 60% of the market in 1976. It holds licenses from R.J. Reynolds.

[k] Imperial Group had 64% of the UK market in 1975.

[l] Loew's (P. Lorillard): 8%.

[m] Tabazaire.

[n] Jointly-owned by BAT (30%) and Rothman's (70%). It is the only cigarette manufacturer.

71

materials (principally leaf tobacco) or other factors of production. Process technology does not constitute a barrier to entry because it is not subject to large economies of scale. Small-scale operations are feasible and as efficient as much larger ones. Bain himself found that the smallest efficient plant scale in cigarettes was 5.5 percent of the total capacity of the U.S. industry (Bain 1956, pp. 72-80). Recent estimates put minimum efficient scale at only 7 to 8 percent of the U.S. cigarette industry; for smaller plant sizes unit costs were still only 1 to 2 percent higher (Henning and Mann 1976, p. 149). The average cigarette plant in even very small markets uses a large number of identical cigarette-making and packing machines. Fidel, Lucangeli, and Shepherd 1977, pp. 3-65). Moreover, the basic process technology is relatively simple as manufacturing techniques go. Technology and engineering technical assistance are readily available to those with the capital to purchase it. And, there is a brisk trade in second-hand machinery. The search for safe, low-tar cigarettes through expensive bio-chemical research and advances in automated production may eventually produce technological barriers to entry, but this is still in the future.

Likewise, supply conditions for the principal inputs (leaf tobacco, paper, filters, packaging materials, labor, etc.) do not pose high barriers to entry. Non-leaf inputs are supplied by large independent manufacturers. With the exception of leaf tobacco, none of these items is costly in industrialized nations. While leaf tobacco is expensive, the basic tendency towards oligopsonistic pressure on growers maintains fairly low prices, so it could be afforded by new entrants in most markets.

The primary barriers to entry may be found, instead, in the factors making for enduring consumer preferences for the products of existing firms: (1) through the location of plants or sales outlets; (2) through the provision of exceptionally good service; (3) by means of physical differences in the product supplied; and, (4) through the creation of a favorable subjective image in the minds of consumers for the product (Scherer 1971, p. 324). All four of these are important in the cigarette industry and they all relate to the demand creation efforts of the firms. The first and second points are the result of important investments in distribution networks, sales forces, and market research. These are barriers to entry for new firms but are probably not decisive in most markets.

With respect to physical differences in products, technology plays an important role, but it is product technology not process technology. For firms on the frontier of product technology, differences in product forms, packaging, etc., do not normally confer lasting advantages mainly because they are relatively easy to copy. The history of the cigarette industry is strewn with examples of firms which developed a new product form first, only to see it copied by a competitor who eventually became the market leader for that type of cigarette (Kellner 1973, pp. 81-106; Shepherd 1983). Such "free riding" limits product form variation (e.g., 85 mm vs. 100 mm cigarettes) as an enduring source of advantage, although firms have specialized somewhat. For the major TNCs, different product forms or packaging are not usually decisive sources of monopoly which will endure. This is a barrier to entry for potential competitors, however.

These product form and packaging differences, slight as they might be, are powerfully reinforced by the creation of subjective brand images through massive advertising and other types of promotion. Existing brands pose a powerful barrier to entry because they have accumulated a stock of "goodwill" or brand loyalty from both previous and current promotional investments. According to fragmentary market research some 50 percent of cigarette smokers in the United States have never changed brands, and 25 to 30 percent have smoked the same brand three years or more (Key 1976, pp. 165-166). Profound product form shake-ups such as the introduction of filters in the 1950s or the current rush to low tar brands do tend to alter brand loyalties, but they are infrequent. Brand loyalty resulting from advertising and market segmentation is a serious barrier to new entry. Potential competitors wishing to enter a given market have to incur advertising expenditure and product form segmentation over and above that of the established firms in order to penetrate the market. These demand creation efforts prevent new entry and permit above competitive profits.

At least a word on financial barriers to entry is in order. The capital requirements for new entry only acquire importance in the context of the demand creation barriers to entry posed by advertising, product-form variation, and other techniques of promotion. A manager at Philip Morris estimated in the late 1960s, that the minimum capital requirements for entry were around $500 million. (Kellner 1973, pp. 77, 98). It is considerably larger today. This enormous sum is required because of the necessity for extensive advertising. This is a substantial deterrent for even large non-tobacco firms that do have the demand creation expertise with which to consider entering the industry. The minimum figure is certainly much larger now with the escalation in cost of new brand launches required for gaining a share of the low tar market and the lower efficiency of non-broadcast media. It would appear that barriers to entry in the U.S. market have climbed rather than declined as a consequence.

Another factor acquires importance over the long run, a factor not adequately explored in the economics literature. This is the role of advertising *quality* or demand creation ability more generally.[1] Where

73

the principal entrepreneurial function is the effective design and employment of demand creation techniques, as it is in the cigarette business, we should not expect quality considerations to be entirely random as the literature does. It is this factor more than any other which accounts for the major changes in U.S. firms' relative positions over the past 35 years. Historically, there have been variations in the quality of demand creation efforts of firms. This has had an important impact despite similar levels of demand creation expenditure across firms and brands, some having had markedly more successful demand creation.

This is not simply a question of intra-oligopoly rivalry, either. It seems likely, for example, that industry barriers to entry have risen because of the increasing importance of demand creation in the industry and the increasingly sophisticated demand creation carried on by the existing firms. It is a long way from the "seat of the pants" sloganeering of "Sooold American!!!" of forty years ago to the complex psycho-demographic market research of today (Shepherd 1983).

Demand creation extends deeply into the design production and packaging of cigarettes. The technology embodied in cigarettes becomes inextricably linked and mixed with the creation and management of demand for them (Shepherd 1977). Most analysts agree that demand creation constitutes the major obstacle to new entry and that "marketing"[2] operations are the most important single source of high concentration in the industry (Cox 1933, pp. 187-219; Tennant 1950, pp. 262-269; Nicholls 1951, pp. 192-203; Kellner 1973, pp. 244-270). In sum, the cigarette industry can be characterized as having rather high barriers to entry resulting from product differentiation[3] that has, in turn, led to high levels of seller concentration.

A HISTORY OF COOPERATION AND COMPETITION IN THE INTERNATIONAL CIGARETTE OLIGOPOLY

In the late nineteenth century most tobacco was consumed in cigars, chewing tobacco, snuff, and smoking tobaccos for pipes and "roll-your-own" cigarettes. Cigarettes—including "roll-your-own" types—only appeared in the U.S. and U.K. in the 1870s. In 1901 U.S. consumption of cigarettes was only 2.8 percent of tobacco consumption by weight. (Tilley 1948, p. 618). Initially, cigarette manufacture was done almost entirely by hand. Only a few firms, all of them small, were engaged in the cigarette business in the 1870s and 1880s on either side of the Altantic. However, in the 1870s firms began to focus on reducing the high cost of labor (Tilley 1948, pp. 568-592). The first practical cigarette-making machine was invented in the early 1880s, and this machine became a crucial element in the success of the eventual leaders in both the U.S. and U.K. industries—James B. Duke and W.D. & H.O. Wills. Machine methods totally altered the industry (Tennant 1950, pp. 20-22; Tilley 1948, pp. 572-575; Alford 1973, pp. 154-157). But mechanization *per se* was not enough for overall success. It led to the need to vastly improve marketing efforts in order to overcome the initial resistance to machine-made goods, open distributors' channels, etc. Machine-made goods also posed the spectre of severe overproduction and declining profit margins if the total demand for cigarettes could not be rapidly expanded. Firms also felt the need to escape the onerous system of "wholesaler domination"[4] which blocked the necessary expansion of demand and to erect barriers to entry. Efforts to rationalize distribution, expand demand and maintain returns quickly led to large-scale advertising in both the U.S. and the U.K. (P. Porter 1969 and 1971; McCurdy 1978).

The situation quickly came to a head in the U.S. Escalating advertising wars among the five cigarette producers cut into the profits of all of them, and consolidation appeared to be the only viable solution to the expropriating effects of cut-throat competition (Eichner 1969, pp. 13-19). Therefore, In 1890 all the existing firms formed the American Tobacco Company (ATC) under James Duke's leadership (Porter 1969; Tennant 1950, pp. 22-25; Tilley 1948, pp. 555-577). With a monopoly of the cigarette industry as its base for cross-subsidization, and with Duke's cut-throat competitive tactics, ATC came to control virtually the entire U.S. tobacco industry—save cigars—over the next twenty years. (U.S. Bureau of Corporations 1909 and 1915; Tennant 1950, pp. 26-57). ATC became one of the largest "Trusts" of the period. It was the second largest U.S. industrial firm (behind U.S. Steel) in capitalization throughout the 1895 to 1904 period and over three times the size of General Electric, the third largest (Nelson 1959, p. 162).

The American Tobacco Company was also one of the earliest and largest of U.S. transnational corporations (Wilkins 1970, pp. 91-93). During the 1880s, in the drive to expand demand, Duke had sent representatives abroad on world tours to drum up business. Exports grew during the 1890s, comprising close to one-third of U.S. cigarette output at the turn of the century, most of which went to the Far East. An important source of the Trust's power was almost complete control of U.S. cigarette exports (Tennant 1950, pp. 40-41). And wherever tariff barriers prevented exports Duke established local manufacturing plants, as in Canada, Japan, Germany, and Australia (BOC 1909, pp. 165-179).

The U.K. cigarette industry also expanded rapidly in this period, though not at the same rate and mainly to British colonial preserves and "spheres or influence" (Alford 1973, pp. 159-247; Corina 1975, pp. 50-89). By the mid-1890s, agents for W.O. & H.O. Wills, now the largest U.K. firm, and ATC were bumping into each other in India, Australia, Japan, and China. (Alford 1973, pp. 247-256). In 1901 Duke boldly invaded the U.K. market itself. (BOC 1909, pp. 166-67). Duke's decision was influenced by adverse conditions in the U.S. at this time: (1) the Trust had consolidated its control of all segments of the U.S. tobacco industry (save cigars); (2) a wave of hostility against cigarettes in the U.S. (including prohibitions against their sale in 14 states) caused a severe depression in sales between 1896 and 1906; and, (3) a change in favor of Turkish tobacco cigarettes led to new competition from small independents. The possibility that the paper cigarette might be obsolete in the U.S. led Duke to hedge his bets in a variety of ways (Tennant 1950, pp. 26-57).

English firms, under the leadership of Wills, retaliated by merging together into the Imperial Tobacco Co. (ITC) to do battle with Duke on more equal terms. Moves and countermoves between the two rapidly spread all over the globe. Imperial was on the verge of a counterinvasion of the U.S. market when, after a year of battle, the two sides came to terms (Corina 1975, pp. 65-108; Alford 1973, pp. 247-279).

The 1903 Cartel

The settlement was a classic cartel. Ogden's was sold to Imperial in exchange for securities of Imperial (14 percent), ATC and ITC agreed to keep out of each other's territories, and a new London based company, British-American Tobacco, Ltd. was organized to take over all the business outside the U.K., the U.S., Cuba, and Puerto Rico. Two-thirds of its initial £5.2 million capital was allocated to ATC and one-third to ITC in exchange for their overseas operations and export trade. There were also agreements to insure consultation and inhibit cheating (BOC 1909, pp. 166-176; Alford 1973, pp. 247-279; Corina 1975, pp. 65-108).

British-American Tobacco was a transnational corporation of impressive proportions. In 1903 BAT compared favorably with even the largest TNCs today in number of overseas operations. By the end of World War I it was the world's largest tobacco company in terms of number of cigarettes. BAT's expansion was especially impressive in China, which was its largest market for many years although some Chinese boycotted the firm's products and fought it by every means available (Cochran 1975; Wang 1960). It also expaned rapidly in Latin America and other markets outside the U.S. and U.K.

The Anti-Trust Case of 1911

Meanwhile, the structure of the industry in the United States was undergoing profound changes. The predatory practices[5] employed by ATC in gaining and maintaining its monopoly position elicited opposition from tobacco growers, leaf traders, small manufacturers, wholesalers, retailers, and organized labor (Tilley 1948, pp. 373-449; BOC 1909 and 1911). These groups wanted better leaf prices for growers, freer entry, increased price competition, and larger margins for retailers and jobbers. (Tennant 1950, pp. 57-60; Cox 1933, pp. 1-17). In a landmark case, the Supreme Court dissolved ATC in 1911 (*U.S. vs. American Tobacco Co.* 221 U.S. 106; Tennant 1950, pp. 57-75; Cox 1933, pp. 1-17; Corina 1975, pp. 108-149), and ordered that it be split up into a number of successor companies: Liggett & Myers, P. Lorillard, a new American Tobacco Co., and R.J. Reynolds. It was required to distribute its stockholdings in BAT and Imperial among individual stockholders, and a number of permanent and temporary injunctions against re-combination were issued. While it probably did not accomplish the domestic results desired, the case did have long-term effects on the international industry. And, whatever the original intent, it upset the structure of the domestic industry sufficiently to stimulate vigorous non-price competition in the domestic industry (Cox 1933).

Several things are important about the anti-trust case: First, the case changed the industry from a near monopoly into a textbook oligopoly. This, in turn, had a variety of effects. Reynolds, which had previously not produced cigarettes, quickly launched a new type of cigarette with flavored burley tobaccos in 1913. This cigarette, Camel, revolutionized the U.S. cigarette business and was quickly imitated by the new ATC (Lucky Strikes) and Liggett & Myers (Chesterfield). The advént of the "American Blend" cigarette stimulated cigarette consumption and set off a long period (1913-1950) of extremely rapid, domestically-oriented growth known as the "Standard Brand" era. Growth in domestic consumption and output was so spectacular over the next four decades that none of the firms showed any real interest in developing foreign operations or exports (Shepherd 1983). Second, the dilution of ATC's two-thirds holding in BAT meant that the concentrated one-third shareholding of Imperial slowly came into working control of BAT. Thus, in the early 1920s, BAT came to be a British-controlled corporation. Third, because U.S. anti-trust law had no jurisdiction over either BAT or Imperial except in their U.S. leaf-buying operations, the BAT-Imperial market allocation agreements of 1903 continued in force until the early 1970s. In the absence of British anti-trust action, Imperial continued to dominate the U.K. domestic market, while BAT held sway abroad outside the U.S. Even after the European Economic Community (EEC) regulations forced the formal repudiation of the BAT/Imperial market division in Europe in the 1970s, BAT/Imperial relations remained close because the British Monopolies Commission did not take remedial action. (Corina 1975, pp. 215-220, 281).

Fourth, brands developed by ATC became the property of BAT outside the U.S. and for export from the U.S. (Cox 1933, pp. 74/n. 27). This severely limited the new American Tobacco Co. in its ability to expand overseas because many of its top-selling domestic brands (Pall Mall, Lucky Strike, etc.) had been ATC brands. As the new American Tobacco Co. came to be one of the major U.S. firms, this constraint powerfully reinforced the domestic orientation already present in the industry. Finally, while the ruling declared the "formal ATC/BAT/ITC cartel illegal, a *de facto* cartel remained intact. With few exceptions the cartel arrangements persisted exactly as before: American firms stayed at home; Imperial ruled the U.K. domestic market; and BAT was the predominant international force outside the U.S. and U.K. well into the 1960s.

The De Facto Cartel of the 1930s and 1940s

After some Anglo-American oligopolistic sparring in the 1920s after BAT became British, a *de facto* cartel evolved. As in a number of other industries at this time, U.S. participation in this pattern of market allocation and mutual forebearance was tacit and indirect (Stocking and Watkins 1948, p. 209). The *quid pro quo* U.S. cigarette firms obtained for not entering foreign markets was protection in exploiting the large, rapidly-growing U.S. market. Without U.S. cooperation the entire structure would have collapsed.

Although World War II provided the opportunity for a tremendous export boom for U.S. firms because European production facilities had been destroyed and American cigarettes became a coveted commodity with the popularization of everything American, U.S. cigarette firms did little to take advantage of this situation. Foreign markets were viewed as unstable and unlikely to provide future growth. The long period of expansive domestic growth had made overseas markets pale in comparison. A near-doubling of sales during the war and the reemergence of overwhelming dominance of the "Big

78

Three" firms (83 percent in 1947—Tennant 1950, pp. 93-95) made the struggle for domestic market shares more important than ever.

Contemporary Rivalry: Stagnation at Home and Growth Abroad

Within the United States changes in the consumption of cigarettes had begun to appear by the late 1940s—before the smoking/health issue was ever broached seriously in the U.S. (Kellner 1973, pp. 136-140). The growth rate of the domestic market began to shrink as the market became relatively saturated at high levels of consumption (see Figure 3.1). It further declined when the smoking/health issue first surfaced as a major public concern in 1952. As a result of publicity about cigarettes and lung cancer in the media sales were down 5 percent in 1954 (Kellner 1973, pp. 54-55).

U.S. Cigarette Consumption
Per capita*, 1900–1980
(in packs of 20)

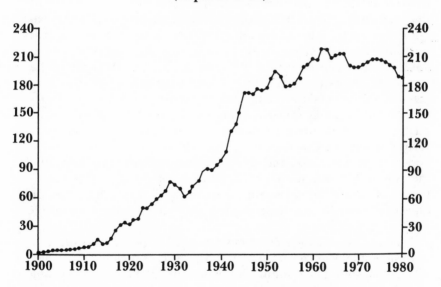

* U. S., Population 18 years and over including U. S. Armed Forces overseas.

Sources: United States Department of Agriculture, *Annual Reports on Tobacco Statistics,* 1937-1951; U. S. Dept. of Agriculture, *Tobacco Situation,* various issues, 1958, 1967, 1971, 1977, 1981.

The decline hit the small firms hardest. The two smallest, Philip Morris and P. Lorillard, began to explore the possibilities of foreign operations and increased exports as a way to hedge against uncertainty (Shepherd 1983). They were particularly concerned that domestic sales might fall below the minimum level required to finance the development and promotion of new filter cigarettes which all firms were introducing in response to the health scare, as it was increasingly clear that these brands would be the future of the industry. Without filter brands it would be impossible to compete. During this time the Big Three firms held their share of the market and did not initiate overseas operations.

Direct Foreign Investment: The U.S. Challenge

The first ventures abroad in the 1950s were tenuous feelers to see how cold the waters of the foreign markets were. The 1952-54 "health scare" coincided with tariff hikes in a number of small, though attractive export markets (Australia, Panama, Philippines, Venezuela). Philip Morris established a partly-owned subsidiary in Australia. But most of the ventures consisted of licensing agreements with local firms. No effort was made to penetrate the European market but these moves were breaches of the long-standing, informal world market allocation. Table 3.3 traces the expansion overseas of U.S. cigarette firms. In the 1950s the domestic orientation was still strong, however, and U.S. producers did not take advantage of the potential popularity of American blend cigarettes overseas. The reason seems to have been the relative success of the introduction of filter cigarettes at home. A revival of high growth rates in the late 1950s made the health scare appear as an aberration and slowed interest in foreign markets. Still, the two smaller firms acquired a continuing interest in foreign operations and were quite successful on a very small scale. Philip Morris, especially, gained a big jump on the rest of the U.S. industry in this way.

The success of filter cigarettes was temporary. In 1964 the U.S. government initiated an inquiry on the hazards of smoking (Fritschler 1975, pp. 37-53). The resulting Surgeon General's Report on Smoking and Health caused considerable fanfare: Smoking was implicated with a variety of serious diseases (Advisory Commission on Smoking and Health 1964). Once again disaster struck the sales figures (see Table 3.3). Although they were 10 years apart, and separated by rapid growth, two health scares made it apparent that the issue would probably continue to affect sales adversely in the future. Whereas between 1900 and 1950 U.S. cigarette sales failed to exceed those of the previous year in only four years (1920, 1931, 1932, 1949), from 1950 to 1977 they had done so on seven years (Table 3.3; Shepherd 1983, Appendix B). After 1964 there was a massive scramble on the part of all U.S. cigarette firms to hedge their bets by acquiring foreign cigarette manufacturing operations and by acquiring domestic firms in non-tobacco areas. As sales continued to stagnate, the scramble intensified. Historical spheres of influence were abandoned under the immense pressure to diversify out of the U.S. cigarette market.

In short, the dramatic upsurge in direct foreign investment and licensing by U.S. cigarette firms was caused by market stagnation in the U.S. related to the smoking/health controversy.[6] This is the context in which all other factors must be understood; it provided the decisive "push" in the search for alternative markets in the 1950s for the smallest firms and, after 1964, for all of them. Although tariff hikes and import prohibitions may have influenced where direct foreign investments or licensing flowed (especially in the 1950s), the dynamics of defensive investment emphasized in product-cycle accounts of direct foreign investment were not basic causes of overseas expansion in the U.S. cigarette industry. Maintenance of export markets and the threat of foreign competition were not significant factors in the overall process of foreign expansion (Shepherd 1983). Nor was the protection of a technologically-based oligopoly position a fundamental motive for overseas investment and licensing. Instead, large-scale demand creation efforts constituted the basic competitive advantage of U.S. cigarette firms. This may have made "on-site" foreign operations especially necessary once the need for alternative markets outside the U.S. became apparent; effective demand creation required the existence of local facilities, close ties with local distributors, local market research, etc. A technologically superior product can be exported profitably, but demand creation advantages can be exploited only imperfectly through exports. Even here, however, the demand creation advantages of U.S. cigarette firms only became important in the context of the relative stagnation of the U.S. domestic market. They were necessary not sufficient causes.

As might be expected in a mad scramble of this sort, there are few discernible patterns in this flow of investment and licensing abroad. Firms did not necessarily search out markets with high growth rates; they figured if the long-run potential was present they could turn the market around with sufficient demand creation. And much direct foreign investment or licensing went to Europe where per capita consumption was already fairly high. Cigarette companies did not necessarily seek large markets; they went everywhere, large and small. They did not penetrate higher income markets and then lower in-

Table 3.3

U.S. Domestic Cigarette Market Growth, Traceable Overseas Subsidiary Investments, Licensing Arrangements Established and Traceable Domestic Non-Tobacco Acquisitions, 1950-1977

	A. U.S. Domestic Cigarette Growth (Annual Percentage Change)		B. Number of Traceable Domestic Non-Tobacco Acquisitions		C. Number of Traceable Subs. Investments & Licensing Arrangements Established	
1950-51	1950	6.4	1950	0	1950	0
1951-52	1951	4.3	1951	0	1951	0
1952-53	1952	-2.9	1952	0	1952	1
1953-54	1952	-5.0	1953	0	1953	0
1954-55	1954	2.8	1954	0	1954	1
1955-56	1955	2.8	1955	0	1955	1
1956-57	1956	4.1	1956	0	1956	4
1957-58	1957	6.3	1957	1	1957	1
1958-59	1958	4.0	1958	1	1958	1
1959-60	1959	3.5	1959	1	1959	1
1960-61	1960	4.0	1960	0	1960	2
1961-62	1961	1.0	1961	0	1961	6
1962-63	1962	3.1	1962	1	1962	5
1963-64	1963	-2.3	1963	2	1963	5
1964-65	1964	3.7	1964	2	1964	2

A. 1950-60 Average: 2.6

B. Total 1950-59: 3

C. Total 1950-59: 10

	A			B		C
1965-66	1.9		1965	4	1965	4
1966-67	1.6	1960-70 Average: 1.3	1966	8	1966	9
1967-68	0.1		1967	6	1967	8
1968-69	−3.7		1968	6	1968	13
1969-70	4.0		1969	8	1969	7
				Total 1960-69: 37		Total 1960-69: 61
1970-71	−1.7		1970	10	1970	4
1971-72	3.7	1970-77 Average: 1.5	1971	3	1971	7
1972-73	6.8		1972	3	1972	10
1973-74	−2.4		1973	2	1973	24
1974-75	2.2		1974	1	1974	11
				Total 1970-76: 25		Total 1970-76: 79
1975-76	5.1		1975	2	1975	18
1976-77	−3.2		1976	4	1976	5
Average Growth 1950-77	2.3		Total 1950-76	65	Total 1950-76	150

Sources: A. United States Department of Agriculture, *Tobacco Situation*, various years, 1950-77;
B. Annual Reports of Companies, 1950-77 (R.J. Reynolds, Philip Morris, American Brands, P. Lorillard, Liggett Group);
C. Annual Reports of the Companies and "Interconnecting Interests of Major Tobacco Manufacturers," *Tobacco Reporter*, various years, 1968-77.

come markets in any order; they went into both simultaneously. Rates of growth, market size, and income were insignificant in comparison with the immediate danger of stagnation in the U.S. (Shepherd 1983).

Given the pressure to diversify quickly out of the U.S. cigarette business, the vast majority of overseas subsidiaries established by these firms were acquired rather than set up *de novo*. In fact, 76 percent of all traceable foreign subsidiary operations established in the 1950 to 1976 period were acquisitions of foreign manufacturing firms (Shepherd 1983, Appendix A). This was advantageous because the firms began foreign operations using established national brands and working through existing distribution networks (Shepherd 1977, pp. 14-15). *De novo* subsidiaries emerged only where the local tobacco industry was so underdeveloped that no local firms were available for acquisition or where TNC competitors already owned 100 percent of the industry. In developing nations, where one might have expected a stronger tendency toward establishment of subsidiaries *de novo*, the pattern of acquisition remained; for example, 77 percent of the 22 subsidiaries established in Latin America were acquired. Precisely how this process took place is considered below.

Diversification

In their efforts to diversify holdings, cigarette firms used the same strategy of acquiring existing firms, rather than establishing new ones. All U.S. cigarette firms now derive a significant and growing share of their sales and income from non-tobacco pursuits; 35 to 50 percent of sales and 10 to 30 percent of earnings are the norm for the larger firms, the proportions being somewhat higher for the smaller ones.[7] This has transformed U.S. cigarette firms into full-fledged, highly-diversified conglomerates engaged in a plethora of non-tobacco activities spanning virtually the entire range of modern economic endeavor. While the crucial center of their activities remains the cigarette business, U.S. cigarette firms are clearly very different economic entities from the "tobacco companies" of the 1950s. In fact, some may even be prototypes of a new form of conglomerate TNC firm.

International Rivalry

One result of the relatively sudden expansion of U.S. cigarette firms abroad after 1964 was an intensification of the competition within the industry, especially with BAT. Although BAT had the advantage of long experience in overseas markets, its complacency was abruptly challenged by the appeal of U.S. cigarettes and the brash, aggressive advertising campaigns of U.S. firms promoting them. To counteract the challenge of U.S. cigarette companies BAT followed the prudent strategy of any existing firm *vis-a-vis* a new entrant, emphasizing its well-known national brands, maintaining high volume-low margin pricing with solid promotional backing and distribution, and judiciously introducing new product forms and brands only when it became necessary. U.S. firms' initial inexperience with consumer preferences abroad also helped BAT maintain its position.

As it worked out, the primary challenge to BAT came from Philip Morris, and, to a lesser extent, R.J. Reynolds. Liggett was almost wholly unsuccessful abroad and P. Lorillard pursued a strategy of overseas licensing (eventually selling the rights to its brands abroad to BAT in 1978). Another firm that did not pose a direct threat to BAT was American, whose brands in overseas markets were largely owned by BAT. American concentrated almost all of its overseas manufacturing in the U.K. domestic market through the acquisition of Gallaher in the late 1960s (Corina 1975, pp. 257-266). Nevertheless, as U.S. firms continued to expand in the 1960s and 1970s it became apparent that the long Anglo-American understanding on separate development was now history. American, through Gallaher, challenged Imperial in the U.K. and Philip Morris and R.J. Reynolds were competing with BAT almost everywhere. In the early 1970s Philip Morris became the world's second largest tobacco company and Marlboro the world's largest-selling brand.

Mutual Forebearance and Spheres of Influence

Despite these developments, some *de facto* spheres of influence have remained. Concentration remains high at least partially because in all but the largest national markets only a few TNCs are usually present. The number of TNCs is limited in all but the largest national markets. Oligopolistic proliferation of subsidiaries has not been common. These historical spheres of influence and patterns of mutual forebearance are most obvious in Asia and Africa where European firms have dominated, apart from U.S. licensing in the Philippines. U.S. firms have tended to restrict their operations to more familiar terrain in Latin America and Western Europe. The larger markets of Western Europe, Canada, and Latin America have been areas of fairly competitive behavior.[8] On the whole, then, both oligopolistic competition and market allocation and restraint have characterized TNC operations.

The character of TNC rivalry also needs to be understood. In general, "cut-throat" competition has been rare. Aggression of this sort has been very limited and temporary. Competition, even when breaking into new overseas markets, is only infrequently without certain rules of the game (Shepherd, forthcoming). Non-price competition, advertising blitzes, etc., have not always been restrained and there is an occasional struggle à outrance. This has taken place in Brazil, Argentina, and a number of other fiercely-contested markets. But the normal pattern has not been entirely aggressive. After several years of ad warfare and new brand launchings, the parties tend to come to terms, demand creation expenses are reduced, and new market shares and a more settled equilibrium evolve.

Toward A New Equilibrium?

By the late 1970s there were persistent signs that a new international equilibrium was once again being established. Successful diversification into non-tobacco areas and the weeding out of the smaller TNCs had been accomplished. The industry was being regrouped on the basis of a two-tiered stratification of firms: The large, truly transnational firms (BAT, Philip Morris, Rupert/Rothmans, and R.J. Reynolds) were allocating among themselves the international business, while the smaller firms such as Liggett & Myers, P. Lorillard and Reemstma, were retiring to their respective national markets, concentrating on increasing their domestic market shares and diversifying into non-tobacco ventures. The positions of American Brands and Imperial are still unclear, but it seems likely that they will be restricted to their domestic markets and one or two others. The marked slowdown in the numbers of new subsidiaries and licensing agreements established since 1977 reflects this new equilibrium. The industry has entered a period of consolidation now that most of the major overseas markets have been allocated.

INTERNATIONAL CONDUCT OF THE CIGARETTE INDUSTRY IN LATIN AMERICA

The most striking thing about the world cigarette industry in the last thirty years has been the virtual disappearance of the private, nationally-owned tobacco company and its replacement by a TNC subsidiary. This has been particularly evident in Latin America, but it has also taken place in Europe, Canada, Asia and wherever there were national tobacco firms to be acquired. This section will discuss how this massive industrial restructuring occurred in Latin America.

Historical Emergence of Latin America Cigarette Industries

In Latin America, tobacco often played an important part in the economic and political struggles of the colonial era. The famous "Comunero" rebellion in Socorro, Colombia in 1781, for example, began as a protest against policies on growing and marketing of tobacco under the Crown monopoly (Leonard 1951). Eventually, the deeply-felt hatred of the colonial monopoly led to the dismantling of most tobacco monopolies (Stein and Stein 1970, pp. 123-157; Harrison 1952). By the mid-nineteenth century most tobacco industries in the region had became at least formally private.

As Latin America was increasingly linked into the international system of trade, nations there experimented with various commodities in which they might enjoy some comparative advantage. Leaf tobacco was one of these primary products and various export booms centered on tobacco took place in some countries. Domestically, tobacco was a crucial factor in government revenue in virtually all Latin American nations both before and after Independence (Stein and Stein 1970, pp. 71-74, 99-106).

The tobacco industry was based on locally-grown, dark tobacco, used for cigars, snuff, and chewing in the pre-cigarette era. Dark, air-cured tobaccos of this type were, and still are, favored in areas of Latin cultural influence. In the late nineteenth century when cigarettes were first introduced, dark leaf production for cigars was already well-established. Thus, it was natural that early Latin American cigarette producers would make cigarettes from these dark cigar-leaf cuttings (Brooks 1952, pp. 257-258).

One of the reasons tobacco firms played such an important role in the early economic development of the region is because tobacco manufacture was a prime candidate for import substitution industrialization (ISI) efforts. Tobacco products were a luxury to import, domestic raw materials were readily available, scale requirements were not large, technology was not unduly difficult to acquire or adapt to local conditions, and leaf production was labor-intensive. Because it provided tax revenue for the state and reduced non-essential imports, the industry frequently received substantial effective tariff protection.

In the largest markets of the region (Argentina, Brazil, Mexico), BAT entered the industry fairly early (often just prior to or after World War I), usually by acquiring a local firm. Aggressively carving out large market shares, BAT often met with opposition from owners of national firms, economic nationalists, and others who feared foreign control of the economy. In some nations, such as Colombia, it was unable to gain a permanent foothold in the market. However, BAT usually followed an accommodating strategy for dealing with economic nationalism, and numerous local firms grew up alongside BAT subsidiaries in some markets. It was only with the wholesale take-over of these firms by other, largely U.S., TNCs in the 1960s that Latin American tobacco industries were effectively "denationalized".

The "Controlled" Product-Cycle

Transnational corporations have a substantial, though imperfect, ability to shape the context in which they operate. An important element in this context is their ability to determine consumption patterns.

The patterns of consumption encouraged by TNCs and their impact on the international "product-cycle" can sometimes be stated with considerable specificity. In the case of the cigarette industry, there has been a remarkable convergence of worldwide consumption patterns toward TNC product forms. These are partly the result of TNC efforts at demand creation and partly the result of the diffusion of industralized nations' life-styles, first to LDC elites, and then to broader portions of the population. These are both aspects of a single process, and consumption trends in the international tobacco industry over the past thirty years provide eloquent testimony to the degree to which TNCs are able to channel consumption patterns in favorable directions for their own success and profitability.

There have been four major, worldwide shifts in the consumption of tobacco products in the last thirty years, all of them influenced by TNCs: (1) from all other tobacco products to cigarettes; (2) from the consumption of dark tobaccos to the consumption of light tobaccos; (3) from the consumption of unfiltered cigarettes to the consumption of filtered cigarettes; and, (4) from the consumption of short (70mm) cigarettes to the consumption of longer cigarettes (85 mm, 100mm, 120mm). In short, the trend has been toward TNC product forms, i.e., longer-length, filtered, light tobacco cigarettes and away from the shorter-length, non-filtered, dark tobacco products of national producers. In particular, there has been a decisive shift to "American Blend" cigarettes, once culturally specific only to the U.S.

To see why particular product forms have tended to give TNCs an advantage, it is necessary to understand that, in the course of attempting to create demand, TNCs have developed a vested interest in channeling demand into products with which they are already familiar. Rather than adjusting to the consumer's existing preferences, TNCs generally find it more profitable to attempt to stimulate in the consumer those responses which would lead him to prefer the products which TNCs already have and which they wish to establish in the market. This is particularly crucial just prior, during, and immediately after TNC entry. The great success of TNCs lies in guiding production and consumption patterns away from local, national idiosyncracies which may reduce appropriability and/or give local firms the decisive advantage, and into "international" patterns. These international consumption patterns form a milieu in which any given national market must operate, one which creates an implicit demand for TNC product forms and brands.

The Role of Contraband

More importantly, protected markets are often softened up prior to TNC entry by contraband cigarettes. Increased smuggling of cigarettes is strongly associated with TNC expansion, especially that of U.S. cigarette firms during the late 1960s (see Table 3.4).

Significant contraband trade in cigarettes is not only evident in Latin America, but in many nations, including relatively developed ones like Italy. For example, it was estimated that up to 200,000 Italians were earning their living smuggling cigarettes in 1978, costing the government an estimated $560 million a year in lost revenue ("Italy: Smuggling on the Rise" 1978, pp. 20, 26).

There are distinct patterns to cigarette smuggling. Cigarettes are first exported from the developed countries to small, intermediary, free trade nations such as Hong Kong, Panama, Netherlands Antilles, Paraguay, Lebanon, Malaysia, Belgium/Luxembourg, and Singapore. U.S. cigarette exports to these destinations outstrip the potential for domestic consumption by a factor of five to ten. For example, the Netherlands Antilles, with a population of 200,000, imported 4,126 million cigarettes from the U.S. in 1976. This equaled 20,630 cigarettes for every single man, woman and child when the estimated 1975 annual per capita consumption in the U.S. was only 2,816 cigarettes! These cigarettes are then re-exported to larger, protected markets close to the entrepôts. The Netherlands Antilles and Panama supply Colombia and the Carribean; Hong Kong, Malaysia, and Singapore supply the Phillipines, Thailand, and Indonesia; Paraguay supplies Brazil and Argentina; and Lebanon supplies much of the Mid-East. The value of this trade is considerable, even at the tax-free, duty-free prices reported at exit from the U.S.: In 1975 it was $50 million for Hong Kong; $37 million for the Netherlands Antilles; and $18 million

Table 3.4
Recorded World Exports and Imports of Cigarettes,
1951-1960ᵃ and 1967-1976ᵇ

Year	Recorded World Exports	Recorded World Imports	Percentage Difference
1951	126,735	106,508	16.0
1952	115,324	95,732	17.0
1953	114,869	90,708	21.0
1954	105,317	91,939	15.1
1955	108,420	92,179	15.0
1956	109,717	85,379	22.2
1957	110,129	92,334	16.2
1958	110,484	93,208	15.6
1959	108,609	86,425	20.4
1960	110,428	84,162	23.8
1967-71ᶜ Average	136,356	92,058	32.5
1972	178,415	126,016	29.4
1973	191,935	133,306	30.5
1974	203,888	153,615	24.7
1975	222,659	170,778	23.2
1976	241,797	177,361	26.6

Sources: U. S. Dept. of Agriculture, *World Tobacco Analysis—Consumer Marketing,* February 1958; *Foreign Agriculture Circulars—Tobacco,* FT 5-60, FT 8-62, FT-3-76, FT-2-77 (July, 1960; May, 1962; July 1976 and 1977)

Notes:
ᵃ In thousands of pounds of cigarettes
ᵇ In millions of cigarettes
ᶜ Unfortunately, the United States Dept. of Agriculture discontinued publishing data on world trade in cigarettes after 1962 and did not resume its international cigarette trade series until 1976 in which the 1967-1972 average was provided. It may be that USDA discontinued the data series since it appeared so unreliable as to be worthless during the 1960s.

for Lebanon, to cite a few examples. The retail value once it reaches the consumer is probably about twice this (Shepherd, forthcoming, Tables 33-34).

Contraband provides an effective, if unorthodox and illegal, method of gaining a foothold in protected foreign markets. Increase in the contraband cigarette trade is highly correlated with attempts of TNCs to take over national cigarette industries. Usually smuggling

90

reaches its peak just prior, during, and after TNC entry into a market. But it may extend for a considerable period of time if resistance by locally-owned firms is prolonged. After TNCs are well established smuggling declines. Colombia provides a good example of this phenomenon. It has one of the last wholly nationally-owned private cigarette industries with a fairly large market (above 20 billion cigarettes annually). Until recently, it also produced almost exclusively dark tobacco cigarettes as was once the norm throughout Latin America. Contraband began to increase in the early 1970s and national producers were severely hurt, forcing them to sign licensing agreements with TNCs to manufacture the two largest selling contraband cigarette brands, Philip Morris' Marlboro and P. Lorillard's Kent. However, these licenses were rescinded and contraband has continued at high levels in Colombia—approximately 4.5 billion cigarettes a year. Thus, domestic production has declined significantly (Republica de Colombia DNP 1975, p. 6; Pérez Vásquez 1975). This illicit trade was nearly as large as all U.S. exports of cigarettes to the EEC in the early 1970s and was worth $40 to $50 million. TNCs are still applying pressure in Colombia.

The process is revealed more clearly by the Argentine experience. Smuggling of cigarettes skyrocketed in the early 1960s, then fell off momentarily when legal imports with low duties were permitted to combat the problem. As a defensive measure, some national firms established themselves as exclusive importers of TNCs brands, beginning dependence on the TNCs. When legal imports were shut off, licensing arrangements were established for local manufacture of TNC brands that had previously been imported. Shortly thereafter, however, all the nationally-owned firms were acquired at bargain prices by TNCs, thus completing the denationalization process. Once TNCs were established and TNC brands were introduced in local versions smuggling rapidly declined to pre-1960 levels. It is estimated that $28 million in government revenue were lost between 1961 and 1967 because of contraband and $54 million in balance of payments. (ORIC 1968, Anexo V, pp. 5, 28).

Government policy toward this issue in both Colombia and Argentina tended to vacillate among various alternatives, none of which provided any real solution to the problem. Decisive government action on behalf of national firms was not forthcoming. Governments were incapable of eradicating corruption or incompetence in customs enforcement and in other crucial sectors of public administration such as the military. Although governments were losing millions of dollars in revenues from cigarette taxes, advertising for TNC brands that could only enter the countries illegally was blatantly apparent along public thoroughfares and in the mass media in both countries (Pérez Vásquez 1975, p. 31; Vilas 1974, p. 12). Assuming that legal imports with low tariffs would cut smuggling and recoup government revenues, import bans and high tariffs on foreign cigarettes were lifted. This only served to consolidate, legitimize, and expand TNCs' positions in the market and did nothing to relieve the pressures on nationally-owned firms. The latter vehemently protested, not without reason, that they had willingly borne the brunt of high taxation on their products to help support the government and were therefore entitled to some support themselves. In fact, during periods of legal imports, the effective rate of taxation on nationally-owned firms' products was actually much higher than that levied on TNC imported brands (Pérez Vásquez 1975, pp. 5-20). Thus, temporary periods of legal imports alternated with increased smuggling when import bans and high tariffs were reimposed until national firms were sufficiently financially crippled to either sell out to TNCs or sign licensing agreements.

Vacillation of public policy also appears to have been the result of the protected status and quasi-monopolistic positions national firms had long held in their markets. Public officials were not sympathetic to the plight of nationally-owned firms. When support did come, governmental action was taken not out of any great sympathy, but rather out of concern for the effects on tax revenues and the economy as a whole. Interviews with policymakers confirm that many viewed national cigarette firms as predatory, oppressive monopolists finally getting a taste of their own medicine. Thus, they tacitly encouraged TNC competiton, legal or illegal (Shepherd 1983). It could be argued that without the debilitating effects of contraband and government vacillation, many nationally-owned firms in Latin America could have survived.

Smuggling patterns suggest that contraband has been an arm of the marketing efforts of TNCs to penetrate foreign cigarette industries.[9] The benefits of smuggling go considerably beyond the simple desire to export more cigarettes. Contraband cigarettes create a demand for certain product forms and brands thereby facilitating TNC licensing and subsidiary operations. Smuggling also cripples local firms which can then be easily acquired. And, with licensing, contraband can be employed to press for equity participation. Contraband is for TNCs in the international economy what covert action is for governments in international politics. Although the precise role of transnational corporations in contraband activities needs clarification, it is obvious they are the primary beneficiaries.

Impact on Industrial Structure: Foreign Dominance and Concentration

"Denationalization" is an apt term for the process of TNC entry into the region's cigarette industries over the past twenty years because it took place largely through the acquisition by TNCs of existing nationally-owned firms. Nearly 80 percent of the traceable U.S. TNC subsidiaries in Latin America were acquisitions (Shepherd 1983, Appendix A). Denationalization has also primarily entailed the expansion of U.S. TNCs into the region. Although some European TNCs entered in the 1960s, BAT is the main European firm and most of its subsidiaries there were set up much earlier. Denationalization has been most aggressively pressed toward complete take-over in the largest markets with considerable growth potential, such as Argentina, Brazil, and Venezuela. In many of the smaller or more sluggish markets, TNCs have been content with licensing arrangements or minority equity positions, as in Peru, Bolivia, and Paraguay.

Transnational corporations are present in every national market in Latin America, save Cuba, and they are the dominating factor in most. As Table 3.5 indicates, their market shares are large, giving them control of most of the major cigarette industries. Nationally-owned tobacco industries survive in only a few nations such as Uruguay, Peru, and Colombia. Even these are tied to the TNCs by licensing arrangements and TNC influence is on the rise.

After cigarette TNCs entered Latin American markets, a radical transformation of the industry frequently took place, especially in the larger markets like Brazil, Argentina, and Mexico. Intense non-price oligopolistic competition for larger market shares immediately broke out. There was a rather short (five-year) cycle of intense, more evenly-divided competition in terms of market shares, followed by a considerable market shake-up (firms with initially large market shares declined and vice versa), and then renewed concentration and consolidation. The Argentine experience after 1966 may be a paradigmatic case. Before TNCs entered the Argentinian market, there were about seven major firms operating there. Around 65 percent of the market was evenly divided among locally-owned firms, the remainder was controlled by BAT's subsidiary. After a short period of intense oligopolistic rivalry following TNC take-overs, however, successive mergers reduced the industry to only two firms, a duopoly in the hands of BAT and Philip Morris. In other words, there was a transition from loose oligopoly to workable competition and then to renewed concentration and consolidation. (Fidel, Lucangeli and Shep-

Table 3.5

Transnational Cigarette Firms in Latin America: Subsidiaries, Licensing
Arrangements, and Non-Tobacco Operations, c. 1976

	British-American %	Philip Morris %	R. J. Reynolds %	Liggett Group %	Rupert/ Rothman's Group %	Reemtsma %	Loew's %	Total Output 1976	Est. TNC[b] Share %
Argentina	S-(42) NT	S-(22)		S-(17)		S-(19)	L	36,800	100
Barbados	S-(100)						L	210	100
Bolivia		L	S-(11)	S-(NI)				1,700	NI
Brazil	S-(75) NT	S-(5)		S^c	S^d	S^e		117,000	91
Colombia		L					S^f/L	18,300	3/15[a]
Costa Rica	S-(57)	S-(16)		L				2,300	75
Chile	S-(100)			L				8,800	100
Dom. Rep.		S-(NI)						3,200	NI
Ecuador		S-(NI)	S-(NI)					3,700	NI
El Salvador	S-(76)	S-(15)						2,200	91
Guatemala		S-(45) NT					L	2,400	50
Guyana	S-(NI)							500	NI
Haiti		L						500	NI
Honduras	S-(100)							1,800	100
Jamaica	S-(27)				S-(70)			1,500	97
Mexico	S-(30) NT	S-(14)	S^g/L-(NI)	L			L	45,000	60
N. Antilles		L						NI	NI
Nicaragua	S-(96)							1,700	96
Panama	S-(55)	S-(43)					L	1,100	98
Paraguay	L							700	NI

Peru	L	L[h]	L	S[i]/L		L	3,800	25
Puerto Rico		S[i]-(NI)	S-(NI)			S[i]-(NI)	NI	100
Trinidad/		L	L					
Tabago							1,200	NI
Uruguay		S-(10)					3,500	10
Venezuela	S-(19) NT	S[k]-(76)	S-(2)			L	18,800	97

Sources: United Nations Conference on Trade and Development, *Marketing and Distribution of Tobacco* (TD/R/C.1205), June 16, 1978. Table 9, p. 31/32; United States Department of Agriculture, *Foreign Agriculture Circular—Tobacco* TI-2-77, July, 1977; and estimates by the author based on various trade sources.

Notes:

[a] In millions of cigarettes (not by value).

[b] Estimates which include cigarettes manufactured under licensing arrangments but *not* export sales (either illicit or legal).

[c] Leaf exporting subsidiary only. Liggett closed its manufacturing subsidiary in 1972.

[d] The Rupert/Rothman Group (Martin Brinkmann) sold this subsidiary (Lopes) to R.J. Reynolds in 1975.

[e] Reemtsma sold this subsidiary (Fumos Santa Cruz) to Philip Morris in 1975.

[f] Leaf tobacco production subsidiary to supply its licensee, Protabacos, S.A.

[g] Reynolds sold its subsidiary (Baloyan) when the Mexican government forced divestiture of majority TNC holdings after 1973.

[h] Licensing agreement signed in 1978.

[i] Liggett sold its subsidiary in 1975.

[j] Apparently selling companies which do not manufacture in Puerto Rico.

[k] May have been sold off in 1976.

[l] TNC sales are only approximately 3% not including contraband; approximately 15% including illicit imports of TNC brands.

LEGEND: S-(%): Subsidiary with significant (20%+) equity holdings. Market share (by volume) is given in parenthesis.

L: Licensing agreement with a local company (either locally-owned or another TNC) in which no equity is held.

NI: No information available.

NT: Non-tobacco subsidiary operations are also present with significant (20%+) equity ownership).

95

herd 1977, pp. 21-39). While there are a number of factors making for high levels of concentration in Latin American cigarette industries, not all of them directly attributable to TNCs, the entry of TNCs has accentuated and further concentrated market structure.

TNC Expansion of Demand.

Another consequence of the expansion of TNCs into Latin American markets was rapid growth rates in total output and per capita consumption. This was often in great contrast to the relatively stagnant growth rates realized by nationally-owned firms. In Argentina, for example, sales of nationally-made cigarettes increased only 38 percent between 1950 and 1966, or an average of 2.4 percent annually, and per capita sales increased 5 percent (averaging .03 percent annually). After TNC entry, however, sales increased 58 percent between 1966 and 1975, an average of 6.4 percent annually, and per capita sales showed even more dramatic increases of 37 percent (4.1 percent annually) (Departmento de Tabaco 1950-1975).

Rapid growth was the result of increases in demand creation, primarily advertising, and the rationalization of distribution, larger sales forces, and other promotional techniques. In Argentina, in the five years prior to TNC entry in 1966, the average annual cigarette advertising expenditure (per 1,000 packs at constant 1960 prices) was 71.6 pesos. In the five years *after* TNC entry (from 1967 to 1971), this figure jumped four-fold to 266.8 pesos. Reported advertising expenditures were actually larger than reported earnings for Philip Morris' subsidiary in 1967, and high levels of advertising produced reported losses for three of the five TNCs in the 1967-1970 period. (Fidel and Lucangeli 1978, p. 18). Once the industrial shake-up had taken place, new brands launched, and old ones repositioned or eliminated, advertising and other promotional expenditures declined.

Initially, the transnational corporations heavily promoted their "international" (read: home market) brands in order to gain acceptance of locally-made versions of these brands formerly made available through smuggling. Over the long run, however, these brands play a somewhat less important role. National brands previously developed by local firms continued to be popular and comprised a large, often major, portion of the market.[10] Philip Morris, for example, reported that about 60 percent of its volume abroad was in regional and national brands. (Philip Morris, Inc. 1976, p. 6). The continued popularity of national brands suggests that TNC footholds in the market with international brands during the contraband period were actually

96

rather fragile and did not provide a secure basis for long-term success. Thus, the acquisition of national firms' brands was critical to their success.

Nationally-owned firms were not simply defeated in a relatively open, fair game of commercial combat with TNCs. Often enough, nationally-owned firms were well established, and their brands had accumulated a large stock of goodwill and market appeal. Most nationally-owned firms put up credible opposition. They did not simply "cave in" or sell out at the first hint of foreign competition. Without the debilitating effects of contraband and governmental vacillation, nationally-owned firms probably could have survived in many markets in Latin America.

EVALUATION OF THE PERFORMANCE OF THE INTERNATIONAL CIGARETTE OLIGOPOLY IN LDCs

Focusing largely on Latin America, but also on less developed nations (LDCs) generally, this section attempts a brief overview of the industrial performance of transnational cigarette firms in a variety of areas: pricing behavior, profitability, technology and employment, trade and balance of payments, linkage effects, income distribution, and product appropriateness, including the smoking/health issue.

Pricing Behavior.

Because of the high levels of concentration manifested in the international cigarette industry durable price competition would seem quite unlikely. Both the past history of the industry and theory suggest that non-price competition through advertising and product form variation would be much more common. Administered prices and oligopolistic price leadership patterns characterize many overseas cigarette markets in both TNC—and non-TNC—markets. But TNCs have an independent impact on prices which functions in addition to market power and concentration *per se*.

Once TNCs enter the market and take over local firms, prices increase substantially. As one example, cigarette prices increased substantially in Argentina after the acquisition of local firms in 1966. The real average price of a pack of cigarettes in Argentina was 12.0 pesos for the five years prior to the entry of TNC firms in 1966; in the five years following entry, however, the price jumped to an average of 15.5 pesos, an increase of 23 percent. It was not until stricter price controls were imposed by the Peron government in 1972 that the real price declined back to pre-1966 levels (Estudio Sur 1975, Table A-3, p. 10).

These price hikes reflected the efforts of TNCs to maintain or increase oligopolistic profit margins in the face of heightened non-price rivalry, e.g., the vast increase in advertising and the launching of new, more expensive product forms and brands. In given product categories there was some minor price shading, largely for new brand launches and brand "repositioning," but there was little true price competition. Whatever price competition existed was either temporary or as much the result of price control changes and rapid inflation as of TNC policy.

The most significant impact of TNCs on prices has been the overall shift toward more expensive, higher-margin product forms and brands. Orthodox oligopoly predicts this behavior (Kaldor 1949), and it is now operating internationally, especially in the form of "international" brands. A survey undertaken in 1976 of retail cigarette prices in thirty-six capital cities around the world found the international brand Marlboro priced higher than the largest selling national brand in all but seven cities. In only one (Brussels), was it lower in price. Of the ten LDC capitals surveyed, Marlboro was priced higher in all but one (Buenos Aires), where it was the same price (UNCTAD 1978, Table 23, p. 76). Differential taxation may account for some of these differences, but the basic pattern of higher prices would likely remain even if taxes were factored out.

Profitability

High levels of concentration and oligopolistic pricing strategies imply excess profits above a competitive profit rate equilibrium. Despite generally higher costs of demand creation and sometimes higher quality products, it seems probable that TNC profitability is usually well above ordinary industrial levels. Extraordinary circumstances aside—such as the price control/inflationary squeeze in Argentina—TNCs have normally earned oligopolistic profits. Unfortunately, it is difficult to evaluate how profitable the foreign operations of transnational corporations are because of the general absence of reliable disaggregated data on profits on individual operations abroad and the creative accounting implicit in the wide discretion TNCs have in where they declare their profits (Moran 1973, p. 381).

The little data available for cigarette TNCs is thus difficult to interpret. In 1978 Philip Morris reported net earnings of 14.9 percent on net assets in its wholly-owned foreign subsidiaries (Philip Morris, Inc. 1978, p. 46). If this figure is accurate and conceptually similar, Philip Morris' level of profitability abroad approached that enjoyed domestically by U.S. firms during the heyday of the American cigarette industry from 1911 to 1950. Tennant characterized this level of profitability as "far above competitive levels and [it] bespeaks a high degree of market control vigorously exercised" (Tennant 1950, 342). Likewise, in the mid-1970s, BAT reported that its Latin American subsidiaries, with only 12 percent of its total net assets, accounted for a full 20 percent of its total turnover, and about 20 percent of its total operating profits (before interest). In fact, in 1974 BAT reported much higher profit rates on its operations in Latin America, Asia, and Africa than in its U.K., European, U.S./Canada, and Australian regions. Operating profits as a percentage of net assets were 29 percent in Latin America, 36 percent in Asia and 29 percent in Africa. The operating profit rate on turnover (including taxes) was 7 percent in Latin America, a hefty 13 percent in Asia, and 14 percent in Africa (BAT, Ltd. 1974, p. 12).[11]

Technology and Employment

In cigarette manufacture there is some substitutability between labor and capital. The range is rather narrow, however, because cigarette production is highly capital-intensive and the labor-absorption potential of cigarette manufacture is rather low with any methods other than the most primitive handrolling techniques. The range of substitutability is not significant for employment creation. When introducing new product forms into Latin America TNCs have usually employed capital-intensive, sophisticated process technologies to replace older, more labor-intensive methods. Licensing of international brands by local firms almost invariably involves the importation of newer, more capital-intensive machinery to produce them as, for example, in Colombia and Peru.

The situation is more complex than this, however. There is no inexorable relationship between products and processes; TNCs have sometimes utilized relatively antiquated technologies and on occasion made imaginative use of local engineering talent and skilled labor to maintain or improve older technologies, as in Argentina in the 1970s (Fidel, Lucangeli and Shepherd 1977).

In terms of saving labor, the performance of TNCs and national firms has been about the same in cigarette manufacturing. The real potential for employment generation is found in agricultural (leaf) production. Here the range of alternative technologies is much broader in terms of labor absorption, and runs from very labor-intensive to highly capital-intensive. Few cigarette firms directly produce leaf tobacco, leaving the farm operations in the hands of growers, at least nominally independent. But all cigarette firms are

99

extensively involved in leaf production, marketing, and processing through the development of technology, extension programs, contracting, financing, and myriad other activities. This involvement is usually more direct and more extensive in developing nations than in developed countries. In general, TNCs have encouraged more capital-intensive agricultural practices with adverse employment effects and have not adapted to local conditions as well as national firms. BAT, with longer experience in the Third World, is an exception.

Concomitant with the introduction of new products and rapid growth in cigarette manufacturing in Latin America has been a substantial transfer of technology in both the industrial and agricultural sectors. Domestic skills have been improved, production quality has been raised, and secondary employment created. Technological dependence, however, continues and is likely to get worse as demand is increasingly tied to the TNCs international product cycle. Virtually no transnational corporate R&D is carried out locally; local products like dark tobacco cigarettes are being phased out; and both industrial and agricultural production is becoming inextricably bound up with imported process and product technology. In these conditions, whatever local industrial and agricultural know-how still exists is likely to atrophy or be confined to local adaptation chores.

Trade and Balance of Payments.

World trade in cigarettes is not large compared to total world production—about 6 percent in 1975 (USDA 1976). This is because most governments reason there are far better ways of spending scarce foreign exchange and have established substantial tariffs and other trade barriers. Trade has also been limited by the dominance of a handful of TNCs which routinely impose territorial restrictions on subsidiaries and licensees not to export their production of international brands. Philip Morris, for example, is not about to export Marlboros from Brazil to Argentina when it also has a subsidiary producing them in Argentina. Nor is it likely to permit subsidiaries and licensees to engage in international trade which is reserved for the home plants in the industrialized nations.

On the other hand, the development of leaf tobacco exports has been supported by TNCs because it is consistent with their interests in lower worldwide leaf prices and because they have often been forced by local content regulations to develop local tobacco supplies. As a consequence they have aided in the emergence of exports in some developing nations which collectively account for 55 percent of total leaf tobacco exports (UNCTAD 1978, p. 96). This trade is highly concentrated and some of the major TNCs are important leaf dealers (BAT and Imperial) (UNCTAD 1978, p. 88-115).

Another important issue concerning balance of payments in developing nations is the propensity of TNCs to import. International brand products and capital—intensive processes tend to require a variety of imported components. It is common for governments to grant a five- to ten-year grace period during which TNCs are allowed to import a progressively declining percentage of foreign tobacco for these brands while local sources of supply are developed. This imported, highly-processed tobacco can be very expensive. Sophisticated imported cigarette-making machinery used by TNCs will usually not run with locally-made cigarette paper, filter rod material, glue, etc. And the quality standards imposed for these international brands often require imported packaging materials, filters, and so forth. Technology fees on these brands and other technical assistance charges further aggravate balance of payments problems.

Transnational corporations may also have a direct pecuniary interest in expanding intrafirm trade—which in turn permits lucrative transfer-pricing strategies. BAT may, for example, suggest the vital necessity of buying new cigarette-making machinery from Molins and imported packaging materials from Mardon (in both of which it holds a substantial interest). Philip Morris noted that it had made a net positive contribution of over $200 million to the U.S. balance of payments through the export of cigarettes, leaf tobacco, and other manufacturing components in 1978 (Philip Morris, Inc. 1978, p. 11). These kinds of imports can thus wipe out any foreign exchange gains from increased tobacco exports, as has reportedly taken place in Zambia (Ross 1980, p. 146). On the other hand, TNCs have not always performed much worse than local firms in some of these areas. Sometimes they have complied better with government local content directives than local firms which tend to resist the investment in local production that these regulations usually imply.

Linkage Effects and Income Distribution.

The most important linkage in this industry is with leaf production. This is a very important question because of the large number of people involved and because leaf growers tend to be low income small farmers, peasants, and sharecroppers in LDCs. Overall, the performance of TNCs with farmers have probably been somewhat better than that of local firms simply because national firms have performed so poorly. National firms have tended to act like robber barons *vis-a-vis* local farmers. In Peru, for example, patron-client relations and

101

monopsonistic exploitation by local firms has been the rule, exploiting them to the hilt.

TNC relations with growers have more often followed the model of their relations with local labor unions, creating "labor aristocracies." If TNCs can be faulted it is for a tendency to work with larger richer, "commercial" farmers. There is also a definite cycle in TNC-farmer relations, a curiously opposite version of the "obsolescing bargain" noted by Moran and others. To foment light tobacco production, TNCs have offered substantial incentives to local farmers such as high leaf prices, low-cost inputs, free technical assistance, low-interest loans, and low-cost infrastructure construction. Once production was well established, however, monopsony power entered the picture and terms hardened. With marketing, technical assistance, and input channels now controlled through exclusive contracts, farmers' costs and income become largely company-dictated. In some nations, such as Argentina, only astute political organization, the slow development of countervailing power, and export markets have enabled growers to partially escape these effects of TNC monopsony/oligopsony.

National firms have probably done better in developing linkages with local suppliers. TNCs tend to import most non-leaf components. Prior to the entry of TNCs, for instance local Argentine firms had developed a wide variety of backward linkages with local suppliers, produced parts themselves, adapted production processes, and even built entire machines from scratch sometimes copying established engineering designs. The situation with respect to local distributors, jobbers, and retailers is less clear. Some TNCs such as BAT have tried to control distribution or squeeze local distributors' margins; others have been less rapacious. National firms have had their own struggles with these sectors, sometimes integrating vertically into wholesaling.

Regarding income distribution, the worst offenders in this industry are governments. Many Latin American governments have antiquated fiscal structures in which highly-regressive cigarette taxes have provide as much as 15 percent of total revenue. These taxes are often the single largest source of internal revenue. Cigarette taxes are highly regressive in their incidence, transferring money out of the pockets of consumers (many of them poor) and into government coffers. Moreover, these revenues are rarely returned to the consumer in the form of public services useful to them. And while cigarette taxation is highly regressive in most nations, it is probably more inequitable in LDCs with their greater inequalities of income distribution.

Apart from the portions going to growers and some part of the distribution force, little income generated by the cigarette industry in Latin America has gone to unskilled labor or farmers. Governments have received as much as 60 percent of the retail price of cigarettes in the form of taxes, manufacturers and distributors have received around 35 percent and farmers 5 to 10 percent. (Republica de Colombia DNP, 1975; Estudio Sur 1975). Nevertheless, the industry's performance in income distribution is almost certainly better than that of many other modern and/or TNC-dominated sectors such as autos and chemicals. This is because there are at least some payments to low-income groups like farmers and the wholesale/retail sales force. With expanding sales under TNCs, this effect has been reinforced.

Product Appropriateness.

For reasons of public health, cigarettes are obviously not a very appropriate product. The case against cigarettes is even stronger in LDCs, where vast sectors of the populace frequently lack the most rudimentary forms of food, clothing, and shelter, and health standards are already low. Furthermore, TNCs are more adept at increasing the per capita consumption of cigarettes than national firms. Hence, TNCs' much-heralded "efficiency" is obviously problematic in industries like cigarettes. In this industry, efficiency in demand creation contradicts basic human needs.

In most developing nations, the smoking/health issue has been almost totally absent from public debate. The adverse health effects of cigarette smoking have not become public knowledge nor the object of governmental action, with the consequence that TNCs often find it much easier to market their products in these areas than at home. ("Third World Market for Cigarettes Expands" 1978, p. 13). A World Health Organization (WHO) survey showed that of 100 governments providing information, 70 had no legislation whatsoever aimed at controlling the promotion or use of cigarettes ("Next Step Toward WHO Tobacco Control" 1976, p. 14). Another survey revealed that over two dozen LDCs (including all 14 Latin American nations surveyed) had taken no action in the regulation of cigarette advertising and the great majority had no warnings on cigarette packs (Pakkala 1976, p. 55).

The public health hazard smoking poses remains a low priority in most LDCs. The health director in Tanzania put it succinctly: "Smoking-related diseases are not regarded as a matter of concern at the present time" ("Third World Tobacco Push Hit" 1978, p. 2). Yet, the World Health Organization reported: "In some developing countries the epidemic of smoking-related disease is already of such magnitude as to rival even infectious disease or malnutrition as a public health problem. In Brazil, lung cancer became the leading cause of male death in 1974 and Brazilians dying of cardiovascular disease linked to smoking has gone up 5 percent since 1970" (Ross 1980, p. 145).

The international cigarette oligopoly has not been eager to raise implicitly the health issue by introducing low tar/low nicotine product forms to LDCs, for to do so would make a fair proportion of their existing products obsolete. In fact, they have tended to hold low tar cigarettes in reserve until such time as the product-cycle for older product forms has run its course in LDCs and health issues surrounding cigarettes become much more publicly controversial than they are at present. Many LDCs have only recently begun to consume substantial quantities of "first generation," 1950s-style filtered cigarettes in place of non-filters. In other markets, variations on the basic "first generation" filter cigarette are still a novelty (e.g., 100mm and 120mm filters, menthol filters, charcoal filters, etc.). Thus, TNCs have usually been careful in their operations in LDCs not to release more advanced product forms than the given national market is "ready for" in the product-cycle.[12]

At this juncture, some kind of normative or political judgment is indispensable. There is no escape from the trite, but frequently-resisted, observation that all goods and services are not equal in importance. Some measure of increased consumer welfare from higher-quality TNC cigarettes simply has to be balanced against the obviously more important and pressing basic needs of the broad mass of the population in LDCs. Since basic needs do not presumably include cigarettes, which have almost universally been classed as an unnecessary luxury by governments, these are not high priority items in a poor society.

GOVERNMENTAL POLICY ALTERNATIVES TO IMPROVE PERFORMANCE

The cigarette industry has not witnessed radical shifts in bargaining power from firms to governments such as the widely-heralded changes that have occurred in extractive sectors. Therefore, the dynamics of "bilateral monopoly" have been considerably different in this industry from those characterizing some raw materials. The basic reason for this is the degree of control the industry retains over demand creation and technology which allows it to control international consumer patterns. Transnational corporations are still very much in the driver's seat at present, although the smoking/health issue may become the "Achilles heel" of the industry in the future. The situation in developing nations is complicated by their inability to fully control access to the market—one of the primary sources of bargaining power *vis-a-vis* TNCs (Haskel 1980). Many LDCs are simply unable to seal off their cigarette markets from TNCs. ISI policies like high tariffs failed in maintaining a national industry in large measure because the domestic cigarette market could not be withheld or guaranteed to national firms. Since tariffs and import prohibitions could not block TNC entry, access to the market was not the trump card it has frequently been for governments in bargaining with TNCs.

One other major difficulty concerns the political will needed to translate potential bargaining power into real capability. As was noted in the analysis of smuggling, this political will was not evident in many Latin American nations. The state in most nations is not a unitary actor, maximizing some perceived national interest. In Latin American nations the political capacity to make and enforce the kinds of decisions necessary to shut out or constrain TNCs is often very low. This is partly the result of the weakness of the state itself and its administrative capability, but the class basis and alliances of the Latin American state are perhaps the major factors (Evans 1979). Furthermore, the state is usually the senior partner in the industry through its tax revenues, making policy even more problematic.

The following analysis of policy options assumes a relatively strong government that would have to have the power to set priorities for the industry, come to agreements about and with TNCs, and then enforce them. It would have to be a state dedicated to some conception of the national interest that goes beyond the narrow class interest of the upper- and upper-middle class, a debatable proposition at present in most nations in the region. Above all, these policy options are predicated on sufficient control of smuggling to regain the crucial power guarding access to the market. Under these conditions the state can change structural and conduct variables of the industry if appropriately designed and enforced policies are brought to bear in a timely fashion.

Policy Options for Industrial Restructuring.

TNC dominance is now a fact of life in Latin America in this industry.[13] It is simply too late to do much serious bargaining over entry conditions in most markets. TNC mutual forebearance and the elimination of smaller TNCs also make it unlikely that an "outsider" can be enticed into the market under different conditions to shake up the local industry. Since cigarette manufacture is not characterized by the large sunk costs and periodic negotiation over new concessions involved in extractive investments, there is little reason to expect much renegotiation over entry conditions.

Although transnational corporations dominate the Latin American cigarette industry and there is very little that can be done to entice new firms into the field, there are measures that could be taken to restructure the industry to improve overall performance. The feasible choices for most nations are three: (1) a highly concentrated oligopoly of TNCs; (2) a high concentrated oligopoly of national firms; and, (3) a state monopoly. A state monopoly would involve expropriation and all the difficulties that portends but this form of industrial structure should not be ruled out entirely. It is not necesarily anticapitalist nor does it necessarily set a precedent for expropriation in other sectors. Many otherwise capitalist nations have state monopolies in tobacco, including France, Japan, Austria, South Korea, Italy, Thailand, Turkey, and Spain. Most of these nations have had considerable success with state monopoly. State monopoly has much to recommend itself in the way of eliminating the social wastes of differentiated oligopoly, curbing the abuses of private market power, controlling tax revenues, and dealing with the smoking-health issue. Moreover, the inefficiencies sometimes associated with a state monopoly are much less troubling in the case of cigarettes. In fact, the somnolent decay of a state monopoly might be just what the doctor ordered.

If a state cigarette firm is set up, it is probably not advisable to allow local private firms to operate as the case of Peru illustrates. There, the Empresa Nacional de Tabaco was confined to the least-expensive and least-profitable end of the market while private firms concentrated on profitable *tabaco rubio* brands. A state enterprise which tries to compete with the private sector must be adequately financed and can become a constant drain on the state without ever becoming truly competitive. Moreover, this structure encourages the state enterprise to engage in all the socially wasteful aspects of oligopolistic competition without reaping the benefits of state monopoly. This "yardstick" approach may allow the state to get a better understanding of the industry and fill some empty space in the market, but this is a high price to pay for limited benefits. The best alternatives are either a complete state monopoly or a restructuring of the private sector to encourage more competition.

A state enterprise may also be the answer to persistent tensions and severe monopsonistic pressures in the agricultural end of the industry. In nations with large leaf exports, for example, governments might consider splitting off leaf export operations from the TNCs by forming joint ventures with the large international leaf trading firms such as been done in the Philippines, Thailand, South Korea, and other capitalist nations with state enterprises. This might avoid trade difficulties by playing the leaf trading oligopolists off against each other. More importantly, state enterprise can reduce the problems associated with monopsony or oligopsony in the domestic leaf market, either from TNCs or rapacious national firms. Mexico's TABAMEX is an attempt to solve the problem along these lines.

If state enterprises are not employed, the creation and promotion of real countervailing power should be used. These "New Deal" type agricultural reform measures would include price supports, government inspecting and grading of leaf, acreage/poundage programs to control supply, cooperatives, the development of effective agricultural extension, research and credit, and perhaps the implementation of an auction system to break the monopsony involved in contract buying. The case of Argentina shows that these measures can improve the tobacco farmer's lot. There, a surcharge on cigarettes was used to pay leaf growers a margin above what TNCs paid. The surcharge slowly became about 50 percent of what growers received and reduced TNC market power. The development of exports through non-TNC channels can also powerfully affect growers' returns, and this aided the development of countervailing power in Argentina.

Measures to Affect Conduct. If a state monopoly is rejected, the governments of developing nations will have to rely on measures to change the conduct of private firms. Frequently, measures dealing with import substitution, trade, prices, and profit repatriation and the like are not industry specific, are overly-formalistic, and are focused on narrow criteria characteristic of the "economism" of much national economic planning in Latin America. A partial, agency-by-agency fragmentation of policy adds up to an *ad hoc* policy environment with conflicting and incoherent rules of the game. What is needed are policies based on a broad, indepth analysis of the industry and its performance. Specifically, policies concerning local content, price controls, competition and demand creation should be reviewed to eliminate conflicting and incoherent regulations that control the operations of cigarette firms.

Local Content Policies. Efforts by governments all over the world to encourage cigarette firms to use locally-grown tobacco to save on scarce foreign exchange have been, for the most part, successful. Local content regulations are therefore somewhat less important than in some other industries. There are, however, possibilities for developing local sources for other requirements of the industry, such as cigarette paper, filter rod materials, and machinery. This is more feasible in some of the larger markets since most of these materials require substantial markets to realize economies of scale in their manufacture. Furthermore, there is still room for using more domestic machinery, especially in agriculture, where firms have frequently imported expensive capital-intensive machinery when simpler, domestically-made or adapted equipment would do. Improved government policies in this area would have a number of benefits for LDCs, such as reducing imports, providing more employment in both making the equipment and using it, and developing local technological capacity.

Price Controls. There are strong precedents in Latin America for the use of price controls to improve performance of the cigarette industry because the commodity has been considered politically sensitive. When these controls have been strictly enforced they have been fairly effective in forcing more competitive and socially beneficial behavior. The political process of revising the controls upward means that price changes almost inevitably tend to lag behind inflation. This keeps prices more in line with what they would be under more competitive conditions. Price controls can have the effect of keeping a firm's profitability closer to what it would be in a competitive equilibrium and forcing it to make decisions regarding technology, etc., along almost neo-classical factor price criteria (Fidel, Lucangeli, and Shepherd, 1977). Thus, all that is needed here is to use existing price controls, make them permanent, and enforce them strictly.

Competition Policy. Regarding competition, there is probably little that can be done to decrease radically concentration in the industry. Governments can, however, abolish the flat rate cigarette tax which discriminates against lower-priced products. Were they to institute *ad valorum* taxes this might allow new entrants to get a foothold in the cheaper end of the market. These taxes would also be more equitable for poorer consumers. The establishment of merger review procedures would also stimulate competition by blocking the uncontrolled takeover of small firms. As was shown earlier, TNCs often entered the market by buying up one national firm and then over the years acquiring others, or by combining among themselves. This has powerfully increased concentration. While there is little that can be done about the past, conscientious merger review with an eye toward blocking further concentration could avoid this being repeated in the future in some markets. Finally, effective anti-trust legislation—including treble damage suits—is sorely needed if competition is to be promoted. This will probably not provide much "free market" competition, any more than it has in the U.S., but it might prevent Latin American oligopolies from evolving into private monopolies and discourage the worst abuses of market power.

Policies Toward Advertising, Product Form Variation and Promotion through Distribution

The key to understanding market power in the cigarette industry is the nexus between demand creation and technology expressed in advertising, product form variation, and distribution strategies. Any coherent policy aimed at improving the performance of the industry must deal with all of these or be ineffectual.

Several possible attacks on demand creation suggest themselves. One is the complete prohibition of advertising of cigarettes including the sponsorship of sports events, coupons, and so forth for all media. A blanket prohibition on all these forms of demand creation would probably be easier to enforce than one with numerous loopholes. The potential uproar this policy might cause could be partially defused by insisting it was industry-specific, promulgated because of the dangers to public health. Another policy might be a stiff *ad valorum* tax on demand creation expenditures of all kinds, particularly advertising, the proceeds of which could be used to finance anti-smoking educational campaigns and public health programs. Still, these measures are not likely to be politically feasible.

A more politically feasible policy would be to escalate existing cigarette taxes to restrict consumption. Given the low per capita income in most Latin American nations, this regressive measure would probably restrict consumption among the vast majority if the tax were stiff enough. At the very least, governments should require that cigarette advertisements and packages contain warnings about the dangers associated with cigarette smoking. Tax revenues from cigarettes should also be used to finance anti-smoking educational campaigns and public health programs. And, finally, governments should pay more attention to restricting the distribution of cigarettes. This could limit demand creation to a certain extent, especially to youth. Limitations on the size of the wholesale and retail sales force involved in cigarette promotion might have a large impact because distribution is still a bottleneck in LDCs and a fair degree of sales pressure is still exercised at that level in these nations. Governments should consider splitting off the distributional end of the business from cigarette firms, many of which are fully integrated into wholesale distribution to improve efficiency and gain market power in this area.

At the same time efforts are being made to reduce demand, policies should be initiated to insure that safer low tar/nicotine product forms are introduced by taxing cigarettes according to tar and nicotine levels (Harris 1980).

There are indications that such measures might be markedly more successful in slowing (or even reducing) cigarette consumption in less developed nations. This is because cigarette smoking is not yet well established in many LDCs as opposed to industrialized countries where it has become an integral part of the political, economic and socio-cultural landscape. Although these policy options are unlikely to be attempted, the potential benefits of restricting primary demand growth are so large LDC governments should consider them. As always, an ounce of prevention is worth a pound of cure.

In sum, governments of developing nations have a variety of policy options available to them to reduce the oligopolistic control of transnational cigarette firms if they choose to use them.

Notes

[1] Industrial organization and the economics of advertising literatures have ignored the quality dimension in favor of a focus on advertising *expenditure*. Despite the complex methodology employed, one suspects that the omission of this simple but crucial factor may account for the widely divergent results obtained (for example, Comanor and Wilson 1974 vs. Schmaleusee, 1972).

[2] The term "marketing" is a gross misnomer for these techniques. It implies some process of adaptation to a given, autonomous market when, in fact, marketing activities are often directed to control and change, or, in effect, *transcend* the market.

[3] The analysis up to this point has studiously avoided the use of the term "product differentiation." For reasons not unlike those presented by Simon (1970, Appendix A), I regard the term as hopelessly confused and conceptually inadequate.

[4] The term is from Kaldor (1949, pp. 16-19) who, in turn, drew much of his analysis from Hawtrey (1926, pp. 15-45). "Wholesalers' domination" functioned in most markets for consumer goods during the nineteenth century in the U.S. until it was transformed at the end of the century by national advertising, transportation improvements, and large-scale manufacturing (Porter and Livesay 1971; McCurdy 1978).

[5] These tactics are exhaustively described in the Bureau of Corporations' investigations of the Trust (1909–1915, Parts I-III) and in testimony recorded in the anti-trust cases *United States vs. American Tobacco Company* 164 Fed. 700 (1908) and *United States vs. American Tobacco Company* 221 U.S. 106 (1911).

[6] The cumulative impact of persistent publicity, supported by other public policies, on U.S. consumption may have been substantial. Warner (1977) estimates that, in the absence of the campaign, per capita consumption would have exceeded its actual 1975 value by 20 to 30 percent.

[7] The diversification experience of this industry is interesting because it seems to contradict some widely-accepted ideas in the IO literature. For reasons of space, these can only be summarized here (Shepherd 1981; Shepherd, forthcomings). First, the cost

on non-tobacco acquisitions and subsequent investment was very large, revealing both the degree of commitment to diversification and the large cash flow/financial leverage for use in cross-subsidization efforts. Second, the variety of non-tobacco businesses was (and is) large. Diversification was not limited to a few demand creation-intensive consumer products similar to cigarettes. Finally, the process of diversification was on the whole, rather successful, though profitability in non-tobacco areas has not matched the extraordinary levels enjoyed in the domestic cigarette industry.

[8] Numbers of overseas subsidiaries and licensing agreements are clearly very imperfect measures, vastly inferior to (largely unavailable) data on investment flows, market shares and the like. Nevertheless, they provide one indication of the geographic distribution of operations (Shepherd 1983, Appendix A). In 1977 U.S. TNC's had 46 percent of their wholly- or partially-owned subsidiaries in Latin America, 28 percent in the U.K. and Western Europe, and only 19 percent in Asia, and only one such operation in Africa. In comparison, Western European firms had 40 percent of their subsidiaries in Asia, 28 percent in Latin America, and 7 percent in Africa (Shepherd forthcoming, Table 29).

[9] It is in this context that the significant upswing in U.S. cigarette exports since the late 1960s should be interpreted. U.S. cigarette exports were 82 billion in 1980, valued at some $1.06 billion. This was over 11 percent of U.S. cigarette output, the largest percentage going abroad (other than to U.S. Armed Services) since 1920. Cigarette exports are now 79 percent of the value of U.S. leaf tobacco exports, traditionally much more important as exports (USDA 1981, p. 8). While a number of factors have influenced increasing exports-oil exporting states' imports, the worldwide trend to "American Blend" cigarettes, and the "multiplier effect" of the presence of U.S. TNCs' operations abroad that is claimed by the industry (Philip Morris 1976, p. 7). Increased smuggling is also a factor.

[10] In Argentina during 1975 the combination of government price controls and extreme rates of inflation had made the more expensive international brands relatively cheap. Even at the height of international brand popularity, however, these brands accounted for only 32.7 percent of the Argentine cigarette market by unit volume (Camara de la Industria del Cigarrillo, 1976).

[11] On the other hand, U.S. TNCs' profitability abroad has apparently not matched that of its domestic business in cigarettes. From 1974 to 1978, for example, Philip Morris reported that between 25.2 and 29.5 percent of its operating revenues come from abroad but only 19.5 to 23.4 percent of its operating income did. Likewise, its ratio of operating income to operating revenue was between 10.4 and 12.0 percent from 1974 to 1978 on international operations vs. a much higher 19.1 to 23.3 percent on its domestic cigarette business (Philip Morris, Inc. 1978). This suggests that, high as overseas subsidiaries' profit rates might be, they still do not rival those of domestic cigarette operations for U.S. firms.

[12] Furthermore, TNC cigarettes made abroad (by either subsidiaries or licensees) are usually much higher in tar and nicotine than their look-alike brands in the U.S. For example, a recent comparison test showed that Marlboro, Chesterfield, Kent, and Kool averaged 17.5 mg. tar in the U.S. while the same brands made in the Philippines averaged 31.8 mg. tar (Ross 1980, pp. 144-145). In part, these differences may be explained by local content regulations, but it seems unlikely that this factor is the primary reason for such wide disparities in tar and nicotine levels.

[13] With the benefit of hindsight it is now possible to see that less developed nations' governments should have struck much better deals with TNCs in the industry in the 1960s and 1970s when the pressure on TNCs to go abroad was at its height. A kind of paranoia about the smoking/health issue gripped the U.S. industry at this time and it

111

seems likely that much more favorable bargains could have been negotiated than are possible now. Unfortunately, many Third World governments did not have monitoring agencies charged with reviewing conditions of entry at that time. Where they did, they were not preoccupied with TNC manufacturing, the focus being on squeezing the large extractive industries.

Richard S. Newfarmer

4.

International Oligopoly in the Electrical Industry

INTRODUCTION*

The use of electricity as a source of power has progressed a long way since the rainy evening when Ben Franklin courageously and somewhat misguidedly flew his kite in a storm. Few people in the industrialized world go through a day without flicking a light switch, turning on an electrical appliance, or using electricity in some way. This chapter traces the circuitous evolution of this complex industry, the rivalry of its dominant firms, and its growth in developing countries, particularly Brazil.

The electrical machinery industry is one of the most important, technically advanced, and fastest growing industries worldwide. Depending on how it is defined[1], it accounts for between 5 and 10 percent of manufacturing value-added in most industrialized and newly industrializing countries. The industry's consumer products are well-known: lamps, electronic equipment, and household appliances. Its capital goods include heavy equipment to generate and distribute electricity, such as turbines, generators, transformers and switch-gear, and specialized industrial equipment, such as motors, drives, and control instrumentation for factories.

Much of the world's production of electrical goods is produced by a score or so of giant firms which have annual sales in excess of $1 billion and produce in most of the industry's sub-branches (see Table 4.1). With growth, the industry has become highly diversified; firms

* This chapter draws on research elaborated in greater detail in *Transnational Conglomerates and the Economics of Dependent Development* Greenwich JAI: 1980. To avoid repetition, internal citations to this work have been omitted.

Table 4.1

Transnational Companies in the Electrical Industry,[a] 1980

| | Sales (millions) | Electrical Machinery | | | | | | Conglomerate |
		Power Machinery	Distribution Equipment	Telecom- munications	Domestic Electrical	Medical Equipment	Lamps	(selected non-electrical industries)
Federal Republic of Germany								
Majors:								
Siemens	17,950	Yes	Yes	Yes	Some	Yes	Yes	defense, locomotives, computers
AEG-Telefunken	6,755		Yes	Some	Yes	Yes	Yes	office equipment, defense
France								
Majors:								
Cie. Générale d'Electricité (CGE)	10,847	Yes	Yes	Yes	Yes	Some	Yes	computers, defense
Cie. Française Thomson-Houston-Hotchkiss-Brandt	8,657	Some	Yes		Yes		Yes	autoparts, radar, broadcasting
Minors:								
Schneider	7,511	(some heavy industrial equipment)						mining, non-electrical machinery, iron and steel
Japan								
Majors:								
Hitachi	12,871	Yes	Yes		Some	Yes		chemicals, machinery, railway equipment
Matsushita Electric	12,684	Yes	Yes	Yes	Yes		Yes	non-electrical appliances
Tokyo Shibaura (Toshiba)	8,146	Yes	Yes	Yes	Yes	Some	Yes	chemicals, nuclear equipment
Mitsubishi Electric	5,065		Some		Yes			shipbuilding, auto electrical
Nissan Electric	3,767			Yes	Some			data processing, computer
Minors:								
Sanyo	4,023				Yes	Yes		non-electrical appliances
Sony	3,789							
Netherlands								
Majors:								
Philips	18,402			Yes	Yes	Yes	Yes	chemicals, computers

Source: Financial Times International Business Yearbook, Fortune Magazine, and public media.
Notes:
[a] Dominant transnational producers in lines of businesses considered in the text.
[b] Ericsson, ASEA and Electrolux have interlocking directories and are affiliated with Sweden's financially powerful Wallenberg family.
[c] Electrolux is affiliated with ASEA in Sweden, but unconsolidated.

Sweden							
Majors:							
ASEA[b,c]	2,969	Yes	Yes	Yes			locomotive
Ericsson[b]	2,878		Yes				
Minors:							
Electrolux[b,c]	5,409		Yes	Yes	Yes		industrial ovens, office equipment
Switzerland							
Majors:							
Brown Boveri	6,005	Yes	Yes	Yes			non-electrical machinery, locomotives
United Kingdom							
Majors:							
General Electric Co., Ltd. (GEC)	6,556	Yes	Yes	Yes	Some	Yes	TV rentals, radar, engineering, musical equipment, recc
United States							
Majors:							
General Electric (GE)	24,959	Yes	Some	Yes	Some	Yes	defense, broadcasting, mining, aerospace
Westinghouse	8,914	Yes	Some	Yes	Some	Yes	soft drinks, wrist watches, broadcasting, records
I.T.T.	18,529	Yes	Yes	Yes	Some	Yes	hotels, rentacar, motion picture, food, insurance
R.C.A.	8,011		Some	Yes	Some		broadcasting, defense, foods, car rental, bookpublishing
Minors:							
Whirlpool	2,243	Yes		Yes			non-electrical appliances
Allis Chalmers	2,063	Yes	Yes				farm machinery

historically spanning the industry and controlling most of its technology have begun to gravitate towards particular branches. To avoid the problem of over-aggregation, this paper focuses on three sub-branches: heavy equipment, televisions, and lamps.

THE ORGANIZATION OF THE INTERNATIONAL
ELECTRICAL INDUSTRY: STRUCTURE AND RIVALRY

History of internationalization

After the invention of the electric lamp in 1879, a handful of firms came to dominate electrical technology in developed countries: General Electric (GE) and Westinghouse of the U.S., AEG and Siemens of Germany, ASEA of Sweden, Brown Boveri of Switzerland, to name a few, rose to preeminence in their home markets. Fierce price and technological competition eliminated many smaller companies in the early stages of the industry so that by the turn of the century, strong price competition had given way to oligopolistic agreements in most national markets; though firms continued to compete vigorously in innovation, marketing, and other non-price ways. In the U.S. in 1896, GE and Westinghouse had entered into patent cross-licensing arrangements that virtually established agreed-upon market shares for most of their products (Passer 1953, pp. 263-265; 323-326) and producers in England and Germany, unencumbered by antitrust legislation, had formed local cartels to set prices and allocate business (Stocking and Watkins 1946, pp. 314-316).

The dominant firms soon tried to expand into international markets. By 1890 the two leading U.S. companies had established marketing subsidiaries and joint ventures in the United Kingdom, Germany, and France. Shortly thereafter Siemens set up a subsidiary in Chicago. However, their efforts were only marginally successful. Foreign parent firms found it difficult to manage subsidiaries at a distance; domestic firms pirated designs or challenged patents before sympathetic national courts; price competition drove earnings down (FTC 1928); direct investments proved only modestly effective; and, producers looked for a reduction of the competitive pressures generated from their international activities. As early as 1883 Werner Siemens was concerned about foreign competition, and had written to his brother William: "I believe it would be a good policy to make peace with Edision *in the whole world*. It will make us ruler of the electrical

116

industry." Yet it took another two decades to quell the heated competition in markets and courts of law.

Around 1900 the leading firms adopted patent licensing agreements. Cross-licenses enabled firms to obtain those parts of a technology they needed in conjunction with their own to complete a process or product and enter into production without violating the patents of a rival. The company with the most patented technology, GE, was therefore in the strongest bargaining position *vis-a-vis* other rivals (FTC 1928). It negotiated contracts with AEG in 1903, Tokyo Electric in 1904, Shibaura Engineering in 1905, and by 1926, it had licensing arrangements with firms in over 19 foreign countries, many of which were joint ventures or wholly-owned subsidiaries. To a lesser extent the other major firms followed suit. Westinghouse had contracts with at least seven overseas firms (FTC 1928). By the 1920s technology agreements covered lamps, most heavy electrical machinery, household appliances, motion picture equipment, phonographs, radio equipment, typewriters, and other products (Hexner 1945, pp. 368-398).

The system of cross-licensing permitted firms to allocate markets among themselves through clauses restricting the use of the licensed technology to well defined territories. For example, GE was accorded a dominant role in Brazil and Mexico in lamps, while Osram and Philips were given privileged positions in Southern and Eastern Europe. In most agreements companies were forbidden to initiate production in the nonproducing areas using the technology covered in the agreement; when production was permitted, the designated firm was commonly empowered to set the market price and other firms agreed to follow the set price if they chose to sell in the market. The agreements usually lasted ten years, and were repeatedly renegotiated and renewed.

The Depression had a dramatic destabilizing effect on the international equilibrium that had been organized under cross-licenses. Since home demand had almost evaporated and new competition was depressing export prices, the largest transnational enterprises turned to collusion to preserve their markets from outside poaching and to maintain prices to nonproducing countries. On December 13, 1930 nine[2] of the world's largest electrical manufacturers met in the Paris office of International General Electric Co., and signed the International Notification and Compensation Agreements (INCA), the basis of a formal cartel to restrain trade in heavy electrical equipment. The INCA followed in the wake of separate cartels for other products, such as lamps (1924) and cables (1928). These agreements did not abrogate existing market allocations established through the cross-licenses among the leading producers, but covered countries not previously included in cross-licenses arrangements, mainly developing countries. By 1936 producers felt the need for a more formal administrative apparatus and so they formed the International Electrical Association (IEA) in Zurich, Switzerland, to administer INCA. The cartel had grown into 16 "sections" of product groups with at least 42 members (FTC 1928, pp. 43-45).

World War II temporarily disrupted the cartel, but the IEA continued to function in a limited way. Some British, U.S., Swiss and other European producers participated on the Allied side, while the German, Italian, and French producers organized a parallel cartel in the Axis area. After the war the cartel in heavy equipment was slowly reconstituted and territories renegotiated in a much changed international environment.

The effects of the restrictive clauses in the licensing agreements were to allocate markets among producers creating near monopolies and to entrench the dominant position of firms in their home markets by raising barriers to entry to other domestic enterprises, which could not go abroad to buy the needed technology (FTC 1928). Developing countries were especially hurt because they could buy from only a few predetermined sellers who often adopted concerted pricing tactics. Moreover, TNCs agreed to impede the spread of manufacturing facilities and technology to the nonproducing countries insuring that these areas would remain importers by raising nearly insurmountable technological barriers to entry to domestic producers.

Post-War and Contemporary International Organization

In the post-war period the industry became considerably more diversified with many new products, especially mass-market consumer products. Technological advances created auxiliary industries that were related to, but grew separately from the electrical industry itself, such as computers, calculators, and copiers. The modern electrical industry thus includes a highly diversified range of products, ranging from heavy electrical supply equipment to producer goods to consumer goods. It is controlled by a relatively small group of very large corporations which produce in nearly all of the industry's branches. Exact measurement of aggregate concentration is impossible because of the absence of world production data and of product-line reporting by company. However, Ayhan Cilingiroglu, writing for the World Bank, gives an idea of the dimensions of international concentration in heavy electrical equipment:

The large international firms predominate in the production of generators, turbines, and switchgear. Certain items like very large steam turbines and generators or high voltage DC trans-'mission equipment are the exclusive domain of a few firms. Even in transformers, which are the most common product of the [capital goods side of the] industry, the large firms take the lion's share. In the world there are about 250 manufacturers of power and distribution transformers, employing altogether about 120,000 people—of these, about 25 firms employ 90,000 (75 percent of the labor force) and account for all the exports (1969, p. 16)

Much the same could be said for large motors, cables, telecommunication equipment, and many consumer products.

Markets in the industry are probably becoming more concentrated. This is clearly the case for heavy electrical equipment, because governments in Western Europe have sponsored industrial reorganization programs and encouraged mergers to insure the viability of this strategic industry in the face of sagging demand and increasing minimal efficient scales. Even in consumer markets of some developed countries, concentration of electronics equipment and domestic electrical appliances has increased slightly. In the Federal Republic of Germany, the four largest firms increased their share of the electronics equipment industry from 45 percent in 1962 to 51 percent in 1973; in France the increase in concentration was from 49 to 68 percent (1972). Concentration in domestic appliances rose in Germany to 75 percent and in Ireland to 61 percent between 1969 and 1973, but remained the same in Denmark at 94 percent (EEC 1975). Concentration across most consumer markets in the U.S. has declined marginally (U.S. Department of Commerce 1972).

The international firms are tied together by a web of contractual arrangements that heighten concentration in the market. A few firms hold substantial blocks of shareholder equity in the others. GE, for example, owns about 10 percent of Japan's Toshiba, and until recently, held nearly 12 percent of Germany's AEG. Other firms engage joint ventures in important markets; for example, Philips and Matsushita together produce electronic products for export from Japan and Allis Chalmers has combined with Siemens to sell power equipment in the United States. And, cross-licensing arrangements are still common. While such ties can have pro- or anti-competitive effects in a specific market, the effect generally is to raise international aggregate concentration.

In sum, the share of the world industry of the largest 20 and probably even the largest 8 firms has increased in the post-war period.

119

The industry has become more diversified and most product markets seem to have remained remarkably stable in concentration at relatively high levels. Many have even increased.

The reasons for this are several. First, in some branches technologically determined minimum efficient scales constitute a large share of the market, and increases in scale have matched or even exceeded growth in the market; the low costs of the few largest firms keep concentration high. Second, size is often linked to technical advance. The largest firms have an advantage in innovation and can set the technological pace. In some heavy equipment markets, such as power generators, the technological trend is towards ever larger products, giving the large leading firms an advantage since only they can better absorb the risks inherent in longer delivery times and wider cyclical business swings. Third, government policy in many home markets, especially in Europe, has promoted consolidation believing that mergers solve the problems raised by excess capacity and slower growth. Fourth, product differentiation plays an important role in maintaining or increasing concentration, especially in some consumer electronics products. Because industry leaders spend large amounts on advertising, potential entrants are disadvantaged in competing for consumer loyalty without comparable or even greater expenditures. Consequently, continued or even increasing concentration in the industry results from a blend of technologically determined economic forces, control of finance capital, tactics of leading firms, and state policy.

International Oligopolistic Rivalry

International rivalry among the dominant transnationals gradually increased after World War II. The world economy had undergone a qualitative transformation as industries grew rapidly, international trade reached new heights, and foreign investment replaced exports of final products as a way of reaching many foreign markets. Much of the new international trade was between parent corporations and their subsidiaries, reaching nearly 25 percent in the electrical industry. Simultaneously, public attitudes towards international cartels became less tolerant in the U.S., and (to a lesser extent) Western Europe and Japan. As a consequence of these changes producers had to adjust strategies they employed in their export activities and direct investments to the new environment. The next section will trace the new patterns of rivalry that evolved in three branches of the industry: heavy equipment, televisions, and lamps.

120

Heavy Equipment. The IEA slowly assumed its pre-war form after reconstruction efforts in Europe were accomplished and covered most heavy equipment (Monopolies Commission 1957). It was weak and probably ineffectual in the years immediately following the war. An antitrust consent decree in the U.S. prevented the participation of U.S. firms, and the U.S. post-war administration in Japan had obtained passage of similar antitrust laws for Japanese firms. The European and British firms after the war were at first occupied with rebuilding domestic electrical installations and factories and they paid less attention to foreign markets. The reconstruction effort soon tapered off and by the early 1950s manufacturers found themselves with expanded capacity and decreased domestic demand. Many of them looked to export markets for sales outlets, generating strong competitive pressures among firms of various nationalities. This probably accelerated the recoalescence of the cartel. By the mid-1950s the IEA had 40 members from all over Europe (Monopolies Commission 1957, pp. 25-31), which slowly expanded to 55 in 1977 (see Table 4.2). The value of production actually under the cartel's auspices grew rapidly because many of the small firms merged with larger members. Throughout the 1960s, then, the cartel appears to have grown in strength, both in breadth of membership and restrictive provisions in contracts (Epstein and Newfarmer 1980).

The entrance of the Japanese into the cartel in the late 1960s further strengthened its control of the market by eliminating the main competitive threat in foreign export markets. Japanese exports of steam turbines averaged 178 MW per year between 1960 and 1967, about 6.4 percent of total world shipments. Between 1968 and 1970, they averaged 1,967 MW, a tenfold increase that accounted for 23 percent of world shipments. European members of IEA viewed the emergence of the Japanese as a serious threat to their export markets and sometimes included special provisions in their agreements to cope with this competition. Sometime in 1967-1968, IEA representatives contacted the Japanese firms, which had already formed their own national export cartel and initiated negotiations for their entrance into the IEA. By 1970 they were in reality all but full members, although they maintained the ruse of independence by keeping their participation secret, by not paying IEA dues in the manner of European firms, and by having code letters rather than numbers. By 1976 they were paying 25 percent of the entire administrative budget and subscribing to agreements in six of ten major product groups (Epstein and Newfarmer 1980).

121

Table 4.2
Membership of IEA and Participation in Product Sections, 1977

Company	Product Section Code Letters[a]									
	A	B	E	F	G	H	K	P	T	W
AEG-Telefunken	X	X	X	X	X		X	X	X	
Alsthom	X	X	X				X	X	X	
Alsthom-Savoisienne						X				
AMN	X									
Ansaldo	X	X	X							X
ASEA		X	X	X	X	X	X			
Bell										X
Bonar Long						X				
Boving										X
Brown Boveri	X	X	X			X	X	X	X	
Creusot-Loire	X									X
Delle-Alsthom					X					
Elin-Union			X	X		X		X		
Escher Wyss										X
Ferranti						X				
Fiat									X	
Franco Tosi	X									X
GEC	X	X	X	X	X	X		X	X	X
Hawker Siddeley						X				
Italtrafo						X				
Jeumont-Schneider						X	X	X		
John Brown									X	
Karlstads										X
Kvaerner Brug										X
KWU	X	X							X	
Legnano						X				
Magrini					X					
MAN	X	X								
Marelli		X	X			b		X		
Merlin Gerin					X					
National Industri			X			X				
Neyrpic										X
Nohab										X
Parsons	X	X								
Parsons Peebles						X				
Reyrolle					X					
Riva Calzoni										X
Secheron						X				
Siemens	X	X	X	X	X		X	X		
Smit Transformatoren						X				
Smit Slikkerveer	X									

Company	A	B	E	F	G	H	K	P	T	W
SOGET (Rateau)	X									
Sprecher & Schuh				X						
Stal-Laval	X	X							X	
Tampella										X
Trafo Union					X					
Turbotechnica									X	
Voith Heidenheim										X
Voith St. Poelten										X
Fuji Electric			X			X	X			X
Hitachi	X	X	X			X	X			X
Meidensha			X			X	X			X
Mitsubishi Electric			X			X	X			
Mitsubishi Heavy	X	X								X
Toshiba	X	X	X			X	X			X

Product Section Code Letters[a]

Source: Epstein and Newfarmer 1980.

Notes:
[a] Equipment lines covered in each coded section are listed in Table 4.3.
[b] Scheduled to resign from this section on June 30, 1977.

Conspicuous for their absence are U.S. producers. In 1947 an antitrust consent decree prohibited U.S. firms from participating in the IEA. Subsequently, there has been little economic incentive to motivate U.S. producers to join it since about one-half of the world market is located in the U.S. As European and Japanese firms penetrate the U.S. market, the incentives for U.S. firms to come to terms with IEA members are greater. When Americans do bid on international inquiries, U.S. firms probably add an element of uncertainty that facilitates discussion of bids in advance so that the collaborating sellers can assess the buyer's willingness to pay and price accordingly.

The two main IEA contracts are the Tendering and Contracting Agreement (TCA) and the Export Notification Agreement (known as Agreement X). The TCA and Agreement X contain general procedures that apply to all product sections. Each product section defines the specific provisions (including definition of product and territories covered) applicable to its members in annexes to the TCA and Agreement X. Frequently, product sections conclude additional agreements that contain more detailed provisions for compensation, pooling, market allocation, and price setting. The five principal restrictive provisions applicable to each of the 10 product sections are summarized in Table 4.3.

Table 4.3
IEA Contracts: Restrictive Provisions in International Agreements,[a] 1974

All Agreements Pertaining to Section:	TCA	Notification	Liabilities, Guarantees	Pricing Provisions	Quota & Allocations	Compensation	Pooling	Pre-Tender Collaboration Procedures	Number of Known Members
A —Steam Turbines	Yes	Yes	Yes	Yes		Yes			17
B —Steam Generators	Yes	Yes	Yes	Yes		Yes			15
E —Water Turbine Driven Generators	Yes	Yes	Yes	Yes	Yes	Yes	Formerly	Yes	15
F —Synchronous Condensers	Yes	Yes	Yes						5
G —Switchgear	Yes	Yes	Yes	Yes				Yes	10
H —Transformers	Yes	Yes	Yes	Yes	Yes	Yes	Yes	Yes	22
K —Rectifiers	Yes	Yes	Yes	Yes				Yes	11
P —Rolling Mill Equipment	Yes	Yes	Yes	Yes	Yes	Yes	Yes	Yes	9
T —Gas Turbines	Yes	Yes	Yes			Yes			8
W—Water Turbines	Yes	Yes	Yes	Yes	Yes	Yes		Yes	20

Source: Epstein and Newfarmer 1980.

Note:
[a] Provisions in each section vary slightly. For a full explanation see Epstein and Newfarmer, 1980.

Under the notification provision of Agreement X every member, upon hearing of an inquiry for heavy electrical equipment, is required to notify the cartel secretary by means of a special card supplied for that purpose. The secretary then advises each notifying member of all other members who had notified the secretary of the bid. This sytem withholds information about the particular purchaser from non-notifying cartel members, since only those who have notified the secretary are advised of others who intend to bid. The effect of notification is to acquaint members with the identities of their competitors.

The ground rules delineated in the TCA provide general procedures governing the behavior of members party of the arrangements. Additional specific rules and procedures for convening and conducting *price-fixing* meetings are sometimes elaborated in the annexes. For example, in the annexes pertaining to Sections A and B (steam turbines and steam turbine generators), members have agreed to be bound by the following provisions: ". . .*any party. . .shall. . .quote not lower than the price determined* from and in accordance with the Price and Heat Consumption Manual multiplied by the factor stated in Appendix I hereto. . ." (A/B Price Memorandum: para. 1, italics; quoted in Epstein and Newfarmer 1980, p. 196).

Members of Sections A and B use the appended schedules of prices, multiplied by a factor that changes with the inflation rate and other business conditions, to set a common minimum price below which they will not bid. The schedules provide detailed adjustment factors for pricing of technologically complex and heterogeneous equipment.[1] In addition, members agree that they will offer no firm price, that they will not state a ceiling on escalation, and that no validity period will be stated (A/B Price Memorandum, para. 4, in Epstein and Newfarmer 1980, p. 197).

Perhaps the most complicated provisions are those involving *quotas and allocation* of bids. The annexes lay out in extreme detail the share of value of orders to be given to each producer and the procedure by which companies decide who will receive the offer. The basic allocation rule is that the producer with the lowest cumulative total toward his annual quota is to receive the bid. *Compensation* is a scheme whereby the winner of an order compensates the unsuccessful participants in a tender with a flat sum of money usually taken as a percentage of the value of the order. Compensation payments are often coupled with allocation and price-fixing arrangements which generally prejudice a buyer regardless of the number of tenderers in the bidding. *Pooling Arrangements* are a second type of payment to unsuccessful tenderers. Most pooling arrangements appear to have a penalty function. For example, the pool in Agreement P(H)C was applied only to those orders won at prices below the reference price contained in the agreement (Agreement P(H)C: para. 5a, in Epstein and Newfarmer 1980, pp. 284-285).

Records kept by IEA members provide a way to measure the success of cartel arrangements. Referring to Table 4.4, the "pool cancelled" column, which most directly approximates the non-collusive situation because buyers could not agree on a separate pricing arrangement, shows the average market value of transformers sold to all countries was 98.3 percent of the reference price. When special circumstances prevailed and the bidding was under a "special arrangement", when members sought to obtain the order regardless of price, the average price was 88 percent of reference price, nearly ten percentage points below the competitive level. In contrast, when tendering cartel members agreed to abide by the pool arrangement, prices paid averaged 116.6 percent of reference price and nearly 18 percentage points above the "pool cancelled", more competitive situation. Finally, the least competitive situation, the case of only one seller, had the highest prices—nearly 50 percent above the competitive situation.

Developing countries paid substantially more than developed importing countries for heavy equipment from the cartel. On the average for all situations, developing countries paid 129.4 percent of reference price compared to 97.2 percent for the importing developed countries. In part, the difference is because developing countries accepted tenders from only one company more often than did developed countries. On these bids, developing countries paid 162.1 percent of reference price on the average versus 114.0 percent for developed countries. In those potentially more competitive situations where the pool was cancelled, developing countries paid 110.1 percent of reference price compared to 88.0 percent for developed countries, undoubtedly a reflection of the different skills of buyers and the success of all bidders—members and non-members—in maintaining higher prices. The presence of a pooling arrangement prior to tender added approximately 11 percent onto the "pool cancelled" situation. According to these data, cartelized transactions to developing countries netted 25 percent more to cartel members than the average price on all sales to all countries in the pool cancelled, more competitive circumstances.[3] Overall, the magnitude of the price increases attributable to the cartel suggested by this data are on the order of 15-25 percent. Of course, it is not known how representative the transformer section is of other sections or how typical was this period of cartel operations. With the entrance of the Japanese and the subse-

Table 4.4

Effects of the IEA Cartel on Prices of Transformers, 1965-1967

| | Average Price[a] as Percent of Reference Price under: | | | | | | | | | |
| | Special Arrangements | | Pool Cancelled | | Pool in Effect | | Only One Tenderer | | All Orders | |
	Price	No.[b]	Price	No.[b]	Price	No.[b]	Price	No.[b]	Price	No.[b]
All Countries:	87.7	4	98.2	40	116.4	58	148.1	31	117.4	133
Developed Countries[c]	93.2	2	87.5	21	106.1	21	114.1	9	99.6	53
Developing Countries[d]	82.3	2	110.0	19	122.2	37	162.0	22	129.3	80

Source: Calculated from IEA records for Agreement p(H)C as shown in Epstein and Newfarmer 1980. For a more detailed statistical analysis, see Epstein and Newfarmer, 1982.

Notes:

[a] Price f.o.b.

[b] Number of bidding situations.

[c] Includes Australia, New Zealand, South Africa, Spain, Denmark, Greece, Israel, and Ireland.

[d] Includes India, Pakistan, Rhodesia, Zambia, Nigeria, Ivory Coast, Hong Kong, Malaysia, Jamaica, Brazil, Paraguay, Chile, Colombia, Venezuela, Panama, Formosa (Taiwan), China, Korea (South), Iran, Kuwait, Iraq, Rumania, Yugoslavia, Philippines, Indonesia, Saudi Arabia, Syria, Lebanon, and Morocco.

127

quent increase activity within sections, it is likely the number of arrangements and collusive tenders increased substantially. To extrapolate a rough estimate on orders of $2 billion annually covered by these arrangements, the amount of excess profits attributable to successful cartelization could range from $300 to 500 million annually, much of which is financed by developing countries.

Televisions. Events in the consumer electronics industry show the limits to oligopolistic stability under pressure from assertive public policy and rapidly changing technology. The international television industry is tightly organized at both the primary (i.e., components) and secondary (i.e., equipment assembly and sales) levels. Contemporary market arrangements are based upon the patent pools of the 1920s, when industry leaders controlling all aspects of the advanced wireless technology, pooled their patent rights, often into a commonly owned firm (UKBT 1947; Frankfurt Institute 1966). These firms then licensed outside manufacturers in exchange for a royalty fee and an agreement to abide by the restrictions of the pool. Many of the pools survived until the 1970s (Greer 1973, p. 64; Kronstein 1978, pp. 123-125).

A series of judicial actions in the U.S. loosened the tight hold of the majors on televisions and the electronics industry in general. RCA, founded as the U.S. patent pool joint venture of GE and Westinghouse, was split off from them by a consent decree in 1932, but continued to administer and collect other patents for the U.S. pool. Successful antitrust suits beginning in the 1950s terminated the pool and committed many of RCA's patents to the public domain in the United States. In Europe international licenses among the majors still buttress the old but rapidly crumbling market allocation arrangements.

During the 1950s and 1960s as RCA's patent control of the U.S. market eroded, the Japanese made substantial technical progress building upon licenses of RCA, Philips, and others. Enjoying an increasingly productive, low-cost labor force, and a protected home market, the Japanese giants inundated the U.S. market, first in radio, then black and white televisions, and finally color receivers. Philips participated but only through its joint venture with Matsushita in Japan. By 1973 less than 5 percent of radio receivers were made in the U.S. and the number of imported Japanese electronic products continued to grow, some claimed, through a policy of dumping financed by profits earned in protected home markets. The response of U.S. producers began to take shape along three lines. The smaller, less diversified firms were driven to sellout. Whirlpool sold its 57 percent interest in Warwick Electronics to Sanyo; Philips purchased Magnavox

128

and a series of other producers between 1969 and 1974; Matsushita bought Motorola's Quasar division. Some large single product-line firms, such as Zenith, filed dumping suits in federal courts. The industry leaders, such as GE and RCA, established joint ventures and licensing arrangements with the Japanese.

The strong international competition among TNCs in televisions and other electronics had immediate consequences for industrial development in some developing countries. In response to the Japanese penetration, U.S. firms were forced to invest abroad in assembly operations where labor was far cheaper; as the competition continued, the price of Japanese labor eventually rose and they too have been compelled to establish export platforms. The future of these industries in developing areas is not completely secure as much R & D in the industry is directed towards increased automation. Still, it is doubtful that such investments would have taken place in the absence of the strong competition among the global giants.

Lamps. The international lamp industry was fully cartelized in 1924, and the cartel lasted into the post-war period. The Phoebus cartel, as it was called, has since been replaced with an informal and perhaps only slightly less stable equilibrium among producers characterized by clear spheres of influence preserved through mutual forbearance in international investment and trade.

Events in Great Britain illustrate how national markets were reorganized after the demise of the Phoebus cartel. In 1956, under a court order from the Monopolies Commission, the lamp association that had collectively fixed prices and quality standards was dissolved. Numerous major and minor manufacturers sold to the four dominant firms, so that the latter's share of the market jumped from 53 percent in 1950 to 89 percent in 1966 (Monopolies Commission 1968, p. 58). In the other European markets, Philips, Osram and several others with close ties to them account for over three quarters of national sales (Locatelli 1967), and in the United States, GE, Westinghouse, and GTE-Sylvania account for about 80 percent of the market. Despite this high concentration, the dominant U.S. firms have made no major direct investments in the European lamp market or vice versa.

Parallel pricing seems to have replaced collusive or cartelized pricing in most national markets. The Monopolies Commission of the U.K. concluded that even after the demise of the British cartel in 1956: "There has been no appreciable increase in price competition" (1968, pp. 22, 23). On the continent prices display a rigidity not associated with competition; within the EEC price discrimination continues despite the lowering of tariffs; and (Locatelli 1967, pp. 58-63) in Canada several companies were successfully prosecuted for collusion and price fixing during the late 1950s and 1960s when bids on government sales were often the same to the exact penny (*Business Week* September 9, 1976).

There are four firms that presently dominate production in the developing countries: GE, Osram, Philips, and GEC of the United Kingdom. Spheres of influence, traceable to the early cross-licenses, still are apparent; GE is the major producer in Latin America, often in conjunction with Philips and Osram. Commonwealth countries are primarily the domain of Philips, GEC, and occasionally other British manufacturers and General Electric. For some Commonwealth markets, such as India and Australia, Osram, Philips, and GEC have formed a joint venture called the Electric Lamp Manufacturers (ELM) to manage the market.

In the mid-1970s the Indian government convicted ELM of parallel pricing and restrictive practices (Dugar 1976, pp. 429-435). Licenses with the parents of ELM effectively tied imports to TNCs of a predetermined home country and proscribed lamp exports to markets controlled by the parent organizations and their rivals (Swann 1973, p. 26). Even after the action of the government, the industry remains concentrated and under foreign leadership.

In sum, these three major branches of the electrical industry represent both the success and limits to international oligopolistic coordination in various forms of market organization. International and national export cartels are found in other branches of the industry, and informal interdependent behavior is probably common. The Federal Cartel Office of West Germany, for example, reported in 1970 that it has registered 12 electrical export cartels, 7 of which were linked to international cartels, presumably the IEA. National electrical export cartels were registered in Japan (6), the Netherlands (20, including other products), and even the U.S.(1) (OECD 1974, pp. 12, 13, 60-70). Informal interdependent behavior, probably covering a much wider range of products, is virtually unquantifiable. Conservatively, all forms of transnational market power (including intrafirm trade) affect at least 35 to 40 percent of international trade in electrical products and a much higher percentage of sales in oligopolistic markets of individual countries (Newfarmer 1980, pp. 115-116).

INTERNATIONAL OLIGOPOLY AND DEVELOPMENT: THE CASE OF BRAZIL

Brazil offers an interesting case study of the expansion of the electrical industry for two reasons. First, its industrial structure is similar to other advanced newly industrializing countries which have followed import substitution programs, such as Mexico, Argentina, and, to a lesser extent, India. Second, the experience of Brazil may also be relevant to countries with a smaller industrial base, such as Peru, Venezuela, Pakistan, and Nigeria, if they pursue similar policies.

History

Prior to 1940 Brazil's domestic electrical industry lagged behind nearly every other dynamic industry, despite a multiplying consumer demand. All heavy equipment was imported as were all lamp components for local assembly. The industry's relative underdevelopment can be traced to the international practices of TNCs as well as the division of labor between foreign and national groups that flourished in the coffee-based political economy. The international practices of the leading TNCs discouraged any industrial growth in most electrical products until after 1945. The international cross-licensing arrangements, patent pools, agreements not to undertake manufacturing operations in nonproducing countries using international technology, and international cartels that covered most electrical products effectively had prevented most independent Brazilian entrepreneurs from obtaining necessary electrical technology. Brazilian firms did break into the low-technology end of the industry after imports subsided in 1930, but their success was limited. Among themselves, TNCs agreed not to undertake manufacturing operations in the non producing countries using the international technology. The few electrical industries that were established in Brazil, such as GE's lamp assembly operations in the 1920s, were founded under the terms of the international accords, and Philips' entry soon after GE was to share the local monopoly, not to disturb it. In fact, GE manufactured all Philips' lamps until the 1940s. The underdeveloped state of the industry was also a consequence of the national economy. Up to this time, Brazilian entrepreneurs were realizing substantial profits in agricultural exports, commerce, and finance. A symbiotic division of labor developed between foreign and Brazilian groups with Brazilians controlling the profitable export sector and foreigners satisfying domestic demand in electrical and other industries primarily through imports. When the Depression brought on import substitution, some Brazilian entrepreneurs moved into manufacturing, but their successes were greater in almost every other industry.

The state intervened after the war to protect these nascent industries by introducing tariffs and import-substitution policies. National firms grew and TNCs, prompted by the threat of international competition in foreign markets and benefiting from preferential import concessions under Instruction 113 of 1955, responded with increases in foreign direct investments. General Electric and other heavy equipment manufacturers opened operations in smaller product lines, such as transformers and motors, to maintain control of the large Brazilian market. The industry grew rapidly, and, under the pressure of state policy, became locally integrated and diversified. By 1960 about two-thirds of the local industry was foreign-owned.

The government had attempted to intervene directly in the heavy equipment industry as early as 1953. President Vargas submitted legislation to Congress in 1953 to create a state-owned utility that would manufacture its own electrical equipment. The legislation did not pass Congress intact, largely because of the intense lobbying of the foreign-owned utilities. By the time Eletrobras, a state-owned utility holding company, actually was formed in 1962, the TNCs had begun manufacturing heavy equipment and the original mandate of Eletrobras to make equipment disappeared. Since 1953 the government has introduced no sector-specific policy initiatives attempting to control TNC activities in the electrical industry.

TNC Growth and Domestic Market Structure

The contemporary Brazilian electrical industry is highly concentrated, despite the entrance of more TNCs after 1960. Nearly one-half of industrial production comes from industries where the four largest plants supply one-half or more of the market (see Table 4.5). Many firms own more than one plant and Brazilian industrial classifications include many non-competing subproducts, so firm-level concentration is actually much higher in product markets, probably averaging between 60 and 70 percent industry wide. For example, in heavy equipment, no product market has a four-firm concentration ratio of less than 50 percent; in lamps, GE and Philips control about 80 percent of the market; and in televisions, Philips and Philco control more than one-half the market.

Market concentration appears to have decreased slightly, but far less precipitously than the product cycle model would suggest for this time of rapid market growth. The four-plant concentration ratio declined in ten comparable industries and rose in five between 1968 and 1973. In fact, in only one industry did new entrance and market share gains by smaller firms transform a concentrated oligopoly into a more competitively structured market. TNCs seem to show a higher affinity for concentrated and differentiated markets than do Brazilian firms. Using a sample of nearly 200 Brazilian and transnational firms

Table 4.5

Plant Concentration Ratios in Brazil's Electrical Markets, 1968, 1970, 1973
(The share of the largest four plants in industrial shipments)

IBGE	Industry	1968	1970	1973
1251	Industrial Machinery, including Drives	34	28	28
1253	Office Machines	90	74	58
1254	Heavy Home Appliances	89	60	64
1311	Generators, Transformers, Switchgear	31	24	22
1319	Equipment Parts, not otherwise classified	a	50	46
1321	Electrical Conductors	67	58	49
1322	Meters and Controls	24	97	76
1323	Electric Motors	a	59	48
1324	Electrical Installations	a	20	18
1325	Batteries	67	99	99
1326	Electrodes	a	0	100
1327	Resisters	a	78	90
1328	Carbon & Graphite Contacts	63	72	61
1329	Electrical Parts, n.o.c.	a	0	73
1331	Lamps	93	90	84
1341	Electrical Materials for Vehicles	61	36	42
1352	Light Home Appliances	39	37	51
1352	Electrical Apparatus for Industrial Use	50	36	38
1353	Medical Equipment	96	38	51
1359	Parts for Electrical Utensils, n.o.c.	a	79	79
1371	Electrical Components	a	52	43
1381	Telephone & Radio Equipment	95	82	72
1382	Transmission Equipment for Radiotelegraph	68	84	100
1383	Electric Signs & Signals	a	63	83
1384	Television Transmission Equipment	a	76	64
1385	TV, Radio & Sound Receivers	50	50	54
1386	Parts for Telephone & Transmission Equipment	a	41	28
1391	Repair of Electrical & Communication Equipment	a	22	66
3042	Phonograph Records	a	74	89
	Weighted Average	n.a.	49	48

Source: Special IBGE Tabulation.

Note:
a Included as part of another industry in 1968 because of change in industrial classification between 1968 and 1970.

133

in 16 electrical sub-industries, a recent study concluded the level of foreign ownership was significantly and positively associated with the level of market concentration and product differentiation. Although imperfect, measures for technological intensity showed no statistically significant association with the level of foreign ownership (Newfarmer and Marsh 1981; Newfarmer 1980).

During the 1960s and 1970s the foreign share of the industry did not decline. To the contrary, the level of foreign ownership increased from 66 to 77 percent between 1960 and 1974, and subsequently has risen to over 80 percent. Conventional explanations attribute their increasing market share to greater technical efficiency. This explanation overlooks conduct in international and domestic markets designed to reinforce local market positions or to restructure markets to their advantage. The next section will explore these issues.

Oligopolistic Tactics to Control Markets

As TNCs enter a market and expand within it, their conduct affects the structure of domestic markets and industrial performance. Tracing briefly six types of market tactics illustrates how the international market power of TNCs manifests itself in the domestic market and what the role of TNCs in shaping market development is.

Interlocking Directorates. Sharing directors is one tactic to coordinate pricing and other strategies in the local market. As Table 4.6 demonstrates, foreign firms showed a higher propensity to establish director interlocks than did Brazilian firms. In fact, 44 of the 49 electrical interlocks among consolidated industrials involved only transnational firms. Only one interlock between two Brazilian enterprises was discovered. Transnational electrical firms also accounted for 19 of 21 ties among electrical firms and financial corporations. Since over one-half of these financial corporations were Brazilian-controlled, international capital has "merged" with domestic Brazilian capital in the industrial-financial links, not within the industry itself.

While interlocks may serve different purposes, they can facilitate various forms of coordinated strategies incompatible with price competition, such as raising barriers to entry facing potential competitors, especially domestic firms. For example, financial interlocks may give the well-situated foreign firm an advantage over domestically controlled outsiders in access to capital. Interlocks among direct competitors affect performance when they result in concerted

134

Table 4.6

Director Interlocks within the Electrical Industry and with other Manufacturers

Interlocks Among:	Total	Industrials			Finance Co's[a]				
		Total	Electrical Firms or Supply-Related	Other Industrials	Total	Investment Banks	Commercial Banks	Insurance Co's	Other
Electrical Industry									
TNCs & TNCs[b]	63	44	17	27	19	8	5	6	0
Brazilian & Brazilian	3	1	1	0	2	1	0	1	0
TNCs & Brazilian	4	4	0	4	0	0	0	0	0
Total	70	49	18	31	21	9	5	7	0
Other Industrials									
TNCs & TNCs	8	6	2	4	2	1	1	0	0
Brazilian & Brazilian	1	1	0	1	0	0	0	0	0
TNCs & Brazilian	4	3	2	1	1	0	0	0	1
Total	13	10	4	6	3	1	1	0	1
Total	83	59	22	37	24	10	6	7	1

Source: Newfarmer, 1980.

Method of Tabulation: If one of the enterprises directed was an electrical firm (defined as on *Visão* or ABINEE list), the interlocks are counted within "electrical industry"; the exception to this is where the primary activity of the interlocked group is in another industry or the electrical firm is less than $500,000 in size. Interlocks between subsidiaries (including finance) of the same parent group are not counted as an interlock, nor are ex-directorships. Family directorships are considered as one individual.

Note:
[a] Finance companies were not distinguished by ownership category; most are Brazilian.
[b] Ownership designation of interlock refers only to industrials. Finance companies are for the most part Brazilian-owned.

pricing tactics. For example, the interlock between Philco and Philips gave the two companies 74 percent of the black and white television market and 67 percent of the color television market, more than enough to control selling prices and the entrance of new, less financially strong, competitors.

Cross subsidization. Firms may choose to absorb losses in certain markets for a period of time in order to drive out less capitalized firms, discipline a competitive fringe, or capture a sizable share of a potentially lucrative market. Such subsidized inefficiency, if it is prolonged, usually results in higher market concentration and, when the cross-subsidizing firms are transnational, in a high level of foreign ownership. Of the 44 electrical firms (27 TNCs and 17 Brazilians) for which data were available between 1966 and 1974, 9 recorded no earnings or losses for at least five of seven years. All were TNCs. Their action raised both the level of concentration and foreign ownership in many of the markets affected, such as televisions, motors, and transformers.

Product Differentiation. A third tactic is the heavy reliance on product differentiation to create demand, either in the form of advertising campaigns or other promotional outlays. These activities raise barriers to entry to would-be competitors because to obtain a share of the market potential entrants must either spend heavily on promotional expenses or forgo profits by pricing below the market level. Statistical analysis of data from nearly 200 electrical firms showed that the demand creation actions of TNCs were a significant factor in explaining the level of industry product differentiation (Newfarmer and Marsh 1981). In turn, this measure of product differentiation was positively correlated with the level of industrial concentration and firm profitability, suggesting that promotional efforts raise a barrier to entry and have an independent structural effect on firm performance. When Matsushata decided to open a television and components subsidiary in Brazil, it spent nearly 50 percent of its total costs on advertising to break into the market.

Formal Collusion. Unlike differentiated consumer electrical products where sellers can adopt informal interdependent pricing tactics with minimal direct collusion, made-to-order electrical machinery often requires careful, explicit agreement to achieve a non-competitive price equilibrium. One example of such an agreement, remarkably similar to those of the IEA, concerns transformers. A cartel of seven transformer companies operated in Brazil from 1965 through the early

136

1970s adversely affecting industrial structure and performance. The agreements contained predatory clauses to "combat" outsiders, and drive small national firms out of the market. The levels of concentration, barriers to entry, and foreign ownership rose during this period. And, real unit prices apparently followed the perverse pattern associated with non-competitive markets, more than tripling between the first quarter of 1968 and one year later; at the same time the quantity index declined from 184 to 96 (Newfarmer 1980).

Acquisitions. Between 1960 and 1974, forty-seven changes in ownership due to acquisitions in the Brazilian electrical industry were traced. All but one of these resulted in a new firm that was foreign controlled. The impacts on market structure were twofold. First, acquisitions of TNCs raised concentration in several product markets, and often had the effect of narrowing supply channels. Second, TNC takeovers raised the level of foreign ownership in the industry especially in televisions and heavy equipment. By separating the effects of rapid growth, entry, and exit from the industry from those due to acquisition, it was discovered that takeovers accounted for over 90 percent of the increase in the foreign share of the electrical industry at this time.[4]

Various combinations of these market tactics were apparent in all three branches of the industry examined here and illustrate the remarkable success of TNCs in creating or taking over domestic oligopoly. The *heavy equipment* producers (GE, Westinghouse, Brown Boveri, ASEA, Siemens, and AEG) initiated production in Brazil over a ten year period between 1955 and 1965, with each company specializing in a different line. While the recession of 1965 to 1967 drove many national firms out of the industry, TNCs cross-subsidized their losses and, according to some claims, sold considerably below cost, driving marginal firms from the markets. Presently, all but one or two product markets are concentrated oligopolies with four-firm concentration ratios greater than 60 percent.

Philips founded the Brazilian *television* industry in the early 1960s. Several national firms competed in the final market into the 1970s, by which time transnationals had acquired more than a dozen national firms and had driven others from the market. Philips maintained control of the components market through strategic acquisitions of successful entrants and AEG cross-subsidized many years of poor profits. The introduction of color television in 1971 consolidated their position in both markets because of their technological strength. Today, Philips, Philco, and AEG-Telefunken have more than 75 per-

137

cent of the color television market, and Philips and Philco have inter-locking directorates.

Ever since GE constructed the first *lamp* factory in Brazil in 1921 and later sold lamps to Philips beginning in 1926, the local lamp oligopoly has never been seriously disturbed, even with the post-war entrance of Osram and GTE-Sylvania. Osram, it will be remembered, was until recently a joint venture of GE, Siemen, and AEG. Market shares have remained stable since the 1950s: GE holds 50 percent of the market, Philips 30 percent, and Osram and GTE-Sylvania share the remainder. The companies met quarterly to decide prices, pro-duction quantities, and discuss market conditions throughout the 1970s.

If these cases are representative, what do these patterns of behav-ior of TNCs imply for the performance of the Brazilian electrical industry?

Firm and Industrial Performance

This section summarizes findings on the performance of the electrical industry in Brazil—and the independent role of TNCs in shaping that performance—in six areas: growth, pricing, trade, tech-nology, employment and income distribution, poverty, and product appropriateness.

Growth and International Competitiveness. After lagging behind other industries prior to 1930, the electrical sector has grown more rapidly than any other Brazilian manufacturing sector in the post-war period. Growth was especially fast after 1966, when physical production ex-panded by more than 15 percent annually. Although hampered by high costs of raw materials, the industry is now one of the largest in the Third World and has become internationally competitive in such products as televisions, lamps, radios, air conditioners, refrigerators, and small machinery lines. The industry's primary advantage is its inexpensive labor. Adjusting for takeovers, TNCs grew only slightly more rapidly than local electrical industries—13.4 percent versus 13.0 percent. Foreign ownership *per se* was apparently not a prime cause of the rapid growth of the industry, though TNCs were integral to growth.

Pricing, Profitability, and Inflation. The examples used to illustrate the behavior of the industry, suggest that formal or informal price coordination may be significant. Given the high level of concentration

138

in all 16 sub-industries of the electrical industry, theory suggests that there might be excess profits and inefficiency attributable to oligopolistic pricing strategies. One indication of this is the degree to which high profits are associated with increasing concentration and product differentiation, controlling for other characteristics of the firm. In fact, the levels of industrial concentration and product differentiation were significantly and positively correlated with profitability on sales, indicating the presence of monopoly profits and suggesting inefficiency.[5]

Brazilian firms recorded higher levels of profitability than foreign firms in the industry, after controlling for various firm characteristics and imperfect market structures. This may be because foreign firms engaged in transfer pricing that reduces their reported profit levels; or it may suggest that TNCs earned their profits through their position in differentiated oligopolies while Brazilian firms did so through greater efficiency in small-scale production and use of more labor-intensive technologies.

Despite inefficiencies attributable to domestic oligopoly, the inflation performance of the industry has been respectable when compared to the rest of the economy. Prices for the electrical industry rose one-sixth less than for all industries between 1969 and 1975. This was due to the substantial gains in productivity, to new technical changes, and to economies of scale. On the other hand it is arguable that real prices would have fallen further if oligopolistic margins had been reduced through competition. Administered pricing in concentrated industries, such as lamps and televisions, can be expected to hamper current anti-inflationary efforts, especially as the economy slows.

Trade and Balance of Payments Effects. The trade performance of the electrical industry has not fulfilled government objectives in reducing the country's trade deficit. The imported share of the domestic supply of electrical products has risen from under 10 percent in 1965 to over 20 percent in the 1970s and exports have not compensated for the huge increase.

TNCs have played a central role in the worsening trade balance. Relative to their sales, they import over twice that of Brazilian firms, other things being equal, and account for nearly 90 percent of the industry's entire import bill. This is to be expected since their product lines are often the newest and most recently substituted in the import-substitution process. An equally powerful reason is the economics of transnational production which often make imports more attractive than local sourcing. It does not appear that there are any significant differences in the export propensities of foreign or domestic firms,

139

suggesting that the apparent advantage TNCs have in this area has not been fully exploited.

Policies of the Brazilian government, particularly on exchange rates and import monitoring have also contributed to the lack of success in reducing the industry's trade deficit. Without revision in these and other policies, market forces (including TNCs) are not likely to reduce the trade deficit.

Technological Appropriateness and Dependence. In the electrical industry, there appears to be some, perhaps narrow, range of substitutability between labor and capital in the various production processes. Comparing statistically foreign and domestic firms, TNCs were found to use proportionately less labor per unit of capital than Brazilian firms. This probably occurs because of institutional biases in the transfer of technology through transnational production. Also, the level of market concentration was found to be inversely correlated with the labor-capital ratio, indicating that oligopolists are less responsive to relative factor prices because they can pass on their higher costs to buyers. These findings suggest that foreign ownership and oligopolistic market structures lessen the direct employment creation that occurs with the industry's growth.

The growth of the electrical industry has changed the nature of technological dependence in Brazil. On the one hand, labor skills have been raised, domestic production is more diversified and integrated locally, and the quality of products has improved. On the other hand, the industry was nearly as dependent on imported product and process technology and industrial know-how in the 1970s as it was a decade or two earlier. There is relatively little local research and development being done in Brazil. Of 102 electrical firms surveyed in 1974, only 2 reported expenditures on R&D; both were Brazilian owned. One was Bardella, a leading turbogenerator firm that had operated under a licensing arrangement from Voith of Germany until Voith wished to assume an equity share. The newly independent firm now operates its own sophisticated research and development program and has acquired other licenses to obtain parts of new technology.

Direct Employment and Income Distribution Effects. Employment in the industry as a whole (not including linkage effects) has expanded at a moderate pace. From 1966 to 1972, a boom period, new employment grew by about 6 percent annually and total wages and salaries paid grew in real terms at 8 percent, about matching the annual real increase in industrial sales. While the industry is more labor-intensive

140

than many other modern industries, employment rose less rapidly than 10 of the 21 other manufacturing industries, even though it was among the 3 most rapidly growing industries by value added. Consideration of secondary employment creation is not likely to improve the industry's ranking appreciably because of the industry's high import content.

Many of the new urban jobs are going to women. The television and other electronics assembly industry has entire work forces that are female because, employers say, their manual dexterity is superior. Also, women cause fewer labor problems and their wage rate is generally lower than for men.

Employment creation, of course, is directly related to income distribution. Those persons who directly benefited from the industry's growth were by and large those in the top 25 percent of the work force. In 1970, for example, most of the jobs created in the industry were highly paid, affecting the top one-third of the work force. At that time, the industry paid out over three-quarters of income payments to workers and managers in the top two income quintiles and only 23 percent of wages and salaries to the lower two quintiles, which comprise over two-thirds of the work force. Only 6.4 percent of wages went to the lowest income category. This performance was superior to some other modern industries, but less positive than the impact of the manufacturing sector as a whole.

Transnational corporations influence income distribution within the industry in at least three ways. First, by virtue of their leadership role they transmit the latest fashionable products originating in the advanced countries to the developing world. These products often involve more sophisticated, capital-intensive, and larger-scale technologies than extent domestic products. They often require more capital and longer production runs to be efficient. Some new products, such as washing machines or dishwashers, substitute capital for labor in the household. To the extent that new products substitute for domestic labor and/or require relatively capital-intensive and fixed production technology, the introduction, promotion, and consumer acceptance of the foreign-born product will lessen the amount of employment creation within the industry. Second, TNCs probably reduce the new income accruing to labor because of the capital-intensive processes they use. Equally important, they employ fewer low-income, unskilled workers in production than Brazilian firms, and rely on highly skilled workers familiar with their latest technologies. Third, the market power of TNCs (and that of domestic firms, for that matter) has a generally adverse effect upon income distribution. Firms producing in oligopolies, especially differentiated oligopolies, were shown to

141

raise prices above the competitive level, transferring income directly from consumers to producers. This has a generally regressive impact on income distribution since part of these profits are paid to upper class owners of capital and their managers. When the oligopolists are foreign-based, the income transfer may be international. Labor in the concentrated industries could conceivably benefit from use of the monopoly power if it were sufficiently powerful to lay a claim to higher wages; this does not appear to have been the case in Brazil.

Proverty, Income Distribution and Product Appropriateness. Two questions are relevant when discussing the industry's implication for poverty and basic needs questions: On the consumption side, do the industry's products meet the essential needs of the poorest income groups? On the production side, does the industry draw in and benefit the lowest income groups in providing training, jobs, and income, thus moving the economy as a whole towards meeting the essential needs of all?

There can be little doubt that, on the consumption side, the industry's consumer products are oriented towards supplying an elite demand. Only about one-half of Brazilians have electricity, almost all of them live in cities. About one-quarter of households have a television or refrigerator. Moreover, production and sales efforts are geared towards diversifying the consumption basket of the relatively rich, not providing products for those without. For example, in 1972, even before three-quarters of households had a black and white television, the industry began producing color sets. These more sophisticated receivers now account for over one-half of revenues in the television industry, and are the high-growth segment of the market. In contrast, the relatively cheap products that have gained wide dissemination such as radios and lamps, are of only secondary interest to the leading manufacturers because growth potentials have been realized.

This pattern of demand stems in large measure from the distribution of wealth and income in Brazil. The interests of industrialists and the dynamics of the product cycle tend to reinforce the pattern, rather than dislodge it. Because it represents their monopoly advantage within the market, TNCs have an interest in introducing the latest fashion, high technology products sold mainly to relatively wealthy consumers. If the foreign product can be successfully marketed, domestic competitors often are compelled to imitate, and so are continually relegated to a follower role in the cycle. Consider again Brazil's television industry: The introduction of color required the import of foreign technology, heavily favoring foreign subsidiaries. Local firms that had maintained sizable shares of the black and white mar-

142

ket found themselves losing in both black and white and color markets because subsidiaries could capitalize on their superior color technology in winning consumer acceptance in both markets. At the same time, domestic firms became again dependent on their TNC competitors for color parts.

On the production side, the bulk of employment and income the industry generates is not among the poorest one-half of income earners. Like other capital-intensive industries, most of the income generated appears to accumulate to the middle and upper classes. As one study concluded:

> . . . Brazil's growth strategy of heavy dependence on modern industries like automobiles and chemicals, and on foreign investment . . . exacerbated the wage-widening effects of growth. Increasing production of simply produced mass consumption goods . . . would be beneficial. A growth strategy in which agriculture, mining, construction, personnel services and maintenance were leading sectors would create a great deal of employment without giving such a bonus wage windfall to the supervisors and technicians who were lucky enough to have the skills and position to capitalize on growth. (Morley, Barbosa, and de Souza 1979, p. 285)

SUMMARY

The experience of this industry shows that, while TNCs have been remarkably flexible and successful in their adaptation to changing policy environments, government policy can have substantial impact on how the industry develops and how market power is exercised. In the U.S. antitrust actions in televisions restructured the components and receiver industry giving producers in several countries the opportunity to compete in a way that they would not have had had RCA been permitted to maintain the patent pools; in heavy equipment, vigilent anticartel policy kept U.S. producers out of the international cartel, creating a destablizing force in the industry; the early lamp consent decrees and anticartel action opened the way for incipient foreign competition in the U.S. market. In Western Europe and Japan antitrust enforcement, more stringent since the establishment of the EEC, has played a secondary role to the creation of "national champions" through incentives to merge and export. Consequently, the industry has become more concentrated and has entered into a symbiotic relationship with home governments.

143

The Brazilian case is representative of the industry's development in advanced developing countries. State policy promoted import substitution and compelled TNCs to establish local production facilities. Brazil now has achieved an impressive industrial park with some advanced, though not independent, technological capability. The same could be said for Mexico, Argentina, and to a lesser extent Pakistan, South Korea, and India. The smaller developing countries have had markedly less success—except perhaps in electronics—because of their smaller markets and lower bargaining power.

These policy initiatives, while often unleashing the forces of competition in selected markets or forcing the international oligopoly to alter its preferred strategy of serving international markets, have not seriously challenged the market power of the dominant major firms. Indeed, TNCs have adopted new international practices to counter them. In lamps, for example, informal recognized spheres of influence minimized the disruptive effects of the demise of the Phoebus cartel internationally; while in national markets leading firms acquired weaker rivals and market concentration increased. In televisions, after the slow erosion of the patent pool system, dominant firms have been less successful in reorganizing the world market, probably because of the rapid pace of technological changes. The heavy equipment industry has shown greater stability largely because of the merger wave in Europe and Japan, the high barriers to entry into most markets, and the recognition of spheres of influence.

The attack on global cartels and restrictive practices in conjunction with national policies of import substitution forced the companies to opt for more foreign direct investment as a way of organizing the world market. Ironically, this seems to have produced a more stable system since small national oligopolies are easier to manage than a global market. Out of the new international rivalry, state policies, and changing technological conditions, the industry has become more globally concentrated in the hands of the few remaining giants. It appears improbable that in the forseeable future either market forces or public policies will alter this trend.

Measures to Affect the Domestic Industrial Structure

This study has shown that governments have valid reason to be concerned with the level of foreignness and concentration in their economies. First, subsidiaries behave differently than their national counterparts in takeover activities, advertising strategies, technological choice, and development. Sometimes their behavior is at odds with national development programs and it makes a great deal of

144

sense to try to sever the structural link which gives the foreign firm legal control over these dimensions of conduct in the developing country. The experience in the natural resource sectors of many developing countries and of industry in Japan tends to confirm the viability of this strategy for at least some strong developing countries. Second, many markets in the electrical industry are concentrated beyond the level necessary to produce efficiently. Careful analysis could lead to a twin strategy: regulation or nationalization of concentrated markets where high minimum efficient scales require concentration for optimal performance; in markets where concentration is founded on pecuniary or product differentiation advantages and is in excess of the socially desirable level, governments must decide if they wish to restructure these markets to permit the market to discipline producers. Let us consider three types of policies to treat structures of foreignness and concentration.

Merger Review. Programs could be set up to monitor and review all substantial mergers and acquisitions. The Brazilian case shows that when a TNC buys a local firm it may not increase employment technological capacities, administrative capabilities, or even augment domestic capital. Moreover, acquisitions raise the level of foreign ownership and often concentration. Merger review can insure that only socially beneficial mergers will occur.

State Financing and Planning. The state must play a more active role in financing national development, if it wants growth in national investments to exceed foreign investments. To insure that such financing is efficient and directed towards development projects, it should be undertaken in the framework of a strengthened national planning apparatus, hopefully accountable to the public through democratic procedures.

Industrial Restructuring. Governments could consider selected industrial restructuring as one tool of national planning. For example, the lamp industry could in many countries be split off from the transnational electrical conglomerates such as has occurred in Japan.

Industrial restructuring can be undertaken through the judicious use of the monopsony buying power of state enterprises. The Brazilian, Mexican, and Venezuelan governments have used the monopsony power of state enterprises in electrical generation to favor domestic firms. Brazil's huge Itaipu complex was awarded to a consortium headed by the most technologically progressive and independent Brazilian firm, Industrias Bardella. Venezuela has used its Guri dam

145

project to build a domestically owned cable industry. Mexico has attempted to use the purchases of the state electrical utility monopoly to compel the TNCs to produce locally what they have customarily imported as well as to negotiate the terms of sale and continued operation in Mexico. The government sought to include provisions for joint ownership, including one-third shares each for transnational, government, and private domestic partners.

The Mexican case is interesting in another respect. One topic of negotiation, besides ownership and local content, was trade behavior. In the negotiations with Brown Boveri for hydrogenerator production, the government succeeded in winning an agreement that would compel the Mexican subsidiary to export its products to selected countries in Latin America, among them Peru. The ironic lesson about international linkages should not be lost: The Mexican government was negotiating global market share agreements with a Swiss multinational that might influence where Peru would be able to buy its imports from Brown Boveri—unbeknown to Peru.

Another way the government could affect industrial structure is to create a state owned enterprise in heavy equipment such as the French have done. Although the Brazilians have successfully used state enterprise in several other advanced industries, they have not followed up on the 1953 congressional initiative to establish a manufacturing enterprise in electrical machinery. The Mexicans have used the bargaining process to secure joint venture participation but no wholly-owned facilities. State enterprise in general in Latin America has been used to "fill empty space" rather than to compete in and discipline tight oligopolies.

Measures to Affect Firm Conduct

Policy measures in Brazil affecting the electrical industry have been limited to those general regulatory measures affecting the manufacturing sector as a whole and have not been specific to the industry. This industry's history points to several areas where general legislation could increase returns and facilitate economic development.

Competition Policy. If a developing country wishes to rely on a market system, experience in the industrialized world has shown that the government must work vigorously at promoting competition. Antitrust laws have an important place in accomplishing this and they are woefully inadequate. While the laws may be on the books, they usually have inadequate sanctions and enforcement procedures. Of particular importance, they often do not carry provisions for private suits for

146

damages; the treble damage provisions of U.S. antitrust laws have provided an important incentive for vigorous enforcement of antitrust laws.

International cross-subsidization deserves the special attention of policymakers. Many important electrical firms in Brazil reported considerable and persistent losses. Their continued growth could only be financed through funds transferred from other high-profit markets. Independent Brazilian firms operated at a disadvantage within the market, even if they were more efficient. While not all international cross-subsidization is deleterious, it can be used to restructure markets towards a higher foreign presence and concentration. The Mexicans reportedly have adopted legislation against such practices and other countries might benefit from examining the frequency and effects of cross-subsidization with an eye to its control.

Policies at entry. Both the Brazilian and Mexican governments have used their control over access to the domestic market to improve the behavior of TNCs. They have granted patent recognition, import priviledges, financing and special permission to produce certain lines in exchange for export quotas, local content agreements, and ownership concessions. Governments have been more successful at obtaining trade concessions and local content agreements than agreements on ownership and technology, but the more sophisticated governments have learned how to play one oligopolist off another.

Examples from Mexico again illustrate the point. In heavy equipment, the TNCs have preferred to supply the market through exports from home bases. However, after Westinghouse agreed to build a joint venture in transformers in conjunction with that national development bank, Brown Boveri attempted to enter the market by matching the concessions. The same occurred in circuit breakers. The government was able to prod General Electric to consider breaking its long-standing policy against joint ventures.

Trade Policies. Governments in the advanced developing countries have had remarkable success in creating import substitution industries, especially in the consumer-producer goods side of the electrical industry. However, in some cases, tariffs and other trade prohibitions are now extraneous or even self-defeating. In Brazil, for example, prohibitions against imports of some consumer products merely protect stable, high-price, foreign oligopolies, such as the lamp and consumer appliance industries. Studies indicate that both industries are internationally competitive. Import competition would not destroy domestic industry but might increase competition and reduce prices.

147

Transfer pricing is another virtually untouched area in most developing countries. The Greek experience has shown that careful monitoring of transfer pricing can raise the share of nationally generated profits acruing in the host country. All electrical firms are heavy importers and warrant the special attention of knowledgeable watchdogs.

These are only some of the areas where government policy can markedly improve industrial performance in developing countries. But government intervention does not automatically guarantee improved performance: state enterprises may prove wasteful and inefficient and regulation may cause distortions that inhibit growth. Nonetheless, governments which recognize the importance of industrial structure and performance and then take appropriate and efficient policy actions are likely to be rewarded with higher returns from transnational investments, even if they are not in a position to affect the broad pattern of development within the international industry.

Notes

According to the Standard International Trade Classification used, the electrical machinery group (Division 72) has 6 major three-digit groups and 18 four-digit subgroups. The main groups are listed below, along with selected four-digit industries of interest in this chapter:

SITC 722 - electrical power machinery and switchgear
        722.1 electric power machinery
        722.2 switchgear, etc.
SITC 723 - equipment for distributing electricity
        723.1 insulated wire and cable
SITC 724 - telecommunications apparatus
        724.1 television receivers
SITC 725 - domestic electrical equipment
SITC 729 - other electrical machinery and apparatus
        729.2 electric lamps

Although the analysis is concerned mainly with these subindustries and product classes, discussion must include power generating equipment (SITC 701) and at times office machinery (SITC 714). The study will also touch on closely related industries in which some of the leading international conglomerates operate. Major electrical TNCs produce certain industrial machinery classified under non-electrical machinery (SITC 718), and traction equipment (such as electrical locomotives in SITC 731).

[2] The nine producers were: AEG and Siemens (Germany) British Thomson-Houston, British Electric Co., The General Electric Co., Metropolitan Vickers (United Kingdom) Brown Boveri (Switzerland) Westinghouse and General Electric (US)

[3] Multiple regression analysis, controlling for number of tenderers, country size, and growth rates, confirmed the significance of cartel procedures in raising prices and bears out these relationships (Epstein and Newfarmer 1982).

[4] One socio-political consequence of the increased foreign participationn in the electrical machinery industry was a more active participation in the manufacturing association that represents the interests of the sector to the government. In 1962 more than two-thirds of the officers of the trade association came from Brazilian companies. By 1974 the leadership role had almost reversed, with TNCs controlling 60 percent of the leadership posts. The industry association has been generally supportive of foreign enterprise in its policy positions made to the government, helping to create a propitious climate for the growth of foreign investment.

[5] It is conceivable that the supply price of the oligopoly could be lower than that of the competitively structured market yielding simultaneously above normal profits and efficiency gains because few plants are able to achieve economies of scale. Nonetheless, since many electrical markets are more concentrated than economies of scale alone would require, and since industrial concentration has no consistent effect on either labor or capital productivity this argument is called into question for all but a few markets. Also, the observed high profits and industrial concentration are closely related to product differentiation, which has only questionable social gains, so it is probable that any efficiency gains due to differentiated oligopoly are negligible (Newfarmer 1980).

David Dale Martin

5.

The Iron and Steel Industry: Transnational Control without TNCs?

INTRODUCTION

The iron and steel industry stands in stark contrast to the general pattern exhibited by other transnational industries. In iron and steel we do *not* see a few transnational corporations operating in parallel throughout the world. In this industry direct foreign investment has played a minor role. On the world level ownership of steel enterprises is highly fragmented and competition appears to be intense. The purpose of this case study is to describe a contrasting pattern of industrial structure and conduct and to explain how and why the iron and steel industry came to be a special case. We shall see that, in spite of the large number of steel enterprises in the developed countries, oligopoly exists not only within each nation but also in the relations among the national industries—albeit, an oligopoly of "industrial policies" and supranational governmental organizations rather than an oligopoly of transnational corporations. The structure of control of this industry is quite complex. To help understand these complexities a historical sketch of the evolution of the industrial structure in the United States, Europe, and Japan precedes the examination of the contemporary global structure and its implications for less developed countries.

Table 5.1 lists the world's leading steel enterprises. Output of crude steel in 1974 and in 1979 reflects their size absolutely and relative to each other, and total sales revenues in 1979 make possible comparison of the size of steel companies relative to other large

Table 5.1

Crude Steel Output 1974 and 1979 and Sales Rank 1979 of
the World's Leading Steel Producers

Company	Crude Steel Output (mil. metric tons)		Rank Among Steel Producers		1979 Sales[a] (million dollars)	Sales Rank Among U.S. Industrial Companies (1979)[b]	Sales Rank Among Industrial Companies Outside U.S. (1979)[c]
	1974	1979	1974	1979			
UNITED STATES							
U. S. Steel	30.8	27.0	2	2	12,929	14	
Bethlehem Steel	20.2	17.6	3	3	7,137	38	
Republic Steel	9.6	9.1	12	12	3,987	85	
National Steel	9.6	9.7	13	11	4,234	76	
Armco Steel	8.1	7.3	17	16	5,035	58	
Inland Steel	7.3	7.5	19	15	3,635	95	
Jones and Laughlin	7.3	10.4	20	10	4,175	e	
Youngstown	5.4	d	23	d	d	d	
Wheeling-Pittsburgh	3.8	3.5	31	35	1,242	243	
Kaiser Steel	2.7	2.4	36	43	975	293	
Allegheny-Ludlum	f	f	g	g	10,569	208	
Interlake	f	f	g	g	1,105	265	
Cyclops	f	f	g	g	915	304	
McLouth Steel	f	f	g	g	725	350	
European Coal & Steel Community							
British Steel (U.K.)	19.3	17.5	4	4	6,385		50
Thyssen (Ger.)	16.3	13.5	5	6	13,637		18

Italsider	13.6	13.0	9	7	3,744	96
Estel (Neth.)	12.2	11.6	10	i	6,503	47
Arbed (BLEU)	11.2	4.6	11	27	1,549	261
Pechiney Ugine Kuhlmann (France)	9.5	f	14	g	7,961	35
Sacilor (France)	9.0	6.3	16	j	3,764	95
Cockerill (Belgium)	6.6	4.2	21	30	3,259	110
Peine-Salzgitten (Ger.)	5.5	4.0	22	31	3,869	89
Mannesmann (Ger.)	5.1	4.3	25	29	6,825	44
Krupp (Ger.)	4.5	4.9	27	24	6,982	41
Klöckner (Ger.)	3.5	4.7	32	26	2,368	159
Halnaut-Sambre (Belgium)	2.7	3.9	35	32	1,468	274
Stahlwerke Röchling-Burbach (Ger.)	f	2.0	g	47	1,319	301
Dillinger-Hüttenwerke (Ger.)	f	f	g	g	1,020	371
Sidmar (Belgium)	f	2.8	g	40	891	416
Falck (Italy)	f	f	g	g	h	h
Usinor (France)	f	7.2	g	17	3,792	94
JAPAN						
Nippon Steel	38.5	33.5	1	1	12,595	23
Nippon Kokan	16.2	14.1	6	5	5,971	57
Kawasaki	14.9	12.9	7	8	4,795	74
Sumimoto	14.6	12.9	8	9	5,342	66
Kobe Steel	9.1	7.6	15	14	4,411	78
Nisshin Steel	3.3	2.9	33	38	1,543	264
Daido Steel	f	f	g	g	1,501	270

Table 5.1 (Continued)

Crude Steel Output 1974 and 1979 and Sales Rank of 1979 of
the World's Leading Steel Producers (by country)

Company	Crude Steel Output (mil. metric tons)		Rank Among Steel Producers		1979 Sales[a] (million dollars)	Sales Rank Among U.S. Industrial Companies (1979)[b]	Sales Rank Among Industrial Companies Outside U.S. (1979)[c]
	1974	1979	1974	1979			
OTHER							
Broken Hill (Australia)	7.8	8.1	18	13	3,206		115
Stelco (Canada)	5.0	5.3	26	24	1,785		225
Iscor (S. Africa)	4.3	6.9	28	18	1,894		210
Vöest-Alpine (Austria)	4.1	4.6	29	28	3,991		86
Steel Authority of India (India)	3.9	6.4	30	19	1,758		228
Dominion Foundries (Canada)	2.8	3.7	34	33	1,225		326
Altos Hornos de Vizcaya (Spain)	2.1	1.2	28	49	754		474
Altos Hornos de Mexico (Mexico)	2.0	2.5	39	42	h		h
Tata Iron & Steel	1.7	1.8	40	48	h		h
Ensidesa (Spain)	f	4.9	g	25	1,546		263
Sandvik Group (Sweden)	f	f	g	g	1,549		260
Sidurgica Nacional (Brazil)	f	2.3	g	44	1,015		374
Usiminas (Brazil)	f	3.2	g	37	908		407

154

SSAB (Sweden)	[f]	2.2	[g]	45	[g] 973	386
Pohang (S. Korea)	[f]	5.6	[g]	21	[g] 1,250 [h]	321 [i]
Sidor (Venezuela)	[f]	[f]	[g]	[g]	[h]	[i]
ES Group (Norway)	[f]	[f]	[g]	[g]	712	494
John Lipaght (Australia)	[f]	[f]	[g]	[g]	[h]	
Algoma (Canada)	[f]	3.2	[g]	16	[h]	[i]

Notes:

[a] Figure represents total company sales. Figures for companies outside the U.S. converted to U.S. dollars using an exchange rate that consists of the average rate in the official exchange market during each company's fiscal year.

[b] *Fortune* 1980, pp. 276-295.

[c] *Fortune* 1980, pp. 190-199.

[d] Youngstown Sheet and Tube was formerly ar part of Lykes-Youngstown Corporation. In 1978, Lykes-Youngstown merged with LTV Corporation. Youngstown Sheet and Tube was subsequently consolidated under the management of Jones and Laughlin Steel, a subsidiary of LTV. Combined Youngstown-Jones and Laughlin Steel sales are shown for Jones and Laughlin Steel.

[e] Subsidiary of LTV Corporation. Figure shown represents steel sales only and was obtained from "The LTV Corporation 1979 Annual Report to Shareholders," p. 9. Total sales for LTV Corporation in 1979 were $7,996 million, placing the company 31st among U.S. industrial corporations.

[f] 1974 - less than 1.7; 1979 - less than 1.0

[g] 1974 - lower than 40th; 1979 - lower than 49th

[h] Not among top 500 industrial companies outside the U.S.

[i] 1979 figures for steel production are a compilation of those reported for two main subsidiaries of Hoesch Werke AG (6.0 mm tons and ranked #20) and Hocgovens Ijmuiden (5.6 mm tons and ranked #22)

[j] 1979 figures for steel production are a compilation of those reported for Sacilor (3.6 mm tons and ranked #34) and main subsidiary Sollac (2.7 mm tons and ranked #41)

industrial companies. The 1974 output data are included to indicate relative magnitudes in that year of peak demand before the recession. Nippon Steel, United States Steel, Bethlehem Steel, and British Steel are the four largest steel enterprises. Although most steel firms obtain some inputs and dispose of some outputs outside their home countries, none is typical of transnational firms that operate the same type of plant in a number of nations. For most steel enterprises transnationalness consists in importing mineral inputs from mines in foreign locations and exporting outputs, with or without vertical integration. For example, United States Steel Company and Nippon Steel, the two largest steel companies, held less than 5 percent of their assets outside their home countries in 1976 (UNCTC 1978, p. 289).

Although steel enterprises are geographically delimited, the steel group includes several very large firms. United States Steel Company in 1979 was ranked fourteenth within *Fortune's* largest U. S. Industrial corporations. Five of the Japanese steel companies and ten of those in the European Community were within the top 100 in *Fortune's* 1979 sales ranking of companies outside the United States. With the exception, perhaps, of Thyssen in the Federal Republic of Germany, these firms are not diversified out of steel to any great extent. They are big because steel is a large part of industrial activity in industrial economies.

Table 5.1 further illustrates that fourteen of the steel producers outside the U.S., Japan, and the European Community were among *Fortune's* top 500 outside the U.S. in 1979 sales. The steel enterprises in the developing countries have come to represent a threat to producers in the developed countries. In 1979 the Steel Authority of India had reached a crude steel output of 6.4 million metric tons making it the nineteenth largest steel enterprise in the world. Pohang of South Korea was close behind with 5.6 million tons, ranking twenty-first. Further growth and entry of the Third World producers into world markets will depend on the rapidly evolving transnational control structure. Whether developing countries are able to increase their rate of production, they surely will increase their rate of consumption of iron and steel products because steel use remains an inherent part of industrialization.

Steel is a basic industry in the sense that the state of the industrial arts coupled with resource scarcities do not permit substitution of other materials for steel in large numbers of uses without prohibitively high costs. Steel products enter as inputs into the production of many consumer goods, but they are sold as intermediate goods by enterprises to enterprises. Production of steel requires the input of such minerals as iron, limestone, coal, or other fossil fuels, as well as nonferrous metals used in alloying. The various mineral inputs are found in many parts of the world, but their geographical distribution no longer corresponds closely with the location of the final consumption of steel products. Thus, the world steel industry consists of labor and capital equipment applied to mining, transportation, and processing of minerals, the reserves of which are exhaustible.

The minimum efficient scale of a steel plant depends upon the location at which it is built. Transportation costs are high relative to value added by production. Relatively high transportation charges exist for both inputs and outputs. Choice of plant size is intricately tied up with choice among alternative technologies, alternative types of inputs, sources of those inputs, size and location of markets, and transportation costs. Thus, it makes no sense to speak of the minimum efficient scale of steel facilities.

No single simple explanation can explain why this industry did not experience the "transnationalization" of production seen in other industries. The products of the steel industry are essentially homogeneous across firms, even though each firm must offer a wide variety of standard product types. Perhaps this absence of product differentiation and the failure of firms in the industrialized countries to make direct foreign investment in each other's home markets in the pre-World War II years played a role. Immediately after the war the market for steel in most developing countries was small. When markets began to grow, as in Japan, India, Brazil, and Mexico, local steelmaking enterprises had already arisen and pre-empted much of the market. Most important in inhibiting foreign direct investment was the inherent conservatism of steel industry management who were unaccustomed to expanding capacity even at home. Since its creation in 1901 United States Steel has built only two basic integrated steel plants. It is easy to see that investments abroad would be unlikely, particularly considering the added risk of expropriation.

The structure of the industry within steel producing nations has long been characterized by oligopoly, cartelization, and/or government ownership. A highly competitive national industrial structure has not existed anywhere since 1901 when United States Steel Corporation was formed through a succession of mergers that combined about 180 formerly independent enterprises engaged in various stages of the industry (Hogan 1971, pp. 235-302). International trade in inputs has been characterized by direct foreign investment in mining—often through joint ventures—and by long-term supply contracts. No organized commodity market exists for any of the major mineral inputs into steelmaking. Competition in international trade in the outputs of the various national steel industries has been much greater, but there, too, restraints on such competition have been common, stemming from both government action and enterprise agreements.

In the period between the two world wars international cartels dominated. After World War II competition increased with the emergence of the Japanese industry as a major exporter and with the creation of the European Coal and Steel Community (ECSC) in 1953. (Stegemann 1977). As the United States became a net importer of steel products pressures arose for protection of this major market of the world's exporters and national governments came to play an increasing role in the regulation of competition in world markets. The formation in 1978 of a permanent Steel Committee of the Organization for Economic Co-operation and Development (OECD) suggests the possibility of some new multinational governmental control structure in the future. The developing countries, be they potential exporters or importers of either mineral inputs, capital equipment, or steel products, will be affected significantly by any changes in the structure of control of the world steel industry that affect prices, technological and financial aid, and access to markets. Before turning to these current developments and the prospects for the future, we will briefly survey the historical development of the transnational control structure.

EVOLUTION OF TRANSNATIONAL STEEL CORPORATIONS

In 1875 the world's total steel production amounted to 1.8 million tons (Warren 1975, p. 19). British, American, and German output accounted for 79 percent. Almost a century later, in 1974, world raw steel production hit a peak of 707.8 million metric tons, of which only 29 percent was produced in those three nations. Rapid growth in world steel output has been accompanied by geographical disbursion of the industry. With an output of 1.9 million metric tons in 1974, South Korea produced more than the whole world in 1875 and yet ranked thirtieth (*Iron Age,* January 2, 1978, p. 93). Competition has been limited, however, by the relatively high cost of transportation, cartelization, and governmental actions. Understanding of current national policies affecting international trade in steel requires knowledge of the basing-point system of pricing steel products which is the key structural characteristic of steel markets in both the United States and Europe.

158

The Basing-Point System in the United States

Before 1901 the steel industry in the United States was characterized by a high degree of competition (Hogan 1971, p. 236). Unlike a number of other manufacturing industries, the steel industry was not brought under the centralized control of a trust. Centralized control was accomplished only after the trust device had been effectively prohibited and the New Jersey holding company had taken its place. Although challenged by the Department of Justice as a combination in restraint of trade, the U.S. Steel Corporation's control of more than half of the United States steel industry was given legal sanction by the Supreme Court in 1920 (*United States* vs. *United States Steel Corp.*, 1920). Writing in 1953, George W. Stocking said:

> Since its organization, the United States Steel Corporation has apparently used its influence in so far as it could lawfully do so (and at times it has apparently transgressed the law) to free prices from the immediate impact of fluctuations in demand, to lessen the rigor of price competition among the leading steel producers, and to insure that at any particular time all steel companies would quote identical prices to any customer. It has done so by precept and example. This is evident in what its leaders have said and what they have done. (1953, p. 42)

The essential elements in the oligopoly pattern of limited competition in the U.S. steel industry were established in the first decade after the formation of the U. S. Steel Corporation. "Stable prices" were attained without overt collusion by using: basing-point pricing, price leadership, and joint determination of a schedule of prices for "extras" (Stocking, p. 47).

The high costs of transportation relative to the other costs of delivering steel products to the location of consumption presents a real problem in even conceiving of the way in which a perfectly competitive market would function. Even with many firms in the nation, there will not be many at every particular location. If each firm sold by quoting F.O.B. mill price, then the transport costs would be the primary determinant of the cost of a steel product. A seller would find local customers and be unable to penetrate more distant territories without either lowering his mill price to all customers or else discriminating among customers on the basis of location. Such freight absorption is sometimes called "dumping" when sales take place across national boundaries. If geographical price discrimination is permitted by law, then competition takes the form of each buyer playing one

159

seller off against another to get a concession from the F.O.B. mill price.

On the other hand, if transport costs were very low relative to other costs of production, a competitive auction market might develop at a particular location where sellers delivered their products and buyers purchased them. The steel industry in the U.S. adopted this strategy using Pittsburgh as the market place, but without actually bringing steel buyers and sellers together there. This is how it worked: a seller would quote a price for the product that included the base price, "extras" to account for product specification, and freight from Pittsburgh to the buyer's location. Each buyer received identical quotations for delivered products no matter where the supplying mill was located. Mills located at the basing point would net the base price on all sales regardless of the customer's location. In times of high demand mills not located at the basing-point could limit sales to nearby customers or those more distant than they from the basing-point and thereby receive a higher average net revenue for output. In times of low demand and excess capacity local mills would seek business at a greater distance and would meet, but not undercut, the price of rivals. With tacit agreement to follow a leader in setting the base price and the price of "extras", and with everyone using the same freight calculation, price competition was effectively eliminated. This system of single basing-point pricing was faulty, however. In good times when all plants were operating at capacity the F.O.B. mill price was used; in bad times price cutting occurred and the whole structure crumbled.

The American steel industry followed the Pittsburgh Plus system until 1924 when the Federal Trade Commission ordered U. S. Steel to abandon it as a violation of the price discrimination provisions of section 2 of the Clayton Act. (*In the Matter of United States Steel Corporation et al.*, 8 FTC Decisions 1, 1924). As a result of the order U. S. Steel and other firms increased the number of bases from which it quoted delivered steel prices (Stocking 1953, pp. 53-54). The multiple basing-point system developed and was used from 1924 until 1948, when the United States Supreme Court held a similar system to be unlawful in the cement industry (*Federal Trade Commission v. Cement Institute* 1948). United States Steel then announced a policy of selling F.O.B. mill only and the other companies followed suit.

The primary effect of the 1948 F.T.C. cement case seems to have been action by the companies to treat each mill as a basing-point. A 1958 Senate committee report quoted the president of U. S. Steel explaining the company's pricing practice as follows:

160

United States Steel offered a delivered price to meet the lowest delivered price it anticipated would be bid on this item. From its prior knowledge of dealings with the Naval Gun Factory and of the market, U. S. Steel could and did expect that Bethlehem would offer a bid on this invitation. Upon evaluation of these competitive circumstances, U. S. Steel found that if Bethlehem bid its announced price for the item at its producing mill at Sparrows Point, Maryland, from which it could be expected to offer to ship, plus freight from that mill to the Naval Gun Factory, its delivery price would be $0.07205 per pound. U. S. Steel accordingly reduced its own delivered price for shipment from its Fairless Works to the Naval Gun Factory by an amount which would enable it to meet the equally low price of its competitor (U.S. Congress, Senate, Subcommittee on Antitrust and Monopoly 1958, p. 122).

Because the price discrimination statute allows the defense of "meeting competition", such pricing results in no violation of the law so long as all mills are used as basing-points in calculating the governing price for each buying location and overt collusion is avoided. In a consent order entered in 1951 that ended an F.T.C. case against the basing-point system in the steel industry, the commission sanctioned freight absorption and delivered pricing "when innocently and independently pursued, regularly or otherwise, with the result of promoting competition." (Stocking 1953, p.178). This oligopoly pattern within the U.S. market was undisturbed until the late 1960s when European and Japanese imports were offered for sale outside the system.

The International Steel Cartel

World War I stimulated the demand for steel but left the European industry in a state of disorganization. In 1926 the Entente Internationale de l'Acier (EIA) was formed which united the steel producers of Germany, the Saar, France, Belgium, and Luxemburg and accounted for one-third of world output and two-thirds of all steel exports (Stocking and Watkins 1946, p. 171). In the absence of any legal prohibition comparable to the American antitrust law, price competition was brought to an end with the establishment of the cartel. The cartel agreement focused on raw steel production. Although no attempt was made directly to control prices or capacity expansion, restriction of output of raw steel did tend to control the prices of finished steel products and lessen incentives for expansion. The mechanism of control of raw steel production was relatively simple. Each country was assigned a quota of the total amount of raw steel to be produced in each forthcoming quarter. The quotas were fixed and based on production in the base period of first quarter 1926. The total quarterly tonnage to be produced was decided by a management committee by a two-thirds vote with each country having votes in proportion to its quota. A fine was levied for each ton produced in excess of the assigned quota and compensation was paid for each ton produced below the quota (Hexner 1943, Appendix III). National associations allocated the quotas among producing firms in each nation. Governments of the participating countries supported the arrangement but were not directly involved.

Although the 1926 agreement was originally set to expire in March 1931, it actually broke down in October 1929. A major factor in the breakdown was the rapid growth in demand in Germany that resulted in German producers exceeding their quota and paying heavy fines. After a succession of temporary agreements a second international steel cartel was established on June 1, 1933. By 1937 this cartel had brought together producers of 90 percent of the iron and steel entering into international trade, including those in the United Kingdom and the United States (Stocking and Watkins 1946, p. 187).

The second international cartel agreement differed significantly from the first one. During the interregnum between the two, the German, French, Belgian, and Luxemburg producers had agreed to stay out of each other's home markets. Their competition focused on export trade to other nations. Therefore, the new agreement made no attempt to control production and domestic sales, but was limited to control of exports. The quota system was applied to the export and price of particular steel products as well as to the total export of steel products measured by crude steel content. Thus, export of any steel product, whether or not subject to a particular product quota, counted against the general export limitation, which was continued until 1936 by which time specific product agreements had been achieved for most products (Hexner 1943, pp. 82-89).

At the outbreak of World War II, the structure of control of the world steel industry was dominated by the cartel. The cartel was administered by a management committee of representatives of national groups and a *comptoir* committee made up of the managing directors of the various export syndicates that controlled each product category. The specific product syndicates unified export sales of all member countries and in some cases licensed distributors in importing countries and imposed resale price maintenance. The syndicates also undertook to discipline domestic nonmember producers in importing countries by reducing prices to induce them to cooperate (Stocking and Watkins 1946, pp. 188-191).

In general the cartel imposed quotas on exports that protected the home markets of members and allocated "third country" markets. The anti-trust laws of the United States placed some limitations on the participation of the U.S. steel industry, but these limitations seem to have been overcome. The Webb-Pomerene Act of 1918 granted exemption from the Sherman Act to export trade associations that avoid any "act which artificially or intentionally enhances or depresses prices within the United States of commodities of the class exported by such associations, or which substantially lessens competition within the United States or otherwise restrains trade therein." In 1928 U. S. Steel and Bethlehem Steel formed the Steel Export Association of America as a Webb-Pomerene association that included many, but not all, of the American exporters. Before joining the cartel in 1938, the Steel Export Association of America had made price and quota agreements with the tin plate, rails, and tubular products syndicates. Representatives of the association agreed to stay out of the exclusive territories of the other members and were given some exclusive export territories, but the domestic American market was explicitly excluded from the formal agreements (United States Congress, Temporary National Economic Committee Hearings 1939, PT. XX, 10930). The cartel was disrupted by the outbreak of World War II when the British naval blockade prevented German steel from reaching the German firms' exclusive territories in South America. When America entered into the war the cartel dissolved (Stocking and Watkins 1946, p. 215).

Direct investment by European and United States steel companies in steel producing plants in third country markets would seem to have been discouraged by the cartel arrangements even if no explicit prohibition was included in the agreement. The high prices made possible by the cartel, the possibility of war, and the threat of expropriation, were substantial enough to make the incurring of high transport charges to distant markets a less risky business strategy than direct investment. The pattern set at this time undoubtedly affected postwar developments in the industry.

Post-War European Reconstruction and the ECSC

World War II left Europe with destroyed steel plants and great demand for steel products. For several years the gap was filled by U.S. Marshall Plan aid and exports of steel products. By 1950, however, recovery had reached the point that renewed competition among the European national steel industries for export markets was just around the corner. A number of economic and political factors combined to bring forth the ECSC which was proposed by France's Robert Schuman in May 1950 and implemented in 1952 by the provisions of the Treaty of Paris (Commission of the European Communities, *Treaties*, 1973, pp. 747-773).

The economic factors included the likelihood of a repetition of the excess capacity, intense competition, and cartelization that followed World War I. None of the post-World War II European nations was self-sufficient in both coal and iron ore and some arrangements for international trade were necessary. The political factors included a desire by the French to solve the economic problems in a way that would forestall the reemergence of an autonomous German industrial warmaking capability. Sentiment in Germany for the regaining of sovereignty favored a move that furthered that goal by removing French fears (Mason 1955, pp. 1-33).

The Treaty of Paris created a supranational governmental organization to regulate the structure and conduct of the coal and steel industries of the Federal Republic of West Germany, France, Italy, Belgium, Luxemburg, and the Netherlands. The organizational structure included the high authority composed originally of nine men with six-year terms who were to be independent of the member governments. The commission of the European Communities took over the functions of the high authority in 1967 when the European Economic Community, the European Atomic Energy Community, and the European Coal and Steel Community were unified. The high authority was made subject to a number of checks and balances by other ECSC institutions, including a council of ministers, a high court, a common assembly (now the European Parliament) and a consultative committee composed of steel industry, labor, and customer representatives (Commission of the European Communities, *Treaties*, 1973).

The ECSC differed from cartel organizations of the inter-war period in several important respects: it was a more permanent organization ; control was not in the hands of the steel industry managers, although they play an important role; the role of the national governments was more formal; tariffs played no part in the trade among the member nations; and, national policies on steel were subject to limitations. Yet some of the features of the pre-war cartel arrangement were reestablished in spite of the adoption of some antitrust provisions.

Article 65 of the Treaty of Paris deals with agreements and concerted practices that might restrain trade in steel products among the member nations. Taken alone it might serve to prohibit the reestablishment of cartel protection of home markets, but not the cartelization of exports to non-member countries. Other provisions of the Treaty, however, make provision for limited protection of home markets of member nations by actually prescribing a multiple basing-point system of pricing. Furthermore, the commission is empowered, under certain circumstances, to regulate investment, output, imports, and prices.

The Treaty prohibited discrimination in general, but provided that a seller may align his price to a particular buyer on a lower delivered price of a competitor. Furthermore, base prices as well as transport rates are made "transparent" to all buyers and sellers by requirements that they be reported to the commission for publication. A seller is allowed to announce its prices as of a basing-point other than the location of its mills (Stegemann 1968).[1]

Of course, even with the basing-point system, price competition can take place, particularly if excess capacity exists, by a breakdown of price leadership. The cohesiveness of the European enterprises has proven to be inadequate to prevent considerably more flexibility in prices than has existed in the United States where a similar, but unofficial, system prevails (Stegemann 1977, pp. 59-62).

The Treaty of Paris did much more than prescribe a multiple basing-point system for the common market. It provided the commission with discretionary powers to regulate and control the market in times of low demand (Martin 1979, pp. 842-848). According to Article 46 the commission is required to:

(1) conduct a continuous study of market and price trends;
(2) periodically draw up programmes indicating foreseeable developments in production, consumption, exports and imports; and,
(3) periodically lay down general objectives for modernization, long-term planning of manufacture and expansion of productive capacity; . . .

Investment in new or improved plant and equipment can be indirectly promoted or discouraged by the commission's power to make loans or loan guarantees. Furthermore, the commission may require advance notification of individual investment programs and deliver an opinion "within the framework of the general objectives provided for in Article 46." An adverse opinion by the commission can stop financial assistance or even result in fines if the investment program of an enterprise involves "subsidies, aids, protection or discrimination" contrary to the treaty.

The Treaty requires the commission to give preference to indirect means of controlling production, but it explicitly provides for a system

165

of production quotas in the event of a massive decline in demand. The indirect means include cooperation with member governments to influence general demand, intervention in regard to prices, and commercial policies affecting trade with "third countries"—that is, exports and imports of the community.

Minimum prices within the common market can be set by the commission under Article 61, but only "if it finds that a manifest crisis exists or is imminent." Prices of exports may also be set by the commission. Quotas on imports from third countries may be imposed upon recommendation by the commission to member governments under three conditions specified in Article 74: (1) third country exporters are "engaging in dumping or other practices condemned by the Havana Charter;" (2) lower prices of imports results from "conditions of competition contrary to this Treaty;" or, (3) if a steel product "is imported into the territory of one or more Member States in relatively increased quantities and under such conditions that these imports cause or threaten to cause serious injury to production within the common market of like or directly competing products." Consent of the council is required under the second criterion. The third requires the conditions of "manifest crisis" laid down in Article 58 which lays out a system of coping with declining demand that is reminiscent of the international cartels of the inter-war period.

It is noteworthy that the production quotas can be enforced by a system of payments for overproduction similar to the systems used in the cartels. The Treaty of Paris envisaged a policy of cartelization as a last resort to be used by the commission only when confronted with a "manifest crisis." As we will see below the commission has recently made use of its powers to enforce output quotas, and, in the face of Japanese competition, to seek extension of this cartel approach to world markets through "voluntary" restraint arrangements and consultations with industry leaders and government policymakers through an OECD steel committee. The emergence of Japan as a steel producer equal to the U.S. and Europe has had a great effect on the nature of competition in world markets.

The Emergence of Japan

In 1929 Japanese steel output amounted to only 2.1 million tons—less than 2 percent of the world total. Rearmament brought an expansion in steel demand and a consolidation of the six largest private firms into the Japan Iron and Steel Company which was taken over by the government during World War II. Steel ingot production reached 7.5 million tons by 1940. This expanded steel industry was based on imported minerals from the Empire and scrap from the United States which were then finished in Japan (Kawahito 1972, p. 4).

The war resulted in the loss of the Empire and a shortage of raw materials and fuel but little damage to the iron and steel facilities in Japan. Because the demand for steel had always been primarily for military uses, the Japanese steel companies found themselves with excess plant capacity after the war. From a peak of 7.65 million metric tons in 1943, crude steel output dropped to a low of 557 thousand metric tons in 1946 and remained below a million in 1947. Although reconstruction and development of the Japanese economy would require much more steel, the occupation forces were threatening the removal of much of the steel industry capacity as reparations. The developing cold war and the cost to the U.S. of relief for Japan, however, led in 1947 to a change in occupation policies from reparation to rapid economic development (Kawahito 1972, pp. 4-9).

The Japanese government-owned Reconstruction Finance Bank provided more than half of the steel industry's capital during the 1946 to 1948 period. Recovery was also assisted by a raw material subsidy and a price subsidy for iron and steel products designed to help steel users as well as steel producers. The United States assisted with the reopening of imports of heavy oil in June 1947 and iron ore and coal in January 1948. Crude steel output reached 1.7 million metric tons in 1948 and 3.1 million in 1949. Net exports amounted to over 9 percent of output in 1949 and 15 percent in 1950 (Kawahito 1972, pp. 6, 11). Thus, Japan became a steel exporter at the beginning of its post-war development.

Just as the ending of post-war subsidies and worldwide recession were threatening an end to steel industry recovery, the Korean War created a new demand boom in 1950 and 1951. Kawahito said:

> The Korean War boom lasted for a short time, but it is still widely considered to have provided the biggest "break" in the post-war development of the Japanese steel industry. It brought industrial production to the prewar scale by 1952. it enabled steel exports to surpass the previous peak of 1936 in 1952, and production to exceed the previous peak of 1943 in 1953. Moreover, it generated the basis for a continuous rise of demand for steel for many years to come, and it provided the industry with funds to be used for modernization (1972, p. 21).

Modernization of the Japanese steel industry was essential if it were to survive after the boom. Its production was dependent on acquisition of iron ore, coal, and fuel oil from distant sources at high costs. Furthermore, in 1952, iron production required seven times as many manhours per ton as in the United States and steel required five times as many. From 1951 through about 1955 the Japanese steel industry was engaged in a modernization program. With the aid of government loans and favorable tax treatment, large capital expenditure programs were undertaken to renovate and expand existing plants. Output of crude steel rose from 4.8 million metric tons in 1950 to 9.4 in 1955, with net exports accounting for 24 percent of output in the latter year. This program included the introduction or dissemination of techniques for sintering and beneficiating iron ore, substituting fuel oil for coal, and continuous casting. Steel production per worker remained lower than in Europe and the U.S., but by 1955, with lower wage rates, Japanese steel production costs began to approach the world level (Kawahito 1972, pp. 22-35).

In October 1955 the Japanese government restricted exports to assure domestic supplies of steel. The industry was pressing capacity and a second five year modernization program was launched which cost four times as much as the first program. It was financed primarily from private sources, but included a loan from the World Bank equal to 8.6 percent of the total investment. It included the construction of a number of new integrated iron and steel works with giant blast furnaces to make iron for basic-oxygen steel furnaces. The new basic-oxygen technology developed by 1953 in Austria not only improved productivity but also allowed expansion of steel output with less reliance on scrap which had become scarce in Japan as the war scrap was depleted. The new technology, however, required more iron ore, most of which had to be imported. In 1955 Japan imported 85 percent of its iron ore and 40 percent of its coking coal. Japanese companies sought to overcome their raw materials problem by negotiating long-term contracts with old suppliers and developing new mines in Malaya, India, and the Philippines. The second modernization program also included construction of giant ore and coal carriers and new steel works located at seaside and equipped with modern harbor and port facilities to lower materials handling costs.

By 1960 the Japanese steel industry had emerged as a viable competitor on the world steel market as well as an important contributor to the industrialization of Japan. With crude steel output reaching 22.1 million metric tons of which 12 percent was exported, Japan had surpassed France and approached the United Kingdom in output (Kawahito 1972, pp. 35-42). The emergence of the Japanese steel industry was accomplished in spite of a clear absence of comparative advantage stemming from resource endowments. Its success was the result of adoption of the best foreign technology at a faster rate than the older industries of the world coupled with development of new technologies, particularly in the area of computerized control systems, materials handling, and ocean shipping. Its rapid development continued in the 1960s and 1970s. By 1980 Japan was the leading exporter of steel in the world, producing 112.0 million metric tons of raw steel compared with 101.0 million in the United States and 128.0 in the European Community (American Metal Market *Metal Statistics,* 1980). At all times the bulk of Japanese steel production has been consumed domestically. In fact, at one time expansion was so rapid that about 15 percent of production was used in expanding the steel industry itself.

Even though the Japanese adopted antitrust laws making collusion unlawful, as in the United States and in Europe, prices are set under conditions in which competition is limited. The firms Yawata and Fuji, which had been split apart during the occupation, were again merged in 1970 into Shin Nippon Steel to become the largest steel producer in the world. Together with four other large integrated companies they produced over 90 percent of Japan's pig iron and over three-fourths of crude steel (Kawahito 1972, p. 56). Most steel is distributed by wholesale trading companies affiliated with the steel producers that operate with the assistance of the Ministry of International Trade and Industry and the tolerance of the Fair Trade Commission. Kawahito described the system as follows:

> . . . all member companies meet monthly with their wholesalers, announce their future-sales price and quantity, and conclude sales contracts at the same time and at the same place so that mutual suspicion may be eliminated. If a producer finds that his intended supply exceeds his wholesaler's demand, he will automatically reduce production by that amount in the following month. The price is supposed to be determined freely and independently by each steel company. In actuality, it is predetermined through negotiations by producers, representatives of dealers and users, and MITI. Therefore, it turns out to be uniform except for some variation on the basis of types of company. Integrated steel producers charge higher prices than nonintegrated, open-hearth furnace and electric-furnace companies. The system also provides a place where steel companies and related parties may discuss various problems affecting the industry (1972, p. 103).

The problem of avoiding differences in price stemming from differences in location of producers and customers is solved in Japan, not by a basing-point system, but by selling to all at uniform delivered prices. All freight costs are absorbed.

169

As this brief historical review has indicated, the world steel industry has been dominated by the three oligopolistic industries in the U.S., Europe, and Japan for the past two decades. The next section will discuss the interrelations among these three groups.

THE STRUCTURE OF CONTROL OF WORLD TRADE IN STEEL

At about the same time that Japan had emerged as a producer of steel capable of competing in world markets the United States lost its post-war dominance. In 1959 the United States imported 4.4 million net tons—6.1 percent of its consumption. By then the European industry had also recovered from the war and was operating under the ECSC rules that permitted cartelization of exports (Kronstein 1973, pp. 134-135). Pressures began to mount for some sort of arrangements for limiting competition in world markets, of which American imports were becoming a significant part. Four important recent developments have influenced the structure of the world steel trade: the 1968 and 1971 voluntary export restraint arrangements to protect the U.S. market; the European Community's reaction to the 1974 worldwide recession with its "Davignon Plan;" the American trigger-price system; and, the creation of a permanent Steel Committee of the OECD. Each will be discussed below.

Voluntary Restraint Arrangements: 1968-1974

The United States has remained an exporter of steel-mill products throughout the post-war period. Measured in short tons the amount has varied between a low of 1.7 million in 1959 to a high of 7.1 million in 1970. Measured in terms of exports relative to industry shipments the figures show no trend down, but fluctuation over the years with a low of 1.9 percent in 1966 to a high of 7.8 percent in 1970. The major change has taken place in imports of steel-mill products into the United States which averaged about 1.9 percent of apparent consumption between 1950 and 1958, and rose to 16.7 percent in 1968. Imports have exceeded exports in every year since 1958 (FTC 1977, p. 70).

As a consequence pressure by business and labor on Congress had become so great in 1968 that the Johnson Administration feared Congressional enactment of compulsary quotas that would jeopardize GATT and the whole post-war effort to achieve expansion of world trade and cause a reversion to isolationism and protection in the

170

legislative branch. To avoid these eventualities the administration developed a scheme that would shift the onus of trade restriction to the exporters. A three-year "voluntary" agreement among American, Japanese, and ECSC steel producers to temporarily commit themselves to a quantitative restriction on aggregate exports of steel-mill products was the result. It limited Japanese and ECSC producers to 5.75 million tons each in 1969 with a 5 percent per year increase in 1970 and 1971. Although it was effective in cutting down the level of exports to the U.S., imports rose to 17.8 percent of U.S. consumption in 1971. The 1968 agreement had been couched in aggregate terms with respect to both product type and geographical section of the U.S. market. Exporters, who used export cartels to coordinate their sales, began to emphasize higher priced and higher profit products and the incidence of the import competition continued to grow in some sections of the United States. The U.K. was outside the initial agreement as were other smaller exporting nations.

When the initial agreement expired a new three year agreement was signed in 1971. This agreement included the U.K. and limited Japanese exports to Europe as well as both Japanese and European exports to the U.S. and set specific product and geographical quotas that were monitored by the U.S. customs officials.

The arrangement was in conflict with the spirit, if not the letter, of the competitive policies in Japan, the United States, and the ECSC. In Japan product-by-product export cartels were formed to allot the quotas among Japanese producers. Collusive restriction on exports from Europe to the U.S. is not prohibited by the Treaty of Paris, but the participation of European enterprises in the three-way arrangement that restricted Japanese exports to Europe might have met disapproval by the competition officials at the Commission. They failed to interfere. In the U.S. the question whether participation of the secretary of state in such a cartelization scheme violates the Sherman Antitrust Act was raised in a private antitrust case (*Consumers Union vs. Rogers*). The U.S. Department of Justice's Civil Division had the job of defending the secretary of state. The district court ruled against the arrangement, but it was sanctioned by the circuit court of appeals after the lawyers for the plaintiff failed to press the antitrust counts in order to expedite the case (*Consumers Union vs. Kissinger*). A way had been found for the U.S., Japan, and Europe to cartelize a large portion of world trade in steel while still adhering to GATT and their own domestic competition policies.

The expiration of the second VER arrangement coincided with the worldwide boom in 1974. Imports into the U.S. were coming in at prices higher than domestic price ceilings and the U.S. industry was pressing capacity. The arrangement was allowed to lapse just before the 1974 downturn in the world economy.

The Davignon Plan for the European Community

The first four months of 1975 brought a record-breaking fall in demand for steel from ECSC producers. Compared with a year earlier orders dropped 34 percent. Prices dropped 25 to 35 percent for sales within the community and 40 to 60 percent for exports (Martin 1979; *Commission of the European Communities Bulletin* 1975, pp. 47, 96). A series of moves were made between 1975 and 1979 by the commission to restrict output and imports and to enhance prices as well as to "rationalize" the industry and reduce capacity.

In 1975 the commission began to revise its "forward programme" quarterly and thereby provide production estimates to each national steel industry. Trade associations in each nation allocated the national output targets among individual companies, which since it was sanctioned by the commission did not violate Article 65 of the Treaty of Paris. The commission also required monthly reporting of actual crude steel output and forecasts by each company of the next month's production. These actions seem to have achieved low levels of output and stable, but low, prices. Thus, revenues dropped and unit costs rose. The effect on profits of the companies led to pressure for stronger actions by the commission to get prices back up to higher levels. The ECSC, however, was a large exporter as well as an importer of steel products. Measures to raise prices within the community would not only invite increased imports but also require either loss of export markets or differentials between export and domestic prices that would trigger anti-dumping actions abroad. "Manifest crisis" measures to set production quotas and minimum domestic prices would have been useless without quantity and price controls on imports and would have required the approval of the council that consisted of representatives of the member governments, all of which were members of the OECD as were most of the countries from which steel imports originated. In the wake of the 1974 oil crisis, the OECD members had adopted a Trade Pledge that obligated them to avoid unilateral actions to restrict imports. Therefore, the commission chose the OECD as the "appropriate setting for international concertation," and consultation on steel took place on November 13, 1975 in Paris at which the participating OECD nations agreed to continue consultation and exchange of information (*OECD Observer* No. 6, 1975, pp. 16-17).

172

Meanwhile, the commission had initiated negotiations with individual countries for voluntary export restraint arrangements. In october 1975 the six largest Japanese steel producers agreed to restrain exports to Europe. This and other VER arrangements succeeded in holding imports down and enabled some improvement in prices as slow recovery from the recession began. By the end of 1976, however, the demand for steel was below the worst levels of 1975 and by Spring 1977 the ECSC industry was operating at about 60 percent of capacity.

In March 1977 the commission adopted new measures that came to be known as the "Davignon Plan" named after Etienne Davignon, the commissioner responsible for industrial policy. The plan consisted of measures to: (1) preserve the "unity and openness of the market;" (2) modernize production capacity; (3) intervene more directly in pricing; and, (4) retrain and redeploy workers (Martin 1979, pp. 869-885). It was designed to assist the community steel industry become more efficient, technologically advanced, and able to compete in a world of freer trade with the Japanese and other emerging steel industries in LDCs. Emphasis was placed on closing obsolete and poorly located plants and investing in cost reducing projects.

The intervention included the continuation of VER arrangements and voluntary restrictions on output and mandatory minimum prices on bars and "guideline" prices on other products. This was the first time Article 61, authorizing the use of mandatory minimum prices during a "manifest crisis, was invoked. The Davignon Plan proposed several measures to member governments to facilitate the imposition of countervailing duties in cases of dumping of imports. These measures strengthened the hand of the commission in negotiating voluntary restraint arrangements while not conflicting with the community's ostensible opposition to protectionism.

Although the plan was a move away from free trade and competition, it was designed to avoid retaliation by substituting negotiation for competition in world markets. It provided an impetus to the development of a permanent institutional arrange..,ent for controlling the world steel industry.

The American Trigger-Price System

The worldwide recession that began in late 1974 coincided with the expiration of the second voluntary export restraint arrangement. The steel industry and labor organizations in the United States attempted to induce the Ford Administration to negotiate another VER. Participation by the U.S. government was essential in order to give some assurance of protection from antitrust actions. After the Ford Administration limited its intervention to quotas on specialty steel imports which were authorized by the 1974 Trade Act, steel interests unsuccessfully attempted to convince the Carter Administration to place quotas on ordinary steel products. Instead, that administration urged the industry to seek enforcement of the anti-dumping provisions of the 1974 Trade Act. The very large number of anti-dumping proceedings then threatened to provoke major problems in relations between the United States and the European Community.

The U.S. market had become particularly attractive to European exports because the structure of control of the industry and the smaller decline in demand kept the price of steel high. The community, with or without dumping, was in a good position to increase its share of the U.S. market and did so. In light of the specialty teel quotas and the increasing threat of countervailing duties resulting from anti-dumping actions, the Europeans sought solutions by negotiation. On November 8, 1977 Davignon met in Washington with Undersecretary of the Treasury Anthony Solomon and Special Trade Representative Robert Strauss to discuss the U.S. government's strategy for the steel industry. Similar discussions were held in Brussels with a Japanese delegation on November 28, 1977 *(Commission of European Communities Bulletin* 1977, pp. 70, 71).

Under the 1974 Trade Act, "dumping" was not limited to price discrimination. Included in the legal definition was exporting to the United States "at prices which represent less than the cost of producing the merchandise in question." The statute gave the secretary of the treasury much discretion in determining the "cost of producing." In response to the domestic pressures and those from our trading partners, in February 1978, the secretary of the treasury announced a new system of dealing with steel industry anti-dumping proceedings. Under this trigger-price system, the secretary used his discretionary powers to ascertain appropriate import prices based on ascertainment of the costs of the most efficient—namely, the Japanese—steel producers. Any imports priced above that level were not challenged but any coming in from any source below the trigger-prices resulted in expedited handling of any anti-dumping actions brought under the 1974 Trade Act. The trigger-prices were raised from time to time to reflect not only cost changes in Japan but also changes in the dollar-yen exchange rate. Thus, a floor was set on import prices. This measure was accepted by the Europeans and Japanese as a desirable solution to the U.S. industry's problem because it served to limit price competition among the exporters. In addition, the trigger-price system had little effect on the exporter's shares of the U.S. market because U.S. producers chose to raise domestic prices and to allow the imports to continue.

The steel companies thus achieved some protection for prices and profits, but the steel workers did not accomplish protection of jobs. The system was also put under stress by changes in foreign exchange rates. In March 1980, after the Department of Commerce refused to accede to industry demands to raise the trigger-prices, the United States Steel Company instituted anti-dumping actions against European exporters. In response, the government briefly suspended the trigger-price system (*Wall Street Journal*, March 24, 1980), but it was soon reinstated (*Wall Street Journal*, October 1, 1980). It was finally abandoned in 1982 by the Reagan Administration after several steel companies again instituted anti-dumping proceedings.

The OECD Steel Committee

In December 1977, just as the American trigger-price system was being formulated, the OECD ad hoc steel group adopted three principles to guide member countries in coping with the steel crisis. First, the burden of adjustments required by reorganization and restructuring should not be shifted to trading partners. Second, quantitative restrictions are harmful in the long-run. Third, no nation can be expected to absorb low priced imports in large quantities to the detriment of its own employment and production. It then established a monitoring system to get early warning of problems and to facilitate rational investment decision in the future (*Commission of the European Communities Bulletin* 1977, p. 84).

In October 1978 the ad hoc steel group became a permanent steel committee consisting of representatives from member nations. The potential role of this new organization is great since the treaty that created the OECD provides that a decision taken unanimously by the council is legally binding on the member governments. Because of the status of treaties in U.S. law, it is quite possible that an OECD arrangement for concerted action on steel crisis measures could not be reached by the Sherman Act prohibitions against cartelization. The OECD steel committee could evolve into something comparable to the ECSC, extending the multiple basing-point system and collusion in pricing to the whole of international trade in steel. In January 1979 the newly elected chairman of the committee, Alan W. Wolff, dismissed the comments of critics:

> . . . who say that the OECD committee will turn into a "world steel cartel," and the complaints of those who would like to see

175

some sort of international agreement on steel production and marketing. The Committee, he said in effect, will steer a course midway between those extremes, and will substitute the concept of "awareness" for the concept of "control." (*American Metal Market*, February 15, 1979, pp. 1, 32)

This middle ground may turn out to be the beginning of a new era of oligopoly on the world level in which the inter-reacting rivals are organizations in which government and business decisionmakers are intertwined as in the ECSC. With steel enterprises under national government control in much of the world industry, the emerging OECD arrangement is likely to be a complex pattern of social control of business and trade that will not fit neatly into the conceptual framework of industrial organization theory or international trade theory.

If development continues in Third World steel industries and if East-West trade continues to expand, then the OECD First World nations will have to cope with the development of steel capacity beyond their organizational bounds. After much debate, the steel committee decided to invite South Korea, India, Brazil, and Mexico, countries with rapidly expanding steel industries, to join the organization: all of them declined the invitation.

In summary, global concentration in the steel industry appears to be increasing. Between 1960 and 1974, the three firm concentration ratios increased in the ECSC from 22 to 34 and in Japan from 52 to 59, while dropping from 52 to 45 in the United States (Stegemann 1977, p. 262). But the cohesiveness of the oligopolies in each of those sectors of the developed world has increased as a result of closer involvement of governments with the corporations and each other in coordinating steel industry decisionmaking.

INTERNATIONAL INDUSTRIAL ORGANIZATION AND DEVELOPING COUNTRIES

The steel industry was identified as one of the priority sectors at the March 1975 Lima conference of the United Nations Industrial Development Organization, which set a target for developing countries to increase their share of the world's industrial production from 7 percent to at least 25 percent by the year 2000 (UNIDO 1976, p. 1). The output of steel in the developing countries which was less than 7 percent of world steel production in 1970, reached 11 percent in 1977 (UNIDO 1978, p. 3). Table 5.2 shows the pattern of recent production

Table 5.2

Raw Steel Production in Selected Countries, 1974-1980

(in mil. metric tons)

Country	1974	1975	1976	1977	1978	1979(p)	1980(p)	1981(f)
United States	132.0	105.9	116.3	113.7	124.3	123.3	101.0	114.6
European Community	155.4	125.2	134.0	126.1	132.4	140.1	128.0	102.2
Japan	117.1	102.3	107.4	102.4	102.1	111.7	112.0	102.0
Eastern Europe	184.8	192.4	198.4	203.9	210.8	208.9	NA	NA
India	7.1	8.0	9.4	10.0	10.1	10.1	NA	NA
South Korea	1.9	2.0	3.5	4.3	5.0	7.6	NA	NA
Taiwan	0.9	1.0	1.6	1.8	3.4	4.3	NA	NA
Argentina	2.4	2.2	2.4	2.7	2.8	3.2	NA	NA
Brazil	7.5	834	9.3	11.3	12.2	13.9	NA	NA
Mexico	5.1	5.3	5.3	5.6	6.7	7.0	NA	NA
Venezuela	1.0	1.1	0.9	0.8	0.8	1.5	NA	NA

Source: American Metal Market, *Metal Statistics*, 1978 and 1980

P —preliminary
F —forecasted
NA—not available

growth in several developing countries as well as in the established steel areas. As the table illustrates the steel industries of the developed countries continued to cope with excess capacity, while those in several developing nations expanded. South Korea's output climbed from 1.9 to 7.6 million metric tons between 1974 and 1979. For Taiwan the increase was from .9 to 4.3 and for Brazil from 7.5 to 13.9 million metric tons. Opportunities for import substitution clearly exist in some LDCs and a repetition of the Japanese entry into the steel export market is not out of the question in spite of the concern of the established steel industry managers with over expansion of world capacity. Yet the opportunities and problems for steel industry development vary greatly among the less developed countries. Three specific cases are examined herein: Mexico, Brazil, and Venezuela. Each has already achieved significant steel production and each has some resource endowments superior to Japan's. In each early entry of private firms into steel production has been overshadowed or superceded by state-owned enterprises. Brief examination of steel industry development in these three countries will give some insights into the reasons for the great role of the public sector.

Mexico

Mexico's steel industry is not new. The Hojalata y Lamina S.A. steel complex in Monterrey began after Isaac Garza and Francisco Sada founded a brewery in 1892 and soon integrated backward into production of glass bottles and steel for bottle caps (*The New York Times*, June 5, 1978, p. D3). In 1950 the Mexican steel industry, located mainly in Monterrey, produced only 337 thousand tons of steel, but that amounted to almost half of the 707 thousand tons consumed in Mexico. By 1965 the domestic market had grown about four-fold to 2.7 million tons of which 2.4 million was produced domestically (Manners 1971, pp. 1-85). The recent boom in Mexican economic growth has accelerated the demand for steel products which, despite major expansion programs is unlikely to be met by domestic production.

After a reorganization of government steel operations begun in 1978, the Mexican industry now consists of one privately owned and controlled company and one government company. Hojalata y Lamina, S.A., which owns the HYLSA direct reduction process, is part of the Grupo Alfa conglomerate. SIDERMEX, a new state enterprise, controls the government-owned plants including one in Monclava near Monterrey with 3.2 million tons capacity, a new steel complex, SICARTSA, built between 1971 and 1976 on the west coast with an initial capacity of 1.1 million tons, the 1.5 million ton plant of Fun-

178

didora de Monterrey in which Nippon Steel owns a 14 percent interest, and the Veracruz plant of Tubos de Acero.

All sectors of the Mexican steel industry are planning rapid expansion, although most projects were suspended temporarily in 1982. HYLSA has a program for expanding from 1.5 million to 2.5 million tons capacity which will include 1.6 million tons of flat products. Tubos de Acero embarked in January 1980 on a six-year, $650 million investment program to double the capacity of its plant in Veracruz to 840 thousand tons per year, of which 520 thousand tons will be pipe for the petroleum industry (*The New York Times*, December 16, 1979, p. F3). SIDERMEX is spending $750 million to increase the capacity of the Altos Hornos Moncolva plant from 3.2 million tons to 4.25 million tons. Plans to begin the second phase of the SICARTSA plant were announced in October 1979 and to develop a new plant somewhere on the Gulf coast. These plans are based on a calculation that the demand for steel will reach 28.6 million tons by 1990 and production will reach 26.7 million from public and private plants, leaving imports of 1.9 million tons. The public share is expected to grow from 64 to 72 percent (*World Business Weekly*, October 22, 1979, p. 10).

Whether the new SIDERMEX organization succeeds in such rapid growth will depend on its ability to overcome many obstacles, such as worker productivity, an inefficient transportation system, and its ability to keep up with technological innovations. Productivity per worker improved from 80 tons in 1977 to 100 tons in 1979, which was better than the U.K. and U.S.S.R. steel industries according to Jorge Leipen Garay, the director general of SIDERMEX (*The New York Times,* December 16, 1979, p. F3). The SICARTSA plant, located at the new port of Lazaro Cardenas, was designed to produce nonflat products such as wire bars. When recession cut the price of wire bars in half just after the plant went into production, its output was largely exported, not only because demand fell but also because there was no way to transport the product to domestic markets. A new railroad, completed in November 1979, and a restructuring of production, should eliminate that problem. (*Hispano,* December 17, 1979, pp. 31-32).

The effort to expand the steel industry may leave Mexico dependent on imported iron ore. Although exploration for new deposits is underway, about two-thirds of the steel production capacity will be located on the coast by 1990 which shall facilitate the importation of iron-ore. So long as the natural gas supplies hold out, production of steel with imported ore would be better than importation of steel, assuming that the expanding Mexican steel industry achieves low enough costs to afford Mexico a comparative advantage in steel production.

To the extent that development of the Mexican steel industry is stimulated by government subsidized prices for electricity, petroleum, and natural gas, the comparative advantage may be temporary. If it continues, steel interests and other consumers may lock Mexico into a price structure that promotes consumption rather than conservation. It appears that government policy was based primarily on a desire to achieve rapid growth in steel products. The major policy question then is whether self-sufficiency in steel will be sustainable.

Brazil

Unlike Mexico, Brazil is a major exporter of iron ore. In 1977 Brazil produced 8.1 percent of the world's iron ore, although its raw steel production was only 1.7 percent of the world total (American Iron and Steel Institute 1978). In 1975 Brazil exported 71 million tons of the 79 million tons of iron ore produced there, primarily to Japan, although the United States imported 7.5 million tons of iron ore which amounted to 16 percent of U.S. iron ore imports and 11 percent of Brazil's iron ore exports (*Minerals Yearbook* 1975, pp. 8, 9). Potentially, Brazil might process much more of its iron ore into semi-finished or finished steel products for export. One impediment to such a strategy is the lack of domestic supplies of either coking coal or natural gas.

The iron industry of Brazil is very old. As early as 1556 a forge was established, but until the late eighteenth century the government of Portugal opposed such industrial development in the colony. Several iron-making plants were established during the nineteenth century. At the beginning of the twentieth century about 70 small plants produced about 2000 tons of pig iron per year, but Brazil continued to rely on imports of steel products (Baer 1969, pp. 48-57).

By 1940 consumption of rolled-steel products in Brazil had risen to 414,519 tons, of which 69 percent were imported. In that year more than half the steel ingot output of Brazil was accounted for by Companhia Siderúrgica Belgo-Mineira. That company was formed in 1921 when ARBED, the Belgium-Luxemburg firm, absorbed a small Brazilian company and in 1940 it opened a small integrated steel mill using charcoal (Baer 1969, pp. 59-65).

Several abortive attempts were made by the government to obtain foreign private direct investment in a large, integrated steel works. The established steel companies in the U.S. and Germany were interested in access to Brazilian iron ore but were reluctant to invest in steel

180

facilities in a steel importing country, but it is not clear whether the existence of the international steel cartel played any role in the failures. As the outbreak of war between Germany and the U.S. approached, President Vargas invited both the German and the U.S. governments to help finance and build a modern integrated steel-making facility at Volta Redonda. The U.S. government's interest in military bases in Brazil and its wish to discourage further German economic penetration in Latin America led to a decision by the Export-Import Bank to help finance the project, which was producing coke and steel ingot by 1946 (Baer 1969, pp. 68-76). This loan by the Export-Import Bank was its first step into the financing of industrial projects in developing countries (Shapiro and Volk, p. 23).

The Volta Redonda project was designed by Arthur G. McKee and Company, an American firm, and Companhia Siderúrgica Nacional (CSN) was created to operate it. CSN common stock was offered to private Brazilian investors with the government standing ready to take whatever amount was necessary. As capitalization was increased with capacity expansion, the government share grew and CSN soon became an essentially government-owned and government-operated company (Baer 1969, p. 76).

By 1952 the Banco do Brasil had attained full control of Aços Especiais Itabira which was organized as a private firm in the 1940s to convert iron ore into steel with electric furnace technology.

In the 1950s two additional coke-using integrated firms were established on the initiative of private groups and local governments but ultimately with Brazilian government participation and control. The Companhia Siderúrgica Paulista was created to operate an integrated coke-using, basic oxygen facility near the markets of São Paulo and Santos (Baer 1969, pp. 80, 81).

Usinas Siderúrgicas de Minas Gerais was created in 1956 to take advantage of the back haul from the export of iron ore from Minas Gerais to the United States. Coking coal could be brought back in the otherwise empty ships and railroad cars if an integrated steel plant were located near the iron mines. The plant was built in a new town near the iron ore mines of Companhia Vale do Rio Doce, the government-owned exporting firm. Construction of the plant was supervised by a Japanese consortium which originally received a 40 percent equity participation. Other participants included the state of Minas Gerais, the Companhia Vale do Rio Doce, and CSN.

Several smaller integrated and non-integrated firms entered or expanded in the 1950s. The German company Mannesmann founded a Brazilian subsidiary in 1952 and built a coke-using blast furnace in the early 1960s. The private Ferro e Aço de Vitoria Companhia was acquired by the Banco Nacional de Desenvolvimento Economico and expanded by the building of a new rolling mill. Ferrostaal A.G., which built the rolling mill, received a small equity participation.

This was the beginning of extensive private and government investments in the industry. By 1966 there were over 25 small pig iron producers and more than 40 steel enterprises. About two-thirds of the steel capacity (around 3.7 million tons annually) was in the hands of a small number of government-controlled firms (Baer 1969, p. 83, Appendices). The use of a mixture of government and private equity participation enabled Brazil to overcome the problems of foreign exchange funding and technology transfer in building a modern steel industry. The period of autonomy of the mixed enterprises ended, however, in 1964 when a revolution brought a military government into power. At a time when Brazil was suffering hyperinflation, balance of payments problems, and recession, the government moved to control steel pricing, output, and investment decisions as instruments of economic policy. The steel industry experienced a crisis of excess capacity and financial losses. Although demand for steel recovered in 1969 and output reached 90 percent of capacity, the three major state-controlled firms were in no position to finance the needed expansion and Brazilian government policies were inadequate to prevent a severe shortage of steel in the early 1970s (Wernecke pp. 28-53). To alleviate the problem a steel consulting group, Conselho Consultivo da Industria Siderúrgica (CONSIDER), was created and given ministerial status in June 1970. It had sole authority to approve federal financial assistance for the three firms, and set about negotiating with the World Bank, the Inter-American Development Bank (IDB), and all countries that would supply equipment for expansion. A ten-year steel plan was announced in January 1971. With assistance from the World Bank and the IDB, another period of rapid expansion of the Brazilian steel industry began. In spite of problems in implementing the plan on schedule, significant expansion was achieved during the 1970s. Yet failure to achieve self-sufficiency in steel products required Brazil to finance not only the external component of the investment in new capacity but also a very large volume of imports. In 1974 imports amounted to 5 million ingot-tons, or 65 percent of domestic production, at a cost of $1.6 billion (Wernecke 1977, p. 89)

In 1973 centralization of control was formalized with the creation of a government holding company, Siderúrgica Brasileira, S.A. (SIDERBRAS). SIDERBRAS now coordinates steel imports as well as acts as an agent for the operating companies in negotiating foreign loans and joint ventures. Two new major steel mills were underway but not yet completed in early 1980. The one at Acominas in Minas Gerais was planned to produce two million tons per year of heavy sections and rails. The other at Tubarao, a new iron ore port, is a joint venture among SIDERBRAS, Kawasaki of Japan, and Finsider, the Italian government-controlled firm. This steel mill was expected to produce three million tons per year of semifinished steel for export by 1982 and eventually reach 12 million tons per year (Shapiro & Volk p. 24)

A new "master plan" for the 1979-1988 period was announced in 1978. This plan calls for investment of over $25 billion in the steel industry, and aims at balanced growth among existing companies. Based on an annual growth rate of 7.3 percent for the Brazilian economy between 1981 and 1988, the plan estimates a rise in steel consumption to 33 million tons by 1988. Industrial expansion would provide sufficient flat rolled products for the domestic market so that by 1988 34 million tons would be produced annually. To reach that goal all that is needed is completion of projects already approved by CONSIDER for the government sector and some expansion of non-flat products by the private sector (*Metal Bulletin,* December 15, 1978, p. 40).

Whether Brazil's current plan will be fulfilled on schedule or flounder a bit as did the 1971 plan, it appears that Brazil is well on its way to becoming self-sufficient, if not a major supplier of world markets in competition with the Japanese and European established producers.

Regional Cooperation in Steel Production. In December 1978 in Rio de Janiero, the Latin American Iron and Steel Institute, ILAFO, recommended that the region adopt policies to insure regional self-sufficiency in steel production. The chairman, Dr. Davis Vallejo Jaramillo, commented that:

> Steelmakers in developed countries were seeking to frustrate the growth in the developing world in order to preserve their markets. He pointed out, for example, that U.S. steelmakers had opposed the granting of financial help for the Trinidad steel project because a large part of its output is destined for the export market. The formation of the steel committee of OECD was also seen as a move to limit the transfer of technology and finance to developing countries.
>
> Jaramillo said that consumption of steel in Ilafa countries had grown from 16.56 million tons (raw steel equivalent) in 1969 to 27.9 million tons in 1977 and was expected to grow to 29 million tons in 1978. The goal set for both consumption and production by 1985 was 55 million tpy, requiring a growth rate of 7% and 11.8% respectively. This was a gigantic challenge for

183

the region, he continued, and meant that in seven years it would have to increase capacity by 30 million tons or 12.5% a year, calling for investments of $33,000 million (*Metal Bulletin*, Dec. 5, 1978, p. 36)

In an editorial a week later, *Metal Bulletin* (December 12, 1978, p. 15) said:

> The expansion that is still taking place around the world, especially in developing countries, does seem to many observers to be somewhat misguided at a time when over-capacity is considerable and when there seems little prospect of the new facilities being fully utilized for some time ahead. For developing countries such thoughts are seen as a disguised way of trying to persuade them to forego their own expansion plans and continue to rely on imports from established producers.
>
> However, there does come a point where preoccupation with steel expansion becomes excessive and thoughts that precious investment finance might be employed in other important sectors begin to surface.

This view was supported by United Nations Industrial Development Organization which reported in 1978 that:

> Increasing cooperation between developed and developing countries in the steel sector has been an indicator of the fact that such arrangements [cooperation on a barter or production compensation basis] are advantageous to both sides. A developing country profits by being able to develop and exploit its natural resources and manufacture value added products while a developed country [profits] by getting the opportunity to manufacture and supply the equipment (capital goods), to transfer technological innovations and professional expertise, to train manpower thereby enabling its manufacturing organizations to make full use of their capacities, experiences and skills. The convergence of interests—developing countries for steel production and developed countries for the export of capital goods, transfer of technology, training, etc. should be fully utilized in the years to come. (1978)

Accomplishment of this degree of cooperation between the developed and developing nations would be much easier if the structure of control of industry in the developed countries were more competitive. Even though the people of the world might benefit from such cooperation, there exists particular groups whose interests are clearly hurt by

184

what Joseph Schumpeter called "creative destruction" of old capital values brought about by innovation and change that benefits society. In a highly decentralized, competitive economy entry of better located and technically more efficient plant capacity for producing the old products or new substitutes would take place in spite of the loss of the vested interests of capital, labor, (and communities generally) that are associated with the older plants. Amelioration of such losses is the primary goal of such governmental intervention as the Davignon Plan and the U.S. trigger-price system. The principle behind trade adjustment assistance is that society gains by allowing the "creative destruction" of vested interests and compensating the losses by subsidies that provide income without perpetuating the old activities. Those with the vested interests, however, will usually treat the latter as secondary solutions to their problem and use what power they possess to interfere with changes that threaten them.

How effective the emerging structure of control of the steel industries of the First World countries will be in protecting the old capital values remains to be seen. The closing of plants in Europe and the United States indicates that the forces of change are strong. United States Steel reported a loss of $561.7 million for the fourth quarter of 1979—the largest quarterly loss ever for an American company—and began closing all or parts of 16 plants eliminating 13,000 jobs. The following year it signed an agreement with Nippon Steel to improve productivity in its remaining facilities (*Wall Street Journal*, February 14, 1980, p. 1).

On January 31, 1980 Lewis W. Foy, president of the American Iron and Steel Institute and chairman of the Board of Bethlehem Steel, referring to the Soviet intervention in Afghanistan, invoked the national defense argument to appeal for government policies to protect the U.S. steel industry. He said: "Our national security demands a build-up in our defense capabilities, and it can't be done without ample domestic supplies of steel products." Steel producers predict that without new government policies, by 1988 U.S. steel production will decline to 130 million tons from 158 million in 1978 and imports will rise to 50 million from 21 million (*The Courier-Journal*, February 1, 1980, p. 1). The suspension of the trigger-price system after the filing of anti-dumping actions by U. S. Steel in March 1980, coincided with the onset of recession in the United States that seems likely to worsen the crisis of the steel industries of the developed countries and stimulate both the threat of a trade war and efforts to avoid it by closer cooperation among governments and companies.

The political climate in the First World steel producing nations does not encourage financial and technical assistance to the expanding Third World steel producing industries. If the old steel companies did not control decisions on such assistance, then competition and the search for profits by developed country steel plant-building companies might override the incentives for the declining steel firms to try to stifle development of overseas competitors.[2] Steel companies as well as financial institutions in the First World have been assisting the development process. Undoubtedly, any effective moves toward closer coordination of OECD member nation's policies on steel can be expected to affect the ease with which development assistance can be obtained for Third World steel projects. It will affect the degree of centralization of control among those companies with capacity to render assistance as well as the policies of both private and public lending institutions.

To the extent that competition among steel plant-building companies is inhibited, the cost if not the availability of their services can be expected to be affected.

Much more information is needed on the structure of control of the markets for the various products and services that are required for steel industry expansion in LDCs. The arrangements for the use of the LDC basic oxygen process in the 1950s and 1960s suggest that competition is far from perfect in the steelmaking technology markets. An Austrian company, VOEST, patented the new process in the late 1940s. Another Austrian company, OAM, and a German company, H. S. Brassert and Company, had been working on similar processes. To avoid patent litigation, they jointly created in Zurich, Switzerland, a company named Brassert Oxygen Technik AG (BOT) to control patent rights to related steel-making processes for all the world. BOT concluded numerous agreements with leading steel firms throughout the world whereby each turned over exclusive world rights to BOT to its own present and future patents in exchange for domestic rights to the new process. Furthermore, any company that acquired a sublicense from one of these leading firms also was required to turn over exclusive rights to foreign countries to any improvement patents. By 1962 BOT had acquired over 720 patents and 290 applications for patents in thirty-eight countries. H. Kronstein concluded that: "BOT was in a position to establish a system of private market regulation in the international steel market." (Kronstein pp. 302-303). So long as such technology cartels do not reach too much of the needed technology or raise its price too much, the process of development can continue. A recent study by Alexander J. Yeats shows that a special French trading arrangement, that limited competition in the sale of steel products to some developing countries

186

resulted in higher import prices than existed for other countries where more competitive conditions prevailed (Yeats pp. 178-180).

Venezuela

In 1950 Venezuela produced only 100 thousand metric tons of iron ore (measured by iron content). By 1960 iron ore output had increased more than a hundred fold. In 1975 Venezuela accounted for more than three percent of total world production (United Nations *Statistical Annual* 1976, Table 56). Venezuela ranked eighth in identified reserves of iron ore in 1975 with one percent of the world total (Bureau of Mines, 1976).

After World War II, United States Steel and Bethlehem Steel invested in iron mining in Venezuela to supply ore primarily to their East Coast tidewater plants. The Orinoco Mining Company was a wholly owned subsidiary of U. S. Steel and the Iron Mines Company of Venezuela was a wholly owned subsidiary of Bethlehem Steel Corporation. Both companies operated mines, railroads and shiploading docks. On January 1, 1975 they were nationalized by the Venezuelan government. With the nationalization and the depressed state of steel output in the United States, Venezuelan iron ore output has declined in the past few years. Output in 1978 was about half that of the peak year, 1974.

In 1950 a private company, Siderúrgica Venezolana, began producing steel from scrap in an electric furnace and the government began plans for an integrated steel mill. Construction began in 1956 on a blast-furnace-open hearth facility on the Orinoco River in Guayana. That plant began production in 1962 with a capacity of 0.7 million tons of crude steel. In 1964 it was placed under a government-owned company, SIDOR, a subsidiary of Corporacion Venezolana de Guayana (CVG). The original plant produced only non-flat and seamless tubular products. A flat products mill was added in the early 1970s and steel capacity was enlarged to 1.2 million tons per year. Until 1975 the SIDOR plant obtained its iron ore from the United States Steel Corporation subsidiary. The nationalized properties were placed under Ferrominera Orinoco, a subsidiary of CVG (West 1979, pp. 138-139).

A National Steel Plan was announced in 1974. It was part of a Venezuelan government policy of using oil revenues to industrialize around the country's domestic raw materials. The aim is to export iron in the form of steel using products rather than as ore. With good supplies of natural gas, dolomite, limestone, and even coal, but not of

187

high grade for coking, Venezuela perceives an opportunity to export finished products with much more value added by local labor than the iron ore activities had been affording (West, p. 140). At 576.4 pounds per year, Venezuela consumes more steel per capita than any other Latin American country. It imported about 2 million tons in 1979 (*World Business Weekly*, October 8, 1979, p. 27).

The National Steel Plan called for crude steel capacity expansion from 1.5 million tons per year in 1975 to 5.5 in 1980, 10.0 in 1985, and 15.0 in 1990. The first phase of the plan is well underway. It consists of 3.6 million tons of crude steel capacity in the form of the most modern direct reduction-electric furnace technology, including a pelletizing plant, eight direct reduction modules, ten electric arc furnaces connected to continuous casting machines, and rolling mills for both flat and non-flat products. Already operating at 50 percent of capacity in 1979, this SIDOR facility is expected to reach 5.3 million tons by 1984. The location of natural gas, hydroelectric power and iron ore in close proximity gave the DR process the advantage over traditional blast-furnace technology in Guyana, but lack of a local labor supply may prove disadvantageous for additional expansion in this area. The DR process was chosen after studies showed it to require 40 percent less capital investment and 20 percent lower operating costs. The blast furnace process would have required importation of $100 million of coke and 700,000 tons of scrap iron a year (*World Business Weekly*, October 8, 1979, p. 27).

The second phase of the 1974 National Steel Plan called for a green-field blast-furnace type facility in the state of Zulia near Maracaibo. The Zulia steel project would be coupled with development of coal reserves at Guasare, which would produce coal of low quality that would require mixing with imported coking coal. The project was placed under Corpozulia, a development corporation of the state of Zulia. After President Luis Herrera Compins replaced Carlos Andres Perez, the National Steel Plan was re-examined. In late 1979 projects not already underway were halted. The Zulia project may yet be allowed to proceed. In the final bidding stage three international consortia were left in the running—one led by Krupp, one by Davy International, and one by a French bank. Under a 1978 law approving the project, foreign financing of at least 25 percent was stipulated. Project design work began in 1976 with a contract for technical assistance from British Steel Corporation. The third phase of the original plan was not specified, but it was to have been either another 5 million ton green-field plant or expansion of the earlier plants either in Zulia or Guayana.

Venezuela, like Brazil, turned to state-owned enterprise for steel industry development after having had both domestic and foreign private sector firms. The private domestic steel industry failed to grow as rapidly as steel consumption and the foreign firms failed to integrate forward from iron mining into steel production. If the Venezuelan economy continues to develop rapidly under the spur of petroleum revenues, the government will continue to have incentive to substitute local production of steel products for imports and also to upgrade the value added by iron ore exports. The pace of expansion of steel output relative to steel consumption remains uncertain.

SUMMARY

The main concern of this case study is the implication of foreign direct investment for development. In the case of iron and steel, foreign direct investment in ore mining was not followed by a second wave of investments in the down stream activities of iron and steel production. Examination of the iron and steel industry affords an opportunity to examine the other side of the coin—*viz.*, the implications of the absence of foreign direct investment for development.

The distribution between rich and poor countries of the gains from transnational trade and investment are clearly affected by the transnational control structure of the world iron and steel industry. The type of growth that occurs is also clearly affected by this transnational structure of control. The iron and steel industry case demonstrates that, even without TNC control of Third World steel industries, developed world industrial policies can bias trade and investment toward developed countries. The success of Third World locally-controlled steel industrial growth sets in motion defensive moves to preserve the developed world's role as importer of minerals and exporter of finished products. The orthodox perspective implicitly assumes that imperfections in competition have a negligible effect on the distribution of the gains from trade. Yet the patterns of trade and the location and amount of investment in steel production capacity in the world is greatly affected by the transnational control structure.

That structure is centered on a legally-sanctioned cartelization in the ECSC, a basing-point system that has the same effects of limiting competition in the United States, and a tight oligopoly with collusive pricing within Japan. Those three developed world centers of power are coordinated in their trade relations by ostensible commitment to

189

GATT and free trade. Actually, however, trade is restricted by three-way collusion that takes the form of industrial policies in each that are aimed at limiting competition: for example, voluntary restraint arrangements and the trigger-price system. Industrial policies originally rationalized as temporary exceptions to free trade, taken to save free trade in times of crisis, have tended to become institutionalized. That process is still going on in the early 1980s.

The developed world steel enterprises would gain much from continued rapid development of Third World economies, if that development took the shape of growing demand for steel without growing supply. A growing steel market in Brazil, Mexico, and Venezuela, for example, could take the competitive pressure off the Japanese, U.S., European rivalry and end the "crises" of those steel industries. The power of the large steel enterprises to affect the state in the developed world is great. Even though the large steel companies are not powerful *vis-a-vis* the Third World they can greatly affect the North-South distribution of the gains from trade by affecting developed world industrial policies and thereby the processes of technological transfer and financing of investment by Third World state-owned enterprises.

In the iron and steel industry international rivalry among the large companies has taken the form of market interpenetration followed by structural changes designed to control competition. This process has continued from the cartel of the 1920s to the establishment of the OECD steel committee. The consequences of that process can be a limiting of access to export markets for all steel producers including the Third World producers as well as worldwide limitations on expansion of world capacity. Steel industry and sympathetic governmental policymakers have long recognized the crucial role of "excess" capacity in making difficult the control of prices. A long-run view requires focus on investment decisions.

The post-World War II transnational expansion that brought TNC control of downstream manufacturing facilities located within Third World countries did not occur in the iron and steel industry for a number of reasons. Perhaps the best explanation is the historical accident. If United States Steel had chosen to build a Brazilian facility in the 1940s, it might have launched a policy of direct foreign investment throughout the world after the war. The post-war period found the Brazilian opportunity preempted by state-owned enterprise. The European firms were caught up in reconstruction and in no position to finance direct foreign investment. The U.S. firms had neither experience with such transnational operations nor much incentive at a time when export markets were strong. Other Third World nations

190

viewed steel as basic to industrialization and moved into production with state-owned enterprises because the developed world companies showed no desire to do so. The existence of the state-owned pattern fed back to affect developed world companies' incentives because of a fear of expropriation. Now the state-owned enterprise has become the dominant form not only in the Third World but even in Europe, where crisis conditions have led to state intervention. That pattern appears likely to continue. Where private ownership continues, as in the U.S., Japan, and Germany, much closer relations between companies and governments seem likely as industrial policies become institutionalized.

The OECD exists to coordinate and harmonize member government policies. Its steel committee was created to achieve such harmonization of member government industrial policies relating to steel. Diversity of interest among the participants will make harmonization very difficult to achieve, but perhaps less difficult than the achievements in Europe that began with the Shuman Plan. The OECD provides a nucleus for First World union comparable to the European Communities. Indeed, the creation of a common market in steel among OECD members with the basing-point system of pricing imposed, would bring order out of the present struggle that threatens a protectionist revival that would force abandonment of even the pretense of free trade among the industrialized nations. It is difficult to say how the developing countries would fare under such a cartelized system, but entry would have to be negotiated and capacity expansion restraint might become a prerequisite of access to developed world markets. Cartels usually allot markets on an historical basis, which hurts the new or expanding participants.

Continuation of relatively free trade and only loose coordination in the First World would clearly be better for LDCs that must depend on external sources of technical services and equipment. Considerable progress has been made in Brazil and Mexico in achieving some capacity to produce such producer goods. Cooperation among Latin American nations to render such services to each other has been sought in ILAFO. Yet the managers of each steel expansion project have incentives to seek the best and cheapest sources without regard to the development interests of their neighbors. Furthermore, any one LDC that succeeds in achieving the capacity to supply technical services and producer goods will tend to be coöpted, like Japan, Australia, and Canada, into the First World.

If Latin American nations should come to view dependence on each other as less undesirable than dependence on the First or the Second World, they might take important steps toward economic unification in the steel sector—not just because it happened that way in Europe, but because steel is indeed an industry that is basic to industrialization. Closer cooperation, for example, could assure Brazil petroleum, Mexico iron ore, and Venezuela markets while improving each nation's chances of surviving successful efforts of the traditional steel producers to restrain world steel capacity expansion.

Notes

[1] This important aspect of the present structure of the European steel industry was succinctly analyzed by Ernst Joachim Mestmacker as follows:

As far as the ECSC is concerned, there can be no doubt that the basing point system originated directly from the practice of the steel cartels. By deliberately including this system in the ECSC Treaty an important, probably the most important part of the past cartel practice was adopted. . . . Even if we take into account that the steel market is an imperfectly competitive market, it is questionable whether the pricing system sanctioned by the ECSC Treaty will permit the degree of price competition required for attaining the objective of Article 2 of the ECSC Treaty, that conditions should be created, which in themselves would be sufficient to guarantee the most rational distribution of the production on the highest level of productivity. The basing point system as operated under the Treaty can hinder the integration of the national industries. It maintains the location conditions of producers and consumers on the level attained in applying the basing point system under the domination of the cartel, and it hinders the planning of production on the basis of the market prices (1961, p. 332).

[2] The chairmen of the boards of both U.S. Steel and Bethlehem sit on the board of J.P. Morgan Co., which holds all the stock of Morgan Guaranty Trust Company.

Douglas C. Bennett and Kenneth E. Sharpe

6.

The World Automobile Industry and its Implications

INTRODUCTION*

As of 1976 the second and fourth largest firms in the world and nine of the largest fifty were motor vehicle manufacturers (Fortune 1976). Three of these—General Motors (GM) Ford, and Chrysler are based in the United States, two are in France—Renault and Peugeot-Citroen, two are in Germany—Volkswagenwerk and Daimler Benz, and two are based in Japan—Toyota and Nissan. With Italy's Fiat and the U.K.'s British Leyland these firms account for over 85 percent of all motor vehicles produced in the world.

Although recent changes in the price of petroleum products have slowed growth and significantly unsettled the industry, motor vehicle manufacture remains a critical sector of the world economy. Because the production of motor vehicles requires substantial quantities of steel, aluminum, glass, rubber, and a large number of sophisticated manufactured components (a total of up to 2500 parts), and because their sale and maintenance require extensive distribution and service networks, the automobile industry has been frequently singled out to pace industrial growth. In the U.S., Europe, and Japan a common estimate is that motor vehicle manufacture accounts for one job in ten when its many forward and backward-linking tentacles are taken together.

Having created several hundred foreign subsidiaries the major transnational auto firms dominate the industry fully as much as devel-

* The authors wish to thank David Moore and Louis Wolf Goodman for their valuable comments and suggestions on earlier drafts of this chapter.

193

oping countries as in the developed ones, but the industry presents quite a different portrait in the two locales. In each of the major producing countries, a small number of firms, seldom more than three or four, most of them domestically-owned, dominate production and sales. In developing countries, however, it is not uncommon to find five or ten manufacturers, nearly all of them foreign-owned subsidiaries of transnational corporations, each bidding for shares of small, if promising, markets. Production in these developing country plants tends to be inefficient by comparison with the standards of the major producing countries, and yet the firms have persisted in the proliferation of models and in the frequent model changes that have become commonplace in the developed countries. In a number of these developing countries there have been vigorous governmental policies to promote the development of an automobile manufacturing industry, but little evidence of any attempts to promote locally-owned "national champions" such as those undertaken by governments in Europe and Japan.

How do we account for the distinctive features of auto industries in developing countries, and how do we explain the differences between these and auto industries in the major producing countries? How do we explain, for example, the larger number of firms in the very much smaller markets of the developing countries? How do we explain the strong tendency to foreign ownership in the developing country auto industries? How do we explain the utilization of the same competitive strategies (model proliferation, frequent model changes, little price competition) by the transnational automobile firms in the very differently structured markets of the developed countries? Finally and most importantly, what are the welfare and development consequences of the auto industries in developing countries as these industries are currently structured?

Over the past fifty years a process of concentration has taken place in the automobile industries of each of the major industrialized countries. Especially since World War II the surviving major firms have become increasingly international in their operations, first in terms of sales and later in terms of manufacturing operation. As the developed country markets began to show signs of saturation these transnational auto firms have increasingly looked to the developing country markets for future sales growth and for the defense of their positions in the world industry. Since 1955, partly for cost considerations and partly under the compulsion of government policies, they have moved from serving these markets through exports of assembled vehicles (or of unassembled kits) to domestic manufacture of automobiles. More recently, and again under some compulsion from government policies, these transnational firms have begun to export vehicles and components from LDCs to other countries, even to the major producing countries. How successful these efforts will be depends on how the world industry emerges from its current crisis.

This chapter will trace the development of the world automobile manufacturing oligopoly and its consequences for developing countries in Latin America.

DEVELOPMENT OF THE AUTOMOBILE INDUSTRY: CONCENTRATION IN DEVELOPED COUNTRY MARKETS

The United States

During the first decades of this century 181 companies manufactured and sold automobiles in the United States.[1] By 1927, 137 had ceased operating. Today, fewer than ten survive, one of these accounting for over half of the motor vehicles manufactured and the largest three for over 90 percent (and for over 98 percent of the automobiles). This increasing concentration has been the result of changes in technology and demand that forced many firms to merge or to close, and raised such substantial barriers to entry that no new firms attempted entry after Kaiser's unsuccessful effort following World War II until Volkswagen's recent entry.

The shift to higher-powered four-cylinder engines, and technical changes associated with axles and transmissions raised production costs and forced out some firms, but Ford's reliance of a single standard model (the model "T")—the low cost, mass production methods that this permitted—was the most important technical change in transforming the industry. Ford's price dropped from $950 in 1909 to $300 in the early 1920s, while its market share soared from under 10 percent to over 55 percent in a rapidly growing market (Lanzillotti 1971, pp. 256-261). Although Ford's production techniques set the standard for the industry, its domination of the market was soon challenged by General Motors and later by Chrysler. General Motors began to offer a variety of makes and models against Ford's single model. Ford was slow to respond to this challenge, not offering the model "A" until the end of the 1920s and a V-8 engine until 1932. General Motors overtook Ford controlling 43 percent of the market in 1931, a position of dominance it has retained every since. Chrysler followed GM's product and marketing strategy, and by 1937 it had overtaken Ford as well. By 1930 General Motors, Ford, and Chrysler

195

had established their dominance of the U.S. motor vehicle industry, and the annual model changes they initiated made it increasingly difficult for other firms, the independents, to achieve the economies of scale necessary to remain competitive in price (Vatter 1952; Menge 1962; White 1971). Of the independent firms only American Motors remains today.

In the mid-1950s imports began claiming a significant share of the U.S. market, the door having been opened by the reluctance of the U.S. Big Three to manufacture small cars. European firms, most notably Volkswagen, spearheaded this import surge but were later overtaken by the Japanese producers whose share of the U.S. market grew from 2 percent in 1969 to nearly 25 percent in the early 1980s. Volkswagenwerk became a fifth U.S. automobile manufacturer when it opened a manufacturing plant in New Stanton, Pennsylvania to recoup its sagging U.S. sales.

Having been the pre-eminent auto firms in the world only a decade ago, the U.S. Big Three suddenly found themselves pushed very hard in their own home market by Japanese firms. Chrysler was driven to within hours of declaring bankruptcy, and Ford and GM suffered considerable losses. All three embarked on investment programs to modernize their production facilities and to reduce the size of their vehicles (the latter partly in response to government-mandated fuel-economy standards). All three now seem certain to survive as major auto firms. The import challenge has been severe enough, particularly in its consequences for domestic employment in the industry, that voluntary export restraints were negotiated with the Japanese government, and further protectionist measures, including a local content requirement championed by the United Auto Workers, have been considered by Congress.

Europe

The development of the motor vehicle industries in Western European countries parrelled that of the U.S.[2] In the early 1920s Great Britain, France, and Germany each had dozens, even hundreds of firms, but by the end of the decade the numbers had declined drastically and three firms accounted for about 70 percent of production in each country (Rhys 1972; Wells 1978). For the most part, the reasons for the concentration were the same as those in the United States. The process of concentration in Europe was accelerated however, by the competition these firms faced from U.S. manufacturers, particularly Ford and GM. The U.S. market grew much more quickly than the European markets, so that by 1929 U.S. companies exported 536,000 vehicles and assembled another 200,000 abroad. The significant cost advantages that this afforded the U.S. firms provided both a further impetus towards the adoption of mass production techniques and government policies to defend fledging national industries.

Although protective policies varied, the basic mechanisms were tariffs or import quotas to protect national industries from cheaper U.S. imports. To overcome protective measures U.S. companies set up local assembly plants or acquired national manufacturers. Ford established assembly operation in the United Kingdom in 1911, in France in 1913, and in Germany in 1929. And predictably new protective policies were instigated against direct foreign investment such as taxes that discriminated against foreign imports on laws that forbade any direct foreign investment (Wells 1978, pp. 232-237).

The years following World War II were years of recovery and reconversion from war production. Competition among firms intensified as pent-up demand began to be satisfied. This demand took new form after the creation of the European Economic Community when tariffs within the community were reduced, trade in motor vehicles increased, and a substantial interpenetration of markets occurred. The problem was augmented by a new wave of foreign investment from the U.S.; Ford bought out the minority shareholders in its British subsidiary in 1960, and Chrysler, which before had lacked a foothold in Europe, gained a minority position in Simca in 1958 and Rootes in 1964. Later it gained control of each, though in 1978 it sold its European operations to Peugeot.

During the 1960s, the successful European firms adopted the patterns of product differentiation that prevailed in the U.S. Renault increased its offering of models from one in 1961 to ten in 1971; Volkswagen expanded its range from two in 1960 to eight in 1971 (Jenkins 1977, pp. 16-47). The move to offer a greater range of models required larger size firms and this encouraged still greater industrial concentration. Abetted by government policies that favored the emergence of a single national firm that would survive the increasingly stiff international competition, a wave of mergers too place.

Some of the same pressures that encouraged increasing concentration also encouraged a search for export markets beyond Europe, in areas that had formerly been the preserve of the U.S. Big Three. The increased size, efficiency, and marketing capability of these surviving European firms made possible the mounting of such an international challenge.

Japan

In Europe a process of extreme concentration in the automobile industries prevailed as it has in the U.S., but in Europe that process was abetted by government policies so that at least one national producer would survive. In Japan the government played a still stronger role in nurturing the emergence of an internationally competitive national industry.[4]

The Japanese industry developed more slowly than in the U.S. or Europe, and until well into the 1950s commercial vehicle manufacture was much more important than production of passenger cars.[3] As the major truck manufacturers (Toyota, Nissan, Diesel Jidosha—later Isuzu—Mitsubishi, Hino Heavy Industries, Prince Jidosha, and Fuji Heavy Industries) moved into automobile production, their major competition came from imports, particularly from the U.S. In 1953 there were 23,719 such vehicles imported, more than three times the domestic production (Duncan 1973, p. 146). Some of these producers sought licenses from European manufacturers for technical assistance to begin to assemble cars and manufacture components: Nissan tied up with Austin, Hino with Renault, Isuzu with Rootes, and Mitsubishi with Willys. Toyota alone elected to develop its passenger car, the Toyopet, independently.

In the early 1950s the Japanese government began moving to protect and insulate the industry from foreign competition. Domestic manufacture of parts was mandated and foreign investment was excluded. The government action was crucial in reserving the consumer demand that was to grow rapidly during the 1960s exclusively for Japanese firms.

The Japanese industry had begun later and as a much more concentrated industry than those in the U.S. and Europe. It was to become still more concentrated again with the government playing a strong hand. For the government with its interest in promoting international trade, the auto industry was a potential source of 'strategic' exports. However, the pressures (particularly from the U.S.) to liberalize trade barriers, threatened to destroy the industry before it was strong enough to compete internationally. The Ministry of International Trade and Industry (MITI) judged, as early as 1961, that if the Japanese motor vehicle industry were to compete successfully in the international market and withstand increased domestic competition from foreign firms, it would have to be reorganized (Duncan 1973, pp. 84-100). Relying more on administrative guidance than legislated sanctions, MITI encouraged the emergence of two major groups around Nissan and Toyota. By the early 1970s these groups accounted for 70 percent of domestic and 90 percent of export sales. Although not all of the firms responded to MITI's shepherding, the rapid expansion of the industry through the early 1970s made it possible for some of the smaller, independent companies to survive and grow. Honda and Fuji (Subaru) remained wholly independent, but three others moved to protect themselves from Nissan and Toyota by linking up with U.S. companies as minority partners: Isuzu with GM, Mitsubishi with Chrysler, and Toyo Kogyo (Mazda) with Ford.

As a result of the reorganization of the industry and the increased sales in the domestic market which permitted scale of economies and cost and price reductions, the industry was well positioned for the export drive that began in the mid-1960s. Actively encouraged by government policies, exports grew from 100,000 units in 1965 to 4,352,817 in 1977. While these exports were actively encouraged by the government, they also took on increasing importance for the firms when the domestic market began to saturate. Foreign sales became the source of future growth and profitability.

Market Structure and Market Power in the Major Producing Countries

By 1972 concentration in the world motor vehicle industry had progressed to the point where two firms, GM and Ford, were responsible for over 40 percent of total world automobile sales and the largest eight companies were responsible for about 85 percent (see table 6.1). In the United States the automobile industry had become the classic example of how a tight oligopoly works. Through the 1960s the industry proved to be one of the most profitable in the U.S., with the three major firms averaging better than 15 percent return on capital.

One of the major barriers to entry into this lucrative industry has been the large capital requirements for realizing the economies of scale inherent in mass production. It has been estimated that the most cost effective integrated auto plant would need to produce 300,000 vehicles per year, which would require an initial investment of $250-500 million, and perhaps an additional $150 million in break-in losses, all with a substantial risk of ultimate failure (Bain 1968, pp. 284-287; Toder 1978, pp. 129-143). Product differentiation, the need for a diversified product line, advertising, and the franchise dealer system constitute further barriers to entry.

Such market power has had a number of unfortunate consequences for American consumers, beginning with higher prices. In 1972 estimates of the extra cost paid by consumers averaged about $1.9 billion (or $200 per vehicle) to pay for the costs of model

Table 6.1

Transnational Operations of the Major World Motor Vehicle Manufacturers

Rank by Sales	Company	Nationality	Government ownership (percentage)	Total consolidated sales (millions of dollars)	Foreign Sales		Foreign assests as percentage of total assets	Foreign earnings as percentage of total earnings	Foreign employment as percentage of total employment
					Exports from home country	Sales of overseas affiliates to third parties			
						As percentage of total consolidated sales			
2	General Motors	United States	—	47,181		24	12	18	—
4	Ford Motor	United States	—	28,840		31	40	45	51
14	Chrysler	United States	—	15,538		28	33	22	47
20	Renault	France	100	9,353		45	—	—	—

24	Daimler-Benz	Germany, Federal Republic of	14[b]	8,938	39		21		—	17[c]
26	Volkswagenwerk	Germany, Federal Republic of	40	8,513		62	—		—	32
34	Toyota Motor	Japan	—	7,696	35		—	2	—	15[c]
38	Peugeot-Citroen	France	—	7,347	19		28		—	16
42	Nissan Motor	Japan	—	6,584	41		25	6	—	15
72	Fiat	Italy	—	4,658[d]	—		—		—	19
82	British Leyland	United Kingdom	100	4,178	36		18		—	12
102	Volvo	Sweden	—	3,615	44		24		—	27

Source: extracted from United Nations Economic and Social Council, Commission on Transnational Corporations, *Transnational Corporations in World Development: A Re-examination*, 1978, Table IV-1, pp. 288-312.

Notes:

a Ranked in descending order of total consolidated sales; rank of major industrial corporations.

b Kuwaiti interest.

c Estimated.

d Parent company sales.

changes, most of this going for cosmetic restyling rather than genuine improvement in performance, fuel efficiency, or safety. (Snell 1973, pp. 13-14). But the consequences extend to the deliberate shaping of public transportation policy to suppress competition with motor vehicles. In the late 1920s General Motors, together with Standard Oil of California and Firestone Rubber, engineered the replacement of over 100 local electric transit systems with GM supplied bus systems in 45 cities (Snell 1973, p. 32). Similar patterns of market structure and firm conduct are evident in the other major producing countries with one difference: whereas the degree of concentration in the motor vehicle industry until recently inclined the U.S. government to consider antitrust action (U.S. Senate 1956; U.S. Senate 1958), it prompted European and Japanese governments to promote concentration, largely to protect their national producers.

The question to which we now turn is how this market power of the major transnational automobile firms translates to developing countries. The same firms that have dominated motor vehicle manufacturer in the developed countries have become dominant in developing countries, but with what consequences?

DEVELOPMENT OF THE AUTOMOTIVE INDUSTRY: INTERNATIONALIZATION TO DEVELOPING COUNTRY MARKETS

Although there was foreign trade and foreign investment in the motor vehicle industry from its earliest days, the emergence of a genuinely international industry, a competitive oligopoly of transnational corporations rather than merely a series of national oligopolies, has occurred in the last two or three decades. What has transpired is a restructuring of global patterns of trade and investment that has affected both developed and developing countries.

In 1950 the United States accounted for 76.2 percent of all world motor vehicle production; by 1978 that percentage had been eroded to 30.4 percent. Dramatically increased production in Europe and then Japan was the major factor in this reorganization of world production, but production in developing countries has increased as well (see Table 6.2). Eight or twelve transnational motor vehicle manufacturers have dominated the world market via the foreign investments in developed countries which lacked their own national firms (Australia, Belgium, Spain) and via, direct investments in developing countries. Substantial changes in trade flows have attended these shifts in investment and production. While the United States has declined as an

202

Table 6.2

Motor Vehicle Manufacture by World Regions
(percent of world output)

Region	1910	1922	1929	1937	1950	1955	1960	1965	1970	1975
North America	73.0	93.8	88.2	78.8	79.5	70.4	51.1	49.0	31.9	31.1
Western Europe	27.0	6.2	11.5	17.5	15.1	23.4	37.5	35.2	39.7	33.0
Eastern Europe/USSR	—	—	0.3	3.4	3.7	3.8	4.5	3.8	5.2	8.2
Japan	—	—	—	0.3	0.3	0.5	2.6	7.7	17.9	20.7
Latin America	—	—	—	—	0.2	0.2	1.6	1.9	2.7	4.6
Australia/South Africa	—	—	—	—	1.2	1.7	2.7	2.4	2.6	2.4
Total	100.0	100.0	100.0	100.0	100.0	100.0	100.0	100.0	100.0	100.0
Number of units (000s)	260	2,820	6,345	6,381	10,563	13,712	16,243	24,469	29,611	33,541

Source: Gerald Bloomfield, *The World Automotive Industry* (Newton Abbot: David and Charles, 1978), p. 146 based on Motor Vehicle Manufacturers Association Data.

exporter of vehicles and parts, European firms have come to export about 50 percent of their home country production, principally to neighboring EEC countries and the US., and Japanese transnationals have undertaken aggressive exports to the U.S. and Europe. The Japanese firms have also been the most reluctant to make foreign direct investments in either developed or developing countries.

By the early 1970s the foreign investments of the major transnational automobile firms had created production networks turning out manufactured components and assembled vehicles at far-flung locales around the world. With sharp competition for market share continuing in the industry and with adjustments being required by the rising price of petroleum products and by government policies, these firms have set about rationalizing and integrating their production facilities on a global scale. Increasingly, these firms have turned to worldwide sourcing of major components, manufacturing such parts in two or three locations to supply all their subsidiaries around the world in order to take full advantage of economies of scale in production. The logical conclusion of this strategy is the "world car": the assembly by a firm in many countries of a single basic-design model, tailored in small ways to fit local conditions, from worldwide sourced components. No longer would even the TNCs' home countries have within their borders the full complement of production facilities to manufacture a vehicle. Where components would be manufactured would depend on considerations of labor cost and skill, raw materials availability, and governmental requirements and incentives. General Motor's Chevette and Ford's Fiesta represented the first steps in the direction of a world car. A different though related trend being relied upon by European manufacturers, is for two or three manufacturers to form a joint venture to manufacture particular major components—four cylinder engines, or transaxels—to share the costs of new investments. This global integration of production will have significant, probably painful, implications for the major producing countries (as can already be seen in the U.S., the U.K., and Italy).[4] In order to understand the consequences of the internationalization of the world automobile industry for developing countries, particularly those in Latin America, it is necessary to look at the forces that have propelled transnational automobile firms to invest abroad in manufacturing facilities and the forms these foreign operations have taken.[5]

Although the technical developments that made possible a motor vehicle industry occurred almost simultaneously in Europe and the United States, the United States proved to be the first mass market for motor vehicles. The production and marketing techniques to which Ford, General Motors, and Chrysler owed their predominance in the

204

U.S. market proved to be the kind of 'unique asset' which Stephen Hymer has identified as providing the basis and the motive for firms to undertake foreign investments (Hymer 1960; Caves 1971). A slowdown in the growth of the U.S. market after 1923 presented the major U.S. firms with a strong incentive to exploit their advantage in foreign markets. The first candidates were those markets which had demand characteristics most similar to those in the U.S.[6] In 1911, just three years after the model-T was introduced, Ford created an assembly operation in Great Britain and soon it had others in France and Germany. General Motors followed suit, establishing its own assembly operations. An attempt by GM to acquire an interest in Citroen in 1919 was rebuffed by the French Government, but within a decade it had acquired Vauxhall, a British producer, and Opel, a German concern (Wells 1978, pp. 230-237). Chrysler followed a strategy different than Ford and GM waiting to make substantial foreign investments until the late 1950s.

The U.S. firms established a secondary market in Latin America. Ford built an assembly plant in Argentina in 1916, and within a decade had operations in all the major Latin American countries; General Motors and Chrysler followed this example, although the latter was inclined to license local firms to assemble its vehicles. In contrast, foreign sales either through export or local assembly were an insignificant portion of the business of European automobile manufacturers, though British and French firms did dominate sales in their respective colonies. In other words, prior to World War II, a distinct pattern of market spheres had become apparent with the U.S. firms focusing on Latin American markets, French and British firms dominating the markets of their colonial possessions, and other producers confined to their home markets.

During the years of recovery following the war firms in each of the major producing countries were preoccupied with meeting pent-up demand in their home markets. But by 1950 European firms began to contest one another's home markets. It was Volkswagen's challenge to U.S. hegemony in the North and South American market in the early 1950s that signalled the end of the pattern of market domination that had prevailed before the war (Jenkins 1977, p. 35). From then on the structure of the automobile industries in Latin America and other developing countries began a dramatic transformation. It proceeded through three stages: (I) a pre-industrialization stage in which vehicles were imported as completely built-up units (CBU) or as semi- or completely knocked-down (CKD or SKD) kits that were assembled by licensees or subsidiaries of foreign manufacturers; (II) an import-substituting stage in which some degree of local

205

manufacture of vehicles for sale in the domestic market was undertaken, and in which wholly-owned subsidiaries tended to displace licensees; and, (III) an exporting stage in which some developing countries have begun exports of vehicles or components to developed and developing countries. Because of differences in levels of development and in sizes of effective markets the various countries in Latin America have proceeded through these stages at different rates. The transition from stage I to stage II took place in the late 1950s and early 1960s, and the transition to stage III began around 1970. The medium-sized countries (Chile, Columbia, Peru, Uruguay, and Venezuela) entered stage II at a lag of up to five years, and are only perhaps now arriving at the transition to stage III. The smallest, poorest countries (particularly those in Central America and the Carribbean) still find themselves in stage I. Because the stages refer as much to strategies of the transnational automobile firms that dominate the world industry as they do to policies of developing countries, some countries find themselves today caught up in a stage III world without having gone through a prior phase of import-substituting industrialization. What is critical to an understanding of the stages and of the motion through them is that stage II arose out of confluence of interest between the auto TNCs and the governments of developing countries, and that stage III has emerged out of a new and different confluence of interest among these same actors that resulted from their distinct experiences under stage II.[7]

The Transition from Stage I to Stage II

The same forces that led to increasing concentration within the automobile industries of the developed countries impelled the surviving motor vehicle firms to expand into foreign markets including markets in developing countries.

Three points require emphasis. First, the major transnational automobile firms found themselves in oligopolistically-structured markets and these markets were beginning to be saturated. Increasingly, new car sales were to consumers who were replacing vehicles, not ones making first-time purchases, and there were consequently smaller growth possibilities. Second, changes in market strategies increased the importance of foreign markets. In order to boost sales by encouraging frequent purchases by consumers, the auto companies began offering a full range of models and making frequent model changes. These same strategies, however, made it difficult to realize the full scale economies possible in automotive manufacture. Thus foreign markets could provide sales opportunities when home country sales began to level off, and could also extend model runs to capture scale economies. Finally, deliberate efforts to promote trade liberalization encouraged foreign sales by the major motor vehicle firms. The U.S.'s championing of such a liberal trade regime following World War II insured low tariff barriers for imports into its markets. Later, the establishment of the EEC made possible the inter-penetration of markets by European manufacturers.

Expansion into markets beyond the home country base thus became a necessity for the large auto firms if they were to survive the increasing national and international competition. At first markets in developing countries figured only minimally in the internationalization of the industry, but soon the firms realized that these would eventually become markets of high growth possibility. The increased attention of the major auto firms to sales possibilities in developing countries were met by a corresponding realization in these countries that an automobile industry might contribute to industrialization. By the 1950s several of the larger developing countries had initiated import substitution policies restricting automotive imports and mandating minimum levels of local content for vehicles sold in the domestic market. It was predominantly in Latin America that the first such policies were to be found: Brazil adopted a local content requirement in 1956, Argentina in 1959, Mexico, Venezuela, and Chile in 1962, and Peru in 1965. Brazil and Argentina mandated nearly complete domestic manufacture, while Mexico, more concerned about holding down prices and with an eye firmly fixed on the geographic and political realities of the long common border with the U.S., initially set its level of required local content at only 60 percent of the cost of production, thus allowing continued importation of exterior sheet metal stampings and other selected components.

The quick and uniform response of the transnational automotive firms to these local content requirements conforms to the "follow-the-leader" pattern of defensive investment that Knickerbocker and others have identified in competitive, product-pioneering manufacturing oligopolies (Knickerbocker 1973; Jenkins 1977, pp. 40-42). As a risk-minimizing strategy firms match one another's moves: they defend their positions in the oligopoly by making similar investments. In the automobile industry in Latin America, the first moves were made not by any individual firm but by governments whose import substituting policies forced the firms to commence manufacturing operations or to risk the possibility of these markets' being conceded to competitors.

Whereas the major producing countries have highly concentrated industries dominated by a few firms, the developing countries find themselves with industries with five to ten firms and with markets that are smaller by a factor of 10 to 100. Given the small size of markets and the large number of firms, the full achievement of scale economies is impossible. The resulting inefficiency in production arises from the dynamics of internationalization in the world automobile industry and not simply from any inherent tendency to inefficiency of import substitution industrialization.

A concomitant of the pattern of defensive investment was a rapid and thorough denationalization of the Latin American automobile industries. Many domestically-owned firms, which had licensed technology from one of the major transnational firms were unable for financial, technological, and/or managerial reasons to make the transition from assembly to manufacture operations. In other cases the transnational automobile firms were unwilling to continue licensing arrangements once vehicle manufacture was to commence. In Mexico only two of the twelve firms assembling vehicles before the 1962 local content decree were foreign-owned, and only three of the ten firms approved to undertake manufacturing operations were foreign-owned. By 1970, however, three of the domestically-owned firms had folded and two others had sold majority equity to their transnational licensor. The process of denationalization was even more thorough in Brazil and Argentina, partly because only the Mexican government was inclined to make efforts to maintain a degree of local ownership in the industry.

The Transition from Stage II to Stage III

One convergence of interests—transnational automobile firms looking to promote sales and secure toeholds in LDC markets and LDC governments looking to promote domestic industrialization through import substitution—led to the establishment of automotive industries manufacturing for domestic markets in Latin America. Another convergence of interests led to the promotion of manufactured exports from some of these newly-created industries.

By the late 1960s the larger Latin American countries had overcrowded and inefficient automobile industries. Although a few firms might withdraw the transnational corporations avoided being eliminated from these markets by subsidizing any losses from the earnings of other operations. In the late 1960s Mexico, Brazil, and Argentina came to see the promotion of exports as a solution to the problem of inefficiency. Brazil and Argentina required very high levels of local content, but the large number of firms in each industry spelled high costs and high prices nearly twice those in countries of origin. The high prices meant a smaller potential domestic market. The Mexican

208

industry was not significantly less overcrowded, but the lower level of mandatory local content (60 percent) meant that certain high-scale efficiency components (particularly exterior body stampings) could be imported, and thus costs and prices were not so high. Nevertheless, the continuing flow of imports constituted a significant burden on the balance of payments. Consequently, Mexico had an interest in promoting automotive exports to compensate its imports, while Brazil and Argentina could hope for export sales to increase the effective markets for their industries. In each case, LDC interest in exports was seen as a solution to the problem of inefficiency (a reversal of the neoclassical dictum that efficiency promotes exports).

The transnational automobile firms had been reticent to undertake domestic manufacture in LDCs because such manufacture would diminish potential production volumes from home country plants which embodied substantial fixed investments. Could these firms be expected to undertake exports from these developing countries that might compete with and further diminish potential production volumes from their home country plants? To understand why the transnational automobile firms were willing now to export products from their overseas subsidiaries it is necessary to consider that import substituting industrialization had led to the creation of a large number of operations, each of which constituted a small-scale replica of the manufacturing facilities of the home country. The higher the level of mandatory local content the less the subsidiary was and could be integrated into a rationalized, worldwide fabric of operations. By 1970 these operations had significant fixed assets and a trained, low-cost labor force. Consequently, it became attractive for some transnational auto firms to favor a relaxing of mandatory local content levels in return for commitments to export. What production was undertaken in the developing country would be at efficient production scales since it would be for domestic and foreign markets, and the transnational firms could rationalize their worldwide operations by setting the production of major components in different countries. Vehicles would be assembled in the country where they were to be sold, but could embody components produced in many different countries. This was the convergence of interests that facilitated the transition from stage II to stage III. It is worth noting that changes in development orthodoxy played a role in these transitions from stage to stage. Local content requirements were implemented while import substitution was in vogue. The shift to a policy that keyed industrialization in the automobile industry to exports rather than the domestic market coincided with a shift in development advice from import substitution to export promotion.

The 1973 tripling of oil prices and the 1974 to 1975 world recession triggered a number of important changes in the automobile industry and reinforced the transnational firms' interest in promoting exports from their developing country plants. They did so partly by altering the motives the firms have in undertaking foreign investments. The rise in the price of oil encouraged a shift away from the production of larger vehicles, and the U.S. government, for example, spurred its domestic manufacturers towards this transition by requiring steadily increasing levels of fuel efficiency (measured by fleet average). The Japanese firms pioneered automated production technology which gave them at least a temporary cost and quality edge. Increased market interpenetration and currency revaluations led the European and Japanese firms to reconsider their exports of built-up units to the United States. Honda and Nissan followed Volkswagen in opening U.S. plants, Renault entered into a long-term agreement with the American Motor Company, and General Motors has contracted to assemble Toyotas in California. In this increasingly competitive environment, the U.S. and European-based transnationals in particular were compelled to make massive investments to manufacture a new generation of vehicles. Latin America, the Asian rim, and the low-wage fringe of Europe emerged as important sites for new components plants. The search for lower labor costs was scarcely a consideration in the first foreign investments of transnational auto firms, but it has now become a major desiderata as have fiscal incentives from host country governments. Increasingly, components are manufactured in widely-spread locations around the globe to be assembled in or near the market of sale.

In 1969 Mexico became the first Latin American country to make the shift to an export promotion policy in the automobile industry. Faced with the choice between higher local content or contemporary exports to take pressure off the balance of payments and give an additional boost to domestic manufacture, the government opted for the export route and the firms were not inclined to disagree with the choice. The policy was reaffirmed in 1972 and,despite an episode of reconsideration after the firms' exports fell below their commitments in the 1974 world industrial recession, was again reaffirmed in 1977. In response, GM, Ford, Chrysler, and Volkswagen made major new investments in Mexico to supply components for U.S. assembly plants (Bennett and Sharpe 1979a).

To enforce compliance with its auto export program, the Mexican government threatened to restrict a firm's access to the domestic market if exports were not forthcoming. The Brazilian government began encouraging automobile exports in 1971 through the Export

Fiscal Benefits Program by offering to relax the high levels of mandatory local content in return for commitments from individual firms to export more than they imported, or to generate an overall balance of payments surplus for the firm's operations in Brazil (Müller and Moore 1978). Argentina, which seriously began promoting exports in 1971, also tied opportunities for increased domestic sales to export performance by each firm. Exports rose dramatically for a few years, but as the domestic market began to shrink and firms lost interest in gaining opportunities for increased domestic sales, export performance slumped as well (Jenkins 1979, pp. 27-30).

Only Brazil, Argentina, and Mexico have managed significant automotive exports, and only Brazil and Mexico seem currently capable of sustaining such exports. Countries with smaller markets—Columbia, Venezuela, Peru—have not yet made this transition from stage II to stage III. Partly this is because the transition from stage I to stage II (manufacture for the domestic market) came earlier and more fully in Brazil and Mexico. These countries had automotive manufacturing plants with excess capacity that could be turned to export production. But partly this is because of the leverage provided by the large and growing domestic markets to which the Brazilian and Mexican governments control access. Not all of the exports from these countries by any means has come from pre-existing plants. In both countries TNCs have installed production facilities for automotive parts that are principally for export. If the U.S. adopts protectionist measures to combat the Japanese challenge, exports for Brazil and Mexico would suffer, however.

The automobile industry has gone through similar evolutionary stages in Latin America and other developing countries. Initially, the major automotive transnationals extended and defended their oligopoly positions. Under the threat of preemptive moves from one another and protectionist government policies these TNCs agreed to manufacture a substantial percentage of each vehicle in the country of sale. What resulted were tiny replicas of home country facilities, only each of these LDC markets had more firms than any of the more developed motor vehicle producing countries. When the industrial structures created proved to be costly and inefficient and to forestall the rationalization of each firm's transnational operation, a different pattern of TNC trade and investment began to emerge, propelled equally by corporate strategy and LDC government policy. Firms began to carry out substantial manufacturing activities in each of these developing countries, though not necessarily for all the parts needed for vehicles sold domestically, and to export a percentage of the product. For the governments this new pattern of industrialization meant a significant measure of domestic manufacture and employment, less drain on the balance of payments, and the possibility of a cost structure in the industry closer to that in the developed countries. For the firms this new pattern meant the possibility of rationalizing their operations in developing countries by sourcing components from many different countries. Developing countries could be used for the manufacture of components whose manufacture by standard techniques was now illegal in developed countries because of anti-pollution legislation, or components (such as manual transmissions) which were being phased out of developed country sales.

Strategic Differences Among the Major TNCs

Within this common pattern there has been substantial variation in the ways that the major transnational automobile firms based in the U.S., Europe, and Japan have responded to the opportunities for domestic automobile manufacture in Latin America and other developing areas, and in the degree of market penetration they have achieved (see Table 6.3).

Before the beginning of domestic manufacture, the U.S. manufacturers of large automobiles dominated the Latin American markets. Since 1955, however, sales demand increased for the smaller vehicles produced by European and Japanese firms. The prime beneficiary of this trend has been Volkswagen, largely because of its domination of the huge Brazilian market. Volkswagen's success has triggered a belated entry into the Brazilian market by Fiat—a principal worldwide competitor within the same market tier. In addition to the large car and small car tiers a third tier exists composed of commercial vehicles. Firms such as Daimler Benz, Volvo, and Saab-Scania have focused their developing countries' operations in this tier. As latecomers to the global competition the Japanese transnationals have concentrated on the Asian rim and their foreign sales have tended to be in countries which still accept CBU and CKD imports.

The location of the firm's home country plants has affected the manner in which they have responded to opportunities in Latin America. In Mexico the U.S. firms insisted on being allowed to import exterior body stampings so that they could continue annual model changes. The European firms have tended to serve small Central American markets from their Latin American plants. Not having manufacturing operations in the U.S., the European firms have also met their export commitments by supplying replacement parts for the U.S. market from their Latin American operations. Volkswagen's con-

Table 6.3

Total Vehicle Production by Firm in Latin America, 1976[a]
(in units)

	Argentina	Brazil	Chile	Colombia	Mexico	Peru	Venezuela	Total	% of Latin American Market
American Motors	—	—	—	—	22,669[b]	—	1,213[c]	23,882	1.4
Chrysler	21,986	27,831	—	15,336	55,929	11,031	43,355	175,468	10.2
Citroen	15,839	—	1,764[b]	—	—	—	—	17,603	1.0
	44,444	8,350	1,439	4,023	—	—	4,510	62,766	3.6
Ford	33,954	171,931	—	—	45,497	—	52,317	303,699	17.7
General Motors	16,195	181,144	960	—	36,757	—	30,238	265,294	15.4
Mercedes Benz	6,682	48,817	—	—	—	—	2,180	57,679	3.4
Nissan	—	—	—	—	30,624	5,453	4,856	40,933	2.4
Peugeot	16,121	—	1,557[c]	—	—	—	—	17,678	1.0
Renault	30,896	—	1,307[c]	15,998	36,894[b]	—	5,266[c]	90,361	5.3
Toyota	—	1,498	—	—	—	6,609	7,326	15,433	0.9
Volkswagen	—	529,636	—	—	70,398	9,628	3,000	612,662	35.7
Others	7,400	16,262	—	—	1,161	1,623	8,471	34,917	2.0
Total	193,517	985,469	7,027	35,357	299,929	34,344	162,732	1,718,375	100.0
Percentage	11.3	57.3	0.4	2.1	17.4	2.0	9.5	100.0	

Source: R.N. Gwynne, "The Motor Vehicle Industry in Latin America," *Bank of London and South America Review* 1978, p. 471.

Notes:
[a] Uruguay, Ecuador, and Costa Rica also assemble small numbers of vehicles.
[b] Joint ventures with respective governments.
[c] One firm produces two different makes.

struction of a U.S. manufacturing plant has opened new possibilities for component exports from its Brazilian and Mexican subsidiaries, particularly in view of the substantial production facilities already installed in these locations. Renault now has similar opportunities.

Some firms, such as Renault, have been willing to participate in joint ventures with local public or private capital as a partner. Others have licensed local enterprises so long as only assembly operations were carried out in the developing countries, but moved to assert ownership and management control once significant manufacturing was commenced. Ford and GM have both insisted upon wholly-owned subsidiaries, but their strategies have differed in other regards on several occasions. Ford was the firm that took the initiative in bargaining with governments over changes in policy. It was Ford that first indicated a willingness to commence domestic manufacture in Argentina and Mexico and to undertake exports from Mexico in 1969: it was Ford, looking for a cost-efficient way to introduce its Maverick into the Brazilian market, which first proposed a loosening of local content requirements in return for export commitments. The dynamics of defensive investment require that some firm must be willing to undertake a new investment; the other firms match the move. In the Latin American motor vehicle industries, Ford has traditionally made the first moves. Recently, however, GM has begun to dominate Ford as fully abroad as at home. When the Mexican government promulgated a new automotive decree which mandated higher levels of exports Ford sought to lead an effort to block implementation. When GM announced a large investment program to comply with the new policy, however, Ford felt compelled to follow suit.

PERFORMANCE

The performance of the automobile industry in developing countries will be evaluated from three complementary perspectives: (1) utilizing the standard industrial organization criteria, with some revision because of the presence of transnational subsidiaries in these markets; (2) assessing performance against the goals of industrial development; and, (3) appraising performance with a view to the satisfaction of basic human needs.

The Standard Industrial Organization Criteria

Although about a dozen major transnational firms based in the United States, Europe, and Japan dominate the world automobile industry, there is no world cartel in the industry nor any evidence of an agreement, formal or informal, by which these major firms divide and share markets, either in developed or developing countries. The oligopolistic structure of the industry does allow the firms to eschew price competition in favor of other forms of competition: product differentiation, model proliferation, and frequent model changes within the markets they already serve, and an agressive search for new markets and increased market share where the industry is still establishing itself.

The developing countries, particularly the more populous ones in Latin America and in Asia, have become sites of aggressive competition among the major transnational automobile firms. Where the major developed producing countries find themselves with three or four firms surviving 50 years of winnowing, these developing countries, with much smaller markets, find themselves with two or three times that number of firms, subsidiaries of transnational automobile firms based in the U.S., Japan, and Europe. These subsidiaries carry with them the same products and the same marketing strategies they have elected in their home country markets. That the structure of the world market has led these firms to an aggressive search for increased market share in LDCs using competitive strategies shaped in their established, developed country bases has consequences for efficiency, costs, prices, and profitability of operations.

In 1977 eleven firms operated in Brazil, eleven in Argentina, twelve in Venezuela and seven in Mexico. Columbia stands out as an unusual case with only three motor vehicle manufacturers. The markets for these firms are highly concentrated, nevertheless. In Argentina and in Mexico, four firms account for nearly 70 percent of production, in Venezuela three firms account for over 75 percent, in Brazil three firms have a market share near 90 percent, and in Columbia two firms account for nearly 90 percent of production. These firms use manufacturing technology perfected in developed country markets with very high economies of scale. It is often argued that the size of the effective market in nearly all the developing countries of Latin America is too small to support auto manufacture that utilizes the economies of scale that characterize production in the U.S., Japan, and the EEC countries and inefficiency is the inevitable result (Behrman 1972). This is a distinctly partial view. Economies of scale are important considerations, and only production runs on the order of 2-300,000 or more vehicles fully exploit these. Of the seventy-odd automotive plants in Latin America, only the Volkswagen plant in Brazil surpasses this level in annual production. The Ford and GM plants in Brazil produce over 100,000 vehicles per year, and

215

six other plants (Ford in Argentina, Mexico, and Venezuela: the Chrysler and Volkswagen plants in Mexico; and the Fiat operation in Argentina) exceed 50,000. It is important to keep in mind, however, that the scale economies vary considerably for the hundreds of components that comprise an automobile: they are highest for exterior body parts, lower for engines, and lower still for assembly operations. Scale economies refer primarily to production runs of a particular model, not to a firm as a whole. Offering a diverse array of models can worsen the problem of inefficient production while extending a particular model over several years can ameliorate it. Consequently, the problem of high cost, inefficient production owes less to the size of these markets than it does to the fragmentation of these markets among a large number of firms, each offering a wide variety of models and changing these models frequently. In the early 1970s ten firms offered a total of 120 models in Argentina, ten firms produced 131 models in Brazil, and nine firms in Mexico manufactured 76 models (Jenkins 1977). The large number of firms and the proliferation of models are characteristics of Latin American automobile industries that stem directly from the structure of the world automobile industry and of the competitive strategies that have come to characterize it.[8]

However the causes are viewed, automotive manufacture in Latin America tends to be inefficient in comparison with developed country production. Higher costs and higher prices to the public are the result. According to an Economic Commission for Latin America (ECLA) survey production costs in Latin American countries range from one and one-half to two times as high as production costs in the country of origin, and prices run one and one-half to nearly four times as high (ECLA 1973, Table I-25; Baranson 1969, Table 3; Salas Vargas 1979).

Export promotion strategies have been implemented in Brazil, Argentina, Mexico, and elsewhere largely to deal with problem of cost and efficiency. The possibility of exports opens up a much wider and larger market (and thus the possibility of longer production runs with greater utilization of scale economies). Moreover, it permits a lower level of mandatory local content by allowing exports to compensate for imported components, and therefore allows importation of those components for which efficient domestic manufacture is not currently feasible. This is a policy strategy so far available only to the countries with the largest markets which can condition access to the local market to satisfactory export performance.

It is difficult to determine if these high prices translate to high levels of profitability for the transnational firms. Profits are reported primarily on global operations, and insofar as there are significant intrafirm transfers (particularly if these transfers are of goods for which there is no price set in arm's length international market transactions) statements of costs and of earnings for individual subsidiaries would be arbitrary in any case. Consequently, even if data on the profitability of individual subsidiaries were available, it would not be a reliable guide to questions of efficiency in resource allocation or to questions of income transfers from consumers to owners of capital within individual LDCs. Undoubtedly, some of the larger subsidiaries in Latin America have paid handsome returns on invested capital, but as GM's withdrawal from Argentina and the closing of several plants in Chile would seem indicate, other subsidiaries, particularly the smaller ones, have yielded disappointing earnings. It would be a mistake, however, to evaluate the performance of the industry strictly in terms of short-term profits. The transnational auto firms have longer run visions. They are interested in gaining a secure footing in Latin America for the day when these markets will be many times larger than they are today, and are willing and able to subsidize unprofitable operations, shielding the subsidiaries from the discipline of the local market in the short-term.

The Goals of Industrial Growth

If transnational corporations require us to revise our ways of assessing performance principally because their conduct is not subject to the discipline of any single market, a consideration of the predicament of developing countries also requires some revision of performance norms. Industrialization is of paramount importance to the governments of many developing countries; frequently they are willing to sacrifice efficiency in the short-run for long-term industrial growth, and to expect efficiency only when an industry reaches maturity. In the pursuit of industrialization, the automobile industry has played a particularly central role because of its exceptionally long forward and backward linkages that would stimulate growth in a number of additional sectors. Compelling domestic manufacture of motor vehicles would mean jobs and investments, foreign exchange savings, and technological development in a number of areas that could serve as a base for industrialization in other sectors. These purposes suggest a number of performance norms against which the automobile industries in Latin America can be evaluated.

Industrial growth. Between 1955 and 1973 production of motor vehicles in Latin America increased twenty-five fold, from 60,000 vehicles to nearly 1,500,000. Brazil accounted for approximately half of that, but substantial growth occurred in Argentina, Mexico, and Venezuela as well. In Brazil between 1961 and 1973 the production in the industry grew at an average annual rate of 16.9 percent per year. In Mexico over the same period production growth averaged 13 percent (see Table 6.4). Since 1973 there has been slower growth in the automobile industry around the world, but on the whole, Latin America has been less affected than the U.S. and other developed countries. In Argentina the industry has stagnated and there has been a significant decline in production in Chile (accompanied by deindustrialization, closing of plants, and loss of jobs), but the industries in the other countries have continued to grow despite some pauses. In each of the countries that has undertaken domestic manufacture of motor vehicles, the automobile industry has grown to a position of prominence in the manufacturing sector and in the economy as a whole. In Brazil and Argentina in the early 1970s the industry directly accounted for about 4 percent of total GNP and 12 percent of total industrial production. In Mexico the industry constituted about 7 percent of manufacturing output while in Venezuela and Chile the figures were correspondingly lower, 4.4 percent and 2.8 percent respectively. (Jenkins 1977, p. 62).

Employment. The rapidly increasing production has dramatically increased employment in these motor vehicle industries. The biggest surge occurred as the shift was made to domestic manufacturing operations when parts supply industries had to be created almost from scratch, but employment has continued to rise with total production. In Mexico, for example, the auto firms employed just over 9,000 people in 1962, on the eve of the transition to domestic manufacture; by 1977 they employed over 39,000. The supplier industry employed an additional 58,000, and the distributors and dealers another 51,000 in 1977 (CANACINTRA 1978, pp. 150,161). And these figures do not count employment in those countries which are suppliers of raw materials and other inputs, such as steel, rubber, glass, and so forth.

Although a substantial number of new jobs have been created through motor vehicle manufacturing in these countries, the promotion of motor vehicle manufacturing can hardly be defended as the most direct route to increase employment opportunities. In nearly all its phases the industry is capital intensive, particularly because the technology has been developed in high cost, scarce labor conditions of the developed world. Its transfer to developing countries via transnational corporations has not been adapted to the different relative factor costs of Latin America countries. Thus, the opportunity cost of

218

job creation in the automobile industry is quite high: the same investments in another industry could have created many more jobs.

Technological development.   With few exceptions, the products and the manufacturing processes in developing countries have been the same as those in the TNCs home country bases. Technical innovation is not to be found in these LDC automobile industries, but innovation may not be the proper norm. Many LDC governments look to their domestic automobile industries to improve the overall technical capability of their manufacturing sectors to bring them up to international standards. In essence, the automobile industry serves as a technical training base for other industries. Local employees hired by the transnational auto firms acquire technical and managerial skills that are transferable to other industries, and insofar as automobile firms purchase their component parts from local manufacturers there will be a flow of technology from these transnational firms to the local ones that may be used in other products. While considerable technological learning occurred, the ownership structure of transnational automobile firms constitutes a barrier against technological innovation in appropriate products or appropriate manufacturing processes in developing countries. The coming of worldwide sourcing and of the world car means that innovation in transnational corporation no longer takes place exclusively in home country bases, but it is unlikely that LDC industries will be a significant enough part of these corporate empires to be a focus of or a site for innovation. (Müller, Baranson, and Moran 1974; Baranson 1971).

Bargaining

The conduct of subsidiaries of transnational automobile corporations—and thus the performance of auto industries—is shaped by the structure and competitive dynamics of the world auto industry. The world industry structure only establishes broad limits, however; what happens within these limits is largely set in the bargaining that transpires between the transnational firms and governments of developing countries which host TNC subsidiaries. The outcomes of the bargaining of the Mexican and Brazilian governments with the auto firms in their countries concerning mandatory exports have had serious consequences for the balance of trade and for the level of export activity in those two countries. A full grasp of such bargaining encounters requires an understanding of (a) the actors involved in the bargaining; (b) their interests and intentions; and, (c) the potential power they can exercise in pursuit of their objectives and the circumstances that lead

219

Table 6.4
Total Vehicle Production by Country in Latin America, 1956-1978

Year	Brazil	Argentina	Mexico	Chile	Venezuela	Colombia	Peru
1956		5,943					
1957		15,635					
1958		27,834					
1959	96,114	32,952		632			
1960	133,041	89,338	55,286	2,317			
1961	145,584	136,188	62,784	3,939			
1962	191,194	129,880	65,153	6,515			
1963	174,191	104,889	76,516	7,939	24,052		
1964	183,707	166,483	94,441	7,797	44,974		
1965	135,187	194,536	97,395	8,570	58,392		2,824
1966	224,609	179,453	114,766	7,096	60,502	1,604	13,170
1967	225,487	175,318	120,379	13,157	58,049	2,407	17,414
1968	279,715	180,976	146,478	18,042	62,868	4,124	10,119
1969	353,693	218,590	165,391	22,069	73,061	9,546	16,860

Year							
1970	416,040	219,599	189,986	24,591	69,976	17,652	14,456
1971	516,067	253,237	211,393	23,470	79,608	22,806	16,639
1972	609,470	268,593	229,791	26,228	88,674	24,015	23,796
1973	729,386	293,742	285,570	17,015	96,951	34,443	31,741
1974	858,479	286,312	359,947	13,852	118,152	45,340	29,719
1975	929,805	240,036	356,624	7,597	143,915	43,407	34,274
1976	985,469	193,517	324,979	7,027	162,732	42,384	34,344
1977	919,242	235,536	280,313		163,297		25,224
1978	1,062,197	179,875	384,127				

Sources: for Brazil: Kenneth Mericle, "The Political Economy of the Brazilian Motor Vehicle Industry," 1979.
for Mexico: Asociación Mexicana de la Industria Automotriz (AMIA), *La Industria Automotriz en Cifras, 1976;* *Boletín,* various numbers.
for Venezuela and Colombia: Camara de la Industria Venzolana Automotriz (CIVA), *La Industria Automotriz en Cifras, 1977.*
for Peru: Corporación Financiera de Desarrollo (COFIDE), *La Industria Automotriz,* 1978.
for Chile: Rhys Jenkins, *Dependent Industrialization in Latin America:* The Automotive Industry in Argentina, Chile and Mexico, 197, p. 286; Motor Vehicle Manufacturers Association, *Motor Vehicle Facts and Figures,* various years.

them to draw more or less fully upon this potential power to realize their ends.

Sometimes the bargaining only involves the state and the TNCs, but other actors may be involved as well. In Mexico the manufacture of auto parts was reserved for Mexican firms, and their presence in recent bargaining has affected outcomes. It is important to explain who is excluded from the bargaining and with what consequences. If labor had not been excluded from the bargaining in virtually all of these Latin American countries, for example, there might have been significantly different outcomes.

The interests of the state are more difficult to identify than those of the TNCs. Certainly we must not presume that the state represents the "national interest;" its viewpoint is more partial. The question of the interest or intentions of the state in these bargaining encounters requires for its answer an understanding of the relationship of the state to various classes and class fractions, and an understanding of the organization and controlling viewpoint of the various agencies of the state that are undertaking the bargaining. (Bennett and Sharpe 1979b; Bennett and Sharpe 1980).

One point that must be stressed about the interests of the state and of the transnational automobile firms is that no matter how contentious or conflictive the actual bargaining may become, it rests upon a foundation of shared or convergent interests—the convergent interests that we underscored in discussing the transition from imports or assembly to domestic manufacture and in discussing the transition from this to exports of automotive products from developing countries. Both the firms and the host governments see net benefits in the participation of TNCs in developing countries; what is being bargained over is the distribution of these various benefits.

The power of the transnational firms rests on their control of the technology, capital, and administrative skills necessary to manufacture motor vehicles. Even though motor vehicle manufacture does not rest upon rapidly changing technology it is a complicated matter, and the capital requirements are quite substantial. The ability of transnational firms to withhold these resources is the principal basis of their power. In addition, they can mobilize influential institutions to support them, particularly their own government, and transnational financial institutions. These allies can bring other sanctions to bear such as withholding trade opportunities, access to loans, and so forth. The bargaining power of the government of the developing nation resides mainly in its control over access to local markets and the labor force. What makes the threat to withhold access to the local market a viable source of power is precisely the pattern of defensive investment that has characterized international competition among the major transnational automobile firms. "When one member of the club makes a move, the others pant to follow," Knickerbocker writes. "By realizing this, the LDC is in a position to demand a high entrance fee" (Knickerbocker 1973, pp. 197-198). This potential power was not immediately apparent to many governments; like many other aspects of bargaining with TNCs it had to be learned (Moran 1974). Officials in Brazil and Argentina did not realize the interest of the transnational automobile firms in their national markets, and therefore made no effort to restrict the number of firms which commenced domestic manufacture. Even with this experience in mind, the Mexican government underestimated the vigor with which the TNCs would press for entry and wound up with twice the number of firms it wanted. Other Latin American nations have learned from the mistakes of these early ventures. During the negotiations for firms to manufacture in the Andean Pact countries, precise requirements were specified (e.g., automobiles with engine displacements between 1500 and 2000 cc.), and firms made offers for the right to produce that product. Learning has taken place in other aspects of bargaining as well. Developing countries have copied one another in their policies regarding technological transfers, formulae for computing local content, and techniques of accounting.

The bargaining leverage provided host country governments by their control of access to a domestic market is affected, of course, by the size of the local market. The smaller countries of Latin America thus lack the power that can be wielded by Brazil, Argentina, and Mexico. Common markets or other regional arrangements may create larger unified markets out of several smaller markets, and thereby increase the bargaining power of all the members if they can settle differences among themselves. The common market arrangement among the Andean Pact countries has been the most significant of such attempts.

SATISFACTION OF BASIC HUMAN NEEDS

A fundamental issue in assessing the performance of any industry is how it serves the interests of the poorest classes of the population in terms of consumption, and in terms of providing jobs, training in skills, and income. In most developed countries automobiles are an item of mass consumption but in most developing countries they are a luxury item, reserved by their price for the wealthiest strata. There is a further consideration concerning "appropriateness of products": the

223

broad array of models offered by the transnational auto firms and the frequency of model changes would not have occurred if these firms had grown up within developing countries. Mass production of one or two models would have been more likely. Unfortunately, only token efforts have been made by the transnational firms to develop vehicles that are designed for the particular needs of developing countries. A more favorable case can be made for the industry's basic human needs performance in attending to the production side. New jobs have been created, there has been some training in skills, and people who might otherwise have had a marginal relationship to the mainstream economy now can count on a sustaining wage.

Beyond these two questions, however, there is a more fundamental issue that concerns the overall shape and character of industrialization in developing countries. The automobile industry has been singled out in many of these countries as the centerpiece of industrial growth. This has caused a restructuring of the patterns of life around the requisites of the industry and these patterns have serious implications with respect to transportation, housing, public sector investments, energy, pollution, income distribution and the general quality of life of the population. The automobile industry has created patterns of urbanization and suburbanization that are particularly suited for those with vehicles and unsuited for those without. It requires substantial public sector investments, including constant repair and improvement of city streets and expressways, parking facilities, and traffic control. The sprawling of urban areas made possible by the automobile put additional strain on expenses for sewer lines, water service, electrical power, and telephone services. Not only are these costs substantial, and a subsidization of the auto industry and of those who are affluent enough to possess automobiles, they represent a diversion of public funds away from alternative expenditures for public transit facilities and for service networks oriented around them.[9] The industry has also created problems associated with the use of fossil fuels. Motor vehicles, especially old and poorly maintained ones, pollute the air. This is especially serious in urban areas in developing countries where the public health hazard is rapidly reaching crisis proportions. Moreover, the rapidly increasing price of oil has put an enormous strain on the economies of most developing countries. Finally, the development of the industry has had significant consequences for income distribution. As Cardoso and Faletto noted: "industrialization in dependent economies enhances income concentration as it increases sharp differences in productivity without generalizing this trend to the whole of the economy. . . . The wages of technicians, managers, and specialized workers, although not directly determined by productivity, are incomparably higher than those earned by peasants or workers employed in traditional sectors. (Cardoso and Faletto 1979, p. xxii). Such "structural heterogeneity" is particularly apparent in the automobile industry. In Brazil in 1974, for example, Finance Minister Mario Henrique Simonsen was quoted as saying that:

> A transfer of income form the richest 20% to the poorest 80% would probably increase the demand for food, but not the demand for automobiles. The result of a sudden redistribution would be merely to generate inflation in the food producing sector and excess capacity in the car industry (Gall 1977, pp. 49-50).

It bears adding that a turn towards export promotion policies may provide a wider market and militate against inefficiency in production, but it may also create a climate in which governments feel the need to hold down wages and maintain labor control in order to attract investments.

SUMMARY

The automobile, $5 to $10,000 dollars worth of iron, steel, glass, aluminum, plastics, textiles, rubber, stamped and machined parts, is a perfect consumer durable around which to promote industrialization. It is difficult to think of another consumer good that could serve as the centerpiece of industrialization quite so well. Certainly there are human costs, but are they not a natural concomitant of industrial growth? This is a difficult question to answer. In part, perhaps, yes: there are costs for growth, but not necessarily these costs, nor assessed in these ways. The automobile industry with its many by-products is a centerpiece of industrialization in the countries we have been considering because they are market economies which place primary reliance on private sector investment and individual choice. Under such conditions, those with more money have more voice concerning the future shape of the society in which all will live. It is a deeply-entrenched, pre-existing pattern of income inequality that allows the automobile industry to play a central role in the industrialization of Latin American countries by providing a sizeable if minority class of automobile consumers whose tastes are in line with those of the more developed world. If consumer choice sets the direction of industrial growth, the needs of the society at large will suffer.

Notes

[1] For discussions of the automobile industry in the United States see White 1971; Lanzillotti 1971; Toder 1978.

[2] For a discussion of the automobile industries in Europe see Wells 1978; Jenkins 1977, pp. 16-47; Krutky 1979; and Bloomfield 1978, pp. 182-225.

[3] On the development of the Japanese motor vehicle industry see Duncan 1973; Bloomfield 1978, pp. 226-234.

[4] On the notion of worldwide sourcing see Adam 1971 and 1972. On the development of the world car see Gooding 1979; *Business Week* 1978. On the implications of these changes in the world motor vehicle industry see Cohen 1979.

[5] There is a growing literature on the motor vehicle industry in Latin America. The indispensable overview is Jenkins 1977; but also Muller, Baransonn and Moran 1974; Gwynne 1978; NACLA Report 1979. On Argentina see Jenkins 1979. For Mexico see Vazquez Tercero 1975; Bennett and Sharpe 1979a; Bennett and Sharpe 1979b. On Chile see Johnson 1967; Jenkins 1977. On Columbia see Fleet 1978. On Venezuela see Naim 1979; Skurski and Coronil 1979. For Brazil see Mericle 1979; Oliveira and Travolo Popoutchi 1979. This last mentioned is the first of a series of studies of Latin American automobile industries being done by the Instituto Latinoamericano de Estudios Transnacionales in Mexico City. For discussions of the overall approach being taken in these studies see Trajtenberg 1977; Lifschitz 1978.

[6] The product cycle model can help us understand the evolving pattern of location of sales and production in the automobile industry, but it is less helpful in other regards. It cannot help us understand whether the foreign production is via direct investment or technical licenses; and the local competitors it predicts will eventually arise to challenge foreign investors have not materialized in the automobile industry and are unlikely to do so. The best introduction to the product cycle approach remains Vernon 1971. For a useful critique see Giddy 1978.

[7] There have been a number of previous attempts to identify stages in the internationalization of the world automobile industry. See, for example, Barannson 1969; Muller, Baranson and Moran 1974; Jenkins 1977; Bloomfield 1978. The delineation of stages offered here differs from previous attempts principally in its attempt to distinguish the interests of the transnational automobile firms from the interests of the LDC governmennts, and to show how these interests have converged in certain key respects to bring about the succession of stages.

[8] On the question of scale economies and efficiency in production in Latin American motor vehicle industries see Johnson 1967; Munk 1969; Baranson 1969; Jenkins 1977, pp. 196-208. Jenkins discussion is particularly recommended in that, like ours, it argues that proliferation of firms and models and the tendency to frequent model changes are direct consequences of the global pattern of oligopolistic competition among the major transnational automobile firms. No purely technical explanation of the inefficiency will suffice.

[9] These considerations are hardly unique to developing countries. On the impact of the automobile on the quality of life in the United States see Rothschild 1973.

Peter J. West

7.

International Expansion and Concentration of Tire Industry and Implications for Latin America

INTRODUCTION

The purpose of this chapter is to examine international expansion and competition in the rubber tire industry and their consequences for Latin American development. The first section surveys the development of the industry since its beginning, focusing on the processes of international expansion and concentration of production. The present levels and causes of concentration are analysed in the second section, while section three examines industry conduct and international oligopolistic rivalry. Then in section four the degree of internationalization of the major firms and the role of the developing countries in their global operations are discussed. The last two sections deal with the Latin American industry. Section five examines direct foreign investment and its effects on industry structure, and section six focuses on the history, conduct, and performance of the Argentinian tire industry.

DEVELOPMENT OF A WORLD INDUSTRY

In the early years of development of the industry there was a rapid growth in output, due to the explosion in vehicle ownership and production. Quickly, a small number of companies emerged as dominant producers. In the U.S. the four leading firms (Goodyear, Firestone, Goodrich, and U.S. Rubber[1]) achieved their dominant position not long after the establishment of the industry at the turn of the century, so that together they controlled 55 percent of the market by 1919 (Weston 1953, p. 41). At the same time the absolute number of producers increased rapidly. In 1921 there were 178 establishments engaged in tire production, and more than 500 firms entered into the industry at one time or another (FTC 1966, p. 2). Meanwhile, in Europe Dunlop of the U.K., Michelin of France, and Pirelli of Italy were emerging as the major companies.

The process of international expansion and competition started soon after the formation of the industry. As can be seen from Table 7.1, eight foreign manufacturing subsidiaries and affiliates were established before World War I. Most of these were formed by Dunlop, which began manufacture in France, Germany, Canada, Australia, and Japan. Nonetheless, at this stage competition tended to be confined within regional boundaries. Thus, companies in Europe principally faced competition from other European companies. Similarly, companies in the United States mainly faced competition from other U.S. firms. It is to be emphasized that this regionalization of competition did not result from any agreement between major companies to divide up markets, and so represented a lower stage of internationalization in comparison with later periods.

World War I interrupted the process of international expansion of European companies, but provided an impetus for U.S. firms to expand into markets around the world (Litchfield 1954). Goodyear, for example, opened a large factory in Canada at this time, while Goodrich established a plant in Japan in association with local investors. After the war, international competition spread out from the regional spheres and took on a more fully international character. Major European and U.S. firms came into direct conflict with one another, not only through trade but also, in the industrialized countries, through cross-investments. Both Dunlop and Michelin erected plants in the United States, and U.S. firms expanded abroad directing their attention primarily toward the U.K. Being the largest European market at the time and unlike many other markets, unprotected by tariffs, it was attractive to U.S. companies, which were now experiencing lower growth at home than in the early days of the industry. They at first attacked the market through exports and by 1920 accounted for 45 percent of total U.K. tire imports. But when a 33½ percent tariff was placed on tire imports in 1927 Goodyear and Firestone, as well as Michelin and Pirelli, set up plants in quick succession. The U.S. companies did not in this period enter extensively into other European countries, but they did move further into Dominion markets such as Canada and Australia formerly dominated by Dunlop.

Table 7.1

Major U.S. and European Tire Companies: Establishment of Overseas Tire Manufacturing Subsidiaries and Affiliates, Classified According to Period of Establishment and Location in Developed or Developing Country[a]

	Pre-1914			1914-1929			1930-1939			1940-1945			1946-1975		
	T[b]	DC[c]	LDC[d]	T	DC	LDC	T	DC	LDC	T	DC	LDC	T	DC	LDC
Dunlop	5	5	—	1	1	—	3	—	3	—	—	—	7	1	6
Pirelli	1	1	—	1	1	—	—	—	—	1	—	1	4	1	3
Michelin	1	1	—	2	2	—	4	2	2	—	—	—	6	3	3
Goodyear	—	—	—	2	2	—	4	1	3	2	—	2	19	5	14
Firestone	—	—	—	2	2	—	5	1	4	1	—	1	19	8	11
Uniroyal	1	1	—	1	1	—	2	1	1	1	—	1	10	5	5
Goodrich	—	—	—	4	4	—	1	—	1	2	—	2	8	4	4
General	—	—	—	—	—	—	2	1	1	3	—	3	16	4	12
TOTAL	8	8	—	13	13	—	21	6	15	10	—	10	89	31	58

Source: Own compilation.

Notes:

[a] In this table both foreign subsidiary (majority-owned) and affiliated (minority-owned) companies have been included. Licensing agreements with no equity stake have also been included when the licensee is entirely or largely dependent on the purchased technology. Subsidiaries and affiliates later sold or closed down have been included, so that it is not possible to read across the table to see how many subsidiaries and affiliates a company has now. Date of establishment has been defined as the date of the start of production in the case of new companies, and the date of association or takeover in the case of already existing companies.

[b] T = Total   [c] DC = developed countries   [d] LDC = less developed countries

During the Depression most of the small tire firms in the United States went out of business. Demand reached a peak in 1928 and declined sharply in the early 1930s, resulting in acute excess capacity. This was in large measure a direct result of the Depression, but in addition was a reflection of the development of longer-lived tires, which reduced replacement demand. Rivalry was also intensified by the entrance of mass distributors into retail tire sales, which began in 1926 when Goodyear signed a contract with Sears containing substantial price discounts.[2] The consequence of all these pressures was a period of intense price competition which hurt the small companies most. As a result in 1935 the share of the four largest firms reached a peak of 81 percent (see Table 7.2), and by 1937 there were only twenty-six companies left in the industry.

In the U.K. the concentration process was somewhat different. Dunlop was the only major producer until foreign companies began manufacturing there in the late 1920s. This resulted in a decrease in industry concentration but contributed to the elimination of smaller companies. In all probability, the investments by major U.S. and continental European firms in the U.K. at this time furthered the process of international concentration in the industry by helping to increase the world market shares of these firms.[3]

During the crisis years of the 1930s, the focus of international investment shifted from the developed to the underdeveloped countries. Table 7.1 illustrates that 15 out of a total of 21 investment entries made by the major producers were in non-industrialized countries. Investments tended to take place in the countries with the largest internal markets, such as Argentina, India, and South Africa. Stagnant market conditions discouraged the major producers from making cross-investments in one another's home territories. There were, in fact, some disinvestments; Michelin pulled out of the U.S. and Goodrich disposed of most of its stake in a U.K. firm. Those investments which occurred in the developed countries in this period were directed at markets without a major national producer such as Belgium, Sweden, Switzerland, and Germany.

The situation in underdeveloped countries was different. Here there were virtually no local tire manufacturers and demand was met entirely through imports. During the Depression the export of tires to these markets became difficult and uncertain, due to currency devaluations, exchange controls, and import restrictions or tariffs. A foreign company forming a manufacturing subsidiary could expect to have monopolistic, or at least oligopolistic, control of the market and be protected from imports either due to existing restrictions or from restrictive measures it could obtain from the government as a

Table 7.2

U.S. Proportion of Output Concentrated in Largest Manufacturing Companies (by Value of Shipments). Tires and Inner Tubes. (Percentage of Shipments)

Year	Top 4 Companies	Top 8 Companies
1935	81	90
1947	77	90
1954	79	91
1963	70	89
1972	73	90

Source: U.S. Department of Commerce, Bureau of the Census: *Statistical Abstract of the United States.* Various years.

condition for investing. Although these markets were stagnating much as were developed country markets, there was still an incentive to invest in them, to defend existing market shares, and to obtain growth locally through import substitution. The investments which took place in this period represented the start of the development of the industry in Latin America and underdeveloped countries in general.

The process of internationalization of the industry came to a halt during World War II. Indeed, the general tendency was towards nationalization as opposed to internationalization, as parent companies lost control of their overseas subsidiaries. Despite this, some U.S. companies did make investments in various Latin American nations, and this resulted in the spread of the industry to a number of additional countries in the region: Peru, Cuba, Colombia, Chile, and Venezuela. But after the war there was a sustained and prolonged process of international expansion by the major tire firms which was more extensive than in all previous periods combined. Referring back to Table 7.1, it can be seen that a total of 89 foreign manufacturing subsidiaries and affiliates were formed by the major companies between 1946 and 1975, compared with a total of 52 in all the previous periods combined. Of the total number of investments, 31 were in developed countries and no less than 58 in developing nations.[4] In Latin America this process of internationalization of production mainly meant the establishment of additional capacity in countries where plants already existed. In Africa and Asia, however, where far fewer countries had a tire industry at the start of the period, it resulted in the extension of the industry to many new countries. In Africa, for example, 11 nations acquired a tire industry between 1960 and 1974. In total, 43 developing countries now have at least one tire plant, 14 being in Latin America and the Caribbean, 14 in Africa, 10 in Asia, and 5 in the peripheral European countries.

The process of concentration in the industry has continued in the post-war period. At the national level it has taken the form of eliminating smaller producers rather than substantially increasing the market share of the top companies. In the case of the United States the share of the top four firms fell somewhat during the 1950s and 1960s, because some medium-sized producers, particularly General Tire, increased their share. Nevertheless, the proportion of output accounted for by the top eight companies has remained virtually unchanged (see Table 7.2). Moreover, the number of manufacturers has continued to decline, falling from 23 in 1945 to 14 in 1965 and 12 in 1979.

The entry of Michelin into manufacture in the U.S. in 1975 is likely to have important consequences for the process of concentration in the U.S. industry, as the company is aiming to capture 10 to 14 percent of the passenger car market (*Business Week* July 26, 1976). In the medium term, the four-firm concentration ratio is likely to fall, as Michelin builds up its production.[5] However, if the company attains its market share goal, it will become one of the four largest producers, and this could result in an increase in the four-firm concentration ratio in the long-term. Indeed, it has been rumored that one or more of the U.S. majors could leave the industry altogether.[6] Furthermore, Michelin's expansion into the U.S. is likely to have significant consequences for concentration at the international level, allowing the company to further increase its world market share.

Three principal conclusions stem from the above analysis. In the first place, a relatively small number of firms came to dominate the tire industry at a comparatively early date and, although there have been periodical changes in their ranking, there have been few fundamental changes in their composition.[7] Second, although the degree of oligopolistic competition has fluctuated, there has been no "cycle from monopoly to oligopoly to workable competition," said by Vernon to characterize many international products (1977, p. 91). Indeed, the tire industry is characterized by a tendency towards increased concentration and a continual elimination of smaller firms. Finally, direct foreign investment has been the principal vehicle for the organization of the world industry. As a result production is highly internationalized, in the sense that the major corporations operate facilities throughout the world.

PRESENT LEVEL AND CAUSES OF CONCENTRATION

As a result of the historical process of concentration described in the last section, the tire industry now exhibits a highly oligopolistic structure, both internationally and in distinct national markets. With respect to international concentration, this is brought out by the data in Table 7.3, which shows the shares of major producers in the capitalist world tire market. As can be seen, in the late 1970s the top four firms accounted for 60 percent of total output, while the top eight firms accounted for 80 percent of output. Table 7.4 gives details on the level of concentration in major developed country markets at this time indicating that in four countries—the U.K., France, Italy, and Japan—the top four companies accounted for no less than 90 percent of output and the total number of manufacturers was very small, varying from five to seven. However, markets in the U.S. and the Federal Republic of Germany, although highly oligopolistic, were somewhat

Table 7.3

Major Producers in World Tire Industry[a], 1979.

Company	Nationality	Percentage market shares
Goodyear	U.S.	23
Michelin	France	16
Firestone	U.S.	14
Bridgestone	Japan	7
Dunlop[b]	U.K.	6
Uniroyal	U.S.	5
B.F. Goodrich	U.S.	4
Pirelli[b]	Italy	4
General Tire	U.S.	4
Continental	Federal Republic of Germany	3
Top 4 companies		60
Top 8 companies		79

Source: Own Compilation

Notes:
[a] Market Economies only
[b] Although Dunlop and Pirelli had merged in 1971 to form the Dunlop-Pirelli Union, they are shown separately here as the Union was dissolved in 1981.

Table 7.4

Level of Concentration in Major Developed Countries, early 1970s.

	4 firm concentration ratio[a] (%)	Number of firms	Year
U.S.	71	13	1972
Federal Republic of Germany	75	9	1975
U.K.	89	6	1972
France	92	7	1972
Italy	92	5	1973
Japan	92	6	1972

Source: Own compilation.

Note:

[a] Figures for France and Italy refer to domestic tire sales, for UK to total tire sales, for USA to tire output, for W. Germany to tire output capacity and for Japan to rubber consumption in tire manufacture.

less concentrated than the other major markets, in terms of both the four-firm concentration ratio and the total number of companies. In the case of West Germany, it would seem that this was due to the fact that the country did not have a strong, indigenous multinational manufacturer, permitting foreign companies to enter in larger numbers and on a more significant scale than in the other countries.

One explanation of the high level of concentration concerns the advantages in innovation and marketing large firms have. The emphasis on innovation might appear paradoxical at first, as the tire industry is not characterized by a particularly high R&D/sales ratio. In the United States, for example, the rubber products industry (principally tires) ranked 12th in 25 industrial groups in terms of R&D expenditures as a percentage of net sales in 1974, while many less concentrated industries, such as pharmaceuticals, had substantially higher research intensities (National Science Foundation 1976). Despite the comparatively low R&D/sales ratio, expenditure by the major firms on R&D is substantial in absolute terms[8] and far in excess of that of smaller companies. This is brought out by the data in Table 7.5, which shows average annual R&D spending by U.S. tire firms in the years from 1975 to 1978. According to one estimate, the major firms devote around 45 percent of their R&D budgets to tire projects (Rubber World 1970).

Table 7.5

Internally-Financed R&D Expenditures of Tire Companies in the U.S., 1975–1978.

	Amount ($ millions)	Percentage of Net Sales
5 Major Firms		
Goodyear	126.2	2.0
Firestone	57.6	1.4
Uniroyal	50.5	2.1
Goodrich	39.9	1.8
General Tire	29.0	1.5
Average	60.6	1.8
4 Minor Firms		
Armstrong	5.4	1.6
Cooper	2.8	1.2
Mansfield	1.3	1.3
Mohawk	1.7	0.9
Average	2.8	1.3

Source: Annual Reports
"Survey of Corporate R&D Spending," *Business Week,* Various

Clearly, the large, multinational corporations have been responsible for the vast majority of innovations in the industry (West 1984). Even in those few cases where significant innovations have been introduced by smaller firms, the major firms have been in a position to rapidly imitate them once their commercial success had become apparent. The classic example of this is the bias-belted tire which was first introduced in the U.S. market by Armstrong, but turned into a resounding commercial success by the industry leader, Goodyear. The pace of technical change has been quite rapid and has been reflected not only in major new tire constructions (tubeless tire, radial tire, bias-belted tire, run-flat tires, etc.), but also in fundamental changes in the materials used in tire construction and a constant improvement in tire design. Generally speaking technical advances apply to all types and sizes of tire. As a result, there are no independent sub-sectors of the market in which small companies could concentrate their activities and they have to keep up with the general pace of technological advance in order to survive, which is neither easy or cheap to do. The major companies protect their inventions with patents that are not easily circumvented. For example, in order to avoid the Michelin patents on the radial tire, the major innovation in the industry in the post-war period, Pirelli had to develop a radial with a completely different carcass material (rayon instead of steel wire). Furthermore, the acquisition of licenses is not in itself sufficient to keep up with the pace of technological change, and must be accompanied by in-house R&D. This is well brought out by the following description of the difficulties in developing steel-belted radials given by the managing director of a small U.K. tire manufacturer, Avon:

> "We spent an awful lot of money and a lot of pain and grief in developing our own specifications for steel braced tyres because Michelin gives you a license to make the things but don't tell you how to do it. So we've had to invent all that ourselves. (Tyres and Batteries 1975).

Large-firm advantages in R&D expenditure and output thus represent an important competitive advantage which makes it difficult for small companies to survive.

The advantages of major firms in innovation are reinforced by their superiority in advertising and marketing. In the original equipment market, where the tire firms sell directly to the vehicle manufacturers, this is of little importance as competition is based almost exclusively on product quality and price. In the replacement market, however, advertising is an essential complement to innovation, and large firms have substantial advantages in this area too. The advertising budgets of the major firms are substantial. Goodyear, for example, spent almost $68 million on advertising in 1975, making it the thirty-fifth largest advertiser in the U.S. (*Advertising Age* August 23, 1976). But the advertising/sales ratio of major firms is not particularly high.[9] Furthermore, this form of large firm advantage is perhaps less important than in many other consumer goods industries, as replacement tires are in a sense a "distress" purchase, and it is relatively difficult to affect consumer choice through product differentiation in the form of styling, novelty, and appearance.

Another major cause of concentration is the advantage which large, established companies possess in tire distribution. Only the major firms are in a position to sell to the vehicle companies in the original equipment market, and this gives them advantages in replacement sales. There is a tendency for replacement purchases to replicate original equipment, although the importance of this is at times exaggerated. More significantly, a position in the original equipment market facilitated the establishment of franchised dealerships and retail outlets for replacement sales that came to represent a significant barrier to entry for small manufacturers. The domination of distribution by the large tire companies is one of the principal reasons for the decline in the number of small producers (FTC 1966 pp. 19-22).

CONDUCT AND INTERNATIONAL OLIGOPOLISTIC RIVALRY

The market power of firms in the tire industry is less than might be expected from the high levels of concentration characterizing the industry, because in both the original equipment and replacement markets the tire companies must contend with other large-scale organizations (vehicle producers and mass distributors such as chain stores). The existence of the countervailing power of large buyers goes a long way towards explaining why severe price competition at times breaks out among tire firms, especially when demand is weak, and why the industry has not been characterized by a high rate of profit, despite its highly concentrated structure. Price competition in the industry is oligopolistic in character, and various studies have documented formal and explicit collusion. In the U.K. the Monopolies Commission found that in the early post-war period regular consultations between all producers resulted in identical prices being charged to the consumer in the replacement market, with Dunlop acting as price leader. Another study undertaken in 1971 indicated that price competition was pervasive, taking the form of discounting from list prices in supplying retail outlets. However, Dunlop still exercised some leadership on list prices, and also a degree of leadership on the basic discounts available (Swann et al. 1973, pp. 182-205). The United States Federal Trade Commission reported in 1962 that the tire manufacturers had agreed on a uniform pricing system, exchanged confidential information about quotations and selling terms, and fixed prices quoted to government and industry customers (*Rubber Age* February 1962). And the same situation existed in developing countries; the Indian Tariff Commission reported in 1955 that tires and tubes of all makers were sold at uniform prices.

Regarding international collusion over prices and other aspects of corporate behavior, cartel arrangements have been far less prevalent than in some other industries. The only formal agreement of this kind for which evidence exists was made in the 1920s when competition was intense and corporations were operating at a loss in export markets. To prevent further losses the major tire producers for a brief

237

period engaged in price collusion. Consultations between Dunlop, representing the European firms, and the Rubber Export Association of America, representing the U.S. companies, resulted in a common price level in all markets where tire prices were not determined by local manufacture. The fact that Dunlop continued to incur losses on export sales between 1925 and 1930 despite the existence of this scheme suggests it was not particularly effective.

The strategies used to establish spheres of influence and control the industry changed in the 1930s to direct foreign investment with some territorial division of investments. Dunlop concentrated on colonial or former colonial areas and the U.S. firms focused on Latin America. This formed the basis of an important reciprocal manufacturing arrangement between Goodyear and Dunlop the leading U.S. and European firms, respectively. Goodyear agreed to make Dunlop tires in countries where it operated but Dunlop did not and vice versa. No change in the production process or in machinery and equipment was necessary in the plants where the agreement was implemented, except for the use of different molds (which imprint the tire tread as well as the brand name and specifications) in the vulcanizing presses. And each company maintained its own selling and distribution channels. The arrangement is still in operation today, although it is far less extensive than previously.

In the post-war period competition among the multinational firms in the developed countries intensified. In the 1950s and early 1960s U.S. firms invested extensively in Europe and to a lesser extent in Japan. These were the years of the American challenge. Starting around the mid-1960s a European counter-challenge was mounted. With the development of the radial-ply tire,[10] technological leadership in the industry passed to European firms. To capture monopoly rents from its lead in radial technology, Michelin in particular mounted a determined attack on the North American market by opening a radial plant in Canada in 1971, much of whose output was destined for the United States. The U.S. Treasury, under pressure from domestic tire companies, quickly placed an extra duty of 6.6 percent on tire imports from Canada but Michelin reacted by establishing large-scale manufacturing operations in the U.S. in 1975. Thus, United States penetration into Europe was countered by European penetration of the U.S. market, spearheaded by Michelin, a decade later. Furthermore, the three smaller U.S. multinationals—Goodrich, General Tire, and Uniroyal—have withdrawn from manufacturing operations in Europe, due to the highly competitive situation which has developed in recent years.[11] More recently a Japanese challenge has been launched,

238

with Bridgestone acquiring a Firestone facility in the U.S. and Sumitomo taking over Dunlop's European operations.

A significant feature of competitive behavior in the industry in the post-war period was the slowness of U.S. firms to introduce the radial tire into their domestic market. This was not due to lack of technology, as they had been producing radials in their European plants since the early 1960s, but rather because radials require new production machinery and their longer life cuts into replacement demand.[12] In the early 1970s, however, they were forced to commence radial manufacture by the penetration of European radials into the U.S. market and by the decision of the automobile firms to use them. It is an open question whether the delaying tactics were in their long-term interest. Offsetting the advantages they derived, their slowness made it easier for Michelin to enter the market. Nevertheless, this is a classic example of the use of market power to slow the pace of innovation in an industry.

Although the internationalization of the tire industry has been linked to that of the automobile industry, this relationship is more tenuous than might be supposed. Indeed, it is often the case that a tire plant is established in a developing country before car manufacture begins. Even though vehicle exports create the market for replacement tires in the first place, and the companies which sell original equipment tires are benefited by having their product introduced to the market through car exports, too much weight should not be placed on this link. Michelin's penetration of the U.S. market had little to do with sales of French cars there; Pirelli was a major manufacturer of tires in Brazil long before Fiat thought of constructing a plant in the country.

The tendency for a large number of foreign firms to enter a small market at the same time has been less prevalent in the tire industry than in some other industries such as motor vehicles. In other words, what Knickerbocker terms oligopolistic reaction is relatively low (Knickerbocker 1973; West 1984). Table 7.6 classifies 57 developed and developing countries according to how many of the nine multinational firms set up subsidiaries or affiliates in them between 1900 and 1975. As can be seen, in only 13 countries did four or more of the nine multinational firms establish manufacturing operations. The tendency towards the entry of a small number of firms was particularly noticeable in the developing areas. Only one firm entered into 21 of the 42 countries, and the entry of four or more companies was confined to 6 countries. The lower degree of oligopolistic reaction in the developing countries would appear to be related to their generally

Table 7.6

57 Developed and Developing Countries Classified According to Number of Multinational Companies which Established Manufacturing Subsidiaries or Affiliates, 1900–1975

Number of Subsidiaries	Number of Countries in which a given Number of Subsidiaries were formed		
	Total	DC	LDC
1	24	3	21
2	11	3	8
3	9	2	7
4	4	1	3
5	5	3	2
6	2	2	—
7	1	—	1
8	1	1	—
9	—	—	—

Source: Own compilation.

small market size. When two or more firms do enter into a given market, however, they tend to do so in quick succession.

INTERNATIONAL DIVISION OF LABOR: THE ROLE OF DEVELOPING COUNTRIES

As a result of the process of international expansion, foreign manufacture accounts for a significant proportion of total operations for most of the major firms in the tire industry. As can be seen in Table 7.7, there are important differences among the companies. For example, foreign sales usually form a larger percentage of total sales for the European companies than the U.S. ones.[13]

The importance of developing country output for the industry has been slowly but steadily increasing. They absorbed about 8 percent of total production in market economies in 1968 and 13 percent in 1977. Moreover, these countries now play a significant role in the global operations of some of the multinationals. Subsidiaries in developing countries accounted for almost 30 percent of the aggregate turnover of the Dunlop-Pirelli Union between 1971 and 1974, and the contribution to profits before interest and tax was even more im-

Table 7.7

Multinational Tire Firms: Sales of Foreign Subsidiaries, 1972 and 1979
(Percentage of Total)

	1972	1979
U.S. Firms		
Goodyear	n.a.	38
Firestone	30	33
Uniroyal	29	37
B.F. Goodrich	26	20
General Tire	20[c]	<10
European Firms		
Dunlop[a]	59	61
Michelin	47[b]	56

Source: Annual Reports

Notes:
[a] Refers to the Dunlop managed firms in the Dunlop-Pirelli Union plus various subsidiaries not included in the Union.
[b] Estimate
[c] 1973

pressive, being 54 percent for the whole period. Latin American subsidiaries alone accounted for practically 30 percent of total group profits in these years. The average rate of return on sales was three times greater in the developing world than in the developed nations, the highest rate being earned by Latin America, followed by Asia and Africa, and then North America and Australia. The low profit of developed countries was because of over-capacity in the European industry.

Developing countries are equally important to the major U.S. multinational tire companies. In 1976 companies in the rubber products sector, which mainly consists of tires, made 36 percent of their overseas sales in developing countries (Chung 1978) which hence represented about 11 percent of the worldwide sales of these companies. There are, however, significant differences among the firms. For Goodyear and Firestone, the two largest U.S. companies, the developing countries, particularly those of Latin America, play an important role in worldwide activities. Goodyear's subsidiaries in Latin America accounted for 11 percent of global sales and about 20 percent of overall operating profits in 1979. In 1977 Firestone's Latin American subsidiaries accounted for almost 10 percent of global sales and 17 percent of operating profits. In 1978 when the company made an operating loss in all the major developed areas, the Latin American firms registered an operating profit of $70 million, representing a return of 14.5 percent on sales (Firestone 1978).

The above analysis suggests that for some of the major firms in the industry the developing countries already play a vital role in their global activities. Furthermore, in the late seventies and early eighties a situation of excess capacity and reduced demand developed in the United States and Europe which led to plant closures: Uniroyal shut two of its five tire factories and Firestone closed five plants in the United States; in the U.K. Dunlop reduced its tire producing capacity by a third and Firestone shut both its plants; and in West Germany there were also substantial plant closures. In contrast, in the developing countries the number of vehicles per person is low and there exists a higher potentiality for rapid demand growth. As Brazier and Pelling of Dunlop have noted:

> "In the home market levels of car ownership are already high, and consequently there will come a time in the future when the growth of tyre demand will slow down. Therefore an international company which wishes to grow must seek to invest in countries whose levels of ownership of vehicles and other durables are so low that rapid growth is likely to continue for a long time." (Brazier and Pelling n.d.).

All the indications are that the moment of slow growth in the developed countries has already arrived and that certain developing countries are becoming important locations for capital accumulation.

FOREIGN INVESTMENT AND INDUSTRIAL STRUCTURE IN LATIN AMERICA

Foreign investment in tires began at a relatively early point in the process of import substituting industrialization in Latin America and spread throughout the continent. Table 7.8 shows the date of establishment of the first plant in each country which now has a tire industry and the number of firms and plants in existence in 1947 and 1980. As can be seen, a tire industry had been established in four countries by 1939, and by 1980 only those countries with the smallest internal markets, such as Paraguay and some of the Central American nations, were without one.

In explaining the early timing and wide geographical spread of foreign investment in the industry available evidence indicates that it is

Table 7.8

Date of Opening of First Tire Plant and Number of Manufacturing Companies and Plants in Existence in 1947 and 1980

Country	Date First Plant Opened	Number of Companies		Number of Plants	
		1947	1980	1947	1980
Argentina	1931	4	4	4	4
Mexico	1933	4	5	4	8
Uruguay	1936	1	1	1	1
Brazil	1939	3	4	3	9
Venezuela	1941	1	4	1	4
Peru	1943	1	2	1	2
Cuba	1943	2	a	2	a
Chile	1944	1	2	1	2
Colombia	1945	2	3	2	3
Guatemala	1958	—	1	—	1
Ecuador	1963	—	1	—	1
Costa Rica	1967	—	1	—	1
Jamaica	1967	—	1	—	1
Trinidad	1968	—	1	—	1

Source: Own compilation.

Note:

[a] The four U.S. tire companies in Cuba were expropriated in 1950. Production continued afterwards, but is is not clear how many plants are in operation today.

possible to design small-scale tire plants which do not have exorbitantly high unit costs of production (Bain 1956). The relative inelasticity of the industry demand curve has contributed to the commercial feasibility of such plants. As a result of this combination of supply and demand characteristics, what might be termed the minimum feasible scale of production in a protected market is quite small in the tire industry, and this has permitted the establishment of plants in countries with a limited market. The comparatively low value to weight ratio of tires has also contributed to the widespread distribution of manufacturing units.

Another essential feature of the Latin American tire industry is the dominant role which foreign capital has played in its development. Excluding Cuba, all 30 currently operating tire manufacturing firms in the region receive technical assistance on a continuous basis from foreign multinational companies. Of these firms, only three do not have some degree of equity participation by the multinationals. And of the 27 with foreign capital participation, 21 are wholly or majority foreign-owned and only 6 minority foreign-owned. As Table 7.9 indicates, 14 of the 30 companies were majority-owned subsidiaries when

Table 7.9

Affiliation between the Multinationals and Tire Manufacturing Firms in Latin America and the Caribbean.

	Originally	Now
Wholly-owned foreign subsidiary[a]	11	13
Joint venture: majority foreign-owned[b]	3	8
Joint venture: minority foreign-owned[c]	9	6
National company with foreign technical assistance[d]	3	3
National company without foreign technical assistance[e]	4	—

Source: Own compilation

Notes:
[a] 95% or more foreign-owned.
[b] 51% to 94% foreign-owned.
[c] 6% to 50% foreign-owned.
[d] 5% or less foreign-owned, with on-going technical assistance.
[e] 5% or less foreign-owned, without on-going technical assistance.

they were founded, while only 4 were nationally-owned firms without technical assistance from a multinational. Furthermore, there have been no significant entries of national firms which were later obliged to close down, although the 4 firms which started production without foreign technical assistance are all associated with multinationals. Thus, the denationalization of capital, a phenomenon noted in other industrial sectors in Latin America, has not been a general feature of the tire industry precisely because the industry has been foreign-dominated from the start.

To understand why foreign capital dominance has always characterized the industry, it is necessary to look at the production process. A key feature of tire production is that the vast majority of the manufacturing process must be located at one site. As a result, plants established in developing countries are highly integrated in contrast to the development pattern of many other industries where the final and generally less complex stages of manufacture are established first and separate from the initial phases. As a result local production has been practically fully integrated from the start, so there is no stage at which it was easier for national firms to enter. Technical change and the difficulty of imitating innovations have constituted an important barrier to entry for unaffiliated national investors.

However, the technology factor alone is not capable of explaining the heavy degree of equity participation by the multinationals; it is also necessary to take into account the policy of these firms with respect to the mode of overseas operation (West 1984, chapter 9). Most of the multinationals, particularly Goodyear, have preferred complete or majority ownership of their subsidiaries. The chief exception is General Tire which has consistently pursued a policy of entering into association with local investors on a minority basis. There are signs that some of the multinationals such as Dunlop and Firestone have recently been relaxing their equity requirements in accordance with the changing environment for foreign firms and demonstrated a willingness to accept minority control of their overseas subsidiaries. In general, though, the multinationals have required and obtained majority ownership of their Latin American affiliates. The primary reason the overseas operations developed this way is because when the expansion occurred in the 1930s and 1940s the industry in the developed countries had attained such a level of concentration that the major firms had sufficient financial resources, in relation to the cost of setting up an overseas plant, to be able to take majority ownership in their subsidiaries.

In conclusion, the low degree of oligopolistic reaction together with the dominance of foreign capital have resulted in a highly con-

245

centrated industrial structure in all countries in the Latin American region. This concentration in Latin America is equal to or greater than that in the developed countries. The comparatively low degree of oligopolistic reaction has meant that only a small number of foreign firms have normally invested in any country of the region (with only one firm entering many of the smaller markets), while the dominance of the multinationals in the industry's development has meant that its structure has by and large been determined by the investment behavior of foreign rather than nationally-owned firms.

THE ARGENTINIAN TIRE INDUSTRY

This section will examine industrial structure, conduct, and performance in Argentina. Particular attention will be paid to technology transfer, adaptation, and learning in the analysis of conduct and performance.

The first sales subsidiaries in Argentina were established by Dunlop in 1911, Goodyear and Firestone in 1915, and U.S. Rubber in 1917. During the 1920s there was a veritable boom in motor vehicle ownership and a corresponding rapid increase in the replacement demand for tires.[14] Ford and General Motors established assembly plants in 1916 and 1925 respectively, and the first commercial tire plants in Latin America were set up in Argentina in the early 1930s by Goodyear (1930), Firestone (1931), and Michelin (1934). Although tire demand had reached almost 2,000 units per day and the minimum feasible scale of output was only 300 tires per day, only three plants were established when the market could have accommodated six. Companies such as Goodrich and U.S. Rubber withdrew, and by 1938 imports represented only 5 percent of apparent consumption in volume terms.

Goodyear began manufacturing Dunlop tires in its Argentinian plant in 1935. The manner in which the two multinationals recognized their mutual interest in forestalling duplicate investments through such off-take arrangements was described by the then President of Goodyear, Paul Litchfield, when he met his counterpart, Eric Geddes of Dunlop:

> "He brought up an interesting question after we started the Argentine plant. 'We were thinking about going in there ourselves,' he said, 'You have beaten us to it. I doubt if the market warrants two factories. What would you think of building tires for us to our specifications in Buenos Aires? We would furnish

246

the molds.' I thought it over . . . could see nothing wrong with it. One large factory would be more efficient than two small ones, would get factory costs down, widen the market. 'Would Dunlop build tires for us, lets say in India or South Africa,' I replied. 'Naturally,' said Sir Eric." (Litchfield 1954, p. 234).

During World War II tire output in Argentina fell sharply when the Japanese invaded Southeast Asia and cut off natural rubber supplies, resulting in a serious shortage in the local market. In response a locally-owned rubber products firm (FATE) started manufacturing tire treads for re-treading used tires, and after the war began tire production. Political as well as economic conditions favored the establishment of a nationally-owned company at this time. This was the period of the Peronist regime and the foreign investment climate was "unfavorable." Moreover, according to local sources foreign tire firms sanctioned the establishment of a nationally-owned firm, as it would shield the whole industry against unwelcome government policies. Under these circumstances, FATE was able to establish itself without technical assistance from any of the multinationals, despite the fact that the quality of its output was initially quite poor. By the mid-1950s, however, circumstances had changed: there was no longer a shortage of tires, the Peronist regime had been overthrown, and the foreign tire firms had initiated various important innovations in their designs. To keep abreast of the market FATE decided to sign a technical assistance agreement with General Tire in 1957.

There were several other changes in the industry in the early post-war period. A new plant jointly owned by Pirelli and U.S. Rubber was established, and the Michelin factory was closed. Pirelli and U.S. Rubber both took a 50 percent share in a firm set up in 1951, but management and technology were supplied by the U.S. company. Each firm had its own sales organization and distribution outlets. However, in 1968 Pirelli bought out U.S. Rubber's share, terminating the only jointly-owned production venture which ever existed in the Latin American tire industry. The structure of the Argentinian tire industry has remained unchanged since then.

Technology Transfer

When examining the conduct and performance of firms in the Argentinian tire industry, an important difference emerges between FATE and the subsidiaries of the multinationals in terms of technology transfer and learning. Table 7.10 shows that royalty fees paid by FATE are considerably less than those paid by the local subsidiaries of

247

Table 7.10

Argentina: Royalty and Technical Assistance Fees Paid

Licensee	Licensor	% Equity of Licensee Held by Licensor	Amount Paid as % of Sales 1972	1973
Neumáticos Goodyear	Goodyear	100	3.2	2.2
Firestone de la Argentina	Firestone	100	n.a.	2.0
Pirelli COPLAN	Pirelli	100[a]	1.6	1.9
FATE	General Tire	0	1.2	1.0

Source: Licensee company balance sheets.

Note:
[a] 60% owned by Pirelli and 40% by Dunlop.

the multinationals. Additional evidence on FATE's relatively low explicit technology payments is provided by information about contractual royalty payments for various Latin American tire firms. Payments are generally fixed at around 3 percent of net sales, but FATE's technology contract with General Tire stipulates a progressively falling rate from 3 percent to 0.5 percent as the value of sales of the licensee increases. By 1974 the rate of payment had been reduced to 0.8 percent of net sales. In contrast another General Tire affiliate in Latin America, Cauchos General of Venezuela, had an average royalty rate of 3.8 percent of net sales in the period from 1975 to 1979.

Before concluding that FATE purchases foreign technology at a relatively low cost, it is necessary to examine possible implicit or indirect payments for imported technology. In this respect, the possibilities for overpricing imported raw material and intermediate goods are limited because the interchange of components and semifinished products between factories in different parts of the world is minimal. Furthermore, many of the raw materials in the tire industry, such as natural and synthetic rubbers and carbon black, are relatively undifferentiated in character and have clearly defined world prices. These considerations do not, of course, rule out overpricing altogether. In his Colombian study, Vaitsos found that a wholly-owned tire subsidiary was paying an inflated price for natural rubber imported from the parent company (Vaitsos 1971). And overpricing of some of the specialized chemicals used in rubber compounds is a distinct possibility. In the specific case of FATE imported raw materials consist mainly of natural rubber and some synthetic rubbers. It seems highly unlikely that any implicit payments are made to General Tire through overpricing of these. There is no clause in the technology contract between the two companies specifying where FATE must purchase its raw materials, and General Tire does not possess its own natural rubber plantations or the capacity to produce significant amounts of synthetic rubber. Furthermore, it is implausible that a firm like FATE, which has shown the ability to develop its own technology (see below) and negotiate a relatively low explicit price for foreign technical assistance, would not be able to prevent significant overpricing.

Another important form of indirect payment for imported technology, the capitalization of know-how, is not relevant in the case of FATE, as it is wholly-owned by Argentinian investors. It is of considerable importance, however, in other tire firms in Latin America, particularly in the case of joint ventures. For example, Goodrich's minority equity investment in Lima Rubber Co. in Peru, representing 25 percent of the total capital of the company, largely took the form of know-how capitalization. In addition to the dividend payments on this capitalized know-how, the U.S. multinational receives an ongoing royalty equivalent to 3 percent of the net sales of its Peruvian affiliate. Thus, if anything, this analysis suggests that FATE makes lower indirect payments for foreign technology than other tire firms in the region for reasons that will become apparent in the following analysis of technology adaptation and learning.

Technology Adaptations and Learning

Although multinationals do make some adaptation of their tire designs to take account of local market conditions, the modifications are generally minor, involving changes in the composition of the rubber compounds and in the design of tire treads and carcasses. In Argentina, for example, truck tires are produced with stronger casings, because they are commonly overloaded and receive extensive wear and tear. With respect to process technology, there have been few significant differences between Latin American and developed countries, with the exception that second-hand machinery is often used in countries like Argentina.[15] As second-hand equipment tends to be more labor-intensive than newer machinery, this has tended to boost

249

employment. Still, the tire industry is quite capital-intensive, and in Argentina provided a total employment of only 7,075 in 1974.

The adaptations introduced by the multinationals have not been sufficiently important to justify the establishment of local R&D facilities in Argentina or other Latin American countries. Generally speaking, all technological development is undertaken in the central research laboratories of the multinationals.[16] The only role which is reserved for the local subsidiary is to road-test the modified tire designs. This applies to joint venture operations as well as to wholly foreign-owned subsidiaries. In the tire industry, multinationals have hence contributed little to the development of host country technological skills through undertaking local R&D activities,[17] but they have contributed to the development of local technical skills by training the labor force and instigating quality control activities in their plants and laboratories.

In contrast with the multinationals, FATE has pursued a strategy of local technological development, which could contain important lessons for other developing countries. As it initially had no technical assistance contract with a foreign firm, the company relied on its ingenuity in copying the tire designs of the local subsidiaries of multinationals, and on information provided by the suppliers of equipment and raw materials and consultants. Quality was poor but invaluable experience was gained. When FATE later entered into a technical assistance agreement with General Tire, it did not allow this to displace its own R&D activities. Using the agreement as a means of keeping abreast of the major innovations in the industry, a strategy was devised whereby information supplied by General Tire is used by the company to develop its own tire designs adapted to the conditions of the Argentinian market. Examples of tires it has developed for Argentinian road conditions are the PCR truck tire, which has a tread specially designed for use on the gravel roads of the Argentinian interior, and the FATE TM, a high speed tire designed for use in motor sports. However, the most outstanding success achieved to date is the FATE radial tire. Work on this started in 1966 and a passenger car radial was launched in 1970, ahead of the three subsidiaries of multinational firms including Pirelli, one of the original innovators of the radial. As was the case in the United States, multinationals operating in Latin America held up the introduction of the radial for many years. This slowing down in the pace of innovation was detrimental to the interests of these countries, because radials have a longer life and better gasoline mileage.

The development strategy used by FATE has paid off. Their share of the market rose to about 27 percent in 1973 compared with only 13 percent in 1961. By 1974 company expenditures on R&D amounted to around 0.5 percent of sales totalling about $0.4 million and employing 18 professionals and 17 technicians. Although the ratio of R&D to sales is less than that for tire firms in the industrialized countries, since expenditure at subsidiary level in Latin America is generally close to zero, there is a sharp difference between FATE and the multinationals in this respect. One interesting consequence of the firms's investment in R&D has been their ability to assist other firms in developing their technical capabilities. FATE was one of the founding members of the Rubber Research Center of the National Institute of Industrial Technology with an objective of testing raw materials and rubber compounds for use by local rubber goods manufacturers.

The strategy of using outside technical help for major innovations but producing minor innovations locally has had a number of beneficial effects from both a private and a social point of view. It is reasonable to conclude that the company's relatively low payment for imported technology is in large measure due to the fact that it developed its own technological capabilities, both before and after signing the assistance agreement with General Tire. When technology is transferred between more or less independent parties, the price paid is largely determined by relative bargaining power, and the negotiating strength of the purchasing firm depends in a fundamental way on the extent of its technological capabilities. Apart from representing a benefit to the company, FATE's low payment for imported technology is also beneficial from a social point of view, as it results in a saving in scarce foreign exchange.

Prices and Costs

Turning briefly to other performance criteria, a study of the Argentinian tire industry found that the list prices recommended by the various manufacturers to their retail distributors were practically identical (Paz and Otero 1970). However, price competition existed at the retail level because firms offered substantial and varied discounts to retailers. In many ways this pattern of pricing is similar to that in the developed countries. With respect to price levels, the study estimated that the average price of a representative group of tires was 37 percent higher in Argentina than in the United States in 1970. Over half of this difference was due to higher raw material and intermediate input costs, the remainder was due to differences in other components of average costs and/or profit margins. The average plant size in Argentina is less than that in the United States and somewhat below the minimum optimal scale, but given the relatively flat plant cost

251

curve in the industry, it is more than probable that this was easily offset by lower labor costs. Hence it is reasonable to assume that part of the difference in price levels was the consequence of higher profitability resulting from greater market power in Argentina. Such market power stems both from the high level of concentration and from the fact that large-scale purchasers are less prevalent in Argentina than the U.S. Tires have begun to be sold in supermarkets in recent years, but small and medium-sized dealerships continue to be the dominant channel of distribution. Thus, there is a lack of concentrated buying power in the replacement market which could push prices towards the competitive level.

This analysis suggests that the higher profit rates earned by the multinationals in the developing countries is in part due to the exercise of greater market power in these countries than in the developed ones. It should be emphasized, however, that the generally more rapid growth of demand in the less developed areas than in Europe and the U.S. and the problems of excess capacity in the latter, are also important in explaining these higher rates of profit.

Exports

As in most other developing countries, the tire industry in Argentina has largely fulfilled an import-substituting role, and exports have generally been only a small fraction of production. Significant exports have only been made under special circumstances. For example, from 1968 to 1970 sales were made to the U.S., mainly by Goodyear, of types and sizes of tire no longer produced in that country, and required for older models of motor vehicles. The possibility of any Latin American country becoming a significant export platform in this industry is made difficult by the state of over-capacity in the U.S. and Europe, the widespread geographical distribution of production facilities, the lack of trade in intermediate products and components, and the dominant position of multinationals in the sector.

Basic Needs

Finally, as regards the pattern of growth in developing nations, since tires are not demanded for their own sake, but only as a component for motor vehicles, the conclusions about product appropriateness are similar to those for the auto industry. Like the auto firms the tire multinationals have a vested interest in the continuance of the process of uneven development, because a skewed income distribution is required in low per capita income countries to create demand for cars and their components. A basic needs strategy would, of course, still require tires for public transport and trucks, but it would in all probability imply a lower level of demand for car tires, which make up a large part of consumption in many countries. For example, in Argentina car tire output represented 64 percent of the total in unit terms on average for the period 1959 to 1973. Moreover, given that certain developing countries are by no means "marginal" or "peripheral" in terms of their contribution to the worldwide sales and profits of the multinationals, any change in development strategy which would result in reduced profit opportunities in these countries could hardly be viewed with magnanimity.

SUMMARY

Addressing the four issues concerning transnational expansion and its effects on development raised in chapter 1 of this book, the following conclusions may be made about the international tire industry. First, as regards foreign expansion, tire production is highly internationalized in the sense that the major corporations operate facilities in many countries throughout the world. The monopolistic advantages of large firms in the form of control over technology and tire distribution have been the main governing factors of direct foreign investment in the sector, but its relatively early timing and wide geographical spread are related to the lack of significant plant scale economies in tire manufacture. The product life cycle theory does not throw much light on the process of overseas expansion by tire firms, partly because it is not clear what is meant by the 'product' in this case. The rubber tire is a mature product and the industry is old, but tire design is still constantly being improved through technical innovation, and there are no signs of the multinationals losing their grip on the industry. Moreover, the success of the U.S. transnationals in resisting the change to radial technology, in both their home market and in the developing countries of Latin America, illustrates that the major corporations have a considerable degree of control over the lives of particular generations of tires. Second, the early expansion overseas by the tire firms indicates that oligopolistic competition has been international in scope during most of the history of the industry. The degree and nature of this rivalry has, however, varied widely in different periods and locations. After the rather unsuccessful attempt at export cartelization in the 1920s, direct foreign investment became the principal vehicle for organizing the world industry. The Great Depression saw the elimination of many smaller firms in the industrialized countries and the start of overseas investment in the non-industrialized nations. Following on this turbulent period, in the postwar years the U.S. majors slowed down the pace of technical change and stepped up their penetration of markets abroad. This American challenge was, however, countered by a European thrust into the U.S. market in the 1970s and, more recently, by Japanese expansion into markets outside Southeast Asia.

Oligopolistic rivalry intensified in the late 1970s as a consequence of economic recession and the effects of the energy crisis, which resulted in a sharp increase in the prices of tire raw materials and a downturn in passenger miles driven. As in the Great Depression, the industry's problems in the present crisis have been exacerbated by the introduction of longer-lasting tires, in this case the switch to the radial. Excess capacity has led to price competition in both the U.S. and Europe. The crisis has also been characterized by a restructuring of capital in the industry at both the national and international levels, and there are signs that this could give rise to more concentration and a more tightly-knit international oligopoly in the future. Various small producers have been forced out of business in Europe and the U.S. and plant closures by many of the major firms have led to a large cutback in industry capacity.[18] It is thought that one or more of the smaller multinationals could shortly be forced out of the industry.[18]

There are already indications that the sharp cutbacks in capacity and market position restructuring among the majors have led to a decline in price competition, as capacity is now more in line with demand (*Wall Street Journal*, August 8, 1981). Hence it is possible that, once the dust settles, the industry will emerge as a more concentrated and tightly-knit international oligopoly, with 'orderly' pricing and higher profitability as vehicle and tire demand enter into the next cyclical upturn.

The experience of this industry indicates that neither neoclassical price theory nor Galbraithian type analyses of corporate power fully capture the essence of oligopolistic rivalry. Competition in the neoclassical model is a serene affair with everyone a price-taker facing fixed conditions as the market establishes equilibrium. This is far removed from the competitive struggle between producers as it actually occurs in industries like tires. For Galbraith planning supersedes the market and price competition all but disappears with the growth of the modern corporation (Galbraith 1967). Although much closer to reality than the neoclassical model, this fails to recognize that, however great the power of large corporations over individual markets, the anarchy of the market in general always eventually imposes itself and, certainly in the case of tires, periods of recession, slack demand, and excess capacity can result in quite fierce price competition.[19] Nevertheless, such periods do not usher in workable competition a la Vernon, but rather lay the basis for a reorganized and perhaps more concentrated oligopoly in the future.

Turning to the impact of transnational expansion on Latin American development, it should first of all be said that the early and widespread establishment of tire manufacturing facilities, coupled with the fact that unit costs in less than optimal scale plants are not in general excessive, signifies that foreign investment has in all probability played a positive role in terms of industrial growth. However, it is equally clear that the tire transnationals are locked into a process of uneven development and a system of mass transportation biased towards the private automobile for the few, in which a skewed income distribution is required to bolster demand for cars and their components. Furthermore, in recent years Latin America and other developing countries have made an increasingly important contribution to the global sales and profits of the tire transnationals, so that any change in development strategy or economic policy affecting profit opportunities is more than ever inimical to their interests. Given this increasing involvement in a process of growth which benefits only a small part of the population, the multinationals cannot be regarded as passively accepting the development strategies adopted by developing countries. On the contrary, as major actors in the leading sectors of capital accumulation, they play a fundamental role in the determination of the path of development followed.

Mutual forbearance in the form of a generally low degree of oligopolistic reaction in foreign investment, and collusion in the form of production off-take agreements, have meant that there has not normally been an excessive and costly duplication of production facilities in the Latin American tire industry, especially in contrast with sectors like autos. But it has also led to very high levels of concentration, boosting the market power and profitability of the transnationals operating in the region.

Although the tire multinationals have contributed to local technical skills in terms of quality control activities, their contribution to technological development through R&D activity, even for minor adaptations of imported technology, has generally been scant. A situation of technological dependence has thus been maintained implying, among other things, a continuing flow of surplus abroad in the form of royalties and technical assistance fees.

Finally, as concerns transnationals, the state, and bargaining, the increased rivalry among major firms characterizing the present period of oligopolistic instability, together with the growing importance of developing country markets, provide host governments with greater opportunities for securing more favorable terms in their negotiations with the transnationals. One indication of this is that various multinationals which previously required majority ownership of overseas affiliates, such as Dunlop and Firestone, are now willing to accept minority stakes.

It might be argued that if less developed countries want modern tire technology, they have no choice but to rely on the transnationals. There is of course some validity in this, but the case of FATE in Argentina demonstrates that there are alternatives. Despite the variety of special circumstances which aided the company, particularly in its early years, its experience suggests that even in this concentrated industry, marked by quite rapid technical change, it is possible for firms in developing countries to both keep abreast of innovations at the world level and develop their own technological capabilities. An important conclusion which arises from this analysis is that elements of the FATE strategy, perhaps in modified form, could advantageously be applied in other developing countries. But a word of caution should be added about who in the developing countries gains from this sort of policy. Though FATE's actions in Argentina have undoubtedly had social benefits in the shape of foreign exchange savings and greater technological development, it is also evident that given the present socio-economic structure of the country, the major beneficiaries have been the small group of local private investors which own and run the firm. These have seen their power and wealth increase as the company has grown to occupy an important position in the Argentinian tire industry. Thus although policies such as those pursued by FATE help to improve the international distribution of gains from transnational production, they do not in themselves do much to alter the process of uneven development within the developing countries.

Notes

[1] U.S. Rubber changed its name to Uniroyal in 1968.

[2] The major firms initially gained most of the business of the mass distributors, putting smaller companies at a disadvantage. Paradoxically, over the longer term their entry was to erode the market power of the majors, as will be seen below.

[3] This provides a good example of the relationship between national and international concentration, and the necessity of taking account of both when analysing industries dominated by multinational enterprises. For further discussion see West 1983.

[4] In addition, the Japanese company Bridgestone opened plants in Singapore, Thailand, Indonesia, and Iran.

[5] By 1979 Michelin's market share had risen to 5 percent. *The Economist*, 3.11.79.

[6] Both Uniroyal and Goodrich have been mentioned as possibilities in this respect.

[7] Indeed, entries have been limited to two cases: General Tire which rose to prominence in the 1930s, but it still very minor in terms of tire sales in relation to the other multinationals; and Bridgestone of Japan, which grew rapidly in the post-war period.

[8] In1975 Goodyear's internally-financed R & D outlay was the 25th largest for all U.S. industrial corporations.

[9] In a study of 41 consumer goods industries in the U.S. in 1958, tires ranked 4th in terms of concentration but 25th according to the advertising sales ratio (L. G. Telser, "Advertising and Competition", *Journal of Political Economy*, December 1964).

[10] The steel belted radial was innovated by Michelin in 1948 and the textile belted radial was introduced by Pirellin in 1959.

[11] General and Goodrich, neither of which had established a strong presence in the European market, had either closed down or sold all their European plants by 1976 and 1977 respectively. The most dramatic withdrawal was that of Uniroyal, which in 1979 sold its entire European tire business, consisting of plants in the U.K., West Germany, France, and Belgium, to the largest West German tire firm, Continental. Meanwhile, the two U.S. majors, Goodyear and Firestone, have been rationalizing their European operations to deal with the situation, and this has involved plant closures, particularly in the case of Firestone.

[12] The rated mileage for a radial is around 40,000 miles, compared with 30,000 for a bias-belted tire and 23,000 for a conventional bias-ply tire (Blank 1979).

[13] Some tire firms are now highly diversified producers, and this raises the question of how accurately the total figures represent the geographical distribution of tire operations. For Goodyear, Firestone, and Michelin this is not a major problem, as tires still account for a high proportion of total sales and profits. For Goodrich and Uniroyal fragmentary additional information suggests that the proportion of tire sales abroad is not all that different to that of total sales. On the other hand, the percentage of Dunlop's tire sales overseas is greater than that for total sales, and the same would also seem to be true of General Tire.

[14] The four tire manufacturing firms in Cuba, all affiliated to U.S. multinationals, were expropriated in 1960.

[15] The vehicle park increased from 47.0 thousand in 1920 to 411.4 thousand in 1929, and tire imports rose from 1.3 to 7.0 million kilos between 1921 and 1929.

[16] Importation of second-hand machinery has declined in recent years because of government legislation against its use, and due to the switchover to radial tires, which require spcialized machinery.

[17] The Pirelli subsidiary in Brazil has recently become an important exception to this general role, as it has established a R & D unit which is contributing on an increasing scale to Pirelli's global research in the tire field.

[18] In the U.S., for example, the number of tire plants fell from 722 in 1975 to 69 in 1977 and only 54 in 1980, while employment in the industry dropped from 114 to 84 thousand between 1977 and 1980.

[19] Following the sale of its entire European operations, Uniroyal's decisions to close two of its five U.S. tire plants was described as a 'last ditch effort to save the company's ailing tire business' (*Business Week*, 11.2.80). It is reported that General Tire might try to merge its tire business with that of another producer. Dunlop's recent decision to sell off most of its European operations, including those in its home market, to Sumitomo of Japan raises the question of how much longer it will be a significant force in the world tire industry.

[20] This of course does not mean that the industry price level falls, or stops increasing in such periods, as this overall price is to a large degree determined by prime costs. Hence,

257

both in 1979 and 1980 the U.S. producer price index for tires rose by 15 percent primarily due to increases in raw material costs. price competition principally affects the mark-up over prime cost, and is reflected in the inability of producers to fully pass on cost increases.

Gary Gereffi

8.

The Global Pharmaceutical Industry and its Impact in Latin America

INTRODUCTION*

Health is a basic human need. Because pharmaceutical products directly affect the health of a nation, they have greater social relevance than the products of almost any other industry. As a result the pharmaceutical industry in all countries has tended to operate in a highly politicized environment subject to an exceptional degree of government scrutiny and control. At a minimum most countries have enacted and enforced legislation setting high standards for drug purity, safety, and efficacy. Many governments also seek to foster the development of pharmaceutical production within their national frontiers in the hope of increasing their self-sufficiency in the supply of essential pharmaceutical products, decreasing the cost of drugs, and promoting the various benefits associated with industrial growth. At the global level the pharmaceutical industry is dominated by a relatively small number of large transnational corporations which have vigorously resisted the expanding range of national demands being placed upon them by developed and less developed countries alike because national priorities and the profit-oriented goals of transnational drug firms are often at odds. Most frequently at issue are divergent and deeply held concerns about drug prices, product selection, and local control.

* The author would like to thank Princeton University Press for permission to use material from sections of his book, *The Pharmaceutical Industry and Dependency in the Third World* (1983). Karin Peedo of Duke University provided valuable research assistance in preparing the final draft of this paper.

259

This chapter focuses on the relationship between pharmaceutical TNCs and Third World nations with a particular emphasis on Latin America in an effort to identify the nature of these conflicts and to indicate the types of accommodations being reached at the national and international levels. Attention is also given to the roles played by local private companies and state-owned firms in the pharmaceutical industry since they, like the TNCs, shape the path of development being followed in each society. Both advanced and less developed countries share some areas of common concern toward drug manufacturers such as assuring product safety and efficacy. Nonetheless this paper argues that the health needs and economic capabilities of industrialized and Third World nations are clearly different and hence varied types of national policies toward pharmaceutical TNCs are called for.

THE INTERNATIONALIZATION OF THE PHARMACEUTICAL INDUSTRY

The modern pharmaceutical industry emerged with the wave of new wonder drugs that were discovered after World War II. In the 1930s it was a commodity business in which major companies manufactured and sold a complete array of all the ingredients the pharmacist needed to compound the doctor's prescriptions. Advertising was done in newspapers and popular magazines, therapeutic advance was slow, and drug companies hardly engaged in research (Clymer 1975, p. 138). By the end of the 1950s the pharmaceutical industry had transformed itself into a research- and advertising-intensive business. Drug firms had grown rapidly and they concentrated on specialty (as opposed to commodity) products whose value could be protected by patents and heavily promoted brand names. The vertically integrated company that combined drug discovery, production, and marketing functions in a single corporate network came to dominate the industry. As government regulations created a class of drugs that could not legally be sold without a prescription, advertising was directed more and more at the medical profession (Temin 1979a and 1979b).

The announcement of the first sulfa drug (sulfanilamide) in 1935 marked the advent of the age of wonder drugs. A family of sulfa drugs (sulfonamides) was soon developed, representing the first effective cure for a variety of bacterial diseases that included pneumonia, scarlet fever, and streptococcal infections among others. The nature of the therapeutic revolution heralded by the sulfa drugs was not appreciated, however, until penicillin was introduced in large quantities during World War II. What set both penicillin and the sulfa drugs apart from all previous discoveries was their mode of therapeutic action. They established with certainty what Paul Ehrlich, the father of modern chemotherapy, had prognosticated at the turn of the century: that man-made drugs could destroy target germs without harming the living host. Whereas previous drug therapy was passive in that it relied on vaccines and antitoxins to help the body build up its natural defenses against disease, Ehrlich's so-called "active therapy" led scientists to try to improve upon man's innate arsenal. In the anti-infectives field sulfa drugs and penicillins were followed by broad-spectrum antibiotics such as the tetracyclines and more recently the cephalosporins which are effective against a much wider range of organisms than penicillin. In the 1950s drugs opening up totally new areas of therapy were discovered: steroids, tranquilizers, oral contraceptives, oral antidiabetic drugs, cardiovascular drugs, etc. The product profile of the pharmaceutical industry thus began to assume its modern form.

Cartels

Prior to and during World War II U.S. and European companies participated in pharmaceutical cartels that regulated the international manufacture and trade of drug products on the basis of patents, technological processes, and trademarks. The specific drugs that were the object of these cartel agreements included aspirin, hormones, vitamins, and a series of medicinal raw materials such as coal tar, quinine, iodine, cocaine, and opium. By 1930 one German firm, I. G. Farben, had become the largest industrial corporation in Europe and the largest chemical company in the world controlling the entire German production of dyes, nearly all the explosives, 90 percent of mineral acids, 65 to 85 percent of synthetic nitrogens, 40 percent of pharmaceuticals, and 30 percent of rayon (Stocking and Watkins 1947, pp. 411-414; Borkin 1978).

In the area of pharmaceutical marketing, I. G. Farben and the Sterling Products Company of the United States signed contracts that effectively designated to the German concern the exclusive rights to manufacture drugs destined for South and Central America and Mexico. With respect to the use of trademarks the famous "Bayer Cross" was the object of a dispute between the Friedrich Bayer Company of Germany and Sterling Products, which at the close of World War I had purchased Bayer's New York interests from the U.S. Alien Property Custodian. Faced with the prospect of prolonged litigation over the rights and titles to this trademark, Bayer and Sterling agreed

261

to pool profits from sales made by either party in South or Central America. In another illustrative case a pact of this type was made between E. Merck of Germany and Merck and Company, the largest manufacturer of pharmaceuticals in the United States. It was decided that between them the two enterprises would allocate the markets in which the trademark "Merck" might be used exclusively: Merck and Company was to have the United States, its dependencies, and Canada, while E. Merck was to have the rest of the world except for Cuba, the Philippines, and the West Indies, where they were to sell jointly. This trademark was to be applied to some four hundred pharmaceutical products in addition to processes specified in the agreement (Hexner 1946, pp. 332-334).

In the post-World War II era pharmaceutical cartels lost their importance. One explanation for this was the disbanding of I. G. Farben after the war and the public sale by the U.S. Alien Property Custodian of many highly valuable German-owned patents that had been confiscated during the war as enemy properties. Probably the main factor, however, was the extremely rapid rate of technological change in the industry. Many of the drugs previously regulated by cartels were essentially commodity items. Once the wonder drugs appeared the technological basis of pharmaceutical production changed rapidly and stable cartel arrangements became well-nigh impossible to maintain. Moreover, during the 1950s and 1960s the United States was the leading source of pharmaceutical innovation and U.S. antitrust laws made cartels a particularly perilous step for American companies to undertake. Finally, pharmaceutical enterprises have been able to utilize other barriers to entry that, like cartels, serve the purpose of effectively protecting them from certain kinds of competition. These barriers to entry include patents, product differentiation techniques, economies of scale, and the government regulatory process that often makes the testing and approval of new drugs prohibitively expensive for smaller companies.

As the major drug firms grew in size in the postwar period they also became increasingly transnational in organization. Sales, production, and especially research were carried out by affiliates located in countries other than that in which the parent was domiciled as the cost of drug development increased and government regulation became more stringent. The trend toward transnationalization came first and is most pronounced in European companies, but U.S.-based drug companies are also highly transnational, with overseas sales representing 40 percent of their global sales of ethical (prescription) pharmaceuticals in 1977 (PMA 1978, p. 3). Profits on foreign sales have been estimated at over 50 percent of the total profits of U.S. drug manufacturers (*Business Week* 1974, p. 73). Japanese pharmaceutical companies, traditionally closely tied to their large national market, also have turned increasingly to transnational activities during the past fifteen years. By the 1970s the world's largest drug firms were all transnational corporations.

World Patterns in Production and Consumption

Worldwide production of pharmaceuticals, estimated at $84 billion in 1980, is concentrated in the developed market economies that account for nearly 70 percent of the industry's total output. The centrally planned economies (the Soviet Union, Eastern Europe, and China) follow with 19 percent, while the developing countries produced just over 11 percent. A closer look reveals that relatively few nations control the bulk of global pharmaceutical production. The three largest drug manufacturing countries—the United States, Japan, and the Federal Republic of Germany—together represent one-half of the world's total output. Over two-thirds of the pharmaceuticals manufactured in the developing world come from a half-dozen nations: India, Brazil, Mexico, Argentina, Egypt, and the Republic of Korea (UNIDO 1980; UNCTC 1981, p. 4).

Pharmaceutical consumption is also highly uneven. The developing countries, where nearly two-thirds of the world's population lives, consumed only 14 percent of world production in 1980. The developed market economies accounted for 70 percent of world consumption and the centrally planned economies for the remaining 14 percent (*SCRIP* July 28, 1980). Within each of the developing regions pharmaceutical consumption is overwhelmingly concentrated in a few nations: Japan consumes 70 percent of the drugs available in Asia; Egypt and Nigeria account for 50 percent of total drug consumption in Africa; and Brazil consumes 36 percent of the pharmaceuticals used in Latin America (Reekie and Weber 1979, p. 29). The two largest national drug markets—the United States and Japan—made up 21 percent and 14 percent respectively of world pharmaceutical sales in 1981, while the combined share of the top four West European markets was just over 19 percent (IMS Pharmaceutical MARKETLETTER January 4, 1982, p. 2).

Globally there are more than 10,000 companies that could be called pharmaceutical manufacturers. Only about 100 of these are major participants in the international market. These firms supply about 90 percent of total world shipments of pharmaceutical products for human use with the top 50 drug companies representing nearly two-thirds of this total (Schaumann 1976, pp. 16-17; Agarwal 1978, p.

6). United States-based corporations are clearly dominant, accounting for just under 50 percent of the sales of the top 50 drug firms in 1977. The United States, the Federal Republic of Germany, and Switzerland are the base of operations for 33 of the 50 largest drug enterprises (23 from the United States, seven from the Federal Republic of Germany, and three from Switzerland). Together they make up almost 80 percent of the pharmaceutical sales of the top 50 companies (UNCTC 1979, p. 112). In 1980 this pattern continues to be evident for the world's 15 largest pharmaceutical firms. The top 13 companies are all American, West German, or Swiss; 7 are from the United States while the Federal Republic of Germany and Switzerland are each represented by 3 major pharmaceutical enterprises (see table 8.1).

The world's 50 largest pharmaceutical companies are all transnational corporations; they sell their products in foreign markets, and usually engage in manufacturing and research and development activities abroad as well. The European drug firms are the most internationalized in terms of foreign sales. Almost all of the principal European companies carry out over 50 percent of their pharmaceutical sales outside their respective home markets, with each of the three Swiss transnationals realizing more than 90 percent of their drug sales abroad. The major U.S.-based pharmaceutical firms sell between one-third and one-half of their output overseas, satisfying the huge demand in their domestic market first. Japanese drug companies are the least internationalized with foreign markets accounting for no more than 7 percent of their total pharmaceuticals (UNCTC 1979, p. 113).

A fuller understanding of the internationalization of the pharmaceutical industry can be gained by looking at when and where TNCs have gone abroad. Before 1950 the 25 largest U.S. pharmaceutical companies had established just 28 foreign subsidiaries, the vast majority of which were located in a few geographically or culturally proximate countries: Canada, Great Britain (including the Commonwealth countries), and Mexico. During the 1950s and 1960s the pace of U.S. expansion picked up sharply, with 152 and 181 pharmaceutical subsidiaries formed in these decades respectively. In the 1950s the outward thrust was primarily directed at Western Europe, the Commonwealth countries, and the relatively advanced nations in Latin America (Mexico, Brazil, and Argentina) whereas in the 1960s interest was concentrated in Africa, Asia, the Middle East, and the lesser developed countries of Latin America and Europe (Katz 1981, p. 62). A significant shift thus took place in the international pharmaceutical industry: local production, generally based on active ingredients imported from the TNC parent, was beginning to substitute for at least some of the direct importation of finished pharmaceutical products in a wide variety of host countries.

264

Table 8.1

The World's 15 Largest Pharmaceutical Companies, 1980

Company	Country of Origin	Pharmaceutical Sales[a] (US$ millions)	Profit (US$ millions)	Profit Margin (percentage)	R & D (US$ millions)	R&D as percentage of sales
1. Hoechst	FRG	2,413	NA	NA	660	4.4
2. Merck and Co.	USA	2,287[b]	607[g]	26.6	234	8.6
3. American Home Products	USA	2,193[c]	603[g]	27.5	102	2.5
4. Bayer	FRG	2,182	NA	NA	630	4.3
5. Warner-Lambert	USA	1,926[d]	271[g]	14.1	72	6.2
6. Bristol-Myers	USA	1,905[c]	379[g]	19.9	129	6.8
7. Ciba-Geigy	SWI	1,805	NA	NA	217	12.0
8. Pfizer	USA	1,664[d]	388[g]	23.6	160	5.3
9. Roche-Sapac	SWI	1,461	130[h]	3.0	389	11.8
10. Eli Lilly	USA	1,426[e]	330[g]	23.2	201	7.8
11. SmithKline	USA	1,376[b]	468[i]	30.1	136	7.7
12. Sandoz	SWI	1,339	114[h]	4.1	170	12.7
13. Boehringer-Ingelheim	FRG	1,267	27[h]	3.5	139	11.0
14. Rhone-Poulenc	FRA	1,255[b]	126[g]	9.9	302	4.5
15. Glaxo	UK	1,214[f]	194[j]	16.0	106	8.8

Source: IMS Pharmaceutical MARKETLETTER, January 11, 1982, p. 4.

a   Sales figures are for human pharmaceutical preparations unless otherwise indicated.
b   Human and animal health.
c   Prescription and packaged medicines.
d   Health care.
e   Human health.
f   Includes food products.
g   Pre-tax segment of operating income.
h   Corporate net profit.
i   Operating income, health care.
j   Trading profit.
NA   Not available.

THE STRUCTURE OF THE PHARMACEUTICAL INDUSTRY

The structure of the pharmaceutical industry refers to such characteristics as seller concentration, barriers to the entry of new firms, the conditions of demand, and buyer concentration (UNCTC 1979, chapter 4). Seller concentration is probably the most commonly mentioned element of market structure because it is closely linked to entry barriers for new firms and to the nature of competition among the leading companies. Generally the higher the degree of concentration (measured by the share of sales accounted for by a small number, usually four to eight, of the largest sellers), the more difficult it is for new firms to successfully enter the market. Furthermore, in concentrated markets with only a few large sellers of a product each company is often reluctant to provoke retaliation by cutting prices. Consequently, large firms tend to eschew price rivalry and turn instead to two other competitive strategies: promotional rivalry based on high advertising expenditures and various product differentiation techniques, and product rivalry based on high R & D expenditures to create new drugs that are in some way different or better than those previously used.

In sales of finished pharmaceuticals the average four-firm concentration ratio for the drug industry in developed countries is 25 to 30 percent, with the figure for developing nations being somewhat higher (Burstall, Dunning and Lake 1981, p. 59; Grabowski and Vernon 1976, p. 195). This degree of concentration is lower than that found in other high-technology industries such as automobiles, aircraft, computers, and chemicals. Overall indicators of concentration are deceptive, however, because the drug industry in fact is fragmented into a number of separate therapeutic markets, and within these markets, concentration levels are quite high. The four-firm concentration ratios for nine major therapeutic categories in the United States in 1973 ranged from a low of 61 percent in sedatives to 96 percent for antiarthritic drugs and 98 percent for antidiabetic drugs (Schwartzman 1976, p. 131). Sales concentration among companies usually reflects a similar concentration among the leading drugs in a given field. In all of the nine U.S. therapeutic markets but one (antibiotics), the five top brand named products contribute over 50 percent of total sales (Schwartzman 1976, p. 129).

The evidence for seller concentration is even more striking in the manufacture of bulk drugs. Of the 550 bulk medicinal chemicals produced in the United States in 1981, only 6 were manufactured by more than three companies while nearly 430 were available from a single domestic source (United States International Trade Commis-

266

sion 1982, pp. 105-122). A recent study prepared by UNIDO on sources of supply for 26 essential bulk drugs, their chemical intermediates, and some raw materials indicates the further back in the production chain one goes, the greater the likelihood of exceedingly high levels of seller concentration. While several of the essential pharmaceuticals were manufactured by only a few companies at the global level, e.g., reserpine and primaquine are produced by just four companies each, a more common pattern shows many manufacturers of the finished drug with only a few producers of the required chemical intermediates or raw materials. Forty-seven companies make tetracycline, for example, but the chemical intermediates used in tetracycline come from just five firms in the world. Overall, 10 of the 26 essential drugs listed in the UNIDO study are manufactured by 6 or fewer firms worldwide at one or more stages in their production process (UNIDO 1982).

The conditions of consumer demand in the pharmaceutical industry shape the ways in which market concentration affects industry performance. The pharmaceutical industry is composed of two distinct sectors: the proprietary drug sector and the ethical drug sector. Proprietary drugs are advertised directly to the consuming public and do not require a prescription so the consumer makes the buying decision for this class of medicines. Ethical drugs require a doctor's prescription and the buying decision in the developed countries is made for the consumer by a doctor. The pharmacist fills the prescription exactly as it is written. In the aphorism made famous by the late U.S. Senator Estes Kefauver, "He who orders (the doctor) does not pay; he who pays does not order." From the consumer's point of view, the main criticism made of this situation is that doctors tend to be insensitive to price differences between substitutable drugs.

The situation is different in most of the Third World where, although a doctor's prescription may be legally required, patients commonly and openly obtain drugs directly from a pharmacist without a prescription. In essence a system of self-medication flourishes not only in the large urban drug supermarkets but also in rural areas and small villages where there may be few or even no health professionals available. Frequently the poorest segments of the population rely on the advice of pharmacists, relatives, and friends, or the directions given in the package leaflets on how to take the drug and what danger signs to watch for. Under these circumstances the information that pharmaceutical companies release in package inserts or labeling material becomes especially important in determining the situations in which a prescription drug should be used because this information often reaches people with little or no medical knowledge against

267

which to evaluate promotional claims. The phenomenon of self-medication in developing countries has little or no effect on the pricing policies of pharmaceutical firms. The intermediary role of doctors is simply replaced by that of pharmacists who become the primary target of the industry's promotional activities. Price insensitivity thus remains an important problem.

THE CONDUCT OF TRANSNATIONAL DRUG FIRMS

Notwithstanding the high degree of concentration in therapeutic markets, rivalry in the pharmaceutical industry does exist and it is often intense. The exact nature of the competition differs from one therapeutic market to another—ranging from product rivalry to promotional rivalry to price rivalry, or combinations thereof—depending upon such characteristics as the state of technology, the existence of patents, the hold of brand names, and the role of government policy. In general, though, competition in pharmaceuticals is based on the development of new products and on promotion.

Product Rivalry

As mentioned previously, the 1950s and early 1960s were a golden age of discovery in the pharmaceutical industry. Research and development productivity in the industry in the United States and elsewhere, however, dropped sharply during the next decade declining by about sixfold between 1960 and 1970 (Grabowski, Vernon, and Thomas 1976, pp. 64-65, 77). One explanation for the decline in new drug discovery is that the underlying stock of research opportunities was depleted by the rapid rate of innovation that occurred in the first part of the post-World War II era (Grabowski 1976, pp. 19-24; Schnee and Caglarcan 1976, p. 33; Cohen, Katz, and Beck 1975, pp. 18-26). In addition, stringent regulatory controls for drugs in the United States—in particular the 1962 Kefauver-Harris Amendments—contributed to the decline in innovational output (Peltzman 1974). At the end of the 1970s the situation reversed when a number of revolutionary drug products were introduced onto the market by pharmaceutical manufacturers, leading many to claim the industry was on the threshold of a new "golden age of research productivity" (*Business Week* 1979; *Dun's Review* 1979; *Newsweek* 1979a and 1979b).

What is significant about these recent drug products is that they seem to reflect new knowledge about how the body functions, how disease is caused, and what chemicals interfere with physiological processes. Perhaps the most revolutionary characteristic of many of them is that, instead of simply treating symptoms, they have a direct effect on the causes of disease. Equipped with a better understanding about the body's immune-response system and about such natural substances as interferon, beta blockers, and prostaglandins, researchers have been able to concoct precise pharmaceutical agents to stop the body from overproducing damaging substances. Closely linked to their revolutionary mode of therapeutic action is a profound change in the strategy used to develop these new drugs. Instead of screening thousands of compounds randomly to discover pharmaceutical products that have significant medical activity and are safe, researchers specify in advance the characteristics desired in a new drug. This is fundamentally a biological approach, since the molecules of the chemical compound are designed, atom by atom, to alter a pretargeted physiological process in the body. Now the job of the chemists is to create compounds with the emphasis on effect rather than chemical structure, which is the reverse of the traditional process.

While the pharmaceutical industry may be on the threshold of a second "golden age" in drug discovery, the commercial benefits of these scientific advances are likely to remain highly concentrated. Merck and Company, the biggest U.S. pharmaceutical firm, increased its sales by 15 percent and its net income by 11 percent in 1978 largely on the basis of five new drugs it marketed in that year. Yet Merck also spent about $750 million during a recent ten-year period without producing a single important drug for the market (*Business Week* 1979). Those enterprises that are lagging behind in the new products race face bleak economic prospects in the industry's innovative track.

The world's 15 largest pharmaceutical companies in 1980 were all research-intensive operations. Only one firm of the 15 spent less than $100 million on R & D and several companies spent more money on new product development than they earned in profits (see table 8.1). Another important indicator of research productivity among drug firms is the number of new products launched. The two most successful pharmaceutical companies in this regard in 1980 were Schering-Plough and Johnson and Johnson, with 48 and 46 new product launches respectively (IMS Pharmaceutical MARKETLETTER June 8, 1981, p. 8).

Promotional Rivalry

Product rivalry and promotional rivalry in the pharmaceutical industry are closely linked by the workings of patent and brand name systems. When a new product is developed by a drug manufacturer, it is normally patented and given a trademarked brand name. The assigned function of a patent is to stimulate inventive activity by impeding the imitation of a new product during a period of legally sanctioned monopoly (e.g., seventeen years in the United States, sixteen in the United Kingdom, and seven in India), thereby allowing the innovating firm the opportunity to recoup or more than recoup its investment. Often the patent system is only partially successful in forestalling competitors, however. Patents do not preclude the development of "me-too" drugs that achieve similar therapeutic ends by means of minor chemical modifications. Furthermore a patented product can be licensed to other manufacturers, which minimizes the competitive barrier of the patent itself.

In these situations, the product brand name system serves as a critical complement to the patent system. A brand name may be effective where a patent is not, e.g., for products that cannot be patented, that are freely licensed, or for which the patent has expired. The brand system is the foundation of the drug industry's extensive promotional activity, just as the patent system is the cornerstone of its intense research activity. In addition to providing doctors with essential scientific information about a wide variety of new products, drug promotion programs aim to gain and maintain market dominance for products through the creation of strong and lasting brand name preferences among prescribing physicians and the consuming public alike. In their positive effects for the drug industry the brand name and patent systems thus are similar: they both insulate the major drug companies from price competition.

The brand name system produces a bewildering array of different names for the same drug. For the 700 active ingredients available in the United States, there exist an estimated 20,000 names (Brooke 1975, p. 19)—an average of 30 names for each drug product. The situation is similar in other nations (UNCTAD 1977, pp. 50-51). Since there are too many drugs to permit a systematic evaluation of quality and price alternatives, doctors probably find it rational to learn about and work with only a few well promoted brands. This makes it more difficult for true price competition to take place among pharmaceuticals.

Price Rivalry

Although some form of governmental price control for drugs exists in most countries (UNCTC 1979, pp. 139-141), it generally has been ineffective because of the patent and brand name systems. To the extent that price rivalry among pharmaceuticals does exist it is most prevalent among multiple-source drugs sold by more than one company, i.e., unpatented generic products and patented items that have been widely licensed.

The potential for price competition is high, though, because generic drugs are a large and rapidly growing part of the pharmaceutical industry. Drug prescriptions written in the United States only using generic names have risen steadily from 6 percent in 1966 to 12.4 percent in 1977. Overall sales of generic drugs in the United States, which includes prescriptions for multiple source pharmaceuticals and generic drugs sold to institutions, amount to about 40 percent of the total sales of multisource ethical pharmaceutical products (UNCTC 1979, pp. 80-81). The principal causes for the expansion of the generic sector of the drug industry are: (1) the increasing insistence of developed and developing country governments alike that generic prescribing and procurement policies be used as a tool for cost containment, if not cost reduction, in pharmaceutical spending; and (2) the rapid rate at which drug patents have expired since the 1960s. Pharmaceutical products no longer under patent protection represented about 45 percent of the total volume of United States ethical drug sales in the late 1970s (*Business Week* 1979, p. 145). By 1989 new patent expiries will have occurred for drugs whose 1979 sales stood at $2.2 billion (ALIFAR 1982b, p. 21).

The generic drug market has two distinct segments: commodity generics and branded generics. The former includes all products sold under their generic name only; no brand name is used nor is the manufacturer's name linked to the name of the product. The latter includes unpatented pharmaceuticals that are marketed under product brand names or labeled with the company's trade name rather than a specific product brand name such as Pfizer's erythromycin called "Pfizer-E". The two segments contrast sharply in terms of size, the type of enterprises participating in each, and the nature of their clients. In the United States branded generics accounted for 93 percent and commodity generics for only 7 percent of generic drug sales totaling $4.4 billion in 1979. While the 500 to 600 firms that make commodity-generic pharmaceuticals are usually small with limited resources and narrow profit margins, four transnational pharmaceutical enterprises—Eli Lilly, American Home Products, Warner-Lambert, and SmithKline—dominate the market with 42 percent of total sales (ALIFAR 1982b, p. 20). Large transnational drug companies also permeate the branded-generic market and promote these products in the same way they market their patented items. The leaders in the United States in 1979 were G. D. Searle ($200 million),

271

Eli Lilly ($170 million), and a Hoffmann-La Roche subsidiary named Roche Laboratories ($160 million) (*SCRIP* August 25, 1980, p. 8). The final contrast relates to clients. Pharmacies, private hospitals, physicians, and the government are all major buyers of commodity generics. The pharmacy is the only significant customer for branded generics, however, accounting for nearly nine-tenths of manufacturers' sales of these products. Usually branded generics are sold at higher prices than non-branded commodity versions of the same drug.

A two-tier operating structure appears to be emerging in the pharmaceutical industry, made up of suppliers of new drugs (product innovators) and broad-line generic suppliers. The former is the province of a select number of research-oriented companies that spend large sums on new drug development primarily for developed country markets, and include the American firms Merck and Company, Eli Lilly, Upjohn, SmithKline, American Home Products, and Pfizer, and European pharmaceutical companies such as Hoffmann-La Roche, Ciba-Geigy, Hoechst-Roussel, Burroughs-Wellcome, and Bayer. The second category of producers will compete mainly on the basis of price in the generic drug market, thus appealing to the cost-conscious sectors in both developed and developing countries. These firms tend to concentrate on over-the-counter products. The largest drug enterprises like Eli Lilly, Hoffmann-La Roche, Ciba-Geigy, and SmithKline probably will operate in both the innovative and generic (particularly branded-generic) tiers of the pharmaceutical market. Some medium-sized companies might opt for a specialty profile, but faced with soaring research costs most of the smaller firms will have little choice but to concentrate on generic supply if they remain in the industry. The large branded segment of the generic market gives the transnational drug companies a distinct edge over small national competitors, especially in developing countries, because the former can use their brand name image as a major source of market power. Thus even in what is potentially the most competitive segment of the pharmaceutical industry in terms of price, transnational firms are becoming the dominant force and national producers seem to be losing out.

THE PERFORMANCE OF PHARMACEUTICAL TNCs

The pharmaceutical industry is one of the most profitable in the world. In the United States and the United Kingdom in the latter part of the 1960s, the industry as a whole earned 21 percent and 26 percent, respectively, on capital employed as compared with 13 percent for all manufacturing in both countries. The larger firms are considerably more profitable than these average figures would indicate. The two leading British companies in 1972, for example, earned 45 percent (Boots) and 41 percent (Beecham) on capital employed. Among the top 100 British firms only one, Rank Xerox, was more profitable that year. Similarly, American drug enterprises frequently earned over 40 percent and even 50 percent profits as a percentage of net worth. The profit rates of pharmaceutical TNCs in the Third World are often higher than in developed countries. Declared profits on capital employed for several TNC subsidiaries operating in Egypt in 1967 came to 115 percent for Hoechst, 53 percent for Pfizer, and 52 percent for a Swiss consortium made up of Ciba, Sandoz, and Wander. In India 33 foreign-controlled drug companies earned 30 percent on capital employed in 1970 as compared to 8 percent for almost 2,000 Indian manufacturing firms (Lall 1975, p. 28; Silverman and Lee 1974, p. 331).

The persistence over an extended period of time of high profit rates for the pharmaceutical industry is a direct consequence of its favorable institutional context. High barriers to the entry of new competitors created by patents and trademarked brand names, substantial seller concentration in therapeutic markets, the captive nature of the consumer, and the traditional price insensitivity of doctors are all grounds to expect that the rate of return in pharmaceuticals (even after accounting adjustments) will be considerably above the manufacturing average. Profitability measures are not sufficient for judging TNC appropriateness, however. The real appropriateness issues for Third World countries center around more detailed manifestations of TNC performance. Are their drug prices fair? Are their products and technologies the ones most in need? Are their marketing practices informative and consistent? Each of these questions will be examined in turn.

Appropriate Prices

Finished drug prices vary considerably from country to country. Because American and Canadian prices for prescription products tend to be the highest in the world while prices in many Third World countries are relatively low, it is sometimes argued that drug prices are likely to be less in the lower-income countries. This does not explain why Bristol's Polycillin was priced at $41.95 in Brazil and $21.84 in the United States or why Ciba's Serpasil was priced at $3.00 in Mexico and less than $1.25 in Switzerland and the Federal Republic of Germany (Silverman and Lee 1974, p. 179). Among the factors that might affect the price of pharmaceuticals in different nations are market size, currency problems, different wage scales, taxes, cost of raw materials, living costs, allocation of research costs, and government regulations. Generally, drug prices in different countries tend to be set at the highest level the traffic will bear.

Whereas international differences in finished drug prices are a feature of the pharmaceutical industry as a whole, the differential pricing of drug intermediates is a problem specifically related to the behavior of TNCs. This practice is known as transfer pricing. Transfer prices are those prices set for intrafirm sales between TNC affiliates located in different countries. When these intrafirm prices are higher than the arm's-length price used in selling to unrelated concerns, the goods in question are overpriced and extra funds are transferred via the pricing channel from the buying to the selling units. Conversely, underpricing transfers additional funds from the seller to the buyer within a single company's transnational network. Whereas this procedure does not directly affect the level of profits made by the TNC, it does affect where and how these profits are to be declared.

Transfer pricing is more common and the gap between transfer and arm's-length prices is more egregious in the pharmaceutical industry than in any other. This is because of the large volume and highly specialized nature of the intermediates that account for most of the intrafirm trade in the industry (Lall 1979, p. 63). Although measures to keep transfer-pricing problems in check have been initiated by some developed countries, the practice is widespread and especially detrimental to the national interests of developing nations. The Colombian government, for example, estimated that the weighted average of overpricing for a wide range of pharmaceutical imports in the late 1960s was between 87 and 155 percent depending on the items and time period covered (Lall 1973, p. 186). One product, diazepam, the active ingredient for Valium, was imported into Colombia at a price that exceeded its lowest available price elsewhere by an astonishing 6,400 percent (Vaitsos 1974). A study in Argentina found the prices of drugs in eight submarkets to be 143 to 3,800 percent higher than the minimum import prices for these same products in the country (Krieger and Prieto 1977, p. 193). A parliamentary inquiry in Brazil found several instances of overpricing ranging from 500 to 1,000 percent of arm's-length prices (Ledogar 1975, p. 54). And in Mexico the average rate of overpricing for five steroid hormone imports in the mid-1970s varied from 214 percent to just under 2,900 percent (Gereffi 1983, pp. 148-149).

Although host country governments have usually assumed primary responsibility for keeping transfer-pricing problems in check, recent investigations indicate that the best monitors of transfer pricing may be the active involvement of indigenous entrepreneurs in local production. In India, for instance, evidence was found that foreign drug companies grossly misrepresented the cost of raw material imports and also the capital cost for manufacturing pharmaceuticals locally. When an indigenous enterprise prepared a feasibility plan for the production of a heart disease drug, its estimated cost for plant and equipment was $25,000 compared to the declared capital cost of $1.2 million by the only TNC making the product in India at that time. This TNC had been importing the basic raw material for this drug from its parent company at approximately $490 per kilogram, whereas the international price of the finished product was about $30 per kilogram (Deolalikar 1980, pp. 84-87).

Overall, the evidence indicates that TNCs have engaged in highly questionable pricing practices. The wide international price differences that have been mentioned are not necessarily related to countries' income levels, as one might expect, and transfer pricing by TNCs has systematically diverted pharmaceutical revenues from many Third World markets. TNC behavior has definitely raised drug prices in Third World societies well above what would be expected from arm's-length transactions among truly competitive firms in the world industry.

Appropriate Products and Technologies

The appropriateness of pharmaceutical products will be assessed according to two criteria: their effectiveness in reducing the mortality and morbidity rates in a nation, and the degree to which the distribution of pharmaceutical sales by therapeutic group matches the disease pattern in a country. Whereas the first criterion relates to the industry's efficacy, the second refers to social equity since it determines whether the industry supplies goods required by the majority of the population. Appropriate technology will be defined as technology that uses inputs (labor, capital, or raw materials) in the same proportion as they are found in the local economy.

Although new drugs have greatly increased the social and economic well-being of almost all nations, Third World nations differ from developed countries in their capacity to utilize new drugs in national health care and in the specific kinds of medicine most needed by their population (McDermott 1980). In Pakistan systemic antibiotics account for 25 percent of all drugs sold through retail pharmacies; the next most popular therapeutic class is vitamins with 13 percent of drugstore sales. Systemic antibiotics are also the most widely used class of drugs in the Philippines (19 percent of retail pharmacy sales), Brazil (14 percent), and Venezuela (14 percent). The next most popular therapeutic categories in each of these countries are vitamins and cough and cold preparations. In the United States, on the other hand, the leading therapeutic classes of drugs are psycholeptics (tranquilizers/sedatives) and analgesics (pain relievers). In the Federal Republic of Germany the two top drug categories are cardiac therapy and psycholeptics, followed by peripheral vasodilators used in controlling high blood pressure. Systemic antibiotics account for only 7 percent of drugstore sales in the United States and 4 percent in the Federal Republic of Germany. The disparities between developing and developed countries in types of drug consumption are even more striking when absolute figures are the basis of the comparison. All of Latin America together, for example, consumes a smaller quantity of antidiabetic drugs than Holland. India consumes only 0.1 percent as many antihypertensive drugs as are used in Belgium although both drug markets are of roughly equal size. The differences are sharper still when the industrialized countries are compared with Africa (Tiefenbacher 1979, pp. 213-214).

When these consumption figures are joined with data on disease patterns and the local production of drugs, it becomes clear that Third World countries are being offered a very inappropriate mix of products by the pharmaceutical industry. The case of India, which has the Third World's most sophisticated drug industry, affords a good illustration of the problem. The most prevalent diseases in India are filariasis, malaria, dysentery, leprosy, and tuberculosis. Pharmaceutical sales reveal a totally different set of priorities, however. Vitamins, cough and cold preparations, and tonics and health restorers account for nearly one-quarter of the total sales of pharmaceuticals in India. And not one of the 15 leading pharmaceutical products by sales in 1978 was used in the treatment of the three major diseases in India: filariasis, dysentery, and leprosy. Ten of the fifteen products were manufactured by subsidiaries of TNCs (Deolalikar 1980, pp. 64-65). Installed capacities for many important drugs in India are far below licensed capacities. The actual utilization of the installed capacity is still less: only 12 percent for antileprosy drugs, 14 percent for thiacetazone (an antituberculosis drug), and 50 percent for insulin. For non-essential items like tonics and vitamins, on the other hand, production in several Indian firms greatly exceeds (sometimes by a factor of ten) the licensed capacities (Agarwal 1978, p. 39).

Why do pharmaceutical firms fail to provide adequate production capacity for essential drugs demanded by a majority of the population in Third World nations? The principal explanation for this phenomenon relates to the highly unequal distribution of income in these countries. Because middle-income and rich consumers represent the main market for modern drugs, pharmaceutical companies concentrate on furnishing remedies for middle class ailments like general fatigue, headaches, and constipation rather than for low-income diseases like leprosy, filariasis, and tuberculosis (Deolalikar 1980, p. 67). Less than 5 percent of the overall R & D effort of the U.S. pharmaceutical industry, for example, is directed to the health problems of the Third World and the amount is growing smaller (Sarett 1979, pp. 134-136; Wescoe 1979). Moreover, research priorities of the TNCs, like those of developed country governments and foundations, are clearly oriented toward the major maladies of the industrialized societies: cancer, heart disease, mental illness, and neurological disorders. Another reason why drug companies do not cater to the needs of the poor may be because there are strict price controls on essential drugs in many nations that greatly reduce the profitability of these items. A final factor is cultural in nature. In an important sense modern medicine not only treats disease, it also "creates" it. Disease-creation as a cultural phenomenon refers to the ways in which medical institutions create more illness by redefining normal human experiences such as pain and anxiety as sickness. This "medicalization of life" has weakened individual autonomy and the capacity of people to "suffer their reality" (Illich 1976; Mendelsohn 1979; Renaud 1975). Third World nations have been encouraged to adopt western medical practices and diseases in large part through the promotional machinery of pharmaceutical TNCs that make and market the remedies. The overwhelming attention that the pharmaceutical industry has given to middle class ailments and specialized diseases of the rich supports the urban orientation common in Third World health services in which 80 percent of the national health expenditure goes for the needs of just 20 percent of the population (Agarwal 1978, p. 65).

With respect to technology the preference of pharmaceutical TNCs for wholly owned operations in the Third World with only a minimal amount of technology transfer and centralized R & D is well known. To use the example of India again, foreign-owned pharmaceutical firms are more capital-intensive and less labor-intensive than local firms (Deolalikar 1980). Since labor is more abundantly available than capital in the Indian economy, this pattern is in direct contrast to the country's relative factor endowments and TNCs can thus be regarded as socially inefficient in this context. Studies have also found that when foreign technology is transferred Indian companies are more likely to adapt and modify the technology for local use than TNCs are. These conclusions are supported by evidence from other Third World countries as well (UNCTC 1983).

Finally, TNCs often do not take advantage of the raw materials in developing nations that could be used in drug manufacture. This is because TNCs with the relevant technology usually have chosen to limit manufacture in the Third World to intermediate chemicals, producing the finished pharmaceutical products at a central plant in the developed countries. This puts some developing countries in the curious position of importing high-priced medicines that they had previously exported at an intermediate stage (Gereffi 1978).

Overall, one has to conclude that the products and technologies of the pharmaceutical industry have been far more appropriate to the capabilities and needs of the developed countries than they have been to the Third World. The imposition of consumption patterns and even specific maladies derived from the middle and upper classes of the industrial societies has served to retard the development of an effective strategy of preventive health care that would meet the needs of the low-income majority in Third World nations.

Appropriate Marketing

The drug promotion of transnational pharmaceutical companies in Latin America has been the subject of detailed investigations and much controversy (Silverman 1976; Ledogar 1975, pp. 25-51). One survey on the promotion of prescription drugs found striking differences in the way drugs are described to physicians in the United States and to physicians in Latin America. In the United States pharmaceutical companies tended to identify only a few diseases for which a drug is recommended while the contraindications, warnings, and potential adverse reactions were given in extensive detail. In Latin America numerous diseases for which the drug might be used were listed, while the hazards were usually minimized, glossed over, or totally ignored. Even more surprising, there were substantial differences in how global enterprises described the same drug product to physicians within Latin America. A transnational pharmaceutical company marketing a prescription drug frequently told one story about it in Mexico, a different one in Guatemala, and gave still other versions in Ecuador, Colombia, or Brazil. If there were corporate or national patterns or policies to account for these variations, they were not readily discernible. This would appear to invalidate one of the most widely used defenses by the industry to explain differences in promotion: namely, that these reflect "honest differences in opinion"

278

between regulators in the exceptionally stringent United States Food and Drug Administration (FDA) and regulators elsewhere.

Much of the controversy surrounding the pharmaceutical industry concerns the marketing of questionable drugs. Most Latin American countries have laws requiring that any drug product that is imported must be approved for marketing in the country of origin. This has not prevented the sale in Latin America of certain prescription pharmaceuticals originally introduced in the United States but later taken off the market by FDA orders, such as fixed-ratio antibiotic products. Companies get away with this by setting up a plant to produce the drug or put it in finished dosage form in an obliging nation which is listed as the country of origin. Until recently, some of the major pharmaceutical exporting nations have had relatively lax drug registration laws that allowed them to satisfy country-of-origin requirements without meeting modern standards of safety or efficacy. The nations that generally have employed the strictest registration criteria for drugs include the United States, Great Britain, the Netherlands, Norway, and Sweden.

It appears that the wasteful, excessive, and even harmful marketing techniques of pharmaceutical TNCs might be overcome in Latin America through action by the pharmaceutical companies themselves. Several months after Silverman's *The Drugging of the Americas* (1976) was published, the council of the International Federation of Pharmaceutical Manufacturers Association adopted a resolution submitted by the United States delegation calling for prescription product labeling to be consistent with "the body of scientific and medical evidence pertaining to that product." Special care was to be taken in appropriately communicating "essential information as to medical products' safety, contraindications and side effects." By 1977 it was evident that some global drug firms had already altered their promotion by limiting claims and disclosing hazards in the labeling of certain products (Silverman 1977, p. 166). In his newest book, Silverman lauds companies like Merck, Eli Lilly, Syntex, SmithKline, and Ciba-Geigy for their consistency and stringency in labeling and promoting their products (Silverman, Lee, and Lydecker 1982, pp. 150-152).

It has been argued that stricter quality control for drugs discriminates in favor of TNCs because they can absorb the higher costs more easily than local firms in Third World countries can (see the comment by a Brazilian doctor in Ledogar 1975, p. 18). To the extent that excessive claims or suppressed warnings for prescription drugs increase the sales of these products, however, local firms as well as TNCs have stood to gain from illegitimate promotion even though this has exposed human beings to unnecessary danger. Lack of state action in the quality control area, therefore, may at times reflect the political influence of drug producers (local or foreign) rather than governmental ignorance of the facts.

THE PHARMACEUTICAL INDUSTRY IN LATIN AMERICA

Latin America is a very diverse region. This diversity is evident with regard to health and development indicators, as well as in the structure and performance of national pharmaceutical industries. Some of these differences, along with important underlying similarities, will be outlined below.

Pharmaceutical consumption per capita in Latin America varies considerably across countries. Nonetheless there appears to be a moderately strong positive correlation between pharmaceutical consumption per capita and gross domestic product (GDP) per capita (see table 8.2). While the biggest countries in the region have the most pharmacies, the relationship between market size and the number of pharmaceutical products and presentational forms is quite uneven. Bolivia offers the second largest number of drug products in Latin America (8,000) even though it has one of the smallest populations and the lowest GDP per capita. Colombia sells more than twice as many dosage-form pharmaceuticals as Argentina yet has fewer inhabitants, while Brazil and Peru offer similar numbers of dosage-form medicines despite the fact that the former nation has over seven times as many people as the latter. All of the Latin American countries import substantial amounts of pharmaceuticals by value, but with the exception of Mexico they export very little.

One of two complementary strategies is normally followed when developing nations begin to establish a local drug industry. The first strategy is vertical integration which, in its usual backwards direction, means increasing the productive capability of the local industry starting with packaging, working up to various kinds of dosage formulation, and ending with the manufacture of bulk drugs or intermediate chemicals. A second approach involves the use of ownership controls, which require domestic production facilities to be at least partly held by national capital (private or governmental). Whereas vertical integration affects the level of development reached by Third World countries, ownership controls try to shape its direction by tempering the global norms of TNCs with the nationalist orientation of local entrepreneurs.

Table 8.3 presents the level of development of the pharmaceutical industry in Latin America in terms of five different stages of vertical

Table 8.2

Latin America: Pharmaceutical Industry Indicators, 1980

Country	Population in thousands, 1980	Gross domestic product per capita, 1980[a] (U.S. dollars)	Pharmaceutical consumption per capita (U.S. dollars)	Number of products	Number of dosage forms	Number of pharmacies[b]	Pharmaceutical exports (millions of U.S. dollars)	Pharmaceutical imports (millions of U.S. dollars)
Argentina	27,900	1,938	68.8[e]	3,400	7,000	7,100	34[b]	479
Bolivia	5,570	494	5.7	8,000	NA	NA	—	24
Brazil	122,320	1,384	12.7	5,043	10,843	12,600	40[c]	215
Colombia	26,894	757	20.8	9,000	15,000	6,000	NA	30
Costa Rica	2,100	750	13.3	6,000	NA	NA	NA	34[d]
Chile	11,104	1,774	17.8	3,300	NA	1,400	—	38
Ecuador	9,021	663	11.9	NA	NA	1,000	3.5	NA
Mexico	69,965	1,294	15.7	NA	14,000	7,800	107	217
Paraguay	3,004	758	13.3	2,993	NA	NA	—	22
Peru	17,625	1,006	11.3	NA	10,500	2,000	NA	NA
Uruguay	2,924	1,743	32.1	2,400	4,300	820	1.9[b]	14[b]
Venezuela	14,930	2,114	18.1	5,200	12,500	2,600	1.2[b]	—

Source: ALIFAR 1981, pp. 3, 12, 15.

Notes:

[a] In 1978 dollars.

[b] 1979.

[c] 1978.

[d] 1977.

[e] These figures should be viewed with caution since they probably reflect the over evaluation of the local currencies.

NA Not available.

Table 8.3

Levels of Development of the Pharmaceutical Industry in Latin America, 1979

Stage of Pharmaceutical Production	Countries
Group 1 Countries which have no manufacturing facilities and therefore are dependent upon imported pharmaceuticals in their finished form. In many of these countries there is insufficient trained personnel, limited public health services and poor distribution channels.	Dominica Grenada Honduras
Group 2 Countries which have started to repack formulated drugs and process bulk drugs into dosage forms.	Bolivia Costa Rica El Salvador Guatemala Haiti
Group 3 Countries which manufacture a broad range of bulk drugs into dosage forms and manufacture some simple bulk drugs from intermediates.	Colombia Ecuador Peru
Group 4 Countries which produce a broad range of bulk drugs from intermediates and manufacture some intermediates using locally produced chemicals.	Chile Cuba Venezuela
Group 5 Countries which manufacture most of the intermediates required for the pharmaceutical industry and undertake local research on the development of products and manufacturing processes.	Argentina Brazil Mexico

Source: IMSworld Publications Ltd. 1979, p. 40, revised and amended by the author.

integration. Each level of development has a distinctive set of constraints (UNIDO 1979, pp. 11-12). At the first or lowest level, the resources made available for health care from the national budget are very limited and there is a serious shortage of trained personnel. Countries at this level tend to have small national markets, unrestricted imports, proliferation of different brand named products, and no national policy concerning the drug industry. Countries that have reached the second and third stages of development have difficulty obtaining suitable formulation technology, bulk drugs and raw materials on reasonable terms and they may also have trouble convincing doctors and patients of the quality of domestically produced drugs. For the nations that have reached the fourth or fifth stages of pharmaceutical industry development, the constraints are essentially the same. In large countries where packaging and chemical industries are already well established, there is a move to begin local production of the equipment and machinery used by the pharmaceutical industry. Manufacturers in Argentina, Brazil, Egypt, India, and Mexico are willing to sell pharmaceutical plants to other Third World nations (UNCTC 1979, p. 91). India is on the forefront of this movement. It has begun to concentrate on producing plants of small-scale capacity (less than one ton per day) that can make a variety of chemically related synthetic drugs on a batch basis.

The degree of domestic ownership in Latin American pharmaceutical industries, like the extent of vertical integration, is relatively low as table 8.4 indicates. In all countries locally owned firms account for less than one-half of domestic drug sales. Nationally owned pharmaceutical laboratories are strongest in Argentina where they nearly match their TNC rivals in sales volume, and weakest in Ecuador and Colombia where local market shares are barely over 10 percent. Brazil and Mexico, which like Argentina have relatively large pharmaceutical markets in terms of sales, nonetheless have a much lower level of participation by locally owned laboratories in total industry output. The strength of domestically owned pharmaceutical firms in the region is further evidenced by their overall size amid all of the top drug firms at the national level. In Chile there are four local laboratories among the top fourteen pharmaceutical enterprises in the country, and in Argentina there are four local companies among the top sixteen drug firms. Uruguay, Venezuela, and Peru also have a number of prominent nationally owned laboratories. The domestic drug industries in Brazil and Mexico are shown to be weak according to this measure, however, with the largest Brazilian-owned laboratory ranking seventh and Mexico's biggest local drug firm standing thirty-first on their respective national lists.

Several additional findings can be gleaned from the table. First, the distribution of medicines in Latin America moves predominantly through private channels. With the exception of Bolivia, at least 70 percent of pharmaceutical sales goes to the private sector. Nevertheless, in several nations like Mexico and Brazil the public sector demand for medicines is growing faster than the private sector market, and a

Table 8.4

Latin America: Pharmaceutical Market Size and Market Share Data, 1980

Country	Pharmaceutical sales (US$ millions)	Number of laboratories	Market share of the 20 largest laboratories (percentage)	Market share of the nationally owned laboratories (percentage)	Rank of the 4 largest nationally owned laboratories	Percentage of total sales: private sector	public sector	Employees
Argentina	1,920	225	52%	47%	1, 3, 10, 16	92%	8%	37,000
Bolivia	32	12	—	NA	NA	50%	50%	NA
Brazil	1,554	489ᵃ	46%	22%	7, 24, 30, 54	80%	20%	62,000
Colombia	560	325	53%	12%	NA	70%	30%	15,000
Costa Rica	28	13	82%ᶜ	18%	NA	70%	30%	NA
Chile	198	41	74%	42%	1, 2, 5, 14	80%	20%	5,970
Ecuador	96	75	62%	11%ᵇ	1, 19, 34, 49	NA	NA	6,000
Mexico	1,100	315	45%	28%	31, 36, 48, 51	77%	23%	43,000
Paraguay	40	24	—	NA	NA	90%	10%	NA
Peru	200	80	61%ᵈ	26%	4, 10, 19, 27	75%	25%	17,000
Uruguay	94	69	71%	39%	10, 12, 15, 18	80%	20%	2,860
Venezuela	270	75	48%	22%	2, 5, 17, 23	74%	26%	7,600

Source: ALIFAR 1981, pp. 12, 15.

Notes:

[a]   1978.
[b]   1979.
[c]   In 1977 only three laboratories accounted for 82 percent of total production.
[d]   The 25 largest laboratories.
NA Not available.

number of the largest local pharmaceutical enterprises are state-owned. Second, the twenty-firm concentration ratios in these countries tend to be higher than the corresponding indices for developed countries, although there is considerable variation within the region with the smaller nations showing much higher levels of concentration. Finally, the data on pharmaceutical employees and the number of laboratories suggest notable differences in productivity and capital intensity. Argentina, Chile, and Uruguay, for example, are far more productive in terms of pharmaceutical sales per employee than Ecuador or Peru.

In order to increase the degree of local ownership, Third World countries have been promoting joint ventures between TNCs and domestic companies. Small and medium-sized firms in the developed countries have started to help developing nations industrialize, particularly through the mechanism of technology transfer. Swedish firms appear to have taken a lead in this area. Astra, a Swedish drug company that already has manufacturing facilities in Argentina, Brazil, and Mexico, has proposed to be a 26 percent joint-owner with an Indian pharmaceutical company and Nitro-Nobel, another Swedish firm, in order to manufacture clofazimine (a leprosy treatment) in India. When Ciba-Geigy, which holds the patents on clofazimine, refused to transfer its rights or knowledge, Astra offered to help develop a production method based on know-how that bypasses the restrictive patents. The project may take one or two years with an annual cost of about $1 million (Developing World Industry and Technology, Inc. 1979, p. 23). While TNCs normally transfer technology only through wholly owned subsidiaries or majority-owned joint ventures, SweDrug Consulting is involved in several projects in Cuba and the Arab countries in which it is either a minority shareholder or has received a lump-sum payment for its expertise (Agarwal 1978, pp. 49-50). The Swedish health ministry is trying to set up another enterprise to provide developing nations with technical assistance to improve the organization, distribution, administration and management of their incipient pharmaceutical supply systems. On the whole, the pharmaceutical industry in Latin America and other developing nations has made a limited contribution to national industrialization. There are signs that this may be changing, however, as smaller firms from the developed countries have begun accommodating demands from the developing nations for increased production capacity.

A wide range of policies has been employed to develop the pharmaceutical industry in Latin America. Although the private sector is generally predominant, the role of the state in the purchasing, production, and distribution of medicines has varied considerably.

285

The cases of Mexico, Brazil, Costa Rica, and Cuba are discussed below because they illustrate the types of state initiatives being undertaken in both large and small countries to assure a continuing supply of essential pharmaceutical products, to reduce the cost of drugs, and to increase local industrialization. With the significant exception of Cuba, most countries of the region have sought to attain these goals without seriously threatening the interests of private pharmaceutical firms.

Mexico

In Mexico, where drug sales totaled over $1 billion in 1980 (75 percent in the private sector and 25 percent in the public sector), local consumption of finished pharmaceuticals was almost fully met by local production. Over half of the raw materials used are still imported, however, and TNCs account for about 85 percent of total sales and an even larger share of Mexico's pharmaceutical exports. Thirty-eight of the forty largest pharmaceutical companies in Mexico are foreign-owned (Gereffi 1982). Despite the fact that Mexico is one of the leading Third World exporters of pharmaceutical products, the absolute level of its drug imports greatly exceeds drug exports and thus the country has experienced a steadily growing negative trade balance in the pharmaceutical sector (de María y Campos 1977, p. 898).

In response to this high level of TNC dominance, the Mexican government has taken a series of measures between 1972 and 1982 to try to reduce the impact of foreign subsidiaries and increase domestic control of the industry. These include three new laws, the creation of two state-owned enterprises (Proquivemex and Vitrium) to control the commercialization of barbasco and the manufacture and distribution of basic pharmaceutical products, the formation of an Intersecretarial Commission for the Pharmaceutical Industry as a technical coordinating organism for public sector activities, and the establishment and initial implementation of an essential drug list to standardize public sector purchases of basic medicines according to their generic name and in the dosages and presentational forms (tablets, capsules, injectable solutions, etc.) most often used.

Of the three laws, the 1972 Technology Transfer Law is generally considered to be the most successful. It established a National Registry of Technology Transfer to review all agreements in which a foreign company charges a Mexican company for technological or marketing know-how. If an agreement is judged too harsh in terms of price, duration, export restrictions, purchase requirements, etc., it is denied registration. Most of the proposed agreements that have been rejected are redrawn and submitted on terms more favorable to Mexico. The 1973 Foreign Investment Law required that all new foreign enterprises have at least 51 percent Mexican capital irrespective of activity. Despite the intent of this law, however, the vast majority of pharmaceutical firms in Mexico remained wholly owned by foreigners as late as 1977 (Gereffi 1982, tables 5 and 6). This apparent anomaly is explained by a "grandfather clause" in the 1973 law which stipulates that companies established prior to the law will not be affected by the Mexicanization requirement unless and until they decide to expand their operations. This expansion will be treated as a new investment, which means it will be approved only if the foreign enterprise sells a majority share of its stock to Mexicans. Since almost all of the principal pharmaceutical firms in Mexico were set up before 1973, the original owners can retain full control of their company. The Mexican market for drugs is growing rapidly, though, and existing TNCs will be forced to increase the size and scope of their activities just to keep pace. Sooner or later, they will have to give up their long-standing resistance to Mexicanization or withdraw from the market altogether.

The 1976 Law on Inventions and Trademarks is a very ambitious piece of legislation that reduces the period of patent protection in Mexico from fifteen years to ten years, and requires that patents be exploited within four years of the date they are issued or they will expire and fall into the public domain. Trademarks, under the 1976 law, will be registered for five-year periods. Registered trademarks may be renewed indefinitely every five years provided that it can be shown they have been in use in the previous period.

Although its ostensible objective is to "promote and regulate the pharmaceutical industry so that its development contributes to solving health problems at the national level," the Intersecretarial Commission for the Pharmaceutical Industry in fact represents the first governmental body entrusted with formulating policy for the industry as a whole in Mexico. The main lines of policy developed and supported by the Intersecretarial Commission are found in the "Program to Promote the Pharmaceutical Industry" (*Diario oficial* April 25, 1980). This program sets forth objectives for the period 1980 to 1983. While the program is quite comprehensive, its main goals can be summarized as follows: to increase the annual output of pharmaceutical firms at a rate of 15 to 20 percent and to export between 5 and 20 percent of this output, the lower percentage in each case referring to finished drugs and the higher percentage to active ingredients; to keep imports of finished drugs at the present level of 3 percent of local consumption and restrict the importation of raw materials; to increase the market share of Mexican firms from 30 to 50 percent and to increase the local equity share of Mexican capital from its current level of 28 percent to at least 51 percent; to raise the share of local inputs to at least 50 percent of the total production cost of pharmaceuticals; to limit royalty payments to a range of 0.5 to 3 percent depending on the type of product and the percentage of equity held by foreign firms; to standardize public-sector purchases through use of the essential drug list; and, to divide the Mexican market for pharmaceutical products into three types—private, public, and social interest (composed of indigent persons who neither work for the government nor are covered by social security)—with lower prices for identical drugs in the latter two markets.

In order to help implement this sectoral program, the Mexican government announced in 1981 that it was setting up a second state pharmaceutical company called Vitrium (*Diario oficial* October 27, 1981). Vitrium is, in a number of respects, a far bolder initiative than Proquivemex whose primary function was to control barbasco supply (Gereffi 1978 and 1983). Capitalized at P $30 million (US$1.2 million), Vitrium will be 75 percent owned by the Mexican government and 25 percent owned by a Swedish state pharmaceutical enterprise, KabiVitrium. The new Mexican firm will be responsible for the manufacture, import, and distribution of basic pharmaceutical products. The decision to create Vitrium was based in part on the findings of a study of pharmaceutical production and requirements in Mexico over the period 1979 to 1986. The study estimated that pharmaceutical consumption in the public sector will grow at twice the rate of that for the private sector and that current installed capacity in the country is insufficient to meet the 1986 demand for drugs (*SCRIP* November 23, 1981, p. 7).

A coordinated, intersectoral effort is being made in Mexico to increase the share of domestically owned firms in pharmaceutical production, to foster the development of local research and technology, and to reduce royalty and technical assistance payments to foreign countries. Mexico's achievements in these areas have required major legislative initiatives at the highest levels (including presidential decrees) in order to promote an integrated plan for the development of the industry. Whether the country will be successful in implementing these objectives remains to be seen.

Brazil

The Brazilian pharmaceutical industry went through a major period of denationalization between 1957 and 1977 when thirty-four of the largest domestic firms were acquired by TNCs. In the hope of increasing the competitiveness of local firms *vis-à-vis* their foreign rivals, Brazil completely abolished patent protection for pharmaceuticals in 1969. A decade after the introduction of the ban, the ten largest national drug companies had increased their share of the market by close to 10 percent. This trend was broken, though, when two of the firms were acquired by TNCs in 1978 and 1979. It is interesting to note that despite the ban on patents, foreign investment in the pharmaceutical sector rose from $113 million in 1971 to $646 million in 1979, one of the highest growth rates of any industry in Brazil. This seems to contradict the argument of those who contend that the absence of patents will keep foreign investors away. In the area of trademarks, Brazil tried to prohibit brand names from being used for drugs containing a single active ingredient. The legal challenge to this measure by TNCs was upheld in the courts and the Brazilian Parliament subsequently enacted a less restrictive bill on trade names in 1977 (UNCTC 1981, pp. 41-42).

The Brazilian "triple alliance" (Evans 1979) between TNCs, the state, and local private capital has led to an unusual compromise arrangement between a rationalized drug list and free market forces involving the state-owned enterprise Central de Medicamentos (CEME) (Evans 1976, pp. 133-136; Ledogar 1975, pp. 61-67). Central de Medicamentos was created in 1971 under the direct responsibility of the president of the republic. CEME's role was elaborated in the four volume Master Plan for Pharmaceuticals. In order to satisfy its original objective of social service for the poor majority in Brazil, CEME set out to rationalize the procurement of medicines for the hospitals and clinics associated with Brazil's system of state medical assistance—the Instituto Nacional de Previdencia Social—and to provide free prescription drugs to the poorest of the institute's clients. In addition, the Master Plan proposed reviving approximately 20 state-owned laboratories and giving preferential treatment to local companies, with the ultimate goal of having the country manufacture most of its own pharmaceutical raw materials by the end of the decade. Other provisions in the plan included tight controls on the sale and promotion of drugs, regulations on the content of drug package inserts, and restrictions on the distribution of free drug samples.

Only part of the Master Plan was ever put into effect and it was done in a way that did not threaten the dominant position or continued growth of private (and especially foreign) drug firms. In 1973 CEME distributed medications to 9 million people. Its target group were those people receiving the official minimum wage or less—in other words, exactly that segment of the population that is normally

289

excluded from the commercial market for medicines. Thus, CEME was not likely to take any customers away from private firms. To the contrary, CEME's activities probably stimulated the expansion of the commercial market. A large share of the medications distributed by CEME was not produced by public laboratories but purchased from private companies, many of them foreign-owned. In 1973 CEME increased private-sector sales by a total of $3.5 million (Evans 1976, p. 135). Furthermore, whereas the logic of profitability for private firms lies in maximizing product differentiation, CEME's strategy was quite the opposite: to limit the number of medicines it deals with, concentrating on those needed for the diseases most prevalent among the population it serves. The Master Plan initially contained a list of 134 pharmaceutical products accounting for about three-quarters of the cost of national drug imports in 1971. To the extent that CEME might try to manufacture these products domestically through its system of public laboratories, the only private enterprises likely to suffer would be locally owned ones whose output is less technologically advanced and not the foreign subsidiaries of TNCs.

CEME's budget has risen from 65 million cruzeiros in 1972 to 11.9 billion cruzeiros (US$192 million) in 1981. CEME coordinates a network of 22 state laboratories that supply it with essentialmedicine, which it distributes in 3,750 of the 3,975 Brazilian municipalities. Drug purchases by CEME in 1981 represented about 12 percent of total pharmaceutical sales in Brazil, although this probably undervalues the state firm's importance because its prices are much lower than those prevailing in the commercial market. Sixty-two percent of the medicines distributed by CEME are supplied by the state laboratories, 31 percent come from private drug companies in Brazil, and the remaining 7 percent are imported (ALIFAR 1982a, pp. 7-8). In addition to compiling the essential drug list that currently contains over 400 products and coordinating the activities of the 22 public sector pharmaceutical units, CEME is responsible for the centrla procurement of medicines, quality control of supplies, the setting of priorities in raw material manufacture, and the modernization of production and distribution facilities. Between 1971 and 1981 CEME spent $1.1 million on state drug research programs (SCRIP March 10, 1982, p. 11). CEME approved eight new research and development projects during 1981 with a total value of nearly $600,000, over half of the amount spent in the previous ten years (ALIFAR 1982a, p. 8). Late in 1981 an Interministerial Group on the Pharmaceutical Industry was established in Brazil to develop the national pharmaceutical industry and to promote greater self-sufficiency (SCRIP January 27, 1982, p. 9).

The case of CEME in Brazil shows how a government-sponsored procurement scheme, if given political support and sufficient financial and technical resources, can simultaneously rationalize drug purchasing and distribution in the public sector as well as contribute to the country's pharmaceutical research capabilities. The purchasing power of CEME can also be used to influence the production profile of Brazil by stimulating national companies to manufacture essential drugs.

Costa Rica

Costa Rica is an example of an ambitious attempt by a small Latin American nation to implement a series of reforms in the importation, distribution, and export of pharmaceutical products (UNCTAD, 1982). In the late 1960s drug imports supplied virtually all of Costa Rica's demand for medicines and local manufacturing was negligible. By 1977 total local production had grown to $21 million and half of this output was exported by TNCs to other Central American countries, thereby making pharmaceutical products Costa Rica's leading manufactured export in 1975. In addition, the Costa Rican Social Security Fund (Caja Costaricense del Seguro Social or CCSS) now provides health care coverage for 85 percent of the population, it is the country's major purchaser of imported finished drugs, it has set up its own quality control laboratory to inspect imported as well as locally produced medicines, and it has achieved considerable foreign exchange savings through public tenders and bulk purchasing. In order to understand the reasons for Costa Rica's apparent success in pharmaceuticals and also some of the attendant shortcomings, one needs to look at the division of labor that has evolved between TNCs, local private capital, and the state.

The national consumption of pharmaceutical products was $36 million ($17 per capita) in 1977. Seventy percent of this domestic demand was met through imports and the remaining 30 percent by local production. Transnational firms are predominant in local production with three foreign-owned laboratories accounting for 82 percent of Costa Rica's total drug output of $21 million in 1977. Although Costa Rica had not been of much interest to TNCs before 1960, several firms came in after the country joined the Central American Common Market (CACM). Besides allowing for the free flow of goods within an enlarged regional market, the CACM offers pharmaceutical companies a generous package of fiscal incentives if they set up manufacturing operations. Three pharmaceutical TNCs use Costa Rica as a base to export between 50 and 85 percent of their production to other CACM countries. Two of the TNCs specialize in the manufacture of ethical drugs, while the third produces over-the-counter pharmaceuticals for the domestic market and makes ethical drugs for export only. The foreign exchange earned from these exports was about $10 million in 1977, but almost all of these export earnings ($9.4 million) were absorbed by imports of raw materials and other inputs required in the production process. Thus the trade balance advantage to Costa Rica from the TNCs' pharmaceutical exports was very small.

The ten domestic pharmaceutical companies in Costa Rica supply 18 percent of all drugs produced locally. The nature of their contribution has changed radically since the entry of the transnationals, however. Unable to cope directly with large-scale foreign production units, Costa Rica's nationally owned laboratories have taken one of three courses of action: (1) most stopped producing drugs as their main activity and instead began making cosmetics under licensing arrangements with TNCs; (2) others specialized in the manufacture of popular remedies that had limited therapeutic effect and did not involve competition with the foreign firms; and (3) a few laboratories began to produce generic drugs for CCSS, thus tying their financial security to the purchasing policies of the state social security agency. In short, national firms in Costa Rica's pharmaceutical industry shifted to cosmetics, over-the-counter products, or generics—if they survived at all. The three TNCs, on the other hand, have limited their production to formulating and packaging imported raw materials and semi-finished drugs despite the larger scale of output made possible by the CACM. As a result, Costa Rica continues to import more than two-thirds of the finished drugs it consumes and up to 95 percent of the raw materials needed for local formulation and packaging (ALIFAR 1981, p. 23).

One of the important lessons that can be learned from the Costa Rican experience is the role played by CCSS in acquiring bulk drugs and in using public tenders for that purpose. Created in 1941, the social security agency has increased its health-related coverage of the population from 47 percent in 1970 to 85 percent in 1979. It has been responsible for the procurement and distribution of bulk and finished drugs, it conducts its own formulation and research activities, and it has adopted a list of essential drugs that serves as a guideline for imports and local production. In 1978 the savings to the public sector made possible by CCSS's public tender purchases of drugs were estimated at $3.2 million—i.e., 27 percent of the total value of 1978 orders. The average market price for imported pharmaceuticals (after adjusting for inflation, wholesale and retail margins, and import tar-

292

iffs) was still three times higher than CCSS's procurement prices. To achieve these savings Costa Rica's social security agency has moved to suppliers of generic drugs whenever possible without sacrificing quality. This is expected to eventually help national firms increase their share of the local market.

Cuba

An examination of the pharmaceutical industry in Cuba illustrates, even more than the Costa Rican case, the profound impact of a strong state sector on pharmaceutical purchasing, production, and distribution. When Costa Rica began to transfer health care to the public sector under the auspices of its social security agency, it did so within a capitalist framework. Cuba, on the other hand, underwent a radical socialist transformation in 1959. This transformation has affected all areas of Cuban society, and the health-pharmaceutical sector is no exception.

According to a recent report prepared by Cuba's Ministry of Public Health for UNCTAD (1980), the health situation in Cuba before 1959 was a dismal one. Life expectancy was between fifty and sixty years, and the infant mortality rate was 70 for every 1,000 live births. Health care was almost totally unavailable in rural areas where it was most needed and instead was concentrated around Havana where the highest profits were to be made. The pharmaceutical industry was dominated by transnational firms that controlled about 70 percent of the market. Seventy to 80 percent of the pharmaceuticals consumed in Cuba were imported as finished products and drug prices were very high. The few drugs produced locally were often of poor quality, there was almost no use of Cuba's raw materials as pharmaceutical inputs, and Cuban technical personnel were badly trained.

This situation has changed considerably. Important steps have been taken in the fight against infectious and parasitic diseases, leading to dramatic reductions in Cuba's mortality and morbidity rates. The annual pharmaceutical consumption per capita in the late 1970s was $37.40 which compares favorably with many highly industrialized countries. The improvements in health conditions within Cuba can be attributed to three main factors: (1) the growth and increased activity of the public health sector; (2) the extension of effective health care to rural areas; and (3) the establishment and expansion of a national pharmaceutical industry. Of particular importance in the Cuban case is the attempt to fuse the pharmaceutical and health sectors into an integrated whole.

As might be expected in a state socialist system, the establishment of a local pharmaceutical industry entailed major bureaucratic realignments. In 1961 the Cuban government consolidated 14 existing drug manufacturing plants to form the state company, Empresa Consolidada de Productos Farmacéuticos. This firm, under the jurisdiction of the Ministry of Industry, was responsible for reorganizing and expanding pharmaceutical production, issuing quality control guidelines, and training (often in other socialist countries) sufficient numbers of Cuban technical personnel. The Ministry of Health decided what pharmaceutical products were needed in the country based on essential drug lists drawn up by the National Formulary Committee that it created in 1962. The Ministry of Foreign Trade was in charge of all imports and exports of medicines. Within this ministry two specialized state trading agencies were set up: Medicuba handled all pharmaceutical imports and exports, including finished drugs, active and inert ingredients, and bulk orders of medicines and medicinal herbs; and Empresa de Suministros Médicos was responsible for a wide range of medical supplies for surgical, clinical, and laboratory use. The distribution of medicines within Cuba came under the jurisdiction of the Ministry of Internal Trade, which established a national network of pharmacies capable of supplying even remote rural areas. This bureaucratic division of labor was in effect until 1968, when all of these activities were centralized under the authority of the Ministry of Public Health.

Of particular importance to the Public Health Ministry is the essential drug list. When the first national formulary was published in 1963, it contained 611 generically named pharmaceutical preparations (compared to the 20,000 registered drug products on the market prior to the revolution). Only drugs listed on the formulary could be produced within the country. By 1979 the national formulary had adopted the new title of "Therapeutic Guide" and contained 689 pharmaceutical products in 855 dosage forms. Medicuba uses this essential drug list in its bulk procurement of medicines, which has produced foreign exchange savings ranging from 30 to nearly 70 percent (UNCTAD 1980, pp. 37-38).

Cuba, in a period of just over twenty years, has moved from a situation of extreme dependency on foreign pharmaceutical products and technology to a position of enhanced autonomy in the industry. Whereas Cuba used to rely on imports for 70 to 80 percent of its pharmaceutical needs, it has advanced to the stage where it now exports both inputs and finished drugs to developing nations in Asia, Africa, and the rest of Latin America. Through cooperation with other socialist countries, Cuba has made efforts to develop a technological infrastructure that is potentially self-sustaining. Cuba's most notable achievements have probably been made in the distribution of health care services. All medical attention, including drugs, is provided free of charge to hospital patients and to certain other groups, such as pregnant women, the physically and mentally handicapped, people residing in homes for the elderly, and low-income families. The evolution of Cuba's state health sector has also generated, however, a large and complex bureaucratic infrastructure. Future successes in the area of public health will no doubt be measured, in part, by how effectively the Cuban state manages to coordinate its ambitious and multifaceted efforts.

CONCLUSIONS

This study leads to a number of generalizations about the consequences of foreign control, local private control, and state control in Third World pharmaceutical industries.

First, many domestic private drug firms in the Third World contribute more to national goals of resource efficiency and equity than TNCs do. The motives underlying this socially desirable behavior are not altruistic, however. It just so happens that the self-interest of local firms and national development objectives often overlap. The tendency of local companies to reduce their reliance on foreign know-how because it compromises management control coincides with the Third World country's interest in technological autonomy. And whereas domestic enterprises favor bulk drug and generic product manufacture because the absence of heavy promotion and established brand names makes competition with TNCs easier, developing nations also prefer this strategy because it leads to increased vertical integration and lower drug prices, especially for essential items required by the poor. If the transfer-pricing behavior of TNCs, to take a final example, tends to lessen a host country's foreign exchange and tax revenues, the profit incentive that leads indigenous entrepreneurs to set up rival local production facilities may also counteract this national problem by generating alternative cost figures through which overinvoicing may come to light.

The main reason why the divergence between private interests and social interests will be narrower for domestic firms than for TNCs lies in the latter's transnational decisionmaking framework. TNCs have a worldwide perspective and seek to maximize their global profits, while the production and research functions of these enterprises are often centralized in their home countries. The situation frequently leads to conflicts between the TNC goal of global efficiency and a Third World country's desire for increased national autonomy. Since the domestic firm's decisions are made in a milieu affected by local scarcities and values, its performance is more likely to reflect these social realities.

There are significant exceptions to the coincidence between local private and societal interests. One such area forms the basis for a second generalization. Neither local private nor foreign pharmaceutical firms can be regarded as having a more socially desirable mix of finished products than the other. There is evidence that TNCs and local companies alike directed their manufacturing efforts overwhelmingly toward drugs desired by upper-income consumers and disregarded products needed by the poor majority of the population.

The third generalization is related. Because the private sector as a whole is frequently unresponsive to important social needs, especially with regard to the poor, a wide variety of Third World nations has decided to rely on state-owned enterprises in the pharmaceutical sector. A number of state firms in Mexico, Brazil, Costa Rica, Cuba, Egypt, and India have played important roles in the procurement, distribution, and production of drugs. The private sector, as a rule, tends to protest the state's entry into drug manufacture far more vehemently than it does state involvement in the purchasing or distribution of pharmaceuticals.

Fourth, many of the larger Third World countries want pharmaceutical TNCs to expand their local production of active ingredients. Some of the TNCs agree, privately if not publicly, that their own interests would be best served by more involvement in active ingredient manufacture. They feel that in the area of finished drugs, government preference for local firms in public sector sales will steadily reduce the TNCs' share of the market.

Fifth, in the countries where the private sector is predominant (such as Argentina, Brazil, and Mexico) product differentiation and promotional expenses tend to be greater than in countries with large public sectors (such as Cuba, Costa Rica, or Egypt). The price of drug products could be lowered and the position of local firms in the industry improved if some of the more pernicious aspects of pharmaceutical marketing were better regulated. Two priority areas can be singled out here. One is the mandatory usage of generic names in advertising and prescribing pharmaceutical products. The institutionalization of essential drug lists, which many Third World nations are adopting, should greatly help generic names to become more widely accepted and used. The other area is the excessive use of free samples by detailmen in promoting their companies' products. For instance, the usual practice when introducing a new drug into the Mexican market is to give away an average of four capsules for each capsule sold in the first year, three capsules for each capsule sold in the second year, and so on until a level of one to one is reached (de María y Campos 1977, p. 901). This heavy reliance on free samples, which usually originates with the TNCs, multiplies the promotional costs for local firms to successfully enter the market. If such practices were restricted, competition would increase and the cost of many drugs would come down.

Sixth, adequate quality control in pharmaceutical production continues to be one of the biggest problems plaguing many Third World drug industries. This is an area in which the TNCs generally excel. If domestic pharmaceutical companies hope to effectively compete with their foreign rivals, they will have to meet stricter quality control standards. TNCs, on the other hand, are also prone to want to relax selected quality standards when these relate to the excessive claims or suppressed warnings for some of the prescription drugs no longer approved in their countries of origin.

Finally, a variety of cases indicate that successful pharmaceutical industry reforms need continued governmental support. In countries like Brazil, Mexico, and Sri Lanka, major reform attempts were overturned or vitiated because of shifting political circumstances and the withdrawal of regime support (Gereffi 1983). Transnational firms, local private laboratories, and the local medical profession tend to band together to preserve the status quo, irrespective of the varying kinds of reform being promoted. Effective change in the industry thus requires, along with technological and organizational capability, a strong commitment by the government to assure full and lasting implementation of new drug policies.

Rhys Jenkins with Peter J. West

9.

The International Tractor Industry and its Impact in Latin America

INTRODUCTION*

The first tractors powered by an internal combustion engine appeared in the United States in the 1890s but it was not until after 1910 when Henry Ford introduced the Fordson tractor that they began to be used extensively. The industry developed rapidly in the inter-war years so that by 1920 tractor sales in the United States reached more than 200,000 units a year. This is more than ten times the maximum output achieved by either Britain or Germany in any year prior to World War II and more than a hundred times the output of France. (Conant 1953, p. 35) Such a predominance of the U.S. industry reflects the early mechanization of agriculture in North America compared with Europe. Nonetheless, the industry did not bloom into an "international" industry until relatively late—the 1960s. Why did this industry's internationalization lag behind the push abroad of other industries?

Not surprisingly, the U.S. also dominated international trade in tractors in the 1920s and 1930s. Although between 1936 and 1939 the U.S. never exported more than 15 percent of its tractor output, the large domestic production meant that U.S. exports dwarfed those of other countries (PEP 1949, p. 49). In 1937 U.S. tractor exports amounted to more than $52 million, over ten times the value of British exports in the same year (PEP 1949, Appendix X and XI).

The inter-war period saw the emergence of the present oligopolistic structure of the tractor industry in the United States. Although in the early 1920s Ford had acquired 80 percent of the

* The authors are grateful to Gerry Helleiner, Richard Newfarmer, and Van Whitting for their comments on an earlier version of this chapter.

tractor market through cutting the price of the Fordson tractor to less than half its 1919 level, its dominance of the market was short-lived and introduction of new models by International Harvester and John Deere in the mid-1920s led to a fall in Ford's sales and in 1928 the Company decided to leave the industry altogether. By 1929 the two firms accounted for over 80 percent of total sales and the seven leading firms accounted for 96 percent of the market (Conant 1953, p. 35).[1] Although by 1937 the two largest firms accounted for just under 70 percent of the market as a result of a significant decline in International Harvester's share, the seven leading firms had increased their share slightly to 98 percent (Conant 1953, p. 36).

In Britain large-scale production of tractors began with the setting up of the Ford plant at Dagenham in 1933. It was not until after World War II that Ferguson challenged Ford's monopoly and the present structure of two dominant firms emerged. In Germany the industry developed after World War I and by 1927 there were some 40 tractor manufacturers operating. However, it was not until the Nazis turned towards agricultural mechanization in the late 1930s that production passed 10,000 units a year (PEP 1949, p. 50).

The period immediately after World War II and into the 1950s saw a substantial growth both of tractor production and use in North America and Western Europe. In North America this reflected the backlog of demand which had built up during the war years while in Western Europe the immediate post-war period saw a rapid extension of agricultural mechanization. In the United States the period of rapid growth was fairly short-lived with sales reaching a peak in the early 1950s (Canada Royal Commission 1971, Table 6.2), whereas in Europe as a whole, tractor sales reached a peak in the late 1950s.

In the early 1960s the international tractor industry was heavily concentrated in North America and the four major European producing countries, which together accounted for the bulk of tractors produced, sold, used, and exported outside the Communist block. As Table 9.1 indicates, in 1962 almost 90 percent of production, more than 95 percent of exports, and almost three-fifths of apparent consumption of tractors in the capitalist world occurred within these six countries, while they also accounted for more than three-quarters of all tractors in use. Major changes took place in the industry by the mid-1970s. The share of apparent consumption of tractors of the six countries has declined to just over a third of non-Communist consumption and less than a quarter of the total worldwide. From a position of virtual complete dominance in production their share of the capitalist world's tractor output had decreased to just over a half, while their share of exports and tractors in use showed similar large declines as traditional markets appeared to reach a saturation level.

Table 9.1

Share of North America, United Kingdom, West Germany, France, and Italy in World Stock, Production, Exports, and Consumption of Tractors, 1962 and 1976

	1962	*1976*
Tractors in Use:		
Worldwide %	64.9	50.1
non-Communist %	77.3	62.5
Tractor Production:		
Worldwide %	57.9	34.1
non-Communist %	88.1	53.9
Tractor Exports ('000):	297.6	393.5
Worldwide %	84.5	56.4
non-Communist %	95.3	69.2
Apparent Consumption ('):	430.7	454.2
Worldwide %	39.7	23.3
non-Communist %	58.5	34.1

Source: Compiled from UN and FAO and country specific data.

These trends reflect the expansion of the industry to a number of new countries producing tractors, the most prominent of which is Japan but which also include Spain, Turkey, India, Brazil, Argentina, and Mexico. The growth of new markets has been even more widespread. The share of Africa, Asia, and Latin America in the apparent consumption of tractors worldwide increased from 8 percent in 1962 to almost a third by 1976, while the shares of all other areas (except the Soviet Union which remained constant) declined.

These trends reflect a number of changes in the world tractor market since the 1960s. Demand in the major industrial countries began to slow down after the attainment of something like a saturation level in terms of the number of tractors in use.[2] The growth of tractor demand in Africa, Asia, and Latin America partly reflects the rapid development of tractor production and sales in Japan in the 1970s, and the increased mechanization of agriculture in the underdeveloped countries which has been associated with the introduction of the Green Revolution in many areas. Between 1962 and 1976 the estimated share of the underdeveloped countries in the apparent consumption of tractors worldwide increased from around 7 percent to over 20 percent.

In the mid-1970s Massey-Ferguson projected that the countries of Latin America, Africa, and Asia (excluding Japan and Eastern Bloc countries) would increase their share of total demand from just over a third in 1975 to 55 percent ten years later. The most spectacular growth is expected in Latin America which by 1985 would absorb more tractors than the whole of Western Europe—over one quarter of all tractors produced (*Agricultural Machinery Journal* August 1976, p. 33).

In the late 1970s the tractor industry internationally was dominated by a small number of large companies. The emergence of Kubota of Japan as one of the six leading companies (see Table 9.2) indicates the way in which recent changes in the international distribution of tractor production and use can lead to the growth of new competitors from those countries with rapidly growing domestic markets. The existing oligopolistic structure of the industry may also be disturbed by the rapid growth of new markets outside the traditional centers of production in which some firms have been able to acquire a favorable position. Thus, the trends projected for the tractor industry are likely to be accompanied by a worldwide struggle between the major oligopolies for control of the new markets.

THE STRUCTURE OF THE TRACTOR INDUSTRY IN THE MAJOR PRODUCING COUNTRIES

In North America and Great Britain a small number of firms had already established a dominant position in the industry by World War II. In the other major producing countries concentration increased in the post-war period as a number of smaller firms were driven out of the industry. In West Germany in the early 1950s it was estimated that as many as thirty-two companies produced tractors[3] but several years later some of the smaller companies and even relatively important producers such as Hanomag, Eicher, and Porsche, which had been among the market leaders in the 1950s, either went out of business or were taken over by foreign firms.[4] The same thing happened in France when Vierzon was taken over by Case in 1959 and Vendeurve by Allis-Chalmers in 1960 (Kudrle 1975, pp. 94-95). In Italy the tractor industry has been dominated by Fiat since the 1950s when three firms owned by the Institute per la Ricontruzione (IRI) saw their share of the market fall from 26 percent in 1951 to 4 percent five years later (Kudrle 1975, p. 100) and Fiat merged with the fourth largest company, O.M., in 1959.

Table 9.2

major Companies in the International Tractor Industry, 1978

	Total Sales ($mn)	Total Assets ($mn)	Agricultural Machinery Sales ($mn)	Tractors Produced	Foreign Sales ($mn)
Deere	4,155	3,887	3,297	100,000	1,239
Massey-Ferguson	2,926	2,547	2,042	146,700	2,048[c]
International Harvester	6,664	4,316	2,348	120,000	1,828
Ford	42,784	22,101	1,000 (est)	107,300	14,985
Fiat	15,477	8,817	898	62,690	n.a.
Kubota[a]	2,452	2,437	964	120,000[b]	255

Source: Company Annual Reports

Notes:
[a] Year to 15 April 1979
[b] 1977
[c] Sales outside North America

In short, tractor production in North America and Western Europe came to be dominated by a small number of firms in the post-war period. In the United States seven firms accounted for virtually all the tractors produced by the 1970s. These were Deere, International Harvester, Massey-Ferguson, Ford, J.I. Case, Allis Chalmers, and White. In Britain three foreign firms, Ford, Massey-Ferguson, and International Harvester, and two local firms, British Leyland and David Brown, dominated the industry. In France only three companies, Massey-Ferguson, Renault, and International Harvester, produce tractors locally.[5] West Germany and Italy have more producers than the other European countries. In West Germany fourteen firms sold locally-produced tractors in 1978 but only six produced on a significant scale, namely International Harvester, Fendt, Deutz, Deere-Lanz, Daimler-Benz, and Eicher (Massey-Ferguson). There was a similar situation in Italy with a number of companies producing small volumes of tractors but four firms, Fiat, Same, Landini, and Lamborghini[6] accounted for the bulk of local production.

The industry is characterized by high levels of concentration. Table 9.3 shows the development of concentration in North America and Western Europe. It can be seen that the level of concentration is high and fairly stable in North America and the United Kingdom throughout the period. In West Germany concentration increased gradually and steadily, whereas in France concentration increased in the 1950s but fell again in the sixties and early seventies associated with increasing import penetration, as will be seen below, and in Italy it increased rapidly in the late fifties and remained at a high level subsequently.

Japan, where tractor production only took off in the 1970s, is also characterized by high levels of concentration. Japanese tractor production, which had been of only 10,000 units in 1965, had still only reached 40,000 by 1970 and 50,000 in 1972. In 1976, however, production reached over 280,000 and Japan became the largest producer of tractors (in volume terms) in the capitalist world (*Japan Statistical Yearbook 1978*). Five firms, Kubota, Yanmar, Iseki, Satoh, and Toyosha, accounted for the bulk of this production.

It is not difficult to find explanations for the high level of concentration in the tractor industry in terms of the traditional analysis of barriers to entry. The most comprehensive study of economies of scale in tractor production concluded that the optimum scale of production is at least 90,000 tractors a year (Canada Royal Commission 1971, Ch. 7). It was estimated that costs fell by 11 percent between 60,000 and 90,000 units.

There appears to be general agreement that economies of scale do exist up to a level of 90,000 units but there is considerable disagree-

Table 9.3

Four-firm Concentration in Major Producing Countries, 1950-1975

	1950	1955	1960	1965	1970	1975
North America	75+	70+	69	72[d]	83[f]	n.a.
U.K.	80+	80+	80+	85+	85+	76
France	52[a]	68	75	64	61	60
West Germany	n.a.	45[b]	49	53	60	67
Italy	52	49[b]	74	77[c]	n.a.	70[e]

Sources: 1950-1970: Kudrle (1975): Table 1-5
1972, U.S.: *Business Week* October 27, 1973, p. 78.
1975, U.K.: EIU (1976), Table 5.
France: Commission des Communates Europeennes
(1978) Table 36
West Germany: *Agricultural Machinery Journal* June 1976,
p. 29.
Italy: *Agricultural Machinery Journal* May 1979, p. 28.

Notes: [a] *1951;*
[b] *1956;*
[c] *1964;*
[d] *1966;*
[e] *1978*
[f] *1972 U.S. only*

ment over the extent of the cost disadvantage of producing at lower levels of output. A study of the British tractor industry argued that there was little cost difference between Massey-Ferguson producing 95,000 tractors and David Brown producing 25,000 tractors (Commission of the European Communities 1975, pp. 159-166). However, this conclusion was not based on an analysis of the cost structure of the two firms but on a comparison of profit margins and prices. As the study suggests, Massey-Ferguson may not have taken advantage of the potential for greater scale economies because it produced a larger number of models and its production runs for each one were not much greater than David Brown's. It is also possible that differences in production costs may be hidden by differences in distribution costs which also affect overall profitability.

It is, however, worth pointing out that if the optimum scale of production of tractors is 90,000 a year, very few plants anywhere in the world attain this level. Indeed, only the United States and Japan among the capitalist economies had sufficient domestic sales to justify more than one optimal sized plant, and the entire capitalist world's production of tractors in the mid-1970s could be produced by a handful of such plants. Even if the optimal scale of production were to prove to be considerably less than 90,000 tractors a year, economies of scale would still be a major obstacle to entry in the industry since a new entrant would either have to attain a significant share of its domestic market or export a high proportion of its output from the outset.

Product demand is also an important determinant of entry conditions in the industry. As mentioned before, demand for tractors is stagnating in many of the major producing countries. Moreover, entry is more difficult in a slowly growing market than in a fast growing one because entry is more likely to lead to retaliation. The instability of demand for tractors which depends on fluctuating farm incomes is also an important barrier to entry since it requires firms to be sufficiently large and diversified to withstand a number of years of unfavorable demand conditions.

The other major barrier to entry is the distribution system. Manufacturers need to have a reliable dealer and service network. To assure the stability of these networks and to exclude other manufacturers tractor companies established early in the history of the business in the United States exclusive dealerships which included interest free credit for up to a year. (Conant 1953, p. 32). Bain identified the tractor industry as having a high product differentiation barrier based on product reputation, customer service, and established dealer systems (Kudrle 1975, p. 55).

In Britain, despite the geographically more concentrated market for tractors, the practice of exclusive dealership also poses a barrier to entry. Deere's attempt to penetrate this market in the mid-1960s illustrates how difficult to surmount this barrier to entry could be. Many of its early dealers were inexperienced and a large number failed. It was only with time and the switching of dealers from other manufacturers that Deere began to establish a foothold in the British market (Commission of the European Communities 1975, pp. 142-144).

THE INTERNATIONALIZATION OF CAPITAL IN THE TRACTOR INDUSTRY

In the post-war years there was a rapid expansion in international trade in tractors. The most spectacular growth of exports was achieved by Britain which by 1951 exported over 100,000 tractors a year, a level that has been maintained subsequently (SMMT, 1976). In fact, exports accounted for around 70 percent total output. Similarly, exports have increased steadily in West Germany so that they exceeded production for the domestic market for the first time in 1972 and have since then run at around 60 percent of total production (Landmaschinen-und Ackerschlepper-Vereinigung). In Italy a rapid expansion of exports began in the late 1950s and by the seventies Italy was exporting the same proportion of its output as West Germany (Fiat, *Annual Report* 1976, 1978). The French tractor industry has been less heavily export oriented than that of other European countries. Although by the 1970s France was exporting over 30 percent of all tractors produced, that country has continued to be a net importer of tractors. Japanese tractor exports have grown from 10,000 in 1975 to 45,000 in 1977 and 70,000 in 1978, accounting for almost a quarter of total output in that year (*Implement and Tractor* April 21, 1979).

It is also interesting in this context to note the pattern of imports of the major tractor producing countries. Throughout the 1950s North America, the U.K. and West Germany imported under 5 percent of tractors sold, while France and Italy, which began the decade as heavy importers of tractors, reduced the share of imports to around 15 and 25 percent respectively by the late fifties (Kudrle 1975, Table 7.2). This suggests that the growth of tractor exports in this period did not involve interpenetration of each other's markets by the major producing countries but was directed towards non-producing countries.

The pattern began to change in the 1960s. The import share in France and West Germany began to rise reflecting the increased interpenetration of each other's markets by the major European producers following the formation of the EEC. In North America imports remained low until the mid-seventies when the rapid growth of Japanese exports of small tractors, an area which had been relatively neglected by North American manufacturers, increased rapidly. In the U.K. tractor imports increased rapidly in the early 1970s, no doubt assisted by a Kennedy round reduction in tariffs from 15 to 7.5 percent in 1972.

The growth of foreign investment by the North American tractor firms began almost immediately after World War II. As Table 9.4 indicates new investment was at first concentrated in Britain and then extended to continental Europe, and eventually about 1960 spread to Southern Europe and the Third World. The earliest foreign subsidiary created by a North American manufacturer outside Western Europe was the Deere plant in Argentina in 1959. In the subsequent two decades the four major North American manufacturers began pro-

Table 9.4

Direct Foreign Investment in Tractor manufacture in the Post-War Period

Period in Which Tractor Production Began

Company	1945-49		1950-59		1960-69		1970-79	
	DC	LDC	DC	LDC	DC	LDC	DC	LDC
Deere	—	—	W. Germany	Argentina	—	Spain Mexico Iran	Australia	Venezuela
Massey-Ferguson (previously Massey-Harris)	U.K.	—	France Italy	—	—	India Brazil Spain Mexico Morocco Argentina	Germany	Peru Libya Egypt
International Harvester	Australia U.K.	—	France W. Germany	—	—	India Mexico Philippines Turkey	Japan	S. Africa
Ford	—	—	—	—	Belgium	Brazil India	—	Turkey Brazil[a]
Fiat	—	—	France	Argentina	—	—	—	Spain
Deutz	—	—	—	Argentina	—	Brazil	—	—

Source: Own investigation

Notes: DC—North America, Western Europe (excluding Spain), and Japan
LDC—Africa, Asia (excluding Japan), Latin America, and Spain
[a]—Ford re-entered the Brazilian tractor market in 1976, having withdrawn in 1967.

308

ducing tractors in twenty-five new countries, of which twenty-one were less developed countries of Southern Europe and the Third World.

In contrast the European owned companies expanded almost entirely through exports. The formation of the EEC enabled European firms to penetrate each other's domestic markets without having to establish new plants which has tended to concentrate production in one country. In fact, Renault, which acquired Porsche in 1963, attempted to supply the German market through exports from France rather than continue production in Germany (Kudrle 1975, p. 98), while Fiat which had a French plant stopped producing tractors there in 1972 in order to concentrate its output in Turin. The European companies have also been less active than North American firms in expanding production outside the traditional centers. Fiat has been most active in this respect, beginning tractor production in Argentina as early as 1954. It also assembles tractors through an associated company in Turkey and recently acquired a small Spanish firm, Motransa. Deutz has only one overseas subsidiary producing tractors, in Argentina, which was set up in 1959 (having closed down its Brazilian plant in the early seventies), while Renault produces all its tractors in France. Of the British tractor firms, British Leyland has an assembly plant in Turkey, while David Brown has no oversease production.

Another important means by which the tractor companies have expanded internationally especially in socialist countries has been through licensing agreements with local firms. Massey-Ferguson had a licensing agreement with a Yugoslav State enterprise as early as 1955 and more recently it has signed an agreement with the Ursus tractor plant in Poland to introduce their parts, transmissions, and designs. Fiat has tractors produced under license in Romania and Yugoslavia and leads a consortium to construct a tractor plant in the Soviet Union.

The growing importance of overseas operations for the principal North American tractor companies, and particularly overseas production as indicated by the share of assets abroad, is summarized in Table 9.5. Deere and Massey-Ferguson have expanded rapidly outside North America since the late fifties and only International Harvester, the least dynamic of the companies, has increased its sales more rapidly in North America than elsewhere. Even International Harvester has increased its share of net assets located outside North America. Deere, the leading firm in North America, has been particularly anxious to establish itself overseas and cross-subsidized losses by its foreign subsidiaries for a decade in order to diversify geographically (*Business Week* October 27, 1973).

Table 9.5

Non-North American Sales and Assets of Major Tractor Companies
(in Percentage)

	Sales			Total Assets		
	Deere	M-F	Int. Harv.	Deere	M-F	Int. Harv.[b]
1958	12[a]	59	23	8[a]	41	17
1968	17	62	19	19	51	19
1978	23	70	20	28	60	23

Sources: Canada Royal Commission (1971), Table 12.3; Annual Reports of the Companies

Notes: [a] 1957;
[b] Data for International Harvester refer to net assets

The other major producers of tractors internationally are large firms either in the motor industry or engineering, only a very small proportion of whose output consists of tractors.[7] This makes it impossible to use company-wide statistics as an indicator of the internationalization of their tractor operations. Nevertheless, some data are available to indicate the extent to which these firms manufacture and sell tractors internationally. Ford's overseas production of tractors increased from 30 percent of total output in 1950 to more than 70 percent ten years later and since then has varied between 60 and 75 percent (Wilkins and Hill 1964, Appendix 4; Ford, *Annual Reports*). In 1978, 23 percent of all Fiat tractors were produced abroad by subsidiaries, associated companies and licensees. Forty-six percent of all employees of the company's tractor sector and 38 percent of its investments were also overseas (Fiat, *Annual Report* 1977).

Sales to the Third World have been an important element in overseas expansion. Massey-Ferguson's sales to the underdeveloped countries increased from less than a tenth of total sales in 1958 to almost a quarter twenty years later. The growth of Third World markets has also been significant for John Deere, whose sales outside of North America and Europe increased from 7.5 percent in 1972 to 11 percent six years later. Similar trends are evident for European companies such as Deutz and David Brown.

A further aspect of the internationalization of capital in the tractor industry is the way major companies plan and integrate the operations of their subsidiaries in different countries. This goes beyond the simple international circulation of commodities since it involves complementary production of different models or parts and components in different locations and the international circulation of

310

products within the same transnational corporation. This may involve the sourcing of particular parts or components in countries where labor is relatively cheap, the production of different parts and components in different centers so that the maximum advantage can be taken of economies of scale rather than duplicating production facilities, or the specialization of subsidiaries in a particular country in the models for which there is greatest demand in that country.

Evidence of the extent to which international trade in the industry takes place within transnational corporations is unfortunately fragmentary. The evidence indicates that in 1975 more than three-quarters of U.S. imports of farm machinery and equipment came from related parties, defined as firms in which there is a 5 percent shareholding (Helleiner 1978, Table 4). In fact, farm machinery ranked third among fifty industries behind electronic components and accessories and motor vehicles and equipment, in terms of the proportion of intra-firm trade. A similar pattern emerges if the exports of U.S. majority owned foreign affiliates are considered. In 1970, 88 percent of the exports of such subsidiaries in the farm machinery and equipment industry went either to the U.S. parent company or affiliates in third countries, placing it second among thirty-two industries considered (Helleiner 1978, Table 5). Finally, in the same year more than half the total U.S. exports of farm machinery and equipment were made up by U.S. transnationals exporting to majority-owned affiliates overseas, again putting it second out of thirty-two industries (Helleiner 1978, Table 3). Although data are not available to permit tractors to be separated from other agricultural machinery, in view of the importance of TNCs in the tractor industry, it seems probable that the share of intrafirm trade would be even higher than for farm machinery as a whole.

Examples of the way in which the major tractor TNCs have integrated their operations in different countries supports the picture that has just been drawn. Two of the major North American companies, Massey-Ferguson and Ford, obtained a substantial proportion of the parts used in their North American tractors from Britain in the fifties and sixties when production was cheaper there.[8] A policy of interchangeability of parts in tractors produced by Massey-Ferguson in different countries began to be developed in the mid-fifties. In the sixties Ford moved towards greater integration of its operations with a new line introduced at the Basildon factory, complemented by assembly operations in Detroit and Antwerp. Detroit manufactured the most sophisticated transmissions while other transmissions and rear axles were produced in Antwerp, and tractor engines and most other parts came from Basildon (Kudrle 1975, pp. 173-174). International Har-

311

vester was not as active as Ford and Massey-Ferguson in integrating its international operations and especially its European operations with those in the U.S., primarily because of the anticipated opposition from the United Auto Workers at the loss of jobs which this would cause. The firm did begin to import a small diesel tractor into the United States from its British subsidiary in the late 1950s and soon after developed a common continental line of tractors with the engine being produced in West Germany and the transmission and cabin in France. The tractor is then assembled in Germany and imported into France (Commission des Communautes Europeennes 1978, p. 65). John Deere was also slow to integrate its operations internationally. It only began to import European-made tractors into the U.S. in 1970 because, unlike other North American companies it lacked a production base in Britain which was generally regarded as the lowest cost area, while its operation in Germany was based on the not very modern plant acquired from Lanz in 1956. Moreover, since European combine and tractor operations were concentrated in West Germany, the kind of European integration adopted by the other U.S. multinationals did not arise for Deere.

The major European producers have not developed international production to such an extent as the North American firms and hence the scope for international integration has been limited. Fiat divided its tractor production between France, which produced large tractors, and Italy, producing small ones and all the engines until the early seventies (Commission des Communautes Europeennes, 1978). Subsequently, however, tractor production was concentrated in Italy. A similar division between Case, producing large tractors (over 100 HP) in the U.S., and David Brown concentrating on smaller tractors produced in the U.K., has developed since the two firms were acquired by Tenneco and their world retail network has been reshaped (*Agricultural Machinery Journal* April 1978, pp. 26-27). Production of the other major European companies has been nationally based and the firms have relied on exports to penetrate international markets.

The major factor underlying the developments described above has been the stagnation of demand for tractors, first in the United States and later in Western Europe. In order to maintain a high rate of growth and accumulation, companies with most of their operations in slow growing markets have been forced to look for new markets. In some cases these have been supplied by exports but in others, where either the large size of the potential market or the requirements imposed by local governments have been such as to tilt the balance in favor of local production, foreign investment has taken place. Demand for tractors reached a peak in all the major producing coun-

312

tries apart from Italy during the 1950s.[9] In the United States domestic sales of agricultural tractors did not exceed their 1951 level at current prices until 1965 (Schwartzman 1970, Table A.3) and in Canada the peak sales of 1950 were not exceeded until 1964 (Canada Royal Commission 1971, Table A.11). The sixties and seventies were also a period of relatively slow growth of tractor sales in Western Europe. Sales in France[10] and West Germany[11] increased at an average annual rate of 5 and 1 percent respectively between 1962 and 1975, while in the United Kingdom the average growth rate was 4 percent per annum for approximately the same period.[12]

The expansion of the North American tractor companies into Britain and the Continent in the late forties and early fifties was partly an attempt to obtain a foothold in markets which promised to continue to be buoyant after the decline of growth in the U.S. and Canadian markets. Investments in the latter part of the fifties by firms such as Deere in Germany and Case and Allis-Chalmers in France may have been prompted by the prospects of the sales the formation of the EEC was likely to create. And the increased interpenetration of European markets in the sixties and the increased imports of tractors to Britain in the seventies was clearly partly a result of tariff reductions.

The changed demand conditions affected the profitability of the major tractor producers in North America. The average return on investment was lower for all five major companies (Deere, Massey-Ferguson, Case, International Harvester, and Allis-Chalmers) in 1957-1967 than in 1947-1956 as were profit margins on sales (Martinusen and Barry 1970, Tables 3.1 and 3.6). In fact, net income as a percentage of sales reached a peak for all five companies in 1950 (Martinusen and Barry 1970, p. 190). Although there are no detailed estimates of capacity utilization in the North American tractor industry available, it is certain that there was considerable excess capacity in the fifties and this must have contributed to the fall in profitability.

Clearly, the prospects for a firm which continued to produce tractors primarily for the domestic market were not good after the early fifties. In addition to expanding internationally, many firms began to diversify into other sectors. Since 90 percent of the total sales of Massey-Ferguson and John Deere depended on farm machinery, these two companies were under the greatest pressure to diversify into other industries (Schwartzman 1970, Table 3.2). Massey-Ferguson began a diversification program in the late fifties acquiring Mid-Western Industries Inc., a company manufacturing light industrial equipment, in 1957 and Perkins in the U.K. in 1959. By 1977 their share of sales in farm machinery had been reduced to less than 70 percent and tractor sales had dropped to 38 percent of total company sales. John Deere followed a similar pattern of diversification. The share of agricultural machinery in total sales fell to 86 percent in 1967 and 79 percent by 1978. Recently, the British tractor company, David Brown, has begun to diversify to reduce its dependence on agricultural machinery. It managed to reduce the share of tractors in total sales from 94 percent in 1971 to 79 percent in 1977 (*Agricultural Machinery Journal* April 1978, p. 26).

In conclusion, it can be said that the falling demand for tractors in terms of units and the slow rate of growth of demand in terms of value is a key element in understanding the dynamics of internationalization in the industry. It appears that the problems posed by market saturation occur much more severely in the tractor industry than in other sectors such as cars where sales continue to show an upward trend. This has resulted in the development internationally of a highly oligopolistic industrial structure. In 1950 it was estimated that the 'big four' in the North American tractor industry accounted for 70 percent of total sales outside the Communist Bloc but this was a reflection of the preponderance of North American production rather than a high level of international concentration. With the decline of North American production in the early 1950s the share of the leading four firms declined to only 59 percent in 1954. It rose again subsequently so that by 1966 the four firm concentration had reached 63 percent and it is estimated that the share of the five largest firms increased even more sharply from 62 percent to 69 percent over the same period (Kudrle 1975, p. 140). Since the mid-sixties the share of the largest four firms has fallen to below 60 percent in the early seventies and less than 50 percent by the late seventies by which time Kubota of Japan had become one of the four leading firms in terms of units produced.

COMPETITIVE BEHAVIOR IN THE INTERNATIONAL TRACTOR OLIGOPOLY

Transnational tractor corporations have avoided price competition in numerous ways. Of primary importance, most of the leading firms have charged similar prices for tractors of the same size. For example, in Canada differences in prices charged by Deere, International Harvester, and Massey-Ferguson within each horsepower group in 1967 were usually less than 5 percent. The same was true in Britain several years later. Obviously, such similar prices would not be possible without some form of price leadership. In North America price leadership was exercised by International Harvester until the late 1950s and subsequently it has passed to Deere. An examination of the timing of price changes for tractors in Canada between 1963 and 1968 indicated that on all but one occasion Deere was the first firm to announce an increase and price changes announced by the other major firms were remarkably similar year after year (Canada Royal Commission 1971, pp. 151-152). In West Germany, Deutz was reported as being the usual price leader in the 1960s (Kudrle 1975, p. 128). In Italy the dominant position of Fiat makes it a likely price leader.

Price competition among the major tractor firms has been insignificant because fixed costs account for approximately 55 percent of the value of sales in the farm machinery industry. In order to offset a reduction in price the firm must expect a substantial increase in the volume of sales at the lower price. But since the market elasticity of demand for tractors is relatively low and since demand has also been growing slowly it has not been possible for a firm to increase its sales through the expansion of the total market. Price cutting by a firm which already had a significant share of the market would probably be followed by its competitors, since otherwise not only their market shares but also their absolute level of sales would decline. Under these circumstances market leaders are unlikely to resort to aggressive price competition.

These conditions also lead one to expect that when the demand for tractors falls, firms will attempt to maintain or even push up prices in order to cover the increased fixed costs per unit. There is some evidence to suggest that this occurred. Between 1951 and 1954, when there was a sharp drop in demand for tractors in the United States, the average price of tractors (as measured by the implicit GDP price deflater for the industry) increased by 8.3 percent, almost twice as much as the average increase in prices. This is particularly significant since there can be little doubt that the reduction in sales in this period was a result of changes in demand as the post-war boom in tractor sales came to an end.

On the other hand, small companies may be able to compete by offering lower prices since their growth is not seen as a threat to the dominant firms in the short-term and will not evoke retaliation. For example, British Leyland and David Brown tractors were sold in the United States at prices up to 15 percent lower than those of the leading firms (Kudrle 1975, p. 86). Fiat and Ford both offered lower prices in West Germany where their share of the market was small (Kudrle 1975, p. 109). East European producers have also competed aggressively on price in foreign markets in recent years. The Czech firm Zetor sold tractors in Britain at a price which is 30 percent below that of equivalent domestically produced tractors (Commission of the European Communities 1975, p. 145).

The ability of the large companies to maintain their dominant position despite charging considerably higher prices than their competitors is a result of the importance of non-price factors particularly the dealership and service network in the industry. As a report on the U.K. agricultural machinery industry commented

"Developing a dealer network is the key to success in this industry. Whereas a strong network can outweigh price and design disadvantages the converse is not true." (Commission of the European Communities 1975, p. 141).

The fact that despite a policy of offering substantially lower prices and including a number of optional extras as standard features on their models, Zetor was only able to gain 5 percent of the U.K. market in the mid-seventies was attributable to inadequate dealer representation rather than any deficiencies in the quality of Czech tractors. Thus the system of distribution in the tractor industry is not only an important barrier to entry, as was seen above, but the acquisition, support, and maintenance of an adequate dealer network is a crucial aspect of non-price competition which can be regarded as a form of product differentiation.

A related aspect of competitive behavior, particularly in North America, has been the practice of financing dealer inventories, known as "floor-planning." This was first introduced by Deere in the fifties in response to the decline in demand in North America and has led to an increased commitment of assets by the leading companies in distribution. It has been estimated by Massey-Ferguson that "floor planning" increased the retail price of one tractor model by 5.5 percent in the mid-sixties (Canada Royal Commission 1971). Firms which failed to offer credit to dealers would find themselves at a disadvantage in building up or retaining a dealership network. The provision of such credit however increases the capital requirements for entry into the industry and hence the disadvantage of small firms which are forced to operate with a limited number of sales outlets. This practice has resulted in an unusual asset structure for the major farm machinery companies which has a very high level of inventories and receivables in relation to sales (Kudrle 1975, pp. 208-215).

Product competition has been another form of non-price competition in the tractor industry. This has taken two main forms in the post-war period. In the first place there has been a steady increase in the size of tractors offered by the manufacturer in all the major producing countries. In North America Deere's acquisition of market

316

leadership in the sixties coincided with its acquiring a lead in the horsepower race (Canada Royal Commission 1971, Table 9.7). Large tractors have consistently been the most profitable segment of the market and Deere's strength in North America has been based on its concentration on the larger end of the market (*Business Week* October 27, 1973).

Secondly, the industry has followed the pattern set in the automobile industry in terms of offering an ever increasing range of models and model variations. This form of competition became particularly acute when tractor demand began to decline. The number of models offered by seven companies in North America increased from thirty-five to forty-one between 1946 and 1956 when demand was high and accelerated to reach fifty-three by 1967. The change is even more marked when model variations are considered. These rose from ninety in 1946 to 142 in 1956 and 535 in 1967 (Schwartzman 1970, pp. 145-147). A similar pattern has been observed in other countries. In the U.K. between 1966 and 1974, when tractor production fell by 25 percent, the number of models offered by the four largest firms increased from fourteen to twenty-five (Commission of the European Communities 1975, pp. 171-177). The West German market was also characterized by a large number of models in the late 1960s, with International Harvester, Deere, Deutz, and Massey-Ferguson offering six models each (Kudrle 1975, p. 149)[13].

Other forms of non-price competition have been relatively unimportant in the tractor industry in the post-war period. Innovation through the introduction of new products which played an important role in changing market shares in the inter-war years[14] has become much less significant in recent years. Indeed, in North America such competition has been muted by a tacit agreement by the firms to license new inventions to their competitors after a short time lag (Canada Royal Commission 1971, p. 149). Nor have styling changes been an important element in competition in the tractor industry with models tending to remain unchanged for a decade or more. Finally advertising, a major competitive weapon in consumer good industries, is of relatively limited importance in the industry. The major North American farm machinery companies spent on the average less than 1.5 percent of sales revenue on advertising during the 1960s (Kudrle 1975, p. 150). And in the U.K. it has been estimated that sales promotion budgets of the major tractor firms were even lower at around a half percent of turnover (Commission of the European Communities 1976, p. 144). The general view in the industry is that advertising is not a very important element in market success and this is supported by the econometric analysis of the U.K. tractor market by Cowling and

Rayner in which advertising expenditure, although statistically significant in the equation for market shares, only increases the explanatory power of the equation slightly (Cowling and Rayner 1970, p. 1301).

The oligopolistic structure of the tractor industry has implications for the behavior of the major firms internationally as well as within national boundaries. A first important question is the effect of oligopolistic interaction on the expansion of international production in the industry. The most striking aspect of the international operations of the major tractor companies is their relatively late development in terms of the chronology of multinational corporation expansion generally and their concentration in a relatively small number of countries.

This can partly be explained by the importance of economies of scale in the industry but this does not constitute an adequate explanation on its own since other industries such as automobiles which are also subject to large-scale economies have expanded internationally much more rapidly. A second crucial factor has, therefore, been the high level of international concentration and stable structure of the industry particularly in the fifties and sixties. This has contributed to a low level of oligopolistic reaction in the industry.

Another aspect of the behavior of the major tractor firms internationally has been the practice of charging very different prices for virtually identical tractors in different countries. This was first discovered when the Canadian Royal Commission on Farm Machinery ascertained that in 1970 the prices of the same tractor varied between 22 and 32 percent lower in Britain than in Canada (Canada Royal Commission 1970, p. 155). In fact, it seems to have been a deliberate policy of the major firms to maintain prices for small and medium tractors in North America above the level in Britain even after allowing for the costs of shipping. Prices in two European countries, West Germany and Sweden, were also well above those in Britain plus shipping costs and import duties (Schwartzman 1970, pp. 130-138). This price discrimination was enforced by a restrictive clause in their contracts with dealers forbidding exports (Canada Royal Commission 1971, p. 159). Such a policy enabled firms exporting from Britain, to earn high profit margins on these exports without disturbing the oligopolistic equilibrium in other markets. While it might have been possible for the two firms with large-scale production in the U.K., Massey-Ferguson and Ford, to have substantially undercut the prices offered by U.S. based firms in the North American market this might have invoked retaliation. They preferred, therefore, to follow the pattern of prices set in the North American market through the price leadership of Deere.[15] This policy of restraint in taking advantage of

318

international cost differences is also consistent with the restraint in expanding overseas production facilities discussed above.

A final aspect of international conduct concerns the international integration of the companies' operations and the possibility of using transfer pricing in order to shift profits from one subsidiary to another. As the Canadian Royal Commission discovered, this makes it extremely difficult to calculate the true profitability of the tractor companies in any one country. The Commission concluded that when the multinational farm machinery companies which operated in Canada declared profits on Canadian sales of $25 million, they earned a further $29 million on such sales which were declared outside the country (Canada Royal Commission 1971, Table 12.16). Import prices for a number of farm machinery companies in Canada varied between 60 and 63 percent of the suggested retail price whereas export prices varied from 60 to 66 percent. For four companies declared profits in 1966 were $34.7 million but these would have been only $24.6 million if all companies had used the least favorable of these transfer prices or $46.9 million if they had used the most favorable transfer prices (Canada Royal Commission 1971, p. 220). This indicates the scope for shifting profits even if transfer pricing is confined within farily narrow margins.

The international scope of their operations gives the multinational corporations considerable flexibility particularly in relation to underdeveloped countries which have exchange control regulations, high import duties and prohibitions on imports of certain products. The following practices reported by John Deere are illustrative in this respect.[16]

1. Payments for exports by a subsidiary were used for corporate expenditure outside the country in violation of exchange control rules.

2. A payment made to a subsidiary 180 days before it became due was not paid over by the Company to the subsidiary until the maturity date but in the meantime was used as collateral for a bank loan to the subsidiary in foreign currency in order to defer the time when the payment would be converted into the rapidly inflating currency.

3. Imports of certain tooling and components which were prohibited by the host government were included in shipments to a customer of John Deere in that country.

4. Prices of certain products to dealers in a number of foreign countries were increased and remittances were made abroad at the request of the dealers.

It is the multinational structure of these companies which makes it possible for them to operate in this way. It is significant that Massey-

Ferguson, in the reorganization of its international operations in 1959, incorporated three 'offshore' companies in countries regarded as tax havens. A subsidiary in Curaçao was responsible for sales of patents and licenses, one in Switzerland for purchasing machinery and equipment from outside suppliers and re-selling them to operating units, and one in Panama for borrowing short-term funds on the international money markets and re-lending them to operating units (Neufeld 1969, p. 229). Such a move obviously increased the company's ability to shift profits and minimize its tax burden substantially.

THE LATIN AMERICAN TRACTOR INDUSTRY

Structure and Growth

The Latin American tractor industry reflects in many ways the structure of the international industry discussed above. Perhaps the most striking of these is that until comparatively recently the industry only existed in the three most industrialized countries of the region—Argentina, Brazil, and Mexico—in sharp contrast to the motor industry which developed in far more countries in the sixties. This can be attributed to the reluctance of the major manufacturers to lose economies of scale through setting up plants in small markets and the limited extent of oligopolistic reaction.

Argentina was the first country in Latin America to develop a local tractor industry when a state-owned firm was authorized to set up a tractor plant in 1952 to produce 1,000 tractors a year under license from Fiat. In 1953 the government called an international tender to produce tractors in Argentina and accepted four proposals by Fiat, Deutz, Fahr, and Hanomag, the first of which acquired control of the state factory. Until 1959 tractors were really only assembled in Argentina but in that year a new decree required an increase in local content from 40 to 80 percent within four years. By 1960, when tractor production reached a peak, there were seven firms in the industry, including John Deere, Rycsa (Case), and the state firm, DINFIA, in addition to the four already mentioned. Falling production and increasing local content requirements led to a rationalization of the industry in the early sixties. DINFIA stopped production in 1962, Rycsa in 1964, and Fahr in 1966, leaving four firms, of which one, Hanomag, was subsequently acquired by Massey-Ferguson. The import content of locally produced tractors was reduced to 14 percent by 1966 and only 8 percent by 1967.

A decree to promote the tractor industry was passed in Brazil in 1959. Subsequently ten firms entered the industry including Massey-Ferguson, Ford, Deutz, and Valmet. Local content was increased so that by the mid-1960s imported materials accounted for only 5 percent of total costs in two Brazilian tractor plants (Carnoy 1972, p. 141). As in Argentina, a sharp decline in production led to a shake-out in the industry with Ford and Pasco stopping production in 1967, Fendt in 1969, and Deutz in the early seventies.

The decision to promote local production of tractors in Mexico was not taken until 1965. Regulations stipulated that local content must equal 60 percent of direct costs and that the majority of shares must be owned by Mexicans. In contrast to Argentina and Brazil, the Mexican tractor industry has continued to be dependent on imported parts and components throughout its history. An estimate made in 1975 indicated that Sidena (Ford), Deere, and International Harvester only just met the Mexican government's local content requirements with an average of 60.1 percent of direct cost within Mexico while Massey-Ferguson had a slightly higher content at 63.1 percent (Davila Reig 1975, Table 12). Mexico also differs from Argentina and Brazil in that imports continue to account for a substantial share of tractor sales (Davila Reig 1975, Appendix V).

The four major North American tractor producers are all active in Latin America, led by Massey-Ferguson which has subsidiaries in all three major countries as well as one in Peru. John Deere has subsidiaries in both Argentina and Mexico but is absent from the largest Latin American market, Brazil. Ford tractors are produced under license in Mexico by the state-owned, Sidena, and in 1976 the company re-started production of tractors in Brazil, while International Harvester is only present in the Mexican market. None of the smaller North American firms produces tractors in Latin America. The major European firm, Fiat, was for a long time the market leader in Argentina where Deutz is also a producer. Finally, the small Finnish firm, Valmet, has a Brazilian subsidiary which produces substantially more tractors than the parent company.

Local capital has until recently played a secondary role in the Latin American tractor industry. In both Argentina and Mexico, state-owned companies participated in the development of the industry. In Argentina, however, DIFIA was always a very small-scale producer and ceased production in the early sixties. In Mexico the state firm, SIDENA, manufacturing Ford tractors under license has been one of the major manufacturers since the mid-sixties.[17] In Brazil the third largest firm in the mid-seventies, Companhia Brasileira de Tractores, was locally-owned. The company began production with a license from the Oliver Corporation in 1960 but subsequently developed its own models. In the mid-seventies with an output of over 10,000 tractors a year the company appeared to be a very successful example of local capital competing with multinationals. However, with the decline in the Brazilian market in the late seventies and the reentry of Ford into the industry in 1976 the company has been particularly badly hit and production fell to less than half the levels of the mid-seventies.[18]

Despite the late start, tractor production in Latin America grew rapidly. Between 1967 and 1977 production increased more than five-fold from 18,375 to 89,874 primarily because of a ten-fold expansion in Brazilian production. Growth in Argentina, where production peaked at over 20,000 units in 1960 and then fell by 1967 to its lowest level since the first years of the industry in the early 1950s, and in Mexico made only a modest contribution to the overall upsurge.

Tractor production in Latin America is highly concentrated as Table 9.6 indicates. In the peak year for tractor production in the region (1976) Massey-Ferguson was the market leader accounting for between 37 and 45 percent of production. The two largest firms account for between 65 and 73 percent of production in each Latin American country compared with between 35 and 57 percent in the developed countries suggesting that the industry is more concentrated in Latin America than in the United States and Europe.

The market leadership of Massey-Ferguson in all three countries gave it a position of complete dominance at the regional level in the mid-seventies. Subsequently, it has lost ground reflecting the difficulties which the company has experienced internationally. In 1979 it sold its Mexican subsidiary to local interests and a year later, along with the other firms operating in Argentina, closed down its local plant. In Brazil it has seen its market share decline by about 10 percentage points mainly to the benefit of Ford.

Competitive Strategies

The competitive strategies employed by the international tractor firms in Latin America are the same as those used in the developed nations, e.g., the provision of a range of tractor models, increasing size of tractors, and product differentiation through a strong system of distribution and after sale service.

Almost the same variety of models are sold in Latin America as in Europe. In Argentina five firms produced thirty different models between them with sixteen different HP offerings in the sixties while

322

Table 9.6

Production by Firm in Principal Latin American Countries, 1976

	Argentina		Brazil		Mexico		Total	
	No.	%	No.	%	No.	%	No.	%
Massey-Ferguson	9,028	37.7	29,271	44.8	3,788	42.6	42,087	42.9
John Deere	4,178	17.5	—	—	1,399	15.7	5,577	5.7
International Harvester	—	—	—	—	1,046	11.8	1,046	1.1
Ford	—	—	5,169	7.9	2,660	29.9	7,829	8.0
Fiat	6,171	28.1	—	—	—	—	6,717	6.8
Deutz	4,000	16.7	—	—	—	—	4,000	4.1
Valmet	—	—	15,071	23.1	—	—	15,071	15.4
Comphania Brasileira de Tractores	—	—	11,653	17.8	—	—	11,653	11.9
Other	—	—	4,146	6.3	—	—	4,146	4.2
TOTAL	23,923	100.0	65,310	100.0	8,893	100.0	98,126	100.0

Source: Own compilation.

in 1975 the four remaining companies produced thirty-one models with twenty different horsepowers (Dagnino Pastore 1966, Table 3.1; and ADEFA).[19] In Mexico the number of models produced by the four firms increased from ten in 1970 to sixteen in 1976 with fourteen different sizes. Similarly, in Brazil the number of models produced increased from nineteen in the early seventies to thirty-four by the end of the decade.

In all these countries the trend has been to produce increasingly powerful tractors. The average size of locally produced tractors in Argentina increased from 46.4 HP in 1960 to 71.2 HP in 1976. In Mexico it increased from 57.7 HP in 1969 to 67.3 by 1976 (Davila Reig 1975, Table 5; and AMIA 1977,p. 150), while in Brazil there has been a shift in production towards larger tractors at least during the seventies, which probably began even earlier (Oliveira 1979, Table 14). Moreover, the rising average size of tractors produced has been accompanied by the disappearance of the smaller models of tractor. In Argenina tractors of 35 HP or less accounted for over a quarter of production in 1960 but by the mid-seventies the smallest tractors available were of over 40 HP (ADEFA). A similar trend was evident in Mexico in the seventies. In 1971 over half the tractors produced were of 55 HP or less but by 1980, only one 55 HP model was still in production. This increasing emphasis on larger tractors and the disappearance of small tractors reduced the prospects of the bulk of the Latin American peasantry ever being able to utilize them.

As was indicated above, one of the most distinctive features of competition in the tractor industry, especially in North America, is the system of distribution and in particular the extension of credit to dealers. As a result of this system the major farm machinery companies have a very high ratio of current assets, both to total assets and to sales, compared with other industries. As Table 9.7 indicates, in 1967 over 80 percent of the assets of six North American farm machinery companies consisted of current assets. The asset structure of three Mexican tractor firms was also very similar, while two of the four Argentinian firms had virtually exactly the same proportion of current assets as the U.S. firms and the other two firms had slightly lower ratios. Current assets were greater than sales in Argentina and Mexico while they were slightly lower in the U.S. In both the United States and Mexico the high share of current assets are primarily due to the importance of credits (accounts receivable) which account for a very similar proportion of total assets and are somewhat higher in relation to sales in Mexico. In the case of Argentina inventories are

Table 9.7

Financial Ratios in the Tractor Industry, Argentina, Mexico, U.S. (in Percentage)

	Argentina (1963)				Mexico (1972) (3 firms)[b]	U.S. (1967) (6 firms)[c]
	Firm A	Firm B	Firm C	Firm D[a]		
Current Assets/Sales	103.1	103.1	101.0	384.6	110.3	90.7
Inventories/Sales	60.2	67.6	59.5	303.0	36.2	29.3
Credit/Sales	41.2	32.8	35.5	84.7	68.1	55.9
Current Assets/Total Assets	74.2	80.4	66.7	80.8	84.0	80.8
Inventories/Total Assets	43.4	52.7	39.3	63.6	27.6	26.1
Credit/Total Assets	29.6	25.6	23.4	17.8	51.9	49.8

Sources: Argentina: Dagnino Pastore (1966), Table 9.34 and own elaboration
  Mexico: Davila Reig (1975), Appendix I and II
  U.S.: Martinusen and Barry (1970), Table 4.1 and Tables C.1—C.6.

Notes:
[a] As can be seen from the Table, one Argentinian firm (D) is way out of line with very high levels of inventories and credits to sales. This probably reflects a very poor sales performance by the firm in that year, a hypothesis that is borne out by the heavy losses which it made. (Pastore 1966, Table 9.37).
[b] Massey-Ferguson, John Deere, International Harvester
[c] Massey-Ferguson, John Deere, International Harvester, J.I. Case, Allis Chalmers, White Motor

more important than credits but this may simply reflect the overall depressed states of the tractor market in the year considered.

In the absence of detailed studies of the system of tractor distribution in the Latin American countries, this evidence from the balance sheets of the tractor companies suggests that the dealer network has played a similar role in the competitive strategies of the firms to that discussed above in the developed countries.

Industrial Performance

Despite the growth of tractor production, levels of output in Latin America have been well below those required for minimum efficient scales of plant. Total production in the region only approached the 90,000 level in the mid-seventies. More importantly, this production is divided between more than a dozen plants in three countries. Consequently, only Massey-Ferguson in Brazil has achieved levels of production of around 20,000 tractors or more a year, whereas in Argentina and Mexico the major firms have been producing less than 10,000 units a year.

This has inevitably meant that locally manufactured tractors have been costly to produce. A study of the industry in Argentina and Brazil in the mid-1960s concluded that prices were approximately 40 percent higher than the cif price of imported tractors from the United States and twice as high as the equivalent British price (Carnoy 1972, p. 148). Despite lower levels of content in Mexico which might have been expected to keep down costs relative to international levels, the average price per HP of locally produced tractors was almost 50 percent higher than in the United States in 1975. (Calculated from AMIA 1977, pp. 150, 181; *Implement and Tractor*, July 11, 1978, p. 64.) The lack of economies of scale was clearly a major factor in the high cost of locally produced tractors. In Argentina in 1963 six firms produced 11,425 tractors between them, an average of less than 2,000 each, with a range of output from 311 for Rycsa to 4,617 for Fiat. At the same time it was estimated that unit costs were over 40 percent higher at an output of 2,000 than would be the case at an output of 20,000 tractors a year (Calculated from Dagnino Pastore 1966, Table 4.17).

Although the growth of production in the region since the mid-sixties has changed the situation somewhat, in the absence of more recent data, these calculations are of some interest. In Argentina in the mid-seventies both John Deere and Deutz were producing at about the same level as the largest producer in the mid-sixties while Fiat and Massey-Ferguson with somewhat higher volumes were still well below the 10,000 mark. In fact, only Valmet and Cia Brasiliera de Tractores were producing at these levels in Brazil, with Massey-Ferguson of course achieving an output which compares with that of companies such as David Brown, British Leyland, and Renault. Moreover, the higher level of local content in Brazil and the increase in Argentinian content since the mid-sixties is likely to have increased the diseconomies of scale.

High costs of locally produced tractors appear to have been compensated for by high prices expect where, as in the case of Mexico in the late sixties and early seventies, rigid price controls have been enforced. As a result the profitability of the major companies operating in Latin America, especially Massey-Ferguson, was high in the mid-seventies. However, as already indicated, declared profit figures for specific countries need to be treated with considerable caution in view of the international integration of the tractor companies and the scope that this gives for transfer pricing. This is particularly true in Mexico which continues to rely heavily on imported components. By way of illustration, had 20 percent of the value of imports for use in tractor production in Mexico in 1974 represented profits to the company, the rate of return on the firm's own capital would have more than doubled from 8 to 20 percent (Davila Reig 1975, pp. 26-27; AMIA 1976, p. 174).

Furthermore, the tractor industry has been characterized by high levels of excess capacity for most of its history in Latin America. In Argentina in 1963 capacity utilization was only 48 percent and although it reached 80 percent in 1976, this followed a long period of under-utilization (Dagnino Pastore 1966, Chapter 10). In Brazil in the late sixties capacity was around 26,000 and utilization only 25 percent to 30 percent; by the mid-1970s capacity had grown to 110,000 units and utilization had increased to about 65 percent. InMexico capacity utilization on a one-shift basis fluctuated between 30 and 60 percent during that period (Davila Reig 1975, Table 8).
30 and 60 percent during that period (Davila Reig 1975, Table 8).

Two factors appear to have contributed to such high levels of excess capacity in the industry. In the first place, oligopolistic markets tend to lead firms to "build ahead of demand" when faced with plant indivisibilities and economies of scale (Steindl 1952, pp. 9-11) and it has been suggested that this is a typical form of operation where international firms, which have finance available to build a larger plant than is justified by the existing size of the market, are the investors (Fajnzylber 1970, pp. 280-298). Second, in oligopolistic industries output tends to be adjusted through variations in capacity utilization rather than through the entry and exit of firms to and from

327

the industry. This gives rise to particularly high levels of excess capacity when demand is depressed. Such under-utilization of capacity must have contributed to increased costs in the industry. In Argentina in the mid-sixties it was estimated that full capacity operation would reduce costs by 15 percent (Dagnino Pastore 1966, Chapter 10).

It would appear that the structure and performance of the Latin American tractor industry has been conditioned by the international tractor oligopoly. First, oligopolistic reaction, although weak, led to a number of TNCs setting up small-scale production facilities with considerable excess capacity. Second, the pricing behavior of the international oligopoly together with high levels of tariff protection granted by host governments enabled the TNCs to be highly profitable in their operations except when stringent price controls were imposed. Third, the non-price forms of competition characteristic of the industry in the developed countries have been carried over to Latin America.

THE TRACTOR INDUSTRY AND THE MECHANIZATION OF LATIN AMERICAN AGRICULTURE

No analysis of the development of the tractor industry in Latin America would be complete without examining its link to agricultural mechanization. In view of the limited research available on this subject, and the recent development of tractor production in the Andean Pact, this section will draw on empirical information not only from those countries which have a history of tractor production but also from the rest of Latin America.

The development of tractor production in the region has tended to reinforce the vested interests which favor agricultural mechanization. Even before local manufacturing develops, importers are an important lobby in favor of mechanization with a view to increasing sales of agricultural machinery.[20] Once major TNCs have established production facilities, often as was seen above with substantial excess capacity, they constitute a significant force pressing for government support of mechanization policies. Both TNCs and landowners press for government subsidies and credit arguing that agricultural costs should not be increased as a result of the higher costs of producing tractors locally.[21] These companies have also sought additional outlets for their output in the non-producing countries of the region where tractors have been exported with the aid of substantial government subsidies. In analyzing the impact of the tractor TNCs in Latin America, therefore, it is also necessary to consider the main implications of agricultural mechanization in the region.

The use of tractors in Latin America has been concentrated in a few geographical areas. In Argentina 70 percent of the tractors are located in the pampas; in Brazil more than 70 percent are in the state of Saõ Paulo and a similar proportion is concentrated in eight (out of twenty-one) departments in Colombia and the north and Pacific north zones of Mexico (Abercrombie 1972, p. 19). In these areas tractor use per cultivated hectare is not far short of North American levels. While topographical factors and the type of crops cultivated partly explain such concentration, a major element is the highly uneven distribution of landownership and farm size in most Latin American countries. To be economically viable a tractor of 40-60 HP (i.e. around the bottom of the range of tractors produced in Latin America) requires an arable acreage of more than 40 to 50 hectares (Abercrombie 1972, p. 19). A study in Guatemala concluded that even a small tractor of 24 HP requires a minimum farm size of 16 hectares (IADB 1978, p. 32). These figures imply that the vast majority of land holdings in Latin America are far too small to use tractors of the kind being produced in the region. In 1970, 88 percent of all agricultural holdings in South America were of less than 50 hectares and the proportion rose to over 95 percent in Peru, the Dominican Republic, El Salvador, and Honduras. In most Latin American countries the majority of farms are of less than 10 hectares (FAO 1981).

The problem is not just one of farm size. It is also that the bulk of the peasantry does not have sufficient income to contemplate buying a tractor. In Guatemala, for example, the required down payment of 40 percent of the price of a 12.5 HP tractor was between eleven and thirty-four times the annual income of a small farmer (IADB 1978, p. 34). It is not surprising that farms of over 50 hectares had 93 percent of all the tractors in Chile, 66 percent in Colombia and 75 percent of all the farm machinery in Mexico in the early sixties (Abercrombie 1972, p. 20).

The fact that tractor ownership is so concentrated and the mass of the rural population is in no position to acquire a tractor is particularly important in view of government policies to promote agricultural mechanization. It is common practice in Latin America for 70 to 100 percent of the purchase price of tractors to be available as credit from government institutions, often at negative rates of interest. For example, in Argentina, Brazil, and Venezuela the real rates of interest varied from 6 to 13 percent so that farmers only had to pay back between 50 and 80 percent of their loans (Abercrombie 1972, p. 32).

This represented a direct subsidy to the largest landowners in these countries.

The extension of credit for agricultural mechanization also has its international dimension. All the Latin American Free Trade Area (LAFTA) countries have received loans for purchases of agricultural machinery either from the World Bank or the U.S. Eximbank or the Agency for International Development (IADB 1978, p. 15). In fact, aid-financed exports of agricultural machinery are particularly important both for U.S. and U.K. producers. It has been estimated that in the sixties 45 percent of U.S. exports of farm machinery to six Latin American countries were financed by foreign aid and there is evidence that a high proportion of British exports of farm machinery is also aid-financed (Canada Royal Commission 1971, p. 274). Tractors were the type of machine most frequently exported in this way. Again, the same conclusion can be drawn that the bulk of this "aid" goes to subsidize the better-off sectors of the rural population and/or the tractor companies themselves.[22]

Not only does the mass of the rural population not benefit directly from agricultural mechanization but it may even be adversely affected as a result of the displacement of labor. Typically a significant proportion of the rural population is either landless or depends on employment on large farms at certain times of the year in order to supplement its income. The impact of mechanization on the demand for labor is therefore crucial in determining the effects for the poorer sectors in the rural areas. It has been estimated that the introduction of one tractor implies a reduction in average labor requirements for the main field crops of about four man years in Chile, six man years in Colombia and seven man years in Guatemala (Abercrombie 1972, p. 26). While there are some factors which work in the opposite direction to increase the total demand for labor, such as the possibility of extending cultivation, releasing land previously required to keep draught animals, the changeover from grazing to arable land, and the possibility of double cropping, it appears that the general effect in Latin America has been to displace labor. Even taking these counteracting factors into account, it has been conservatively estimated that the tractors in use in Latin America in 1969 had displaced about 2.5 million jobs in the region (Abercrombie 1972, p. 27).

Not surprisingly it appears that agricultural mechanization has increased inequality in the rural areas. In the conditions which generally prevail in Latin America the main beneficiaries have been large landlords and a few tractor drivers. In Brazil, for example, despite the much higher level of mechanization in the south compared to the

330

north-east of the country, wages only reflect the higher productivity to a small degree and income distribution is even less equitable in the south than the north-east (Abercrombie 1972, p. 22). A simulation exercise to evaluate the impact of subsidizing farm mechanization in Colombia also concluded that the policy accentuated inequality through increasing the share of income appropriated by owners of capital (large landowners) at the expense of labor and small farmers (Thirsk 1972).

Although it is sometimes argued that the development of the agricultural machinery industry is an important offsetting factor to the displacement of labor by mechanization, the employment created by the industry is minimal. An estimate for eleven LAFTA countries in the late sixties indicated that total employment was only 140,000 of which half was in the distribution, maintenance and repair sectors (Abercrombie 1972, Table IV). In the mid-seventies the total number directly employed in the tractor industry in Argentina, Brazil, and Mexico was less than 20,000. Moreover, the creation of these jobs required considerable capital investment: investment per job created in Argentina and Brazil in the late sixties was of the order of $10,000 and each job at the new Deere plant in Venezuela would have cost over $60,000 (Abercrombie 1972, p. 22; and own investigation).

The overall impact of the development of a local tractor industry in Latin America and the agricultural mechanization that this implies has been aptly summarized by the Inter-American Development Bank:

> It would appear that if current mechanization policies and trends in many Latin American countries continue the outcome will be greater concentration of land use in the hands of a few, greater unemployment in the rural areas and probably little, if any, increases in food production levels (IADB 1978, p. 35).

That this is not an inevitable consequence of mechanization is clear from the Cuban example. In Cuba extensive mechanization of agriculture, especially sugar cane, has been possible without the adverse effects on labor observed in other countries because the state guarantees employment elsewhere (Aurori 1977). Indeed, it is possible to devise programs of selective mechanization for Latin America which would minimize the displacement of labor or even increase the demand for labor. The problem is that these run counter to the logic of capital accumulation, not only of the tractor TNCs but also of large landowners in Latin America.[23]

THE CREATION OF THE ANDEAN PACT TRACTOR
INDUSTRY

While tractor production on any scale in Latin America has been confined to Argentina, Brazil, and Mexico, recent developments in the Andean Pact involving negotiations with the major TNCs to develop the industry in the region are of particular interest in analysing the relation between host governments and foreign capital. The contract signed between Venezuela and John Deere to set up a local tractor plant illustrates both the opportunities for the state to take advantage of intra-capitalist competition to obtain favorable terms from the TNCs and the pitfalls of such a strategy.

Despite its relatively small size, the Andean Pact market for tractors has been the scene of intense competition between the multinational producers in recent years. This rivalry has been particularly keen in the bidding process to establish local production facilities in the region, reflecting the growing importance of the developing countries in world tractor demand and the destabilization of the oligopolistic structure of the international industry, which were analyzed in detail earlier in this paper.

The comparatively small size of the Andean Pact market in the early 1970s is brought out by the figures in Table 9.8 below, which shows the imports of agricultural tractors by the countries in the region for the years 1970-1974. As the local manufacture of tractors did not commence until 1974, and then in only one country at an initially low level of output, these figures may be taken as a reasonable approximation of the demand for tractors in the region at the time. As can be seen, imports of agricultural tractors in these years average around 6,000 units per year, or 5,000 per year excluding Chile. Demand has increased since then, primarily due to the dynamism of the Venezuelan market following the 1973 increase in world oil prices. Imports of agricultural tractors in this country were more than 5,000 units per year in 1975 and 1976 and further growth in the market to 8,700 units is foreseen by 1985. Venezuela has thus reinforced its position as the principal consuming country in the Andean Pact region, and it is hardly surprising that it is precisely in this country that rivalry to establish local manufacturing operations has been most intense.

However, it was not Venezuela but rather Peru which was the first country in the region to set up a tractor manufacturing plant. Having obtained agreement from the other members of the Pact (which at the time did not include Venezuela) that it should be assigned tractor production under the regional automotive program, Peru reached an agreement with Massey-Ferguson at the end of 1972 for the establishment of local manufacturing facilities. A company called Tractores Andinos SA was formed as a joint-venture between Massey-Ferguson with 49 percent of the equity and the Peruvian government with 51 percent, held by the state agencies Industrias del Peru and La Corporacion Financiera de Desarollo. Assembly of Massey-Ferguson tractors commenced in temporary facilities in 1974, and a manufacturing plant with an annual capacity of 2,000 units was opened in Trujillo in the north of the country in 1976. The level of local integration was only 22 percent initially but was planned to rise to 62 percent within three years of the opening of the plant (*Grupo Andino*, 1975 and 1976; Massey-Ferguson Ltd. *Annual Report*, 1975). For the production of diesel engines a separate company known as Motores Diesel Andinos was formed. Apart from Perkins engines for Massey-Ferguson tractors, this company's plant is also designed to produce Volvo heavy diesel engines. The company is 52 percent owned by the Peruvian government with Perkins and Volvo each having 24 percent of the equity. Production began in late 1977 with an initial capacity of 10,000 units per year and a level of local integration of 18 percent. Capacity is subsequently intended to be expanded to 15,000 units and it is hoped that the level of local integration will reach 70 percent (*Grupo Andino*).

Table 9.8

Average Annual Imports of Agricultural Tractors by Andean Pact Countries, 1970–1974

	No. of Units	% of Units
Bolivia	92	1.6
Chile[a]	742	12.7
Colombia	1,620	27.7
Ecuador	424	7.3
Peru	365	6.2
Venezuela[b]	2,605	44.5
TOTAL	5,848	100.00

Source: Based on partner country export data.
Notes: [a] Left the Pact in 1976
[b] Joined the Pact in 1973

Meanwhile, negotiations were being undertaken in Venezuela for the establishment of a tractor plant in that country. In 1970 Renault presented a project to the Corporacion Venezolana de Guayana, the government development corporation for the Guayana region, for the

333

construction of a plant with an annual capacity of 2,000 units. It then called for bids from other firms and offers were received from Massey-Ferguson, Ford, and Deutz. These were passed to two interministerial committees for evaluation but no decision was made. News that Peru was going ahead with its project in association with Massey-Ferguson seems to have stirred the Venezuelans into action, particularly after the country had entered the Andean Pact in 1973, meaning that most of its market could have been supplied from the Peruvian plant. New bids were called for and offers were received from a substantial number of companies, the principal contenders seeming to have been Deere, Ford, International Harvester, and Deutz. A contract was signed with Deere in 1974 and, as an official document notes, after all seemed to have been lost due to the start of the Peruvian project, Venezuela was able to obtain an agreement that it be assigned tractor production as well as Peru in the Pact's automotive program. The anxiety of the Venezuelans to establish their own tractor plant is not surprising given their dominant position in the Andean Pact tractor market and the rapid growth of demand in the country.

The Venezuelan tractor company, called Fabrica Nacional de Tractores y Motores SA (FANATRACTO), is a joint-venture between Deere with 20 percent of the equity and the Corporacion Venezolana de Guyana and private Venezuelan investors with 45 percent and 35 percent shares respectively. One of the private sector investors is Deere's importing and distributing agent in Venezuela, Aco, which has a 15 percent participation.[24] Assembly in temporary facilities began in 1978 while construction was underway of the manufacturing plant in Ciudad Bolivar in the Guayana region. The plant will have an initial capacity of 5,500 tractors and 7,500 diesel engines. At present local integration is only 12 percent but when the new plant is completed this will rise to 60 percent.

The Venezuelans were able to obtain favorable conditions in their negotiations with Deere, and it will be argued that this was related to the rivalry between the multinational tractor producers and the relatively weak position of Deere in the fast growing Latin American market, particularly in relation to its major competitor in the world tractor market, Massey-Ferguson. In the first place, as was mentioned above, Deere agreed to participate in the Venezuelan project with an equity participation of only 20 percent. This is particularly significant given that the company has shown a preference for virtually 100 percent ownership of its overseas manufacturing companies.

The evidence suggests that Venezuela was able to negotiate a relatively low price for technical assistance and know-how from Deere. A package of three contracts were signed between FANATRACTO and Deere. The first of these is a licensing agreement under which Deere grants to FANATRACTO the right to manufacture its tractors and to use its trademark. It also grants to FANATRACTO all patents held by Deere in Venezuela. The most significant feature of this contract is that it stipulates a zero royalty rate. The other two contracts are for the supply of technical assistance by Deere to FANATRACTO for the construction of the plant in Ciudad Bolivar and the production of John Deere tractors. In these contracts payments are related to the actual amount of technical assistance supplied, as they take the form of professional fees at stipulated rates per man-hour of services rendered. This is in stark contrast with the normal type of technological contract in the Andean Pact, or Latin American countries in general, whereby payment is fixed as a proportion of sales (or less commonly as a given amount per unit of production) and is hence not directly related to the technical assistance services received. The forecast amounts of payments during the five years of operation of the contract are shown in Table 9.9 As can be seen, the payments diminish sharply after the second year and in the fifth year represent a very small percentage of estimated sales.

Table 9.9

Forecast Technical Assistance Payments by FANATRACTO of Venezuela to Deere and Co.

	Amount ($, 000s)	% of Net Sales
Year 1	750	2.8
2	1,000	2.6
3	750	1.5
4	450	0.7
5	100	0.2
Total	3,050	1.3

Source: Superintendencia de Inversiones Extranjeras

The technical assistance arrangement with Deere may be contrasted with the proposal made by Deutz, which was one of the principal contenders for the Venezuelan project. Deutz asked for an initial lump sum payment of $712 thousand and annual payments of $200 per tractor produced, equivalent to 3 percent of the CKD value of the German produced tractor. This is the more traditional type of arrangement whereby payment is not directly related to the services actually received.

335

A final advantage gained by Venezuela in its negotiations with Deere is that the U.S. firm has agreed to purchase 25,000 tons per year of parts from a foundry to be constructed in Venezuela. This foundry is also to be located in the Guayana region and will supply the tractor plant. The project has however run into delays, although a feasibility study has been undertaken by British Leyland. As Venezuela can in no way be considered as a low cost source of supplies it would appear that the export arrangement is more advantageous to the country rather than to Deere.

A word of caution is in order concerning the apparently favorable terms obtained by the Venezuelan government in its tractor negotiations. It is important to see such arrangements not simply as a once and for all deal but as a continuing process. Thus, whether or not a negotiation can be regarded as successful depends on the extent to which apparently favorable terms on paper are actually complied with in practice. It is of course too early to say whether or not the Venezuelan government will prove to be successful in this sense. An extremely important question here is whether Deere will be able to make substantial profits through selling parts and components to FANATRACTO at inflated prices. There will obviously be considerable scope for this since it has been estimated that during the first five years of the project 15,600 tractor kits will be imported from Deere factories in Argentina, Germany, Spain, and France at a total cost of $84.8 million. Thus, the success of the negotiations from the point of view of the Venezuelan government will depend crucially on how far transfer pricing can be controlled.

To understand why the Venezuelans were apparently able to obtain unusually favorable terms in their negotiations with Deere, it is necessary to take account of the growing importance of Latin America in the world tractor market, and the competition between the major international firms to maintain and strengthen their positions in the region. As we saw above, according to estimates made by Massey-Ferguson in the mid-seventies, Latin America is expected to increase its share in total tractor consumption in non-Communist countries from 14 percent in 1975 to 27 percent in 1985, making it the area with the fastest growing demand in the western world. Evidently, the extent to which the major firms are able to participate in this rapidly growing market will be a major determinant of their international competitive position in coming years.

However, the major companies were very unevenly placed to take advantage of this forecasted growth in the Latin American market, making it almost inevitable that the quite dramatic change in the geographical distribution of world tractor demand would upset what-

336

ever oligopolistic equilibrium existed between the multinationals. In particular Massey-Ferguson would, if it could maintain its dominant position in the region, benefit considerably. Deere has reasonable shares in the Argentinian and Mexican markets, but has no plant in Brazil. The company was considering investing in Brazil in the mid-1970s,[25] but seems to have been outmaneuvered by Ford which opened a new tractor plant in the country in 1976. Subsequently in 1979 Deere entered the Brazilian combine harvester market, taking a 20 percent shareholding in Schneider-Logeman, the country's largest combine manufacturer, thus insuring a foothold in Brazil.

After Massey-Ferguson clinched the deal with Peru, giving rise to the possibility that it might capture most of the Andean Pact market, it can easily be understood why the focus of international competition in the region switched to Venezuela—a rapidly growing market in which local production facilities had still not been established. Deere must have been particularly anxious to win the Venezuelan contract, not only because of its relatively weak position in the three major Latin American markets in comparison with Massey-Ferguson, but also because it was the market leader in Venezuela itself. As Table 9.10 shows, Deere accounted for 25 percent of industry sales of agricultural tractors in Venezuela in 1975, followed by Ford with 17 percent and Massey-Ferguson with 10 percent. Deere was also the market leader between 1972-1974, with Ford in second place and International Harvester third. It hence had more to lose than the other firms had it failed to win the contract.

Thus, in one sense it may be said that international competition between the major world tractor producers has had the beneficial effect of allowing a country like Venezuela to negotiate favorable terms for the establishment of local manufacturing facilities. But on the grounds of economies of scale such competition has had detrimental effects as, coupled with rivalry between the Andean Pact nation states to have production based in their territories, it has led to the setting up already of two quite integrated plants in a relatively small regional market. The tractor industry is characterized by very important plant economies of scale. As was mentioned above, it has been estimated that a level of output of at least 20,000 units per year is necessary to guarantee international competitiveness, while some studies indicate that all potential economies of scale are not exhausted until capacity reaches 90,000 units per year. But Andean Pact demand in the early 1970s was only 6,000 tractors per year and now, with the growth of the Venezuelan market, may be around 8,000 units per year. The establishment of two—and possibly more—plants in such a relatively small although growing market is bound to lead to increased

337

unit costs of production, loss of international competitiveness, and higher prices for domestic consumers.

Table 9.10

Venezuela: Sales of Agricultural Tractors by Company, 1975

Company	Nationality	No. of Units	% of Units
Deere	U.S.	975	25
Ford	U.S.	646	17
Massey-Ferguson	Canada	410	10
International Harvester	U.S.	298	8
David Brown[a]	U.K.		
White Oliver	U.S.	498	13
Leyland	U.K.		
Case[a]	U.S.	472	12
Others[b]	—	577	15
Total	—	3,876	100

Source: Own survey

Notes:
[a] David Brown and Case are both owned by Tenneco of the U.S.
[b] Fiat and Same of Italy, Ebro of Spain, and Ursus of Poland

Indeed the most recent estimates presented by FANATRACTO to the Venezuelan government indicated that even in the most favorable case, when 60 percent local integration is achieved, nationally produced tractors will cost 33 percent more than the equivalent imported models on the assumption of capacity output. With more pessimistic assumptions about the price of bought-in local parts the cost will rise to 62 percent above the import price even with full capacity operation. As a result a 50 percent nominal tariff is at present being proposed to allow FANATRACTO to operate profitably, and the company has stated that it will be necessary to provide financial assistance to tractor buyers to compensate for the higher price they will face when local production starts.[26]

CONCLUSION

This chapter has analyzed the structure of the tractor industry in the post-war period focusing on the transition it made from an industry

338

dominated by North American production, to one where production was concentrated in a small number of developed countries with high levels of exports and finally, since the 1960s, to one that included a number of Third World countries. As was seen, the industry is characterized by high levels of concentration both within countries and at the international level. The principal multinational firms in the industry have, therefore, been highly conscious of the moves made by their main competitors. They have evolved competitive strategies which avoid price competition and emphasize the provision of services through a strong dealer network, the proliferation of a range of models and a continuous upward trend in the average size of the tractors which they offer. Until fairly recently the major firms in the industry have preferred to expand internationally through exports and have been relatively reluctant to establish production facilities overseas compared with other industries. However, lately intensified international competition has led firms to show considerable interest in entering even very small but promising markets.

Latin American tractor production has until recently been confined to Argentina, Brazil, and Mexico. By international standards production levels have been small with the exception of Massey-Ferguson's Brazilian operation. As a result tractor costs in these countries have been significantly higher than in the developed countries, a problem which is accentuated by the firms' following the same competitive strategies as in their domestic markets. Despite high costs the available data suggests that the TNCs have earned good profits in Latin America, a finding that is consistent with the high level of concentration in all the major countries. High profitability does not appear to have been associated with rapid productivity growth at least as far as Brazil and Mexico are concerned. Profits have also been maintained despite lengthy periods when the industry has operated with substantial excess capacity.

The recent growth of the Japanese tractor industry and the emergence of large companies such as Kubota, as well as the development of the tractor industry in the socialist countries, is likely to intensify international competition even further in the 1980s. Already this is occurring in the United States and Western Europe, but so far its impact in Latin America has been limited. Production in all three major countries is dominated by North American and European capital with local firms playing a secondary role in Brazil and Mexico. The overseas expansion of the Japanese manufacturers has so far been confined almost entirely to exports, although Kubota has a subsidiary producing motorized cultivators in Brazil. In the future the tractor industry is likely to approach more closely the situation of the motor industry which for the past two decades has been characterized by intense competition to enter new markets.

This makes it all the more important that free entry should not be granted to foreign firms wishing to invest in local production of tractors. It is possible, as the Venezuelan case indicated, for competition to enter new markets to be exploited by the host government in order to obtain better terms from the TNCs, rather than allowing the market to be fragmented between a large number of firms with substantial excess capacity. Such negotiations can cover local content, models to be produced, plant capacity, involvement of local firms in the construction of the plant, the capital structure of the tractor company, royalty and technical assistance payments, and export commitments, to name only some. The number of possible areas for negotiation is itself an indicator of the dangers of leaving everything to the market, particularly where the firms involved will inevitably have considerable market power.

As has been stressed in this paper, however, it is not sufficient to focus merely on the international structure of the tractor industry within Latin America without also considering the whole question of agricultural mechanization. It is, therefore, crucial that decisions concerning the development and scale of a local tractor industry should be made in the light of an overall policy on mechanization. While some of the adverse effects on income distribution of subsidizing large farmers through cheap credit for mechanization might be offset by changes in policy, the crucial questions of who gains from increasing use of tractors are much more intractable. In brief, the existing structures of land tenure and political power in Latin America are at the root of the problem and radical changes in policy are unlikely without changes in political power. Recommendations for more selective mechanization, increased emphasis on cooperative or collective organization of the peasantry, redistribution of land, etc., immediately run up against powerful vested interests. It is here that one reaches the limits of focusing on a single industry at an international level and the analysis must pass to a study of the political economy of particular countries.

Notes

[1] International Harvester had 60 percent of the market and Deere and Company 21 percent. The other five firms were J.I. Case, Allis-Chalmers, Oliver, Minneapolis-Moline, and Massey-Ferguson.

[2] The size of tractors tends to increase so that measured in terms of HP tractor usage is still rising.

[3] Kudrle (1975: 95) quoting United Nations, *European Tractor Industry*. There is an apparent inconsistency between this figure and the 85 firms producing tractors in 1956 mentioned by Kudrle on p. 128 since he indicates that there were no new entrants between 1950 and 1956.

[4] Porsche by Renault in 1962 and Eicher by Massey-Ferguson in 1970.

[5] Fiat stopped producing tractors in France in 1972.

[6] Lamborghini was acquired by Same in 1978.

[7] Ford's farm machinery sales in the mid-1960s were estimated at 3 percent of total company sales (Martinusen and Berry (1970), p. 11, n.1.) Fiat's sales of tractors in 1978 were 5 percent of the group's turnover (Fiat, *Annual Report*, 1978). Renault's agricultural materials division accounts for between 1 percent and 2 percent of the company's turnover (Commission des Communantes Europeennes, 1978).

[8] Kudrle (1975, p. 185) estimates that half the value of Massey-Ferguson's tractors produced in North America and three-quarters of the value of Ford's were imported in the 1960s. For a discussion of Massey-Ferguson's decision to source from the U.K., see Neufeld (1969), p. 175.

[9] This refers to units sold. This was partly offset by the tendency for the size of tractors to increase.

[10] The figures for France include sales of motor-hoes and motor-cultivators as well as tractors. Calculated from Institut National de la Statistique, *Annuaire Statistique de la France,* various issued deflated by the wholesale price index for industrial products.

[11] Calculated from Landmaschinen—und Ackerschlepper Vereinigung data deflated by the index of industrial wholesale prices.

[12] Calculated from Commission of the European Communities (1975) Table 10.2 deflated by the wholesale price index of manufactured goods.

[13] It should be pointed out that Kudrle interprets the increased number of models offered in North America as a response to consumer demand rather than a deliberate competitive strategy followed by the firms, althoug his arguments for doing so are not very convincing.

[14] The most spectacular example was the success of Ford which re-entered the U.S. tractor market in 1939, introducing the "Ferguson System" there for the first time and achieving a 30 percent share of the market for tractors under 30 HP within four years (Conant 1953, pp. 35-36).

[15] A specific example of this was in 1967 when following a 14.3 percent devaluation of sterling the international tractor companies exporting from Britain did not reduce their prices in Canada to take advantage of their lower dollar costs. (Schwartzman 1970, pp. 137-138).

[16] What follows is summarized from John Deere's SEC-10K form for 1976.

[17] In 1979 Massey-Ferguson sold its holding in Mexico to the local industrial group Alfa. In 1982 a new joint-venture was set up between NAFINSA (60 percent) and Ford (40 percent) to produce Ford tractors.

[18] There is no evidence that locally owned firms in the Latin American tractor industry have behaved in significantly different ways from foreign firms and they will not therefore be discussed separately in the sections which follow on competitive strategies and performance. This contrasts with the situation reported in India where a public enterprise, Punjag Tractors, produces a tractor specifically developed for Indian conditions which is smaller than those manufactured under foreign license. (Bhatt 1978).

[19] Since this paper was first written the tractor industry in Argentina has ceased production with all four plants closing down in the course of 1980 following the adoption of a more liberal trade regime by the military government.

[20] In the early seventies it was reported that government proposals for more selective

mechanization of agriculture in Colombia were strongly attacked by agricultural machinery importers (Abercrombie, 1972: 41).

[21] This is not inconsistent with opposition to the development of a local tractor industry by landowners who prefer to continue importing tractors, but once local production is established and cheap imports are no longer a realistic alternative, then there is a considerable coincidence of interest between the tractor TNCs and landowners.

[22] Burch (1980) has estimated that aid-financed tractor exports to Sri Lanka accounted for nearly 10 percent of Massey-Ferguson's profits in Britain in the early 1970s.

[23] It is interesting to note that Massey-Ferguson in its analysis of the benefits of farm mechanization cites among other advantages the "encouragement to the farmer to be more independent of social unrest spreading from the town to the countryside" and the "promise of a greater degree of freedom from constraints associated with other factors of production" (Massey-Ferguson Ltd., 1974).

[24] Around 40 percent of the shares of Aco are in turn owned by the U.S. transnational company, ALCOA.

[25] For example, in 1976 it was reported that Deere, in association with the Schneider-Logeman group of Rio Grande do Sul, was planning an investment of over $200 million in a tractor plant with an initial capacity of 3,000 units, rising eventually to 14,000 per year (*Bank of London and South America Review*, Vol. 10, No. 11, November 1976).

[26] Since this was written FANATRACTO has been liquidated following the Venezuelan government's decision not to offer tariff protection of more than 25 percent. Opposition by local landowners to the constitution of a local tractor monopoly and the higher cost of a locally produced tractor was a key factor in the government's decision.

Van R. Whiting, Jr.
10.
Transnational Enterprise in the Food Processing Industry

INTRODUCTION*

As the world makes the transition from predominantly rural agricultural societies to urban industrializing societies, fewer people grow their own food, more food is industrially processed, and more food processing is done by transnational enterprises. In Mexico City as in New York, in rural Oaxaca as in Des Moines, consumers buy the branded food products of leading food processing enterprises: Carnation and Nestlé, Del Monte and Campbells, and other familiar firms. Contrary to some predictions,[1] foreign firms have not faded from the scene; rather, large international firms have become even more prominent.

A study of the food processing industry in Mexico presents one of the toughest cases for the international industrial organization approach. Food processing is one of the least concentrated manufacturing industries. Mexico is one of the strongest, most stable, and most developed of the developing countries. It should be a likely case for the reduction of transnational market power. If powerful states can erode the market strength of transnational enterprises in manufacturing industries, it should happen for food in Mexico. If foreign firms maintain their positions, it should indicate general structural and

* Special thanks go Arthur Domike of the United Nations Center on Transnational Corporations for his continued help, advice, and generous sharing of data and materials. Tom Ganiatsos, Chris Baron, and Francois Chesnais all shared their time and/or manuscripts with me. Richard Newfarmer was an exemplary editor and the comments of D. Caldwell, G. Gereffi, D. Martin, and R. Vernon on drafts were most helpful. Anne Lutz's assistance with revisions is also appreciated.

behavioral characteristics of transnational investment. In large part, the continued importance of large international firms in the food industry can be explained by the shift in the scale of oligopolistic competition.

The classic advantages of foreign investors—capital, technology, and access to foreign markets—are relatively unimportant in food processing. The food processing industry has, for the most part, low scale requirements in production, a widely-available technology, and a limited export potential. According to the "obsolescing bargain" model, foreign ownership in food processing should be obsolete. Yet foreign-owned enterprises continue to be prominent in the food processing industries of Mexico and other developing countries. The position of the foreign firms has not eroded, although there have been some changes in the regulatory environment. The actual pattern might be better termed a "renewable bargain" for transnational enterprise.

The main argument of this study is that the structure and conduct of leading food enterprises have influenced their investment behavior and consequently the structure, conduct, and performance of the food industry in developing countries. In the case of Mexico, the government has adopted regulatory policies in an attempt to modify structures, control behavior, and influence performance, but has not forced out the foreign firms.

THE TRANSNATIONAL ENTERPRISES

Food processing enterprises are large, diversified, and predominantly American-owned. Taken as a whole, the food processing industry accounts for about 15 percent of manufacturing output in developed market economies and over 23 percent in developing countries. The developed countries employ some 8 million workers in food and beverage industries, 10.5 percent of all manufacturing employment; in the developing world, 9.7 million workers are employed, almost 19 percent of manufacturing employment. It is estimated that 188 large enterprises, almost all based in the developed market economies, account for about one-third of total world food processing (UN-CTC 1980, pp. 6-8).[2]

In terms of revenue, food processing dwarfs many other industries. Worldwide, at least 60 firms had food and beverage sales over one billion dollars in 1976 (see Table 10.1). Though generally smaller than the oil companies and auto manufacturers in overall size, 20 of the largest 100 U.S. firms listed in the *Fortune 500* were engaged in

Table 10.1

Leading Food and Beverage Processing Firms with 1976 Food Sales Over $1 Billion[a]

Rank	Parent Company[b]	Home Country	Food Processing Revenue ($US M)	Total Firm Revenue ($US M)	Foreign Proportion of Total firm Revenues (%)	Production in Number of food sectors (of 9 total)[c]
1	Unilever	NLD/U.K.	8,741.2	17,638.4	40.0	9
2	Nestlé Alimentana SA	SWISS	6,247.8	7,247.8	95.0	9
3	Kraft, Inc.[1]	U.S.	4,775.8	4,977.0	15.1	6
4	General Foods Corp.	U.S.	4,401.6	4,910.0	25.8	6
5	Esmark, Inc.	U.S.	3,955.2	5,300.6	16.0	4
6	Beatrice Foods Co.	U.S.	3,943.0	5,289.0	21.2	8
7	Coca-Cola Co., Inc.	U.S.	2,911.5	3,032.8	44.0	5
8	Greyhound Corp.	U.S.	2,384.9	3,738.1	n/a	5
9	Ralston Purina Co.	U.S.	2,365.5	3,393.8	24.4	5
10	Borden	U.S.	2,336.3	3,381.1	16.0	7
11	United Brands Co.	U.S.	2,130.4	2,276.6	25.6	5
12	Iowa Beef Processors, Inc.[2]	U.S.	2,077.2	2,077.2	0.0	1
13	Imperial Group, Ltd.	U.K.	2,070.5	5,789.9	11.7	8
14	Archer-Daniels-Midland Co.	U.S.	2,065.5	2,118.5	26.7	4
15	Pepsico, Inc.	U.S.	2,051.2	2,727.6	20.8	6
16	Associated British Foods[3]	U.K.	2,050.5	3,011.9	n/a	7
17	Carnation Co.	U.S.	2,004.5	2,167.0	15.3	5

Table 10.1 (continued)

Rank	Parent Company[b]	Home Country	Food Processing Revenue ($US M)	Total Firm Revenue ($US M)	Foreign Proportion of Total firm Revenues (%)	Production in Number of food sectors (of 9 total)[c]
18	CPC International, Inc.	U.S.	1,968.1	2,696.0	54.7	7
19	LTV Corp.	U.S.	1,919.4	4,496.9	n/a	3
20	H. J. Heinz Co.	U.S.	1,882.0	1,882.0	40.7	3
21	The Seagram Co., Ltd.	CAN	1,873.7	2,048.8	94.0	2
22	Ranks Hovis McDougall, Ltd.	U.K.	1,801.1	1,860.6	13.0	7
23	Proctor & Gamble Co.	U.S.	1,800.5	7,349.0	25.0	3
24	Nabisco, Inc.[4]	U.S.	1,780.2	2,027.3	29.0	5
25	General Mills	U.S.	1,734.7	2,909.4	16.3	6
26	Grand Metropolitan	U.K.	1,704.1	2,974.0	n/a	4
27	Unigate, Ltd.	U.K.	1,640.4	1,743.4	10.0	4
28	Campbell Soup Co.	U.S.	1,590.9	1,635.0	11.0	6
29	Cadbury Schweppes, Ltd.	U.K.	1,522.6	1,589.9	40.0	6
30	Associated Milk Producers	U.S.	1,500.0	1,623.0	0.0	1
31	Mars, Inc.	U.S.	1,500.0	1,500.0	60.0	4
32	BSN-Gervais Danone, SA	FRA.	1,444.8	2,641.3	41.0	5
33	Allied Breweries, Ltd.[5]	U.K.	1,430.3	1,787.9	15.0	3
34	Anderson Clayton	U.S.	1,425.0	1,557.0	n/a	7

35	ITT	U.S.	1,422.0	11,764.0	49.0	4
36	Standard Brands, Inc.[4]	U.S.	1,411.8	1,810.0	33.0	8
37	Kellogg Co.	U.S.	1,385.5	1,385.5	20.3	4
38	Canada Packers, Ltd.	CAN	1,382.5	1,634.9	14.6	5
39	Anheuser-Busch, Inc.	U.S.	1,357.4	1,441.0	0.0	2
40	Cargill, Inc.[6]	U.S.	1,355.0	10,800.0	n/a	6
41	Central Soya Co., Inc.	U.S.	1,348.6	1,839.9	11.1	4
42	Mitsui & Co., Ltd.	JPN	1,320.6	12,993.3	n/a	4
43	Heublein, Inc.	U.S.	1,291.2	1,550.9	14.5	4
44	Union International Co.	U.K.	1,274.3	1,592.9	n/a	3
45	Del Monte Corp.[7]	U.S.	1,270.9	1,483.8	27.4	6
46	Suntory	JPN	1,200.0	1,376.5	n/a	2
47	Spillers, Ltd.	U.K.	1,189.9	1,254.5	7.0	2
48	Norton Simon, Inc.	U.S.	1,159.6	1,807.7	16.7	6
49	Consolidated Foods Corp.[8]	U.S.	1,154.4	2,754.9	13.0	5
50	J. Lyons & Co., Ltd.[5]	U.K.	1,147.5	1,466.7	57.0	6
51	Brooke Bond Liebig, Ltd.	U.K.	1,119.4	1,193.9	61.0	5
52	Snow Brand Milk Products	JPN	1,101.6	1,324.7	n/a	3
53	George A. Hormel & Co.	U.S.	1,094.8	1,094.0	2.1	2
54	Oscar Mayer & Co., Inc.	U.S.	1,087.8	1,133.1	n/a	2
55	Quaker Oats Co.	U.S.	1,070.2	1,551.3	29.5	7
56	Amstar Corp.	U.S.	1,034.0	1,118.5	n/a	3
57	Land O'Lakes	U.S.	1,022.2	1,241.6	0.0	4
58	United Biscuits Holdings	U.K.	1,012.1	1,053.0	n/a	4

Table 10.1 (continued)

Rank	Parent Company[b]	Home Country	Food Processing Revenue ($US M)	Total Firm Revenue ($US M)	Foreign Proportion of Total firm Revenues (%)	Production in Number of food sectors (of 9 total)[c]
59	Bass Charrington	U.K.	1,010.1	1,619.6	n/a	2
60	Tate & Lyle, Ltd.[9]	U.K.	1,005.5	5,169.1	35.0	2

Source: U. N. Center on Transnational Corporations, ST/CTC/19 (1980), pp. 219–220.

Notes:

* n/a = not available.

[a] $1 billion in 1976 food processing revenues is an arbitrary cutoff that happens to include 60 firms around the world, excluding firms in centrally planned economies. The UN-CTC chose $300 million as a cutoff point, and included 188 firms.

[b] A number of mergers and acquisitions by these parent firms have occurred since 1976; the most notable are given below in the notes. In addition, some mergers of firms too small to be included on this list, with the combined firm larger than some firms included here. For example, in 1978 Pillsbury (#88 on the UN-CTC list, with 1976 food revenues of $700 million) acquired Green Giant (#165, with 1976 food revenues of $382.7 million).

[c] Arthur Domike, author of a major study for the United Nations Centre on Transnational Corporations, identified the following nine commodity systems: 1) meats, 2) dairy products, 3) fishery products, 4) fruits and vegetables, 5) cereals, 6) oils and fats, 7) sugar and related products, 8) alcoholic beverages, and 9) tropical beverages. These commodity systems, not the nine "three-digit" industries of the U.S. Industrial Code, are the basis for this column.

[1] Kraft (#3) merged with Dart Industries, the drug store empire, in 1980.

[2] Iowa Beef Packers (#12) was reportedly acquired by Occidental (a diversified energy company) in 1981.

[3] Majority ownership of both Associated British Foods (#16) and Geo. Weston Ltd. of Canada (#87) is held by the Weston family trusts.

[4] Nabisco (#24) and Standard Brands (#36) merged to form Nabisco Brands in 1981.

[5] Allied Breweries (#33) acquired the British firm J. Lyons & Co. (#50) in 1979.

[6] Cargill (#40) acquired Missouri Beef Packers-MBPXL (#79, with 1976 food revenues of $757.8 million) in 1979.

[7] Del Monte (#45) merged with R. J. Reynolds, the tobacco firm, in 1979.

[8] Consolidated Foods (#49) acquired the Dutch firm Douwe Egberts (#136, with 1976 food revenues of $478 million) in 1977.

[9] Tate & Lyle (#60) is a partner in the holding company that has the largest share of stock in the French firm Beghin Say (#115 in the UN-CTC list of large food processors).

349

processing food and beverages. Although some firms are primarily involved in a single food commodity, most of the major firms are diversified across the food industry, participating in a variety of commodity systems. Of the nine commodity systems identified in a study by the United Nations Centre on Transnational Corporations (UN CTC 1980), the ten largest firms participate, on average, in six of the nine; the top thirty firms, in five; and the second thirty firms, in four commodity systems each (see Table 10.1). The two largest firms, Unilever and Nestlé, are active in all nine systems. At the other extreme, Iowa Beef Processors and Associated Milk Producers both rank in the top thirty firms but are involved in only one commodity: meat and dairy products, respectively.

Large international food processing firms are usually based in the developed countries. While over half of them originate in the United States, two of the largest are European: Nestlé is Swiss and Unilever has a split Dutch/British nationality. Of the 60 leading transnational enterprises listed in Table 10.1, 38 are from the United States, 15 from the United Kingdom, 3 from Japan, 2 from Canada, and 1 each from Switzerland and France.

Among the leading firms, most enterprises have been primarily food processors, avoiding a high degree of conglomeration (investment outside the primary industry of the firm). As Table 10.1 indicates, all but nine of the 60 largest food processing firms derived a majority of their total revenues from foods and beverages. Although conglomeration has been increasing (the tobacco firm R. J. Reynolds acquired Del Monte in 1979; and Kraft, the largest U.S. food processor in 1976, with 96 percent of its sales in food processing, merged with the drugstore empire of Dart Industries in 1980), conglomerates are still the exception, not the rule. Mergers more often take place within the food industry, such as the dramatic merger of Nabisco and Standard Brands in July 1981, moving the combined Nabisco Brands into the top rank of large U.S. food processors.[3]

The leading food processors show much more diversity with respect to internationalization. At one extreme, firms specializing in undifferentiated perishable commodities, such as fresh milk or beef, had few if any foreign sales. Foreign sales by breweries were also low, reflecting the difficulty of large-scale exports for a product with low value per unit of weight.[4] At the other extreme, diversified producers of highly differentiated and processed products such as dry milk or instant coffee are more likely to have a high proportion of sales outside the home country. Nestlé, whose home market is small, sells 95 percent of its products abroad. Few large U.S. firms had foreign

350

sales over 25 to 30 percent of the total, however, reflecting the larger domestic market in the United States.

Compared to other major manufacturing industries, the food processing industry is relatively unconcentrated. The world's leading food firms number in the hundreds, not in the tens, and those leaders account for little more than one-third of global production. Yet as we shall see, oligopoly in particular product lines has been an important factor influencing the behavior of transnational food processors.

Food processing is part of the food system that includes all economic activities by which people produce, process, and distribute nutritive biological and chemical materials needed to sustain life (as well as some non-nutritive stimulants and depressants). Specifically, the food processing industry performs three functions: the transformation of products of the biosphere into edible form; the industrial preservation of foods and beverages; and, the reduction or elimination of home preparation time.[5] Technological advances have made it possible to transport foods more easily and to store them longer which, in turn, favored the growth of large firms by facilitating economies of scale and product differentiation.

The food industry (used hereafter as synonymous with the food processing industry) is quite complex. The Standard Industrial Code of the United States lists 47 product lines that comprise 9 more general groupings within the industry.[6]

Despite this diversity of products, the industry can be treated as a unit, because the major firms share common industrial processes and, as a study by the United Nations Industrial Development Organization (UNIDO) pointed out, have common objectives, problems, technology, engineering, regulations, and packaging and marketing methods. The study described typical food processing as follows:

> The raw material is received, inspected, cleaned, graded, separated (from peel, etc.), cut up or ground, mixed with other food ingredients and chemical additives, formed into the desired shape and size, and packaged. It is subjected to heat, refrigeration, or dehydration, sometimes is coated . . . Fermentation, smoking, curing and extraction may also be employed (1969, p. 6).

These common elements of food processing, once performed primarily in the home and later in many small specialized family enterprises, today are carried out by some of the largest firms in the world.[7] The next section will explore the factors that contributed to the development of the industry.

351

History of Food Processing

Though foods have long been traded, sometimes from afar, and processed in the home, food processing as an industrial activity dates only from the last century. As long as most societies were predominantly rural and towns were small, food requirements could be satisfied by nearby farmers. Sailors used long-lasting foods such as potatoes. East-West trade in foods and stimulants included such items as sugar, coffee, tea, cocoa, spices and occasionally grains (Derry and Williams 1961, pp. 66-67). But preservation and preparation of food was done locally, or not at all. The development of food processing as a modern industry awaited the concentration of people in large numbers, far from sources of fresh foods.

Demand Factors The clearest social change that has contributed to the development of the food processing industry is urbanization. As more people come to live in cities and no longer can grow their own food, food from the countryside needs to be preserved, stored, and transported to them. Moreover, because urban women are more likely to become involved in activities outside the home, alternatives to home food preparation become more socially accepted and desired.

Another stimulus to the development of the food industry in the last one hundred and fifty years came from armies, which need food that is easily transported, preserved, and prepared. At the end of the eighteenth century, Napoleon offered a reward for an easily transported food to be used by his armies. Though Pasteur would not establish the scientific basis for sterilization for another fifty years, a French scientist, François Alpert, won Napoleon's price of 12,000 francs after working fifteen years to develop, in 1810, a method of preserving foods by immersing glass containers in boiling water and tightly closing them, thus destroying and sealing out enzymes and bacteria that cause deterioration. The example is not exceptional: armies have continued to provide a major market and hence a demand-generated source of innovation and growth for the industry.[8]

One author has hypothesized that industrialization and the growth of factory work encouraged the production and consumption of products which can be consumed more rapidly in a variety of locations and with a high input of energy, though not necessarily of nutrition (Mintz 1980). Although this argument referred particularly to the consumption of sugar and sugar products by factory workers, it could be extended to coffee or soft drinks with their caffeine stimulants and various other "quick energy" processed food products.

The growth of national income, and especially per capita income, has been an important stimulus to the growth of the industry as well.

In countries with a relative scarcity of labor such as the United States, the demand for labor-saving food products rose as wages rose. Wage earners had the disposable income needed to purchase a wider variety of food products than they had previously used, and they were able to acquire the consumer durables such as refrigerators and freezers that permitted the further development of food processing.

Changes outside the food industry, especially in transportation and communication and in the chemical industry, have helped shape the growth of the food industry. In transportation, the extension of the railroad networks across the United States made possible the expansion of food firms from regional to national markets, and the development of refrigerated rail cars facilitated national and international shipments of frozen foods. More recently, construction of the national highway system has led to increased reliance on trucking, in part displacing the railroad as the carrier of food products. Lined tank trucks developed for chemicals permit the long distance transportation of bulk liquids such as corn syrups or fruit juice concentrates. Containerized shipping has made possible the integration of truck, rail, sea, and air transport for bulk shipments of all kinds. Communications technology has been important not only for mass advertising but also for communications between home offices and subsidiaries of transnational corporations and for rapid worldwide transmission of information on the prices of raw material commodities.

In short, changes in developed societies such as urbanization and larger armies and high-cost labor and technological changes in other industries combined to shape the demand for processed foods and the growth of the industry. But the emergence of large firms was due to other factors.

Growth The growth of major food processors has been characterized by two kinds of expansion: geographical spread from local to national to international production; and diversification of production, mostly within the food industry. While many food processing firms got their start with a single product line, an increasing number are now in the food business rather than in the milk business (Nestlé) or the pickle business (Heinz).[9] As a manager of the British firm Dalgety commented, food enterprises are "positioned between the farm gate, the restaurant door and the supermarket floor" (*The New York Times*, September 6, 1979, D1).

As firms have grown, they have moved from specialization in single product lines (e.g., canned milk at the four-digit level) to a complete commodity sector (e.g., dairy products at the three-digit level), and more recently, to a wide range of processed food products (the two-digit level). The period of early growth of large food firms prior to 1950 generally involved national growth and expansion within a primary commodity sector, while internationalization and diversification across the food industry (and outside it) better characterize the last thirty years.[10] Though changes in society established the pattern of demand for processed foods, three factors within the industry influenced the early growth of large firms: technological improvements affecting production; advertising and promotion; and mergers and acquisitions.

Technological change Technological advances in the food industry are influenced by the availability and perishability of the product and the ratio of value to weight. For example, fresh milk and most bakery foods are highly perishable, making decentralized production important and inventories limited. Other food products require a specific raw material: butter requires milk, steak requires beef, and catsup requires tomatoes. Overcoming the limitations of these basic conditions by reducing perishability and weight and by developing raw materials substitutes has constituted the major technical challenge in the industry.

The development and patenting of a particular technology, such as Henri Nestlé's invention of powdered milk or Appert's process for sterilizing canned goods, initially provided a competitive advantage for the discoverer. But soon other firms adopted the technologies and grew and prospered. More recent advances in freezing, drying, packaging, and other techniques have enabled companies to diversify their product lines, to expand production and to establish themselves firmly in their home markets.[11]

Advertising As technology evolved and food firms diversified into other food product lines, advertising of trademarked brand names was used to promote a greater variety of products.[12] Trademarks are the basis for product identification by risk-averse consumers. Brand-loyal consumers constitute the core of purchasers for trademarked items and hence represent the market share that advertising creates for a product. Unlike the advantage of a patented technology that can be copied after a time, trademark protection is a permanent corporate asset. This was recognized long ago by Henri Nestlé when it was suggested that he should change his trademark. He replied:

> I regret that I am unable to allow you to change my nest for a Swiss Cross. My product must be recognizable at first glance. Not only is the nest my trademark; it is also my coat of arms (Nestlé means "little nest" in German dialect) . . . *I cannot have a different trademark in each country*; anybody can make use of a

cross, but no one else has the right to use my coat of arms" (Heer 1966, p. 43, emphasis added).

As in other consumer-goods industries, the advertising and promotion of trademarked products has played a key role in the growth of large food firms.

Mergers and Acquisitions Concomitant with the growth of food firms was an increase in competition. In response, mergers and acquisitions became an important mechanism for the continued growth of the largest firms. The example of Nestlé and its long standing rival, the Anglo-Swiss Milk Company, is a good illustration of this phenomenon. When Anglo-Swiss began to produce powdered milk in 1878 Nestlé responded by introducing a line of condensed milk, previously an Anglo-Swiss specialty. Both firms expanded into chocolates. The competition continued in overseas markets, especially in the U.S., until the two firms merged in 1905. Similar combinations occurred in other branches of the food industry, such as fruits and vegetables.[13] This first wave of mergers and acquisitions in the early part of this century saw many large enterprises grow from their base as leaders in a single (four digit) product line by combining with other enterprises in similar product lines, forming consolidated companies in particular (three digit) product sectors. In the post-World War II period, a second wave of mergers and acquisitions has resulted in diversified food companies with interests across the entire (two-digit) food industry.[14] Technological advances, aggressive marketing, and mergers and acquisitions all contributed to the growth of large firms that would soon outgrow their home markets.

Contemporary Industrial Structure

The historical pattern of growth has resulted in a contemporary industry that is segmented, but with concentration high in particular segments and growing in the industry as a whole as the industry continues to change. Concentration, specialization and diversification, mergers and acquisitions, and marketing barriers to entry are all elements of current structure. A look at these aspects of industrial structure will help explain the behavior of firms that have expanded abroad.

Concentration In the United States and other developed countries, concentration in food processing has been increasing, especially through the growth of the major firms that lead the industry.[15] Concentration in the U.S., measured by control of assets by 50 of the largest food processors, grew from 41 percent in 1950 to 56 percent in 1974; in sales the average four-firm concentration ratio in food processing increased from 47 percent in 1958 to 52 percent in 1972 (Albrecht and Locker 1979). About one quarter of the value of shipments of the entire food processing industry (including, in this case, manufacturers of agricultural raw materials) are found in categories with four-firm concentration ratios over 50 percent.

Compared to other manufacturing industries the food industry is still relatively unconcentrated. But oligopolies are common in many sub-sectors. Concentration is reflected in the disappearance of firms. The total number of food processing firms in the U.S. has dropped at a rate of 3.2 percent annually, from 41,000 in 1947 to 23,000 in 1972 (Connor 1979, p. 11). At the same time, concentration has increased. Of 51 sub-sectors of the U.S. food industry in 1972, according to an OECD study using Bain's (1968) classification, only 10 were "unconcentrated"; 5 were "very highly concentrated oligopolies"; 12 were "highly concentrated"; 13 were "high moderate concentrated"; and 11 were "low-grade oligopolies."[16]

Specialization and Diversification Within the general trend of growing concentration, variation has occurred in specialization and diversification patterns, in mergers and acquisitions, and in barriers to entry in various sectors of the industry. Most diversification has been within the food industry rather than into unrelated industries.[17] As mentioned before, leading firms worldwide operate in more than four of the nine commodity system sectors. Comparing changes over time in the average number of product lines per firm, table 10.2 shows that, in 1950, at the four digit sub-sector level, 14 of the 25 largest firms were involved in only one to five sub-sectors, and one was in over 20 of the 47 food sub-sectors. By 1975 none of the top 25 U.S. firms was in as few as five sub-sectors. Thirteen companies were in six to ten grocery product lines; nine firms were in 11 to 20 lines, and three were in over 20 lines (Connor 1979, p. 21).

Diversification across the food industry has not necessarily meant less specialization in food products. Connor (1979, p. 68) has shown that among the 200 largest food and tobacco manufacturing firms in the U.S., 162 were primarily food firms; 69.4 percent of their total sales were in food and tobacco. The other 38 manufacturing firms that had expanded into food products had a much lower percentage of total sales in food products. From 1963 to 1972, most growth by food processing firms was within the food sector. Employment outside food and tobacco increased 13 percent; but employment outside manufacturing slightly declined (Connor 1979, p. 51). In both 1963 and

Table 10.2

Diversification of 25 Leading Food Processing Companies, 1950-1975

Number of 4-digit SIC Grocery product lines produced by each company*	1950	1966	1975
		Number of Companies	
1 to 5	14	5	0
6 to 10	8	14	13
11 to 20	3	6	9
over 20	0	0	3

Source: Connor 1979:21, from The National Commission on Food Marketing, *The Structure of Food Manufacturing* (June 1966) and Economic Information Services, Inc. For 1950 and 1966, only industries with $500,000 in sales by company are counted; for 1975, the cutoff was $1,000,000.

*See Appendix C for listing of U.S. SIC industry codes.

1972 about one-quarter of employment by food firms was outside manufacturing.

When food companies diversify out of food products, they are most likely to do one of three things: (1) diversify within the food system, backward into agriculture or forward into food distribution, especially restaurants;[18] (2) diversify into other highly differentiated consumer goods industries, thereby utilizing experience in marketing and economies of scale in the purchase of media advertising; or, (3) diversify into related industries such as packaging or chemicals. Especially as research in food focuses more on the development of substitutes for raw materials through biochemical research (such as the development of corn syrup as a substitute for sugar), the synergy of the food and chemical industries increases.[19] As leading firms diversify into related products, concentration in the structure of the food processing industry as a whole tends to increase.

Acquisitions and Mergers Since World War II, diversification into different product lines in the industry has been accomplished largely by acquisitions of and mergers with other firms. Almost as many acquisitions took place between 1961 and 1965 as had occurred in the previous twelve years, and the absolute number doubled in the second half of the 1960s. While the total number of acquisitions slowed down from 1971 to 1975, the share of all manufacturing acquisitions represented by the food processors shows that these firms have been among the U.S. firms most likely to engage in acquisitions in these years.[20]

The structure of the food industry varies for firms that have traditionally specialized in staples—relatively undifferentiated and little promoted commodities for which there is large and relatively constant demand—and for those that specialized in branded, highly-promoted differentiated products for which demand is created. Diversifying mergers across product lines were more common for differentiated-product firms where growth and market position were largely based on advertising and product differentiation with high levels of value added. Horizontal acquisitions of producers of a single product, on the other hand, were most common in less differentiable products, particularly fluid milk, flour, and bread. These products are highly perishable, and therefore production tends to be limited to regional markets.[21]

Barriers to Entry Marketing and advertising, not plant scale or R&D, have provided the most powerful barriers to entry in the industry, especially in differentiated products. In differentiated product lines with high value added, advertising-to-sales ratios ranged from 1.82 to 6.49 (Connor 1979, p. 74). Advertising increased market share and concentration; diversification facilitated massive advertising; and competition among large firms in the food processing industry made it difficult for a new entrant to establish a significant market share without spending large sums on advertising. The largest food processors thus have a special advantage in advertising, where there are pecuniary advantages to scale, since advertising and media firms give discount rates for national advertising volume even when production or distribution are regional.

Neither plant size nor technological sophistication seem to be crucial explanations of industrial concentration. In most sectors of the industry plant size is not large and multi-plant operations predominate. Research and development in the food industry is concentrated in the largest firms and for years has been primarily oriented to the differentiation of existing products. A study of innovation in the food processing industry (Buzzell and Nourse 1967) showed that few new foods have been developed, while new brands are frequent and differentiated items proliferate. That study indicated that in the early 1960s a new product cost $68,000 for research and development, $26,000 for market research, and $248,000 for test marketing. *The Wall Street Journal* (August 26, 1978) reported that research and development costs for an extension of an existing product are low ($20,000-$50,000) while those for developing a new product may be as high as $1 million for research alone. Even for the largest 100 firms, research and development expenditures are low, averaging between 0.4 and 0.5 percent of sales, compared to about 4 percent for all manufacturing firms (Horst 1974). Major innovations have tended to come from other industries, and in-house research of product variations allows oligopolistic competition while forcing small competitors off the shelves.[22]

In short, concentration of the food industry in home markets is increasing. Mergers and acquisitions are still speeding that process, as well as increasing diversification of firms across the industry and in related fields. As some firms grow, other potential entrants are kept out not so much by production scale economies or by the benefits of R&D, but by the necessity for ample experience and large budgets for advertising. This evolving industrial structure helps us to understand the international behavior of firms as they expand beyond their home markets.

International Expansion of Firms in the Food Processing Industry

The food processing industry already counts most U.S. citizens among its customers, and the drive for further expansion has led many firms to invest abroad. Firms first moved abroad in a "spillover" from home markets, then more consciously entered new markets, first by means of exports and finally, usually in the face of exclusionary tariffs, by direct investment. In a consumer goods industry, it is natural that firms should seek investments in countries with an attractive potential market: it is in countries with high per capita income that food firms are most likely to invest. As total U.S. foreign investment in food and tobacco has grown, the share in Latin America has declined dramatically from 62 percent in 1929 to 15 percent in 1976, to be replaced by Canada and Europe, which each doubled their shares, from 13 to 28 percent and from 20 to 43 percent, respectively (Connor 1979, p. 25). Mexico, the largest single host country for U.S. food investments at the turn of the century, had fallen to fifth place by 1970 (Horst 1974, p. 115), but still ranks highest among developing countries.

Many of the factors that led to a concentration of the food industries in the home market contributed to their expansion abroad. Food firms whose primary products are heavily advertised (drugs and toiletries as well as foods) have a significant share of their business abroad. Likewise, firms whose primary products have high value added have much larger foreign sales than the commodity oriented firms. The exceptions to this—beer, canned fruits and vegetables, and bread, rolls, and cake—tend to be dominated by local industries.[23] For U.S. food companies, the share of foreign sales to total sales averages 13.4 percent, ranging from zero for poultry, eggs, and beer to 27.8 percent for breakfast cereals (Connor 1979, p. 67). Connor's evidence largely supports the hypothesis of Horst (1974) that producers of highly differentiated products are most likely to invest abroad.

Large firms are more likely to invest abroad. Table 10.3 ranks the largest 170 firms by global sales volume and gives data on locations of the foreign subsidiaries. The largest six firms, for example, had investments in 21 countries each, on average; the smallest of these large firms, with sales of at least $500 million, had only four foreign subsidiaries, on average.

Lastly, the size of the home market influences the degree of foreign expansion. Commonly, food firms from home countries with small markets (Switzerland, France, United Kingdom) are likely to have a high share of foreign production, while firms from large countries (U.S., Japan) tend to have lower foreign shares. The Swiss firm Nestlé, which is an extreme example of this phenomenon, sells 89 percent of its dairy products sales in 41 countries outside of Switzerland. More typically, Kraft, Carnation, and Bristol-Meyers had 20 to 25 percent of their dairy sales abroad. In sum, large firms, firms from small countries, and firms that specialize in differentiated, highly advertised products are most likely to invest abroad. These structural characteristics of the home markets are the most important explanatory variables for international investment behavior.

Transnational food firms are likely to earn higher rates of profits abroad than at home. Profit rates from international ventures have been reported as much as 50 percent higher than from home markets, reaching as much as 25 percent of total corporate sales (Albrecht and Locker 1979, p. 23). According to *Survey of Current Business*, earnings of U.S. foreign affiliates in 1975 were higher in food processing than in all other manufacturing activities (12.5 percent vs. 11.1 percent of assets); and were higher in developing countries than in developed nations (15.0 percent vs. 11.9 percent of assets) (Lall 1977, p. 5).

Foreign investment changed the structure of the food industry around the world. As U.S. firms expanded abroad, European and Canadian firms invested in the U.S. food industry.[24] The expansion of food firms abroad has challenged local firms to new competition, but the competition has not made for less concentrated markets, in part because subsidiaries of transnational corporations are often formed by the acquisition of local firms.[25]

Although firms from large developed countries have penetrated each other's markets, "oligopolistic reaction" seems limited to the

360

Table 10.3

Subsidiary Activities of Leading Food Industry Transnational Corporations by Size Groups

Number of Countries

Firm Scale*	No. of Firms	Other Developed Market Economies	Less Developed Countries			Total	No. of countries per firm, average
			Total	Latin America			
Over 5 billion	6	48	86	30	124		21
$3 - 5 billion	17	155	96	32	253		14
$2 - 3 billion	21	140	108	46	248		11
$1.5 - 2 billion	20	99	60	11	159		8
$1.0 - 1.5 billion	33	181	129	69	310		9
$0.75 - 1.0 billion	25	88	87	39	175		7
$0.5 - 0.75 billion	47	116	89	34	205		4
Total	170	827	655	261	1,474		9

Source: UN CTC, preliminary data. Data for 40 firms are unavailable, and for 8 firms incomplete.

*Total revenues.

Table 10.4

Number of Transnational Dairy Industry Affiliates by Size of Local Food Processing Market in Developing Countries

Number of transnational firms with local affiliates	Number of Countries			
	Small Markets[a]	Medium Markets[b]	Large Markets[c]	Total
One firm	8	10	5	23
Two firms	1	8	3	12
Three firms	—	2	5	7
Four firms	—	—	1	1
Five firms	—	1	—	1
Seven firms	—	—	1	1
				45

Source: UN-CTC, preliminary data.

Notes:
[a] Small markets: 1975 sales of all processed foods, less than $200 million.
[b] Medium markets: 1975 sales of all processed foods, $220-$1,000 million.
[c] Large markets: 1975 sales of all processed foods, over $1,000 million.

countries with the largest markets. Elsewhere, *de facto* market sharing seems to prevail. Table 10.4 shows the number of dairy firms in 45 developing host countries, aggregated by size of the market for processed foods. Eight of nine countries with small markets hosted only one transnational dairy firm. As expected, larger markets attracted more firms, but even among large markets, five countries hosted only one transnational dairy firm.[26]

In sum, structural change in home markets has contributed to foreign investment by leading firms, and especially by producers of differentiated, high value added food products. This investment behavior has, in turn, influenced the structure, conduct, and performance of the food industry in developing countries such as Mexico.

INTERNATIONAL INDUSTRIAL ORGANIZATION AND THE CASE OF MEXICO

Mexico is a good case for the study of foreign investment by food firms. Not only is foreign investment important in Mexico, but as one of the most advanced countries of the Third World, political consequences of foreign investment observed there will be likely to occur elesewhere. The organization of the international food industry affects the structure, conduct, and performance of the Mexican industry, and raises important policy issues.

Industry Structure

Foreign food firms have invested in Mexico since the turn of the century, but since 1950, as manufacturing investment in general increased, foreign investment in food and beverages accelerated significantly, from about $20 million in 1950, to $235 million in 1970. Nevertheless, foreign firms in Mexico represent a small share of all food processing (not including beverages): only 8.6 percent of production and 6.1 percent of value added in 1970. This was only about one-third of the manufacturing average, and a small fraction of the levels for other sectors with large absolute levels of foreign investment such as chemicals, electrical machinery, or automobiles where foreigners account for two-thirds to over three-quarters of production (Sepúlveda and Chumacero 1973, Appendix, Table 15 and Table 17). Food processing also has the lowest four plant concentration ratio of major manufacturing industries (Fajnzylber and Martínez Tarragó 1976, p. 186).

These figures would seem to belie the notion commonly held in Mexico that the food processing industry is highly concentrated and

363

foreign-dominated. The seeming paradox of high absolute levels of foreign investment in an industry in which foreign firms do not dominate is resolved by considering the larger absolute size of the industry, and by disaggregating; foreign firms do indeed dominate some specific product markets.

To again take examples from the dairy industry, there were no foreign milk pasteurizers or bottlers, and only one foreign ice cream firm in 1970. But ten out of twelve evaporated and canned milk producers were foreign, and they controlled 96 percent of invested capital, 98 percent of value added and production, and 99 percent of profits.[27]

Though there is no evidence of formal market sharing, there does seem to be mutual forbearance in particular market segments. Even with foreign and domestic competitors present, foreign dairy firms seem to specialize. Nestlé and Carnation both produce canned dairy products, but do not produce directly competing products. Nestlé for a time sold baby food in Mexico, but later dropped it, leaving Gerber as the sole producer. This forbearance behavior in the food industry contrasts with industries such as automobiles, in which oligopolistic reaction has led to competition among many foreign firms in spite of inefficiencies due to the size of the market.

Levels of concentration vary from product to product in the food processing industry. Processed milks, flans and gelatins, and "cajeta" and yogurts, as well as dried fruits and vegetables and soups and sauces, are all concentrated with four-firm concentration ratios over 60 percent. Most though not all of these industries have high levels of foreign participation. In those product lines where foreign firms are important, a common pattern can be observed. The foreign companies account for a small percentage of the number of plants, but a much larger share of all employees, since they tend to be much larger operations. The foreign share of total capital and of production tends to be even larger than the share of employment; the foreign firms are more capital-intensive than domestic firms. In most cases the foreign share of salaries paid is greater than the share of employees, indicating higher wages paid by the transnationals. The pattern of capital-intensive industry developed in the home market is duplicated in Mexico, despite the difference in factor endowments. If the experience of the home countries is any guide, in the absence of state intervention, the large firms may be expected to grow larger through merger and acquisition, advertising and product differentiation; and the total number of firms will fall substantially.

Ownership Most food processing firms are private national firms; state-owned firms are of little importance except in fishing and sugar.

Foreign firms tend to dominate in specific products which are highly concentrated. Among the foreign-owned firms, majority-owned firms predominate: the 1973 Foreign Investment Law requiring 51 percent local ownership was not retroactive, and most major international food processing firms were already in Mexico prior to that date.

There is wide variation in the patterns of foreign affiliation in Mexico. Some parent firms own all of their affiliates and subsidiaries directly, while others "pyramid," having one affiliate own another. Some firms have only food-related affiliates; others are diversified in their holdings. Table 10.5 lists parent firms and their subsidiaries in the milk, fruits, and vegetables sectors.

In 1977 the National Registry of Foreign Investment in Mexico listed 136 food processing enterprises with foreign equity of at least 20 percent (Registry of Foreign Investment, Mexico). Twenty-six foreign parent firms with direct investments of at least $1 million each controlled 85 percent of the total direct foreign investment in the food industry. Only five of the enterprises in which the parent firms had direct investments showed foreign investment of 49 percent or less. Six more had foreign investment between 49 and 50 percent; all the rest were owned primarily (over 50 percent) by foreign investors. From 1973 through 1976 no cases of new foreign investment by firms which did not already have existing investments in Mexico were reported, to my knowledge, to the Registry on Foreign Investment.

Conduct

The structure of the food industry in Mexico influences the conduct of the firms. In advertising, research and development, acquisitions, technology transfer, and trademarks the disproportionate importance of marketing by foreign firms is readily apparent. Each of these issues will be discussed below.

Advertising and R&D Advertising is only recently being studied in Mexico. Bernal Sahagún (1974, p. 111) reported that the leading food processing advertisers were General Foods, Nabisco, and Kraft and that each of these used the same advertising agency used by the parent corporation (Young and Rubicam, McCann Erickson, and J. Walter Thompson, respectively). The same products were being marketed and the same marketing strategies were used.

Information concerning research and development is also scanty. Foreign food firms register few patents and many trademarks, confirming the marketing emphasis observed in developed countries. Only 2.2 percent of all patents but 11.4 percent of all trademarks registered in the Fajnzylber sample of foreign firms were in food

365

Table 10.5

Major Foreign Investors in the Mexican Milk Products, Fruit, and Vegetable Industries, c. 1976

Parent Company (home country) (rank by size of investment in Mexico) Subsidiaries in Mexico	Foreign Ownership % (if known)	Year of Founding of Parent	Year of First Mexican Investment
1. Nestlé (Swiss)		1905	1935
Industrias Alimenticias Club, SA	100%		
Alimentos Findus, SA	100%		
Compania Nestlé, SA	100%		
Synfleur			
Wagons-Lits			
Autoparadores de México			
Chiguahuapan (agua mineral)			
2. Anderson Clayton (U.S.)		1904	1934
Anderson, Clayton & Co., SA	60.8%		
Inmobiliaria ACOMEX, SAdeCV	100%		
Productors API-Aba, SA	100%		
Reproductoras Shaver, SA	100%		
Granjas Progenitoras, SAdeCV	100%		
Comercial Bernal, SdeRL	100%		
Nacional de Dulces, SAdeCV	50%		
Promociones San Andres, SA	100%		
Operadora de Granjas de Gomez Palacio, SdeRL	100%		
Operadora de Granjas de La Laguna, SdeRL	100%		
Operadora de Granjas del Norte, SdeRL	100%		

Company	Ownership		
Operadora de Granjas del Monterrey, SdeRL			
Productora de Aves, SdeRL	100%		
Nacional Pecuaria, SAdeCV	100%		
Terrenos Agrícolas, SC	100% (?)		
Promotora Pecuaria, SAdeCV	100% (?)		
Mercantil Altamira, SdeRL	100% (?)		
3. General Foods (U.S.)		1922	
General Foods de México, SA	99.55%		
Birds Eye de México, SAdeCV	99.93%		1959
4. Campbell Soup Company (U.S.)			
Campbell's de México, SAdeCV	96.4%		1965
5. Richardson Merrell (U.S.)			
Leche Mexicana, SA	99.86%		
Ribot, SA	99.86%		
Richardson Merrell, SAdeCV	99.99%		
J.T. Baker, SAdeCV	100% (?)		
Ulay de México, SAdeCV	100% (?)		
Merrell de México, SAdeCV	100% (?)		
6. Carnation (U.S.)		1920	
Carnation de México, SA	99.99%		1947
7. C.P.C. International (U.S.)		1906	
Productos de Maíz, SA	98.6%		1930

Table 10.5

Major Foreign Investors in the Mexican Milk Products, Fruit, and Vegetable Industries, c. 1976

Parent Company (home country) (rank by size) Subsidiaries in Mexico	Foreign Ownership % (if known)	Year of Founding of Parent	Year of First Mexican Investment
8. Del Monte Corp. (U.S.)		1916	1953
Productos Del Monte, SAdeCV	93.99%		
Frutas y Verduras Selectas, SdeRLdeCV	99.6%		
Papas y Fritos Monterrey, SAdeCV	49.97%		
Productos Bali, SAdeCV	99.40%		
Alimentos Mexicanos Selectos, SAdeCV	59.87%		
9. Kraftco Corp.* (U.S.)		1923	1955
Kraft Foods de México, SAdeCV	99.99%		
10. Warner-Lambert Co. (U.S.)			1936
Colonial Distribuidora, SA	80% (?)		
La Compania Colonial, SA	79.96%		
Toficos, SA	76.68%		

368

Chicle Adams, SA	99.97%
Ahmex, SA	100% (?)
American Optical de México, SA	100% (?)
Cia. Medicinal La Campaña, SAdeCV	100%⁻ (?)
Parke Davis y Cia. de México, SAdeCV	100% (?)
11. McCormick (U.S.)	
McCormick de México, SA	49.99%
12. Compagnie BSN-Gervais Danone (France)	1972
Xalpa Industrial, SA	88.50%
Danone de México, SA	

Sources: Annual Reports of parent companies; corporate and governmental interview in Mexico.

(?) = ownership share uncertain

* Kraftco is now part of Dart-Kraft (see text).

369

(Fajnzylber and Martinez Tarrago 1976, pp. 348-349). From what little evidence is available it would appear that foreign food firms are primarily interested in the urban middle class market. The Mexican government, for example, invited Nestlé to develop an infant milk for distribution through a national parastatal company (CONASUPO). Nestlé declined. When the National Nutrition Institute developed an inexpensive nutritious formula (*CONLAC*) for distribution, the home office of Nestlé reportedly chastized the Mexican subsidiary for the foregone opportunity.[28] A similar situation was reported for the development of a soy-based breakfast food that the government wanted to mass-distribute. Here again a foreign-owned firm, Nabisco, was invited to produce the product, but declined. Rather than investing in research and development of new products for the poor, foreign firms invest in advertising existing products for the well-to-do.

Acquisitions Foreign food firms have expanded into Mexico by either forming new subsidiaries or acquiring local businesses. Most firms affiliated with U.S. companies since 1965 have been acquired. Affiliates established in the early years were more likely to have been newly-formed than acquired, while three-quarters of recent subsidiaries (1966 to 1973) have been acquired (Newfarmer and Mueller 1975, pp. 187-188). Among U.S.-owned firms, almost two-thirds of the food subsidiaries were acquired, compared to half of all manufacturing affiliates. Even more striking, more than half of the acquired food subsidiaries were acquired indirectly, through the acquisition of another company. This is a clear example of how changes in concentration in the home country (acquisition of one parent firm by another) lead to change in concentration in developing host countries.[29] When R. J. Reynolds acquires Del Monte or when Standard Brands and Nabisco merge, concentration in Mexico increases.

Performance in the Mexican Food Industry

Performance may be measured normatively, in terms of economic criteria such as profits and trade impacts; or in terms of national policy goals. Normatively, the debate revolves around value preferences and the viability of alternatives. In practice, foreign food firms respond to criticism by admitting that their products are luxury items. "We don't aim for the lower end of the market, although we know many poor people buy our products," one manager in a fruit and vegetable firm told me. Another tried to justify purchases of expensive processed food by the poor: "Some people buy our product to get

370

a shot of good nutrition for their children once in a while." Foreign firms seem best suited to satisfying the demand of that portion of the population able to translate need into purchasing power.

Profits We have seen that profits in the U.S. food industry are relatively high and are comparable to those of corporations in other oligopolistic industries. When transnational food firms in Mexico are members of oligopolistically-concentrated sectors of the food processing industry, then even if the industry as a whole is not concentrated, one would expect them to earn an "oligopoly rent" comparable to the profits in other concentrated industries. Unfortunately, profit data are not released by the transnationals at the country level, so it is difficult to evaluate profits, let alone to compare advertising-intensive firms with commodity-oriented firms. However, some data from the Senate Special Survey of firms in Brazil and Mexico are available (Newfarmer and Mueller 1975, p. 90). Looking at after-tax earnings as a percentage of equity, the food processing industry in 1972 showed a 9.1 percent return, compared to 13.8 percent for chemicals, 16.1 percent for electrical machinery, and 10.0 percent for the transportation industry. This would seem to contradict the concentration hypothesis. But when royalties, licenses, and technical assistance are included in the earnings, the profit levels of the four industries equalize at 19 to 20 percent, compared to a 16.2 percent average for the entire manufacturing industry. It is possible to conclude, then, that the food processing industry may be receiving oligopoly rents if international transfer payments are included.[30]

Performance in Exports and Imports Mexico exports food, but not processed foods. Food exports, including beef, coffee, sugar, and tomatoes, are an important source of foreign exchange earnings, constituting about one-quarter of total exports. But since the 1970s per capita agricultural production declined and food imports increased. Foreign food processing firms are net importers. An unpublished survey of trade balances of foreign firms operating in Mexico revealed that from 1971 through 1976 foreign-owned food processing firms had large negative trade balances, with imports roughly twice the value of exports. In 1972 a sample of U.S. food processing affiliates operating in Mexico reported exports of only 2 percent of sales, compared to 4 percent for chemicals, 9 percent for electrical machinery, and 8 percent for transportation, among other leading sectors. This poor export performance is probably because processed and convenience foods are already produced by the transnational firms in their home markets; added transportation costs

371

partially offset lower labor costs, and firms have little incentive to export.

Impact on Agricultural Producers Food processing firms rely on a steady supply of high quality agricultural raw materials. In the U.S., firms have integrated backwards into agriculture and have also used production contracts with independent producers. In developing countries such as Mexico, foreign firms are often prohibited from land ownership, so the use of production contracting becomes essential. In a small sample of vegetable processors in Mexico, all eight of the international firms used production contracts. Only 10 of the 16 local firms did so (Morrissy 1974).

Through production contracting, foreign firms introduce modern techniques and increase incomes of suppliers. But the increased efficiency for some growers menas that others who previously found subsistence work may lose their jobs due to increased productivity. In a situation where the foreign processor enjoys a monopsony position, crops are tailored to the buyers' specifications, and both subsistence crops and hand labor are often replaced.

Poor relations with suppliers can be hazardous to firms, especially for firms that fail to adapt to local conditions in dealing with contract farmers. Heinz, which withdrew from Mexico in 1973, is a case in point. Having come to Mexico by acquiring several ailing and disorganized fruit and vegetable packing companies, the company tried to implant their standard operating procedures, including contract farming. Their inexperience, as well as the condition of the firms they acquired, led to failure. When Heinz left Mexico its affiliates were purchased by the Mexican government[31] (Williams and Miller 1975). Effective use of contract farming characterizes successful foreign investors.

PUBLIC POLICY IN MEXICO

In the 1970s a series of regulations governing foreign investment were promulgated. They included a Law on Foreign Investment in 1973, a Law on Technology Transfer in 1972 (reformed in 1982) and a Law on Inventions and Trademarks in 1976. None was specific to food, but all represented an increase in state regulation and intervention in the economy. These regulations were undertaken by one of the oldest, most stable, and by most accounts, one of the strongest states in the developing world. What were the results of this regulatory confrontation of the state and the transnational enterprises in Mexico?

Foreign Investment Regulation

Under the Foreign Investment Law direct acquisition of Mexican firms has been effectively stopped. But already existing firms are able to increase their production up to the limit of their existing capacity. Since processed food products in Mexico are not considered to be a priority industry, new foreign investment in this area is not encouraged, but investment can be increased without the permission of the Foreign Investment Commission, as long as the relative shares of foreign and national capital are not changed. It appears that regulation will not have significant effects on the structure of oligopoly and the concentration of production for specific food product lines. A few cases drawn from the experiences of the major foreign-owned food firms serve to illustrate the point.

In one case, the Foreign Investment Commission authorized the purchase by one transnational enterprise of the subsidiary of another, resulting in an increase in concentration of the product in question. The former owner, a totally foreign firm, declared its intention to cease its operations in the breeding and production of chickens. A second firm, 60 percent foreign-owned, offered to buy the subsidiary enterprise, and the proposal was submitted to the Foreign Investment Commission. The Coordinating Commission for Agriculture, an official dependency of the Ministry of the Presidency, was contacted and asked its opinion. The commission explored the possibility of locating a Mexican purchaser for the firm; no Mexican investors came forward. Because the enterprise in question was losing money and its original owner threatened to close the operation altogether, a speedy decision was reached. Fifty-one percent of the shares of the enterprise to be transferred were put in a trust fund which, within seven years, would be sold to Mexican investors. The acquiring transnational enterprise then took over operation of the firm. Mexicanization of the subsidiary would thus eventually be accomplished. After the approval, the Ministry of Agriculture, which had not been consulted, protested the action on the grounds that the acquiring firm would be able to increase its share of the market for chickens and would achieve a greater degree of vertical integration by increasing its intrafirm consumption of another product, animal feeds, which it also produced. Although 51 percent of the shares and thus 51 percent of the dividends from this enterprise will eventually go to Mexicans, the position of the transnational enterprise *vis-a-vis* domestic Mexican producers of chickens and of animal feeds was strengthened.

In another case, Del Monte, one of the largest producers of canned fruits and vegetables in Mexico, was given permission to open a new plant which was predominantly foreign-owned, to produce tomato paste in Culiacán, Sinaloa. The plant was authorized because the product was intended for export and Mexico wanted to increase the low levels of processed food exports. In addition, the parent firm argued that new employment would be generated, technical assistance to tomato producers would result in increased yields, and waste would be reduced by the utilization of tomatoes for paste that were not suitable for the fresh market. A trade-off was made by accepting majority foreign ownership and an increase in the share of the national production of canned fruits and vegetables by the transnational enterprise, in return for an increase in employment and in exports.

In both of these cases, decisions were handed down rapidly; and the development of alternatives by national capital or by state-owned enterprises which existed in both fields at the national level were only briefly explored (in the case of national firms) or apparently were not explored at all (in the case of state-owned firms). In both cases, the structural position of transnational enterprises in the food processing industry in Mexico was, if anything, strengthened. But the Foreign Investment Commission complied with its mission to encourage Mexicanization or to allow exceptions in return for an increase in exports. As suggested above, since extremely few cases of majority foreign ownership have been approved, the ability to affect the balance of trade of foreign-owned firms is slight (Whiting 1981).

In the food industry, the major barrier to the entry of new firms is the ability to promote consumption of and consumer loyalty to branded food products, by trademarks and through heavy advertising. The regulation of foreign direct investment is clearly not the appropriate instrument to regulate advertising and trademarks. Product differentiation—that is, the production of many similar products with minor variations in color, form, texture, or packaging—could, however, be regulated as part of the regulation of foreign investment. Participants in the drafting of the Law to Promote Mexican Investment and to Regulate Foreign Investment indicated that they hoped to be able to limit the proliferation of differentiated products by transnational enterprises. But point four of article 12 of the law only authorizes the National Foreign Investment Commission "to decide on the proportion of existing foreign investment in Mexico to be admitted in new fields of economic investment or in new production lines." This regulation only provides the authority to regulate the diversification of foreign-owned firms into products completely different from those they had produced in the past.[32] In September 1977 the Foreign Investment Commission finally issued a lengthy resolution containing an elaborate classification at the four-digit level in order to define new lines of economic activity and new product lines. Even after the publication of that resolution, however, product differentiation did not fall within the scope of the mandate of the Foreign Investment Commission. Thus, a firm that produced breakfast cereals could still introduce new cereals; a firm that produced canned dog food could produce dry dog food; a firm that produced a powdered mix for orange drink (Tang) could produce flavored powdered mixes for soft drinks (Kool-Aid). All of these products are now produced by firms affiliated with transnational enterprises in Mexico.

Ironically, the diversification of firms into new product lines could potentially increase the level of competition in Mexican industry, while product differentiation decreases competition by strengthening the market position of the leading firms. Yet it is diversification, not product differentiation, that the Foreign Investment Commission is authorized to regulate. The analysis of foreign investment in the food processing industry in Mexico suggests that the regulations of foreign investment adopted in 1973 were too late to control the entry of most major foreign enterprises and were not designed to control market distortions on inappropriate products in the food industry.

Technology Transfer in the Food Industry

Technology imports in the food and beverage industries are concentrated in foreign affiliated firms. A recent analysis of all contracts registered for firms in the food industry indicates that 90 percent of all beverage payments and 93 percent of all food payments were made by foreign firms. Payments were more likely to be made for a package including technology assistance rather than for trademarks alone. In a 1975 sample of 618 contracts in 20 different industrial sectors, all involving trademark licenses, 32 percent of the contracts were in the food and drink industries. However, of the 198 contracts in these industries, only 38 specified known payments for trademarks, 12 contracts did not contain information on payments, and 148 specified that the trademark licenses were free. Clearly, trademarks are important to firms because of the goodwill and the market share that they represent, not because of royalties (Alvarez 1979, pp. 22-25). Table 10.6 summarizes data on technology contracts of recipient firms in the food processing industry, for contracts registered in Mexico between 1973 and 1977. The data cover 170 contracts involving 122 licensing firms.

Table 10.6

Technology Contracts Registered in Mexico for Recipient Firms in Food Processing, 1978–1977

Ownership of Recipient Firms, with Nationality of Licensor	Number of firms	Number of Firms* That			Number of Contracts* That Included												
		Reported Sales Data	Reported R&D Expenditures	Reported Licensing of Trademarks	Number of Contracts	Coverage					Duration			Specified Payment As % of Sales (After negotiations)			
						Patents	Trademarks	Know-How	Technical Assistance	Administrative Services	Indefinite	Specified Duration	If Specific, Average	0-2.0	>2.0	Decrease	No Decrease
0-24.9% foreign																	
Contract with foreign	27	19	12	9	42	5	12	31	27	3	7	33	7 yrs	8	8	3	13
Contract with national	28	14	1	9	29	1	9	3	3	17	13	15	4 yrs	6	2	2	4
25-49.9% foreign																	
Contract with foreign	14	10	2	9	16	3	10	13	10	2	5	11	7 yrs	6	3	4	5
Contract with national	5	1	0	0	6	0	0	0	0	6	1	4	5 yrs	0	1	1	0
50-100% foreign																	
Contract with foreign	38	36	18	31	64	3	45	45	29	5	28	36	9 yrs	24	7	14	17
Contract with national	10	10	1	5	13	1	7	4	3	3	10	3	10 yrs	1	3	1	3
Total	122	90	34	63	170	13	83	96	72	36	64	102	7 yrs	45	24	25	42

Source: Research by author.

* The reporting was incomplete. Only 90 of the 122 firms reported sales and profit data as required for the five years preceding the date of registration. Only 34 of the firms reported whether or not they incurred expenditures for research and development. And only 69 of the 1970 firms reported specific data on payments as a percentage of sales. Nearly complete data are included for the coverage of the contracts and for their duration.

Significant differences exist between recipient firms that are majority foreign-owned and recipient firms that are predominantly or wholly national. Most striking is the importance of trademarks for foreign-owned licensees. Thirty-six of the 48 majority foreign recipient firms reported contracts including trademark licenses, while only 18 of the 55 firms with zero to 24.9 percent foreign ownership reported trademark licenses. Fifty-two of the 77 contracts of majority foreign subsidiaries involved trademarks, while only 31 of the 93 majority national recipients did so. And only 13 of the 170 contracts included patents. Know-how and technical assistance were much more important than patents for both national and foreign-owned licensees. Provision of administrative services was especially prominent in the contracts between two national firms. With respect to the duration of the contracts, a majority of firms in all categories specified an exact number of years of duration. Among foreign subsidiaries, the average duration was more likely to approach the maximum ten year limit. Over one-third of all firms left the duration of the contract indefinite, however; contracts of this sort usually specified that the agreement would continue until cancelled by either party. Among foreign subsidiaries, almost half used this indefinite form, while only 26 of the 93 majority national licensees left the duration open-ended. By leaving the duration of the contract open-ended, the contract become self-perpetuating. Several foreign subsidiaries that had originally specified a duration exceeding the required ten year limit revised their contracts to include an indefinite duration.

Of the relatively few contracts that specified payments in the contracts summarized in Table 10.6, 24 out of 69 involved payments (after final negotiations were completed) that exceeded 2 percent. Interestingly enough, these were proportionately more likely among majority national firms than among the contracts with foreign subsidiaries. More importantly, the contracts with national recipients were more likely to remain the same after negotiations (only 5 of 22 showed decreased payments) than contracts with majority foreign-owned firms, which showed decreases in 15 of the 35 reported cases. These data suggest that majority foreign-owned firms could more easily reduce the level of their payments for technology transfer than national recipient firms. This is consistent with the argument that foreign subsidiaries have alternative avenues for the repatriation of profits.

In summary, the law establishing the National Registry on Technology Transfer which required all technology contracts to be registered permitted state intervention at the negotiation stage of the technology acquisition process. As a consequence payments stipulated in the contracts were reduced in many cases and a number of restrictive clauses were eliminated, but the effectiveness of these regulations was limited. Freedom from exchange controls, made necessary in part by the extensive border with the United States, limited the ability of this regulation to reduce the total foreign remittances by subsidiaries of transnational enterprises. The utilization of an indefinite term of duration, resulting in an essentially self-perpetuating contract, reduced the effectiveness of the ten year limit on the duration of contracts. For firms in the food processing industry and in other consumer goods industries in which trademarks represent an important element of oligopoly power, these regulations could only reduce or eliminate the payment for trademark licenses but could not restrict the use of foreign trademarks by local firms and transnational subsidiaries.

The Law on Inventions and Trademarks was the most controversial of the three laws here considered, probably due to the novelty of some of the provisions for the transnational enterprises and the absence of short-term tangible benefits for national businesses. It revised a 1942 law governing patents, trademarks, and other industrial property rights, and incorporated some new and controversial provisions. According to the new law, no patents were allowed in the chemical-pharmaceutical, food and beverage, fertilizer, pesticide, and nuclear energy industries. In these areas a new legal entity known as the Certificate of Intervention conveyed certain nonexclusive rights on its holder, whereby anyone could exploit the invention, but all users would be required to pay royalties to the holder of the certificate. Both patents and trademarks must be used within specific periods of time in order to remain valid; and "use" was defined as production in national territory, not merely selling imported articles. A maximum ten year term was established for patents, and a five year renewable term was allowed for trademarks. The most novel aspect of the law stipulated that a foreign trademark would have to be displayed at all times with a second trademark, originally registered in Mexico, of equal size and prominence, on all products bearing that brand.

The Law on Inventions and Trademarks fared less well than the technology law. Although the Certificates of Inventions have been accepted for use in those areas where patents are disallowed, private reports suggest that the newest technology is not being transferred in those areas, a claim that is difficult to assess as yet. Regarding the trademark link, an international protest resulted in the indefinite postponement of the measure in 1979. Unlike the regulations of foreign direct investment or the registration of technology transfer contracts, this measure would have set an international precedent undermining the central control of trademarks and their value to the home office. The Mexican law was closely watched in international organizations such as the United Nations Conference on Trade and Development and the World Intellectual Property Organization. The U.S. government even sent a diplomatic note of protest, although this probably accounts for the fact that the measure was only postponed instead of being overturned: in the nationalist environment of Mexico where the tradition of the Calvo Clause is nearly sacred, direct pressure by a foreign government is likely to be counterproductive. The regulatory measure that was the greatest departure from international norms and that would have touched an important source of market power of firms in consumer good industries was never applied. The increased role of the state in regulating foreign investment was real enough, but was limited in its contribution to Mexico's development goals.

Policies regulating foreign investment in food processing in Mexico were too late to effectively control transnational corporations. The central elements of transnational market power—especially advertising and product differentiation of branded consumer goods—were not affected by the rules and ten years after the foreign investment law, no specific investment policy for food processing had been declared. That this is so in Mexico, where the state is strong and where concentration is lower than elsewhere, suggests that such state regulation in the Third World is unlikely to substantially alter structure and conduct in the food industry.

CONCLUSIONS

This study showed how the structure and conduct of food processing firms in home markets led to increased concentration and firm size. In businesses with differentiated, highly advertised products, these factors tended to increase foreign direct investment. In developing countries like Mexico, international food processors compete with each other, introducing products, marketing methods, and production patterns from the home market. While the Mexican government adopted laws to limit acquisitions and foreign payments, these laws have been insufficient to restrict the strategic behavior of transnational food processors. The relationship between transnational enterprises and the state in Mexico, far from resulting in an "obsolescing bargain," has resulted in a "renewable bargain" for the transnational firms.[33]

Notes

[1] Raymond Vernon (1971, p. 66) described the thesis as a process of erosion of strength of foreign firms. Theodore Moran (1974) illustrated that process for copper firms in Chile, and Vernon (1977) argued that it applied to manufacturing enterprises as well. The argument implies that the original bargain between state and firm becomes obsolete—hence the expression "obsolescent bargain."

[2] This figure from the United Nations Centre on Transnational Corporations excludes production in centrally-planned economies. Other estimates place the share of large transnational firms at 40 percent (UNIDO 1977). These figures are based on estimates for the mid-1970s; mergers of some of the largest firms since then have almost surely increased the share of the largest firms.

[3] Nabisco Brands was established to have food sales over $5 billion in 1981. Some of these conglomerate mergers, though not joining two food firms, have been in related industries: R. J. Reynolds' tobacco products share both marketing strategies and agricultural origins with Del Monte's food products. Dart Industries builds on experience with chemicals and with the marketing of highly advertised, non-durable consumer goods in combining with Kraft. Non-food conglomerates seem to have a taste for acquiring beefpacking firms: LTV owns Wilson; Greyhound Corporation owns Armour, Esmark owns Swift; and in 1981 Occidental was reported to have acquired Iowa Beef Processors (ranked twelfth in Table 10.1). Milk and beef firms have been prohibited from domestic expansion in the U.S. by anti-trust measures, and the perishability of the products made foreign experience in exporting less likely. As profits accumulated, the firms became attractive take-over targets.

[4] The difficulty of exporting also makes foreign direct investment less likely, as the "product cycle" argument of Vernon, Wells, Horst and other has shown.

[5] A recent study by the OECD challenges the traditional definition of food processing as limited to the transformation of biological products and suggests that increasing complementarity of the food and chemical industries will generate increased usage of products of the geosphere as well as of the biosphere in food (OECD 1979, p. 61).

[6] The 47 groupings are often referred to as four-digit industries; the 9 groups of products as three-digit industries. Food processing is a two-digit industry. [Appendix C lists the product groupings of the U.S. Standard Industrial Code at two-, three-, and four-digit levels.] These groupings give some idea of the complexity of the industry. However, the U.S. codes are not universal: there is also an International Standard Industrial Code, and many countries, including Mexico, have their own code. Moreover, none of these classifications captures crucial distinctions such as the difference between staple products (commodities with low value added) and differentiated products (with high value added).

[7] In contrast to food processing, "agroindustry" may be used to refer to all industries based on the transformation of any agricultural raw material (UNIDO 1979, pp. 19, 55). Explicitly or implicitly, use of the concept of agro-industry implies a primary concern with the agricultural producer, the farmer or the peasant. An even broader concept, "agribusiness," was first introduced by Ray Goldberg of the Harvard Business School in 1957, who offers the following definition:

> Agribusiness . . . includes all the farm inputs, farm production, food and fiber processing, and distribution entities utilized in the production and ultimate distribution of food and fiber products to . . . consumers and to . . . export markets (1977, p. 65).

380

[8] Mr. Gail Borden's canned sweetened evaporated milk, developed in the 1850s in the United States, found a ready market in the armies during the American Civil War (Derry and Williams 1961, pp. 691-693). Another Frenchman, the chemist Hippolyte Mege-Mouries, developed margarine in response to a call by Napoleon III for an edible table fat; it was patented in 1869. The rapid pace of innovation in the late nineteenth century was not matched again until World War II. The needs of the U.S. army to transport large quantities of food over long distances contributed to the development of dehydrated potatoes, which greatly reduced their weight, and of nonfat dry milk and frozen juice concentrates, reducing spoilage (Buzzell and Nourse 1967, pp. 42-45). Most recently, the development of a new method of preserving food by introducing gases into a vacuum (called "gaspac") has been financed by the U.S. government (Departments of Agriculture and Energy) (*New York Times* November 15, 1979). The Defense Department is now a major purchaser of light-weight prepared and dried meals to replace "K-rations" for its rapid deployment forces.

[9] Heinz now produces over 1250 varieties of processed foods, compared to the original "57 varieties" (Heinz Annual Report).

[10] Neither in the first edition (1951) nor in the fifth edition (1977) of Walter Adam's *The Structure of American Industry* did food processing earn a chapter. Agriculture, food distribution, beer, and tobacco were included. Other industry studies have examined tomatoes, fluid milk, meat packing, cereals, and so on, but studies of the food processing industry *per se* are recent and relatively few. Yet there were some early indications of the common bases of the industry. As early as 1928, the industry had a journal of its own (*Food Engineering*); this was followed by two others, *Food Processing* (1940) and *Food Technology* (1946).

[11] Historical data for individual companies in this and subsequent sections have been obtained from annual reports; from Buzzell and Nourse 1967; Horst 1974; *Food Processing*, 10/79; Hampe and Wittenberg 1964; and from the following corporate histories or reports: Heer 1966 (Nestlé); Eames and Landis 1974 (Del Monte); Foley 1972 (General Foods): McCann 1976 (United Brands): Wilson, 1968 and CIS, n.d. (Unilever); and Alperts 1973 (Heinz).

[12] The motto of the British company Alfred Bird (later part of General Foods) went: "Early to bed, early to rise; stick to your work . . . and *advertise*." In one example of aggressive product promotion, Wrigley's twice sent chewing gum samples to everyone listed in the telephone directory in the United States.

[13] For example, eleven of the strongest canning firms in California combined in 1899 to form the California Fruit Canners Association; in 1916 the CFCA combined with two other canners to form the California Packing Association, later Del Monte (Eames and Landis 1974).

[14] In the first wave, the National Biscuit Company (Nabisco) was formed at the suggestion of their lawyer by joining over 100 baking enterprises. Standard Brands is an outstanding example of an early consolidator in the food processing industry. Standard Brands was formed in 1929 and grew through the distribution of Fleischmann's Yeast. The merger of Nabisco and Standards Brands in 1981 produced one of the largest diversified food companies. The firm already had leading positions in several market lines before it merger with Nabisco: Standard Brands owned Curtis Candies, Fleischmann's Yeasts and Margarines, and Clinton Corn Processing, as well as Planters Peanuts and Pinata Foods.

[15] Concentration of the U.S. food industry is discussed by Horst (1974) and, with better data, by Conner (1979) and Albrecht and Locker (1979). Albrecht and Locker's work is a directory of more than 200 large agribusiness firms, with 1976 data on each firm. The OECD (1979) study reviews what data is available for its member countries.

[16] The situation in Europe is variable. Although data for sub-sectors are scant, data for the food processing industry as a whole indicate the United Kingdom and Denmark have highly concentrated food industries, while in Germany, France and Italy the industry is relatively unconcentrated. But the EEC reports that, for all countries, "The degree of industry concentration is below the degree of concentration in individual product markets, which are generally oligopolistic and frequently almost monopolistic" (OECD 1979, pp. 172-175).

[17] The exceptions to the general rule of expansion within the food industry have usually involved other consumer goods, particularly tobacco and drugs.

[18] For example, Pillsbury, Ralston Purina, and others own fast-food chains. It is worth noting that some grocery store chains are integrating backwards into processing. This has helped create a segmentation of the market by price. Now processed foods are sold through a three tiered price structure: national brands, "house" brands of the grocery chain, and "no-name" generic products.

[19] Diversification of food firms is dealt with at length by Chesnais in the OECD study (1979, pp. 206-225); particular attention is paid throughout that study to growing links between the food and chemical industries. Chemical firms are exploring new technologies for breaking down biological raw materials into interchangeable building blocks. As with earlier innovations, major changes in the food industry are likely to originate in other industries (Connor 1979, p. 55 and *passim*; Nichols and Veblen 1978, p. 54; UN-CTC 1980).

[20] Large manufacturing acquisitions by food and tobacco processing firms in the period from 1948 to 1960 numbered 58; for 1961 to 1965, 56; for 1966 to 1970, 96; and for 1971 to 1975, the number was 76. In the latter period, food acquisitions were 28.1 percent of all large manufacturing acquisitions; the average for the period was 18.4 percent.

[21] In the United States, merger of staple-product companies in the same product line have been slowed by anti-trust actions. The Federal Trade Commission prohibited the merger of Continental Baking, General Baking, and Ward in the 1920s, and vetoed takeovers in the dairy industry in the 1960s (OECD 1979, p. 167). Firms that acquire companies in other product lines within the food industry face fewer obstacles. Among the more highly differentiated industries, the control of mergers and acquisitions, and hence of concentration, has been relatively unsuccessful, despite a much-commented anti-trust suit brought against the major breakfast cereal manufacturers.

[22] The OECD (1979) study suggests that the general rise in raw materials prices in the early 1970s encouraged basic research by the largest firms. Although this research may provide new barriers to entry in the future, market structure in the past has been most influenced by advertising and product differentiation.

[23] Most foreign investments were preceded by exports; products such as beer, fresh milk, or meat with high weight-to-value and perishable products were unlikely to be exported, enabling local industries to be established elsewhere. In highly advertised product lines (associated with high value-added), foreign sales are high; foreign investments followed exports.

[24] Most rapid expansion of foreign investment in the U.S. took place in the years following World War II; by 1959 investments in food represented 38 percent of all foreign investment in U.S. manufacturing. With the major firms established, that percentage declined to 15 percent by 1976, as interpenetration spread to other industries, U.S. foreign direct investment in food and tobacco was valued at 2.2 billion in 1976; the corresponding figure by foreign firms in the U.S. in the same year was 1.9 billion (Connor 1979).

[25] Since 1948 the number of subsidiaries has been increasing, but the percentage formed from scratch has been declining. Well over half of all subsidiaries of 23 large U.S. food processing firms between 1948 and 1967, and over two-thirds in the most recent part of that period, were acquired rather than newly formed (Horst 1974, p. 111). This pattern has been reproduced in developing country markets.

[26] One country, Mexico, hosts seven firms. Foreign dairy product firms in Mexico sell evaporated, condensed, and dried milk, infant formula preparations, yogurt and cheeses. In all of these product lines except cheeses, the transnational firms compete primarily with each other.

[27] A similar situation holds in the fruit and vegetable industry, with high levels of foreign participation in canning and packing and in soups and sauces, but no foreign investment in the traditional dried products or in jellies and regional sweets (Domike and Rodríguez 1977, various annexes).

[28] In contrast to Nestlé's practices of promoting infant formula as an alternative to breast feeding (only discontinued in response to public pressure in the U.S. and elsewhere) the Mexican government distributed CONLAC as a supplement to breast feeding, and is able to offer instruction in infant nutrition as well. Under Mexican President José Portillo, advertising was developed to promote the benefits of breast feeding.

[29] Of all U.S. food processors in the 1975 sample of the Harvard Multinational Enterprise project, 31 percent entered Mexico by forming new firms; 4 percent were the result of a merger or break-up of subsidiaries; 29 percent were directly acquired; and 36 percent were acquired via another acquisition.

[30] Though these measures of profitability are of limited utility in isolation, cross-industry comparisons do have some usefulness, since the same standard is applied.

[31] The president of Del Monte was perhaps making an indirect reference to this failure when he indicated the importance, for a firm with a perishable raw material, of building its operations from scratch, thus insuring that the physical plant is suitable and the local managers familiar with local conditions (Eames 1974). Del Monte has been quite successful at the introduction of contract farming in Mexico.

[32] For four years after the establishment of the foreign investment commission, the terms "new fields of economic investment" and "new product lines" were not defined. During this time, foreign-owned food processors seemed to operate under the assumption that any food product fell within its traditional activities. Some firms voluntarily reported new products to the Registry of Foreign Investment, while others proceeded without either requesting permission or reporting their new activities. One firm expanded from the production of pet foods into the production of accessories, such as dog collars, for pets; another introduced pet foods to complement foods for humans. A chocolate manufacturer requested and received permission to produce an "instant breakfast" bar. Few expansions into new food product lines were denied.

[33] The distinction between the renewable bargain in manufacturing is contrasted both with the "obsolescing bargain" dominant in extractive industries and with the "transnational bargain" in the production and assembly of components for export (Whiting 1983).

Gary Gereffi
and
Richard S. Newfarmer
11.
International Obligopoly and Uneven Development: Some Lessons from Industrial Case Studies

The writings of Stephen Hymer, Celso Furtado, Osvaldo Sunkel, and others have argued that the expansion of the large transnational corporation would integrate the peripheral economies into a global division of labor in a subordinate, dependent position. A regime of TNCs, they contended, would transfer decisionmaking about production, investment, and growth to a few capital cities in the developed countries; authority, status, income, and consumption patterns would radiate outwards towards the less developed regions. The result was seen to be uneven development. Only the emergence of strong national planning in peripheral countries presented an alternative organization of global production. National planning, Hymer and Furtado argued, could organize production horizontally across many markets in one country to replace the vertical organization of many countries under the direction of TNCs. We examine these broad propositions by comparing the role of TNCs in the generation and use of investment funds in eight transnational industries.

This chapter is organized around four conceptual themes relating to the power of TNCs to control investment funds and thereby affect the course of development. First, we consider the monopolistic advantage enjoyed by TNCs which permits them to gain ascendence in foreign markets. Without such advantages, domestic firms with their superior knowledge of local conditions could readily imitate foreigners and undermine their position. It is thus important to understand these advantages. Competition from other transnationals can erode the monopolistic advantage of any leading firm, so in the second section we consider the role of international rivalry in changing international industrial structure. The process of internationalization affects not only the global organization of an industry, but also the structure and performance of domestic industry in developing countries. The third section, therefore, looks at the consequences of foreign ownership for patterns of industrial development in Latin America. As TNCs expand into a recipient economy, they generate and use potential investment surplus. This can affect development in two ways. First, TNCs can repatriate part of their funds as profits which are no longer available for local growth.[1] Second, TNCs can reinvest locally and, to the extent that TNCs "grow differently" from national economic entities, transnational control of investment changes the path of growth in developing countries. Since nation-states play an important role in setting parameters to private sector growth, the complex interaction between the TNCs and the state is considered in a fourth section.

The comparative discussion points to four general conclusions, paralleling each section. These conclusions should be recognized as preliminary—perhaps even stated as hypotheses—because they emerge inductively from the eight case studies. Moreover, they are subject to some important qualifications set forth in the following discussion. Nonetheless, let us present the broad outlines of four arguments to provide a set of focal points for discussion.

First, the studies demonstrate that the positions of dominance of TNCs in international markets are rooted in monopolistic advantages protected by barriers to entry at home and abroad. These barriers are not based solely on advanced technology but on combinations of several advantages, including scale barriers related to particular product designs and product differentiation barriers. They are an important determinant of international and national concentration.

Second, the international rivalry of TNCs based in different home countries has not seriously eroded these industry-specific barriers to entry or markedly reduced global concentration, though it may have promoted strong competition in certain markets for limited periods. Concentration and other international market structures give rise to particular forms of international oligopolistic behavior, most of which create market structures that in turn reduce the share of gains from investment and trade going to developing countries.

Third, the growth of foreign investment in developing countries in the context of a particular international industrial organization has had two consequences inside these nations. Transnational corporations tend to be associated with concentrated markets and international rivalry has generally not created the conditions for sustained price competition in local markets; to the contrary, a strong case can be made that in fact the activities of foreign investors have promoted imperfect markets. Also the transnational presence clearly alters the path of development through their influence on the type of investment and other dimensions of firm behavior. These include the generation and use of technology, trade behavior, exercise of market power, and investment in a particular product mix. In many cases, the effects of transnationals in rivalry with each other or in interaction with domestic actors are to move the economy away from satisfaction of basic human needs, accentuating uneven development.

Fourth, the growth of TNCs in developing countries as part of capitalist development has tended to provide a set of parameters within which TNC-host country bargaining over the gains from foreign investment takes place. Contrary to the bargaining in natural resources where host governments generally gain in relative power *vis-à-vis* TNCs, the growth of foreign investment in manufacturing does not appear to have shifted bargaining power in favor of host governments. This is partly because continual innovation in products and technologies flows from the parent company rendering previous flows obsolete and partly because new class interests emerge as foreign investment occurs in manufacturing, producing strong allies for TNCs, including managers, middle class consumers, domestic labor, and even domestic competitors. Ironically, the overall effect of negotiating conflict between TNCs and host countries has often been to create a new, more enduring alliance between the two parties. The following sections will explore each of these points in greater detail.

MONOPOLISTIC ADVANTAGES AND SOURCES OF TRANSNATIONAL MARKET POWER

Transnationals have established positions of dominance in world markets because, according to Richard Caves (1971), they have some monopolistic advantage. This has two important implications to be explored in subsequent sections. First, local firms cannot easily enter TNC markets and erode their long-term market position through the normal course of growth, explaining in part the continued high levels of observed international concentration. Second, firms having a monopolistic advantage usually have the opportunity to capture higher rates of returns than firms in competitive markets.

Hymer, Charles Kindleberger, and later Caves reasoned that this monopolistic advantage is predicated on some combination of "intangible assets," e.g., a differentiated product, a new technology, and management capabilities. This combination is not easily imitated by local firms in host countries because barriers to entry prevent other firms from obtaining or replicating this package of intangible assets. The eight industrial case studies allow us to disaggregate monopolistic advantages and the barriers to entry protecting them. Consider three sources of monopolistic advantages.

Technology

The most commonly identified component of the package of intangible assets is technology. Patented technology in product design and/or production processes does give dominant transnationals an absolute cost advantage in several industries: pharmaceuticals, tires, electrical machinery, and, to a lesser extent, electronics. Unpatented technology is becoming more important in auto production, though for many years before the oil crisis technology was virtually absent as a barrier to entry. Technology does not appear to be particularly important in tractors and is almost nonexistant in most food products and cigarettes.

Other barriers to entry may supplement or supplant the patent system in protecting a technological monopolistic advantage. For example scale and pecuniary economies are an important barrier in large, heavy electrical equipment which, together with patent protection, impedes the spread of technology to outside firms; in pharmaceuticals and tires, product differentiation in the form of sales networks also contributes to impeding the spread of technology.

Economies of Scale

Economies of scale relative to market size give TNCs a monopolistic advantage worldwide and in some countries. Economies of scale, as the case studies show, can take several forms, including production economies, pecuniary economies, advertising economies, and the economies of information marketing and warehousing. Scale economies can also be a barrier to entry when the minimum efficient scale of production amounts to a large percent of the whole market and when firms smaller than the minimum efficient scale suffer higher costs.

For the advanced industrializing countries of Latin America, production economies of scale appear to constitute an advantage for large firms only in autos, tractors, and steel. Certain very large machines in electrical equipment also experience a scale barrier simply because only a few of these machines usually fulfill demand each year. In pharmaceuticals, cigarettes, food, and tires, minimum efficient scales are relatively small and cost penalties at lower volumes are generally not severe. In most branches of these industries, markets could readily support a larger number of firms than they now do and still attain most production economies. This implies that at least in these transnational industries production technology is *not* the primary determinant of market concentration for the advanced industrializing countries of Latin America. In smaller countries, however, production economies of scale may be an important determinant of concentration.

Production economies of scale can also occur globally if firms are highly integrated in production across national markets and the world is seen as the relevant geographical market. Only one industry shows any indication of experiencing global production economies of scale: autos. Recently, under the pressure of the intense international rivalry caused by the oil crisis and its effects on demand, TNCs have begun to exploit the potential for worldwide integration of production to produce a "world car." These efforts have yet to be wholly successful. In the heavy electrical equipment industry, world demand for very large machines is satisfied by only a few firms, and so global scale barriers are also appearing in these lines as well. The tractor industry may eventually move in the same direction. In these industries, governments everywhere will struggle to obtain a share of the global market.[2]

Economies of scale other than in production—such as in advertising, finance, and information exchange—are also of varying importance. These economies, while real to the firm, may or may not have social benefits corresponding to production economies because it is not clear whether they result in increased output for the same level of social resources. This question warrants greater attention empirically than it has received.

Product Differentiation

One recurring source of transnational monopolistic advantages and barriers to entry is product differentiation. Product differentiation takes on several forms. First, heavy advertising in the mass media was found to be important in autos, cigarettes, consumer electronics, many transnational food products, and to a lesser extent, pharmaceuticals. Second, model changes that attempt to convince

389

consumers to buy the latest, most fashionable products were important in autos, cigarettes, food, and televisions. Model proliferation, a variant of this form of differentiation, is important in these same industries and also tractors. Third, servicing and follow-up on sales are essential in heavy electrical machinery, tractors, and to a lesser extent, autos. Fourth, extensive sales networks and/or dealerships are required to compete in autos, cigarettes, heavy equipment, consumer appliances, tractors, and pharmaceuticals.

Of these forms of product differentiation, it is arguable that only distribution and servicing networks have social benefits commensurate with their private and social costs in developing countries, and this only in heavy electrical equipment and tractors. Heavy promotional outlays and model changes in other industries often serve only to increase social consumption at the expense of savings. At best, advertising passes on some product knowledge at a high cost such as in pharmaceuticals; at worst, advertising outlays simply create images, even misinformation, among consumers such as in cigarettes. In industries where this characterization is valid, then at least part of the transnational transfer of marketing skills in fact promotes inefficient production and waste.

Monopolistic Advantages: A Recapitulation

Monopolistic advantages explain why certain firms can and do take advantage of the opportunity to invest abroad. They also explain how TNCs can establish positions of dominance in many foreign markets protected, however imperfectly, from domestic competition. Finally, they explain how TNCs, partially insulated from price competition, can obtain high returns on their overseas investments with their implications for development.

Three points about monopolistic advantages merit restatement. First, these case studies provide ample evidence that the monopolistic advantage of transnationals is not predicated solely on one factor, for example, technology. In every industry, various and changing combinations of institutions and firm behavior—patented technology, product differentiation, or economics of scale—were found to be important. Often they interacted, as in the case of product differentiation through model changes and economies of scale in autos. Second, monopolistic advantages of TNCs are by and large created institutionally, not technologically. Governments have sometimes been the key institutional force, such as in the case of the patent system or import controls. More often, however, TNCs either by their own design or in rivalry with other TNCs have been the central force in raising barriers to entry. For example, TNCs in the pharmaceutical industry have by design invested heavily in drug creation, an important social contribution; to protect their newfound discoveries, however, they often spend heavily in creating and patenting near substitutes "around" the first discovery to protect their monopolistic advantages. An example of the effects of strong rivalry on barriers is when nonprice competition among transnationals produces high barriers to entry. Non-price competition in tractors, for example, compels firms to establish extensive networks of dealerships and proliferation of models, even when greater economies of scale could be obtained with only one model; this forces the cost structure of the industry upwards while raising a product differentiation barrier. Non-price competition through saturation advertising among cigarette manufacturers prevents all but other powerful transnationals from entering the market. Finally, by disaggregating the sources of monopolistic advantages of TNCs and the barriers to entry for each country, it is possible to lay the foundation for substantive hypotheses about industrial structure, international rivalry, and industrial performance.

INTERNATIONAL INDUSTRIAL ORGANIZATION AND GLOBAL RIVALRY

Knowing the various sources of monopolistic advantages allows us to begin an examination of determinants of industrial structure and oligopolistic behavior at an international level. Monopolistic advantages protected by certain barriers to entry, together with the historical development of capitalism, offer explanations for common patterns of international rivalry. This section traces the industry-specific forces giving rise to foreign activities and relates them to changes in contemporary international industrial organization and to five types of international oligopolistic rivalry, each with important consequences for developing countries.

Impulses Toward Foreign Activities

Firms and industries moving heavily into foreign activities shared at least two characteristics in common. All were associated with imperfect market structures at home and most feared some saturation and stagnation of demand in the home market, either because of market saturation, recession, or threats to the market. For example, the early cigarette maker, the American Tobacco Company (ATC), after mechanizing production, introducing demand creation marketing, and rapidly consolidating the U.S. market under its control, turned to foreign investments to expand its market as the United States became inundated with the wave of quasi-moralistic anti-cigarette publicity in the 1890s. The ATC tried to penetrate the British market where ten to fifteen small domestic firms competed. Fearing the powerful ATC, British firms quickly banded together to form the Imperial Tobacco Company (ITC). The electrical manufacturers in the United States provide a second example. They controlled a new technology in a tight oligopoly, and they wished to control and exploit the technology in international markets. After some early attempts at foreign direct investment failed, they turned to cross-licensing agreements with other dominant firms abroad, both to protect their home markets from new foreign and domestic competition and to gain rents from further use of the technology. The auto industry too feared saturation of domestic demand and increasingly turned to demand creation tactics and to exports in the 1920s. The European tire makers, confronting no particular scale barrier, jumped tariffs with foreign investment in Europe, and some European firms even invested in the United States as their markets slowed in growth. United States firms, meanwhile, began investing in Europe for the same reason around 1920. Later, when the Depression hit, all firms moved into developing countries via foreign directo investment. By 1930 cigarettes, electrical machinery, tires, and autos were transnationally structured industries, though the patterns of control varied considerably.

The post-1945 period witnessed a new wave of foreign activity. The new wave took the form of heavy foreign direct investment in the advanced developing countries of Latin America because of changes the Depression and World War II had wrought on the organization and power of nation-states. States had gained new authority, centralization, and fiscal power to take charge of international economic dealings that had previously been left to the market. The temporary disruption of trading patterns between North and South had created effective protection for incipient domestic industry and propelled import substitution. The new industrialists, workers, and incipient urban middle class formed a powerful coalition to support the state's use of tariffs after 1945 to continue the import substitution process. Transnational corporations in many industries were forced to acquire local production facilities to jump tariff walls.

Much as with the first wave of foreign activity, the foreign expansion of the 1950s was prompted in some measure because of slowing or saturated domestic demand or threatened home markets. Auto firms in the United States experienced another drop in demand once the post-war boom faded; they reacted by expanding into selected European countries and into developing countries to an unprecedented extent. Similar declines in the tire industry forced more expansion into developing countries, prompted many mergers, and compelled diversification into other product lines. The tractor industry, a relatively young transnational industry, experienced its first wave during this same period as large North American firms expanded into Europe and Latin America because of slowing demand and the threat of stagnation. The electrical machinery industry increased its production in advanced developing countries in consumer goods and light equipment, though heavy equipment production was internationalized only in a select few.

In the 1960s, of course, European companies expanded abroad for many of the same reasons that U.S. firms had sought positions in their markets. Auto manufacturers moved into the United States market, first through Volkswagen's export of small cars. The 1970s, however, brought the oil crisis, recession, and new heated competition for fewer consumer dollars in major markets around the world and intensified the struggle for global market shares. Tractor, pharmaceutical, and tire firms began investing heavily in the United States during the 1970s. Recession and market saturation was not the only form the threat to domestic markets took. The increasingly powerful Japanese attempted to reach the United States and Western Europe through exports and were most successful at first in consumer electronics. This competition prompted U.S. giants in televisions to move labor-intensive processes to cheap labor areas, such as Taiwan, and later to establish joint production arrangements in many products. The same activity may now be happening in the auto industry.

Consumer safety concerns in the United States were another threat that firms sought to get around in certain industries. Consider the cigarette industry. After the break-up of the tobacco trust in 1911, American producers continued to produce primarily for the United States market, and the newly independent British-American Tobacco (BAT) continued to serve several tariffed markets in the rest of the world. Medical reports linking smoking to cancer, however, created a health scare in the United States between 1952 and 1954. This was later followed by the Surgeon General's report in 1964. Both precipitated sharp reductions in consumption of cigarettes. Philip Morris, R. J. Reynolds, and the other manufacturers frantically began investing in foreign markets and diversifying at home. Over 90 percent of the 150 overseas sub-divisions of U.S. cigarette manufacturers were established after 1965. In the pharmaceutical industry, firms moved abroad to establish alternative testing facilities when the U.S. Food and Drug

Administration enacted regulations governing the testing and introduction of new drugs. In electrical machinery, the concern for safe nuclear power has curtailed demand in the United States for nuclear equipment since the 1970s, forcing firms to market more intensely abroad.

The steel industry, which was never to become controlled by transnationals, is the exception to these patterns for several reasons. First, growing home markets and high transportation costs prompted monopolistic firms to concentrate in industrialized countries until the mid-1920s. When export markets in developing countries became important after 1925, firms entered into tight international cartel agreements in 1926 to control competition outside home markets and to prevent poaching in each others' home markets. These cartels broke down under the pressure of the Depression, but were re-established and strengthened in 1933. The high fixed costs of investment and scale barriers rendered foreign investment risky and usually uneconomical throughout the 1930s and 1940s. However, the advent of World War II convinced planners in the larger developing countries that domestically controlled steel production was vital to national security interests; so Mexico, Brazil, Argentina, and other countries sought to buy international technology and build their own plants in a state-operated sector. This preempted a foreign investment strategy for the large steel firms when later during the 1950s they might otherwise have invested abroad. Consequently, the influence of the giant steel firms of the industrialized countries in the industry's foreign development has been limited to licensing arrangements and isolated investments in smaller markets. This would have implications for the structure of the global industry later in the 1970s as these new state firms eventually became competitive on the global market.

In summary, the experience of these several industries suggests that the dynamics of growth in the home market merit far greater concern in explaining the expansion of transnationals than they have received so far. The product cycle model, which has come closest to this issue, considers technological progress to be the motor of change and focuses on deteriorating firm-specific advantages. These studies suggest that the expansionary characteristics of capitalism itself offer a fuller explanation: recession, the tendency for markets to become saturated, threats to home bases from cross-penetrating foreign investment and from consumer concerns have played a role equal to, or perhaps more important than, pure technological change in explaining why oligopolists expand abroad. To this list, we must add oligopolistic rivalry, considered below.

Changing International Industrial Structures

One striking consequence of new rivalry and the dynamics of business expansion has been the absence of a trend in any of the industries towards diminished global concentration. If anything, the evidence in cigarettes, heavy electrical equipment, autos, tires, and tractors points to increased concentration of the global marketplace under the dominance of a handful of transnational majors. The data are fairly clear about the direction of changes in most industries, if not the exact magnitudes. In these industries firms have apparently expanded their share of global production relative to what it was in the 1960s (see Table 1.1).

Accompanying this process of concentration in the hands of a few firms is the relative decline of the market share of the dominant firm in most countries. General Motors has lost market share globally (though not in the United States) in autos; General Electric in heavy electrical equipment; Goodyear in tires; Nestlé in foods; Merck & Co. in pharmaceuticals; BAT in cigarettes; Massey-Ferguson in tractors; and U.S. Steel in steel production. The erosion of the dominant position in some industries, such as autos and tires, has been only marginal, however, and most of the dominant firms still maintain a position of leadership within the industry. Still, rivalry among the leading eight firms has in most cases become more equally based.

Acquisitions and mergers in all industries have played a central role in increasing global concentration. Some industrial leaders, such as Philip Morris in cigarettes and Philips in consumer electrical products, routinely used acquisitions to diversify and consolidate their hold on a market. In other industries, such as the auto and electrical equipment industries in Europe, government-sponsored "rationalization" programs promoted mergers to eliminate excess capacity; yet in others, pressures of foreign competition and slowly growing demand have forced smaller rivals out of business or to merge with larger firms, as in autos, tractors, and, to a lesser extent, tires. But mergers and acquisitions among domestic firms have not been the only cause of increased global concentration. Acquisitions were major vehicles of entry in cross-penetrating investments among industrialized countries in nearly every industry (except steel where foreign investment rarely occurred). Takeovers played an equally important role in developing countries, especially in industries where technological and scale barriers did not completely impede entry of domestic firms, such as cigarettes, small electrical equipment and electronics, auto assembly, pharmaceuticals, tires, and food.

Table 11.1

Structural Characteristics of Eight International Industries
(Plus and minus signs indicate direction of change over time; slashes indicate different patterns among industry sub-products)

	Cigarettes	Electrical Equipment Consumer Goods	Electrical Equipment Capital Goods	Steel	Autos	Tires	Pharmaceuticals	Tractors	Food Commodities	Food Processed Consumer Goods
Transnational Control	High+	Medium+	High+	Low	High+	High	Medium	High	Medium	Medium
Concentration[a]: International	High+	Medium	High+	Medium	High+	High+	Low	High+	High	High
National	High	Medium−	High	High	Medium	High	Low/Medium[a]	High	Variable	Variable
Product Differentiation[b]	High	High	Medium	Low	High	Medium	High	Medium	Low	High
Advertising	High	High	Low	Low	High	Medium	High	Medium	Low	High
Product Form Variation	High	High	Low	Low	High	Low	High	Medium	Low	High
Servicing	Low	Low	High	Medium	High	Low	Low	High	Low	Low
Distribution/ Sales Force/ Dealer Networks	High	Medium	High	Low	High	High	High	High	Low	Low

396

Barriers to Entry[c]									
Capital	High	Low/High[d]	Med/High[d]	High	High	Medium	Medium	High	Low	Low
Absolute Cost[e]	Low	Low/High	Med/High	High	High	High	Low/High	Medium	Variable	Variable
Econ. of Scale	Low/High[f]	Low	Low/High[f]	High	High	Low	Low/High[f]	High	High	Medium
Demand Creation	High +	High	Medium	Low	Medium	Medium	High −	Medium	Low	High
Diversification/ Conglomeration	High +	High	High	Low +	Medium −	Medium −	High	High/Low +	Medium	Medium

Source: Preceding case studies. These are impressionistic characterizations designed to give a comparative overview of industry structures. For a more precise description, the reader is referred to the case studies.

Notes:

a In developed countries concentration tends to be low, while in developing countries it is medium.

b This represents the overall importance of the product differentiation effort.

c This refers to the cost disadvantage faced by potential entrants outside the market or the extent to which established firms can raise their price above the minimum average costs without inducing new entry.

d This depends on the degree of vertical integration and industry demand-creation patterns.

e This includes disadvantages due to costs of potential technology, raw materials, distribution channels or finance.

f Production scale economies are low; demand-creation/marketing scale economies are high.

Besides acquisitions, the expansion of TNCs into new markets has brought under their control a wider segment of the world market. The markets of the advanced developing countries after the mid-1960s usually grew more rapidly than those of the developed countries, so by capturing a large share of these markets, the majors' share of the total global market has generally increased.

The effects at entry of cross-penetrating investments on industrial concentration in the developed countries appear mixed. In some industries, such as cigarettes, autos, and tires in the United States, national concentration has been reduced. In others, acquisitions have been virtually the sole vehicle of entry, negating any concentration-reducing effects that might otherwise have occurred. This has been the case for lamps, heavy electrical equipment, tractors, and pharmaceuticals. It should be noted that this cross-penetrating investment has not usually signalled an erosion of the monopoly advantage of the largest four or so firms. More often than not, the local leaders in a domestic oligopoly become absorbed and integrated, through takeovers or behavioral imitation, into the structure of global oligopoly.[3]

Global Interdependence and Oligopolistic Conduct

High levels of industrial concentration raise the possibility that firms will recognize their global interdependence and modify their behavior to account for the strategies of other large rivals. This section relates the dimensions of industrial organization, including global concentration, to five forms of international oligopolistic conduct, each with different implications for development. These patterns of conduct are not mutually exclusive in any time period and moreover since industrial organization changes, firms in any industry may abandon one set of practices for another. Nonetheless, the five conduct forms are presented in chronological order of when they were the prevalent form of international practice. The task at hand is to understand the role of international industrial structure in causing or facilitating certain patterns of conduct (see Table 11.2).

Restrictive Licenses and Cartel Restraints. Restrictive cross-licenses among TNCs from different home countries were seen to be an early and important type of interdependent activity. They were and are prevalent in the electrical machinery and steel industries and, to a far lesser degree, in cigarettes, pharmaceuticals, and tires. In these industries, major firms historically controlled much of the leading patented technology and used their cross-licenses to restrict participants to

398

Table 11.2

Forms of International Interdependence in Eight Industries

	Cigarettes	Electrical Equipment – Consumer Goods	Electrical Equipment – Capital Goods	Steel	Autos	Tires	Pharmaceuticals	Tractors	Food – Commodities	Food – Processed Consumer Goods
Cross-licenses and Cartelization	Medium	Med/Low	High	High	Low	Low	Low	Low	Low	Low
Spheres of Influence and Mutual Forbearance	Medium	Medium−	High−	High+	Low	Medium	Medium	Medium	Medium	Medium
Oligopolistic Reaction	Low	Medium	Low	Low	High	Low	Medium	Low	Low	Medium
Joint Ventures	Medium	Low/High	High+	High+	Low+	Low	Low	Low	Low	Low

Source: Preceding case studies; see Table 11.1.

specified geographical markets, to dictate the selling prices of the products, to prevent new entry of domestic firms in the home markets, and to curtail the number of competitors in foreign markets. Companies have also used licenses as a way of restricting export activities of independent firms and subsidiaries in developing countries, thus restricting some international trade. None of the studies of industries that currently employ this practice—electrical machinery, steel, and cigarettes—presented quantitative estimations of their impact, but presumably their effects are not insignificant.

Formal international cartel behavior was evident historically in cigarettes, steel, electrical machinery, tires, and pharmaceuticals. These cartels—with the notable exceptions of steel and electrical machinery—were generally of limited duration and effect. The tobacco trust was broken up by the United States antitrust action in 1911, though subsequent global market allocation arrangements obviated the need for cartels. Cartels in pharmaceuticals and tires were less successful, apparently because of the number of potential producers, the speed of technological change, and the viability of reaching small, segmented national markets through foreign direct investment. Small markets were often protected by tariffs and exclusive patents. For both industries, foreign investment probably provided a more efficient manner of organizing the world market because smaller national markets are easier to coordinate than the whole world. Foreign direct investment could replace export cartels, even in small protected markets, because of the absence of a scale barrier.

The steel industry, like the electrical equipment industry, requires advanced technology, large fixed investments, and a relatively large market. As discussed above, by the time the steel cartel broke down in the 1940s, many of the most promising markets had been preempted by state enterprises founded by governments concerned about their security during the war years. Often these new enterprises confronted the restrictions on technology transfers imposed by the cartel, but with large amounts of capital, governments of large developing countries could shop for the production technology and pay the high costs of entering the industry. After the war and a period of domestic prosperity because of war reconstruction, producers increasingly turned to their home governments to aid in controlling world trade. This pattern has persisted and intensified as new Japanese competition added to capacity worldwide. Governments have generally been responsive since they see the industry as vital to national defense. The result is now a home government-business partnership negotiated in the framework of an international quasi-cartel.

The European-based cartel in the electrical industry, although having some of the same economic characteristics, does not enjoy official sponsorship. This cartel has been forced to remain clandestine and, under pressures of recent public exposure, has been under investigation in three counties for possible violation of antitrust and tax laws. Nonetheless, economic causes are parallel: excess capacity in the world industry, the need to reach growing markets abroad because of slow growth at home, and high fixed costs with scale barriers preventing foreign direct investments as an alternative to exports. The alternatives open to European and later Japanese producers to reach smaller markets with infrequent orders are either to compete vigorously in prices or to form cartels.

Spheres of Influence and Mutual Forbearance. Geographical spheres of influence were most evident in the tightest international oligopolies: electrical machinery, tires, cigarettes, steel, and tractors. These were usually begun through formal licensing and cartel arrangements, as in electrical machinery, cigarettes, and perhaps pharmaceuticals and tires, though they often became informal after the disintegration of the cartels. For example, tire manufacturers turned to joint production agreements after 1930 as a way to divide up world markets. Joint ventures were used in much the same way in the lamp industry throughout the developing world. The other industries, autos and tractors, evolved in informal spheres. In autos, the early post-war direct investments of U.S. firms were in European countries that lacked their own national firms in the dominions, and in the developing countries, particularly Latin America. This apparent mutual forbearance took on another form besides geography: car size. European and later Japanese firms for many years tended to specialize in small car production while U.S. firms specialized in large cars, creating a two-tier market effect. This undoubtedly lessened the disruptive effects of initial cross-penetrating investments that were to occur later.

The evolution of these spheres coincided with the territories originally allocated under the cross-licenses in industries such as pharmaceuticals, electrical machinery, steel, and cigarettes. These territories were closely linked to former political divisions apparent under nineteenth century colonialism. Although it is known that territories are the subject of intense negotiations in certain industries, it is impossible simply by looking at the geographic distribution of investments to distinguish the effects of mutual forbearance relative to other potential causes, such as currency regimes, tariff preferences, taxes, or cultural familiarity.

In almost all of these industries, the traditional spheres of influence showed signs of erosion under quite different sets of economic pressures in the late 1960s and 1970s. In the electrical industry, the gradual termination of cross-licenses signed in the 1950s and the increasing scrutiny of restrictive clauses in the licenses by the U.S. Department of Justice has limited the control that majors have been able to exert on limiting the use of technology. This is especially true for television production. In addition, the heavy equipment industry has continued to experience excess capacity and slow growth, forcing all companies to look for new markets; the stronger firms are beginning to poach on the territories of weaker members of the international oligopoly. Thus, after many years of mutual forbearance, the giant electrical companies have begun moves towards crossing into each other's markets. Many of the same forces were at work in the tire industry. Excess capacity and slow growth prompted the more technologically advanced European firms to begin selling in the traditionally safe American territory. American consumers quickly saw the advantages in radial technology, but American manufacturers at first resisted production of radial tires and tried to slow their introduction through advertising and other promotional techniques. Only after Michelin seriously penetrated the United States market and the United States auto manufacturers began requesting radials on new cars did American companies move swiftly to produce the new products. The slow response of U.S. companies left them at a competitive disadvantage in Europe and the developing countries and probably contributed to their eventual withdrawal from Europe. The oil crisis has destabilized the international auto oligopoly and caused a reduction in demand in most major markets. This has prompted new cross-penetrating investments and sped the erosion of traditional spheres of influence, including the two-tier division within the United States market. Like the United States tire manufacturers and radial technology, U.S. auto manufacturers at first mistakenly resisted the turn toward smaller cars. In cigarettes, the destabilizing factor was not technology, but the health scares of 1952 and 1964. U.S. producers had to move abroad into the traditional territory of BAT because the domestic market was threatened by new consumer information. The tractor industry also shows signs of weakening mutual forbearance. This has occurred because of the slowing of market growth at home and the successive elimination of rivals in home markets. The merger of major manufacturers has reduced the total number of firms competing in world markets.

In sum, industries with the most enduring informal geographical market allocations appear to be those characterized by high global concentration, tight oligopolistic patterns of behavior in the home markets, rather stable patterns of demand and technological development, and either relatively high scale barriers or very low scale barriers. Home government policy has played a pivotal role in steel and is becoming more important in autos.

Oligopolistic Reaction. Another form of international interdependence is when one home country oligopolist sets up facilities in a foreign market in reaction to the foreign investment behavior of another. The automobile industry, for example, has exhibited strong non-price rivalry predicated upon advertising, model changes, distribution networks, consumer loyalty, large market share, declining costs, and a scale barrier. So if one rival should succeed in establishing a production facility abroad and capturing a major share of the market, other rivals risk losing ready access to the market. In deciding about how and when to serve a market, the current profitability and size of local markets take a back seat to the estimations of corporate planners about future market growth and profit potential and the strategies of rivals.

Patterns of oligopolistic reaction were less evident in industries with higher levels of concentration and more stable patterns of international rivalry, including the cigarette, tire, and tractor industries. In these industries, concentration appeared to be sufficiently high that competitive forces were too weak to provoke retaliatory moves. The cigarette industry has been a tight oligopoly since the turn of the century; cartel agreements and then informal spheres of influence dictated the pattern of expansion. When these agreements finally did break down under the pressures of the health scares, the U. S. companies moved abroad not because of oligopolistic rivalry, but because they realized their vulnerability to consumer knowledge about the product. The tire industry also did not show reaction patterns. Instead, mutual forbearance dominated investment strategies as firms tended to invest in their former political blocs after the demise of the 1925 to 1930 cartel. Market sharing was more common than aggressive cross-penetrating investments. Pharmaceuticals and food firms appear to be sufficiently differentiated so that the follow-the-leader pattern has not emerged as strongly as in other industries. Tractor companies, perhaps the most likely candidate to exhibit oligopolistic reactions because of the scale barrier, appear not to have done so because of the highly stable patterns of conduct in a concentrated market.

These experiences suggest that students of international oligopoly should pay more attention to patterns of behavior in rather stable, tightly knit oligopolies. This conclusion is reinforced with two other pieces of information. First, Frederick Knickerbockr's (1973) results showed that oligopolistic reaction faded in intensity after reaching higher levels of market concentration, suggesting that many more tightly knit oligopolies engaged in other patterns. As industrial concentration in global industries increases, presumably there will be more industries with higher levels of concentration, leading one to suspect a dissipation of oligopolistic reaction. Second, as the spread of giant firms around the world integrates several regional oligopolies into their world network, the rate of formation of new subsidiaries attenuates and so this form of non-price rivalry may diminish in importance. If this is correct, countries will have less opportunity to play off one international oligopolist against the other in negotiations over the terms of new entry. Negotiations will instead have to focus on the more difficult distinction of subsidiary expansion into new product lines.

Joint Ventures. As concentration has increased and traditional spheres of influence have begun to break down, many industries are starting to look to joint ventures among dominant firms as a kind of negotiated solution to intense rivalry. (This pattern had been successfully used much earlier in different circumstances in cigarettes, tires, and lamps.) Thus, in the automobile industry, General Motors has just concluded an agreement with Toyota to produce small cars in California, Chrysler continues to talk with Volkswagen, American Motor Company has already established an agreement with Renault as has Mitsubishi with Chrysler. Similar patterns, though not as pronounced, are occurring in heavy electrical equipment as seen in Siemens' joint venture with Allis Chalmers and Westinghouse's arrangement with Mitsubishi, and in television electronics, such as General Electric's attempt to establish a joint venture with Hitachi to make televisions for the U.S. market. This pattern has not generally occurred in the steel industry, except between state-owned firms in developing countries and some Japanese firms, such as in the case of USIMINAS in Brazil. Other industries where this pattern has not been so evident include food and pharmaceuticals, probably because low fixed costs, high differentiation, and low minimum efficient scales permit several firms to remain in the market even if demand falls.

International Oligopoly and Pricing Behavior. When the same leading transnationals come to control a high share of the global industry as well as large shares in national markets around the world, the possibility arises that their recognized mutual interdependence will extend to pricing practices in local oligopolies. Supporting evidence for this is found in the case studies. First, it is conceivable that firms in an established local oligopoly will react differently to the threat of new entry if both they and the new entrant are foreign and have established patterns of international price behavior. Gereffi notes that pricing structures in the foreign dominated British pharmaceutical industry remained virtually unchanged with the entrance of U.S. drug houses in the early 1970s. On the other hand, when the foreign dominated electrical machinery industry in Brazil was threatened with new domestic expansion in transformers, TNCs cut prices under agreements worked out in a local cartel agreement. Some TNCs in related machinery products even cross-subsidized extensive losses. This juxtaposition suggests new foreign entrants will have an easier time because transnational insiders will respect their "long purse"; independent domestic firms, however, might well face higher barriers to entry because established foreign oligopolists might be willing to cut prices to defer entry.

A second case involves the pricing effects when oligopolistic national markets are linked by the same transnationals. Jenkins and West recount that the tractor manufacturers located in Britain did not pass on a 14 percent devaluation to Canadian buyers in 1967, but opted instead for maintaining the price structure in Canada. Noting the new 14 percent price difference between the two markets, independent dealers in Canada attempted to purchase the lower priced tractors in Great Britain, but dealers in Britain were prevented from selling abroad by contracts with the tractor manufacturers.

A third case involves international price discrimination. Transnational corporations controlling different markets can set prices in accordance with demand elasticities and other local factors and, if tariffs do not protect the discriminated market, they can attempt to frustrate international commodity arbitrage through restrictive trade provisions. Such international discriminatory pricing was reported for lamps, televisions, tractors, cigarettes, and food processed products at various times. Price discrimination probably explains higher rates of foreign profitability found in the auto, tire and other industries of many developing countries. As the tractor examples highlight, such price discrimination and price unresponsiveness to government trade policy raises serious concerns about international oligopoly and intra-firm trade.

International Concentration and Rivalry: Implications for the Distribution of Gains from Trade and Investment

This review of five types of international oligopolistic conduct and their associated market structures illustrates the importance of

405

international organization in determining the forms rivalry in international markets will take. Table 11.3 summarizes these elements together with their effects on developing economies and presents them as illustrative hypotheses.

The limited historical evidence from the experience of cartels indicates that prices of cartelized items were usually higher (Stocking and Watkins 1946). In Newfarmer's study of the electrical equipment industry in this volume, successful cartelization of international exports was found to raise prices more than 15 percent over the competitive rate. Likewise, Martin notes overcharges were also found in the steel industry on sales from France to its former colonies as a consequence of regulated sales.

Equally important are restrictions in international technology markets. Firms in electrical machinery, drugs, and to a lesser extent steel have at various times attempted to limit the spread of technology and raise its price to developing countries. Although in heavy electrical equipment and steel a central purpose of the cross-licensing arrangements of patented technology was to raise a barrier to entry to outside competition, the pharmaceutical firms were concerned that drug prices adequately reflect a monopoly premium attributable to their R&D activities. Similarly, the history of patent pools in television shows that restrictions in the markets for technology were used to raise the price of technology and final products.

High concentration, in combination with high- and low-scale barriers, also facilitated market allocation arrangements, either formally with the active participation of governments, as in steel, or informally through mutual forbearance in foreign investment strategies, such as in cigarettes and, to a lesser extent, tires. These forms of conduct usually lead to higher concentration in developing countries than under competitive circumstances because international rivals in effect grant each other quasi-monopoly positions in particular national markets, a fact that helps explain some domestic industrial structures.

Moderate international concentration and high product differentiation, as well as a high-scale barrier, seemed to be most conducive to oligopolistic reaction, especially evident in autos. The consequences for developing countries may include lower concentration, either higher or lower price-cost margins depending on how strong the struggle for the market is, and usually higher prices and costs associated with industries saddled with excess capacity.

High concentration, high technology barriers, and moderate to high-scale barriers can lead to joint ventures. This seems especially likely (1) when excess capacity and falling demand threaten the profitability of firms in high fixed-cost industries, such as electrical machinery and autos, and, (2) in industries with only moderate scale barriers and stable patterns of rivalry, such as tires, cigarettes, and lamps, where joint ventures already exist to share foreign markets and avoid competition. These two types of joint ventures have different performance consequences for developing countries: the latter type reduces competition because the joint venture partners might otherwise enter the market individually and compete; the former type might aid a rival which would otherwise be forced out of the market.

These five sets of structure-conduct-performance hypotheses are not all inclusive, either of relevant structures or forms of oligopolistic conduct in many national markets. However, this review does point towards a broader, more central conclusion: *A variety of industrial structures in international markets, especially international concentration, accord economic power to relatively few corporations and these imperfections tend to result in oligopolistic conduct that works to the disadvantage of developing countries. In most cases, these multiple forms of international oligopolistic behavior bias the gains from trade and investment in favor of the transnationals and their home country stockholders since they facilitate higher prices for traded products and higher returns to their factors of production, and create or entrench dominant positions in overseas markets.*

This proposition will be examined further in the next section by tracing the effects of foreign investment on industrial structure and performance in developing countries.

INTERNATIONALIZATION AND LOCAL INDUSTRIAL STRUCTURE IN DEVELOPING ECONOMIES

The changing international organization of industry has brought about changes in local industrial structure and performance. The foreign expansion of large corporations induced changes in industrial concentration, level of foreign ownership, barriers to entry, and product differentiation. And transnational corporate investment and growth has influenced domestic industrial performance in terms of profitability, technology, trade, and basic needs issues.

Concentration and Foreign Ownership

Some industries, such as lamps, tires, and tractors, were "born foreign"—that is, the interaction between TNCs wishing to reach and control foreign markets and state tariff policy aimed at building up local industry were conducive to the establishment of foreign subsidiaries, few domestic firms, and little or no opportunity to enter. For

Table 11.3
International Structure, Oligopolistic Conduct and Industrial Performance in Developing Countries: Some Hypotheses

International Structures	Oligopolistic Conduct	Industrial Performance[a] in Developing Countries
High concentration High scale and technology barriers Limited differentiation High fixed costs	Cartels in export markets Cartels in technology markets Foreign investment limited to largest markets	Cartels probably raise prices on imports to developing countries Cartels in technology reduce competition and sometimes industrial growth Cartels may restrict competition in foreign investment activity
High concentration High or low scale barriers	Formal or informal market allocation in exports Mutual forbearance in foreign direct investment activities	Higher domestic concentration in developing countries

408

Moderate concentration High differentiation High scale barriers	Oligopolistic reaction in foreign direct investment	Lower concentration Higher or lower profit margins depending on oligopolistic stability High prices and costs inefficient industry
High concentration High technology barrier Medium-high scale barrier	Joint ventures among rival TNCs in foreign investment	Increases supply of investors, provided none would undertake investment individually Reduces competition among rivals, provided one or more would take investment individually
High concentration Leaders meet in several national oligopolies	Price discrimination and restrictions on commodity arbitrage	Higher than competitive prices on imports Reduced effectiveness of foreign exchange policy

Source: Preceding case studies.

Note:

a This compares performance in industrial oligopolies with workably competitive situations where market imperfections are largely absent; government policy can accentuate or mitigate these outcomes in a given national market.

example, General Electric established a lamp subsidiary in Brazil in 1921 because of reduced transportation costs; the worldwide control of lamp technology was cartelized under the cross-licenses and subsequent product cartel, and this constituted an insurmountable barrier to entry facing potential domestic entrants. Similarly, the tire firms moved preemptively into the developing countries right after the demise of their cartel in 1930. Only in the rare case, such as FATE in Argentina, did a national firm break into the industry. FATE apparently did so only because the local transnationals wanted a domestic firm in the industry to represent their interests to the nationalistic Peronist government. These industries for the most part were thus "born foreign" and international oligopolistic interdependence kept them highly concentrated by discouraging new foreign or domestic entry.

The auto industry's experience is unique in several regards. With its substantial scale barrier, strong non-price rivalry, its high visibility and strategic importance, yet relatively low technology, the industry afforded governments an unusual opportunity to bargain with the international oligopoly through its various developmental stages. In the first stage of import substitution, TNCs exported to assembly firms, often domestically-owned licensees. Later, they acquired these licensees and home-country oligopolists reacted to each other's foreign direct investment strategies, attempting to check each other's moves into new, potentially important markets.This produced a domestic industrial structure far less concentrated than in most home countries, and one with far higher production costs because of low volumes and the proliferation of models. During the second stage, governments of the larger countries, such as Argentina, Brazil, and Mexico, began to appreciate the inefficiencies and social costs of an industrial structure based upon transnational oligopolistic reaction and import substitution and began to "rationalize production" by insisting on local content requirements. The governments of these three large countries succeeded in narrowing the number of producers from a dozen or more down to three to five. Smaller countries rationalized their industries through competitive bids. Thus, the cycle of industrial development, in both large and small countries, went from a phase of no industry to incipient industrialization based upon assembly to a phase of foreign direct investment and low industrial concentration to tight foreign oligopoly with the government playing an active role.

Tractor firms illustrate what happened when oligopolistic reaction was not present. Since the tractor industry is more concentrated, forbearance and spheres of influence have tended to keep down the

410

number of producers in any given market and rarely has the industry gone beyond the highly concentrated stage. Also, pricing and non-price conventions in the international markets tend to carry over into the local market more readily. Thus, even though it was "born foreign," competitive pressures through new foreign entrants have not been strong enough to diminish the oligopoly.

The other industries—cigarettes, electrical machinery, food, and pharmaceuticals—have slightly different experiences because domestic entrepreneurs successfully overcame barriers to entry during the 1930s and 1940s. Because the tobacco industry was a prime target for early import-substitution industrialization, domestic cigarette producers began operations in several markets of Latin America, such as in Argentina, Brazil, Mexico, Colombia, and Peru. BAT subsequently established a strong position in nearly all important Latin American markets, both those with an existing industry and those without one. Nonetheless, under the umbrella of BAT's high prices, a handful of national firms producing the traditional blends survived in several markets of Latin America, and this market structure predominated until the 1960s. The push effect of the health scare in the United States caused Philip Morris, R. J. Reynolds and other U.S. firms to invest abroad. New entry, while it did temporarily destabilize local price structures and competitive patterns, did not markedly reduce the level of industrial concentration because most transnationals entered by takeover. It appears that for most of Latin America, transnationalization of production meant that the oligopolistic structure of dominant foreign firms with domestic followers was transformed to an exclusive foreign oligopoly as foreign firms replaced domestic ones and BAT experienced some loss of market share. The push effect of the United States firms had consequences in those Latin American markets controlled tightly by domestic oligopolists, such as in Colombia. The simultaneous increase in heavy advertising for transnational blends and the mysterious increase in huge volumes of smuggled brands were enough to later convince authorities that TNCs should be allowed to produce locally. Takeovers soon created a foreign oligopoly.

In pharmaceuticals, mixed foreign and domestic oligopolies quickly became foreign dominated as incoming TNCs adopted a similar strategy in acquiring domestic manufacturers. Some of this was a consequence of acquiring former licensees. Thus, the moderately concentrated industries remained so despite new foreign entrance. But measures of concentration in this industry are notably weak because of competing products in therapeutic sub-fields, so we must be wary of international comparisons. In any case, it appears that at least some pharmaceutical markets began as nationally dominated

411

oligopolies, experienced new TNC competition and takeovers, and then regained a certain level of industrial concentration under foreign ownership.

This same pattern of market development occurred in the electrical machinery industry. As the Brazilian case shows, many new domestic firms had been founded in the 1930s and 1940s in light electrical machinery and then later in television. Most of these were acquired in the wave of foreign expansion during the 1950s and 1960s, transforming domestic oligopolies into slightly more concentrated foreign oligopolies. Because competitive pressures were often strong in Brazil, many TNCs were compelled to cross-subsidize losses in the foreign market until excess capacity was eliminated. Most of this excess capacity was owned by domestic firms which could not afford the prolonged cross-subsidization and fell to takeover bids or left the market entirely.

The food industry appears to be undergoing a similar fate in major markets of Latin America. With new products, intense marketing, and strong financial capabilities transnational corporations are moving into the industry largely by acquisition. What was a competitive industry with low-level differentiation is now becoming highly concentrated in certain product classes.

Barriers to Entry and Product Differentiation

Besides changes in industrial concentration, changes in other dimensions of market structure have occurred with the entry of foreign firms into developing countries. These case studies shed light on two questions raised in the opening chapter: Does an increasing foreign share of production produce more competitive market behavior? Are the new market structures more open to domestic entry? The evidence generally points to a negative answer for both questions. Consider product differentiation and other entry barriers.

The cigarette industry perhaps offers the purest example of the power of product differentiation. The cigarette industry is now the leading industry in terms of advertising expenditures in most countries of Latin America. It has not always been so. Evidence suggests that BAT's initial organization of markets in Latin America was predicated largely on expanding distribution channels; advertising levels did not increase dramatically until U.S. firms decided to enter the market. The advertising blitz that accompanied new transnational entrance was sufficiently severe to push back the market share of unacquired domestic firms making the traditional *tabaco negro* (dark

412

blends). While consumers may feel better satisfied, the result has been to raise the cost structure of the industry, to build up consumer loyalties, to make it more difficult and costly for new firms to enter, and to increase the final price of the product.

Transnational pharmaceutical companies appear to have adopted a similar strategy. Their advertising of over-the-counter drugs and promotional expenditures in selling to pharmacists and doctors are often quite high, and there is reason to believe that these levels have increased with the penetration of foreign drug houses. They have also relied heavily on patents to protect their market position, although many governments have not recognized these patents.

The electrical industry has relied on several barriers, including product differentiation. Differentiating strategies take the form of advertising the firm names of diversified manufacturers in consumer goods and heavy promotional expenditures through an elaborate sales force. For Brazil, the advertising and promotional activities of TNCs were seen to have a significant influence on the industrial levels of product differentiation. In addition, TNCs used their excess capacity, large scale, and financial power to limit the market share of independents.

In food processing TNCs also appear to be restructuring the industry using product differentiation techniques found in the home countries. New processed foods are being heavily promoted in a way previously limited to select product categories.

Transnationals that make autos, tractors, and tires have effectively used the same strategies in developing countries that they employ in their home markets. Auto producers have buttressed the industry's scale barrier with heavy spending on promotion and model proliferation. Tractor manufacturers, despite apparently failing to capture all production economies of scale, have opted for several models produced at high unit-costs. In tires, producers have tried advertising without great success and rely on control of patented technology to keep barriers high.

What can be said, then, about transnationalization of production and changes in competition? Market structures with low concentration and patterns of increased competition seem to be transition phases tied to the initial entry of foreign oligopolists. For autos, tractors, and tires, price competition seems to have been waged over the initial market shares only, but once new entry was accomplished and accommodated, more traditional oligopolistic equilibria ensued. This battle was most prolonged in the auto industry where oligopolistic reaction was strong, but this industry was the exception, not the rule, and the final result after government intervention is a more

413

"rational" international oligopoly. For industries that encountered existing national firms, e.g., electrical machinery, food, cigarettes, and pharmaceuticals, the acquisition and other market restructuring strategies seem to have accompanied a transition from domestically controlled oligopoly through a transnational, more competitive period as foreign and domestic firms battled for market share, and then reconcentrated in a new foreign oligopoly. There is not much evidence that transnationals, once having established a new structure of leadership in the market, are any more price competitive than their national counterparts were.

As regards the second question, whether the new market structures are more open to domestic entry, the progressive extension of foreign control to these industries did not bring falling barriers to entry facing domestic firms. The foreign controlled share of most industries studied here actually increased during the 1960s and 1970s or was already at such high levels that foreign domination persisted. There are some important exceptions to this: FATE in Argentina's tire industry, Bardella in Brazil's heavy equipment industry, some of the large domestic food processing firms, and Laboratorios Bagó in Argentina's pharmaceutical industry. In most of these exceptions, the new domestic entry was attributable in part to favorable government intervention in market processes that offset the rather substantial advantage transnationals would have otherwise commanded. It appears that other than for the short-term disruption of some new entries, TNCs have generally made markets imperfect rather than more competitive in these industries.

Foreignness, Local Market Structure, and Economic Performance

Once having established operations in the host market, the next relevant question is: Do TNCs use locally garnered investment capital to "grow differently" from domestic economic actors, and if so, how does their investment affect the pattern of development? Let us consider their performance in this regard in four areas: profitability, technology, trade, and basic human needs.

Profitability. As has been demonstrated previously, cross-sectional studies of market structure and firm profitability show a strong and fairly consistent association between differentiated oligopoly and higher profitability. In other words, as markets become less competitive, firm profitability tends to increase, other things being equal. The case studies, although not a large sample, tend to confirm these findings in two respects. First, the international practices of transna-

414

tionals in their export sales from home countries to developing countries have often heightened existing market imperfections in product and factor markets. These practices, as discussed above, contributed to significantly higher international prices on traded products and probably technology. A second dimension of profitability concerns earnings of subsidiaries. Most of the industries reported higher-than-average rates of profitability in the host market. The exceptions seem to be tire operations in certain countries where downstream major distributors exercised some countervailing power, or when price controllers succeeded in keeping prices low, such as tractors in Argentina. Jenkins and West suggest this exception may have been offset by high transfer prices because of the heavy import component of the industry. This is not to say that firms are immune from the business cycle or that oligopolistic reaction and inefficient scales do not impinge on margins; rather, it does suggest that market power, both global and domestic in origin, eventually translates into higher profits for the power-wielding corporation. Several studies reported higher profits abroad than at home: autos, tractors, food, pharmaceuticals, and tires. This highlights the importance of foreign operations to the growth and continued profitability of most of the transnationals.

Another aspect of profitability, not discussed in most studies, is whether foreign firms in an industry are more profitable than any domestic firms. Some authors have found that TNCs are more profitable, and suggest their higher profitability reflects their greater efficiency (Reuber et al. 1973). However, the literature also shows that TNCs have a higher affinity for concentrated markets, which in turn suggests a strong role for market power as a determinant of profitability. In fact, in the electrical machinery industry transnational firms were found to earn their high profits solely through the effects of market structure; controlling for market structure, Brazilian electrical firms were as profitable. Pharmaceutical TNCs show rather consistently higher rates of return than their domestically-owned counterparts. The evidence is far from conclusive on this point and is clouded further by limited disclosure, transfer pricing, and unstandardized accounting conventions.

In summary, transnationals do appear to exercise their market power in both international sales to developing countries and in local sales of subsidiaries to obtain high profits. This is undoubtedly true for domestic firms as well, although as a group they seem to have less scope to establish oligopolistic positions in manufacturing. The difference for development is that because they are foreign-owned, TNCs (a) accumulate a portion of their high profits abroad at the expense of local growth, and (b) can use a portion of retained local profits to invest in a different fashion from local firms. Both the extent of these differences and their developmental consequences still need to be evaluated. Two qualifications, however, must be interjected. Governmental policies, particularly the level of effective protection extended through tariffs and nontariff barriers, are crucial to maintaining the monopolistic position of firms in the market. These policies usually have a long-term rationale; they are undertaken, of course, to create domestic industries. But they do so at the expense of high profits for concentrated industries, some of which are foreign dominated. Second, high price-cost margins may be offset by lower transaction prices on internal trade of the package of assets—such as the transfer of technology, management expertise, or the like. Nonetheless, one must remain agnostic about the degree to which this offsets high profits stemming from market power because there is virtually no evidence on these transaction prices.

Technology. The case studies shed additional light on the three issues raised in chapter 1 concerning technology: the cost of technology to the local economy, the choice of technique and technological appropriateness, and the issue of technological dependence.

The question of whether the costs of technology are lower for domestic firms than for TNCs is complex because many of the transfers between parent and subsidiary may not be visible or recorded. While technology is hardly a homogeneous term and quality differences are difficult to assess, experiences of the food, tire, and electrical industries suggest that domestic firms in the same industries tend to pay lower rates for the technology they purchase than subsidiaries of TNCs. This was brought out clearly in the case of Argentina's FATE, a domestically controlled tire enterprise, that obtained international technology at a consistently lower rate than subsidiaries of TNCs, apparently because the national firm bargained more effectively with the sellers of international technology. On the other hand, the problem of measuring both the amount of technology transferred and the size of payments makes any conclusion tenuous.

The issue of technological choice and particularly the substitution of capital for labor was addressed only indirectly by most of the studies. In all industries the design of the final product determines to a great extent minimum efficient scales, the ratio of machines to labor, and the amount of capital required to create a job. In other words, if the desired output is a Volvo 168B station-wagon with air conditioning, there are greater limits to technical choice than if the desired output is specified as motorized transportation.

416

Autos, steel, tires, and tractors have fairly rigid production technologies and display considerable unresponsiveness to the relative price of labor and capital in the market, once product designs are specified. The same is less true for the cigarette, electrical machinery, pharmaceutical, and food industries which have greater latitude for small changes in product design that can affect the labor-capital ratio. Indeed, domestic firms in India's pharmaceutical industry have adapted imported technology to use less capital relative to labor. There appears to be some permissible range of substitution in the electrical industry because TNCs generally employed less labor per unit of capital, even controlling for size, vertical integration, and other environmental factors. Transnational corporations also tend to build larger sized plants than domestically-owned firms. This seems to indicate that, after specifying the product output, only in about half the industries could producers choose among a limited range of alternative technologies, and in these domestic firms generally chose more labor-intensive processes.

Celso Furtado, among others, has argued that the incapacity of developing countries to generate their own inventions and innovations has been a critical factor explaining their unequal relationship to the international system, their continuing vulnerability to economic changes initiated in the center, and their technological dependence. Transnational corporations have sought to control the spread of new technology through various tactics, including licensing arrangements, cartels, or foreign direct investment. Let us recount the evidence that leads to this conclusion from the case studies.

The longest historical evidence from a technology-intensive industry comes from the electrical industry. General Electric, Westinghouse, Siemens, AEG, Brown Boveri, Philips, and others sought various ways to control competition in their markets. It was relatively easy to raise a barrier to entry in the industry by denying potential entrants access to the technology by exchanging it and agreeing not to let outsiders use it. The majors did exactly that from the late 1890s to the 1940s; they even went so far in some accords as to agree not to transfer production facilities to developing countries using the international technology. However, the transformation brought about in the 1930 to 1950 period—new industrialization in the South and antitrust actions in the North—forced a change in their strategy.

The steel industry had adopted similar agreements in the 1930s, but the war years prompted governments to take actions to establish local facilities since the transnationals would or could not build local plants. The technological barriers to entry were broken down mainly because governments in Mexico, Brazil, and Argentina were determined to enter the industry and finance any losses in part because the governments of the United States and other home countries wanted their key allies to have steel plants in the face of the Axis threat.

Cross-licensing and cartels were adopted by TNCs in tires and pharmaceuticals as well, but low minimum efficient scales meant that overseas plants could be set up without substantially higher costs. So when the Depression came in 1930, it was feasible for producers to set up foreign operations as they sought to expand overseas.

After World War II, the leading TNCs (except in the steel industry) increasingly chose to invest in production facilities overseas rather than to license technology. Direct ownership allowed firms to control prized technology and to control the development of the market in two senses: Only through direct ownership could firms capture all the gains from their monopolistic advantage and unique package of intangible assets, and maintain or raise additional barriers to entry to new entrants both at home and abroad. Some firms, especially the smaller, weaker members of oligopolies, did license independent companies in developing countries, thus allowing the presence of domestic firms in the high technology branches of some industries such as Bardella in Brazil and FATE in Argentina. But by and large, where firms in high technology industries could afford to invest abroad, they did so in preference to licensing. It should also be noted that some parent TNCs in the electrical and food industries first licensed domestic firms in developing countries and then later acquired their former licensees after these had become successful in the developing market and were in need of more capital.

Finally, the degree of control that TNCs exercise in certain industries—tires, advanced heavy equipment, consumer electronics, and certain pharmaceutical products—may have dampened as much as stimulated the independent innovative spirit of managers in foreign countries, though this is a difficult calculation at best. By integrating the most talented managers, engineers, and would-be entrepreneurs into its transnational organization, the TNC in technologically sophisticated industries integrated these people into an international division of labor where basic R&D was centralized in the home countries. The pharmaceutical industry does have advanced R&D facilities outside the home countries because of U.S. regulations on testing new products, but these are rarely located in developing countries. And by promoting new products TNCs have often stimulated the "imitative" behavior of local industrialists who have sought to enter industries where entry barriers permitted.

Even if TNCs did locate their R&D facilities in developing countries, it is not completely evident that they would direct their innovational efforts into activities needed there for the following reasons: (a) the largest markets from a global perspective still are in the developed countries; and, (b) firms are likely to invest in technology creation where they can raise barriers to entry in addition to patents to ensure they will obtain full monopoly rents. Perhaps the clearest example of this inappropriate product technology comes from the pharmaceutical industry in India. Although the most prevalent diseases are parasitic illnesses that afflict the poor, the distribution of pharmaceutical sales by therapeutic group reveals that vitamins, cough and cold preparations, and tonics and health restorers account for nearly one-quarter of pharmaceutical sales. Drugs treating the three major diseases in India did not even figure among the 15 leading pharmaceutical products in the Indian market. This behavior was common to domestic firms as well, suggesting the problem may emanate as much from uneven growth as from transnational corporate behavior.

The research and development activities of transnational corporations in developing countries are limited and quite distinct from those in the home countries, using different inputs and/or smaller scales than at home. For example, in autos local R&D facilities in Brazil are geared to fostering the substitution of local inputs because firms have had to vertically integrate backwards under pressure of local content rules. What little R&D is undertaken by transnationals in Brazil's electrical industry is also directed at local material inputs. Transnationals apparently do almost no research and development in tires in developing countries. In the cigarette and food industries local R&D efforts concentrate on improving product differentiation based on consumer taste patterns.

That there are economically viable alternatives to these patterns of limited research is evident from the few isolated cases of strong independent firms. In Brazil's electrical industry, only one firm had sizable expenditures in R&D in the early 1970s and it was Bardella, a firm which purchased international technology and invested in its own turbogenerator research facilities. The example of FATE in Argentina's tire industry illustrates that independent firms have an interest in buying international technology and then doing substantial additional research to increase their technological capacities. No comparable activity was undertaken by transnationals in the same industry. Moreover, FATE's efforts extended beyond its own offices: the firm encouraged other interprises to solicit government funds to sponsor R&D and technological improvement efforts in an industrywide trade association. Interestingly, transnationals showed no interest in the project. An example of an alternative technological pattern, this time based on public sector intervention, comes from the pharmaceutical industry in Brazil. The government created a state-owned drug firm, CEME, to improve the distribution of drugs to the poor and stimulate local R&D in public laboratories. While the objectives of the drug program were never fulfilled for domestic political reasons, CEME does hold the possibility of reducing technological dependence. Also, in Mexico privately owned Syntex was a clear standout in R&D during the 1940s and 1950s before it was acquired by a U.S. firm in 1956.

Trade Behavior. The case studies raised extremely important questions about the way transnationals affect the structure and performance of the trade sector. Let us consider three overlapping issues: the direction and magnitude of trade, income effects and transfer pricing, and the role of the state in altering trade patterns.

The transnational organization of the industries studied indicates that TNCs organize world trade along lines different from those predicted by orthodox theories of international trade that assume independent actors. Historically, cigarette and electrical firms actively attempted to divide up world markets via licensing arrangements and cartels to channel trade from certain countries towards others. Similar patterns of market allocation appear to have occurred with varying degrees of clarity in pharmaceuticals, tires, and even autos. Patterns of trade reflecting colonial ties probably have persisted far longer than they would have had firms not endeavored to impede competing trade.

After World War II, TNCs played an important role in opening up markets to imports from the developed countries. The most vivid example is the case of U.S. tobacco firms seeking to establish a presence in the Argentine and Colombian markets, despite active opposition of domestic cigarette manufacturers and protective tariffs. Evidence implicates U.S. firms in the late 1960s in massive advertising campaigns within these countries to create demand with simultaneous increases in smuggling. Contraband cigarettes eventually captured a sizable share of the local market. Once the government, under pressure from the smoking public, finally permitted international brands to be produced locally, the contraband cigarettes suddenly fell off.

The experience of the electrical industry, although less dramatic, is no less consequential. Statistical analysis indicates that foreign firms have a much higher propensity to import than do domestic firms, even controlling for firm size, vertical integration, etc. These findings are applicable to other industries, even though there may be no local firms with which to make a comparison. TNCs are integrated into the global network of trade of the parent and wish to constantly introduce the latest fashion or product into the local market. Parent companies are anxious to capture suppliers' profits, ensure quality and consistency, and convince labor and governments at home that they are not transferring jobs abroad. TNC subsidiaries have less incentive, except when pressured by host governments, to find domestic suppliers; they may even have a disincentive to the extent that the creation of domestic suppliers might facilitate new entry into the final product market. All this suggests that import propensities will be greater under TNCs than under domestic control.

On the export side, firms in the food industry in Mexico recorded much lower rates of exports than their domestic counterparts. It stands to reason that an independent firm such as Carta Blanca would have an interest in exporting to the United States beer market and that Coors or Schlitz would not (if they were producing in Mexico). Cigarette firms have used licensing and other arrangements to prevent the export of brands to compete in other subsidiaries' markets abroad. Transnational electrical firms in Brazil did not report higher rates of exports compared with domestic firms, controlling for other factors. However, some evidence does suggest that in Mexico's foreign-dominated electrical equipment industry, TNCs will eventually export more than their much weaker domestic counterparts, mainly because the government is following a negotiating strategy of export promotion similar to that used in the auto industry.

Some fragmentary evidence also points to the possibility that transnationals might aid the development of semi-peripheral economies through their trade decisions, often under pressure from the host governments. The government permitted Mexico's auto industry to import several lines of components as long as firms exported an equivalent amount of other products. TNCs could satisfy this requirement by transferring labor-intensive production processes to Mexico and producing selected parts for the United States market. Similarly, Brown Boveri had proposed to the Mexican government that its Mexican subsidiary supply all of Peru's power-generator markets. These kinds of TNC-host country agreements as well as intrafirm allocations of international markets generally may make trading patterns less responsive to market forces.

The steel industry offers a case of a state-owned industry expanding rapidly into international markets in the 1970s. Would the Brazilian, Venezuelan, and Mexican industries have exported as aggressively to the industrialized countries had they been owned by TNCs in those countries?

Few of the case studies were able to investigate in depth the extent of overpricing of imports to developing countries and the underpricing of their exports. While some reports of transfer pricing did arise in the pharmaceutical, tire, and tractor industries, it is nearly impossible to come up with systematic estimates of the effects of transfer pricing without access to company records. Aspects of trade in these industries, however, do highlight once again the importance of the problem: the large volume of intrafirm trade that occurs in pharmaceuticals, autos, tires, tractors, and electrical machinery; the high degree of centralized decisionmaking in these industries; and the extent of market power among final product manufacturers which facilitates unregulated transfer of profits outside the country via transfer prices. Food and cigarettes, which usually have low volumes of intrafirm trade because of the high degree of local vertical integration, are compelled to use other vehicles such as technical assistance fees, royalties, and trademark fees to transfer profits abroad. The pharmaceutical case offers a particularly good illustration of the problem's importance. In the early 1970s antitrust authorities in Germany and the United Kingdom ordered Hoffmann-LaRoche to reduce its selling prices by 35 to 75 percent for Librium and Valium. Similarly the Colombian government found import overpricing to amount to 87 to 155 percent of the world price.

The state has had significant influence over the pattern of trade that has evolved in many industries. Nearly all the industries were established behind high levels of effective protection. This meant that the structure of trade shifted from the import of final goods to the import of intermediate products, a pattern that held for autos, electrical machinery, and pharmaceuticals. Tires, and to a lesser extent, cigarettes were established as integrated production facilities largely because of the low minimum efficient scale factor. Tractors became an international industry later so foreign investment occurred during a period when local suppliers already existed; thus they too were more vertically integrated from the outset.

Besides tariffs, however, the state has bargained vigorously over the terms of domestic industrialization. In the auto industry the Argentinian and Brazilian governments successfully compelled firms to reduce the number of models and producers even though their markets were comparatively small. The Mexican government followed a slightly different strategy. Taking advantage of a proposal by Ford, the government decided to opt for equalization in the trade balance. This provided an incentive for manufacturers to select those parts of

422

the production process which could take advantage of the local market and achieve economies of scale. The Andean Pact countries have also limited the number of models and sought to promote exports. Similar negotiations are occurring in Mexico now in the electrical equipment industry. In pharmaceuticals, the Brazilian and Mexican governments are using their control over domestic patent legislation to compel the local production of certain items and reduce the cost of other imports. This too will affect the pattern of trade in their favor. The steel industry is another example of the state's impact on trade. By modifying the terms of ownership and establishing state enterprises, it appears that the Brazilians and perhaps the Mexicans and Venezuelans are in a position to become major exporters in the international market. Under transnational or even domestic private ownership, it is arguable that these plants would not have competed in international markets. Indeed they might not have been built in the first place.

Distribution, Employment, Poverty. The distributional consequences of the transnationalization of production can be summarized at three levels of historical and analytical abstraction. The first is at the most basic and static level and stems from TNCs' association with local imperfect markets. As we have seen from the analysis of profitability, the market power of TNCs usually allows them to raise prices well above their long-term costs of production and above the rate of competitively structured industries. When this power is exercised—and evidence from the literature review and case studies shows that it often is—consumers are forced to pay more for the transnational products than they would if these were sold in competitive markets. These monopoly profits accrue by and large to the owners of capital and privileged managers. A portion of these profits is repatriated.

To the extent that market power is used in these ways, conventional economics suggests it exerts a regressive impact on income distribution and works against the interests of the poor. But two qualifications are in order. First, if labor is sufficiently strong in the monopolistic sector, it may be able to capture a portion of the monopoly profits for itself. The redistributive effects could well be positive (measured in terms of a Gini coefficient), depending on which classes purchase the monopolized products; in autos, for example, well organized workers might exert a progressive effect, while in cigarettes the effect could be to heighten inequality. In either case, owners of capital rarely suffer large relative losses because they can usually pass on higher wage bills to the consumers; the poor rarely gain. A second qualification concerns the relationship of scale efficiency to market power. For those industries where production economies of scale reduce unit costs at higher output levels, the oligopoly price may be lower than the price in an atomistically structured industry. This may be the case for autos, tractors, steel, and very large electrical machinery; the optimal policy is one which taxes away the excess profits, regulates the enterprise to capture the rents, or creates the condition for new competition, perhaps through lowering the degree of effective protection.

A second level of analysis, historical and dynamic in character, considers the distributional effects of how TNCs invest their retained profits and grow. Consider first the distributional implications of the growth of transnationals in comparison to domestic firms in the same industry, and the cumulative effects of these behavioral differences for an industry's development. In all industries with some domestically controlled firms to use as a comparative standard—cigarettes, electrical machinery, steel, tires, pharmaceuticals, and food—transnationals do grow differently than their local counterparts. Their expansion into the local economy raises the barriers to entry in the affected industries and usually increases the market power of surviving firms. Advertising is especially important in the consumer industries as it makes entry more difficult and steers demand into consumption patterns that mirror those in the industrialized countries. Moreover, in all of these industries except cigarettes, the reported cost of imported technology was higher, their research and development activities lower, and often their choice of technology was less responsive to the widespread availability of labor. Evidence on relative trade performance was mixed. Transnationals did apparently have higher import propensities, though detailed statistical analysis was only available for electrical machinery. There was no evidence that TNCs exported more than their domestic counterparts. It is clear that only TNCs can manipulate prices on intrafirm trade with the effect of separating the global allocation of income from the allocation of production. Reported profits of transnationals appear to be higher in tires, pharmaceuticals, and food, though no difference was reported in electrical machinery after allowing for the effects of market power. *On the basis of this narrow comparison and in light of the evidence recounted in the literature review of chapter 2, there is strong reason to believe that the net benefits accruing to low-income groups are probably substantially less under transnationally organized production than under domestic ownership. That is, domestic firms offer a package of behavioral and structural traits that tend to capture for the nation a greater share of the benefits of growth and transmit them to lower income groups—domestic firms are unlikely to avoid taxes through transfer pricing and they tend to operate in more competitive markets, to rely*

424

less heavily on advertising, and to behave in their technology and trade activities in a way that has greater domestic linkages.

This conclusion must be tempered by certain qualifications. First, it is difficult to gauge the positive externalities of transnational control that may lead to the creation of a more technologically advanced industry as a whole. This could come in the form of training managers and workers that later move into the domestic sector, stimulating the rate of technological innovation in the domestically controlled sector through the demonstration effect, and so forth. Examples of such effects are found in the pharmaceutical, electrical, tire and other industries. Second, there is no conclusive evidence about the relative technical efficiency of the foreign and domestic sectors; part of the difficulty lies in separating out the influence of other factors such as market power, and using appropriate shadow prices. Third, there remains the problem of those industries with few or no domestic firms for comparison—such as autos and tractors. One can only evaluate these through counterfactual analysis or comparisons with other countries. Fourth, government policy is instrumental in creating the conditions of domestic competition and distribution, and policy failures on this score require a separate analysis.

Comparing the behavior of foreign to domestic firms to assess foreign influence is enlightening, but also limited. In some industries, as already noted, there may be no domestic firms to serve as a comparative standard; in others, domestic firms may have imitated foreign behavior (or vice versa) so that at times their behavior is nearly alike. More importantly, domestic firms themselves may not offer the best standard against which to judge development performance. A third level of analysis is therefore necessary to capture the broader nature of dependent capitalism: how transnationals fit into an industry's pattern of growth and how this affects the poor.

At any point in time, wealth and income distribution have an important effect on the composition of aggregate output, especially the broad division between luxury items and basic needs goods. If wealth is highly concentrated the demand for luxury goods will obviously be relatively higher. In a dynamic sense, however, as an economy grows the very process of capital accumulation and investment decisionmaking influences what products are manufactured, what technologies are employed, how many and what kinds of jobs will be created, and what the distribution of new income will be between labor and owners of capital. To the extent that producers can influence this cumulative, causal chain at any point, they can influence the form that investment takes and shape productive structure and the distribution of wealth in subsequent periods. Let us illustrate these

425

phenomena first in consumer industries, then in the investment goods industries.

In all the consumer industries, it was seen that firms actively influence consumers' buying decisions by biasing information flows about products to attempt to steer their purchases into high margin products which can be protected with high barriers to entry. Firms used a variety of tactics to expand consumer choices in some areas while foreclosing them in others. Recall the specific case of transnational pharmaceutical firms in India. They promoted highly differentiated drugs serving the relatively wealthy, while essential drugs to treat the most prevalent diseases of the poor accounted for only a minor portion of the total production of pharmaceuticals. At a more general level (and speaking euphemistically), the industry's demand-creation activities have stressed "disease creation": marketing of new, differentiated drugs to treat newly perceived illnesses of the wealthy rather than preventive medicine which could reduce the total social cost of medical care. Obviously, transnationals are not the sole cause of these distortions; however, as they grow, they reinforce the entrenched health care delivery system and create powerful interest group allies that would oppose any reorganization of the system, including doctors who receive product information in promotional campaigns of companies, pharmacists who sell the drugs, and middle-class consumers who wish to maintain their access to items like tranquilizers and cold pills.

In the cigarette industry, the most relevant basic needs choice is to smoke or not to smoke. It probably makes little difference if producers are domestic firms selling *tabaco negro* or foreign firms selling *tabaco rubio*. However, TNCs have been the leaders in pioneering marketing techniques through expensive investments in advertising to convince people to smoke. As advertising outlays are increased, the anti-smoking case is rarely presented to consumers in developing countries. When the hazards of smoking are known and publicized, as they have been on occasion in some developed countries, the rate of increase in cigarette consumption has dropped sharply; this would indicate that the industry's continued rapid growth in developing countries requires a considerable measure of consumer ignorance. Nonetheless, after the industry is implanted, its growth creates powerful allies in the broadcasting industry, the media generally, and even the state (the industry often generates 15 to 20 percent of indirect domestic tax revenues).

In food, consumers obviously can choose among several products, but the successful firms have usually expanded their markets

426

through extensive advertising. Basic foods—often more nutritious and lower in cost—do not have a powerful and active constituency propounding their advantages. One does not become a member of the Pepsi generation by drinking milk or chicha. As brought out sharply in the Nabisco case in Mexico, TNCs have little interest in making more nutritious products, even when subsidized, if these might compete with their high margin differentiated products. As large segments of the buying public gradually change their dietary habits, producers can increase the price between the new processed foods and the basic needs basket with less fear of losing consumers to the latter. Domestic firms are likely to follow this lead. The structure of production generally is oriented to the new items as manufacturers of traditional products suffer slower growth or are forced to leave the business. Even if short-term relative prices change in their favor, producers who have left the traditional business lines often cannot easily reenter.

Changes in Brazil's television market also illustrate how the interaction between successful marketing strategies and production technologies affects the structure of production in subsequent periods. After the growth of black and white television production in the 1960s, TNCs began to lobby for the introduction of color television in Brazil. Philips moved into components production where scale and technology barriers were relatively high. When the government approved the introduction of color televisions, the TNCs were better situated to begin production and to control the growth of the market. Domestic firms quickly followed suit. Since TNCs controlled the advanced patented technology, domestic firms were at an absolute cost disadvantage by an amount equal to the royalty payment and any discriminatory price Philips charged for its parts. The structure of consumption and production moved farther away from wider dissemination of the cheaper product which would have better served the needs of the poor.

In auto production, the interaction between sales and production illustrates the point more clearly. Transnational producers found they could promote their products most effectively through style changes, model proliferation, and other forms of product differentiation. Defining the product in this way sets up a particular relation between economies of scale for a model and technological choice. If models are continually changing, economies of scale create a barrier to entry in most markets of Latin America because only the largest firms will produce enough units to reduce costs towards the minimum. Smaller countries often do not have a big enough market to support even

427

one firm. In the case of Mexico, product differentiation economies have even influenced trade patterns. Under an agreement with the Mexician government, TNCs can import stamped parts from the United States and elsewhere where costs are lower due to the large unit volume, provided they export in a like amount. Many of these major parts are those that change with new models. Whatever its short-term merit, the agreement entrenches a particular organization of production. Domestic firms cannot hope to enter the industry because they cannot import differentiating parts; even if they could, they would be prevented from doing so because they could not export to other markets to satisfy government regulations. With such a barrier to entry, foreign firms are in a position to control not only the form of local development and domestic selling prices, but also the price and terms of exchange of an important segment of Mexico's trade in manufactures. Moreover, any linkage effects in the creation of new upstream supplier industries are severely limited. But since investment in this particular productive structure esists and trade patterns have been established, it is difficult to even imagine an alternative way to organize the industry.

Much of the same occurred in the heavy electrical equipment industry. Transnational heavy equipment manufacturers reportedly altered the relative price structure to favor their largest, most technologically sophisticated hydrogenerating equipment—raising the price slightly on older machines and lowering the price on the newest machines. The objective was to steer the market into larger size categories where they had a comparative technological advantage and where barriers to entry made it more difficult for national producers to enter this high margin, upper end of the market. This process is continual as new production capacity is installed to serve the newly created demand, eventually replacing the old technologies with the new. Scale of production is pushed ever upwards as larger products dominate the market. The active promotion of transnational firms appears to have played a role in insuring that eventual cost relationships would favor large equipment over small. The few remaining domestic firms have to follow the lead of TNCs into the larger size categories, even though the employment-creation effects in the production and use of the large machines are less.

The history of the tractor industry's development in Latin America further illustrates this point. Once the TNCs established local sales and production facilities, they became a major force advocating agricultural mechanization. Yet 85 percent of farms in Latin America are too small to use even small tractors and most farmers are too poor to afford the cost. Large farms, on the other hand, have used tractors to replace labor, often through subsidized credits from local governments. This process tends to widen income inequality and benefit the owners of large land holdings. This situation is not inevitable as countries with agrarian reforms have used tractors to increase productivity and overall income levels of the entire rural sector. In the absence of a major land reform, however, the mechanization of agriculture tends to strengthen those who are already powerful and to widen income and wealth inequality.

In summary, as the level of investment in the productive capacity of an underdeveloped capitalist economy grows, additional investments in transnational luxury products mesh more readily with existing productive capacity than do basic needs goods. For example, it is easier and cheaper to satisfy the demand for motorized transportation through increases in capacity for auto production than through mass transit and railway expansion because of the huge sunk investment in highways, auto production, and supplier industries. In the food industry it is easier and more profitable to market a new cereal brand than invest in research to produce a nutritious biscuit and then market it; in the pharmaceutical industry it is less costly to add sales agents to existing private networks and import new product technology than it is to create products more appropriate to the local diseases of the poor and to set up a distribution network to reach them. Equally important, powerful interest groups, transnational and domestic, will use their political influence to fight any change in the organization of production if their private interests are threatened.

This discussion on three levels of analysis—an extension of the conventional industrial organization model to take account of the distributional consequences of market power, the discussion of how foreign firms grow differently from local companies, and the broader historical perspective on the growth process—suggests that the expansion of foreign enterprise tends to feed into existing patterns of wealth and production and channels development toward accentuating inequalities rather than ameliorating them. The poor are largely unaffected by transnationally led growth. This is clearly not the fault of TNCs in a volitional sense; the very conditions of international rivalry often impede any one of them from acting much differently. Nor is the government solely at fault, although governmental policies have frequently contributed to accentuating domestic inequalities at the same time that vigorous bargaining and local development policies have narrowed the gaps between them and the industrialized countries. The essence of the problem is systemic and requires purposeful government action sustained over decades. Let us end with a consideration of the governmental role.

TRANSNATIONALS AND THE STATE

Governments in both home countries and host countries have played an important role in shaping almost every industry's development. The industrial histories point to three preliminary generalizations about state-TNC interactions in developing countries. First, in most cases at least some industrial growth preceded public policy as market forces propelled development of an incipient industrial base, and so policy development occurred dialectically and interactively with industrial growth. Second, bargaining power over the gains from trade and investment in these manufacturing industries appears not to have shifted dramatically in favor of host governments as has been argued for natural resource industries. Third, it appears that the very process of bargaining over firm conduct does alter the performance of the sector, but the subsequent arrangements lead to durable alliances that shape and constrain further government initiatives.

To set the context for a consideration of state-TNC bargaining, it is important to realize that government policy was rarely aimed at developing a specific industry *de novo*. Rather policy was usually directed at the manufacturing sector as a whole, such as in the case of import substitution or technological policies. When policy was directed towards an industry it almost always grew iteratively with industry itself, usually after the industry had been established and in reaction to perceived inadequacies in the industry's development. For example, the pharmaceutical industry had been established in major markets of Latin America for nearly 30 years before governments began to take action on restrictive patent policy. The cigarette industry has existed in most countries for over half a century and, contrary to the situation in the United States and some of the other developed countries, is still not the subject of industrial policy in Latin America. The auto industry, aside from the high levels of protection established in the 1950s in Brazil and Argentina, only became the subject of vigorous industrial policy in the 1960s. This implies that certain parameters for bargaining had already been implanted within the host countries: productive investments and their transnational ties had been established, a domestic managerial class had developed, and a labor force organized. Thus, usually before alternative industrial policies were articulated in debates within the government, a broad-based constituency of actors was in place that favored some form of existing institutional arrangements. An exception to this is the steel industry where the structure of transnational control was not established in the advanced Latin American countries for reasons noted above. The growth of this industry independent of the transnational control structure arguably has produced considerable benefits for the state controlled steel companies, particularly in their assertive penetration of international markets. In some of the industries not studied here, such as petrochemicals and air transport equipment, governments have more recently taken the lead in establishing the industry.

In contrast to the situation in natural resources, host governments have been reluctant to move aggressively against the structure of transnational control in manufacturing industries. Policies have been directed mainly at the conduct dimensions of manufacturing activities, not ownership or even conventional market structure. In the automobile industry, for example, the Brazilian and Argentine governments imposed local content requirements on the companies to generate backward linkages and domestic employment and the Mexican government moved aggressively in requiring that TNCs match their high levels of imports with high levels of exports. Local content rules have also been instituted in the lamp, consumer electronics and heavy equipment branches of the electrical industry by various governments at various times. The Andean Pact has tried to compel similar conduct in the tractor industry, with less success. In the pharmaceutical industry, governments have sought to reduce payments for imported drugs by invalidating product and process patents that would have reduced the number of international suppliers of these items. Other efforts have been undertaken in the area of consumer labeling and product innovation.

These governmental measures have been remarkably successful in improving the benefits accruing locally from transnational trade and investment. In the process, however, the policies rarely have affected the structural elements of transnational control. To the extent that transnational ownership makes no difference in subsidiary behavior from national ownership, this policy omission is not important. However, the weight of the evidence suggests differences are common and merit policy scrutiny.

Why are there not more examples of assertive government policies towards modifying the transnational structure of control such as those found in mining and petroleum cases? Two factors may help explain this absence. First, in industries with technological barriers, such as electrical machinery, tires, and pharmaceuticals, the control of R&D by the home office has meant that any attempt to increase national control over the industry will run the risk of severing the lifeline of new innovations so crucial to the industry's progressive development. Even when novel technology is secondary to product

431

differentiation, as in food, the continual stream of new products onto the market radiates out from the parent company and this has a similar but perhaps weaker effect.

This reason, taken by itself, is probably not sufficient to explain the absence of structural policies. As seen above, technology is often a minor part of the unique package of intangible assets inhibiting entry. A second reason of perhaps greater consequence is the nature of class alliances that spring up in the manufacturing sector but do not appear in natural resource, "enclave" investments. In manufacturing, foreign investment establishes close ties with a managerial and technical class, a labor force and, most importantly, a wide constituency among the middle class which consumes the transnational products.

Tangible evidence of these alliances are presented in the studies. In Brazil's electrical industry, the pattern of interlocking directorates between foreign-owned manufacturing enterprises and domestically controlled investment banks and financial companies is widespread. The industry's trade association is the main private sector advocate of its policy perspective, and data show that representatives of foreign firms among association officers increased from 33 percent in 1962 to 60 percent in 1974, a growth reflective of the increasing foreign share of the industry. In cigarettes, there is a symbiotic relationship between the government and the industry: the industry collects a high percentage of total government taxes through cigarette taxes. Even domestic industrialists competing with transnational firms become allies in representing the industry's case to the government. Recall the foreign tire manufacturers in Argentina encouraging FATE's entry into production precisely so they would have a domestic ally in their conflicts with Perón. This is not to say that these interest groups formulate industrial policy. Rather, the shifting alliances upon which government support rests require an articulation and mediation of these private interest groups and this has circumscribed the "political will" of the state in its bargaining with TNCs over the structural dimensions of their participation in the market.

Finally, bargains struck in the manufacturing sector on the basis of state-TNC negotiations may be more stable than the "obsolescing bargains" in natural resources. For example, Mexico's negotiations with the auto companies produced an agreement to expand exports concomitant with imports. This had the effect of integrating the sector's development even more tightly into the transnational system of production. There are strong reasons to believe that these arrangements are more durable. First, there are scale barriers of such proportions in autos that any national industry in the developing world not integrated into the transnational structure would experience either high costs of producing for a small protected national market or great costs of entry into international markets. Second, increased government negotiating capacity and knowledge, a prime determinant of strong bargaining positions in the natural resource case, is less important in autos because technology and knowledge is not the primary barrier to entry in world markets. Third, government planners, by virtue of the auto industry's wide acceptance among middle class consumers, parts suppliers, and distributors, are confined politically from taking any action that would alter the priorities in ground transportation in favor of alternative modes of transit. Agreements such as the export promotion policies give both sides a new incentive to see the industry develop. Similar outcomes may prevail in other industries with high-scale barriers and transnational control of global production, such as tractors and heavy electrical equipment.

On the other hand, the issues are far from resolved in some industries. In pharmaceuticals, government negotiation is continuing in India and Brazil over the exact terms of supplying the host market. It is likely that new conduct regulations will be imposed, and these should not preclude other policies later. In food, conduct measures may eventually become popular to control acquisition and advertising behavior, and these too do not prevent subsequent structural measures.

SUMMARY

The industrial case studies in this volume illustrate the complexity surrounding an evaluation of the role of TNCs in development. On the one hand, the weight of the evidence suggests that the international marketplace in which TNCs operate is often biased against developing countries in the distribution of gains from trade investment, and related activities. On the other hand, there are still gains to both parties in most cases and there are many instances where oligopolistic conduct does not prejudice developing countries.

The evidence in this volume strongly indicates that transnational capitalism does play an influential role in orienting the structure of production and consumption in developing countries. Transnational corporations are particularly important and often dominant actors in influencing the type of growth that occurs in these countries. This is not to say that a purely national capitalism would always reduce the degree of unevenness in the development process, though there is evidence that it sometimes does. Rather the linkages and symbiosis between the two on balance tend to reinforce each other so that international oligopoly and uneven development are usually twin characteristics of the same process.

But these tendencies are not immutable or unalterable. Assertive public policy can substantially increase the benefits of transnational trade and investment accruing to developing countries. While the recession of the 1980s has weakened the capacities for states to raise their share of gains from foreign investment, the long-run trend will be for vigorous bargaining between governments and TNCs to continue. Converging interests have created narrower parameters of bargaining, parameters which appear to be more stable than in decades past. But the bargaining itself is still conflictual, and it is probable that governments will continue to push TNCs in directions which counter short-term market signals and firm objectives but which are seen to serve national development objectives.

It is more difficult to make predictions regarding the internal distribution of gains from transnational investment. Government policy has not adequately offset the tendency for capitalist development to concentrate the benefits of rapid growth in the hands of the relatively well-off; to the contrary, in many cases policy has worked to reinforce these same tendencies. Policies on wages, subsidies, taxation, and even industrial and macroeconomic issues have all too frequently favored the relatively wealthy over the poor and cities over rural areas. Of course these policies cannot be isolated from domestic political forces, where transnationals and their close allies are increasingly important. Ultimately, the development task of the future is to build domestic political coalitions favoring the emergence of appropriate policies that do redress the worsening inequalities in many Latin American societies.

Retrospective on the Reagan Initiatives

This book began with a sketch of the Reagan Administration's program toward developing countries—its emphasis on the private sector, the market, and its attempts to free foreign investment from regulation abroad. These studies point to fundamental flaws in the philosophical foundations of the Reagan Administration's approach. Developing countries have much to gain from intervening in market processes and from using the power of the state to reorganize domestic economic activity in order to confer a greater share of the gains upon the host societies. At the same time, of course, inefficiencies in public policies can create costly distortions that detract from the rate

434

of development. Since World War II, the gains from public sector policies have generally outweighed their costs: Growth rates for most of the continent have exceeded five percent annually; industrialization has proceeded even more rapidly; and domestic skills have deepened profoundly. To be sure, the costs of protection during the import substitution phase have been high, and the slow adjustment to high energy and capital costs have cut deeply into current growth. But many industries throughout the region are becoming internationally competitive, including some high-skilled, labor-intensive industries, and these hold the greatest promise for future growth.

This conclusion has two implications for the general posture the U.S. government assumes *vis-a-vis* investment and development. First, U.S. interests lie in relatively unfettered access to the markets and resources of Latin America. But a sophisticated representation of those interests requires beginning with the explicit acknowledgment that regulation at times can increase the Latin American share of the gains from transnational trade and investment. Using the current crisis to pressure developing countries into programs of deregulation, divestiture of state enterprises, or signing bilateral investment treaties either as a condition of obtaining new debt finance or access to the U.S. market will be ineffectual and counterproductive. Such a posture undermines the credibility of all economic analysis the U.S. presents in its policy dialogues with developing countries. A more sensible stance would avoid blanket positions, distinguish among regulatory policies, and emphasize the gains to both the U.S. and Latin American economies if the most costly and ill-considered public policies were revised.

Second, U.S. policy is quite right to be concerned with investment issues at the multilateral level. International rules curbing competition among governments in offering incentives or in mandating exports are fundamental to the health of an international trading regime that will foster an expanding international economy. But initiatives to establish such rules must begin with an understanding of the pervasiveness of the influence of foreign ownership—especially when the gaps in wealth, technology, and foreign holdings are as large as they are between the North and the South. Given the asymmetry in competitive capability between the private sectors of both regions, multilateral policies must recognize the disadvantaged position of developing countries and their right to enact industrial policies promoting industrialization and national enterprise. Nonetheless, as developing countries become internationally competitive and the gaps in technology and income close, developing countries will be expected to play by rules agreed upon by all trading partners. Thus, in exchange for

435

preferential treatment in the early stages of industrialization, developing countries will be asked to recognize the principle of graduation to full acceptance of international rules.

As the current crisis abates and bargaining over the distribution of gains from investment resumes with full intensity, new international rules will become increasingly urgent. Protectionist sentiment may hold up investment regulations as an ever more visible target and threaten access of developing countries' exports to the markets of the industrialized countries. Ironically, the advanced developing countries will find it in their interest to establish these rules: increasingly Brazil, Argentina, and to a lesser extent, Mexico, are spawning outward foreign investment themselves. In the meantime, however, the United States should recognize the legitimacy of selective government interventions to achieve industrialization goals while striving to lay the groundwork for multilateral discussions on investment issues.

Notes

[1] This is in conventional analysis the social cost of foreign capital (Morley and Smith 1977). This is not to say that countries would grow faster without foreign capital; just that repatriated profits are not available for growth.

[2] It should be noted that production economies are inseparable from technological choice, product design, and location of plants. Production economies often can be achieved in ways other than observed in some industries. For example, most of the economies in autos and tractors are obtained through long production runs in the stamping and metalworking phases of production. If the number of models are reduced and if models are changed less frequently, then the same molds can be used over a large output because the output is spread over many years. Thus, observed production economies of scale are intimately bound up with model changes and other product differentiation strategies of international rivalry.

[3] This tends to corroborate and extend a thesis presented by Bergsten, Horst, and Moran (1978) that the overseas operation of TNCs tends to reinforce their monopolistic position at home. They note that TNCs within a worldwide network can spread joint costs, achieve economies of vertical integration, balance diversification, and take advantage of differing tax regimes. An equally important benefit of global operations is the ability to cross-subsidize losses in bad times or to restructure the market to favor their greater control. No more visible example is available than that of the Ford Motor Company: It reportedly lost nearly $1 billion on its U.S. operations in 1979, but overseas profits just managed to keep the company in the black. Low profits or even losses at home have been offset by high earnings abroad at several points in other industries studied as well: heavy electrical equipment (especially nuclear power equipment), cigarettes, tires, and tractors. All this indicates that foreign operations are increasingly essential to transnationals' continued growth and profitability, and that foreign operations sustain and reinforce any monopolistic position in the home market.

Appendix A

A completely different approach to the growth problem is the multicountry, cross-sectional method analyzing the effects of resource inflows upon domestic savings, investment, and growth. Beginning with the attempts of MacDougall (1960) and Rosenstein-Rodan (1961), orthodox economists have argued that foreign investment may make a new contribution to capital formation in the host country and thus increase the rate of growth. The underlying assumption was that a dollar of "foreign resources" would result in an increase of one dollar in imports and local investment. Investment, the secret of growth, was seen to be constrained by inadequate local savings. To this elementary Harrod/Domar formulation were added other explanatory variables of growth besides investment, such as capacity to import and changes in the capital-output ratio. This gave rise to the "two-gap" analysis in which new foreign investment inflows and aid were seen to cover the shortfalls of domestic savings and foreign exchange earnings.

In the early 1970s a series of cross-sectional studies began to challenge this view (Griffin and Enos 1970; Griffin 1970; Rahman 1968; Weisskopf 1972). These writings argued that foreign resource inflows, especially aid, make little contribution to economic growth because they augment consumption and have a new negative rather than positive effect on local savings. The effect occurs because: (a) foreign resources mainly fund consumption rather than investment items; and, (b) foreign investment may preempt local investment opportunities, causing a shift from local savings to local consumption, since it is investment opportunity that generates savings.

The evidence, summarized by Papanek (1972, p. 937), takes the savings rate as a dependent variable in a large sample of countries with cross-sectional or time series data. In four of five studies, the effect of one dollar of new foreign inflows was associated with declines of domestic savings ranging from 23 to 73 cents. In the fifth study (Chenery and Eckstein 1970), 12 of 16 countries showed a negative relationship and only one country had a "substantially" positive result. Papanek (1975) himself presented further evidence of this for a cross-sectional and longitudinal sample of 34 countries for the 1950s and 51 countries in the 1960s, though he discounted his own results as a "statistical artifact" (1975, p. 126). Still, the weight of the cross-sectional evidence seems to be on the side of Griffin, that inflows of foreign resources are negatively associated with the domestic savings rate.

But does this mean that inflows of investment are negatively associated with economic growth? It could be (as Griffin argues) that income is increased because of net additions to consumption. Indeed, Papanek (1975, p. 127) found a weak positive correlation between foreign investment inflows and growth rates, controlling for income per capita and population in his sample. Voivadas (1973), testing the simple relationship between resource inflows and growth for 22 countries, found no significant relationship. He did find a strong positive relationship between exports and increases in growth rates.

Even if some association were established between foreign investment inflows and rates of growth, the direction of causation is not immediately clear. It is possible that rapid growth rates in the host country attract foreign investment, as some authors have argued when seeking to explain the global pattern of foreign investment.

All in all, this approach tells us very little about the role of TNCs in contributing to growth in general, to a certain type of growth, or to stagnation. First, findings on both sides are ambiguous in part because of the lack of sufficiently complex models as well as the high level of aggregation of the data. Often they have low explanatory powers. More importantly, Newlyn (1977) presents a fairly strong critique of the econometrics underlying the analysis, arguing among other things that the tests do not address the behavioral relations being studied. Second, few studies try to distinguish the effects of foreign investment, foreign aid, and other transfers. Only Papanek (1975) makes this distinction, but his definition of foreign investment includes a mixed bag of net foreign direct investment and long-term foreign loans obtained by private borrowers (including presumably state-owned and private domestic enterprises). There is no reason to assume that this aggregate has any relationship to the actual performance of foreign-controlled enterprise. Third, the studies ignore economic activities of ongoing foreign subsidiaries inside the local economy—yet foreign firms retain earnings, borrow locally, repatriate profits, and take over other ongoing enterprises. Until these activities are considered, the multicountry, cross-sectional, and longitudinal statistical endeavors raise more questions than they answer about foreign direct investment, savings, and growth in income.

Appendix B

As with the literature on the effects of foreign direct investment on growth, the cross-sectional studies attempting to measure the influence of foreign investment on dependency make the leap from international behavior to host country foreign macroeconomic performance. The literature provides a sharp contrast to the industrial organizational approach. Two thorough reviews of this literature, one by Bornschier, Chase-Dunn, and Rubinson (1978) and the other by Gereffi (1979), present the results of the nearly 20 studies and consider critically their conclusions. Criticisms of this literature can be divided into two categories: theoretical and methodological.

At the most abstract level, the central thrust of the early *dependistas* (A. G. Frank 1969; Bodenheimer 1971) concentrated heavily on the perceived negative effects of foreign growth rates of developing countries. Other writers (Dos Santos 1970; Furtado 1970) placed greater emphasis on the distortions accompanying the situation of dependence, including technological dependence and internal inequalities within developing countries. Since all these writers stressed the interrelationship of these phenomena—growth, inequality, technological dependence, and foreign direct investment, as well as class and political conflict—and not the unilinear, uni-causality implicit in most econometric models, the school of writers is better seen as a model or even methodology (Palma 1976) rather than a theory with strictly posited economic relationships. Consequently, abstracting simple positivistic relationships without considerable theoretical refinement at a lower level of abstraction is on tenuous ground. Some of these criticisms are brought out by Duvall (1978) and Caporoso (1978).

Most cross-sectional studies have taken as their dependent variable either the growth rate of per capita income or the degree of inequality in specific countries. The idea of using the growth rates receives theoretical support from only a few of the early dependency theorists, particularly A. G. Frank. More recent theorists, such as Dos Santos, Furtado, and Cardoso and Faletto (1979), argue that, at least by the 1970s, growth in the periphery had become consistent with the goals of international capital and in the interests of TNCs. These later

439

formulations are more consistent with the Marxist heritage of dependency theory, which emphasized the unevenness of capitalist growth, temporally, geographically, and among classes (Lenin 1914; Baran 1957).

A more interesting line of argument coming out of almost all *dependistas* is that TNCs distort local development in ways that increase inequality, social stratification, and militate against decentralization of political power and political participation. In their own terms, foreign investment serves and entrenches local ruling elites to the detriment of mass development. Several studies have used measures of internal inequality in income distribution to capture these phenomena. Two criticisms are in order: First, the distortions potentially associated with foreign investment—as this survey has shown—are multiple and complex, and not limited to income distribution. Second, accepting income distribution as the sole dependent variable for the moment, the theoretical underpinnings of the model are not clear and warrant far greater elaboration. Why do increases in foreign direct investment cause increases in inequality? Is it because foreign investment creates highly paid jobs and this causes segmentation in the labor market and/ or increases in economic growth? If so, is foreign investment or growth the independent variable (Gereffi 1979)?

In any event, Bornschier, et al. (1978, p. 652) conclude from their extensive review that "foreign direct investment and aid have the long-term effect of decreasing the rate of economic growth and of inequality" as long as foreign investment and aid are measured by stocks, rather than flows. But before accepting this conclusion, one should examine carefully the methodology.

Gereffi's (1979) excellent review presents six criticisms on empirical and methodological grounds. First, "dependency" is conceptualized too simplistically by considering the stock or flow of foreign direct investment plus aid; this misses the important sectoral characteristics of both. Even though foreign investment tends to settle in common industries, distinctions should be made at lease among mining, manufacturing and petroleum because sectors differ in their impact on national economic growth. When this is done, Bornschier, et al. (1978, p. 677) and Chase-Dunn (1975, p. 734) find that foreign investment in manufacturing has the largest negative effects on economic growth, while foreign investment in extractive industries has positive effects. Theory offers minimal guidance as to why this might be the case. One might second Gereffi's criticism by suggesting the substitution of relative measures, such as the share of an industry or sector controlled by TNCs. These would have a greater theoretical relevance.

440

One attempt to specify intervening variables and carefully analyze the relationship is the study of Evans and Timberlake (1980) with their inclusion of a tertiary sector. They find a positive relation between foreign investment dependence, growth of the tertiary sector, and inequality. Nonetheless, one would like to see more complex models to explain such a complicated relationship. Second, Gereffi points out that there is no "reason to assume *a priori* as the . . . studies do, that direct foreign investment and foreign aid . . . have the same effects on economic growth and inequality." Control over the incoming capital is in the hands of the local government, not foreign investors. Third, Gereffi notes that measures of income inequality usually are cross-sectional, but are often used in the studies as to make inferences about changes over time. Unfortunately time series data are not usually available for income distribution. Fourth, other variables may intervene to make the relationship more complex; increases in income levels appear to widen inequalities (Adelman and Morris 1973; Horvat 1976) and when this is not controlled for in the models, the relationship of foreign direct investment to income distribution is unclear. Fifth, the cross-sectional studies fail to account for the substantial shift of foreign capital into national hands, especially the state. In many developing countries the government nationalized or otherwise assumed ownership of several sectors, yet this process of industrial reorganization is unaccounted for in the analysis. Finally, the analyses make no distinction of the strength of the host state, notes Gereffi. With the exception of Kaufman, Chernotsky, and Geller (1975) and Rubinson (1976 and 1977), most studies make no attempt to quantify the impact of strong host country governments in negotiating with TNCs to increase the host county share of benefits from foreign investment.

Both the Kaufman and the Rubinson studies suffer from theoretical and empirical problems. While it is intuitively appealing that stronger states are likely to strive to promote economic development, it is far less clear that they will promote economic equality. One can think of several counter examples. Even if one could posit a plausible relationship, problems of measurement are formidable: How does one measure the "strong" state? Rubinson uses the value of government revenues as a per cent of GNP and the amount of foreign reserves of a country as measures of strength and the size of external public debt as a measure of weakness. These are far from convincing; a casual appraisal of the strongest states in developing countries (Brazil, Mexico, and Argentina) suggests they usually have the highest external debt. Admittedly, this appraisal is no more than a subjective evaluation about a host government's ability to control successfully locally situated foreign direct investment, manage its economic policy through some sort of centralized decisionmaking authority, and maintain political stability.

Reading this literature leaves us much less sanguine about its usefulness than either Bornschier or Gereffi. If the theoretical underpinnings of the hypotheses tested are muddied and contradictory, if the measures employed are dubious, and if the methodology itself is open to question because of the failure to include theoretically powerful explanatory variables, one must question the usefulness of this approach to analyze dependency questions. On the other hand, the consistency of some findings over various studies is sufficient to command our attention as the literature evolves.

Appendix C

The Food Processing Industry: U.S. Standard Industrial Code

20 Food Processing

201 Meat Products
  2011 Meat packing plants
  2013 Sausages and other prepared meat products
  2016 Poultry dressing plants
  2017 Poultry & egg processing

202 Dairy Products
  2021 Creamery butter
  2022 Cheese, natural & processed
  2023 Condensed and evaporated milk
  2024 Ice cream and frozen desserts
  2026 Fluid milk

203 Fruits and Vegetables
  2032 Canned specialties
  2033 Canned fruits, vegetables, preserves, jams, and jellies
  2034 Dried and dehydrated fruits and vegetables & soup mixes
  2035 Pickled fruits and vegetables, vegetable sauces and seasonings, and salad dressings
  2037 Frozen fruits, fruits juices, and vegetables
  2038 Frozen specialties

204 Grain Mill Products
  2041 Flour and other grain mill products
  2043 Cereal breakfast foods
  2044 Rice milling
  2045 Blended and prepared flour
  2046 Wet corn milling
  2047 Dog, cat & other pet food
  2048 Prepared feeds & feed ingredients for animals & fowls, not elsewhere classified

205 Bakery Products
  2051 Bread and other bakery products, except cookies and crackers
  2052 Cookies and crackers

206 Sugar Products
2061 Cane sugar, except refining only
2062 Cane sugar refining
2063 Beet sugar
2065 Candy and other confectionery products
2066 Chocolate and cocoa products
2067 Chewing gum.

207 Fats and Oils Processing
2074 Cottonseed oil mills
2075 Soybean oil mills
2076 Vegetable oil mills, except corn, cottonseed, & soybean
2077 Animal & marine fats & oils
2079 Shortening, table oils, margarine & other edible fats & oils, not elsewhere classified

208 Beverages (inc. alcoholic)
2082 Malt beverages
2083 Malt
2084 Wines, brandy, and brandy spirits
2085 Distilled, rectified, and blended liquors
2086 Bottled and canned soft drinks and carbonated waters
2087 Flavoring extracts and flavoring syrups, not elsewhere classified

209 Other Food Preparations (inc. fish products, spices)
2091 Canned and cured fish and seafoods
2092 Fresh or frozen packaged fish and seafoods
2095 Roasted coffee
2097 Manufactured ice
2098 Macaroni, spaghetti, vermicelli, and noodles
2099 Food preparations, not elsewhere classified

Comment on Appendix C:

Although no classification system has been universally adopted, these selections from the U.S. Standard Industrial Code give some idea of the complexity of the food industry. Food processing (20) is a "two-digit industry"; dairy products (202) constitute a "three-digit industry"; and condensed and evaporated milk products (2023) are a "four-digit industry." Concentration is greater at the four-digit level. Large modern transnational firms are likely to be diversified across the food processing industry, producing in many three and four-digit industries. As concentration and oligopoly increase at the four-digit level, competition shifts to the three-digit and the two-digit level. Regulation is difficult because the two-digit industry is complex and relatively unconcentrated, and because it includes many local firms (in spite of transnational dominance of certain four-digit industries).

Bibliography

Abercrombie, K.C. 1972. Agricultural Mechanisation and Employment in Latin America. *International Labour Review.* 106, No. 1.

Ablin, Eduardo. 1979. Technology Exports from Developing Countries: Afterthoughts in Light of the Argentine Case. Paper read at the Nordic Symposium on Development Strategies in Latin America, University of Lund, Sweden.

Adam, Gyorgy. 1971. New Trends in International Business: Worldwide Sourcing and Domiciling. *Acta Economica.* 7: 349-367.

————. 1972. Some Implications and Concomitants of Worldwide Sourcing. *Acta Economica.* 8: 2-3.

Adams, Walter. 1977. *The Structure of American Industry.* 5th edition. New York: Macmillan Publishing Co., Inc.

Adelman I. and Morris, C.T. 1973. *Economic Growth and Social Equity in Developing Countries.* Stanford: Stanford University Press.

Advertising Age. August 23, 1976.

Advisory Commission on Smoking and Health, U.S. Surgeon General's Office. 1964. *Smoking and Health.* Washington, D.C.: U.S. Government Printing Office.

Agarwal, Anil. 1978. *Drugs and the Third World.* London: Earthscan.

Agricultural Machinery Digest. August 1976, April 1978.

Albrecht, Stephen and Locker, Michael, eds. 1979. *CDE Stock-Ownership Directory: No. 2.* New York: Corporate Data Exchange, Inc.

Alford, B.W.E. 1973. *W.D. & H.O. Wills and the Development of the U.K. Tobacco Industry, 1786-1965.* London: Methuen.

Alperts, Robert C. 1973. *The Good Provider: H.J. Heinz and His 57 Varieties.* Boston: Houghton Mifflin.

Alvarez Soberanis, Jaime. 1979. *La regulación de las invenciones y marcas y de la transferencia de technología.* Mexico: Editorial Porrúa.

American Brands, Inc. (formerly American Tobacco Company) *Annual Reports.* 1950-1977.

American Iron and Steel Institute. *Annual Statistical Report.* Washington, D.C.

American Metal Market. February 15, 1979.

American Metal Market. *Metal Statistics.* 1978, 1979, and 1980.

Amjad, R. 1977. Profitability and Industrial Concentration in Pakistan. *Journal of Development Studies.* April: 181-198.

Asociación latinoamericana de industrias farmacéuticas (ALIFAR). 1981. "La industria farmacéutica en América Latina: aspectos económicos." Mimeograph. Buenos Aires.

———. 1982a *Industria farmacéutica latinoamericana.* 1: 1. Buenos Aires.

———. 1982b. *Industria farmacéutica latinoamericana.* 1: 2. Buenos Aires.

Asociacíon Mexicana de la Industria Automotriz. 1977. *La Industria Automotriz de México en Cifras, 1976.* Mexico, D.F.: AMIA.

Aurori, C. 1977. Mecanisation agricole: le modele europeen et l'Amerique Latine. *Le fin des outils: technologie et domination.* Paris: Presses Universitaires de France.

B.F. Goodrich. *Annual Report.* Various years.

Baer, Werner. 1969. *The Development of the Brazilian Steel Industry.* Nashville: Vanderbilt University Press.

———. 1973. The Changing Role of the State in the Brazilian Economy. *World Development.* 1:11.

———. 1976. Technology, Employment and Development: Empirical Findings. *World Development.* 4: 121-130.

Bain, Joe. 1956. *Barriers to New Competition.* Cambridge: Harvard University Press.

———. 1966. *International Differences in Industrial Structure.* New Haven: Yale University Press.

———. 1968. *Industrial Organization.* New York: John Wiley and Sons.

Baldwin, Charles C. 1948. Germany's Major Industrial Combines. Office of Military Government, U.S. Department of State.

Baran, Paul. 1957. *The Political Economy of Growth.* New York: Monthly Review Press.

Baranson, Jack. 1969. *Auto Industries in Developing Countries.* World Bank Occasional Staff Papers, No. 8.

———. 1971. *The International Transfer of Automotive Technology to Developing Countries.* New York: UNITAR Research Report, No. 8.

Barnet, R.S. and Muller, R.E. 1974. *Global Reach: The Power of Multinational Corporations.* New York: Simon and Schuster.

Behrman, Jack N. 1972. *The Role of International Companies in Latin American Integration; Autos and Petrochemicals.* Lexington: D.C. Heath and Co.

Bennett, Douglas C. and Sharpe, Kenneth E. 1979a. Transnational Corporations and the Political Economy of Export Promotion: The Case of the Mexican Automobile Industry. *International Organization.* 33(2): 177-201.

————. 1979b. Agenda Setting and Bargaining Power: The Mexican State vs. Transnational Automobile Corporations. *World Politics* 32(1): 57-89.

————. 1980. The State as Banker and Entrepreneur; the Last Resort Character of the Mexican State's Economic Intervention, 1917-1976. *Comparative Politics.* 12(2): 165-189.

Bergsten, C. Fred, Horst, Thomas and Moran, Theodore H. 1978. *American Multinationals and American Interests.* Washington, D.C.: The Brookings Institution.

Bernal Sahagún, Victor M. 1974. *Anatomía de la Publicidad en México: Monopolios, enajenación y desperdicio.* Mexico, D.F.: Editorial Nuestro Tiempo.

Bhatt, V.V. 1978. Decision making in the Public Sector: Case Study of Swaraj Tractor. *Economic and Political Weekly.* 13 (2).

Blank, D.H. 1979. *Nature and Structure of the U.S. Auto Tire Industry.* U.S. Department of Commerce.

Bloomfield, Gerald. 1978. *The World Automotive Industry.* Newton Abbot: David and Charles.

Bodenheimer, Susanne. 1971. Dependency and Imperialism: The Roots of Latin American Underdevelopment. In *Readings in U.S. Imperialism,* eds. K.T. Fann and Donald C. Hodges, pp. 155-181. Boston: Porter Sargent Publisher.

Borkin, Joseph. 1978. *The Crime and Punishment of I. G. Farben.* New York: Free Press.

Bornschier, Volker, Chase-Dunn, Christopher and Rubinson, Richard. 1978. Crossnational Evidence of the Effects of Foreign Investment and Aid on Economic Growth and Inequality: A Summary of Findings and a Reanalysis. *American Journal of Sociology.* 84(3).

Brazier, A.F. and Pelling, G.F. n.d. The Establishment of Rubber Manufacture in Developing Countries. Mimeographed.

British American Tobacco Company, Ltd. 1974. *Report and Accounts.*

Brooke, M.Z. and Remmers, H. Lee. 1970. *The Strategy of Multinational Enterprise.* New York: American Elsevier Publishing Co.

Brooke, Paul A. 1975. *Resistant Prices: A Study of Competitive Strains in the Antibiotic Markets.* New York: Council on Economic Priorities.

Brooks, Jerome E. 1952. *The Mighty Leaf: Tobacco Through the Centuries.* Boston: Little, Brown and Co.

Brozen, Yale. 1974. Entry Barriers: Advertising and Product Differentiation. In *Industrial Concentration: The New Learning,* eds. H.J. Goldschmidt, H.M. Mann and J.F. Weston. Boston: Little, Brown and Co.

447

Bruton, Henry J. 1974. Economic Development and Labor Use: A Review. In *Employment in Developing Nations*. Ed. Edgar O. Edwards. New York: Columbia University Press.

Buckley, Peter and Casson, Mark. 1976. *The Future of the Multinational Enterprise*. New York: Holmes & Meier.

Buckley, Peter and Dunning, John H. 1980. The Industrial Structure of U.S. Indirect Investment in the U.K. *Journal of International Business Studies*. 5-13.

Burch, D. 1980. Overseas Aid and the Transfer of Technology: A Study of Agricultural Mechanization in Sri Lanka. *Development Research Digest*. 3.

Bureau of Mines, U. S. Department of Interior. 1976. *Commodity Data Summaries*. Washington, D.C.

Burstall, Michael L., Dunning, John H. and Lake, Arthur. 1981. *Multinational Enterprise, Governments and Technology: Pharmaceutical Industry*. Paris: Organization for Economic Co-operation and Development.

Business International. 1973. *Setting Intercorporate Pricing Policies*. New York.

Business Week. November 23, 1974, June 28, 1976, July 26, 1976, September 9, 1976, October 4, 1976, November 20, 1978, June 11, 1979, October 29, 1979, November 2, 1980.

Buzzell, Robert D. and Norse, Robert E. 1967. *Production Innovation in Food Processing 1954-1964*. Boston: Harvard University Graduate School of Buisness Administration.

Cámara de la Industria del Cigarrillo. 1976. *Síntesis estadística anual, 1975*. Buenos Aires.

Cámara de la Industria Venezolana Automotriz. 1977. *La Industria Automotriz en Cifras*. Caracas.

Cámara Nacional de Industrias de Transformación. 1978. *Memoria: Primer Simposium de Actualización Operacional de la Industria Automotriz en México*. Mexico, D.F.

Canada Royal Commission. 1971. *Report of the Royal Commission on Farm Machinery*. Ottawa: Information Canada.

Caporaso, James A. 1978. Dependence and Dependency in the Global System. *International Organization*. 32(1): 1-12.

Cardoso, Fernando H. and Faletto, Enzo. 1979. *Dependency and Development in Latin America*. Berkeley: University of California Press.

Carnoy, M. 1972. *Industrialisation in a Latin American Common Market*. Washington, D.C.: The Brookings Institution.

Casson, Mark. 1979. *Alternatives to the Multinational Corporation*. New York: Holmes & Meier.

448

Caves, Richard E. 1971. International Corporations: The Industrial Economics of Foreign Investment. *Economica*. 38 (149).

————. 1974a. Industrial Organization. In *Economic Analysis and the Multinational Enterprise,* ed. J.H. Dunning, New York: Praeger Publishers.

————. 1974b. Causes of Direct Investment: Foreign Firms' Shares in Canadian and United Kingdom Manufacturing Industries. *Review of Economics and Statistics.* 56: 279-293.

————. 1974c. Multinational Firms, Competition and Productivity in Host-Country Markets. *Economica.* 41: 176-193.

————. 1974d. International Trade, International Investment, and Imperfect Markets. Special Paper in International Economics No. 10, Princeton University, Princeton, New Jersey.

Caves, Richard E. and Uekusa, Masu. 1976. *Industrial Organization in Japan.* Washington, D.C.: Brookings Institution.

————. 1980. Industrial Organization, Corporate Strategy and Structure. *The Journal of Economic Literature.* 18:1: 64-92.

Central de Medicamentos. 1981. *Relatório 1981.* Brazil.

Chase-Dunn, Christopher. 1977. The Effects of International Economic Dependence on Development and Inequality: A Cross-national Study. *American Sociological Review.* 40.

Chenery, Hollis and Eckstein, Peter. 1970. Development Alternatives for Latin America. *Journal of Political Economy.* July/August.

Chudnovsky, Daniel. 1974. Foreign Manufacturing Firms' Behavior in Colombia: A Study of the Influence of Technology, Advertising and Financing Upon Profitability, 1966-70. *Empresas Multinacionales y Ganancias Monopolicas.* Buenos Aires.

Chung, W.K. 1978. Sales by Majority-Owned Foreign Affiliates of U.S. Companies. *Survey of Current Business.* March.

Cilingiroglu, Ayhan. 1969. Manufacture of Heavy Electrical Equipment in Developing Countries. World Bank Staff Occasional Papers, No. 9.

CIS Antireport No. 11 (sic), n.d. *Unilever's World.* Nottingham: Russell Press Ltd. Produced in collaboration with SOMA (Amsterdam) and the Transnational Institute.

Clymer, Harold A. 1975. The Economic and Regulatory Climate: U. S. and Overseas Trends. In *Drug Development and Marketing,* ed. Robert B. Helms, pp. 137-154. Washington, D.C.: American Enterprise Institute.

Coase, R.H. 1937. The Nature of the Firm. *Economica.* 4: 386-405.

Cochran, Sherman G. 1975. Big Business in China: Sino-American Rivalry in the Tobacco Industry 1890-1930. Ph.D. dissertation, Yale University.

449

Cohen, Benjamin I. 1973. Comparative Behavior of Foreign and Domestic Export Firms in a Developing Economy. *Review of Economics and Statistics*. 55: 190-197.

———. 1975. *Multinational Firms and Asian Exports*. New Haven: Yale University Press.

Cohen, Benjamin I., Katz, Jorge and Beck, William T. 1975. Innovation and Foreign Investment Behavior of the U.S. Pharmaceutical Industry. New York: National Bureau of Economic Research, Working Paper No. 101.

Cohen, Robert B. 1979. Economic Crises, National Industrial Strategies and Multinational Corporations: The Case of the Auto Industry. October. United Nations Industrial Development Organization, Vienna.

Comanor, William S. and Wilson, Thomas A. 1974. *Advertising and Market Power*. Cambridge: Harvard University Press.

———. 1979. The Effect of Advertising on Competition: A Survey. *Journal of Economic Literature*. 17:1.

Commission of the European Communities. *Bulletin of the European Communities*. No. 6, 1975, No. 11, 1977 and No. 12, 1977. Luxembourg.

———. 1978. *Etude de l'evolution de la concentration dans l'industrie du machinisme agricole en France*. Luxembourg.

———. 1975. *A Study of the Evolution of Concentration in the Mechanical Engineering Sector for the United Kingdom*. Luxembourg.

———. 1973. *Treaties Establishing the European Communities*. Luxembourg.

Conant, M. 1953. Competition in the Farm-Machinery Industry. *Journal of Business*. 26.

Conceiçao Tavares, Maria 1978. *Estrutura Industrial e Empresas Lideres*. Rio de Janeiro: FINEP.

Connor, John M. 1977. *The Market Power of Multinationals*. New York: Praeger.

———. 1979. *Competition and the Role of the Largest Firms in the U.S. Food and Tobacco Industries*. Economics, Statistics, and Cooperatives Service of the U.S.D.A. and the Food Systems Research Group of North Central Regional Project NC-117 (Preliminary Draft).

Connor, John M. and Mueller, William F. 1977a. *Market Power and Profitability of Multinational Corporations in Brazil and Mexico*. Report to the Senate Subcommittee on Multinational Corporations. Washington, D.C.: Government Printing Office.

———. 1977b. The Shaping of Market Structures by Multinationals: Brazil, Mexico, and the United States. Staff Paper Series, No. 120, Agricultural Economics. Madison, University of Wisconsin.

Consumers Union vs. Kissinger. 1974. 506 Fed 2d 136.

Consumers Union vs. Rogers. 1973. 352 F. Supp. 1319.

Cooper, Richard N. 1977. A New International Economic Order for Mutual Gain. *Foreign Policy.* 26.

Corina, Maurice. 1975. *Trust in Tobacco: The Anglo-American Struggle for Power.* London: Michael Joseph.

Corporacion Financera de Desarrollo. 1978. *Peru: La Industria Automotriz.* Lima.

The Courier-Journal. February 1, 1980.

Cox, Reavis. 1933. *Competition in the American Tobacco Industry, 1911-1932: A Study of the Effects of the Partition of the American Tobacco Company by the United States Supreme Court.* New York: Columbia University Press.

Craven, J. (Ed.) 1983. *Industrial Organization, Antitrust and Public Policy.* Boston: Klwer-Nijhoff.

Dagnino Pastore, J.M. 1966. *La Industria del tractor en la Argentina.* Buenos Aires: Instituto di Tella.

Davila Reig, L. et al. 1975. *La Industria de Tractores Agrícolas en México y su Proyección a 1982.* Mexico, D.F.

de María y Campos, Mauricio. 1977. La industria farmacéutica en México. *Comercio Exterior* 27(8): 888-912.

Demsetz, H. 1973a. Industry Structure Market Rivalry and Public Policy. *Journal of Law and Economics.* 16: 1-10.

––––––. 1973b. *The Market Concentration Doctrine.* Washington, D.C.: The American Enterprise Institute.

Deolalikar, Anil B. 1980. Foreign Technology in the Indian Pharmaceutical Industry: Its Impact on Local Innovation and Social Equity. Paper prepared for the Council on International and Public Affairs, New York.

Departamento de Tabaco, Secretaría de Estado de Agricultura y Ganadería. 1950. 1975. *Estadística Anual.* Buenos Aires.

Derry, T.K. and Williams, Trevor I. 1961. *A Short History of Technology from the Earliest Times to A.D. 1900.* New York: Oxford University Press.

Developing World Industry and Technology, Inc. 1979. Changes in the Terms and Conditions of Technology Transfer by the Pharmaceutical Industry to Newly Industrializing Nations: An Overview of the Past Ten Years. Paper prepared for the U.S. Agency for International Development, Washington, D.C.

Diario Oficial. Various years: Mexico, D.F.

Díaz-Alejandro, Carlos. 1976. International Markets for Exhaustible Resources: Less Developed Countries and Transnational Corporations. Yale University Economic Growth Center Paper No. 256.

Domike, Arthur and Rodriguez, Gonzalo, 1977. Agroindustria en México: Estructura de los sistemas y oportunidades para empresas campesinas. 2 vols. Mexico, D.F.: Unpublished manuscript, CIDE.

dos Santos, Theotonio. 1970. The Structure of Dependence. *American Economic Review.* 60(9): 231-236.

Dugar, S. M. 1976. *Law of Restrictive Trade Practices.* New Delhi: A Taxmann Publication.

Duncan, William Chandler. 1973. *U.S.-Japan Automobile Diplomacy: A Study in Economic Concentration.* Cambridge: Ballinger Publishing Company.

Dunlop. *Annual Report.* Various years.

Dunning, John H. 1975. Multinational Enterprises, Market Structure, Economic Power, and Industrial Policy. *Journal of World Trade Law.* 575-613.

————. 1979. Explaining Changing Patterns of International Production: In Defense of the Eclectic Theory. *Oxford Bulletin of Economics and Statistics.* November: 269- 295.

Dunning, John H. and Pierce, R. 1975. Profitability and Performance of the World's Largest Industrial Companies. *Financial Times* Advisory Group.

Dun's Review. 1979. Prescription for Profits. January: 39-41.

Duvall, Raymond D. 1978. Dependence and Dependency Theory: Notes Toward Precision of Concept and Argument. *International Organization.* 32(1): 51-78.

Eames, Alfred W. Jr. and Landis, Richard G. 1974. *The Business of Feeding People: The Story of Del Monte Corporation.* New York: Newcomen Society in North America.

Economic Commission for Latin America. 1973. *Perspectivas y Modalidades de Integración Regional de la Industria Automotrize en América Latina.* New York.

————. 1977. *Las Empresas Transnacionales entre las Mil Mayores Empresas del Brasil.* Documento de Trabajo No. 5. New York.

Commission of the European Communities. 1975. *Fourth Report on Competition Policy.* Brussels.

The Economist. November 3, 1979.

Economist Intelligence Unit. 1976. The United Kingdom Agricultural Tractor Industry. *Motor Business.*

Edwards, Corwin. 1964. *Cartelization in Western Europe.* Bureau of Intelligence and Research U.S. Department of State.

————. 1971. The Impact of International Cartels on International Trade. In *On Economic Concentration.* Ed. H. Arendt. Berlin: Dunker.

Eichner, Alfred S. 1969. *The Emergence of Oligopoly: Sugar Regining as a Case Study.* Baltimore: The Johns Hopkins University Press.

Emmanuel, Arghiri. 1973. *Unequal Exchange: A Study of the Imperialism of Trade.* New York: Monthly Review Press.

Empresa Nacional de Tabaco. 1974. La industria tabacalera nacional y la participacion del estado dentro de su desarrollo. Lima. Mimeographed.

Epstein, Barbara and Newfarmer, Richard S. 1980. *The Continuing Cartel: Report on the International Electrical Association.* Report to the Committee on Interstate and Foreign Commerce, U.S. House of Representatives, June.

————. 1982. Imperfect International Markets and Monopolistic Prices to Developing Countries: A Case Study. *Cambridge Journal of Economics.* March.

Estudio Sur. 1975. *Estudio de la demanda de tabaco national.* Buenos Aires. Mimeographed.

Evans, Peter B. 1976. Foreign Investment and Industrial Transformation: A Brazilian Case Study. *Journal of Development Economics.* 3: 119-139.

————. 1977a. Direct Investment and Industrial Concentration. *Journal of Development Studies.* 13 (4): 373-386.

————. 1977b. Multinationals, State-Owned Corporations, and the Transformation of Imperialism: A Brazilian Case Study. *Economic Development and Cultural Change.* 26 (1): 43-64.

————. 1979. *Dependent Development: The Alliance of Multinational, State, and Local Capital in Brazil.* Princeton: Princeton University Press.

Evans, Peter B. and Gereffi, Gary. 1982. Foreign Investment and Dependent Development: Comparing Brazil and Mexico. In *Brazil and Mexico: Patterns in Late Development.* Eds. Sylvia Hewlett and Richard Weinert, pp. 111-168. Philadelphia, Pa.: Institute for the Study of Human Issues.

Evans, Peter B. and Timberlake, Michael. 1980. Dependence, Inequality, and the Growth of the Tertiary: A Comparative Analysis of Less Developed Countries. *American Sociological Review.* 45: 531-552.

Fajnzylber, Fernando 1970. *Estrategia Industrial y Empresas Internacionales: Posición Relativa de América Latina y Brasil.* New York: Economic Commission for Latin America.

————. 1970. Sistema Industrial e Exportaçao de Manufacturas. Rio de Janeiro, Economic Commission for Latin America, Instituto de Planejamento Económico e Social.

Fajnzylber, Fernando and Martínex-Tarragó, Trinidad. 1976. *Las Empresas Transnacionales.* Mexico, D.F.: Fondo De Cultura Económica.

453

Federal Trade Commission. 1928. *Report on the Radio Corporation of America*. Washington, D.C.: Government Printing Office.

———. 1948. *Report on International Electrical Equipment Cartels*. Washington, D.C.: Government Printing Office.

———. 1966. *Economic Report on the Manufacture and Distribution of Automotive Tires*. Washington, D.C.: Government Printing Office.

———. 1977. *Report on the United States Steel Industry and Its International Rivals*. Washington, D.C.: Government Printing Office.

Federal Trade Commission vs. Cement Institute. 1949. 333 U.S. 683.

Fidel, Julio and Lucangeli, Jorge. 1978. Cost-Benefit of Different Technological Options in the Context of a Differentiated Oligopoly: The Case of the Argentine Cigarette Industry. Buenos Aires: IDB/ECLA Research Program in Science and Technology Working paper No. 18.

Fidel, Julio, Lucangeli, Jorge and Shepherd, Phil. 1977. Perfil y comportamiento tecnológico de la industria del cigarrillo en la Argentina. Buenos Aires: Programa BID/CEPAL de Investigaciones en Temas de Ciencia y Tecnologiá, Monografía de Trabajo No. 7.

Financial Times. August 14, 17 and 20, 1979.

Firestone. *Annual Report*. Various years.

Flamm, Kenneth. 1979. Technology, Employment and Direct Foreign Investment Evidence from the Mexican Manufacturing Sector. Ph.D. dissertation, Massachusetts Institute of Technology.

Fleet, Michael. 1978. Host Country-Multinational Relations in the Columbian Automobile Industry. *Inter-American Economic Report*. Summer.

———. 1979. Bargaining Relations in the Columbian Automobile Industry. Mimeographed.

Foley, John. 1972. *The Food Makers: A History of General Foods Ltd*. Banbury, Oxon, England: General Foods, Ltd.

Food and Agriculture Organization. 1971. *Report of the 1960 World Census of Agriculture, Volume V*. Rome.

Food Processing. October 1979.

Fortune. 1976, 1980.

Frank, A.G. 1967. *Capitalism and Underdevelopment in Latin America*. New York: Monthly Review Press.

Frank, Isaiah. 1980. *Foreign Enterprise in Developing Countries*. Baltimore: The Johns Hopkins University Press.

Frankfurt Institute. 1966. *Study on the Adverse Effects of Specific Restrictive Business Practices on International Trade*. Frankfurt.

Fritschler, A. Lee. 1975. *Smoking and Politics: Policymaking and the Federal Bureaucracy*, 2nd edition. Englewood Cliffs, N.J.: Prentice-Hall.

454

Fung, Shing K. and Cassiolato, Jose E. 1976. The International Transfer of Technology to Brazil through Technology Agreements—Characteristics of the Government Control System and the Commercial Transactions. Cambridge: Center for Policy Alternatives, MIT.

Furtado, Celso. 1970. The Concept of External Dependence in the Study of Underdevelopment. In *The Political Economy of Development and Underdevelopment*. Ed. Chrles K. Wilber. New York: Random House.

Galbraith, J.K. 1967. *The New Industrial State*. London: Hamilton.

Gall, Norman. 1977. The Rise of Brazil. *Commentary*. 63: 49-50.

Gan, W.B. and Tham, S.Y. 1977. Market Structure and Price-Cost Margins in Malaysian Manufacturing Industries. *The Developing Economies*. 15(3): 280-289.

General Tire. *Annual Report*. Various years.

Gereffi, Gary. 1978. Drug Firms and Dependency in Mexico: The Case of the Steroid Hormone Industry. *International Organization*. 32(1): 237-286.

———. 1980. "Wonder Drugs" and Transnational Corporations in Mexico: An Elaboration and Limiting-Case Test of Dependency Theory. Ph.D. dissertation, Yale University.

———. 1982. Transnational Corporations and the Pharmaceutical Industry in Mexico. Mimeographed.

———. 1983. *The Pharmaceutical Industry and Dependency in the Third World*. Princeton: Princeton University Press.

Giddy, Ian H. 1978. The Demise of the Product Cycle Model in International Business Theory. *Columbia Journal of World Business*. Spring: 90-97.

Girvan, N. 1976. Corporate Imperialism in the Caribbean Bauxite Industry. In *Corporate Imperialism: Conflict and Expropriation*. Ed. N. Grivan. White Plains: Sharpe.

Goldberg, Ray A. 1977. The Agribusiness Market Structure and Controls. In *The Lessons of Wage and Price Controls—TheFood Sector*. Eds. John T. Dunlop and Kenneth T. Fedor, pp. 63-106. Cambridge: Harvard University Press.

Gonzales-Vigil, Fernando, Fernandez-Baca Llamosas, Jorge and Portocarrera Maisch, Felix. 1979. *El Complejo Automotor en el Perú*. Lima: ILET-INP.

Goodman, Louis Wolfe. 1981. *Small Countries and Large Firms*. Unpublished manuscript.

Goodyear. *Annual Report*. Various years.

Government of India Tariff Commission. 1955. *Report on the Fair Prices of Rubber Tyres and Tubes, 1955*. New Delhi: Government of India Press.

Grabowski, Henry G. 1976. *Drug Regulation and Innovation: Empirical Evidence and Policy Options.* Washington, D.C.: American Enterprise Institute.

Grabowski, Henry G., and Vernon, John M. 1976. Structural Effects of Regulation on Innovation in the Ethical Drug Industry. In *Essays on Industrial Organization in Honor of Joe S. Bain.* Eds. Robert T. Masson and P. David Qualls, pp. 181-205. Cambridge, Mass.: Ballinger.

Grabowski, Henry G., Vernon, John M. and Thomas, Lacy G. 1976. The Effects of Regulatory Policy on the Incentives to Innovate: An International Comparative Analysis. In *Impact of Public Policy on Drug Innovation and Pricing.* Eds. Samuel A. Mitchell and Emery A. Link, pp. 47-82. Washington, D.C.: American Enterprise Institute.

Greer, Douglas F. 1973a. The Case Against Patent Systems in Less-Developed Countries. *Journal of International Law and Economics.* December: 223-266.

———. 1973b. United States of America. In *Restrictive Business Practices: Studies on the United Kingdom of Great Britain and Northern Ireland, and the United States of America and Japan.* Geneva: UNCTAD.

———. 1979. Control of Terms and Conditions for International Transfers of Technology to Developing Countries. Paper read at Conference on International Regulations of Restrictive Business Practices, November, at Columbia University School of Law, New York.

———. 1980. *Industrial Organization and Public Policy.* New York: Macmillan.

Griffin, K.B. 1970. Foreign Capital, Domestic Savings and Economic Development. *Bulletin,* Oxford University, Institute of Economics and Statistics, May.

———. 1973. The Effect of Aid and Other Resource Transfers on Savings and Growth in Less Developed Countries: A Comment. *Economic Journal.* September: 863-66.

Griffin, K.B. and Enos, J.L. 1970. Foreign Assistance: Objectives and Consequences. *Economic Development and Cultural Change.* 18(3).

Grupo Andino. 1975. Carta Informativa Oficial de la Junta del Acuerdo de Cartagena, No. 51. Noviembre. No. 54. Avril y Mayo.

Gupta, V. 1968. Cost Functions, Concentration, and Barriers to Entry in Twenty-Nine Manufacturing Industries of India. *Journal of Industrial Economics.* 17-18: 57-72.

Gwynne, R.N. 1978. The Motor Vehicle Industry in Latin America. *Bank of London and South America Review.* 12: 462-471.

Hampe, Edward C., Jr. and Wittenberg, Merle. 1964. *The Lifeline of America: Development of the Food Industry.* New York: McGraw Hill.

Hansen, James S. 1975. Transfer Pricing in the Multinational Corporation: A Critical Appraisal. *World Development.* 3:11-12.

Harris, Jeffrey E. 1980. Taxing Tar and Nicotine. *American Economic Review.* 70: 300-312.

Harrison, John P. 1952. The Evolution of the Colombian Tobacco Trade to 1875. *Hispanic American History Review.* 33: 163-174.

Haskel, Barbara G. 1980. Access to Society: A Neglected Dimension of Power. *International Organization.* 34: 89-121.

Hawtrey, R.G. 1926. *The Economic Problem.* London: Longmans, Green.

Heer, John. 1966. *World Events 1866-1966: The First Hundred Years of Nestlé.* Switzerland: Chateau de Glerolles-Rivaz.

Helleiner, G.K. 1973. Manufactured Exports from Less-Developed Countries and Multinational Firms. *Economic Journal.* 83: 21-47.

————. 1975a. Transnational Enterprise in the Manufacturing Sector of the Less Developed Countries. *World Development.* 3(9): 641-650.

————. 1975b. The Role of Multinational Corporations in the Less Developed Countries' Trade in Technology. *World Development.* 3(4): 161-189.

————. 1976. Multinationals, Manufactured Exports and Employment in the Less Developed Countries. International Labour Office, Tripartite World Conference on Employment, Income Distribution and Social Progress and the International Division of Labour, Background Papers, Vol. II, Geneva.

————. 1978. Transnational Corporations and Trade Structure: The Role of Intra-Firm Trade. Paper read at the Conference on Intra-Industry Trade, Institut fur Weltwirtschaft an der Universistat Kiel.

————. 1979a. Intra-firm Trade and the Developing Countries: An Assessment of the Data. *Journal of Development Economics.*

————. 1979b. Structural Aspects of Third World Trade: Some Trends and Some Prospects. *Journal of Development Studies.* 15(3): 70-89.

————. 1979c. World Market Imperfections and the Developing Countries. In *Policy Alternatives for a New International Economic Order.* Ed. W.R. Cline. New York: Praeger Publishers.

Helleiner, G.K. and Lavergne, Real. 1979. Intra-firm Trade and Industrial Exports to the US. *Oxford Bulletin of Economics and Statistics.* 41(4).

457

Henning, J.A. and Mann, H. Michael. 1976. Advertising and Concentration: A Tentative Determination of Cause and Effect. In *Essays on Industrial Organization in Honor of Joe S. Bain.* Eds. Robert T. Masson and P. David Qualls, pp. 143-155. Cambridge: Ballinger.

Hexner, Irvin. 1943. *The International Steel Cartel.* Chapel Hill: The University of North Carolina Press.

————. 1946. *International Cartels.* Chapel Hill: The University of North Carolina Press.

Hirschman, Albert O. 1968. The Political Economy of Import-Substituting Industrialization in Latin America. *Quarterly Journal of Economics.* February.

Hispano. December 17, 1979.

————. 1970, *Exit, Voice, and Loyalty: Responses to Decline in Firms, Organizations, and States.* Cambridge: Harvard University Press.

Hogan, William Thomas. 1971. *Economic History of the Iron and Steel Industry in the United States.* Lexington, Mass.: Heath.

Horst, Thomas. 1971. The Theory of the Multinational Firm: Optimal Behavior under Different Tariff and Tax Rates. *Journal of Political Economy.* 79:5.

————. 1972. Firm and Industry Determinants of the Decision to Invest Abroad: An Empirical Study. *Review of Economics and Statistics.* 54: 258-266.

————. 1974. *At Home Abroad: American Corporations and the Food Industry.* Cambridge: Ballinger.

Horvat, Brako. 1976. The Relation between Rate of Growth and Level of Development. *Journal of Development Studies.* 10(344).

House, W.J. 1973. Market Structure and Industry Performance: The Case of Kenya. *Oxford Economic Papers.* 25: 405-419.

————. 1976. Market Structure and Industry Performance: The Case of Kenya Revisited. *Journal of Economic Studies.* November: 117-132.

Hymer, Stephen. 1976. *The International Operation of National Firms: A Study of Direct Foreign Investment.* Cambridge: MIT Press.

Illich, Ivan. 1976. *Medical Nemesis: The Expropriation of Health.* New York: Bantam Books.

Implement and Tractor. April 12, 1979; July 11, 1978.

IMS Pharmaceutical MARKETLETTER. Various issues. London.

IMSworld Publications Ltd. 1979. Health, Pharmaceutical and Development Indicators World-Wide: A Statistical Survey. London: IMSworld Publications Ltd.

In the Matter of the United States Steel Corporation et al. 1924. 8.

Instituto Nacional de Promoción Industrial y Banco Industrial del Perú. 1965. *La industria del tabaco en el Perú.* Lima.

Inter-American Development Bank. 1978. *Agro-mechanical Technologies in Latin America: a Survey of Applications in Selected Countries.* Washington, D.C.

Interconnecting Interests of Major Tobacco Manufacturers. 1968-1977. *Tobacco Reporter.*

International Metalworkers' Federation. 1976. 2nd IMF Latin American and Caribbean Automobile and Agricultural Implement Conference, Report.

Italy: Smuggling on the Rise. 1978. *Tobacco Reporter.* 20: 26.

Iron Age. January 2, 1978.

Jacquemin, A.P. and de Jong, H.W. 1976. *Markets, Corporate Behavior, and the State: International Aspects of Industrial Organization.* The Hague: Martinus Nijhoff.

———. 1977. *European Industrial Organization.* New York: John Wiley & Sons.

James, Jeffrey and Lister, Stephen. 1980. Galbraith Revisited: Advertising in Non-Affluent Societies. *World Development.* 8-1: 87-96.

Japan Statistical Yearbook. 1978.

Jenkins, Rhys. 1977. *Dependent Industrialization in Latin America; The Automotive Industry in Argentina, Chile and Mexico.* New York: Praeger Publishers.

———. 1979a. The Export Performance of Multinational Corporations in Mexican Industry. *Journal of Development Studies.* 15(3).

———. 1979b. The Rise and Fall of the Argentinian Motor Vehicle Industry. University of East Anglia Development Studies Discussion Paper No. 56.

Jo, Sung-Hwan. 1976. The Impact of Multinational Firms on Employment and Incomes: The Case of South Korea. World Employment Programme Research, Working Papers, WEP2-28, WP12, Geneva: International Labour Office.

Johnson, Leland J. 1967. Problems of Import Substitution: The Chilean Automobile Industry. *Economic Development aand Cultural Change.* 15: 202-216.

Kaldor, Nicholas. 1949. Economic Aspects of Advertising. *Review of Economic Studies.* 18(45): 1-28.

Katz, Jorge M. 1973. Industrial Growth, Royalty Payments and Local Expenditure on Research and Development. In *Latin America in the International Economy.* Eds. V. Urquide and P. Thorp. New York: Wiley.

———. 1976. *Importatión de Technología Aprendizaje e Industrialización Dependiente.* Mexico, D.F.: Fondo de Cultura Economica.

459

————. 1981. Estadios de desarrollo e industria químico-farmacéutica. *Cuadernos médico sociales.* 18: 53-75.

Kaufman, Robert R., Chernotsky, Harry I. and Geller, Daniel S. 1975. A Preliminary Test of the Theory of Dependency. *Comparative Politics.* 7(3): 303-330.

Kawahito, Kiyoski. 1972. *The Japanese Steel Industry.* New York: Praeger Publishers.

Kellner, Irwin L. 1973. The America Cigarette Industry: A Re-Examination. Ph.D. dissertation, New School for Social Research.

Key, Wilson Bryan. 1976. *Media Sexploitation.* Englewood Cliffs: Prentice-Hall.

Kindleberger, Charles P. 1969. *American Business Abroad: Six Lectures on Direct Investment.* New Haven: Yale University Press.

Knickerbocker, Frederick T. 1973. *Oligopolistic Reaction and Multinational Enterprise.* Boston: Division of Research, Graduate School of Business Administration, Harvard University.

————. 1976. Market Structure and Market Power Consequences of Foreign Direct Investment by Multinational Corporations. Center of Multinational Studies, Occasional Paper No. 8.

Krieger, Mario and Prieto, Norma. 1977. Comercio exterior, sustitución de importaciones y technología en la industria farmaceútica argentina. *Desarrollo económico.* 17(65): 179-210.

Kronstein, H. 1973. *The Law of International Cartels.* Ithaca: Cornell University Press.

Krutky, Judy. 1979. Building 'National Champions': Government-Auto Industry Relations in France. Paper read at the International Studies Association.

Kudrle, R. 1975. *Agricultural Tractors: A World Industry Study.* Cambridge: Ballinger.

Lall, Sanjaya. 1971. Balance of Payments and Income Effects of Private Foreign Investment in Manufacturing: Case Studies of India and Iran. Geneva: Trade & Development Board. Mimeographed.

————. 1973. Transfer-Pricing by Multinational Manufacturing Firms. *Oxford Bulletin of Economics and Statistics.* 35(3): 173-195.

————. 1975. Major Issues in Transfer of Technology to Developing Countries: A Case Study of the Pharmaceutical Industry. Geneva: United Nations Conference on Trade and Development.

————. 1977a. Private Foreign Investment and the Transfer of Technology in Food Processing. Prepared for Technology and Employment Branch, International Labour Office, Geneva.

————. 1977b. Transfer Pricing in Assembly Industries: A Preliminary Analysis of the Issues in Malaysia and Singapore. Prepared for the Commonwealth Secretariat, London.

460

————. 1978. Transnationals, Domestic Enterprises, and Industrial Structure in Host LDCs: A Survey. *Oxford Economic Papers*. 30(2): 217-248.

————. 1979a. Multinationals and Market Structure in an Open Developing Economy: The Case of Malaysia. *Weltwirtschaft Archiv*. June.

————. 1979b. Transfer Pricing and Developing Countries: Some Problems of Investigation. *World Development*. 1(7): 59-71.

————. 1980. Monopolistic Advantages and Foreign Involvement by US Manufacturing Industry. *Oxford Economic Papers*. 32(1).

Lall, Sanjaya and Streeten, Paul. 1977. *Foreign Investment, Transnationals and Developing Countries*. Boulder, Colorado: Westview Press.

Lanzillotti, Ralph F. 1971. The Automobile Industry. In *The Structure of American Industry*. Ed. Walter Adams. pp. 256-261. New York: MacMillan.

League of Nations. 1947. *International Cartels*. New York.

Ledogar, Robert J. 1975. *Hungry for Profits: U. S. Food and Drug Multinationals in Latin America*. New York: IDOC/North America.

Leff, Nathanial H. 1979. Monopoly Capitalism and Public Policy in Developing Countries. *Kyklos*. 32(4).

————. 1980. Advertising Expenditures in the Developing World. *Journal of International Business Studies*. Fall: 64-77.

Lenin, V.I. 1914. *Imperialism, The Highest Stage of Capitalism*, In *Essential Works of Lenin*. Ed. Henry M. Christman. New York: Bantam Books.

Leonard, David P. 1951. *The Comunero Rebellion of New Granada in 1781: A Chapter in the Spanish Quest for Social Justice*. Ann Arbor: University of Michigan Press.

Lifschitz, Edgardo. 1978. Bases Para el Estudio de la penetración Transnacional en el Complejo Sectorial Automotor. Mexico, D.F.: Instituto Latinoamericano de Estudios Transnacionales. July.

Liggett Group, Inc. (formerly Liggett & Myers Tobacco Co., Inc.). *Annual Reports*. 1950-1977.

Litchfield, P.W. 1954. *Industrial Voyage: My Life as an Industrial Lieutenant*. New York: Doubleday.

Locatelli, Rinaldo. 1967. *La concurrence dans le Marche Commun des Lampes Electriques*. Bellinzona.

MacDougall, G.D.A. 1960. The Benefits and Costs of Private Investment From Abroad. *Bulletin of the Oxford University Institute of Statistics*. 22: 189-211.

Magee, Stephen P. 1977. Information and Multinational Corporation: An Appropriability Theory of Direct Foreign Investment. In *The New International Economic Order: The North-South Debate*. Ed. Jagdish N. Bhagwati. Cambridge: MIT Press.

Mann. H. Michael. 1974. Advertising, Concentration and Profitability: The State of Knowledge and Directions for Public Policy. In *Industrial Concentration: The New Learning*. Eds. H.J. Goldsmith, H.M. Mann and J.F. Weston. Boston: Little, Brown and Co.

Manners, Gerald. 1971. *The Changing World Market for Iron Ore, A Descriptive Supplement Covering the Years 1950-1965*. Washington, D.C.: Resources for the Future, Inc.

Martin, David Dale. 1979. The Davignon Plan: Whither Competition Policy in the ECSC? *The Antitrust Bulletin*. 24: 837-887.

Martinusen, D. and Barry, B.P. 1970. *Revenues, Costs and Profits in the Farm Machinery Industry*, Canada Royal Commission on Farm Machinery Study No. 11. Ottawa: Information Canada.

Mason, Henry L. 1955. *The European Coal and Steel Community: Experiment in Supranationalism*. The Hague: Martinus Nijhoff.

Mason, R. Hal. 1973. Some Observation on the Choice of Technology by Multinational Firms in Developing Countries. *Review of Economics and Statistics*. 55: 349-355.

Massey-Ferguson Ltd. 1974. *The Pace and Form of Farm Mechanisation in the Developing Countries*. Toronto.

May, Herbert. 1970. *The Contribution of U.S. Private Investment to Latin America's Growth*. New York: The Council for Latin America, Inc.

McCann, Thomas. 1976. *An American Company: The Tragedy of United Fruit*. New York: Crown Publishers, Inc.

McCurdy, Charles W. 1978. American Law and the Marketing Structure of the Large Corporation 1875-1890. *Journal of Economic History*. 38: 631-649.

McDermott, Walsh. 1980. Pharmaceuticals: Their Role in Developing Societies. *Science*. 209: 240-245.

McGreevery, William P. 1971. *An Economic History of Colombia, 1845-1930*. Cambridge: Cambridge University Press.

Mellor, Patricio. 1977. *The Pattern of Industrial Concentration in Latin America*. Santiago: CIEPLAN-CHILE and National Bureau of Economic Research.

Mendelsohn, Robert S. 1979. *Confessions of a Medical Heretic*. Chicago: Contemporary Books.

Menge, John A. 1962. Style Change Costs as a Market Weapon. *Quarterly Journal of Economics*. 76: 632-647.

Mericle, Kenneth. 1979. The Political Economy of the Brazilian Motor Vehicle Industry. Paper read at the Conference on the

Political Economy of the Latin American Automobile Industry, Social Science Research Council, May 1979, at New Haven, Connecticut.

Mestmacher, Ernst Joachim. 1961. The Prohibition Against Discrimination in the European Coal and Steel Community Treaty. *Cartel and Monopoly in Modern Law.* Karlsruhe: Verlag C. F. Muller.

Metal Bulletin. December 5, 12, 15, 1978.

Michelin. *Annual Report.* Various years.

Minerals Yearbook. 1975.

Mintz, Sidney W. 1980. Choice and Occasion: Sweet Moments. Paper read at the Symposium Psychobiology of Human Food Selection, 27-28 March 1980, at Baylor University Medical Center.

Monopolies Commission. 1973. *Report on the Supply of Chloradiazepoxide and Diazepam.* London: Her Majesty's Stationery Office.

———. 1955. *Report on the Supply and Export of Pneumatic Tyrs.* London: Her Majesty's Stationary Office.

———. 1957. *Report on the Supply and Export of Electrical and Allied Machinery and Plant.* London: Her Majesty's Stationery Office.

———. 1968. *Second Report on the Supply of Electric Lamps.* London: Her Majesty's Stationery Office.

Moran, Theodore H. 1973. Foreign Expansion as an "Institutional Necessity" for U.S. Corporate Capitalism: The Search for a Radical Model. *World Politics.* 25(3): 369-386.

———. 1974. *Multinational Corporations and the Politics of Dependence: Copper in Chile.* Princeton: Princeton University Press.

———. 1977. The International Political Economy of Cuban Nickel Development. *Cuban Studies/Estudios Cubanos.* 7(2).

———. 1978. Multinational Corporations and Dependency: A Dialogue for Dependentistas and Non-Dependentistas. *International Organization.* 32(1): 79-100.

Morley, Samual A., Barbosa, Milton and de Souza, Maria Christina C. 1979. Evidence on the International Labor Market During a Process of Rapid Economic Growth. *Journal of Development Economics.* 6(2): 261-286.

Morley, Samuel A. and Smith, Gordon W. 1974. The Choice of Technology: Multinational Firms in Brazil. Houston: Rice University.

———. 1977. The Choice of Technology: Multinational Firms in Brazil. *Economic Development and Cultural Change.* 25 (2): 239-264.

Morrissy, J. David. 1974. *Agriculture Modernization through Production Contracting: The Role of the Fruit and Vegetable Processor in Mexico and Central America.* New York: Frederick A. Praeger.

Motor Vehicle Facts and Figures. Various years.

Mueller, W.F. and Rogers, R. 1980a. Advertising and Competition. *Review of Economics and Statistics.* Forthcoming.
463

Muller, Ronald, Baranson, Jack and Moran, Theodore. 1974. Regulation Policies Toward Multinational Corporations for Host Countries Within the Organization of American States: Generalizations from the Analysis of Issues in the Automotive Sector. Washington, D.C.: Mimeographed.

Muller, Ronald and Moore, David. 1978. Brazilian Bargaining Success in Befiex Export Promotion Program with the Transnational Automotive Industry. United Nations Centre on Transnational Corporations. Mimeographed.

Muller, Ronald and Morgenstern, Richard. 1974. Multinational Corporations and Balance of Payments Impacts in LDCs: An Econometric Analysis of Export Pricing Behavior. *Kyklos.* 27.

Munk, B. 1969. The Welfare Costs of Content Production: The Automotive Industry in Latin America. *Journal of Political Economy.* 77.

Murray, Robin. 1979. Transfer Pricing, Multinationals and the State. University of Sussex. Mimeographed.

————. 1981. *Multinationals Beyond the Market: Intra-Firm Trade and the Control of Transfer Pricing.* Sussex: The Harvester Press Limited.

Mytelka, Lynn K. 1979. *Regional Development in a Global Economy.* The Multinational Corporation Technology and Andean Integration. New Haven: Yale University Press.

Naim, Moises. 1979. Bargaining Between States and Transnational Corporations: The Case of the Venezuelan Motor Vehicle Industry. Paper read at the Conference on the Political Economy of the Latin American Automobile Industry, Social Science Research Council, May 1979, at New Haven, Connecticut.

Nam, Woo H. 1975. The Deeterminants of Industrial Concentration: The Case of Korea. *The Malaysian Economic Review.* 20 (1): 37-48.

North American Congress on Latin America. 1979. 12 (4).

National Science Foundation. 1976. *Research and Development in Industry in 1974.* Washington, D.C.: Government Printing Office.

Nayyar, D. 1978. Transnational Corporations and Manufactures Exports from Poor Countries. *Economic Journal.* 88.

Nelson, Richard L. 1959. *Merger Movements in American Industry, 1895-1956.* Princeton: Princeton University Press.

Neufeld, F.P. 1969. *A Global Corporation.* Toronto: University of Toronto Press.

The New York Times. June 5, 1978, August 6, 1979, November 15, 1979, December 16, 1979, February 1, 1980, February 18, 1982.

Newfarmer, Richard S. 1978a. *The International Market Power of Transnationals.* Geneva: UNCTAD.

————. 1978b. TNC Takeovers in Brazil: The Uneven Distribution of Benefits in the Market for Firms. *World Development.* 6(12).

464

————. 1979. Oligopolistic Tactics to Control Markets and the Growth of TNCs in Brazil's Electrical Industry. *Journal of Development Studies.* 15(3).

————. 1980. *Transnational Conglomerates and the Economics of Dependent Development.* Greenwich: JAI Press.

————. 1983. Multinationals and Marketplace Magic in the 1980s. In C. Kindleberger and D. Audretsch. Eds. *Multinationals in the 1980s.* Cambridge: MIT Press.

Newfarmer, Richard S. and Marsh, Lawrence C. 1981a. Foreign Ownership, Market Structure and Industrial Performance: Brazil's Electrical Industry. *Journal of Development Economics.* 8: 47-75.

————. 1981b. *Industrial Interdependence and Development: A Study of International Linkages and Industrial Performance in Brazil.* Report to the U.S. Commission on Trade. July.

Newfarmer, Richard S. and Mueller, W.F. 1975. *Multinational Corporations in Brazil and Mexico: Structural Sources of Economic and Noneconomic Power.* Report to the Subcommittee on Multinational Corporations. Washington, D.C.: U.S. Government Printing Office.

Newlyn, W. 1977. *The Financing of Development.* Oxford: Clarendon Press.

Newsweek. September 10, 1979, November 12, 1979.

Next Step Toward WHO Tobacco Control. 1976. *Tobacco Reporter.* 14.

Nicholls, William H. 1951. *Price Policies in the Cigarette Industry: A Study of "Concerted Action" and Its Social Control, 1911-1950.* Nashville: Vanderbilt University Press.

Nichols, Michael J. and Veblen, Thomas C. 1978. *The Outlook for Change in the U.S. Food System.* Menlo Park: Stanford Research Institute.

Oficina de Relaciones Industriales del Cigarrillo. 1968. *La industria del cigarrillo en la Argentina.* Buenos Aires.

Organización de Estados Americanos. 1974. *América en Cifras, 1974: Situación Económica: (2) Industria.* Washington, D.C.: Unión Panamericana.

Organization for Economic Co-operation and Development. 1974. *Export Cartels.* Report of the Committee of Exports on Restrictive Practices. Paris.

————. 1975. *Observer.* No. 6.

————. 1977. *Restrictive Business Practices of Multinational Enterprises.* Paris.

————. 1979a. *Concentration and Competition Policy.* Paris.

————. 1979b. *Impact of Multinational Enterprises on National Scientific and Technical Capacities: Food Industry.* DSTI/SPR/79.23-MNE. Paris.

Ornstein, S. 1977. *Industrial Concentration and Advertising Intensity.* Washington, D.C.: American Enterprise Institute.

P. Lorillard Co., Inc. *Annual Reports.* 1950-1977.

Pack, Howard. 1976. The Substitution of Labour for Capital in Kenyan Manufacturing. *The Economic Journal.* 86: 45-58.

Pakkala, A.L. 1976. Living Standard Influences Degrees of Cigarette Smoking. *Tobacco Reporter.* July: 55-72.

Palma, Gabriel. 1976. Dependency: A Formal Theory of Underdevelopment or a Methodology for the Analysis of Concrete Situations of Underdevelopment? *World Development.* 6(7&8): 881-924.

Papanek, G. 1972. The Effect of Aid and Other Resource Transfers on Savings and Growth in Less Developed Countries. *Economic Journal.* 82.

———. 1973. Aid, Foreign Private Investment, Savings and Growth in Less Developed Countries. *Journal of Political Economy.* January-February.

Parry, Thomas G. and Watson, J.F. 1977. Technology Flows and Foreign Investment in the Australian Manufacturing Sector. Reprint from *Australian Economic Papers.* 1979: 103-118.

Passer, H.D. 1953. *The Electrical Manufacturers: 1875-1900.* Cambridge: Harvard University Press.

Paz. R. and Otero, R. 1970. Análisis de la Industria del Neumático en la Republica Argentina: Evolución y Perspectivas. Mimeograph.

Peltzman, Sam. 1974. *Regulation of Pharmaceutical Innovation: The 1962 Amendments.* Washington, D.C.: American Enterprise Institute.

Penrose, Edith. 1973. International Patenting and the Less Developed Countries. *Economic Journal.* 83.

Pérez Vásquez, Jorge. 1975. Comentarios sobre el estudio denominado 'Consumo de cigarrillos rubios nacionales y extranjeros.' Medellin: Compania Colombiana de Tabaco, S.A.

Pharmaceutical Manufacturers Association. 1978. Annual Survey Report: Ethical Pharmaceutical Industry Operations 1977-1978. Washington, D.C.

Philip Morris Co., Inc. *Annual Reports.*

PEP. 1949. *Agricultural Machinery.* London.

Porter, Patrick G. 1969. Origins of the American Tobacco Company. *Business History Review.* 43: 59-76.

———. 1971. Advertising in the Early Cigarette Industry: W. Duke, Sons & Company of Durham. *North Carolina Historical Review.* 48: 31-43.

R.J. Reynolds Industries Inc. (Formerly R.J. Reynolds Tobacco Co.). *Annual Reports.* Various Years.

Radhu, Ghulam M. 1973. Transfer of Technical Know-How Through Multinational Corporations in Pakistan. *Pakistan Development Review.* 12(4): 361-374.

Rahl, J.A. 1979. International Cartels and their Regulation. Paper read at Conference on International Regulation of Restrictive Business Practices, November 1979 at Columbia University. New York.

Rahman, M. 1968. Foreign Capital and Domestic Savings: A Test of Haavelmo's Hypothesis with Cross-country Data. *Review of Economics and Statistics.* 50(1).

Rayner, A.J. and Cowling, K. 1970. Price, Quality and Market Share. *Journal of Political Economy.*

Reekie, Duncan, and Weber, Michael H. 1979. *Profits, Politics and Drugs.* New York: Holmes and Meier.

Registry of Foreign Investment Mexico, D.F.

Renaud, Marc. 1975. On the Structural Constraints to State Intervention in Health. *International Journal of Health Services.* 5(4): 559-571.

República de Colombia, Departamento Nacional de Planeación. 1975. Consumo de cigarrillos rubios nacionales y extranjeros. Bogotá.

Reuber, Grant L., Crookell, H., Emerson, M. and Gallais Hamonno, G. 1973. *Private Foreign Investment in Development.* Oxford: Clarendon Press.

Rhoades, Stephen A. 1974. A Further Evaluation of the Effect of Diversification on Industry Profit Performance. *Review of Economics and Statistics.* 56: 553-560.

Rhys, D.G. 1972. *The Motor Industry: An Economic Survey.* London: Butterworth.

Riedel, J. 1975. The Nature and Determinants of Export-Oriented Direct Foreign Investment in a Developing Country: A Case Study of Taiwan. *Weltwirtschaft Archiv.* 3.

Robbins, Sidney M. and Stobaugh, Robert B. 1973. *Money in the Multinational.* New York: Basic Books.

Robinson, Richard D. 1976. *National Control of Foreign Business Entry: A Survey Of Fifteen Countries.* New York: Praeger Publishers.

Roncaglioli, Rafael and Janus, Norean. 1978. A Survey of the Transnational Structure of the Mass Media and Advertising. Instituto Latinoamericano de Estudios Transnacionales.

Rosenstein-Rodan, Paul N. 1961. International Aid for Underdeveloped Countries. *Review of Economics and Statistics.* May.

Rosenthal, Gert. 1975. The Expansion of the Transnational Enterprise in Central America: Acquisition of Domestic Firms. Mimeographed.

467

Ross, Walter S. 1980. Let's Stop Exporting the Smoking Epidemic. *Readers Digest.* May: 143-147.

Rothschild, Emma. 1973. *Paradise Lost: The Decline of the Auto-Industrial Age.* New York: Random House.

Roumeliotis, Panayotis V. and Golemis, Charalambos P. 1978. Transfer Pricing and the Power of Transnational Enterprises in Greece. Paper read at UNCTAD-IDS Conference on Transfer Pricing, Nov. Brighton, England.

Rubber Age. February 1962.

Rubber World. February 1970.

Rubinson, Richard. 1976. The World-economy and the Distribution of Income within States: A Cross-national Study. *American Sociological Review.* 41(4): 638-654.

————. 1977. Dependence, Government Revenue, and Economic Growth, 1955-1970. *Studies in Comparative International Development.* 12(2): 3-28.

Safarian, A.E. 1966. *Foreign Ownership of Canadian Industry.* Toronto: McGraw Hill Co.

Salas Vargas, Guillermo. 1979. Political Industrial e Industria Automotriz en México, 1947-78, Ph.D. dissertation, El Colegio de Mexico.

Sands, Saul. 1961. Changes in the Scale of Production in U.S. Manufacturing Industry, 1904-1947. *Review of Economics and Statistics.* 43: 365-368.

Sarett, Lewis H. 1979. Current Programs for Development of Pharmaceuticals: The United States Pharmaceutical Industry. In *Pharmaceuticals for Developing Countries,* pp. 130-135. Washington, D.C.: National Academy of Sciences.

Sawhney P. and Sawhney, B. 1973. Capacity-Utilization; Concentration, and Price-Cost Margins: Results on Indian Industries. *Journal of Industrial Economics.* April: 145-153.

Schaumann, Leif. 1976. *Pharmaceutical Industry Dynamics and Outlook to 1985.* Menlo Park, Ca.: Stanford Research Institute.

Scherer, F.M. 1975. *The Economics of Multi-Plant Operation: An International Comparisons Study.* Cambridge: Harvard University Press.

————. 1980. *Industrial Market Structure and Economic Performance.* Chicago: Rand McNally.

Schiller, H. 1971. Madison Avenue Imperialism. *Transaction.* March-April.

Schmalensee, Richard. 1972. *The Economics of Advertising.* Amsterdam: North-Holland.

Schnee, Jerome and Caglarcan, Erol. 1976. The Changing Pharmaceutical R & D Environment. *Business Economics.* 11(3): 31-38.

Schwartzman, David. 1976. *Innovation in the Pharmaceutical Industry.* Baltimore: The Johns Hopkins University Press.

———. 1900. *Oligopoly in the Farm Machinery Industry.* Canada Royal Commission on Farm Machinery Study No. 12, Ottawa, Information Canada.

SCRIP. Various issues. Richmond: England.

Sourrouille, Juan. 1979. *El Complejo Automotor en Argentina.* Mexico, D.F.: Roncaglioli.

Sepúlveda, Bernardo and Chumacero Antonio. 1973. *La inversión extranjera en México.* Mexico D.F.: Fondo de Cultura Económica.

Shapiro, Helen and Volk, Steven. 1979. Steelyard Blues: New Structures in Steel, *NACLA Report on the Americas.* 13(1).

Shepherd, Philip L. 1977. Toward a Synthesis of Product-Cycle and Demand Creation Theories of Multinational Corporate Expansion: Some Introductory Notes and Comments. Paper read at a meeting of the Working Group on Latin America and the International System: Multinational Corporations in Latin America, Social Science Research Council, December 16, New York.

———. 1983. 'Soooold American!!!'—A Study of the Development of the Foreign Operations of the American Cigarette Industry. Ph.D. dissertation, Vanderbilt University.

———. forthcoming. *The Dynamics of the International Cigarette Oligopoly.*

Sierra, Luis F. 1971. *El tabaco en la economía colombiana del siglo XIX.* Bogotá: Universidad Nacional de Colombia.

Simon, Julian L. 1970. *Issues in the Economics of Advertising.* Urbana; Il.: University of Illinois Press.

Silverman, Milton. 1976. *The Drugging of the Americas: How Multinational Drug Companies Say One Thing About Their Products to Physicians in the United States, and Another Thing to Physicians in Latin America.* Berkeley: University of California Press.

———. 1977. The Epidemiology of Drug Promotion. *International Journal of Health Services.* 7(2): 157-166.

Silverman, Milton, and Lee, Philip R. 1974. *Pills, Profits, and Politics.* Berkeley: University of California Press.

Silverman, Milton, Lee, Philip R. and Lydecker, Mia. 1982. *Prescriptions for Death: The Drugging of the Third World.* Berkeley: University of California Press.

Skurski, Julie and Coronil, Fernando. 1979. 'The Motors War': The Power of Motors or the Motors of Power; Public Planning of Automobile Manufacturing in Venezuela. Paper read at the Latin American Studies Association Convention, April 1979.

SMMT. 1975. *The Motor Industry of Great Britain.* London: Society of Motor Manufacturers and Traders.
469

Snell, Bradford C. 1973. *American Ground Transport: A Proposal for Restructuring the Automobile, Truck, Bus, and Rail Industries.* Washington, D.C. U.S. Senate, Subcommittee on Antitrust and Monopoly, Hearings on S.1167. Part 4A. GPO.

Standard and Poor. 1979. *Industry Survey.*

Stegemann, Klaus. 1968. Three Functions of Basing-Point Pricing and Article 60 of the ECSC Treaty. *The Antitrust Bulletin.* 13: 395-432.

———. 1977. *Price Competition and Output Adjustment in the European Steel Market.* Tubingen: J.C.B. Mohr.

Stein, Stanley J. and Stein, Barbara H. 1970. *The Colonial Heritage of Latin America: Essays on Economic Dependence in Perspective.* New York: Oxford University Press.

Steindl, J. 1952. *Maturity and Stagnation in American Capitalism.* Oxford: Blackwell.

Stepan, Alfred. 1978. *State & Society: Peru in Comparative Perspective.* Princeton: Princeton University Press.

Stevens, Guy V.G. 1974. The Determinants of Investment. *Economic Analysis and the Multinational Enterprise,* ed. J.H. Dunning. New York: Praeger Publishers.

Stewart, Frances. 1972 Choice of Technique in Developing Countries. *Journal of Development Studies.* 9(1): 99-121.

Stocking, George W. 1953. *Basing Point Pricing and Regional Development: A Case Study of the Iron and Steel Industry.* Chapel Hill: University of North Carolina Press.

Stocking, George W. and Watkins, Myron W. 1946. *Cartels in Action: Case Studies in International Business Diplomacy.* New York: Twentieth Century Fund.

———. 1948. *Cartels or Competition.* New York: Twentieth Century Fund.

Stopford, John and Wells, Louis T. 1972. *Managing the Multinational Enterprise.* New York: Basic Books.

Strassman, W. Paul. 1970. Construction Productivity and Employment in Developing Countries. *International Labor Review.* 10(5): 503-518.

Streeten, Paul. 1974. The Theory of Development Policy. In *Economic Analysis and the Multinational Enterprise.* Ed. J.H. Dunning. New York: Praeger Publishers.

Subrahamanian, K.K. and Pillai, P. Mohana. 1977. Transnationalization of Production and Marketing Implications of Trade: Some Reflections on Indian Experience. Paper read at IDS/UNCTAD seminar: Intra-firm Transactions and their Impact on Trade and Development.

470

Sunkel, Osvaldo. 1969. National Development Policy and External Dependence in Latin America. *Journal of Development Studies.* 6(1): 23-48.

———. 1972. Big Business and "Dependencia": A Latin American View. *Foreign Affairs.* 50(3): 517-531.

Swann, Dennis. 1973. United Kingdom of Great Britain and Northern Ireland: *Restrictive Business Practices,* Prepared for the United Nations, New York.

Swann, Dennis et al. 1973. *Competition in British Industry: Case Studies of the Effects of Restrictive Practices Legislation.* Dept. of Economics, Lougborough Univ. of Technology.

Telser, L.G. 1964. Advertising and Competition. *Journal of Political Economy.* December.

Temin, Peter, 1979a. The Origin of Compulsory Drug Prescriptions. *Journal of Law and Economics.* 22(1): 91-105.

———. 1979b. Technology, Regulation, and Market Structure in the Modern Pharmaceutical Industry. *Bell Journal of Economics.* 10(2): 429-446.

Tennant, Richard B. 1950. *The American Cigarette Industry: A Study in Economic Analysis and Public Policy.* New Haven: Yale University Press.

Third World Market for Cigarettes Expands. 1978. *Tobacco Reporter.* 13-14.

Third World Tobacco Push Hit. 1978. *Nashville Tennessean.* 2.

Thirsk, W.R. 1972. The Economics of Columbian Farm Mechanisation. Ph.D. dissertation, Yale University.

Tiefenbacher, Max P. 1979. Problems of Distribution, Availability, and Utilization of Agents in Developing Countries: Industry Perspectives. In *Pharmaceuticals for Developing Countries,* pp. 211-227. Washington, D.C.: National Academy of Sciences.

Tilley, Nannie May. 1948. *The Bright Tobacco Industry, 1860-1929.* Chapel Hill: University of North Carolina Press.

Tironi, E. 1978. "Latin American Economic Integration" UNCTAD Conference on TNCs and Integration, Lima, Peru. June.

Tobacco's Contributions. 1981. *Tobacco Reporter.* January: 38-43.

Toder, Eric J. et al. 1978. *Trade Policy and the U.S. Automobile Industry.* New York: Praeger Publishers.

Trajtenberg, Raul, 1977. A Sectorial Approach for the Study of Transnational Penetration in Latin America. Instituto Latinoamericano de Los Transnacionales.

Tsurumi, Yoshi. 1976. *The Japanese are Coming.* Cambridge: Ballinger.

Forget Those Rumours, Avon Stays in the Tyre Business. 1975. *Tyres and Batteries.*

Uniroyal. *Annual Report.* Various years.

United Kingdom Board of Trade (UKBT). 1947. *Survey of International and Internal Cartels 1944-1946.* London.

———. 1975. *Survey of International and Internal Cartels 1944-1946.* vol. 2, Part III. London.

United Nations. 1976. *Statistical Annual.*

United Nations Centre on Transnational Corporations. 1978. *Transnational Corporations in World Development: A Re-examination,* New York.

———. 1979. *Transnational Corporations and the Pharmaceutical Industry.* New York.

———. 1980. *Transnational Corporations in Food and Beverage Processing.* New York.

———. 1981. *Transnational Corporations in the Pharmaceutical Industry of Developing Countries.* New York.

———. 1983. *Transnational Corporations in the Pharmaceutical Industry of Developing Countries: A Technical Study.* New York.

United Nations Conference on Trade and Development. 1978a. *Dominant Positions of Market Power of Transnational Corporations: Use of Transfer-pricing Mechanisms.* New York.

———. 1978b. *Marketing and Distribution of Tobacco.* New York.

———. 1980. *Technology Policies in the Pharmaceutical Sector in Cuba.* Geneva.

———. 1982. *Technology Policies in the Pharmaceutical Sector in Costa Rica.* Geneva.

United Nations Economic and Social Council. 1978. *Transnational Corporations* in World Development: A Re-examination.

United Nations Industrial Development Organization. 1969. *Industrialization of Developing Countries: Problems and Prospects in the Food-Processing Industry.* New York.

———. 1976. *Summary of the Draft World-Wide Study of the Iron and Steel Industry.* New York.

———. 1977a. *Draft World-Wide Study on Agroindustries 1975-2000.* Vienna.

———. 1977b. *The Impact of Trade Marks on the Development Process of Developing Countries.* Geneva.

———. 1978. *Note on the Changing Pattern of World Steel Production.* New York.

———. 1979. *The Cairo Declaration.* Vienna.

———. 1980. *Global Study of the Pharmaceutical Industry.* Vienna.

———. 1982. *Directory of Sources of Supply of 26 Essential Bulk Drugs, Their Chemical Intermediates and Some Raw Materials.* Vienna.

United States Bureau of Corporations. 1909-1915. *Report of the Commissioner of Corporations on the Tobacco Industry Parts I-III.* Washington, D.C.: Government Printing Office.

United States Congress, Temporary National Economic Committee. 1939. *Hearings,* 76th Congress, 2d sess., Part XX.

United States Department of Agriculture Economic Research Service. 1967. *Tobacco Situation.* Washington, D.C.: Government Printing Office.

———. 1982. *Tobacco Outlook & Situation.* Washington, D.C.: Government Printing Office.

———. 1976. Foreign Agricultural Service. *Foreign Agriculture Circular-Tobacco.* Washington, D.C.: Government Printing Office.

———. 1977. Foreign Agricultural Service. *Foreign Agriculture Circular-Tobacco.* Washington, D.C.: Government Printing Office.

———. 1978. Foreign Agricultural Service. *Foreign Agriculture Circular-Tobacco.* Washington, D.C.: Government Printing Office.

———. 1981. Foreign Agricultural Service. *Foreign Agriculture Circular-Tobacco.* Washington, D.C.: Government Printing Office.

United States Department of Commerce. 1972. *Annual Survey of Manufacturers, 1970.* Washington, D.C.: Government Printing Office.

U.S. Department of Commerce, Bureau of the Census. Various Years. *Statistical Abstract of the United States.* Washington, D.C.: Government Printing Office.

U.S. Department of Commerce, Bureau of International Commerce. 1973. *The Multinational Corporation: Studies on U.S. Foreign Investment,* vol. ii. Washington, D.C.: Government Printing Office.

United States Department of Health, Education and Welfare. Public Health Service. 1979. *Smoking and Health: A Report of the Surgeon General.* Washington, D.C.: Government Printing Office.

United States International Trade Commission. 1982. *Synthetic Organic Chemicals: United States Production and Sales, 1981.* Washington, D.C.: Government Printing Office.

United States Senate, Committee on Finance. 1973. *Implication of Multinational Firms for World Trade and Investment and for US Trade and Labour.* Washington, D.C.: Government Printing Office.

United States Senate, Subcommittee on Antitrust and Monopoly. 1956. *Bigness and Concentration of Economic Power—A Case Study of General Motors Corporation.* Washington, D.C.: Government Printing Office.

United States Senate, Subcommittee on Antitrust and Monopoly. 1958. *Administered Prices: Automobiles.* Washington, D.C.: Government Printing Office.

United States Senate, Subcommittee on Antitrust and Monopoly. 1958. *Administered Prices in Steel.* Washington D.C.: Government Printing Office.

United States vs. American Tobacco Company. 1908. 164 Fed. 700.

United States vs. American Tobacco Company. 1911. 221 U.S. 106.

United States vs. United States Steel Corporation. 1920. 251 U.S. 417.

Vaitsos, Constantine V. 1970. Transfer of Resources and Preservation of Monopoly Rents. Harvard Center for International Affairs Economic Development Report No. 168.

————. 1973. Exports, Foreign Capital Inflow and Economic Growth. *Journal of International Economics.* 3: 337-349.

————. 1974a. *Intercountry Income Distribution and Transnational Enterprises.* Oxford: Clarendon Press.

————. 1974b. Employment Effects of Foreign Direct Investments in Developing Countries. In *Employment in Developing Nations.* Ed. Edgar O. Edwards. New York: Columbia University Press.

————. 1976a. Employment Problems and Transnational Enterprises in Developing Countries: Distortions and Inequalities. World Employment Programme Research, Working Papers, WP2-28/WP 11. Geneva: International Labour Office.

————. 1976b. The Revision of the International Patent System: Legal Considerations for a Third World Position. *World Development.* February: 85-99.

————. 1978. The Role of Transnational Enterprise in Latin American Economic Integration Efforts: Who Integrates and with Whom, How and for Whose Benefit? Prepared for UNCTAD secretariat, United Nations Conference on Trade and Development.

————. 1979. The Visible Hand in World Production and Trade: Corporate Integration. Paper read at the Conference on Integration and Unequal Development: The Case of Western Europe, at the Institute of Development Studies, Sussex University.

Vatter, H.G. 1952. The Closure of Entry in the American Automobile Industry. *Oxford Economic Papers.* 4: 213-234.

Vaupel, J.W. and Curhan, J.P. 1973. *The World's Multinational Enterprises.* Cambridge: Harvard Business School.

Vazquez Tercero, Hector. 1975. *Una Decada de Politica Sobre la Industria Automotriz.* Mexico, D.F.: Editoral Tecnos.

Vernon, Raymond. 1966. International Investment and International Trade in the Product Cycle. *Quarterly Journal of Economics.* 190-207.

————. 1971. *Sovereignty at Bay: The Multinational Spread of U.S. Enterprises.* New York: Basic Books.

474

————. 1974a. The Location of Economic Activity. In *Economic Analysis and the Multinational Enterprise*. Ed. J.H. Dunning. New York: Praeger Publishers.

————. 1974b. *Big Business and the State: Changing Relations in West Europe*. Cambridge: Harvard University Press.

————. 1977. *Storm over the Multinationals: The Real Issues*. Cambridge: Harvard University Press.

Vilas, Carlos M. 1974. Estructura de la propiedad y control en el mercade argentino de cigarrillos. Buenos Aires: Mimeographed.

The Wall St. Journal. August 26, 1978, August 8, 1981, March 24, 1980, February 14, 1980, October 1, 1980.

Wang, Y.C. 1960. Free Enterprise in China: The Case of a Cigarette Concern, 1905-1953. *Pacific Historical Review*. 29: 395-414.

Warner, Kenneth E. 1977. The Effects of the Antismoking Campaign on Cigarette Consumption. *American Journal of Public Health*. 67: 645-650.

Warren, Kenneth. 1975. *World Steel: An Economic Geography*. New York: Crane, Russak and Col.

Weiss, Leonard. 1974. The Concentration-Profits Relation and Anti-Trust. In *Industrial Concentration: The New Learning*. Ed. H.J. Goldschmidt et al. Boston: Little, Brown and Co.

Weisskopf, T.E. 1972. The Impact of Foreign Capital Inflow on Domestic Savings in Underdeveloped Countries. *Journal of International Econnomics*. 2: 25-38.

Wells, Louis T. 1972. *The Product Life Cycle and International Trade*. Cambridge: Harvard Graduate School of Business Administration.

————. 1978. Automobiles. In *Big Business and the State*. Ed. Raymond Vernon. Cambridge: Harvard University Press.

Wernecke, William A., Jr. 1977. The Mixed Corporation Model in Brazil: A Case Analysis of Three State Steel Firms 1964/1976. Unpublished Manuscript, Stanford University Library.

Wescoe, W. Clarke. 1979. "Constraints on Expanding the Role of the U.S. Pharmaceutical Industry: United States Industry Perspective. In *Pharmaceuticals for Developing Countries*, pp. 179-186. Washington, D.C.: National Academy of Sciences.

West, Peter J. 1977. The Tyre Multinationals: A Study of Foreign Investment and Technology Transfer in Latin America. Ph.D. dissertation. University of Sussex, England.

————. 1979. Venezuela: The Iron an Steel Industry. *Bank of London & South America Review*. 13.

————. 1984. *Foreign Investment and Technology Transfer: The Tire Industry in Latin America*. Greenwich: JAI Press.

Weston, J.F. 1953. *The Role of Mergers in the Growth of Large Firms.* Berkeley: University of California Press.

White, Eduardo with Feldman, S. 1981. *Latin America Joint Ventures: A New Way to Strengthen the Bargaining Power of Developing Countries vis-a-vis Transnational Corporations?* Geneva: United Nations Center on Transnational Corporations.

White, Lawrence J. 1971. *The American Automobile Industry Since 1945.* Cambridge: Harvard University Press.

————. 1974. *Industrial Concentration and Economic Power in Pakistan.* Princeton: Princeton University Press.

————. 1976. Appropriate Factor Proportions for Manufacturing in LDC's: A Survey of the Evidence. Princeton: Woodrow Wilson School, Research Projects in Development Studies, No. 64.

————. 1981. What Has Been Happening to Aggregate Concentration in the United States? *The Journal of Industrial Economics.* 29: 223-230.

Whiting Jr., Van R. 1981. Transnational Enterprise and the State in Mexico, Ph.D. dissertation. Harvard University.

Wilkins, M. 1970. *The Emergence of Multinational Enterprise: American Business Abroad from the Colonial Era to 1914.* Cambridge: Harvard University Press.

Wilkins, M. and Hill, F.E. 1900. *American Business Abroad.* Detroit: Wayne State University Press.

Williams, Simon and Miller, James A. 1973. *Credit Systems for Smallscale Farmers: Case Histories from Mexico.* Austin: University of Texas Press.

Wilmore, Larry. 1976. Direct Foreign Investment in Central American Manufacturing. *World Development.* 4(6): 499-517.

Wils, Frits. 1979. *Industrialization, Industrialists, and the Nation-State in Peru.* Berkeley: Institute of International Studies.

Wilson, Charles. 1968. *The History of Unilever: A Study in Economic Growth and Social Change,* three volumes. Volume 1, 1851-1929: *The Study of Lever Brothers.* Volume 2, 1854-1929: *The Study of Jergens and Vandenbergh's.* Volume 3, *Unilever, the Last 20 Years* (1945-1965).

World Business Weekly. October 8, 22, 1979.

Yeats, Alexander J. 1978. Monopoly Power, Barriers to Competition and the Pattern of Price Differentials in International Trade. *Journal of Development Economics.* 5: 167-180.

Subject Index

478

479

Authors Index

485

487

Index of Major Companies

489

491